Numerical Methods
Using MATLAB
Fourth Edition

John. H. Mathews
California State University, Fullerton

Kurtis D. Fink
Northwest Missouri State University

PEARSON
Prentice Hall

Upper Saddle River, New Jersey 07458

Library of Congress Cataloging-in-Publication Data
    Numerical methods using MATLAB/John H. Mathews,
    Kurtis D. Fink—4th ed.
        p. cm.
    Includes index
    ISBN 0-13-065248-2
    1. Numerical analysis–Data processing. 2. MATLAB. I. Fink, Kurtis D.
    II. Title.

  QA297.M39   2004
  518–dc22   2003061022

Editor-in-Chief: *Sally Yagan*
Acquisitions Editor: *George Lobell*
Production Editor: *Lynn Savino Wendel*
Vice President/Director of Production and Manufacturing: *David W. Riccardi*
Senior Managing Editor: *Linda Mihatov Behrens*
Assistant Managing Editor: *Bayani Mendoza de Leon*
Executive Managing Editor: *Kathleen Schiaparelli*
Assisant Manufacturing Manager/Buyer: *Michael Bell*
Manufacturing Manager: *Trudy Pisciotti*
Marketing Manager: *Halee Dinsey*
Marketing Assistant: *Rachael Beckman*
Art Director: *Jayne Conte*
Editorial Assistant: *Jennifer Brady*
Cover Designer: *Bruce Kenselaar*
Cover Photo Credits: *Fans Quilt, Quiltmaker unidentified, initialed "PM" Indiana 1925–1935*
Cotton, wool, and rayon, with cotton embroidery 82 × 71 1/2"
Collection American Folk Art Museum, New York Gift of David Pottinger 1980.37.86

© 2004, 1999 by Pearson Education, Inc.
Pearson Prentice Hall
Pearson Education, Inc.
Upper Saddle River, New Jersey 07458

Formerly published under the title Numerical Methods for Mathematics,
Science, and Engineering, © 1992, 1987 by John H. Mathews.

Pearson Prentice Hall® is a trademark of Pearson Education, Inc.

Printed in the United States of America
10 9 8 7 6 5 4 3 2 1

ISBN 0-13-065248-2

Pearson Education LTD., *London*
Pearson Education Australia PTY, Limited, *Sydney*
Pearson Education Singapore, Pte. Ltd
Pearson Education North Asia Ltd, *Hong Kong*
Pearson Education Canada, Ltd., *Toronto*
Pearson Educacion de Mexico, S.A. de C.V.
Pearson Education - Japan, *Tokyo*
Pearson Education Malaysia, Pte. Ltd

Contents

Preface

This book provides a fundamental introduction to numerical analysis suitable for undergraduate students in mathematics, computer science, physical sciences, and engineering. It is assumed that the reader is familiar with calculus and has taken a structured programming course. The text has enough material fitted modularly for either a single-term course or a year sequence. In short, the book contains enough material so that instructors will be able to select topics appropriate to their needs.

Students of various backgrounds should find numerical methods quite interesting and useful, and this is kept in mind throughout the book. Thus, there is a wide variety of examples and problems that help to sharpen one's skill in both the theory and practice of numerical analysis. Computer calculations are presented in the form of tables and graphs whenever possible so that the resulting numerical approximations are easier to visualize and interpret. MATLAB programs are the vehicle for presenting the underlying numerical algorithms.

Emphasis is placed on understanding why numerical methods work and their limitations. This is challenging and involves a balance between theory, error analysis, and readability. An error analysis for each method is presented in a fashion that is appropriate for the method at hand, yet does not turn off the reader. A mathematical derivation for each method is given that uses elementary results and builds the student's understanding of calculus. Computer assignments using MATLAB give students an opportunity to practice their skills at scientific programming.

Shorter numerical exercises can be carried out with a pocket calculator/computer, and the longer ones can be done using MATLAB subroutines. It is left for the instructor to guide the students regarding the pedagogical use of numerical computations. Each instructor can make assignments that are appropriate to the available computing resources. Experimentation with the MATLAB subroutine libraries is encouraged. These materials can be used to assist students in the completion of the numerical analysis component of computer laboratory exercises.

In this edition a section on Bézier curves has been added to the end of the chapter on curve fitting. Additionally, the chapter on numerical optimization has been expanded to include an introduction to both direct and derivative based methods for optimizing functions of one or more variables. A listing of the MATLAB programs in this textbook is available upon request from the authors (*http://math.fullerton.edu/mathews/numerical.html*). An instructor's solution manual for the exercise sets is available from the publisher.

Previously, we took the attitude that any software program that students mastered would work fine. However, many students entering this course have yet to master a programming language (computer science students excepted). MATLAB has become the tool of nearly all engineers and applied mathematicians, and its newest versions have improved the programming aspects. So we think that students will have an easier and more productive time in this MATLAB version of our text.

Acknowledgments

We would like to express our gratitude to all the people whose efforts contributed to the various editions of this book. I (John Mathews) thank the students at California State University, Fullerton. I thank my colleagues Stephen Goode, Mathew Koshy, Edward Sabotka, Harris Schultz, and Soo Tang Tan for their support in the first edition; additionally, I thank Russell Egbert, William Gearhart, Ronald Miller, and Greg Pierce for their suggestions for the second edition. I also thank James Friel, Chairman of the Mathematics Department at CSUF, for his encouragement.

Reviewers who made useful recommendations for the first edition are Walter M. Patterson, III, Lander College; George B. Miller, Central Connecticut State University; Peter J. Gingo, The University of Akron; Michael A. Freedman, The University of Alaska, Fairbanks; and Kenneth P. Bube, University of California, Los Angeles. For the second edition, we thank Richard Bumby, Rutgers University; Robert L. Curry, U.S. Army; Bruce Edwards, University of Florida; and David R. Hill, Temple University.

For the third edition we wish to thank Tim Sauer, George Mason University; Gerald M. Pitstick, University of Oklahoma; Victor De Brunner, University of Oklahoma; George Trapp, West Virginia University; Tad Jarik, University of Alabama, Huntsville; Jeffrey S. Scroggs, North Carolina State University; Kurt Georg, Colorado State University; and James N. Craddock, Southern Illinois University at Carbondale.

Reviewers for the fourth edition were Kevin Kreider, University of Akron; Demetrio Labate, Washington University at St. Louis; Lee Johnson, Virginia Tech; and Azmy Ackleh, University of Louisiana at Lafayette. We are grateful to the reviewers for their time and recommendations.

Suggestions for improvements and additions to the book are always welcome and can be made by corresponding directly with the authors.

John H. Mathews
Mathematics Department
California State University
Fullerton, CA 92634
mathews@fullerton.edu

Kurtis D. Fink
Department of Mathematics
Northwest Missouri State University
Maryville, MO 64468
kfink@mail.nwmissouri.edu

1

Preliminaries

Consider the function $f(x) = \cos(x)$, its derivative $f'(x) = -\sin(x)$, and its antiderivative $F(x) = \sin(x) + C$. These formulas were studied in calculus. The former is used to determine the slope $m = f'(x_0)$ of the curve $y = f(x)$ at a point $(x_0, f(x_0))$, and the latter is used to compute the area under the curve for $a \leq x \leq b$.

The slope at the point $(\pi/2, 0)$ is $m = f'(\pi/2) = -1$ and can be used to find the tangent line at this point (see Figure 1.1(a)):

$$y_{\text{tan}} = m\left(x - \frac{\pi}{2}\right) + 0 = f'\left(\frac{\pi}{2}\right)\left(x - \frac{\pi}{2}\right) = -x + \frac{\pi}{2}.$$

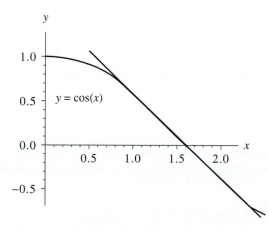

Figure 1.1 (a) The tangent line to the curve $y = \cos(x)$ at the point $(\pi/2, 0)$.

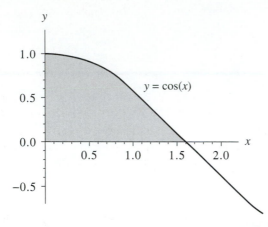

Figure 1.1 (b) The area under the curve $y = \cos(x)$ over the interval $[0, \pi/2]$.

The area under the curve for $0 \leq x \leq \pi/2$ is computed using an integral (see Figure 1.1(b)):

$$\text{area} = \int_0^{\pi/2} \cos(x)\,dx = F\left(\frac{\pi}{2}\right) - F(0) = \sin\left(\frac{\pi}{2}\right) - 0 = 1.$$

These are some of the results that we will need to use from calculus.

1.1 Review of Calculus

It is assumed that the reader is familiar with the notation and subject matter covered in the undergraduate calculus sequence. This should have included the topics of limits, continuity, differentiation, integration, sequences, and series. Throughout the book we refer to the following results.

Limits and Continuity

Definition 1.1. Assume that $f(x)$ is defined on an open interval containing $x = x_0$, except possibly at $x = x_0$ itself. Then f is said to have the *limit* L at $x = x_0$, and we write

(1) $$\lim_{x \to x_0} f(x) = L,$$

if given any $\epsilon > 0$ there exists a $\delta > 0$ such that $|f(x) - L| < \epsilon$ whenever $0 < |x - x_0| < \delta$. When the h-increment notation $x = x_0 + h$ is used, equation (1) becomes

(2) $$\lim_{h \to 0} f(x_0 + h) = L. \qquad \blacktriangle$$

Definition 1.2.   Assume that $f(x)$ is defined on an open interval containing $x = x_0$. Then f is said to be **continuous at $x = x_0$** if

$$(3) \qquad\qquad \lim_{x \to x_0} f(x) = f(x_0).$$

The function f is said to be continuous on a set S if it is continuous at each point $x \in S$. The notation $C^n(S)$ stands for the set of all functions f such that f and its first n derivatives are continuous on S. When S is an interval, say $[a, b]$, then the notation $C^n[a, b]$ is used. As an example, consider the function $f(x) = x^{4/3}$ on the interval $[-1, 1]$. Clearly, $f(x)$ and $f'(x) = (4/3)x^{1/3}$ are continuous on $[-1, 1]$, while $f''(x) = (4/9)x^{-2/3}$ is not continuous at $x = 0$.   ▲

Definition 1.3.   Suppose that $\{x_n\}_{n=1}^{\infty}$ is an infinite sequence. Then the sequence is said to have the *limit L*, and we write

$$(4) \qquad\qquad \lim_{n \to \infty} x_n = L,$$

if given any $\epsilon > 0$, there exists a positive integer $N = N(\epsilon)$ such that $n > N$ implies that $|x_n - L| < \epsilon$.   ▲

When a sequence has a limit, we say that it is a **convergent sequence**. Another commonly used notation is "$x_n \to L$ as $n \to \infty$." Equation (4) is equivalent to

$$(5) \qquad\qquad \lim_{n \to \infty} (x_n - L) = 0.$$

Thus we can view the sequence $\{\epsilon_n\}_{n=1}^{\infty} = \{x_n - L\}_{n=1}^{\infty}$ as an **error sequence**. The following theorem relates the concepts of continuity and convergent sequence.

Theorem 1.1.   Assume that $f(x)$ is defined on the set S and $x_0 \in S$. The following statements are equivalent:

$$(6)$$
(a) The function f is continuous at x_0.

(b) If $\lim_{n \to \infty} x_n = x_0$, then $\lim_{n \to \infty} f(x_n) = f(x_0)$.

Theorem 1.2 (Intermediate Value Theorem).   Assume that $f \in C[a, b]$ and L is any number between $f(a)$ and $f(b)$. Then there exists a number c, with $c \in (a, b)$, such that $f(c) = L$.

Example 1.1.   The function $f(x) = \cos(x - 1)$ is continuous over $[0, 1]$, and the constant $L = 0.8 \in (\cos(0), \cos(1))$. The solution to $f(x) = 0.8$ over $[0, 1]$ is $c_1 = 0.356499$. Similarly, $f(x)$ is continuous over $[1, 2.5]$, and $L = 0.8 \in (\cos(2.5), \cos(1))$. The solution to $f(x) = 0.8$ over $[1, 2.5]$ is $c_2 = 1.643502$. These two cases are shown in Figure 1.2.   ■

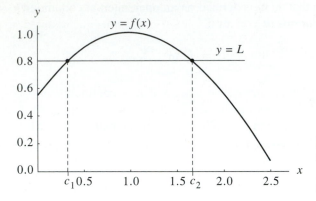

Figure 1.2 The intermediate value theorem applied to the function $f(x) = \cos(x - 1)$ over $[0, 1]$ and over the interval $[1, 2.5]$.

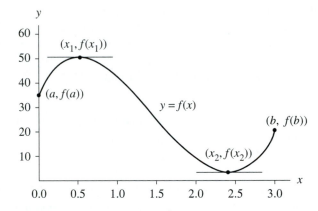

Figure 1.3 The extreme value theorem applied to the function $f(x) = 35 + 59.5x - 66.5x^2 + 15x^3$ over the interval $[0, 3]$.

Theorem 1.3 (Extreme Value Theorem for a Continuous Function). Assume that $f \in C[a, b]$. Then there exists a lower bound M_1, an upper bound M_2, and two numbers $x_1, x_2 \in [a, b]$ such that

(7) $$M_1 = f(x_1) \leq f(x) \leq f(x_2) = M_2 \quad \text{whenever } x \in [a, b].$$

We sometimes express this by writing

(8) $$M_1 = f(x_1) = \min_{a \leq x \leq b}\{f(x)\} \quad \text{and} \quad M_2 = f(x_2) = \max_{a \leq x \leq b}\{f(x)\}.$$

Differentiable Functions

Definition 1.4. Assume that $f(x)$ is defined on an open interval containing x_0. Then f is said to be *differentiable* at x_0 if

(9) $$\lim_{x \to x_0} \frac{f(x) - f(x_0)}{x - x_0}$$

exists. When this limit exists, it is denoted by $f'(x_0)$ and is called the **derivative** of f at x_0. An equivalent way to express this limit is to use the h-increment notation:

$$(10) \qquad \lim_{h \to 0} \frac{f(x_0 + h) - f(x_0)}{h} = f'(x_0).$$

A function that has a derivative at each point in a set S is said to be **differentiable** on S. Note that the number $m = f'(x_0)$ is the slope of the tangent line to the graph of the function $y = f(x)$ at the point $(x_0, f(x_0))$. ▲

Theorem 1.4.   If $f(x)$ is differentiable at $x = x_0$, then $f(x)$ is continuous at $x = x_0$.

It follows from Theorem 1.3 that if a function f is differentiable on a closed interval $[a, b]$, then its extreme values occur at the endpoints of the interval or at the critical points (solutions of $f'(x) = 0$) in the open interval (a, b).

Example 1.2.   The function $f(x) = 15x^3 - 66.5x^2 + 59.5x + 35$ is differentiable on $[0, 3]$. The solutions to $f'(x) = 45x^2 - 123x + 59.5 = 0$ are $x_1 = 0.54955$ and $x_2 = 2.40601$. The maximum and minimum values of f on $[0, 3]$ are:

$$\min\{f(0), f(3), f(x_1), f(x_2)\} = \min\{35, 20, 50.10438, 2.11850\} = 2.11850$$

and

$$\max\{f(0), f(3), f(x_1), f(x_2)\} = \max\{35, 20, 50.10438, 2.11850\} = 50.10438$$

(see Figure 1.3). ■

Theorem 1.5 (Rolle's Theorem).   Assume that $f \in C[a, b]$ and that $f'(x)$ exists for all $x \in (a, b)$. If $f(a) = f(b) = 0$, then there exists a number c, with $c \in (a, b)$, such that $f'(c) = 0$.

Theorem 1.6 (Mean Value Theorem).   Assume that $f \in C[a, b]$ and that $f'(x)$ exists for all $x \in (a, b)$. Then there exists a number c, with $c \in (a, b)$, such that

$$(11) \qquad f'(c) = \frac{f(b) - f(a)}{b - a}.$$

Geometrically, the mean value theorem says that there is at least one number $c \in (a, b)$ such that the slope of the tangent line to the graph of $y = f(x)$ at the point $(c, f(c))$ equals the slope of the secant line through the points $(a, f(a))$ and $(b, f(b))$.

Example 1.3.   The function $f(x) = \sin(x)$ is continuous on the closed interval $[0.1, 2.1]$ and differentiable on the open interval $(0.1, 2.1)$. Thus, by the mean value theorem, there is a number c such that

$$f'(c) = \frac{f(2.1) - f(0.1)}{2.1 - 0.1} = \frac{0.863209 - 0.099833}{2.1 - 0.1} = 0.381688.$$

The solution to $f'(c) = \cos(c) = 0.381688$ in the interval $(0.1, 2.1)$ is $c = 1.179174$. The graphs of $f(x)$, the secant line $y = 0.381688x + 0.099833$, and the tangent line $y = 0.381688x + 0.474215$ are shown in Figure 1.4. ■

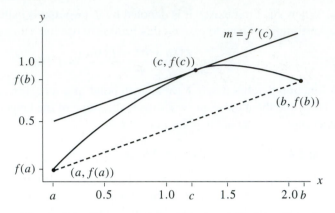

Figure 1.4 The mean value theorem applied to $f(x) = \sin(x)$ over the interval $[0.1, 2.1]$.

Theorem 1.7 (Generalized Rolle's Theorem). Assume that $f \in C[a, b]$ and that $f'(x), f''(x), \ldots, f^{(n)}(x)$ exist over (a, b) and $x_0, x_1, \ldots, x_n \in [a, b]$. If $f(x_j) = 0$ for $j = 0, 1, \ldots, n$, then there exists a number c, with $c \in (a, b)$, such that $f^{(n)}(c) = 0$.

Integrals

Theorem 1.8 (First Fundamental Theorem). If f is continuous over $[a, b]$ and F is any antiderivative of f on $[a, b]$, then

$$(12) \qquad \int_a^b f(x)\, dx = F(b) - F(a) \qquad \text{where } F'(x) = f(x).$$

Theorem 1.9 (Second Fundamental Theorem). If f is continuous over $[a, b]$ and $x \in (a, b)$, then

$$(13) \qquad \frac{d}{dx} \int_a^x f(t)\, dt = f(x).$$

Example 1.4. The function $f(x) = \cos(x)$ satisfies the hypotheses of Theorem 1.9 over the interval $[0, \pi/2]$; thus by the chain rule

$$\frac{d}{dx} \int_0^{x^2} \cos(t)\, dt = \cos(x^2)(x^2)' = 2x \cos(x^2). \qquad \blacksquare$$

Theorem 1.10 (Mean Value Theorem for Integrals). Assume that $f \in C[a, b]$. Then there exists a number c, with $c \in (a, b)$, such that

$$\frac{1}{b - a} \int_a^b f(x)\, dx = f(c).$$

The value $f(c)$ is the average value of f over the interval $[a, b]$.

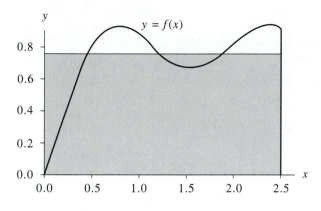

Figure 1.5 The mean value theorem for integrals applied to $f(x) = \sin(x) + \frac{1}{3}\sin(3x)$ over the interval $[0, 2.5]$.

Example 1.5. The function $f(x) = \sin(x) + \frac{1}{3}\sin(3x)$ satisfies the hypotheses of Theorem 1.10 over the interval $[0, 2.5]$. An antiderivative of $f(x)$ is $F(x) = -\cos(x) - \frac{1}{9}\cos(3x)$. The average value of the function $f(x)$ over the interval $[0, 2.5]$ is

$$\frac{1}{2.5 - 0} \int_0^{2.5} f(x)\,dx = \frac{F(2.5) - F(0)}{2.5} = \frac{0.762629 - (-1.111111)}{2.5}$$

$$= \frac{1.873740}{2.5} = 0.749496.$$

There are three solutions to the equation $f(c) = 0.749496$ over the interval $[0, 2.5]$: $c_1 = 0.440566$, $c_2 = 1.268010$, and $c_3 = 1.873583$. The area of the rectangle with base $b - a = 2.5$ and height $f(c_j) = 0.749496$ is $f(c_j)(b - a) = 1.873740$. The area of the rectangle has the same numerical value as the integral of $f(x)$ taken over the interval $[0, 2.5]$. A comparison of the area under the curve $y = f(x)$ and that of the rectangle can be seen in Figure 1.5.   ∎

Theorem 1.11 (Weighted Integral Mean Value Theorem). Assume that $f, g \in C[a, b]$ and $g(x) \geq 0$ for $x \in [a, b]$. Then there exists a number c, with $c \in (a, b)$, such that

(14)
$$\int_a^b f(x)g(x)\,dx = f(c) \int_a^b g(x)\,dx.$$

Example 1.6. The functions $f(x) = \sin(x)$ and $g(x) = x^2$ satisfy the hypotheses of Theorem 1.11 over the interval $[0, \pi/2]$. Thus there exists a number c such that

$$\sin(c) = \frac{\int_0^{\pi/2} x^2 \sin(x)\,dx}{\int_0^{\pi/2} x^2\,dx} = \frac{1.14159}{1.29193} = 0.883631$$

or $c = \sin^{-1}(0.883631) = 1.08356$.   ∎

Series

Definition 1.5.   Let $\{a_n\}_{n=1}^{\infty}$ be a sequence. Then $\sum_{n=1}^{\infty} a_n$ is an infinite series. The nth partial sum is $S_n = \sum_{k=1}^{n} a_k$. The infinite series **converges** if and only if the sequence $\{S_n\}_{n=1}^{\infty}$ converges to a limit S, that is,

$$(15) \qquad \lim_{n \to \infty} S_n = \lim_{n \to \infty} \sum_{k=1}^{n} a_k = S.$$

If a series does not converge, we say that it **diverges**.   ▲

Example 1.7.   Consider the infinite sequence $\{a_n\}_{n=1}^{\infty} = \left\{ \dfrac{1}{n(n+1)} \right\}_{n=1}^{\infty}$. Then the nth partial sum is

$$S_n = \sum_{k=1}^{n} \frac{1}{k(k+1)} = \sum_{k=1}^{n} \left(\frac{1}{k} - \frac{1}{k+1} \right) = 1 - \frac{1}{n+1}.$$

Therefore, the **sum** of the infinite series is

$$S = \lim_{n \to \infty} Sn = \lim_{n \to \infty} \left(1 - \frac{1}{n+1} \right) = 1.$$ ■

Theorem 1.12 (Taylor's Theorem).   Assume that $f \in C^{n+1}[a, b]$ and let $x_0 \in [a, b]$. Then, for every $x \in (a, b)$, there exists a number $c = c(x)$ (the value of c depends on the value of x) that lies between x_0 and x such that

$$(16) \qquad f(x) = P_n(x) + R_n(x),$$

where

$$(17) \qquad P_n(x) = \sum_{k=0}^{n} \frac{f^{(k)}(x_0)}{k!} (x - x_0)^k$$

and

$$(18) \qquad R_n(x) = \frac{f^{(n+1)}(c)}{(n+1)!} (x - x_0)^{n+1}.$$

Example 1.8.   The function $f(x) = \sin(x)$ satisfies the hypotheses of Theorem 1.12. The Taylor polynomial $P_n(x)$ of degree $n = 9$ expanded about $x_0 = 0$ is obtained by evaluating

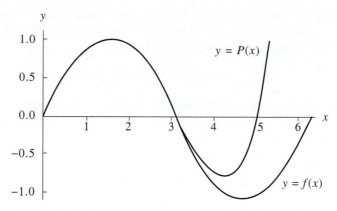

Figure 1.6 The graph of $f(x) = \sin(x)$ and the Taylor polynomial $P_9(x) = x - x^3/3! + x^5/5! - x^7/7! + x^9/9!$.

the following derivatives at $x = 0$ and substituting the numerical values into formula (17).

$$
\begin{aligned}
f(x) &= \sin(x), & f(0) &= 0, \\
f'(x) &= \cos(x), & f'(0) &= 1, \\
f''(x) &= -\sin(x), & f''(0) &= 0, \\
f^{(3)}(x) &= -\cos(x), & f^{(3)}(0) &= -1, \\
&\ \ \vdots & &\ \ \vdots \\
f^{(9)}(x) &= \cos(x), & f^{(9)}(0) &= 1,
\end{aligned}
$$

$$
P_9(x) = x - \frac{x^3}{3!} + \frac{x^5}{5!} - \frac{x^7}{7!} + \frac{x^9}{9!}.
$$

A graph of both f and P_9 over the interval $[0, 2\pi]$ is shown in Figure 1.6.   ∎

Corollary 1.1. If $P_n(x)$ is the Taylor polynomial of degree n given in Theorem 1.12, then

$$
(19) \qquad P_n^{(k)}(x_0) = f^{(k)}(x_0) \quad \text{for } k = 0, 1, \ldots, n.
$$

Evaluation of a Polynomial

Let the polynomial $P(x)$ of degree n have the form

$$
(20) \qquad P(x) = a_n x^n + a_{n-1} x^{n-1} + \cdots + a_2 x^2 + a_1 x + a_0.
$$

Horner's method or **synthetic division** is a technique for evaluating polynomials. It can be thought of as nested multiplication. For example, a fifth-degree polynomial can be written in the nested multiplication form

$$P_5(x) = ((((a_5x + a_4)x + a_3)x + a_2)x + a_1)x + a_0.$$

Theorem 1.13 (Horner's Method for Polynomial Evaluation). Assume that $P(x)$ is the polynomial given in equation (20) and $x = c$ is a number for which $P(c)$ is to be evaluated.

Set $b_n = a_n$ and compute

$$(21) \qquad b_k = a_k + cb_{k+1} \qquad \text{for } k = n - 1, \ n - 2, \ \ldots, \ 1, \ 0;$$

then $b_0 = P(c)$. Moreover, if

$$(22) \qquad Q_0(x) = b_n x^{n-1} + b_{n-1}x^{n-2} + \cdots + b_3 x^2 + b_2 x + b_1,$$

then

$$(23) \qquad P(x) = (x - c)Q_0(x) + R_0,$$

where $Q_0(x)$ is the quotient polynomial of degree $n - 1$ and $R_0 = b_0 = P(c)$ is the remainder.

Proof. Substituting the right side of equation (22) for $Q_0(x)$ and b_0 for R_0 in equation (23) yields

$$
\begin{aligned}
P(x) &= (x - c)(b_n x^{n-1} + b_{n-1}x^{n-2} + \cdots + b_3 x^2 + b_2 x + b_1) + b_0 \\
(24) \qquad &= b_n x^n + (b_{n-1} - cb_n)x^{n-1} + \cdots + (b_2 - cb_3)x^2 \\
&\quad + (b_1 - cb_2)x + (b_0 - cb_1).
\end{aligned}
$$

The numbers b_k are determined by comparing the coefficients of x^k in equations (20) and (24), as shown in Table 1.1.

The value $P(c) = b_0$ is easily obtained by substituting $x = c$ into equation (22) and using the fact that $R_0 = b_0$:

$$(25) \qquad P(c) = (c - c)Q_0(c) + R_0 = b_0. \qquad \bullet$$

The recursive formula for b_k given in (21) is easy to implement with a computer. A simple algorithm is

```
b(n) = a(n);
for k = n - 1: -1: 0
    b(k) = a(k) + c * b(k + 1);
end
```

Table 1.1   Coefficients b_k for Horner's Method

x^k	Comparing (20) and (24)	Solving for b_k
x^n	$a_n = b_n$	$b_n = a_n$
x^{n-1}	$a_{n-1} = b_{n-1} - cb_n$	$b_{n-1} = a_{n-1} + cb_n$
$\vdots$	$\vdots$	$\vdots$
x^k	$a_k = b_k - cb_{k+1}$	$b_k = a_k + cb_{k+1}$
$\vdots$	$\vdots$	$\vdots$
x^0	$a_0 = b_0 - cb_1$	$b_0 = a_0 + cb_1$

Table 1.2   Horner's Table for the Synthetic Division Process

Input	a_n	a_{n-1}	a_{n-2}	$\cdots$	a_k	$\cdots$	a_2	a_1	a_0
c		xb_n	xb_{n-1}	$\cdots$	xb_{k+1}	$\cdots$	xb_3	xb_2	xb_1
	b_n	b_{n-1}	b_{n-2}	$\cdots$	b_k	$\cdots$	b_2	b_1	$b_0 = P(c)$
									Output

When Horner's method is performed by hand, it is easier to write the coefficients of $P(x)$ on a line and perform the calculation $b_k = a_k + cb_{k+1}$ below a_k in a column. The format for this procedure is illustrated in Table 1.2.

Example 1.9.   Use synthetic division (Horner's method) to find $P(3)$ for the polynomial

$$P(x) = x^5 - 6x^4 + 8x^3 + 8x^2 + 4x - 40.$$

	a_5	a_4	a_3	a_2	a_1	a_0
Input	1	-6	8	8	4	-40
$c = 3$		3	-9	-3	15	57
	1	-3	-1	5	19	$17 = P(3) = b_0$
	b_5	b_4	b_3	b_2	b_1	Output

Therefore, $P(3) = 17$.   ■

Exercises for Review of Calculus

1. (a) Find $L = \lim_{n \to \infty}(4n+1)/(2n+1)$. Then determine $\{\epsilon_n\} = \{L - x_n\}$ and find $\lim_{n \to \infty} \epsilon_n$.

(b) Find $L = \lim_{n \to \infty}(2n^2+6n-1)/(4n^2+2n+1)$. Then determine $\{\epsilon_n\} = \{L - x_n\}$ and find $\lim_{n \to \infty} \epsilon_n$.

2. Let $\{x_n\}_{n=1}^{\infty}$ be a sequence such that $\lim_{n \to \infty} x_n = 2$.

(a) Find $\lim_{n \to \infty} \sin(x_n)$.   **(b)** Find $\lim_{n \to \infty} \ln(x_n^2)$.

3. Find the number(s) c referred to in the intermediate value theorem for each function over the interval indicated and for the given value of L.

(a) $f(x) = -x^2 + 2x + 3$ over $[-1, 0]$ using $L = 2$

(b) $f(x) = \sqrt{x^2 - 5x - 2}$ over $[6, 8]$ using $L = 3$

4. Find the upper and lower bounds referred to in the extreme value theorem for each function over the interval indicated.

(a) $f(x) = x^2 - 3x + 1$ over $[-1, 2]$

(b) $f(x) = \cos^2(x) - \sin(x)$ over $[0, 2\pi]$

5. Find the number(s) c referred to in Rolle's theorem for each function over the interval indicated.

(a) $f(x) = x^4 - 4x^2$ over $[-2, 2]$

(b) $f(x) = \sin(x) + \sin(2x)$ over $[0, 2\pi]$

6. Find the number(s) c referred to in the mean value theorem for each function over the interval indicated.

(a) $f(x) = \sqrt{x}$ over $[0, 4]$

(b) $f(x) = \dfrac{x^2}{x+1}$ over $[0, 1]$

7. Apply the generalized Rolle's theorem to $f(x) = x(x-1)(x-3)$ over $[0, 3]$.

8. Apply the first fundamental theorem of calculus to each function over the interval indicated.

(a) $f(x) = xe^x$ over $[0, 2]$

(b) $f(x) = \dfrac{3x}{x^2+1}$ over $[-1, 1]$

9. Apply the second fundamental theorem of calculus to each function.

(a) $\dfrac{d}{dx} \int_0^x t^2 \cos(t)\, dt$ **(b)** $\dfrac{d}{dx} \int_1^{x^3} e^{t^2}\, dt$

10. Find the number(s) c referred to in the mean value theorem for integrals for each function, over the interval indicated.

(a) $f(x) = 6x^2$ over $[-3, 4]$

(b) $f(x) = x \cos(x)$ over $[0, 3\pi/2]$

11. Find the sum of each sequence or series.

(a) $\left\{\dfrac{1}{2^n}\right\}_{n=0}^{\infty}$

(b) $\left\{\dfrac{2}{3^n}\right\}_{n=1}^{\infty}$

(c) $\displaystyle\sum_{n=1}^{\infty}\dfrac{3}{n(n+1)}$

(d) $\displaystyle\sum_{k=1}^{\infty}\dfrac{1}{4k^2-1}$

12. Find the Taylor polynomial of degree $n = 4$ for each function expanded about the given value of x_0.

    (a) $f(x) = \sqrt{x}$, $x_0 = 1$

    (b) $f(x) = x^5 + 4x^2 + 3x + 1$, $x_0 = 0$

    (c) $f(x) = \cos(x)$, $x_0 = 0$

13. Given that $f(x) = \sin(x)$ and $P(x) = x - x^3/3! + x^5/5! - x^7/7! + x^9/9!$, show that $P^{(k)}(0) = f^{(k)}(0)$ for $k = 1, 2, \ldots, 9$.

14. Use synthetic division (Horner's method) to find $P(c)$.

    (a) $P(x) = x^4 + x^3 - 13x^2 - x - 12$, $c = 3$

    (b) $P(x) = 2x^7 + x^6 + x^5 - 2x^4 - x + 23$, $c = -1$

15. Find the average area of all circles centered at the origin with radii between 1 and 3.

16. Assume that a polynomial, $P(x)$, has n real roots in the interval $[a, b]$. Show that $P^{(n-1)}(x)$ has at least one real root in the interval $[a, b]$.

17. Assume that f, f', and f'' are defined on the interval $[a, b]$; $f(a) = f(b) = 0$; and $f(c) > 0$ for $c \in (a, b)$. Show that there is a number $d \in (a, b)$ such that $f''(d) < 0$.

1.2   Binary Numbers

Human beings do arithmetic using the decimal (base 10) number system. Most computers do arithmetic using the binary (base 2) number system. It may seem otherwise, since communication with the computer (input/output) is in base 10 numbers. This transparency does not mean that the computer uses base 10. In fact, it converts inputs to base 2 (or perhaps base 16), then performs base 2 arithmetic, and finally, translates the answer into base 10 before it displays a result. Some experimentation is required to verify this. One computer with nine decimal digits of accuracy gave the answer

(1)
$$\sum_{k=1}^{100,000} 0.1 = 9999.99447.$$

Here the intent was to add the number $\frac{1}{10}$ repeatedly 100,000 times. The mathematical answer is exactly 10,000. One goal is to understand the reason for the computer's apparently flawed calculation. At the end of this section it will be shown how something is lost when the computer translates the decimal fraction $\frac{1}{10}$ into a binary number.

Base 2 Numbers

Base 10 numbers are used for most mathematical purposes. For illustration, the number 1563 is expressible in *expanded form* as

$$1563 = (1 \times 10^3) + (5 \times 10^2) + (6 \times 10^1) + (3 \times 10^0).$$

In general, let N denote a positive integer; then the digits $a_0, a_1, \ldots, a_k$ exist so that N has the base 10 expansion

$$N = (a_k \times 10^k) + (a_{k-1} \times 10^{k-1}) + \cdots + (a_1 \times 10^1) + (a_0 \times 10^0),$$

where the digits a_k are chosen from $\{0, 1, \ldots, 8, 9\}$. Thus N is expressed in decimal notation as

(2) $$N = a_k a_{k-1} \cdots a_2 a_1 a_{0\text{ten}} \qquad \text{(decimal)}.$$

If it is understood that 10 is the base, then (2) is written as

$$N = a_k a_{k-1} \cdots a_2 a_1 a_0.$$

For example, we understand that $1563 = 1563_{\text{ten}}$.

Using powers of 2, the number 1563 can be written

(3)
$$\begin{aligned}
1563 = &(1 \times 2^{10}) + (1 \times 2^9) + (0 \times 2^8) + (0 \times 2^7) + (0 \times 2^6) \\
&+ (0 \times 2^5) + (1 \times 2^4) + (1 \times 2^3) + (0 \times 2^2) + (1 \times 2^1) \\
&+ (1 \times 2^0).
\end{aligned}$$

This can be verified by performing the calculation

$$1563 = 1024 + 512 + 16 + 8 + 2 + 1.$$

In general, let N denote a positive integer; the digits $b_0, b_1, \ldots, b_J$ exist so that N has the base 2 expansion

(4) $$N = (b_J \times 2^J) + (b_{J-1} \times 2^{J-1}) + \cdots + (b_1 \times 2^1) + (b_0 \times 2^0),$$

where each digit b_j is either a 0 or 1. Thus N is expressed in binary notation as

(5) $$N = b_J b_{J-1} \cdots b_2 b_1 b_{0\text{two}} \qquad \text{(binary)}.$$

Using the notation (5) and the result in (3) yields

$$1563 = 11000011011_{\text{two}}.$$

Remarks. The word "two" will always be used as a subscript at the end of a binary number. This will enable the reader to distinguish binary numbers from the ordinary base 10 usage. Thus 111 means one hundred eleven, whereas 111_{two} stands for seven.

It is usually the case that the binary representation for N will require more digits than the decimal representation. This is due to the fact that powers of 2 grow much more slowly than do powers of 10.

An efficient algorithm for finding the base 2 representation of the integer N can be derived from equation (4). Dividing both sides of (4) by 2 yields

(6)
$$\frac{N}{2} = (b_J \times 2^{J-1}) + (b_{J-1} \times 2^{J-2}) + \cdots + (b_1 \times 2^0) + \frac{b_0}{2}.$$

Hence the remainder, upon dividing N by 2, is the digit b_0. Now determine b_1. If (6) is written as $N/2 = Q_0 + b_0/2$, then

(7)
$$Q_0 = (b_J \times 2^{J-1}) + (b_{J-1} \times 2^{J-2}) + \cdots + (b_2 \times 2^1) + (b_1 \times 2^0).$$

Now divide both sides of (7) by 2 to get

$$\frac{Q_0}{2} = (b_J \times 2^{J-2}) + (b_{J-1} \times 2^{J-3}) + \cdots + (b_2 \times 2^0) + \frac{b_1}{2}.$$

Hence the remainder, upon dividing Q_0 by 2, is the digit b_1. This process is continued and generates sequences $\{Q_k\}$ and $\{b_k\}$ of quotients and remainders, respectively. The process is terminated when an integer J is found such that $Q_J = 0$. The sequences obey the following formulas:

$$N = 2Q_0 + b_0$$
$$Q_0 = 2Q_1 + b_1$$

(8)
$$\vdots$$

$$Q_{J-2} = 2Q_{J-1} + b_{J-1}$$
$$Q_{J-1} = 2Q_J + b_J \qquad (Q_J = 0).$$

Example 1.10. Show how to obtain $1563 = 11000011011_{\text{two}}$.

Start with $N = 1563$ and construct the quotients and remainders according to the equations in (8):

$$
\begin{aligned}
1563 &= 2 \times 781 + 1, & b_0 &= 1 \\
781 &= 2 \times 390 + 1, & b_1 &= 1 \\
390 &= 2 \times 195 + 0, & b_2 &= 0 \\
195 &= 2 \times 97 + 1, & b_3 &= 1 \\
97 &= 2 \times 48 + 1, & b_4 &= 1 \\
48 &= 2 \times 24 + 0, & b_5 &= 0 \\
24 &= 2 \times 12 + 0, & b_6 &= 0 \\
12 &= 2 \times 6 + 0, & b_7 &= 0 \\
6 &= 2 \times 3 + 0, & b_8 &= 0 \\
3 &= 2 \times 1 + 1, & b_9 &= 1 \\
1 &= 2 \times 0 + 1, & b_{10} &= 1.
\end{aligned}
$$

Thus the binary representation for 1563 is

$$1563 = b_{10}b_9b_8 \cdots b_2b_1b_{0\text{two}} = 11000011011_{\text{two}}. \qquad \blacksquare$$

Sequences and Series

When rational numbers are expressed in decimal form, it is often the case that infinitely many digits are required. A familiar example is

(9)
$$\frac{1}{3} = 0.\overline{3}.$$

Here the symbol $\overline{3}$ means that the digit 3 is repeated forever to form an infinite repeating decimal. It is understood that 10 is the base in (9). Moreover, it is the mathematical intent that (9) is the shorthand notation for the infinite series

(10)
$$S = (3 \times 10^{-1}) + (3 \times 10^{-2}) + \cdots + (3 \times 10^{-n}) + \cdots$$
$$= \sum_{k=1}^{\infty} 3(10)^{-k} = \frac{1}{3}.$$

If only a finite number of digits is displayed, then an approximation to $1/3$ is obtained. For example, $1/3 \approx 0.333 = 333/1000$. The error in this approximation is $1/3000$. Using (10), the reader can verify that $1/3 = 0.333 + 1/3000$.

It is important to understand the expansion in (10). A naive approach is to multiply both sides by 10 and then subtract.

$$10S = 3 + (3 \times 10^{-1}) + (3 \times 10^{-2}) + \cdots + (3 \times 10^{-n}) + \cdots$$
$$-S = -(3 \times 10^{-1}) - (3 \times 10^{-2}) - \cdots - (3 \times 10^{-n}) - \cdots$$
$$\overline{9S = 3 + (0 \times 10^{-1}) + (0 \times 10^{-2}) + \cdots + (0 \times 10^{-n}) + \cdots}$$

Therefore, $S = 3/9 = 1/3$. The theorems necessary to justify taking the difference between two infinite series can be found in most calculus books. A review of a few of the concepts follows, and the reader may want to refer to a standard text on calculus to fill in all the details.

Definition 1.6.   The infinite series

(11)
$$\sum_{n=0}^{\infty} cr^n = c + cr + cr^2 + \cdots + cr^n + \cdots,$$

where $c \neq 0$ and $r \neq 0$, is called a ***geometric series*** with ratio r. $\blacktriangle$

Theorem 1.14 (Geometric Series).   The geometric series has the following properties:

(12) $$\text{If } |r| < 1, \text{ then } \sum_{n=0}^{\infty} cr^n = \frac{c}{1-r}.$$

(13)   If $|r| > 1$, then the series diverges.

Proof.   The summation formula for a finite geometric series is

(14) $$S_n = c + cr + cr^2 + \cdots + cr^n = \frac{c(1 - r^{n+1})}{1 - r} \quad \text{for } r \neq 1.$$

To establish (12), observe that

(15) $$|r| < 1 \quad \text{implies that} \quad \lim_{n \to \infty} r^{n+1} = 0.$$

Taking the limit as $n \to \infty$, use (14) and (15) to get

$$\lim_{n \to \infty} S_n = \frac{c}{1-r}\left(1 - \lim_{n \to \infty} r^{n+1}\right) = \frac{c}{1-r}.$$

By equation (15) of Section 1.1, the limit above establishes (12).

When $|r| \geq 1$, the sequence $\{r^{n+1}\}$ does not converge. Hence the sequence $\{S_n\}$ in (14) does not tend to a limit. Therefore, (13) is established.   ●

Equation (12) in Theorem 1.14 represents an efficient way to convert an infinite repeating decimal into a fraction.

Example 1.11.

$$0.\overline{3} = \sum_{k=1}^{\infty} 3(10)^{-k} = -3 + \sum_{k=0}^{\infty} 3(10)^{-k}$$

$$= -3 + \frac{3}{1 - \frac{1}{10}} = -3 + \frac{10}{3} = \frac{1}{3}. \qquad ■$$

Binary Fractions

Binary (base 2) fractions can be expressed as sums involving negative powers of 2. If R is a real number that lies in the range $0 < R < 1$, there exist digits $d_1, d_2, \ldots, d_n, \ldots$ so that

(16) $$R = (d_1 \times 2^{-1}) + (d_2 \times 2^{-2}) + \cdots + (d_n \times 2^{-n}) + \cdots,$$

where $d_j \in \{0, 1\}$. We usually express the quantity on the right side of (16) in the binary fraction notation

(17) $$R = 0.d_1 d_2 \cdots d_n \cdots_{\text{two}}.$$

There are many real numbers whose binary representation requires infinitely many digits. The fraction 7/10 can be expressed as 0.7 in base 10, yet its base 2 representation requires infinitely many digits:

(18)
$$\frac{7}{10} = 0.1\overline{0110}_{\text{two}}.$$

The binary fraction in (18) is a repeating fraction where the group of four digits 0110 is repeated forever.

An efficient algorithm for finding base 2 representations can now be developed. If both sides of (16) are multiplied by 2, the result is

(19)
$$2R = d_1 + ((d_2 \times 2^{-1}) + \cdots + (d_n \times 2^{-n+1}) + \cdots).$$

The quantity in parentheses on the right side of (19) is a positive number and is less than 1. Therefore, d_1 is the integer part of $2R$, denoted $d_1 = \text{int}(2R)$. To continue the process, take the fractional part of (19) and write

(20)
$$F_1 = \text{frac}(2R) = (d_2 \times 2^{-1}) + \cdots + (d_n \times 2^{-n+1}) + \cdots,$$

where $\text{frac}(2R)$ is the fractional part of the real number $2R$. Multiplication of both sides of (20) by 2 results in

(21)
$$2F_1 = d_2 + ((d_3 \times 2^{-1}) + \cdots + (d_n \times 2^{-n+2}) + \cdots).$$

Now take the integer part of (21) and obtain $d_2 = \text{int}(2F_1)$.

The process is continued, possibly ad infinitum (if R has an infinite nonrepeating base 2 representation), and two sequences $\{d_k\}$ and $\{F_k\}$ are recursively generated:

(22)
$$d_k = \text{int}(2F_{k-1}),$$
$$F_k = \text{frac}(2F_{k-1}),$$

where $d_1 = \text{int}(2R)$ and $F_1 = \text{frac}(2R)$. The binary decimal representation of R is then given by the convergent geometric series

$$R = \sum_{j=1}^{\infty} d_j (2)^{-j}.$$

Example 1.12.   The binary decimal representation of 7/10 given in (18) was found using the formulas in (22). Let $R = 7/10 = 0.7$; then

$2R = 1.4$	$d_1 = \text{int}(1.4) = 1$	$F_1 = \text{frac}(1.4) = 0.4$
$2F_1 = 0.8$	$d_2 = \text{int}(0.8) = 0$	$F_2 = \text{frac}(0.8) = 0.8$
$2F_2 = 1.6$	$d_3 = \text{int}(1.6) = 1$	$F_3 = \text{frac}(1.6) = 0.6$
$2F_3 = 1.2$	$d_4 = \text{int}(1.2) = 1$	$F_4 = \text{frac}(1.2) = 0.2$
$2F_4 = 0.4$	$d_5 = \text{int}(0.4) = 0$	$F_5 = \text{frac}(0.4) = 0.4$
$2F_5 = 0.8$	$d_6 = \text{int}(0.8) = 0$	$F_6 = \text{frac}(0.8) = 0.8$
$2F_6 = 1.6$	$d_7 = \text{int}(1.6) = 1$	$F_7 = \text{frac}(1.6) = 0.6$

Note that $2F_2 = 1.6 = 2F_6$. The patterns $d_k = d_{k+4}$ and $F_k = F_{k+4}$ will occur for $k = 2$, $3, 4, \ldots$. Thus $7/10 = 0.1\overline{0110}_{\text{two}}$. ∎

Geometric series can be used to find the base 10 rational number that a binary number represents.

Example 1.13. Find the base 10 rational number that the binary number $0.\overline{01}_{\text{two}}$ represents. In expanded form,

$$0.\overline{01}_{\text{two}} = (0 \times 2^{-1}) + (1 \times 2^{-2}) + (0 \times 2^{-3}) + (1 \times 2^{-4}) + \cdots$$

$$= \sum_{k=1}^{\infty} (2^{-2})^k = -1 + \sum_{k=0}^{\infty} (2^{-2})^k$$

$$= -1 + \frac{1}{1 - \frac{1}{4}} = -1 + \frac{4}{3} = \frac{1}{3}.$$ ∎

Binary Shifting

If a rational number that is equivalent to an infinite repeating binary expansion is to be found, then a shift in the digits can be helpful. For example, let S be given by

$$(23) \qquad\qquad S = 0.00000\overline{11000}_{\text{two}}.$$

Multiplying both sides of (23) by 2^5 will shift the binary point five places to the right, and $32S$ has the form

$$(24) \qquad\qquad 32S = 0.\overline{11000}_{\text{two}}.$$

Similarly, multiplying both sides of (23) by 2^{10} will shift the binary point 10 places to the right and $1024S$ has the form

$$(25) \qquad\qquad 1024S = 11000.\overline{11000}_{\text{two}}.$$

The result of naively taking the differences between the left- and right-hand sides of (24) and (25) is $992S = 11000_{\text{two}}$ or $992S = 24$, since $11000_{\text{two}} = 24$. Therefore, $S = 8/33$.

Scientific Notation

A standard way to present a real number, called *scientific notation*, is obtained by shifting the decimal point and supplying an appropriate power of 10. For example,

$$0.0000747 = 7.47 \times 10^{-5},$$
$$31.4159265 = 3.14159265 \times 10,$$
$$9{,}700{,}000{,}000 = 9.7 \times 10^9.$$

In chemistry, an important constant is Avogadro's number, which is 6.02252×10^{23}. It is the number of atoms in the gram atomic weight of an element. In computer science, $1\text{K} = 1.024 \times 10^3$.

Table 1.3   Decimal Equivalents for a Set of Binary Numbers with 4-Bit Mantissa and Exponent of $n = -3, -2, \ldots, 3, 4$

Mantissa	Exponent							
	$n = -3$	$n = -2$	$n = -1$	$n = 0$	$n = 1$	$n = 2$	$n = 3$	$n = 4$
0.1000_{two}	0.0625	0.125	0.25	0.5	1	2	4	8
0.1001_{two}	0.0703125	0.140625	0.28125	0.5625	1.125	2.25	4.5	9
0.1010_{two}	0.078125	0.15625	0.3125	0.625	1.25	2.5	5	10
0.1011_{two}	0.0859375	0.171875	0.34375	0.6875	1.375	2.75	5.5	11
0.1100_{two}	0.09375	0.1875	0.375	0.75	1.5	3	6	12
0.1101_{two}	0.1015625	0.203125	0.40625	0.8125	1.625	3.25	6.5	13
0.1110_{two}	0.109375	0.21875	0.4375	0.875	1.75	3.5	7	14
0.1111_{two}	0.1171875	0.234375	0.46875	0.9375	1.875	3.75	7.5	15

Machine Numbers

Computers use a normalized floating-point binary representation for real numbers. This means that the mathematical quantity x is not actually stored in the computer. Instead, the computer stores a binary approximation to x:

$$(26) \qquad\qquad x \approx \pm q \times 2^n.$$

The number q is the **mantissa** and it is a finite binary expression satisfying the inequality $1/2 \le q < 1$. The integer n is called the **exponent**.

In a computer, only a small subset of the real number system is used. Typically, this subset contains only a portion of the binary numbers suggested by (26). The number of binary digits is restricted in both the numbers q and n. For example, consider the set of all positive real numbers of the form

$$(27) \qquad\qquad 0.d_1 d_2 d_3 d_{4two} \times 2^n,$$

where $d_1 = 1$ and $d_2, d_3,$ and d_4 are either 0 or 1, and $n \in \{-3, -2, -1, 0, 1, 2, 3, 4\}$. There are eight choices for the mantissa and eight choices for the exponent in (27), and this produces a set of 64 numbers:

$$(28) \quad \{0.1000_{two} \times 2^{-3}, 0.1001_{two} \times 2^{-3}, \ldots, 0.1110_{two} \times 2^4, 0.1111_{two} \times 2^4\}.$$

The decimal forms of these 64 numbers are given in Table 1.3. It is important to learn that when the mantissa and exponent in (27) are restricted, the computer has a limited number of values it chooses from to store as an approximation to the real number x.

What would happen if a computer had only a 4-bit mantissa and was restricted to perform the computation $\left(\frac{1}{10} + \frac{1}{5}\right) + \frac{1}{6}$? Assume that the computer rounds all real numbers to the closest binary number in Table 1.3. At each step the reader can look at the table to see that the best approximation is being used.

$$\begin{array}{c} \frac{1}{10} \approx 0.1101_{\text{two}} \times 2^{-3} = 0.01101_{\text{two}} \times 2^{-2} \\ (29) \qquad \frac{1}{5} \approx 0.1101_{\text{two}} \times 2^{-2} = \underline{0.1101_{\text{two}} \;\; \times 2^{-2}} \\ \frac{3}{10} \qquad\qquad\qquad\qquad 1.00111_{\text{two}} \times 2^{-2}. \end{array}$$

The computer must decide how to store the number $1.00111_{\text{two}} \times 2^{-2}$. Assume that it is rounded to $0.1010_{\text{two}} \times 2^{-1}$. The next step is

$$\begin{array}{c} \frac{3}{10} \approx 0.1010_{\text{two}} \times 2^{-1} = 0.1010_{\text{two}} \;\; \times 2^{-1} \\ (30) \qquad \frac{1}{6} \approx 0.1011_{\text{two}} \times 2^{-2} = \underline{0.01011_{\text{two}} \times 2^{-1}} \\ \frac{7}{15} \qquad\qquad\qquad\qquad 0.11111_{\text{two}} \times 2^{-1}. \end{array}$$

The computer must decide how to store the number $0.11111_{\text{two}} \times 2^{-1}$. Since rounding is assumed to take place, it stores $0.10000_{\text{two}} \times 2^0$. Therefore, the computer's solution to the addition problem is

$$(31) \qquad\qquad \frac{7}{15} \approx 0.10000_{\text{two}} \times 2^0.$$

The error in the computer's calculation is

$$(32) \qquad \frac{7}{15} - 0.10000_{\text{two}} \approx 0.466667 - 0.500000 \approx 0.033333.$$

Expressed as a percentage of $7/15$, this amounts to 7.14%.

Computer Accuracy

To store numbers accurately, computers must have floating-point binary numbers with at least 24 binary bits used for the mantissa; this translates to about seven decimal places. If a 32-bit mantissa is used, numbers with nine decimal places can be stored. Now, again, consider the difficulty encountered in (1) at the beginning of the section, when a computer added $1/10$ repeatedly.

Suppose that the mantissa q in (26) contains 32 binary bits. The condition $1/2 \leq q$ implies that the first digit is $d_1 = 1$. Hence q has the form

$$(33) \qquad\qquad q = 0.1d_2d_3 \cdots d_{31}d_{32\text{two}}.$$

When fractions are represented in binary form, it is often the case that infinitely many digits are required. An example is

$$(34) \qquad\qquad \frac{1}{10} = 0.0\overline{0011}_{\text{two}}.$$

When the 32-bit mantissa is used, truncation occurs and the computer uses the internal approximation

$$(35) \qquad \frac{1}{10} \approx 0.11001100110011001100110011001100_{two} \times 2^{-3}.$$

The error in the approximation in (35), the difference between (34) and (35) is

$$(36) \qquad 0.\overline{1100}_{two} \times 2^{-35} \approx 2.328306437 \times 10^{-11}.$$

Because of (36), the computer must be in error when it sums the 100,000 addends of $1/10$ in (1). The error must be greater than $(100,000)(2.328306437 \times 10^{-11}) = 2.328306437 \times 10^{-6}$. Indeed, there is a much larger error. Occasionally, the partial sum could be rounded up or down. Also, as the sum grows, the latter addends of $1/10$ are small compared to the current size of the sum, and their contribution is truncated more severely. The compounding effect of these errors actually produced the error $10,000 - 9999.99447 = 5.53 \times 10^{-3}$.

Computer Floating-Point Numbers

Computers have both an ***integer mode*** and a ***floating-point mode*** for representing numbers. The integer mode is used for performing calculations that are known to be integer valued and has limited usage for numerical analysis. Floating-point numbers are used for scientific and engineering applications. It must be understood that any computer implementation of equation (26) places restrictions on the number of digits used in the mantissa q, and that the range of possible exponents n must be limited.

Computers that use 32 bits to represent single-precision real numbers use 8 bits for the exponent and 24 bits for the mantissa. They can represent real numbers with magnitudes in the range

$$2.938736E - 39 \quad \text{to} \quad 1.701412E + 38$$

(i.e., 2^{-128} to 2^{127}) with six decimal digits of numerical precision (e.g., $2^{-23} = 1.2 \times 10^{-7}$).

Computers that use 48 bits to represent single-precision real numbers might use 8 bits for the exponent and 40 bits for the mantissa. They can represent real numbers in the range

$$2.9387358771E - 39 \quad \text{to} \quad 1.7014118346E + 38$$

(i.e., 2^{-128} to 2^{127}) with 11 decimal digits of numerical precision (e.g., $2^{-39} = 1.8 \times 10^{-12}$).

If the computer has 64-bit double-precision real numbers, it might use 11 bits for the exponent and 53 bits for the mantissa. They can represent real numbers in the range

$$5.562684646268003E - 309 \quad \text{to} \quad 8.988465674311580E + 307$$

(i.e., 2^{-1024} to 2^{1023}) with about 16 decimal digits of numerical precision (e.g., $2^{-52} = 2.2 \times 10^{-16}$).

Exercises for Binary Numbers

1. Use a computer to accumulate the following sums. The intent is to have the computer do repeated subtractions. Do not use the multiplication shortcut.

   (a) $10,000 - \sum_{k=1}^{100,000} 0.1$

   (b) $10,000 - \sum_{k=1}^{80,000} 0.125$

2. Use equations (4) and (5) to convert the following binary numbers to decimal (base 10) form.

   (a) 10101_{two}

   (b) 111000_{two}

   (c) 11111110_{two}

   (d) 1000000111_{two}

3. Use equations (16) and (17) to convert the following binary fractions to decimal (base 10) form.

   (a) 0.11011_{two}

   (b) 0.10101_{two}

   (c) 0.1010101_{two}

   (d) 0.110110110_{two}

4. Convert the following binary numbers to decimal (base 10) form.

   (a) 1.0110101_{two}

   (b) 11.0010010001_{two}

5. The numbers in Exercise 4 are approximately $\sqrt{2}$ and π. Find the error in these approximations, that is, find

   (a) $\sqrt{2} - 1.0110101_{two}$ (Use $\sqrt{2} = 1.41421356237309\ldots$)

   (b) $\pi - 11.0010010001_{two}$ (Use $\pi = 3.14159265358979\ldots$)

6. Follow Example 1.10 and convert the following to binary numbers.

   (a)   23   **(b)**   87   **(c)**   378   **(d)**   2388

7. Follow Example 1.12 and convert the following to a binary fraction of the form $0.d_1 d_2 \cdots d_{n\,two}$.

   (a)   7/16   **(b)**   13/16   **(c)**   23/32   **(d)**   75/128

8. Follow Example 1.12 and convert the following to an infinite repeating binary fraction.

   (a)   1/10   **(b)**   1/3   **(c)**   1/7

9. For the following seven-digit binary approximations, find the error in the approximation $R - 0.d_1 d_2 d_3 d_4 d_5 d_6 d_{7\,two}$.

   (a) $1/10 \approx 0.0001100_{two}$

   (b) $1/7 \approx 0.0010010_{two}$

10. Show that the binary expansion $1/7 = 0.\overline{001}_{two}$ is equivalent to $\frac{1}{7} = \frac{1}{8} + \frac{1}{64} + \frac{1}{512} + \cdots$. Use Theorem 1.14 to establish this expansion.

11. Show that the binary expansion $1/5 = 0.\overline{0011}_{two}$ is equivalent to $\frac{1}{5} = \frac{3}{16} + \frac{3}{256} + \frac{3}{4096} + \cdots$. Use Theorem 1.14 to establish this expansion.

12. Prove that any number 2^{-N}, where N is a positive integer, can be represented as a decimal number that has N digits, that is, $2^{-N} = 0.d_1 d_2 d_3 \cdots d_N$. *Hint.* $1/2 = 0.5$, $1/4 = 0.25, \ldots$.

13. Use Table 1.3 to determine what happens when a computer with a 4-bit mantissa performs the following calculations.

    (a) $\left(\frac{1}{3} + \frac{1}{5}\right) + \frac{1}{6}$ (b) $\left(\frac{1}{10} + \frac{1}{3}\right) + \frac{1}{5}$

    (c) $\left(\frac{3}{17} + \frac{1}{9}\right) + \frac{1}{7}$ (d) $\left(\frac{7}{10} + \frac{1}{9}\right) + \frac{1}{7}$

14. Show that when 2 is replaced by 3 in all the formulas in (8), the result is a method for finding the base 3 expansion of a positive integer. Express the following integers in base 3.

    (a) 10   (b) 23   (c) 421   (d) 1784

15. Show that when 2 is replaced by 3 in (22), the result is a method for finding the base 3 expansion of a positive number R that lies in the interval $0 < R < 1$. Express the following numbers in base 3.

    (a) 1/3   (b) 1/2   (c) 1/10   (d) 11/27

16. Show that when 2 is replaced by 5 in all the formulas in (8), the result is a method for finding the base 5 expansion of a positive integer. Express the following integers in base 5.

    (a) 10   (b) 35   (c) 721   (d) 734

17. Show that when 2 is replaced by 5 in (22), the result is a method for finding the base 5 expansion of a positive number R that lies in the interval $0 < R < 1$. Express the following numbers in base 5.

    (a) 1/3   (b) 1/2   (c) 1/10   (d) 154/625

1.3 Error Analysis

In the practice of numerical analysis it is important to be aware that computed solutions are not exact mathematical solutions. The precision of a numerical solution can be diminished in several subtle ways. Understanding these difficulties can often guide the practitioner in the proper implementation and/or development of numerical algorithms.

Definition 1.7. Suppose that $\widehat{p}$ is an approximation to p. The ***absolute error*** is $E_p = |p - \widehat{p}|$, and the ***relative error*** is $R_p = |p - \widehat{p}|/|p|$, provided that $p \neq 0$.   ▲

The absolute error is simply the difference between the true value and the approximate value, whereas the relative error expresses the error as a percentage of the true value.

Example 1.14. Find the error and relative error in the following three cases. Let $x = 3.141592$ and $\widehat{x} = 3.14$; then the error is

(1a) $$E_x = |x - \widehat{x}| = |3.141592 - 3.14| = 0.001592,$$

and the relative error is

$$R_x = \frac{|x - \hat{x}|}{|x|} = \frac{0.001592}{3.141592} = 0.00507.$$

Let $y = 1,000,000$ and $\hat{y} = 999,996$; then the error is

(1b) $$E_y = |y - \hat{y}| = |1,000,000 - 999,996| = 4,$$

and the relative error is

$$R_y = \frac{|y - \hat{y}|}{|y|} = \frac{4}{1,000,000} = 0.000004.$$

Let $z = 0.000012$ and $\hat{z} = 0.000009$; then the error is

(1c) $$E_z = |z - \hat{z}| = |0.000012 - 0.000009| = 0.000003,$$

and the relative error is

$$R_z = \frac{|z - \hat{z}|}{|z|} = \frac{0.000003}{0.000012} = 0.25.$$ ∎

In case (1a), there is not too much difference between E_x and R_x, and either could be used to determine the accuracy of $\hat{x}$. In case (1b), the value of y is of magnitude 10^6, the error E_y is large, and the relative error R_y is small. In this case, $\hat{y}$ would probably be considered a good approximation to y. In case (1c), z is of magnitude 10^{-6} and the error E_z is the smallest of all three cases, but the relative error R_z is the largest. In terms of percentage, it amounts to 25%, and thus $\hat{z}$ is a bad approximation to z. Observe that as $|p|$ moves away from 1 (greater than or less than) the relative error R_p is a better indicator than E_p of the accuracy of the approximation. Relative error is preferred for floating-point representations since it deals directly with the mantissa.

Definition 1.8. The number $\hat{p}$ is said to **approximate** p to d significant digits if d is the largest nonnegative integer for which

(2) $$\frac{|p - \hat{p}|}{|p|} < \frac{10^{1-d}}{2}.$$ ▲

Example 1.15. Determine the number of significant digits for the approximations in Example 1.14.

(3a) If $x = 3.141592$ and $\hat{x} = 3.14$, then $|x - \hat{x}|/|x| = 0.000507 < 10^{-2}/2$. Therefore, $\hat{x}$ approximates x to two significant digits.

(3b) If $y = 1,000,000$ and $\hat{y} = 999,996$, then $|y - \hat{y}|/|y| = 0.000004 < 10^{-5}/2$. Therefore, $\hat{y}$ approximates y to six significant digits.

(3c) If $z = 0.000012$ and $\hat{z} = 0.000009$, then $|z - \hat{z}|/|z| = 0.25 < 10^{-0}/2$. Therefore, $\hat{z}$ approximates z to one significant digit. ∎

Truncation Error

The notion of truncation error usually refers to errors introduced when a more complicated mathematical expression is "replaced" with a more elementary formula. This terminology originates from the technique of replacing a complicated function with a truncated Taylor series. For example, the infinite Taylor series

$$e^{x^2} = 1 + x^2 + \frac{x^4}{2!} + \frac{x^6}{3!} + \frac{x^8}{4!} + \cdots + \frac{x^{2n}}{n!} + \cdots$$

might be replaced with just the first five terms $1 + x^2 + \frac{x^4}{2!} + \frac{x^6}{3!} + \frac{x^8}{4!}$. This might be done when approximating an integral numerically.

Example 1.16. Given that $\int_0^{1/2} e^{x^2} dx = 0.544987104184 = p$, determine the accuracy of the approximation obtained by replacing the integrand $f(x) = e^{x^2}$ with the truncated Taylor series $P_8(x) = 1 + x^2 + \frac{x^4}{2!} + \frac{x^6}{3!} + \frac{x^8}{4!}$.

Term-by-term integration produces

$$\int_0^{1/2} \left(1 + x^2 + \frac{x^4}{2!} + \frac{x^6}{3!} + \frac{x^8}{4!}\right) dx = \left(x + \frac{x^3}{3} + \frac{x^5}{5(2!)} + \frac{x^7}{7(3!)} + \frac{x^9}{9(4!)}\right)\Bigg|_{x=0}^{x=1/2}$$

$$= \frac{1}{2} + \frac{1}{24} + \frac{1}{320} + \frac{1}{5376} + \frac{1}{110,592}$$

$$= \frac{2,109,491}{3,870,720} = 0.544986720817 = \widehat{p}.$$

Since

$$10^{-5}/2 > |p - \widehat{p}|/|p| = 7.03442 \times 10^{-7} > 10^{-6}/2,$$

the approximation $\widehat{p}$ agrees with the true answer $p = 0.544987104184$ to five significant digits. The graphs of $f(x) = e^{x^2}$ and $y = P_8(x)$ and the area under the curve for $0 \le x \le 1/2$ are shown in Figure 1.7. ∎

Round-off Error

A computer's representation of real numbers is limited to the fixed precision of the mantissa. True values are sometimes not stored exactly by a computer's representation. This is called **round-off error**. In the preceding section the real number $1/10 = 0.0\overline{0011}_{\text{two}}$ was truncated when it was stored in a computer. The actual number that is stored in the computer may undergo chopping or rounding of the last digit. Therefore, since the computer hardware works with only a limited number of digits in machine numbers, rounding errors are introduced and propagated in successive computations.

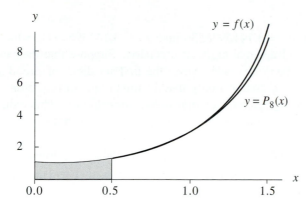

Figure 1.7 The graphs of $y = f(x) = e^{x^2}$, $y = P_8(x)$, and the area under the curve for $0 \le x \le \frac{1}{2}$.

Chopping Off versus Rounding Off

Consider any real number p that is expressed in **normalized decimal form**:

$$(4) \qquad p = \pm 0.d_1 d_2 d_3 \cdots d_k d_{k+1} \cdots \times 10^n,$$

where $1 \le d_1 \le 9$ and $0 \le d_j \le 9$ for $j > 1$. Suppose that k is the maximum number of decimal digits carried in the floating-point computations of a computer; then the real number p is represented by $fl_{\text{chop}}(p)$, which is given by

$$(5) \qquad fl_{\text{chop}}(p) = \pm 0.d_1 d_2 d_3 \cdots d_k \times 10^n,$$

where $1 \le d_1 \le 9$ and $0 \le d_j \le 9$ for $1 < j \le k$. The number $fl_{\text{chop}}(p)$ is called the **chopped floating-point representation** of p. In this case the kth digit of $fl_{\text{chop}}(p)$ agrees with the kth digit of p. An alternative k-digit representation is the **rounded floating-point representation** $fl_{\text{round}}(p)$, which is given by

$$(6) \qquad fl_{\text{round}}(p) = \pm 0.d_1 d_2 d_3 \ldots r_k \times 10^n,$$

where $1 \le d_1 \le 9$ and $0 \le d_j \le 9$ for $1 < j < k$ and the last digit, r_k, is obtained by rounding the number $d_k d_{k+1} d_{k+2} \cdots$ to the nearest integer. For example, the real number

$$p = \frac{22}{7} = 3.142857142857142857\ldots$$

has the following six-digit representations:

$$fl_{\text{chop}}(p) = 0.314285 \times 10^1,$$
$$fl_{\text{round}}(p) = 0.314286 \times 10^1.$$

For common purposes the chopping and rounding would be written as 3.14285 and 3.14286, respectively. The reader should note that essentially all computers use some form of the rounded floating-point representation method.

Loss of Significance

Consider the two numbers $p = 3.1415926536$ and $q = 3.1415957341$, which are nearly equal and both carry 11 decimal digits of precision. Suppose that their difference is formed: $p - q = -0.0000030805$. Since the first six digits of p and q are the same, their difference $p - q$ contains only five decimal digits of precision. This phenomenon is called *loss of significance* or *subtractive cancellation*. This reduction in the precision of the final computed answer can creep in when it is not suspected.

Example 1.17.   Compare the results of calculating $f(500)$ and $g(500)$ using six digits and rounding. The functions are $f(x) = x\left(\sqrt{x+1} - \sqrt{x}\right)$ and $g(x) = \dfrac{x}{\sqrt{x+1} + \sqrt{x}}$. For the first function,

$$f(500) = 500\left(\sqrt{501} - \sqrt{500}\right)$$
$$= 500(22.3830 - 22.3607) = 500(0.0223) = 11.1500.$$

For $g(x)$,

$$g(500) = \frac{500}{\sqrt{501} + \sqrt{500}}$$
$$= \frac{500}{22.3830 + 22.3607} = \frac{500}{44.7437} = 11.1748.$$

The second function, $g(x)$, is algebraically equivalent to $f(x)$, as shown by the computation

$$f(x) = \frac{x\left(\sqrt{x+1} - \sqrt{x}\right)\left(\sqrt{x+1} + \sqrt{x}\right)}{\sqrt{x+1} + \sqrt{x}}$$
$$= \frac{x\left(\left(\sqrt{x+1}\right)^2 - \left(\sqrt{x}\right)^2\right)}{\sqrt{x+1} + \sqrt{x}}$$
$$= \frac{x}{\sqrt{x+1} + \sqrt{x}}.$$

The answer, $g(500) = 11.1748$, involves less error and is the same as that obtained by rounding the true answer $11.174755300747198\ldots$ to six digits.   ∎

The reader is encouraged to study Exercise 12 on how to avoid loss of significance in the quadratic formula. The next example shows that a truncated Taylor series will sometimes help avoid the loss of significance error.

Example 1.18.   Compare the results of calculating $f(0.01)$ and $P(0.01)$ using six digits and rounding, where

$$f(x) = \frac{e^x - 1 - x}{x^2} \quad \text{and} \quad P(x) = \frac{1}{2} + \frac{x}{6} + \frac{x^2}{24}.$$

The function $P(x)$ is the Taylor polynomial of degree $n = 2$ for $f(x)$ expanded about $x = 0$.

For the first function

$$f(0.01) = \frac{e^{0.01} - 1 - 0.01}{(0.01)^2} = \frac{1.010050 - 1 - 0.01}{0.001} = 0.5.$$

For the second function

$$P(0.01) = \frac{1}{2} + \frac{0.01}{6} + \frac{0.001}{24}$$
$$= 0.5 + 0.001667 + 0.000004 = 0.501671.$$

The answer $P(0.01) = 0.501671$ contains less error and is the same as that obtained by rounding the true answer $0.50167084168057542\ldots$ to six digits.   ∎

For polynomial evaluation, the rearrangement of terms into nested multiplication form will sometimes produce a better result.

Example 1.19.   Let $P(x) = x^3 - 3x^2 + 3x - 1$ and $Q(x) = ((x - 3)x + 3)x - 1$. Use three-digit rounding arithmetic to compute approximations to $P(2.19)$ and $Q(2.19)$. Compare them with the true values, $P(2.19) = Q(2.19) = 1.685159$.

$$P(2.19) \approx (2.19)^3 - 3(2.19)^2 + 3(2.19) - 1$$
$$= 10.5 - 14.4 + 6.57 - 1 = 1.67.$$
$$Q(2.19) \approx ((2.19 - 3)2.19 + 3)2.19 - 1 = 1.69.$$

The errors are 0.015159 and -0.004841, respectively. Thus the approximation $Q(2.19) \approx 1.69$ has less error. Exercise 6 explores the situation near the root of this polynomial.   ∎

$O(h^n)$ Order of Approximation

Clearly, the sequences $\left\{\dfrac{1}{n^2}\right\}_{n=1}^{\infty}$ and $\left\{\dfrac{1}{n}\right\}_{n=1}^{\infty}$ are both converging to zero. In addition, it should be observed that the first sequence is converging to zero more rapidly than the second sequence. In the coming chapters some special terminology and notation will be used to describe how rapidly a sequence is converging.

Definition 1.9.   The function $f(h)$ is said to be **big Oh** of $g(h)$, denoted $f(h) = O(g(h))$, if there exist constants C and c such that

$$(7) \qquad\qquad |f(h)| \le C|g(h)| \qquad \text{whenever } h \le c. \qquad\qquad ▲$$

Example 1.20.   Consider the functions $f(x) = x^2 + 1$ and $g(x) = x^3$. Since $x^2 \le x^3$ and $1 \le x^3$ for $x \ge 1$, it follows that $x^2 + 1 \le 2x^3$ for $x \ge 1$. Therefore, $f(x) = O(g(x))$.   ∎

The big Oh notation provides a useful way of describing the rate of growth of a function in terms of well-known elementary functions (x^n, $x^{1/n}$, a^x, $\log_a x$, etc.).

The rate of convergence of sequences can be described in a similar manner.

Definition 1.10.   Let $\{x_n\}_{n=1}^{\infty}$ and $\{y_n\}_{n=1}^{\infty}$ be two sequences. The sequence $\{x_n\}$ is said to be of order big Oh of $\{y_n\}$, denoted $x_n = O(y_n)$, if there exist constants C and N such that

$$(8) \qquad\qquad |x_n| \le C|y_n| \qquad \text{whenever } n \ge N. \qquad\qquad \blacktriangle$$

Example 1.21. $\dfrac{n^2 - 1}{n^3} = O\left(\dfrac{1}{n}\right)$, since $\dfrac{n^2 - 1}{n^3} \le \dfrac{n^2}{n^3} = \dfrac{1}{n}$ whenever $n \ge 1$.   ∎

Often a function $f(h)$ is approximated by a function $p(h)$ and the error bound is known to be $M|h^n|$. This leads to the following definition.

Definition 1.11.   Assume that $f(h)$ is approximated by the function $p(h)$ and that there exist a real constant $M > 0$ and a positive integer n so that

$$(9) \qquad\qquad \frac{|f(h) - p(h)|}{|h^n|} \le M \qquad \text{for sufficiently small } h.$$

We say that $p(h)$ **approximates** $f(h)$ with order of approximation $O(h^n)$ and write

$$(10) \qquad\qquad f(h) = p(h) + O(h^n). \qquad\qquad \blacktriangle$$

When relation (9) is rewritten in the form $|f(h) - p(h)| \le M|h^n|$, we see that the notation $O(h^n)$ stands in place of the error bound $M|h^n|$. The following results show how to apply the definition to simple combinations of two functions.

Theorem 1.15.   Assume that $f(h) = p(h) + O(h^n)$, $g(h) = q(h) + O(h^m)$, and $r = \min\{m, n\}$. Then

$$(11) \qquad\qquad f(h) + g(h) = p(h) + q(h) + O(h^r),$$
$$(12) \qquad\qquad f(h)g(h) = p(h)q(h) + O(h^r),$$

and

$$(13) \qquad \frac{f(h)}{g(h)} = \frac{p(h)}{q(h)} + O(h^r) \qquad \text{provided that } g(h) \ne 0 \text{ and } q(h) \ne 0.$$

It is instructive to consider $p(x)$ to be the nth Taylor polynomial approximation of $f(x)$; then the remainder term is simply designated $O(h^{n+1})$, which stands for the presence of omitted terms starting with the power h^{n+1}. The remainder term converges to zero with the same rapidity that h^{n+1} converges to zero as h approaches zero, as expressed in the relationship

(14) $$\boldsymbol{O}(h^{n+1}) \approx Mh^{n+1} \approx \frac{f^{(n+1)}(c)}{(n+1)!}h^{n+1}$$

for sufficiently small h. Hence the notation $\boldsymbol{O}(h^{n+1})$ stands in place of the quantity Mh^{n+1}, where M is a constant or "behaves like a constant."

Theorem 1.16 (Taylor's Theorem).   Assume that $f \in C^{n+1}[a, b]$. If both x_0 and $x = x_0 + h$ lie in $[a, b]$, then

(15) $$f(x_0 + h) = \sum_{k=0}^{n} \frac{f^{(k)}(x_0)}{k!}h^k + \boldsymbol{O}(h^{n+1}).$$

The following example illustrates the theorems above. The computations use the addition properties (i) $\boldsymbol{O}(h^p) + \boldsymbol{O}(h^p) = \boldsymbol{O}(h^p)$, (ii) $\boldsymbol{O}(h^p) + \boldsymbol{O}(h^q) = \boldsymbol{O}(h^r)$, where $r = \min\{p, q\}$, and the multiplicative property (iii) $\boldsymbol{O}(h^p)\boldsymbol{O}(h^q) = \boldsymbol{O}(h^s)$, where $s = p + q$.

Example 1.22.   Consider the Taylor polynomial expansions

$$e^h = 1 + h + \frac{h^2}{2!} + \frac{h^3}{3!} + \boldsymbol{O}(h^4) \quad \text{and} \quad \cos(h) = 1 - \frac{h^2}{2!} + \frac{h^4}{4!} + \boldsymbol{O}(h^6).$$

Determine the order of approximation for their sum and product.
For the sum we have

$$e^h + \cos(h) = 1 + h + \frac{h^2}{2!} + \frac{h^3}{3!} + \boldsymbol{O}(h^4) + 1 - \frac{h^2}{2!} + \frac{h^4}{4!} + \boldsymbol{O}(h^6)$$

$$= 2 + h + \frac{h^3}{3!} + \boldsymbol{O}(h^4) + \frac{h^4}{4!} + \boldsymbol{O}(h^6).$$

Since $\boldsymbol{O}(h^4) + \dfrac{h^4}{4!} = \boldsymbol{O}(h^4)$ and $\boldsymbol{O}(h^4) + \boldsymbol{O}(h^6) = \boldsymbol{O}(h^4)$, this reduces to

$$e^h + \cos(h) = 2 + h + \frac{h^3}{3!} + \boldsymbol{O}(h^4),$$

and the order of approximation is $\boldsymbol{O}(h^4)$.

The product is treated similarly:

$$e^h \cos(h) = \left(1 + h + \frac{h^2}{2!} + \frac{h^3}{3!} + O(h^4)\right)\left(1 - \frac{h^2}{2!} + \frac{h^4}{4!} + O(h^6)\right)$$

$$= \left(1 + h + \frac{h^2}{2!} + \frac{h^3}{3!}\right)\left(1 - \frac{h^2}{2!} + \frac{h^4}{4!}\right)$$

$$+ \left(1 + h + \frac{h^2}{2!} + \frac{h^3}{3!}\right)O(h^6) + \left(1 - \frac{h^2}{2!} + \frac{h^4}{4!}\right)O(h^4)$$

$$+ O(h^4)O(h^6)$$

$$= 1 + h - \frac{h^3}{3} - \frac{5h^4}{24} - \frac{h^5}{24} + \frac{h^6}{48} + \frac{h^7}{144}$$

$$+ O(h^6) + O(h^4) + O(h^4)O(h^6).$$

Since $O(h^4)O(h^6) = O(h^{10})$ and

$$-\frac{5h^4}{24} - \frac{h^5}{24} + \frac{h^6}{48} + \frac{h^7}{144} + O(h^6) + O(h^4) + O(h^{10}) = O(h^4),$$

the preceding equation is simplified to yield

$$e^h \cos(h) = 1 + h - \frac{h^3}{3} + O(h^4),$$

and the order of approximation is $O(h^4)$.   ∎

Order of Convergence of a Sequence

Numerical approximations are often arrived at by computing a sequence of approximations that get closer and closer to the answer desired. The definition of big Oh for sequences was given in Definition 1.10, and the definition of order of convergence for a sequence is analogous to that given for functions in Definition 1.11.

Definition 1.12.   Suppose that $\lim_{n\to\infty} x_n = x$ and $\{r_n\}_{n=1}^{\infty}$ is a sequence with $\lim_{n\to\infty} r_n = 0$. We say that $\{x_n\}_{n=1}^{\infty}$ *converges* to x with the order of convergence $O(r_n)$, if there exists a constant $K > 0$ such that

$$\frac{|x_n - x|}{|r_n|} \le K \qquad \text{for } n \text{ sufficiently large.}$$

This is indicated by writing $x_n = x + O(r_n)$, or $x_n \to x$ with order of convergence $O(r_n)$.   ▲

Example 1.23.   Let $x_n = \cos(n)/n^2$ and $r_n = 1/n^2$; then $\lim_{n\to\infty} x_n = 0$ with a rate of convergence $O(1/n^2)$. This follows immediately from the relation

$$\frac{|\cos(n)/n^2|}{|1/n^2|} = |\cos(n)| \le 1 \qquad \text{for all } n.$$ ∎

Propagation of Error

Let us investigate how error might be propagated in successive computations. Consider the addition of two numbers p and q (the true values) with the approximate values $\widehat{p}$ and $\widehat{q}$, which contain errors ϵ_p and ϵ_q, respectively. Starting with $p = \widehat{p} + \epsilon_p$ and $q = \widehat{q} + \epsilon_q$, the sum is

$$(16) \qquad p + q = (\widehat{p} + \epsilon_p) + (\widehat{q} + \epsilon_q) = (\widehat{p} + \widehat{q}) + (\epsilon_p + \epsilon_q).$$

Hence, for addition, the error in the sum is the sum of the errors in the addends.

The propagation of error in multiplication is more complicated. The product is

$$(17) \qquad pq = (\widehat{p} + \epsilon_p)(\widehat{p} + \epsilon_q) = \widehat{pq} + \widehat{p}\epsilon_q + \widehat{q}\epsilon_p + \epsilon_p\epsilon_q.$$

Hence, if $\widehat{p}$ and $\widehat{q}$ are larger than 1 in absolute value, the terms $\widehat{p}\epsilon_q$ and $\widehat{q}\epsilon_p$ show that there is a possibility of magnification of the original errors ϵ_p and ϵ_q. Insights are gained if we look at the relative error. Rearrange the terms in (17) to get

$$(18) \qquad pq - \widehat{pq} = \widehat{p}\epsilon_q + \widehat{q}\epsilon_p + \epsilon_p\epsilon_q.$$

Suppose that $p \neq 0$ and $q \neq 0$; then we can divide (18) by pq to obtain the relative error in the product pq:

$$(19) \qquad R_{pq} = \frac{pq - \widehat{pq}}{pq} = \frac{\widehat{p}\epsilon_q + \widehat{q}\epsilon_p + \epsilon_p\epsilon_q}{pq} = \frac{\widehat{p}\epsilon_q}{pq} + \frac{\widehat{q}\epsilon_p}{pq} + \frac{\epsilon_p\epsilon_q}{pq}.$$

Furthermore, suppose that $\widehat{p}$ and $\widehat{q}$ are good approximations for p and q; then $\widehat{p}/p \approx 1, \widehat{q}/q \approx 1$, and $R_p R_q = (\epsilon_p/p)(\epsilon_q/q) \approx 0$ (R_p and R_q are the relative errors in the approximations $\widehat{p}$ and $\widehat{q}$). Then making these substitutions into (19) yields the simplified relationship

$$(20) \qquad R_{pq} = \frac{pq - \widehat{pq}}{pq} \approx \frac{\epsilon_q}{q} + \frac{\epsilon_p}{p} + 0 = R_q + R_p.$$

This shows that the relative error in the product pq is approximately the sum of the relative errors in the approximations $\widehat{p}$ and $\widehat{q}$.

Often, an initial error will be propagated in a sequence of calculations. A quality that is desirable for any numerical process is that a small error in the initial conditions will produce small changes in the final result. An algorithm with this feature is called *stable*; otherwise, it is called **unstable**. Whenever possible we shall choose methods that are stable. The following definition is used to describe the propagation of error.

Definition 1.13. Suppose that ϵ represents an initial error and $\epsilon(n)$ represents the growth of the error after n steps. If $|\epsilon(n)| \approx n\epsilon$, the growth of error is said to be *linear*. If $|\epsilon(n)| \approx K^n \epsilon$, the growth of error is called **exponential**. If $K > 1$, the exponential error grows without bound as $n \to \infty$, and if $0 < K < 1$, the exponential error diminishes to zero as $n \to \infty$. ▲

Table 1.4   Sequence $\{x_n\} = \{1/3^n\}$ and the Approximations $\{r_n\}$, $\{p_n\}$, and $\{q_n\}$

n	x_n	r_n	p_n	q_n
0	$1 = 1.0000000000$	0.9999600000	1.0000000000	1.0000000000
1	$\frac{1}{3} = 0.3333333333$	0.3333200000	0.3333200000	0.3333200000
2	$\frac{1}{9} = 0.1111111111$	0.1111066667	0.1110933330	0.1110666667
3	$\frac{1}{27} = 0.0370370370$	0.0370355556	0.0370177778	0.0369022222
4	$\frac{1}{81} = 0.0123456790$	0.0123451852	0.0123259259	0.0119407407
5	$\frac{1}{243} = 0.0041152263$	0.0041150617	0.0040953086	0.0029002469
6	$\frac{1}{729} = 0.0013717421$	0.0013716872	0.0013517695	-0.0022732510
7	$\frac{1}{2187} = 0.0004572474$	0.0004572291	0.0004372565	-0.0104777503
8	$\frac{1}{6561} = 0.0001524158$	0.0001524097	0.0001324188	-0.0326525834
9	$\frac{1}{19,683} = 0.0000508053$	0.0000508032	0.0000308063	-0.0983641945
10	$\frac{1}{59,049} = 0.0000169351$	0.0000169344	-0.0000030646	-0.2952280648

The next two examples show how an initial error can propagate in either a stable or an unstable fashion. In the first example, three algorithms are introduced. Each algorithm recursively generates the same sequence. Then, in the second example, small changes will be made to the initial conditions and the propagation of error will be analyzed.

Example 1.24.   Show that the following three schemes can be used with infinite-precision arithmetic to recursively generate the terms in the sequence $\{1/3^n\}_{n=0}^{\infty}$.

(21a) $\qquad r_0 = 1 \quad$ and $\quad r_n = \frac{1}{3}r_{n-1}$ $\qquad\qquad\qquad$ for $n = 1, 2, \ldots,$

(21b) $\qquad p_0 = 1, p_1 = \frac{1}{3}, \quad$ and $\quad p_n = \frac{4}{3}p_{n-1} - \frac{1}{3}p_{n-2} \qquad$ for $n = 2, 3, \ldots,$

(21c) $\qquad q_0 = 1, q_1 = \frac{1}{3}, \quad$ and $\quad q_n = \frac{10}{3}q_{n-1} - q_{n-2} \qquad$ for $n = 2, 3, \ldots.$

Formula (21a) is obvious. In (21b) the difference equation has the general solution $p_n = A(1/3^n) + B$. This can be verified by direct substitution:

$$\frac{4}{3}p_{n-1} - \frac{1}{3}p_{n-2} = \frac{4}{3}\left(\frac{A}{3^{n-1}} + B\right) - \frac{1}{3}\left(\frac{A}{3^{n-2}} + B\right)$$

$$= \left(\frac{4}{3^n} - \frac{3}{3^n}\right)A - \left(\frac{4}{3} - \frac{1}{3}\right)B = A\frac{1}{3^n} + B = p_n.$$

Table 1.5   Error Sequences $\{x_n - r_n\}$, $\{x_n - p_n\}$, and $\{x_n - q_n\}$

n	$x_n - r_n$	$x_n - p_n$	$x_n - q_n$
0	0.0000400000	0.0000000000	0.0000000000
1	0.0000133333	0.0000133333	0.0000013333
2	0.0000044444	0.0000177778	0.0000444444
3	0.0000014815	0.0000192593	0.0001348148
4	0.0000004938	0.0000197531	0.0004049383
5	0.0000001646	0.0000199177	0.0012149794
6	0.0000000549	0.0000199726	0.0036449931
7	0.0000000183	0.0000199909	0.0109349977
8	0.0000000061	0.0000199970	0.0328049992
9	0.0000000020	0.0000199990	0.0984149998
10	0.0000000007	0.0000199997	0.2952449999

Setting $A = 1$ and $B = 0$ will generate the sequence desired. In (21c) the difference equation has the general solution $q_n = A(1/3^n) + B3^n$. This too is verified by substitution:

$$\frac{10}{3}q_{n-1} - q_{n-2} = \frac{10}{3}\left(\frac{A}{3^{n-1}} + B3^{n-1}\right) - \left(\frac{A}{3^{n-2}} + B3^{n-2}\right)$$

$$= \left(\frac{10}{3^n} - \frac{9}{3^n}\right)A - (10 - 1)3^{n-2}B$$

$$= A\frac{1}{3^n} + B3^n = q_n.$$

Setting $A = 1$ and $B = 0$ generates the sequence required.   ∎

Example 1.25.   Generate approximations to the sequence $\{x_n\} = \{1/3^n\}$ using the schemes

(22a) $r_0 = 0.99996$ and $r_n = \frac{1}{3}r_{n-1}$ for $n = 1, 2, \ldots,$

(22b) $p_0 = 1, p_1 = 0.33332,$ and $p_n = \frac{4}{3}p_{n-1} - \frac{1}{3}p_{n-2}$ for $n = 2, 3, \ldots,$

(22c) $q_0 = 1, q_1 = 0.33332,$ and $q_n = \frac{10}{3}q_{n-1} - q_{n-2}$ for $n = 2, 3, \ldots.$

In (22a) the initial error in r_0 is 0.00004, and in (22b) and (22c) the initial errors in p_1 and q_1 are 0.0000013. Investigate the propagation of error for each scheme.

Table 1.4 gives the first ten numerical approximations for each sequence, and Table 1.5 gives the error in each formula. The error for $\{r_n\}$ is stable and decreases in an exponential manner. The error for $\{p_n\}$ is stable. The error for $\{q_n\}$ is unstable and grows at an exponential rate. Although the error for $\{p_n\}$ is stable, the terms $p_n \rightarrow 0$ as $n \rightarrow \infty$, so that the error eventually dominates and the terms past p_8 have no significant digits. Figures 1.8, 1.9, and 1.10 show the errors in $\{r_n\}$, $\{p_n\}$, and $\{q_n\}$, respectively.   ∎

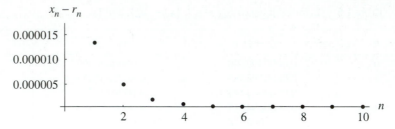

Figure 1.8   A stable decreasing error sequence $\{x_n - r_n\}$.

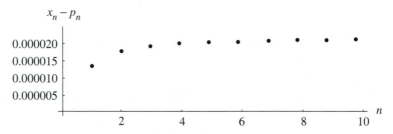

Figure 1.9   A stable error sequence $\{x_n - p_n\}$.

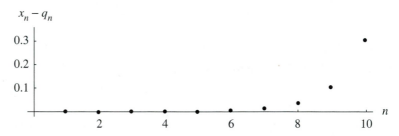

Figure 1.10   An unstable increasing error sequence $\{x_n - q_n\}$.

Uncertainty in Data

Data from real-world problems contain uncertainty or error. This type of error is referred to as *noise*. It will affect the accuracy of any numerical computation that is based on the data. An improvement of precision is not accomplished by performing successive computations using noisy data. Hence, if you start with data with d significant digits of accuracy, then the result of a computation should be reported in d significant digits of accuracy. For example, suppose that the data $p_1 = 4.152$ and $p_2 = 0.07931$ both have four significant digits of accuracy. Then it is tempting to report all the digits that appear on your calculator (i.e., $p_1 + p_2 = 4.23131$). This is an oversight, because you should not report conclusions from noisy data that have more significant digits than the original data. The proper answer in this situation is $p_1 + p_2 = 4.231$.

Exercises for Error Analysis

1. Find the error E_x and relative error R_x. Also determine the number of significant digits in the approximation.
   (a) $x = 2.71828182, \widehat{x} = 2.7182$
   (b) $y = 98, 350, \widehat{y} = 98, 000$
   (c) $z = 0.000068, \widehat{z} = 0.00006$

2. Complete the following computation:

$$\int_0^{1/4} e^{x^2}\, dx \approx \int_0^{1/4} \left(1 + x^2 + \frac{x^2}{2!} + \frac{x^6}{3!}\right) dx = \widehat{p}.$$

   State what type of error is present in this situation. Compare your answer with the true value $p = 0.2553074606$.

3. (a)   Consider the data $p_1 = 1.414$ and $p_2 = 0.09125$, which have four significant digits of accuracy. Determine the proper answer for the sum $p_1 + p_2$ and the product $p_1 p_2$.
   (b)   Consider the data $p_1 = 31.415$ and $p_2 = 0.027182$, which have five significant digits of accuracy. Determine the proper answer for the sum $p_1 + p_2$ and the product $p_1 p_2$.

4. Complete the following computation and state what type of error is present in this situation.
   (a) $$\frac{\sin\left(\frac{\pi}{4} + 0.00001\right) - \sin\left(\frac{\pi}{4}\right)}{0.00001} = \frac{0.70711385222 - 0.70710678119}{0.00001} = \cdots$$
   (b) $$\frac{\ln(2 + 0.00005) - \ln(2)}{0.00005} = \frac{0.69317218025 - 0.69314718056}{0.00005} = \cdots$$

5. Sometimes the loss of significance error can be avoided by rearranging terms in the function using a known identity from trigonometry or algebra. Find an equivalent formula for the following functions that avoids a loss of significance.
   (a) $\ln(x + 1) - \ln(x)$ for large x
   (b) $\sqrt{x^2 + 1} - x$ for large x
   (c) $\cos^2(x) - \sin^2(x)$ for $x \approx \pi/4$
   (d) $\sqrt{\dfrac{1 + \cos(x)}{2}}$ for $x \approx \pi$

6. *Polynomial evaluation.* Let $P(x) = x^3 - 3x^2 + 3x - 1$, $Q(x) = ((x - 3)x + 3)x - 1$, and $R(x) = (x - 1)^3$.
   (a)   Use four-digit rounding arithmetic and compute $P(2.72)$, $Q(2.72)$, and $R(2.72)$. In the computation of $P(x)$, assume that $(2.72)^3 = 20.12$ and $(2.72)^2 = 7.398$.
   (b)   Use four-digit rounding arithmetic and compute $P(0.975)$, $Q(0.975)$, and $R(0.975)$. In the computation of $P(x)$, assume that $(0.975)^3 = 0.9268$ and $(0.975)^2 = 0.9506$.

7. Use three-digit rounding arithmetic to compute the following sums (sum in the given order):

(a) $\displaystyle\sum_{k=1}^{6} \frac{1}{3^k}$

(b) $\displaystyle\sum_{k=1}^{6} \frac{1}{3^{7-k}}$

8. Discuss the propagation of error for the following:

(a)   The sum of three numbers:

$$p + q + r = (\widehat{p} + \epsilon_p) + (\widehat{q} + \epsilon_q) + (\widehat{r} + \epsilon_r).$$

(b)   The quotient of two numbers: $\dfrac{p}{q} = \dfrac{\widehat{p} + \epsilon_p}{\widehat{q} + \epsilon_q}.$

(c)   The product of three numbers:

$$pqr = (\widehat{p} + \epsilon_p)(\widehat{q} + \epsilon_q)(\widehat{r} + \epsilon_r).$$

9. Given the Taylor polynomial expansions

$$\frac{1}{1-h} = 1 + h + h^2 + h^3 + \boldsymbol{O}(h^4)$$

and

$$\cos(h) = 1 - \frac{h^2}{2!} + \frac{h^4}{4!} + \boldsymbol{O}(h^6),$$

determine the order of approximation for their sum and product.

10. Given the Taylor polynomial expansions

$$e^h = 1 + h + \frac{h^2}{2!} + \frac{h^3}{3!} + \frac{h^4}{4!} + \boldsymbol{O}(h^5)$$

and

$$\sin(h) = h - \frac{h^3}{3!} + \boldsymbol{O}(h^5),$$

determine the order of approximation for their sum and product.

11. Given the Taylor polynomial expansions

$$\cos(h) = 1 - \frac{h^2}{2!} + \frac{h^4}{4!} + \boldsymbol{O}(h^6)$$

and

$$\sin(h) = h - \frac{h^3}{3!} + \frac{h^5}{5!} + \boldsymbol{O}(h^7),$$

determine the order of approximation for their sum and product.

12. *Improving the quadratic formula.* Assume that $a \neq 0$ and $b^2 - 4ac > 0$ and consider the equation $ax^2 + bx + c = 0$. The roots can be computed with the quadratic formulas

$$(1) \qquad x_1 = \frac{-b + \sqrt{b^2 - 4ac}}{2a} \quad \text{and} \quad x_2 = \frac{-b - \sqrt{b^2 - 4ac}}{2a}.$$

Show that these roots can be calculated with the equivalent formulas

$$(2) \qquad x_1 = \frac{-2c}{b + \sqrt{b^2 - 4ac}} \quad \text{and} \quad x_2 = \frac{-2c}{b - \sqrt{b^2 - 4ac}}.$$

Hint. Rationalize the numerators in (1). *Remark.* In the cases when $|b| \approx \sqrt{b^2 - 4ac}$, one must proceed with caution to avoid loss of precision due to a catastrophic cancellation. If $b > 0$, then x_1 should be computed with formula (2) and x_2 should be computed using (1). However, if $b < 0$, then x_1 should be computed using (1) and x_2 should be computed using (2).

13. Use the appropriate formula for x_1 and x_2 mentioned in Exercise 12 to find the roots of the following quadratic equations.

(a) $x^2 - 1,000.001x + 1 = 0$
(b) $x^2 - 10,000.0001x + 1 = 0$
(c) $x^2 - 100,000.00001x + 1 = 0$
(d) $x^2 - 1,000,000.000001x + 1 = 0$

Algorithms and Programs

1. Use the results of Exercises 12 and 13 to construct an algorithm and MATLAB program that will accurately compute the roots of a quadratic equation in all situations, including the troublesome ones when $|b| \approx \sqrt{b^2 - 4ac}$.

2. Follow Example 1.25 and generate the first 10 numerical approximations for each of the following three difference equations. In each case a small initial error is introduced. If there were no initial error, then each of the difference equations would generate the sequence $\{1/2^n\}_{n=1}^{\infty}$. Produce output analogous to Tables 1.4 and 1.5 and Figures 1.8, 1.9, and 1.10.

(a) $r_0 = 0.994$ and $r_n = \frac{1}{2} r_{n-1}$, for $n = 1, 2, \ldots$
(b) $p_0 = 1$, $p_1 = 0.497$, and $p_n = \frac{3}{2} p_{n-1} - \frac{1}{2} p_{n-2}$, for $n = 2, 3, \ldots$
(c) $q_0 = 1$, $q_1 = 0.497$, and $q_n = \frac{5}{2} q_{n-1} - q_{n-2}$, for $n = 2, 3, \ldots$

2

Solution of Nonlinear Equations $f(x) = 0$

Consider the physical problem that involves a spherical ball of radius r that is submerged to a depth d in water (see Figure 2.1). Assume that the ball is constructed from a variety of longleaf pine that has a density of $\rho = 0.638$ and that its radius measures $r = 10$ cm. How much of the ball will be submerged when it is placed in water?

The mass M_w of water displaced when a sphere is submerged to a depth d is

$$M_w = \int_0^d \pi(r^2 - (x-r)^2)\,dx = \frac{\pi d^2(3r - d)}{3},$$

and the mass of the ball is $M_b = 4\pi r^3 \rho/3$. Applying Archimedes' law, $M_w = M_b$, produces the following equation that must be solved:

$$\frac{\pi(d^3 - 3d^2 r + 4r^3 \rho)}{3} = 0.$$

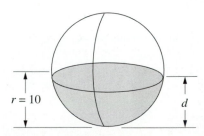

$r = 10$

d

Figure 2.1 The portion of a sphere of radius r that is to be submerged to a depth d.

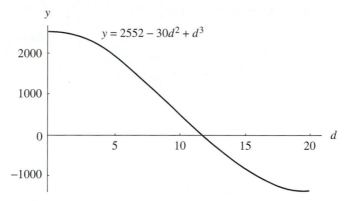

Figure 2.2   The cubic $y = 2552 - 30d^2 + d^3$.

In our case (with $r = 10$ and $\rho = 0.638$) this equation becomes

$$\frac{\pi(2552 - 30d^2 + d^3)}{3} = 0.$$

The graph of the cubic polynomial $y = 2552 - 30d^2 + d^3$ is shown in Figure 2.2 and from it one can see that the solution lies near the value $d = 12$.

The goal of this chapter is to develop a variety of methods for finding numerical approximations for the roots of an equation. For example, the bisection method could be applied to obtain the three roots $d_1 = -8.17607212$, $d_2 = 11.86150151$, and $d_3 = 26.31457061$. The first root d_1 is not a feasible solution for this problem, because d cannot be negative. The third root d_3 is larger than the diameter of the sphere and it is not the solution desired. The root $d_2 = 11.86150151$ lies in the interval $[0, 20]$ and is the proper solution. Its magnitude is reasonable because a little more than one-half of the sphere must be submerged.

2.1   Iteration for Solving $x = g(x)$

A fundamental principle in computer science is *iteration*. As the name suggests, a process is repeated until an answer is achieved. Iterative techniques are used to find roots of equations, solutions of linear and nonlinear systems of equations, and solutions of differential equations. In this section we study the process of iteration using repeated substitution.

A rule or function $g(x)$ for computing successive terms is needed, together with a starting value p_0. Then a sequence of values $\{p_k\}$ is obtained using the iterative rule

$p_{k+1} = g(p_k)$. The sequence has the pattern

$$p_0 \qquad \text{(starting value)}$$
$$p_1 = g(p_0)$$
$$p_2 = g(p_1)$$

(1)
$$\vdots$$

$$p_k = g(p_{k-1})$$
$$p_{k+1} = g(p_k)$$

$$\vdots$$

What can we learn from an unending sequence of numbers? If the numbers tend to a limit, we feel that something has been achieved. But what if the numbers diverge or are periodic? The next example addresses this situation.

Example 2.1.   The iterative rule $p_0 = 1$ and $p_{k+1} = 1.001 p_k$ for $k = 0, 1, \ldots$ produces a divergent sequence. The first 100 terms look as follows:

$$p_1 = 1.001 p_0 = (1.001)(1.000000) = 1.001000,$$
$$p_2 = 1.001 p_1 = (1.001)(1.001000) = 1.002001,$$
$$p_3 = 1.001 p_2 = (1.001)(1.002001) = 1.003003,$$

$$\vdots \qquad\qquad \vdots \qquad\qquad\qquad \vdots$$

$$p_{100} = 1.001 p_{99} = (1.001)(1.104012) = 1.105116.$$

The process can be continued indefinitely, and it is easily shown that $\lim_{n \to \infty} p_n = +\infty$. In Chapter 9 we will see that the sequence $\{p_k\}$ is a numerical solution to the differential equation $y' = 0.001 y$. The solution is known to be $y(x) = e^{0.001x}$. Indeed, if we compare the 100th term in the sequence with $y(100)$, we see that $p_{100} = 1.105116 \approx 1.105171 = e^{0.1} = y(100)$. ∎

In this section we are concerned with the types of functions $g(x)$ that produce convergent sequences $\{p_k\}$.

Finding Fixed Points

Definition 2.1.   A *fixed point* of a function $g(x)$ is a real number P such that $P = g(P)$. ▲

Geometrically, the fixed points of a function $y = g(x)$ are the points of intersection of $y = g(x)$ and $y = x$.

Definition 2.2.   The iteration $p_{n+1} = g(p_n)$ for $n = 0, 1, \ldots$ is called *fixed-point iteration*. ▲

Theorem 2.1.   Assume that g is a continuous function and that $\{p_n\}_{n=0}^{\infty}$ is a sequence generated by fixed-point iteration. If $\lim_{n\to\infty} p_n = P$, then P is a fixed point of $g(x)$.

Proof.   If $\lim_{n\to\infty} p_n = P$, then $\lim_{n\to\infty} p_{n+1} = P$. It follows from this result, the continuity of g, and the relation $p_{n+1} = g(p_n)$ that

$$(2) \qquad\qquad g(P) = g\left(\lim_{n\to\infty} p_n\right) = \lim_{n\to\infty} g(p_n) = \lim_{n\to\infty} p_{n+1} = P.$$

Therefore, P is a fixed point of $g(x)$.   •

Example 2.2.   Consider the convergent iteration

$$p_0 = 0.5 \quad \text{and} \quad p_{k+1} = e^{-p_k} \quad \text{for } k = 0, 1, \ldots.$$

The first 10 terms are obtained by the calculations

$$p_1 = e^{-0.500000} = 0.606531$$
$$p_2 = e^{-0.606531} = 0.545239$$
$$p_3 = e^{-0.545239} = 0.579703$$
$$\vdots \qquad\qquad \vdots$$
$$p_9 = e^{-0.566409} = 0.567560$$
$$p_{10} = e^{-0.567560} = 0.566907$$

The sequence is converging, and further calculations reveal that

$$\lim_{n\to\infty} p_n = 0.567143\ldots.$$

Thus we have found an approximation for the fixed point of the function $y = e^{-x}$.   ∎

The following two theorems establish conditions for the existence of a fixed point and the convergence of the fixed-point iteration process to a fixed point.

Theorem 2.2.   Assume that $g \in C[a, b]$.

(3) If the range of the mapping $y = g(x)$ satisfies $y \in [a, b]$ for all $x \in [a, b]$, then g has a fixed point in $[a, b]$.

(4) Furthermore, suppose that $g'(x)$ is defined over (a, b) and that a positive constant $K < 1$ exists with $|g'(x)| \le K < 1$ for all $x \in (a, b)$; then g has a unique fixed point P in $[a, b]$.

Proof of (3).   If $g(a) = a$ or $g(b) = b$, the assertion is true. Otherwise, the values of $g(a)$ and $g(b)$ must satisfy $g(a) \in (a, b]$ and $g(b) \in [a, b)$. The function $f(x) \equiv x - g(x)$ has the property that

$$f(a) = a - g(a) < 0 \quad \text{and} \quad f(b) = b - g(b) > 0.$$

Now apply Theorem 1.2, the intermediate value theorem, to $f(x)$, with the constant $L = 0$, and conclude that there exists a number P with $P \in (a, b)$ so that $f(P) = 0$. Therefore, $P = g(P)$ and P is the desired fixed point of $g(x)$.

Proof of (4).   Now we must show that this solution is unique. By way of contradiction, let us make the additional assumption that there exist two fixed points P_1 and P_2. Now apply Theorem 1.6, the mean value theorem, and conclude that there exists a number $d \in (a, b)$ so that

(5)
$$g'(d) = \frac{g(P_2) - g(P_1)}{P_2 - P_1}.$$

Next, use the facts that $g(P_1) = P_1$ and $g(P_2) = P_2$ to simplify the right side of equation (5) and obtain

$$g'(d) = \frac{P_2 - P_1}{P_2 - P_1} = 1.$$

But this contradicts the hypothesis in (4) that $|g'(x)| < 1$ over (a, b), so it is not possible for two fixed points to exist. Therefore, $g(x)$ has a unique fixed point P in $[a, b]$ under the conditions given in (4).   ●

Example 2.3.   Apply Theorem 2.2 to show rigorously that $g(x) = \cos(x)$ has a unique fixed point in $[0, 1]$.

Clearly, $g \in C[0, 1]$. Also, $g(x) = \cos(x)$ is a decreasing function on $[0, 1]$; thus its range on $[0, 1]$ is $[\cos(1), 1] \subseteq [0, 1]$. Thus condition (3) of Theorem 2.2 is satisfied and g has a fixed point in $[0, 1]$. Finally, if $x \in (0, 1)$, then $|g'(x)| = |-\sin(x)| = \sin(x) \leq \sin(1) < 0.8415 < 1$. Thus $K = \sin(1) < 1$, condition (4) of Theorem 2.2 is satisfied, and g has a unique fixed point in $[0, 1]$.   ■

We can now state a theorem that can be used to determine whether the fixed-point iteration process given in (1) will produce a convergent or a divergent sequence.

Theorem 2.3 (Fixed-Point Theorem).   Assume that (i) $g, g' \in C[a, b]$, (ii) K is a positive constant, (iii) $p_0 \in (a, b)$, and (iv) $g(x) \in [a, b]$ for all $x \in [a, b]$.

(6) If $|g'(x)| \leq K < 1$ for all $x \in [a, b]$, then the iteration $p_n = g(p_{n-1})$ will converge to the unique fixed point $P \in [a, b]$. In this case, P is said to be an attractive fixed point.

(7) If $|g'(x)| > 1$ for all $x \in [a, b]$, then the iteration $p_n = g(p_{n-1})$ will not converge to P. In this case, P is said to be a repelling fixed point and the iteration exhibits local divergence.

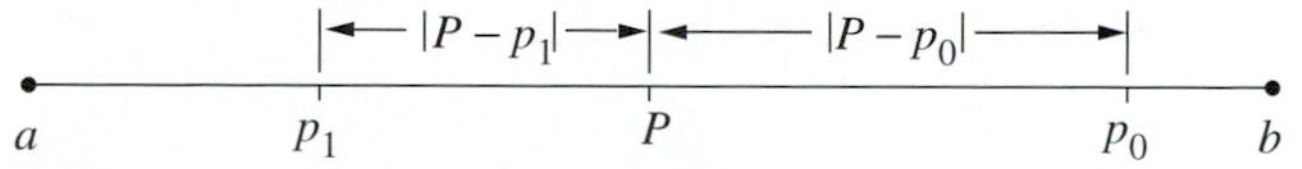

Figure 2.3 The relationship among P, p_0, p_1, $|P - p_0|$, and $|P - p_1|$.

Remark 1. It is assumed that $p_0 \neq P$ in statement (7).

Remark 2. Because g is continuous on an interval containing P, it is permissible to use the simpler criterion $|g'(P)| \leq K < 1$ and $|g'(P)| > 1$ in (6) and (7), respectively.

Proof.   We first show that the points $\{p_n\}_{n=0}^{\infty}$ all lie in (a, b). Starting with p_0, we apply Theorem 1.6, the mean value theorem. There exists a value $c_0 \in (a, b)$ so that

$$
(8) \qquad \begin{aligned}
|P - p_1| &= |g(P) - g(p_0)| = |g'(c_0)(P - p_0)| \\
&= |g'(c_0)||P - p_0| \leq K|P - p_0| < |P - p_0|.
\end{aligned}
$$

Therefore, p_1 is no further from P than p_0 was, and it follows that $p_1 \in (a, b)$ (see Figure 2.3). In general, suppose that $p_{n-1} \in (a, b)$; then

$$
(9) \qquad \begin{aligned}
|P - p_n| &= |g(P) - g(p_{n-1})| = |g'(c_{n-1})(P - p_{n-1})| \\
&= |g'(c_{n-1})||P - p_{n-1}| \leq K|P - p_{n-1}| < |P - p_{n-1}|.
\end{aligned}
$$

Therefore, $p_n \in (a, b)$ and hence, by induction, all the points $\{p_n\}_{n=0}^{\infty}$ lie in (a, b).

To complete the proof of (6), we will show that

$$
(10) \qquad \lim_{n \to \infty} |P - p_n| = 0.
$$

First, a proof by induction will establish the inequality

$$
(11) \qquad |P - p_n| \leq K^n |P - p_0|.
$$

The case $n = 1$ follows from the details in relation (8). Using the induction hypothesis $|P - p_{n-1}| \leq K^{n-1}|P - p_0|$ and the ideas in (9), we obtain

$$
|P - p_n| \leq K|P - p_{n-1}| \leq K K^{n-1}|P - p_0| = K^n|P - p_0|.
$$

Thus, by induction, inequality (11) holds for all n. Since $0 < K < 1$, the term K^n goes to zero as n goes to infinity. Hence

$$
(12) \qquad 0 \leq \lim_{n \to \infty} |P - p_n| \leq \lim_{n \to \infty} K^n |P - p_0| = 0.
$$

The limit of $|P - p_n|$ is squeezed between zero on the left and zero on the right, so we can conclude that $\lim_{n \to \infty} |P - p_n| = 0$. Thus $\lim_{n \to \infty} p_n = P$ and, by Theorem 2.1, the iteration $p_n = g(p_{n-1})$ converges to the fixed point P. Therefore, statement (6) of Theorem 2.3 is proved. We leave statement (7) for the reader to investigate.   •

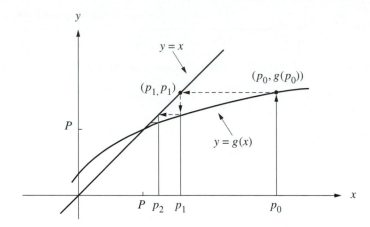

Figure 2.4   (a) Monotone convergence when $0 < g'(P) < 1$.

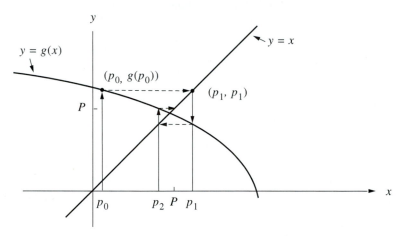

Figure 2.4   (b) Oscillating convergence when $-1 < g'(P) < 0$.

Corollary 2.1.   Assume that g satisfies the hypothesis given in (6) of Theorem 2.3. Bounds for the error involved when using p_n to approximate P are given by

(13) $$|P - p_n| \le K^n |P - p_0| \quad \text{for all } n \ge 1$$

and

(14) $$|P - p_n| \le \frac{K^n |p_1 - p_0|}{1 - K} \quad \text{for all } n \ge 1.$$

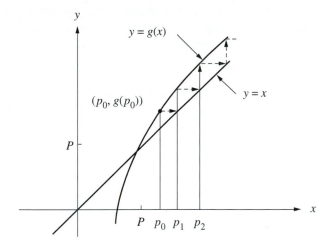

Figure 2.5   (a) Monotone divergence when $1 < g'(P)$.

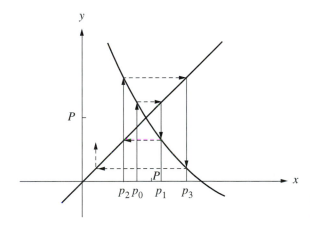

Figure 2.5   (b) Divergent oscillation when $g'(P) < -1$.

Graphical Interpretation of Fixed-Point Iteration

Since we seek a fixed point P to $g(x)$, it is necessary that the graph of the curve $y = g(x)$ and the line $y = x$ intersect at the point (P, P). Two simple types of convergent iteration, monotone and oscillating, are illustrated in Figure 2.4(a) and (b), respectively.

To visualize the process, start at p_0 on the x-axis and move vertically to the point $(p_0, p_1) = (p_0, g(p_0))$ on the curve $y = g(x)$. Then move horizontally from (p_0, p_1) to the point (p_1, p_1) on the line $y = x$. Finally, move vertically downward to p_1 on the x-axis. The recursion $p_{n+1} = g(p_n)$ is used to construct the point (p_n, p_{n+1}) on the graph, then a horizontal motion locates (p_{n+1}, p_{n+1}) on the line $y = x$, and then a vertical movement ends up at p_{n+1} on the x-axis. The situation is shown in Figure 2.4.

If $|g'(P)| > 1$, then the iteration $p_{n+1} = g(p_n)$ produces a sequence that diverges away from P. The two simple types of divergent iteration, monotone and oscillating, are illustrated in Figure 2.5(a) and (b), respectively.

Example 2.4.   Consider the iteration $p_{n+1} = g(p_n)$ when the function $g(x) = 1 + x - x^2/4$ is used. The fixed points can be found by solving the equation $x = g(x)$. The two solutions (fixed points of g) are $x = -2$ and $x = 2$. The derivative of the function is $g'(x) = 1 - x/2$, and there are only two cases to consider.

Case (i):	$P = -2$		*Case (ii):*	$P = 2$
Start with	$p_0 = -2.05$		Start with	$p_0 = 1.6$
then get	$p_1 = -2.100625$		then get	$p_1 = 1.96$
	$p_2 = -2.20378135$			$p_2 = 1.9996$
	$p_3 = -2.41794441$			$p_3 = 1.99999996$

$$\lim_{n \to \infty} p_n = -\infty.$$

$$\lim_{n \to \infty} p_n = 2.$$

Since $|g'(x)| > \frac{3}{2}$ on $[-3, -1]$, by Theorem 2.3, the sequence will not converge to $P = -2$.

Since $|g'(x)| < \frac{1}{2}$ on $[1, 3]$, by Theorem 2.3, the sequence will converge to $P = 2$.
∎

Theorem 2.3 does not state what will happen when $g'(P) = 1$. The next example has been specially constructed so that the sequence $\{p_n\}$ converges whenever $p_0 > P$ and it diverges if we choose $p_0 < P$.

Example 2.5.   Consider the iteration $p_{n+1} = g(p_n)$ when the function $g(x) = 2(x-1)^{1/2}$ for $x \geq 1$ is used. Only one fixed point $P = 2$ exists. The derivative is $g'(x) = 1/(x-1)^{1/2}$ and $g'(2) = 1$, so Theorem 2.3 does not apply. There are two cases to consider when the starting value lies to the left or right of $P = 2$.

Case (i): Start with $p_0 = 1.5$,			*Case (ii):* Start with $p_0 = 2.5$,	
then get	$p_1 = 1.41421356$		then get	$p_1 = 2.44948974$
	$p_2 = 1.28718851$			$p_2 = 2.40789513$
	$p_3 = 1.07179943$			$p_3 = 2.37309514$
	$p_4 = 0.53590832$			$p_4 = 2.34358284$

$$p_5 = 2(-0.46409168)^{1/2}.$$

$$\lim_{n \to \infty} p_n = 2.$$

Since p_4 lies outside the domain of $g(x)$, the term p_5 cannot be computed.

This sequence is converging too slowly to the value $P = 2$; indeed, $P_{1000} = 2.00398714$.
∎

Absolute and Relative Error Considerations

In Example 2.5, case (ii), the sequence converges slowly, and after 1000 iterations the three consecutive terms are

$$p_{1000} = 2.00398714, \qquad p_{1001} = 2.00398317, \qquad \text{and} \qquad p_{1002} = 2.00397921.$$

This should not be disturbing; after all, we could compute a few thousand more terms and find a better approximation! But what about a criterion for stopping the iteration? Notice that if we use the difference between consecutive terms,

$$|p_{1001} - p_{1002}| = |2.00398317 - 2.00397921| = 0.00000396.$$

Yet the absolute error in the approximation p_{1000} is known to be

$$|P - p_{1000}| = |2.00000000 - 2.00398714| = 0.00398714.$$

This is about 1000 times larger than $|p_{1001} - p_{1002}|$ and it shows that closeness of consecutive terms does not guarantee that accuracy has been achieved. But it is usually the only criterion available and is often used to terminate an iterative procedure.

Program 2.1 (Fixed-Point Iteration). To approximate a solution to the equation $x = g(x)$ starting with the initial guess p_0 and iterating $p_{n+1} = g(p_n)$.

```
function [k,p,err,P]=fixpt(g,p0,tol,max1)
% Input  - g is the iteration function input as a string 'g'
%        - p0 is the initial guess for the fixed point
%        - tol is the tolerance
%        - max1 is the maximum number of iterations
%Output - k is the number of iterations that were carried out
%        - p is the approximation to the fixed point
%        - err is the error in the approximation
%        - P contains the sequence {pn}
P(1)= p0;
for k=2:max1
    P(k)=feval(g,P(k-1));
    err=abs(P(k)-P(k-1));
    relerr=err/(abs(P(k))+eps);
    p=P(k);
    if (err<tol) | (relerr<tol),break;end
end
if k == max1
    disp('maximum number of iterations exceeded')
end
P=P';
```

Remark. When using the user-defined function `fixpt`, it is necessary to input the M-file g.m as a string: 'g' (see the Appendix).

Exercises for Iteration for Solving $x = g(x)$

1. Determine rigorously if each function has a unique fixed point on the given interval (follow Example 2.3).
   - **(a)** $g(x) = 1 - x^2/4$ on $[0, 1]$
   - **(b)** $g(x) = 2^{-x}$ on $[0, 1]$
   - **(c)** $g(x) = 1/x$ on $[0.5, 5.2]$

2. Investigate the nature of the fixed-point iteration when

$$g(x) = -4 + 4x - \frac{1}{2}x^2.$$

   - **(a)** Solve $g(x) = x$ and show that $P = 2$ and $P = 4$ are fixed points.
   - **(b)** Use the starting value $p_0 = 1.9$ and compute p_1, p_2, and p_3.
   - **(c)** Use the starting value $p_0 = 3.8$ and compute p_1, p_2, and p_3.
   - **(d)** Find the errors E_k and relative errors R_k for the values p_k in parts (b) and (c).
   - **(e)** What conclusions can be drawn from Theorem 2.3?

3. Graph $g(x)$, the line $y = x$, and the given fixed point P on the same coordinate system. Using the given starting value p_0, compute p_1 and p_2. Construct figures similar to Figures 2.4 and 2.5. Based on your graph, determine geometrically if fixed-point iteration converges.
   - **(a)** $g(x) = (6 + x)^{1/2}$, $P = 3$, and $p_0 = 7$
   - **(b)** $g(x) = 1 + 2/x$, $P = 2$, and $p_0 = 4$
   - **(c)** $g(x) = x^2/3$, $P = 3$, and $p_0 = 3.5$
   - **(d)** $g(x) = -x^2 + 2x + 2$, $P = 2$, and $p_0 = 2.5$

4. Let $g(x) = x^2 + x - 4$. Can fixed-point iteration be used to find the solution(s) to the equation $x = g(x)$? Why?

5. Let $g(x) = x \cos(x)$. Solve $x = g(x)$ and find all the fixed points of g (there are infinitely many). Can fixed-point iteration be used to find the solution(s) to the equation $x = g(x)$? Why?

6. Suppose that $g(x)$ and $g'(x)$ are defined and continuous on (a, b); p_0, p_1, $p_2 \in (a, b)$; and $p_1 = g(p_0)$ and $p_2 = g(p_1)$. Also, assume that there exists a constant K such that $|g'(x)| < K$. Show that $|p_2 - p_1| < K|p_1 - p_0|$. *Hint.* Use the mean value theorem.

7. Suppose that $g(x)$ and $g'(x)$ are continuous on (a, b) and that $|g'(x)| > 1$ on this interval. If the fixed point P and the initial approximations p_0 and p_1 lie in the interval (a, b), then show that $p_1 = g(p_0)$ implies that $|E_1| = |P - p_1| > |P - p_0| = |E_0|$. Hence statement (7) of Theorem 2.3 is established (local divergence).

8. Let $g(x) = -0.0001x^2 + x$ and $p_0 = 1$, and consider fixed-point iteration.
   - **(a)** Show that $p_0 > p_1 > \cdots > p_n > p_{n+1} > \cdots$.
   - **(b)** Show that $p_n > 0$ for all n.

(c)   Since the sequence $\{p_n\}$ is decreasing and bounded below, it has a limit. What is the limit?

9. Let $g(x) = 0.5x + 1.5$ and $p_0 = 4$, and consider fixed-point iteration.
    (a)   Show that the fixed point is $P = 3$.
    (b)   Show that $|P - p_n| = |P - p_{n-1}|/2$ for $n = 1, 2, 3, \ldots$.
    (c)   Show that $|P - p_n| = |P - p_0|/2^n$ for $n = 1, 2, 3, \ldots$.

10. Let $g(x) = x/2$, and consider fixed-point iteration.
    (a)   Find the quantity $|p_{k+1} - p_k|/|p_{k+1}|$.
    (b)   Discuss what will happen if only the relative error stopping criterion were used in Program 2.1.

11. For fixed-point iteration, discuss why it is an advantage to have $g'(P) \approx 0$.

Algorithms and Programs

1. Use Program 2.1 to approximate the fixed points (if any) of each function. Answers should be accurate to 12 decimal places. Produce a graph of each function and the line $y = x$ that clearly shows any fixed points.
    (a) $g(x) = x^5 - 3x^3 - 2x^2 + 2$
    (b) $g(x) = \cos(\sin(x))$
    (c) $g(x) = x^2 - \sin(x + 0.15)$
    (d) $g(x) = x^{x - \cos(x)}$

2.2 Bracketing Methods for Locating a Root

Consider a familiar topic of interest. Suppose that you save money by making regular monthly deposits P and the annual interest rate is I; then the total amount A after N deposits is

$$(1) \qquad A = P + P\left(1 + \frac{I}{12}\right) + P\left(1 + \frac{I}{12}\right)^2 + \cdots + P\left(1 + \frac{I}{12}\right)^{N-1}.$$

The first term on the right side of equation (1) is the last payment. Then the next-to-last payment, which has earned one period of interest, contributes $P(1 + I/12)$. The second-from-last payment has earned two periods of interest and contributes $P(1 + I/12)^2$, and so on. Finally, the last payment, which has earned interest for $N - 1$ periods, contributes $P(1 + I/12)^{N-1}$ toward the total. Recall that the formula for the sum of the N terms of a geometric series is

$$(2) \qquad 1 + r + r^2 + r^3 + \cdots + r^{N-1} = \frac{1 - r^N}{1 - r}.$$

We can write (1) in the form

$$A = P\left(1 + \left(1 + \frac{I}{12}\right) + \left(1 + \frac{I}{12}\right)^2 + \cdots + \left(1 + \frac{I}{12}\right)^{N-1}\right),$$

and use the substitution $r = (1 + I/12)$ in (2) to obtain

$$A = P \frac{1 - \left(1 + \dfrac{I}{12}\right)^N}{1 - \left(1 + \dfrac{I}{12}\right)}.$$

This can be simplified to obtain the annuity-due equation,

$$(3) \qquad\qquad A = \frac{P}{I/12}\left(\left(1 + \frac{I}{12}\right)^N - 1\right).$$

The following example uses the annuity-due equation and requires a sequence of repeated calculations to find an answer.

Example 2.6.   You save \$250 per month for 20 years and desire that the total value of all payments and interest is \$250,000 at the end of the 20 years. What interest rate I is needed to achieve your goal? If we hold $N = 240$ fixed, then A is a function of I alone; that is, $A = A(I)$. We will start with two guesses, $I_0 = 0.12$ and $I_1 = 0.13$, and perform a sequence of calculations to narrow down the final answer. Starting with $I_0 = 0.12$ yields

$$A(0.12) = \frac{250}{0.12/12}\left(\left(1 + \frac{0.12}{12}\right)^{240} - 1\right) = 247{,}314.$$

Since this value is a little short of the goal, we next try $I_1 = 0.13$:

$$A(0.13) = \frac{250}{0.13/12}\left(\left(1 + \frac{0.13}{12}\right)^{240} - 1\right) = 282{,}311.$$

This is a little high, so we try the value in the middle $I_2 = 0.125$:

$$A(0.125) = \frac{250}{0.125/12}\left(\left(1 + \frac{0.125}{12}\right)^{240} - 1\right) = 264{,}623.$$

This is again high and we conclude that the desired rate lies in the interval $[0.12, 0.125]$. The next guess is the midpoint $I_3 = 0.1225$:

$$A(0.1225) = \frac{250}{0.1225/12}\left(\left(1 + \frac{0.1225}{12}\right)^{240} - 1\right) = 255{,}803.$$

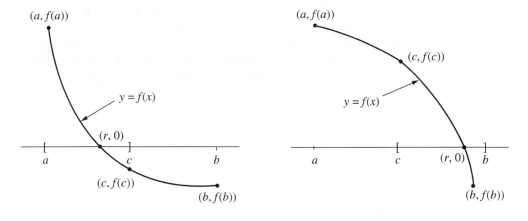

(a) If $f(a)$ and $f(c)$ have
opposite signs, then
squeeze from the right.

(b) If $f(c)$ and $f(b)$ have
opposite signs, then
squeeze from the left.

Figure 2.6   The decision process for the bisection process.

This is high and the interval is now narrowed to $[0.12, 0.1225]$. Our last calculation uses
the midpoint approximation $I_4 = 0.12125$:

$$A(0.12125) = \frac{250}{0.12125/12} \left(\left(1 + \frac{0.12125}{12} \right)^{240} - 1 \right) = 251{,}518.$$

Further iterations can be done to obtain as many significant digits as required. The
purpose of this example was to find the value of I that produced a specified level L of the
function value, that is, to find a solution to $A(I) = L$. It is standard practice to place the
constant L on the left and solve the equation $A(I) - L = 0$.   ∎

Definition 2.3.   Assume that $f(x)$ is a continuous function. Any number r for which
$f(r) = 0$ is called a ***root of the equation*** $f(x) = 0$. Also, we say that r is a ***zero of
the function*** $f(x)$.   ▲

For example, the equation $2x^2 + 5x - 3 = 0$ has two real roots $r_1 = 0.5$ and
$r_2 = -3$, whereas the corresponding function $f(x) = 2x^2 + 5x - 3 = (2x - 1)(x + 3)$
has two real zeros, $r_1 = 0.5$ and $r_2 = -3$.

Bisection Method of Bolzano

In this section we develop our first bracketing method for finding a zero of a continuous
function. We must start with an initial interval $[a, b]$, where $f(a)$ and $f(b)$ have
opposite signs. Since the graph $y = f(x)$ of a continuous function is unbroken, it will

cross the x-axis at a zero $x = r$ that lies somewhere in the interval (see Figure 2.6). The bisection method systematically moves the endpoints of the interval closer and closer together until we obtain an interval of arbitrarily small width that brackets the zero. The decision step for this process of interval halving is first to choose the midpoint $c = (a + b)/2$ and then to analyze the three possibilities that might arise:

(4)   If $f(a)$ and $f(c)$ have opposite signs, a zero lies in $[a, c]$.

(5)   If $f(c)$ and $f(b)$ have opposite signs, a zero lies in $[c, b]$.

(6)   If $f(c) = 0$, then the zero is c.

   If either case (4) or (5) occurs, we have found an interval half as wide as the original interval that contains the root, and we are "squeezing down on it" (see Figure 2.6). To continue the process, relabel the new smaller interval $[a, b]$ and repeat the process until the interval is as small as desired. Since the bisection process involves sequences of nested intervals and their midpoints, we will use the following notation to keep track of the details in the process:

(7)

$[a_0, b_0]$ is the starting interval and $c_0 = (a_0 + b_0)/2$ is the midpoint.

$[a_1, b_1]$ is the second interval, which brackets the zero r, and c_1 is its midpoint; the interval $[a_1, b_1]$ is half as wide as $[a_0, b_0]$.

After arriving at the nth interval $[a_n, b_n]$, which brackets r and has midpoint c_n, the interval $[a_{n+1}, b_{n+1}]$ is constructed, which also brackets r and is half as wide as $[a_n, b_n]$.

It is left as an exercise for the reader to show that the sequence of left endpoints is increasing and the sequence of right endpoints is decreasing; that is,

(8) $$a_0 \le a_1 \le \cdots \le a_n \le \cdots \le r \le \cdots \le b_n \le \cdots \le b_1 \le b_0,$$

where $c_n = (a_n + b_n)/2$, and if $f(a_{n+1})f(b_{n+1}) < 0$, then

(9) $[a_{n+1}, b_{n+1}] = [a_n, c_n]$ or $[a_{n+1}, b_{n+1}] = [c_n, b_n]$ for all n.

Theorem 2.4 (Bisection Theorem).   Assume that $f \in C[a, b]$ and that there exists a number $r \in [a, b]$ such that $f(r) = 0$. If $f(a)$ and $f(b)$ have opposite signs, and $\{c_n\}_{n=0}^{\infty}$ represents the sequence of midpoints generated by the bisection process of (8) and (9), then

(10) $$|r - c_n| \le \frac{b - a}{2^{n+1}}   \text{ for } n = 0, 1, \ldots,$$

and therefore the sequence $\{c_n\}_{n=0}^{\infty}$ converges to the zero $x = r$; that is,

(11) $$\lim_{n \to \infty} c_n = r.$$

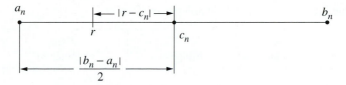

Figure 2.7   The root r and midpoint c_n of $[a_n, b_n]$ for the bisection method.

Proof.   Since both the zero r and the midpoint c_n lie in the interval $[a_n, b_n]$, the distance between c_n and r cannot be greater than half the width of this interval (see Figure 2.7). Thus

(12) $$|r - c_n| \le \frac{b_n - a_n}{2} \quad \text{for all } n.$$

Observe that the successive interval widths form the pattern

$$b_1 - a_1 = \frac{b_0 - a_0}{2^1},$$

$$b_2 - a_2 = \frac{b_1 - a_1}{2} = \frac{b_0 - a_0}{2^2}.$$

It is left as an exercise for the reader to use mathematical induction and show that

(13) $$b_n - a_n = \frac{b_0 - a_0}{2^n}.$$

Combining (12) and (13) results in

(14) $$|r - c_n| \le \frac{b_0 - a_0}{2^{n+1}} \quad \text{for all } n.$$

Now an argument similar to the one given in Theorem 2.3 can be used to show that (14) implies that the sequence $\{c_n\}_{n=0}^{\infty}$ converges to r and the proof of the theorem is complete.   ●

Example 2.7.   The function $h(x) = x \sin(x)$ occurs in the study of undamped forced oscillations. Find the value of x that lies in the interval $[0, 2]$, where the function takes on the value $h(x) = 1$ (the function $\sin(x)$ is evaluated in radians).

   We use the bisection method to find a zero of the function $f(x) = x \sin(x) - 1$. Starting with $a_0 = 0$ and $b_0 = 2$, we compute

$$f(0) = -1.000000 \quad \text{and} \quad f(2) = 0.818595,$$

so a root of $f(x) = 0$ lies in the interval $[0, 2]$. At the midpoint $c_0 = 1$, we find that $f(1) = -0.158529$. Hence the function changes sign on $[c_0, b_0] = [1, 2]$.

Table 2.1   Bisection Method Solution of $x \sin(x) - 1 = 0$

k	Left endpoint, a_k	Midpoint, c_k	Right endpoint, b_k	Function value, $f(c_k)$
0	0	1.	2.	−0.158529
1	1.0	1.5	2.0	0.496242
2	1.00	1.25	1.50	0.186231
3	1.000	1.125	1.250	0.015051
4	1.0000	1.0625	1.1250	−0.071827
5	1.06250	1.09375	1.12500	−0.028362
6	1.093750	1.109375	1.125000	−0.006643
7	1.1093750	1.1171875	1.1250000	0.004208
8	1.10937500	1.11328125	1.11718750	−0.001216
⋮	⋮	⋮	⋮	⋮

To continue, we squeeze from the left and set $a_1 = c_0$ and $b_1 = b_0$. The midpoint is $c_1 = 1.5$ and $f(c_1) = 0.496242$. Now, $f(1) = -0.158529$ and $f(1.5) = 0.496242$ imply that the root lies in the interval $[a_1, c_1] = [1.0, 1.5]$. The next decision is to squeeze from the right and set $a_2 = a_1$ and $b_2 = c_1$. In this manner we obtain a sequence $\{c_k\}$ that converges to $r \approx 1.114157141$. A sample calculation is given in Table 2.1.   ■

A virtue of the bisection method is that formula (10) provides a predetermined estimate for the accuracy of the computed solution. In Example 2.7 the width of the starting interval was $b_0 - a_0 = 2$. Suppose that Table 2.1 were continued to the thirty-first iterate; then, by (10), the error bound would be $|E_{31}| \leq (2 - 0)/2^{32} \approx 4.656613 \times 10^{-10}$. Hence c_{31} would be an approximation to r with nine decimal places of accuracy. The number N of repeated bisections needed to guarantee that the Nth midpoint c_N is an approximation to a zero and has an error less than the preassigned value δ is

$$(15) \qquad N = \text{int} \left(\frac{\ln(b - a) - \ln(\delta)}{\ln(2)} \right).$$

The proof of this formula is left as an exercise.

Another popular algorithm is the ***method of false position*** or the ***regula falsi method***. It was developed because the bisection method converges at a fairly slow speed. As before, we assume that $f(a)$ and $f(b)$ have opposite signs. The bisection method used the midpoint of the interval $[a, b]$ as the next iterate. A better approximation is obtained if we find the point $(c, 0)$ where the secant line L joining the points $(a, f(a))$ and $(b, f(b))$ crosses the x-axis (see Figure 2.8). To find the value c, we write down two versions of the slope m of the line L:

$$(16) \qquad m = \frac{f(b) - f(a)}{b - a},$$

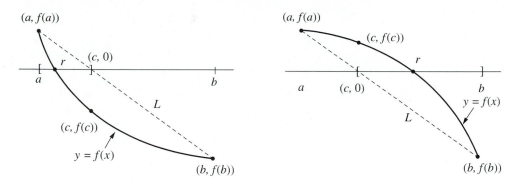

(a) If $f(a)$ and $f(c)$ have
    opposite signs, then
    squeeze from the right.

(b) If $f(c)$ and $f(b)$ have
    opposite signs, then
    squeeze from the left.

Figure 2.8   The decision process for the false position method.

where the points $(a, f(a))$ and $(b, f(b))$ are used, and

$$(17) \qquad m = \frac{0 - f(b)}{c - b},$$

where the points $(c, 0)$ and $(b, f(b))$ are used.

Equating the slopes in (16) and (17), we have

$$\frac{f(b) - f(a)}{b - a} = \frac{0 - f(b)}{c - b},$$

which is easily solved for c to get

$$(18) \qquad c = b - \frac{f(b)(b - a)}{f(b) - f(a)}.$$

The three possibilities are the same as before:

(19)   If $f(a)$ and $f(c)$ have opposite signs, a zero lies in $[a, c]$.

(20)   If $f(c)$ and $f(b)$ have opposite signs, a zero lies in $[c, b]$.

(21)   If $f(c) = 0$, then the zero is c.

Convergence of the False Position Method

The decision process implied by (19) and (20) along with (18) is used to construct a sequence of intervals $\{[a_n, b_n]\}$ each of which brackets the zero. At each step the approximation of the zero r is

$$(22) \qquad c_n = b_n - \frac{f(b_n)(b_n - a_n)}{f(b_n) - f(a_n)},$$

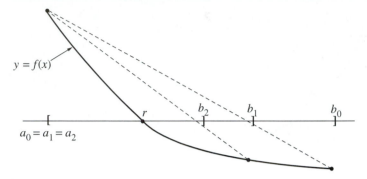

Figure 2.9   The stationary endpoint for the false position method.

and it can be proved that the sequence $\{c_n\}$ will converge to r. But beware; although the interval width $b_n - a_n$ is getting smaller, it is possible that it may not go to zero. If the graph of $y = f(x)$ is concave near $(r, 0)$, one of the endpoints becomes fixed and the other one marches into the solution (see Figure 2.9).

Now we rework the solution to $x \sin(x) - 1 = 0$ using the method of false position and observe that it converges faster than the bisection method. Also, notice that $\{b_n - a_n\}_{n=0}^{\infty}$ does not go to zero.

Example 2.8.   Use the false position method to find the root of $x \sin(x) - 1 = 0$ that is located in the interval $[0, 2]$ (the function $\sin(x)$ is evaluated in radians).

Starting with $a_0 = 0$ and $b_0 = 2$, we have $f(0) = -1.00000000$ and $f(2) = 0.81859485$, so a root lies in the interval $[0, 2]$. Using formula (22), we get

$$c_0 = 2 - \frac{0.81859485(2 - 0)}{0.81859485 - (-1)} = 1.09975017 \quad \text{and} \quad f(c_0) = -0.02001921.$$

The function changes sign on the interval $[c_0, b_0] = [1.09975017, 2]$, so we squeeze from the left and set $a_1 = c_0$ and $b_1 = b_0$. Formula (22) produces the next approximation:

$$c_1 = 2 - \frac{0.81859485(2 - 1.09975017)}{0.81859485 - (-0.02001921)} = 1.12124074$$

and

$$f(c_1) = 0.00983461.$$

Next $f(x)$ changes sign on $[a_1, c_1] = [1.09975017, 1.12124074]$, and the next decision is to squeeze from the right and set $a_2 = a_1$ and $b_2 = c_1$. A summary of the calculations is given in Table 2.2.   ∎

The termination criterion used in the bisection method is not useful for the false position method and may result in an infinite loop. The closeness of consecutive iterates and the size of $|f(c_n)|$ are both used in the termination criterion for Program 2.3. In Section 2.3 we discuss the reasons for this choice.

Table 2.2   False Position Method Solution of $x \sin(x) - 1 = 0$

k	Left endpoint, a_k	Midpoint, c_k	Right endpoint, b_k	Function value, $f(c_k)$
0	0.00000000	1.09975017	2.00000000	−0.02001921
1	1.09975017	1.12124074	2.00000000	0.00983461
2	1.09975017	1.11416120	1.12124074	0.00000563
3	1.09975017	1.11415714	1.11416120	0.00000000

Program 2.2 (Bisection Method). To approximate a root of the equation $f(x) = 0$ in the interval $[a, b]$. Proceed with the method only if $f(x)$ is continuous and $f(a)$ and $f(b)$ have opposite signs.

```
function [c,err,yc]=bisect(f,a,b,delta)
%Input   - f is the function input as a string 'f'
%         - a and b are the left and right endpoints
%         - delta is the tolerance
%Output - c is the zero
%         - yc=f(c)
%         - err is the error estimate for c
ya=feval(f,a);
yb=feval(f,b);
if ya*yb>0,break,end
max1=1+round((log(b-a)-log(delta))/log(2));
for k=1:max1
    c=(a+b)/2;
    yc=feval(f,c);
    if yc==0
        a=c;
        b=c;
elseif yb*yc>0
        b=c;
        yb=yc;
    else
        a=c;
        ya=yc;
    end
    if b-a < delta, break,end
end
c=(a+b)/2;
err=abs(b-a);
yc=feval(f,c);
```

Program 2.3 (False Position or Regula Falsi Method). To approximate a root of the equation $f(x) = 0$ in the interval $[a, b]$. Proceed with the method only if $f(x)$ is continuous and $f(a)$ and $f(b)$ have opposite signs.

```
function [c,err,yc]=regula(f,a,b,delta,epsilon,max1)
%Input   - f is the function input as a string 'f'
%         - a and b are the left and right endpoints
%         - delta is the tolerance for the zero
%         - epsilon is the tolerance for the value of f at the zero
%         - max1 is the maximum number of iterations
%Output  - c is the zero
%         - yc=f(c)
%         - err is the error estimate for c
ya=feval(f,a);
yb=feval(f,b);
if ya*yb>0
    disp('Note: f(a)*f(b)>0'),
    break,
end
for k=1:max1
    dx=yb*(b-a)/(yb-ya);
    c=b-dx;
    ac=c-a;
    yc=feval(f,c);
    if yc==0,break;
    elseif yb*yc>0
        b=c;
        yb=yc;
    else
        a=c;
        ya=yc;
    end
    dx=min(abs(dx),ac);
    if abs(dx)<delta,break,end
    if abs(yc)<epsilon,break,end
end
c;
err=abs(b-a)/2;
yc=feval(f,c);
```

Exercises for Bracketing Methods

In Exercises 1 and 2, find an approximation for the interest rate I that will yield the total annuity value A if 240 monthly payments P are made. Use the two starting values for I and compute the next three approximations using the bisection method.

1. $P = \$275$, $A = \$250{,}000$, $I_0 = 0.11$, $I_1 = 0.12$

2. $P = \$325$, $A = \$400{,}000$, $I_0 = 0.13$, $I_1 = 0.14$

3. For each function, find an interval $[a, b]$ so that $f(a)$ and $f(b)$ have opposite signs.
   (a) $f(x) = e^x - 2 - x$
   (b) $f(x) = \cos(x) + 1 - x$
   (c) $f(x) = \ln(x) - 5 + x$
   (d) $f(x) = x^2 - 10x + 23$

In Exercises 4 through 7, start with $[a_0, b_0]$ and use the false position method to compute c_0, c_1, c_2, and c_3.

4. $e^x - 2 - x = 0$, $[a_0, b_0] = [-2.4, -1.6]$

5. $\cos(x) + 1 - x = 0$, $[a_0, b_0] = [0.8, 1.6]$

6. $\ln(x) - 5 + x = 0$, $[a_0, b_0] = [3.2, 4.0]$

7. $x^2 - 10x + 23 = 0$, $[a_0, b_0] = [6.0, 6.8]$

8. Denote the intervals that arise in the bisection method by $[a_0, b_0]$, $[a_1, b_1]$, $\ldots$, $[a_n, b_n]$.
   (a)   Show that $a_0 \leq a_1 \leq \cdots \leq a_n \leq \cdots$ and that $\cdots \leq b_n \leq \cdots \leq b_1 \leq b_0$.
   (b)   Show that $b_n - a_n = (b_0 - a_0)/2^n$.
   (c)   Let the midpoint of each interval be $c_n = (a_n + b_n)/2$. Show that

$$\lim_{n \to \infty} a_n = \lim_{n \to \infty} c_n = \lim_{n \to \infty} b_n.$$

   Hint. Review convergence of monotone sequences in your calculus book.

9. What will happen if the bisection method is used with the function $f(x) = 1/(x - 2)$ and
   (a)   the interval is $[3, 7]$?   (b)   the interval is $[1, 7]$?

10. What will happen if the bisection method is used with the function $f(x) = \tan(x)$ and
   (a)   the interval is $[3, 4]$?   (b)   the interval is $[1, 3]$?

11. Suppose that the bisection method is used to find a zero of $f(x)$ in the interval $[2, 7]$. How many times must this interval be bisected to guarantee that the approximation c_N has an accuracy of 5×10^{-9}?

12. Show that formula (22) for the false position method is algebraically equivalent to

$$c_n = \frac{a_n f(b_n) - b_n f(a_n)}{f(b_n) - f(a_n)}.$$

13. Establish formula (15) for determining the number of iterations required in the bisection method. *Hint.* Use $|b - a|/2^{n+1} < \delta$ and take logarithms.

14. The polynomial $f(x) = (x-1)^3(x-2)(x-3)$ has three zeros: $x = 1$ of multiplicity 3 and $x = 2$ and $x = 3$, each of multiplicity 1. If a_0 and b_0 are any two real numbers such that $a_0 < 1$ and $b_0 > 3$, then $f(a_0)f(b_0) < 0$. Thus, on the interval $[a_0, b_0]$ the bisection method will converge to one of the three zeros. If $a_0 < 1$ and $b_0 > 3$ are selected such that $c_n = (a_n + b_n)/2$ is not equal to 1, 2, or 3 for any $n \geq 1$, then the bisection method will never converge to which zero(s)? Why?

15. If a polynomial, $f(x)$, has an odd number of real zeros in the interval $[a_0, b_0]$, and each of the zeros is of odd multiplicity, then $f(a_0)f(b_0) < 0$, and the bisection method will converge to one of the zeros. If $a_0 < 1$ and $b_0 > 3$ are selected such that $c_n = (a_n + b_n)/2$ is not equal to any of the zeros of $f(x)$ for any $n \geq 1$, then the bisection method will never converge to which zero(s)? Why?

Algorithms and Programs

1. Find an approximation (accurate to 10 decimal places) for the interest rate I that will yield a total annuity value of \$500,000 if 240 monthly payments of \$300 are made.

2. Consider a spherical ball of radius $r = 15$ cm that is constructed from a variety of white oak that has a density of $\rho = 0.710$. How much of the ball (accurate to eight decimal places) will be submerged when it is placed in water?

3. Modify Programs 2.2 and 2.3 to output a matrix analogous to Tables 2.1 and 2.2, respectively (i.e., the first row of the matrix would be $\begin{bmatrix} 0 & a_0 & c_0 & b_0 & f(c_0) \end{bmatrix}$).

4. Use your programs from Problem 3 to approximate the three smallest positive roots of $x = \tan(x)$ (accurate to eight decimal places).

5. A unit sphere is cut into two segments by a plane. One segment has three times the volume of the other. Determine the distance x of the plane from the center of the sphere (accurate to 10 decimal places).

2.3   Initial Approximation and Convergence Criteria

The bracketing methods depend on finding an interval $[a, b]$ so that $f(a)$ and $f(b)$ have opposite signs. Once the interval has been found, no matter how large, the iterations will proceed until a root is found. Hence these methods are called **globally convergent**. However, if $f(x) = 0$ has several roots in $[a, b]$, then a different starting interval must be used to find each root. It is not always easy to locate these smaller intervals on which $f(x)$ changes sign.

    In Section 2.4 we develop the Newton-Raphson method and the secant method for solving $f(x) = 0$. Both of these methods require that a close approximation to the root be given to guarantee convergence. Hence these methods are called **locally convergent**. They usually converge more rapidly than do global ones. Some hybrid algorithms start with a globally convergent method and switch to a locally convergent method when the iteration gets close to a root.

If the computation of roots is one part of a larger project, then a leisurely pace is suggested and the first thing to do is graph the function. We can view the graph $y = f(x)$ and make decisions based on what it looks like (concavity, slope, oscillatory behavior, local extrema, inflection points, etc.). But more important, if the coordinates of points on the graph are available, they can be analyzed and the approximate location of roots determined. These approximations can then be used as starting values in our root-finding algorithms.

We must proceed carefully. Computer software packages use graphics software of varying sophistication. Suppose that a computer is used to graph $y = f(x)$ on $[a, b]$. Typically, the interval is partitioned into $N + 1$ equally spaced points: $a = x_0 < x_1 < \cdots < x_N = b$ and the function values $y_k = f(x_k)$ computed. Then either a line segment or a "fitted curve" is plotted between consecutive points (x_{k-1}, y_{k-1}) and (x_k, y_k) for $k = 1, 2, \ldots, N$. There must be enough points so that we do not miss a root in a portion of the curve where the function is changing rapidly. If $f(x)$ is continuous and two adjacent points (x_{k-1}, y_{k-1}) and (x_k, y_k) lie on opposite sides of the x-axis, then the intermediate value theorem implies that at least one root lies in the interval $[x_{k-1}, x_k]$. But if there is a root, or even several closely spaced roots, in the interval $[x_{k-1}, x_k]$ and the two adjacent points (x_{k-1}, y_{k-1}) and (x_k, y_k) lie on the same side of the x-axis, then the computer-generated graph would not indicate a situation where the intermediate value theorem is applicable. The graph produced by the computer will not be a true representation of the actual graph of the function f. It is not unusual for functions to have "closely" spaced roots; that is, roots where the graph touches but does not cross the x-axis, or roots "close" to a vertical asymptote. Such characteristics of a function need to be considered when applying any numerical root-finding algorithm.

Finally, near two closely spaced roots or near a double root, the computer-generated curve between (x_{k-1}, y_{k-1}) and (x_k, y_k) may fail to cross or touch the x-axis. If $|f(x_k)|$ is smaller than a preassigned value ϵ (i.e., $f(x_k) \approx 0$), then x_k is a tentative approximate root. But the graph may be close to zero over a wide range of values near x_k, and thus x_k may not be close to an actual root. Hence we add the requirement that the slope change sign near (x_k, y_k); that is, $m_{k-1} = \dfrac{y_k - y_{k-1}}{x_k - x_{k-1}}$ and $m_k = \dfrac{y_{k+1} - y_k}{x_{k+1} - x_k}$ must have opposite signs. Since $x_k - x_{k-1} > 0$ and $x_{k+1} - x_k > 0$, it is not necessary to use the difference quotients, and it will suffice to check to see if the differences $y_k - y_{k-1}$ and $y_{k+1} - y_k$ change sign. In this case, x_k is the approximate root. Unfortunately, we cannot guarantee that this starting value will produce a convergent sequence. If the graph of $y = f(x)$ has a local minimum (or maximum) that is extremely close to zero, then it is possible that x_k will be reported as an approximate root when $f(x_k) \approx 0$, although x_k may not be close to a root.

Table 2.3   Finding Approximate Locations for Roots

	Function values		Differences in y		Significant changes in $f(x)$ or $f'(x)$
x_k	y_{k-1}	y_k	$y_k - y_{k-1}$	$y_{k+1} - y_k$	
−1.2	−3.125	−0.968	2.157	1.329	
−0.9	−0.968	0.361	1.329	0.663	f changes sign in $[x_{k-1}, x_k]$
−0.6	0.361	1.024	0.663	0.159	
−0.3	1.024	1.183	0.159	−0.183	f' changes sign near x_k
0.0	1.183	1.000	−0.183	−0.363	
0.3	1.000	0.637	−0.363	−0.381	
0.6	0.637	0.256	−0.381	−0.237	
0.9	0.256	0.019	−0.237	0.069	f' changes sign near x_k
1.2	0.019	0.088	0.069	0.537	

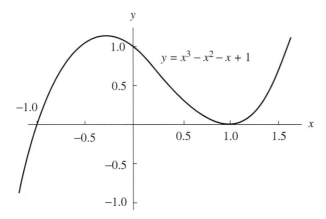

Figure 2.10   The graph of the cubic polynomial $y = x^3 - x^2 - x + 1$.

Example 2.9.   Find the approximate location of the roots of $x^3 - x^2 - x + 1 = 0$ on the interval $[-1.2, 1.2]$. For illustration, choose $N = 8$ and look at Table 2.3.

The three abscissas for consideration are -1.05, -0.3, and 0.9. Because $f(x)$ changes sign on the interval $[-1.2, -0.9]$, the value -1.05 is an approximate root; indeed, $f(-1.05) = -0.210$.

Although the slope changes sign near -0.3, we find that $f(-0.3) = 1.183$; hence -0.3 is not near a root. Finally, the slope changes sign near 0.9 and $f(0.9) = 0.019$, so 0.9 is an approximate root (see Figure 2.10). ■

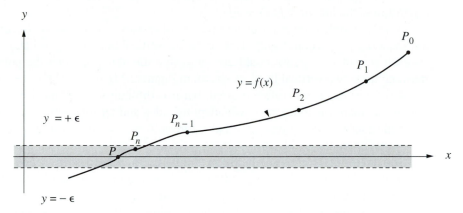

Figure 2.11   (a) The horizontal convergence band for locating a solution to $f(x) = 0$.

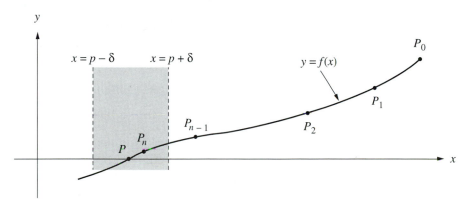

Figure 2.11   (b) The vertical convergence band for locating a solution to $f(x) = 0$.

Checking for Convergence

A graph can be used to see the approximate location of a root, but an algorithm must be used to compute a value p_n that is an acceptable computer solution. Iteration is often used to produce a sequence $\{p_k\}$ that converges to a root p, and a termination criterion or strategy must be designed ahead of time so that the computer will stop when an accurate approximation is reached. Since the goal is to solve $f(x) = 0$, the final value p_n should have the property that $|f(p_n)| < \epsilon$.

The user can supply a tolerance value ϵ for the size of $|f(p_n)|$ and then an iterative process produces points $P_k = (p_k, f(p_k))$ until the last point P_n lies in the horizontal band bounded by the lines $y = +\epsilon$ and $y = -\epsilon$, as shown in Figure 2.11(a). This criterion is useful if the user is trying to solve $h(x) = L$ by applying a root-finding algorithm to the function $f(x) = h(x) - L$.

Another termination criterion involves the abscissas, and we can try to determine if the sequence $\{p_k\}$ is converging. If we draw the vertical lines $x = p + \delta$ and $x = p - \delta$ on each side of $x = p$, we could decide to stop the iteration when the point P_n lies between these two vertical lines, as shown in Figure 2.11(b).

The latter criterion is often desired, but it is difficult to implement because it involves the unknown solution p. We adapt this idea and terminate further calculations when the consecutive iterates p_{n-1} and p_n are sufficiently close or if they agree within M significant digits.

Sometimes the user of an algorithm will be satisfied if $p_n \approx p_{n-1}$ and other times when $f(p_n) \approx 0$. Correct logical reasoning is required to understand the consequences. If we require that $|p_n - p| < \delta$ **and** $|f(p_n)| < \epsilon$, the point P_n will be located in the rectangular region about the solution $(p, 0)$, as shown in Figure 2.12(a). If we stipulate that $|p_n - p| < \delta$ **or** $|f(p_n)| < \epsilon$, the point P_n could be located anywhere in the region formed by the union of the horizontal and vertical stripes, as shown in Figure 2.12(b). The size of the tolerances δ and ϵ are crucial. If the tolerances are chosen too small, iteration may continue forever. They should be chosen about 100 times larger than 10^{-M}, where M is the number of decimal digits in the computer's floating-point numbers. The closeness of the abscissas is checked with one of the criteria

$$|p_n - p_{n-1}| < \delta \qquad \text{(estimate for the absolute error)}$$

or

$$\frac{2|p_n - p_{n-1}|}{|p_n| + |p_{n-1}|} < \delta \qquad \text{(estimate for the relative error)}.$$

The closeness of the ordinate is usually checked by $|f(p_n)| < \epsilon$.

Troublesome Functions

A computer solution to $f(x) = 0$ will almost always be in error due to round off and/or instability in the calculations. If the graph $y = f(x)$ is steep near the root $(p, 0)$, then the root-finding problem is well conditioned (i.e., a solution with several significant digits is easy to obtain). If the graph $y = f(x)$ is shallow near $(p, 0)$, then the root-finding problem is ill conditioned (i.e., the computed root may have only a few significant digits). This occurs when $f(x)$ has a multiple root at p. This is discussed further in the next section.

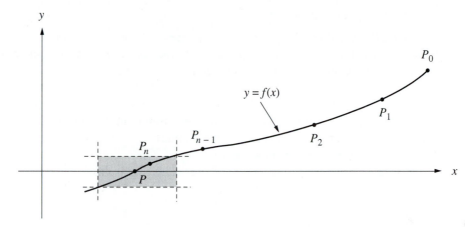

Figure 2.12 (a) The rectangular region defined by $|x - p| < \delta$ AND $|y| < \epsilon$.

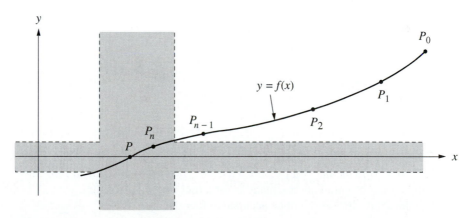

Figure 2.12 (b) The unbounded region defined by $|x - p| < \delta$ OR $|y| < \epsilon$.

Program 2.4 (Approximate Location of Roots). To roughly estimate the locations of the roots of the equation $f(x) = 0$ over the interval $[a, b]$, by using the equally spaced sample points $(x_k, f(x_k))$ and the following criteria:

  (i) $(y_{k-1})(y_k) < 0$, or

  (ii) $|y_k| < \epsilon$ and $(y_k - y_{k-1})(y_{k+1} - y_k) < 0$.

That is, either $f(x_{k-1})$ and $f(x_k)$ have opposite signs or $|f(x_k)|$ is small and the slope of the curve $y = f(x)$ changes sign near $(x_k, f(x_k))$.

```
function R = approot (X,epsilon)

% Input   - f is the object function saved as an M-file named f.m
%         - X is the vector of abscissas
%         - epsilon is the tolerance
% Output - R is the vector of approximate roots

Y=f(X);
yrange = max(Y)-min(Y);
epsilon2 = yrange*epsilon;
n=length(X);
m=0;
X(n+1)=X(n);
Y(n+1)=Y(n);

for k=2:n,
    if Y(k-1)*Y(k)<=0,
        m=m+1;
        R(m)=(X(k-1)+X(k))/2;
    end
    s=(Y(k)-Y(k-1))*(Y(k+1)-Y(k));
    if (abs(Y(k)) < epsilon2) & (s<=0),
        m=m+1;
        R(m)=X(k);
    end
end
end
```

Example 2.10. Use approot to find approximate locations for the roots of $f(x) = \sin(\cos(x^3))$ in the interval $[-2, 2]$. First save f as an M-file named f.m. Since the results will be used as initial approximations for a root-finding algorithm, we will construct X so that the approximations will be accurate to four decimal places.

```
>>X=-2:.001:2;

>>approot (X,0.00001)

ans=

-1.9875 -1.6765 -1.1625 1.1625 1.6765 1.9875
```

Comparing the results with the graph of f, we now have good initial approximations for one of our root-finding algorithms.   ■

Exercises for Initial Approximation

In Exercises 1 through 6, use a computer or graphics calculator to graphically determine the approximate location of the roots of $f(x) = 0$ in the given interval. In each case, determine an interval $[a, b]$ over which Programs 2.2 and 2.3 could be used to determine the roots (i.e., $f(a)f(b) < 0$).

1. $f(x) = x^2 - e^x$ for $-2 \le x \le 2$

2. $f(x) = x - \cos(x)$ for $-2 \le x \le 2$

3. $f(x) = \sin(x) - 2\cos(x)$ for $-2 \le x \le 2$

4. $f(x) = \cos(x) + (1 + x^2)^{-1}$ for $-2 \le x \le 2$

5. $f(x) = (x - 2)^2 - \ln(x)$ for $0.5 \le x \le 4.5$

6. $f(x) = 2x - \tan(x)$ for $-1.4 \le x \le 1.4$

Algorithms and Programs

In Problems 1 and 2 use a computer or graphics calculator and Program 2.4 to approximate the real roots, to four decimal places, of each function over the given interval. Then use Program 2.2 or Program 2.3 to approximate each root to 12 decimal places.

1. $f(x) = 1{,}000{,}000x^3 - 111{,}000x^2 + 1110x - 1$ for $-2 \le x \le 2$

2. $f(x) = 5x^{10} - 38x^9 + 21x^8 - 5\pi x^6 - 3\pi x^5 - 5x^2 + 8x - 3$ for $-15 \le x \le 15$.

3. A computer program that plots the graph of $y = f(x)$ over the interval $[a, b]$ using the points $(x_0, y_0), (x_1, y_1), \ldots$, and (x_N, y_N) usually scales the vertical height of the graph, and a procedure must be written to determine the minimum and maximum values of f over the interval.

    (a) Construct an algorithm that will find the values $Y_{\max} = \max_k\{y_k\}$ and $Y_{\min} = \min_k\{y_k\}$.

    (b) Write a MATLAB program that will find the approximate location and value of the extreme values of $f(x)$ on the interval $[a, b]$.

    (c) Use your program from part (b) to find the approximate location and value of the extreme values of the functions in Problems 1 and 2. Compare your approximations with the actual values.

2.4   Newton-Raphson and Secant Methods

Slope Methods for Finding Roots

If $f(x)$, $f'(x)$, and $f''(x)$ are continuous near a root p, then this extra information regarding the nature of $f(x)$ can be used to develop algorithms that will produce sequences $\{p_k\}$ that converge faster to p than either the bisection or false position method. The Newton-Raphson (or simply Newton's) method is one of the most useful and best known algorithms that relies on the continuity of $f'(x)$ and $f''(x)$. We shall introduce it graphically and then give a more rigorous treatment based on the Taylor polynomial.

Assume that the initial approximation p_0 is near the root p. Then the graph of $y = f(x)$ intersects the x-axis at the point $(p, 0)$, and the point $(p_0, f(p_0))$ lies on the curve near the point $(p, 0)$ (see Figure 2.13). Define p_1 to be the point of intersection of the x-axis and the line tangent to the curve at the point $(p_0, f(p_0))$. Then Figure 2.13 shows that p_1 will be closer to p than p_0 in this case. An equation relating p_1 and p_0 can be found if we write down two versions for the slope of the tangent line L:

$$(1) \qquad m = \frac{0 - f(p_0)}{p_1 - p_0},$$

which is the slope of the line through $(p_1, 0)$ and $(p_0, f(p_0))$, and

$$(2) \qquad m = f'(p_0),$$

which is the slope at the point $(p_0, f(p_0))$. Equating the values of the slope m in equations (1) and (2) and solving for p_1 results in

$$(3) \qquad p_1 = p_0 - \frac{f(p_0)}{f'(p_0)}.$$

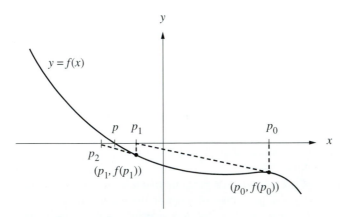

Figure 2.13   The geometric construction of p_1 and p_2 for the Newton-Raphson method.

The process above can be repeated to obtain a sequence $\{p_k\}$ that converges to p. We now make these ideas more precise.

Theorem 2.5 (Newton-Raphson Theorem).   Assume that $f \in C^2[a, b]$ and there exists a number $p \in [a, b]$, where $f(p) = 0$. If $f'(p) \neq 0$, then there exists a $\delta > 0$ such that the sequence $\{p_k\}_{k=0}^{\infty}$ defined by the iteration

(4) $$p_k = g(p_{k-1}) = p_{k-1} - \frac{f(p_{k-1})}{f'(p_{k-1})} \quad \text{for } k = 1, 2, \ldots$$

will converge to p for any initial approximation $p_0 \in [p - \delta, p + \delta]$.

Remark. The function $g(x)$ defined by the formula

(5) $$g(x) = x - \frac{f(x)}{f'(x)}$$

is called the ***Newton-Raphson iteration function***. Since $f(p) = 0$, it is easy to see that $g(p) = p$. Thus the Newton-Raphson iteration for finding the root of the equation $f(x) = 0$ is accomplished by finding a fixed point of the function $g(x)$.

Proof.   The geometric construction of p_1 shown in Figure 2.13 does not help in understanding why p_0 needs to be close to p or why the continuity of $f''(x)$ is essential. Our analysis starts with the Taylor polynomial of degree $n = 1$ and its remainder term:

(6) $$f(x) = f(p_0) + f'(p_0)(x - p_0) + \frac{f''(c)(x - p_0)^2}{2!},$$

where c lies somewhere between p_0 and x. Substituting $x = p$ into equation (6) and using the fact that $f(p) = 0$ produces

(7) $$0 = f(p_0) + f'(p_0)(p - p_0) + \frac{f''(c)(p - p_0)^2}{2!}.$$

If p_0 is close enough to p, the last term on the right side of (7) will be small compared to the sum of the first two terms. Hence it can be neglected and we can use the approximation

(8) $$0 \approx f(p_0) + f'(p_0)(p - p_0).$$

Solving for p in equation (8), we get $p \approx p_0 - f(p_0)/f'(p_0)$. This is used to define the next approximation p_1 to the root

(9) $$p_1 = p_0 - \frac{f(p_0)}{f'(p_0)}.$$

When p_{k-1} is used in place of p_0 in equation (9), the general rule (4) is established. For most applications this is all that needs to be understood. However, to fully comprehend what is happening, we need to consider the fixed-point iteration function and apply Theorem 2.2 in our situation. The key is in the analysis of $g'(x)$:

$$g'(x) = 1 - \frac{f'(x)f'(x) - f(x)f''(x)}{(f'(x))^2} = \frac{f(x)f''(x)}{(f'(x))^2}.$$

By hypothesis, $f(p) = 0$; thus $g'(p) = 0$. Since $g'(p) = 0$ and $g'(x)$ is continuous, it is possible to find a $\delta > 0$ so that the hypothesis $|g'(x)| < 1$ of Theorem 2.2 is satisfied on $(p - \delta, p + \delta)$. Therefore, a sufficient condition for p_0 to initialize a convergent sequence $\{p_k\}_{k=0}^{\infty}$, which converges to a root of $f(x) = 0$, is that $p_0 \in (p - \delta, p + \delta)$ and that δ be chosen so that

(10) $$\frac{|f(x)f''(x)|}{|f'(x)|^2} < 1 \quad \text{for all } x \in (p - \delta, p + \delta). \qquad \bullet$$

Corollary 2.2 (Newton's Iteration for Finding Square Roots).   Assume that $A > 0$ is a real number and let $p_0 > 0$ be an initial approximation to $\sqrt{A}$. Define the sequence $\{p_k\}_{k=0}^{\infty}$ using the recursive rule

(11) $$p_k = \frac{p_{k-1} + \dfrac{A}{p_{k-1}}}{2} \quad \text{for } k = 1, 2, \ldots.$$

Then the sequence $\{p_k\}_{k=0}^{\infty}$ converges to $\sqrt{A}$; that is, $\lim_{n \to \infty} p_k = \sqrt{A}$.

Outline of Proof.   Start with the function $f(x) = x^2 - A$, and notice that the roots of the equation $x^2 - A = 0$ are $\pm\sqrt{A}$. Now use $f(x)$ and the derivative $f'(x)$ in formula (5) and write down the Newton-Raphson iteration formula

(12) $$g(x) = x - \frac{f(x)}{f'(x)} = x - \frac{x^2 - A}{2x}.$$

This formula can be simplified to obtain

(13) $$g(x) = \frac{x + \dfrac{A}{x}}{2}.$$

When $g(x)$ in (13) is used to define the recursive iteration in (4), the result is formula (11). It can be proved that the sequence that is generated in (11) will converge for any starting value $p_0 > 0$. The details are left for the exercises. $\bullet$

An important point of Corollary 2.2 is the fact that the iteration function $g(x)$ involved only the arithmetic operations $+$, $-$, $\times$, and $/$. If $g(x)$ had involved the calculation of a square root, we would be caught in the circular reasoning that being able to calculate the square root would permit you to recursively define a sequence that will converge to $\sqrt{A}$. For this reason, $f(x) = x^2 - A$ was chosen, because it involved only the arithmetic operations.

Example 2.11.   Use Newton's square-root algorithm to find $\sqrt{5}$.
Starting with $p_0 = 2$ and using formula (11), we compute

$$p_1 = \frac{2 + 5/2}{2} = 2.25$$

$$p_2 = \frac{2.25 + 5/2.25}{2} = 2.236111111$$

$$p_3 = \frac{2.236111111 + 5/2.236111111}{2} = 2.236067978$$

$$p_4 = \frac{2.36067978 + 5/2.236067978}{2} = 2.236067978.$$

Further iterations produce $p_k \approx 2.236067978$ for $k > 4$, so we see that convergence accurate to nine decimal places has been achieved.   ∎

Now let us turn to a familiar problem from elementary physics and see why determining the location of a root is an important task. Suppose that a projectile is fired from the origin with an angle of elevation b_0 and initial velocity v_0. In elementary courses, air resistance is neglected and we learn that the height $y = y(t)$ and the distance traveled $x = x(t)$, measured in feet, obey the rules

(14) $$y = v_y t - 16t^2 \quad \text{and} \quad x = v_x t,$$

where the horizontal and vertical components of the initial velocity are $v_x = v_0 \cos(b_0)$ and $v_y = v_0 \sin(b_0)$, respectively. The mathematical model expressed by the rules in (14) is easy to work with, but tends to give too high an altitude and too long a range for the projectile's path. If we make the additional assumption that the air resistance is proportional to the velocity, the equations of motion become

(15) $$y = f(t) = (Cv_y + 32C^2)\left(1 - e^{-t/C}\right) - 32Ct$$

and

(16) $$x = r(t) = Cv_x \left(1 - e^{-t/C}\right),$$

where $C = m/k$ and k is the coefficient of air resistance and m is the mass of the projectile. A larger value of C will result in a higher maximum altitude and a longer range for the projectile. The graph of a flight path of a projectile when air resistance is considered is shown in Figure 2.14. This improved model is more realistic but requires the use of a root-finding algorithm for solving $f(t) = 0$ to determine the elapsed time until the projectile hits the ground. The elementary model in (14) does not require a sophisticated procedure to find the elapsed time.

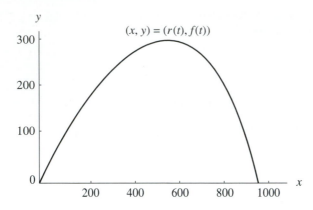

Figure 2.14 The path of a projectile with air resistance considered.

Table 2.4 Finding the Time When the Height $f(t)$ Is Zero

k	Time, p_k	$p_{k+1} - p_k$	Height, $f(p_k)$
0	8.00000000	0.79773101	83.22097200
1	8.79773101	−0.05530160	−6.68369700
2	8.74242941	−0.00025475	−0.03050700
3	8.74217467	−0.00000001	−0.00000100
4	8.74217466	0.00000000	0.00000000

Example 2.12. A projectile is fired with an angle of elevation $b_0 = 45°$, $v_y = v_x = 160$ ft/sec, and $C = 10$. Find the elapsed time until impact and find the range.

Using formulas (15) and (16), the equations of motion are $y = f(t) = 4800(1 - e^{-t/10}) - 320t$ and $x = r(t) = 1600(1 - e^{-t/10})$. Since $f(8) = 83.220972$ and $f(9) = -31.534367$, we will use the initial guess $p_0 = 8$. The derivative is $f'(t) = 480e^{-t/10} - 320$, and its value $f'(p_0) = f'(8) = -104.3220972$ is used in formula (4) to get

$$p_1 = 8 - \frac{83.22097200}{-104.3220972} = 8.797731010.$$

A summary of the calculation is given in Table 2.4.

The value p_4 has eight decimal places of accuracy, and the time until impact is $t \approx 8.74217466$ seconds. The range can now be computed using $r(t)$, and we get

$$r(8.74217466) = 1600\left(1 - e^{-0.874217466}\right) = 932.4986302 \text{ ft.} \quad \blacksquare$$

Division-by-Zero Error

One obvious pitfall of the Newton-Raphson method is the possibility of division by zero in formula (4), which would occur if $f'(p_{k-1}) = 0$. Program 2.5 has a procedure to check for this situation, but what use is the last calculated approximation p_{k-1} in this case? It is quite possible that $f(p_{k-1})$ is sufficiently close to zero and that p_{k-1} is an acceptable approximation to the root. We now investigate this situation and will uncover an interesting fact, that is, how fast the iteration converges.

Definition 2.4.   Assume that $f(x)$ and its derivatives $f'(x), \ldots, f^{(M)}(x)$ are defined and continuous on an interval about $x = p$. We say that $f(x) = 0$ has a ***root of order M*** at $x = p$ if and only if

(17) $f(p) = 0, \quad f'(p) = 0, \quad \ldots, \quad f^{(M-1)}(p) = 0, \quad \text{and} \quad f^{(M)}(p) \neq 0.$

A root of order $M = 1$ is often called a *simple root*, and if $M > 1$, it is called a *multiple root*. A root of order $M = 2$ is sometimes called a *double root*, and so on. The next result will illuminate these concepts.   ▲

Lemma 2.1.   If the equation $f(x) = 0$ has a root of order M at $x = p$, then there exists a continuous function $h(x)$ so that $f(x)$ can be expressed as the product

(18) $$f(x) = (x - p)^M h(x), \qquad \text{where } h(p) \neq 0.$$

Example 2.13.   The function $f(x) = x^3 - 3x + 2$ has a simple root at $p = -2$ and a double root at $p = 1$. This can be verified by considering the derivatives $f'(x) = 3x^2 - 3$ and $f''(x) = 6x$. At the value $p = -2$, we have $f(-2) = 0$ and $f'(-2) = 9$, so $M = 1$ in Definition 2.4; hence $p = -2$ is a simple root. For the value $p = 1$, we have $f(1) = 0$, $f'(1) = 0$, and $f''(1) = 6$, so $M = 2$ in Definition 2.4; hence $p = 1$ is a double root. Also, notice that $f(x)$ has the factorization $f(x) = (x + 2)(x - 1)^2$.   ■

Speed of Convergence

The distinguishing property we seek is the following. If p is a simple root of $f(x) = 0$, Newton's method will converge rapidly, and the number of accurate decimal places (roughly) doubles with each iteration. On the other hand, if p is a multiple root, the error in each successive approximation is a fraction of the previous error. To make this precise, we define the ***order of convergence***. This is a measure of how rapidly a sequence converges.

Definition 2.5.   Assume that $\{p_n\}_{n=0}^{\infty}$ converges to p and set $E_n = p - p_n$ for $n \geq 0$. If two positive constants $A \neq 0$ and $R > 0$ exist, and

(19) $$\lim_{n \to \infty} \frac{|p - p_{n+1}|}{|p - p_n|^R} = \lim_{n \to \infty} \frac{|E_{n+1}|}{|E_n|^R} = A,$$

Table 2.5   Newton's Method Converges Quadratically at a Simple Root

k	p_k	$p_{k+1} - p_k$	$E_k = p - p_k$	$\dfrac{|E_{k+1}|}{|E_k|^2}$
0	−2.400000000	0.323809524	0.400000000	0.476190475
1	−2.076190476	0.072594465	0.076190476	0.619469086
2	−2.003596011	0.003587422	0.003596011	0.664202613
3	−2.000008589	0.000008589	0.000008589	
4	−2.000000000	0.000000000	0.000000000	

then the sequence is said to converge to p with **order of convergence** R. The number A is called the *asymptotic error constant*. The cases $R = 1, 2$ are given special consideration.

(20)   If $R = 1$, the convergence of $\{p_n\}_{n=0}^{\infty}$ is called **linear**.

            If $R = 2$, the convergence of $\{p_n\}_{n=0}^{\infty}$ is called **quadratic**.   ▲

If R is large, the sequence $\{p_n\}$ converges rapidly to p; that is, relation (19) implies that for large values of n we have the approximation $|E_{n+1}| \approx A|E_n|^R$. For example, suppose that $R = 2$ and $|E_n| \approx 10^{-2}$; then we would expect that $|E_{n+1}| \approx A \times 10^{-4}$.

Some sequences converge at a rate that is not an integer, and we will see that the order of convergence of the secant method is $R = (1 + \sqrt{5})/2 \approx 1.618033989$.

Example 2.14 (Quadratic Convergence at a Simple Root).   Start with $p_0 = -2.4$ and use Newton-Raphson iteration to find the root $p = -2$ of the polynomial $f(x) = x^3 - 3x + 2$. The iteration formula for computing $\{p_k\}$ is

(21) $$p_k = g(p_{k-1}) = \frac{2p_{k-1}^3 - 2}{3p_{k-1}^2 - 3}.$$

Using formula (19) with $R = 2$ to check for quadratic convergence, we get the values in Table 2.5.   ■

A detailed look at the rate of convergence in Example 2.14 will reveal that the error in each successive iteration is proportional to the square of the error in the previous iteration. That is,

$$|p - p_{k+1}| \approx A|p - p_k|^2,$$

where $A \approx 2/3$. To check this, we use

$$|p - p_3| = 0.000008589 \quad \text{and} \quad |p - p_2|^2 = |0.003596011|^2 = 0.000012931$$

and it is easy to see that

$$|p - p_3| = 0.000008589 \approx 0.000008621 = \frac{2}{3}|p - p_2|^2.$$

Table 2.6   Newton's Method Converges Linearly at a Double Root

k	p_k	$p_{k+1} - p_k$	$E_k = p - p_k$	$\dfrac{\lvert E_{k+1} \rvert}{\lvert E_k \rvert}$
0	1.200000000	−0.096969697	−0.200000000	0.515151515
1	1.103030303	−0.050673883	−0.103030303	0.508165253
2	1.052356420	−0.025955609	−0.052356420	0.496751115
3	1.026400811	−0.013143081	−0.026400811	0.509753688
4	1.013257730	−0.006614311	−0.013257730	0.501097775
5	1.006643419	−0.003318055	−0.006643419	0.500550093
⋮	⋮	⋮	⋮	⋮

Example 2.15 (Linear Convergence at a Double Root).   Start with $p_0 = 1.2$ and use Newton-Raphson iteration to find the double root $p = 1$ of the polynomial $f(x) = x^3 - 3x + 2$. Using formula (20) to check for linear convergence, we get the values in Table 2.6.   ∎

Notice that the Newton-Raphson method is converging to the double root, but at a slow rate. The values of $f(p_k)$ in Example 2.15 go to zero faster than the values of $f'(p_k)$, so the quotient $f(p_k)/f'(p_k)$ in formula (4) is defined when $p_k \neq p$. The sequence is converging linearly, and the error is decreasing by a factor of approximately $1/2$ with each successive iteration. The following theorem summarizes the performance of Newton's method on simple and double roots.

Theorem 2.6 (Convergence Rate for Newton-Raphson Iteration).   Assume that Newton-Raphson iteration produces a sequence $\{p_n\}_{n=0}^{\infty}$ that converges to the root p of the function $f(x)$. If p is a simple root, convergence is quadratic and

$$(22) \qquad \lvert E_{n+1} \rvert \approx \frac{\lvert f''(p) \rvert}{2 \lvert f'(p) \rvert} \lvert E_n \rvert^2 \quad \text{for } n \text{ sufficiently large.}$$

If p is a multiple root of order M, convergence is linear and

$$(23) \qquad \lvert E_{n+1} \rvert \approx \frac{M-1}{M} \lvert E_n \rvert \quad \text{for } n \text{ sufficiently large.}$$

Pitfalls

The division-by-zero error was easy to anticipate, but there are other difficulties that are not so easy to spot. Suppose that the function is $f(x) = x^2 - 4x + 5$; then the sequence $\{p_k\}$ of real numbers generated by formula (4) will wander back and forth from left to right and not converge. A simple analysis of the situation reveals that $f(x) > 0$ and has no real roots.

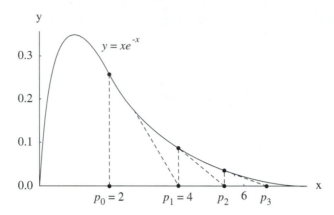

Figure 2.15 (a) Newton-Raphson iteration for $f(x) = xe^{-x}$ can produce a divergent sequence.

Sometimes the initial approximation p_0 is too far away from the desired root and the sequence $\{p_k\}$ converges to some other root. This usually happens when the slope $f'(p_0)$ is small and the tangent line to the curve $y = f(x)$ is nearly horizontal. For example, if $f(x) = \cos(x)$ and we seek the root $p = \pi/2$ and start with $p_0 = 3$, calculation reveals that $p_1 = -4.01525255$, $p_2 = -4.85265757, \ldots$, and $\{p_k\}$ will converge to a different root $-3\pi/2 \approx -4.71238898$.

Suppose that $f(x)$ is positive and monotone decreasing on the unbounded interval $[a, \infty)$ and $p_0 > a$; then the sequence $\{p_k\}$ might diverge to $+\infty$. For example, if $f(x) = xe^{-x}$ and $p_0 = 2.0$, then

$$p_1 = 4.0, \qquad p_2 = 5.333333333, \qquad \ldots, \qquad p_{15} = 19.723549434, \qquad \ldots,$$

and $\{p_k\}$ diverges slowly to $+\infty$ (see Figure 2.15(a)). This particular function has another surprising problem. The value of $f(x)$ goes to zero rapidly as x gets large, for example, $f(p_{15}) = 0.0000000536$, and it is possible that p_{15} could be mistaken for a root. For this reason we designed the stopping criterion in Program 2.5 to involve the relative error $2|p_{k+1} - p_k|/(|p_k|+10^{-6})$, and when $k = 15$, this value is 0.106817, so the tolerance $\delta = 10^{-6}$ will help guard against reporting a false root.

Another phenomenon, **cycling**, occurs when the terms in the sequence $\{p_k\}$ tend to repeat or almost repeat. For example, if $f(x) = x^3 - x - 3$ and the initial approximation is $p_0 = 0$, then the sequence is

$$p_1 = -3.000000, \qquad p_2 = -1.961538, \qquad p_3 = -1.147176, \qquad p_4 = -0.006579,$$
$$p_5 = -3.000389, \qquad p_6 = -1.961818, \qquad p_7 = -1.147430, \qquad \ldots$$

and we are stuck in a cycle where $p_{k+4} \approx p_k$ for $k = 0, 1, \ldots$ (see Figure 2.15(b)). But if the starting value p_0 is sufficiently close to the root $p \approx 1.671699881$, then $\{p_k\}$

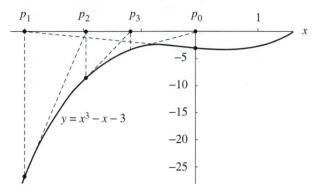

Figure 2.15   (b) Newton-Raphson iteration for $f(x) = x^3 - x - 3$ can produce a cyclic sequence.

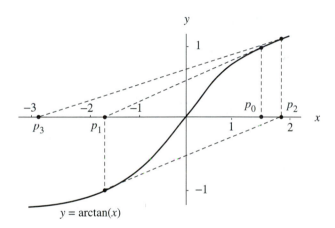

Figure 2.15   (c) Newton-Raphson iteration for $f(x) = \arctan(x)$ can produce a divergent oscillating sequence.

converges. If $p_0 = 2$, the sequence converges: $p_1 = 1.72727272$, $p_2 = 1.67369173$, $p_3 = 1.671702570$, and $p_4 = 1.671699881$.

When $|g'(x)| \geq 1$ on an interval containing the root p, there is a chance of divergent oscillation. For example, let $f(x) = \arctan(x)$; then the Newton-Raphson iteration function is $g(x) = x - (1 + x^2) \arctan(x)$, and $g'(x) = -2x \arctan(x)$. If the starting value $p_0 = 1.45$ is chosen, then

$$p_1 = -1.550263297, \qquad p_2 = 1.845931751, \qquad p_3 = -2.889109054,$$

etc. (see Figure 2.15(c)). But if the starting value is sufficiently close to the root $p = 0$,

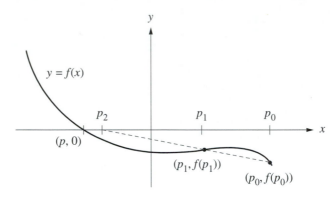

Figure 2.16   The geometric construction of p_2 for the secant method.

a convergent sequence results. If $p_0 = 0.5$, then

$$p_1 = -0.079559511, \qquad p_2 = 0.000335302, \qquad p_3 = 0.000000000.$$

The situations above point to the fact that we must be honest in reporting an answer. Sometimes the sequence does not converge. It is not always the case that after N iterations a solution is found. The user of a root-finding algorithm needs to be warned of the situation when a root is not found. If there is other information concerning the context of the problem, then it is less likely that an erroneous root will be found. Sometimes $f(x)$ has a definite interval in which a root is meaningful. If knowledge of the behavior of the function or an "accurate" graph is available, then it is easier to choose p_0.

Secant Method

The Newton-Raphson algorithm requires the evaluation of two functions per iteration, $f(p_{k-1})$ and $f'(p_{k-1})$. Traditionally, the calculation of derivatives of elementary functions could involve considerable effort. But with modern computer algebra software packages, this has become less of an issue. Still many functions have nonelementary forms (integrals, sums, etc.), and it is desirable to have a method that converges almost as fast as Newton's method yet involves only evaluations of $f(x)$ and not of $f'(x)$. The secant method will require only one evaluation of $f(x)$ per step and at a simple root has an order of convergence $R \approx 1.618033989$. It is almost as fast as Newton's method, which has order 2.

The formula involved in the secant method is the same one that was used in the regula falsi method, except that the logical decisions regarding how to define each succeeding term are different. Two initial points $(p_0, f(p_0))$ and $(p_1, f(p_1))$ near the point $(p, 0)$ are needed, as shown in Figure 2.16. Define p_2 to be the abscissa

Table 2.7   Convergence of the Secant Method at a Simple Root

k	p_k	$p_{k+1} - p_k$	$E_k = p - p_k$	$\dfrac{\lvert E_{k+1}\rvert}{\lvert E_k\rvert^{1.618}}$
0	-2.600000000	0.200000000	0.600000000	0.914152831
1	-2.400000000	0.293401015	0.400000000	0.469497765
2	-2.106598985	0.083957573	0.106598985	0.847290012
3	-2.022641412	0.021130314	0.022641412	0.693608922
4	-2.001511098	0.001488561	0.001511098	0.825841116
5	-2.000022537	0.000022515	0.000022537	0.727100987
6	-2.000000022	0.000000022	0.000000022	
7	-2.000000000	0.000000000	0.000000000	

of the point of intersection of the line through these two points and the x-axis; then Figure 2.16 shows that p_2 will be closer to p than to either p_0 or p_1. The equation relating p_2, p_1, and p_0 is found by considering the slope

$$(24) \qquad m = \frac{f(p_1) - f(p_0)}{p_1 - p_0} \quad \text{and} \quad m = \frac{0 - f(p_1)}{p_2 - p_1}.$$

The values of m in (25) are the slope of the secant line through the first two approximations and the slope of the line through $(p_1, f(p_1))$ and $(p_2, 0)$, respectively. Set the right-hand sides equal in (25) and solve for $p_2 = g(p_1, p_0)$ and get

$$(25) \qquad p_2 = g(p_1, p_0) = p_1 - \frac{f(p_1)(p_1 - p_0)}{f(p_1) - f(p_0)}.$$

The general term is given by the two-point iteration formula

$$(26) \qquad p_{k+1} = g(p_k, p_{k-1}) = p_k - \frac{f(p_k)(p_k - p_{k-1})}{f(p_k) - f(p_{k-1})}.$$

Example 2.16 (Secant Method at a Simple Root).   Start with $p_0 = -2.6$ and $p_1 = -2.4$ and use the secant method to find the root $p = -2$ of the polynomial function $f(x) = x^3 - 3x + 2$.

In this case the iteration formula (27) is

$$(27) \qquad p_{k+1} = g(p_k, p_{k-1}) = p_k - \frac{(p_k^3 - 3p_k + 2)(p_k - p_{k-1})}{p_k^3 - p_{k-1}^3 - 3p_k + 3p_{k-1}}.$$

This can be algebraically manipulated to obtain

$$(28) \qquad p_{k+1} = g(p_k, p_{k-1}) = \frac{p_k^2 p_{k-1} + p_k p_{k-1}^2 - 2}{p_k^2 + p_k p_{k-1} + p_{k-1}^2 - 3}.$$

The sequence of iterates is given in Table 2.7.   ■

There is a relationship between the secant method and Newton's method. For a polynomial function $f(x)$, the secant method two-point formula $p_{k+1} = g(p_k, p_{k-1})$ will reduce to Newton's one-point formula $p_{k+1} = g(p_k)$ if p_k is replaced by p_{k-1}. Indeed, if we replace p_k by p_{k-1} in (29), then the right side becomes the same as the right side of (22) in Example 2.14.

Proofs about the rate of convergence of the secant method can be found in advanced texts on numerical analysis. Let us state that the error terms satisfy the relationship

$$(29) \qquad |E_{k+1}| \approx |E_k|^{1.618} \left| \frac{f''(p)}{2f'(p)} \right|^{0.618}$$

where the order of convergence is $R = (1 + \sqrt{5})/2 \approx 1.618$ and the relation in (30) is valid only at simple roots.

To check this, we make use of Example 2.16 and the specific values

$$|p - p_5| = 0.000022537$$
$$|p - p_4|^{1.618} = 0.001511098^{1.618} = 0.000027296,$$

and

$$A = |f''(-2)/2f'(-2)|^{0.618} = (2/3)^{0.618} = 0.778351205.$$

Combine these and it is easy to see that

$$|p - p_5| = 0.000022537 \approx 0.000021246 = A|p - p_4|^{1.618}.$$

Accelerated Convergence

We could hope that there are root-finding techniques that converge faster than linearly when p is a root of order M. Our final result shows that a modification can be made to Newton's method so that convergence becomes quadratic at a multiple root.

Theorem 2.7 (Acceleration of Newton-Raphson Iteration). Suppose that the Newton-Raphson algorithm produces a sequence that converges linearly to the root $x = p$ of order $M > 1$. Then the Newton-Raphson iteration formula

$$(30) \qquad p_k = p_{k-1} - \frac{Mf(p_{k-1})}{f'(p_{k-1})}$$

will produce a sequence $\{p_k\}_{k=0}^{\infty}$ that converges quadratically to p.

Table 2.8   Acceleration of Convergence at a Double Root

k	p_k	$p_{k+1} - p_k$	$E_k = p - p_k$	$\dfrac{\|E_{k+1}\|}{\|E_k\|^2}$
0	1.200000000	−0.193939394	−0.200000000	0.151515150
1	1.006060606	−0.006054519	−0.006060606	0.165718578
2	1.000006087	−0.000006087	−0.000006087	
3	1.000000000	0.000000000	0.000000000	

Table 2.9   Comparison of the Speed of Convergence

Method	Special considerations	Relation between successive error terms
Bisection		$E_{k+1} \approx \frac{1}{2}\|E_k\|$
Regula falsi		$E_{k+1} \approx A\|E_k\|$
Secant method	Multiple root	$E_{k+1} \approx A\|E_k\|$
Newton-Raphson	Multiple root	$E_{k+1} \approx A\|E_k\|$
Secant method	Simple root	$E_{k+1} \approx A\|E_k\|^{1.618}$
Newton-Raphson	Simple root	$E_{k+1} \approx A\|E_k\|^2$
Accelerated Newton-Raphson	Multiple root	$E_{k+1} \approx A\|E_k\|^2$

Example 2.17 (Acceleration of Convergence at a Double Root).   Start with $p_0 = 1.2$ and use accelerated Newton-Raphson iteration to find the double root $p = 1$ of $f(x) = x^3 - 3x + 2$.

Since $M = 2$, the acceleration formula (31) becomes

$$p_k = p_{k-1} - 2\,\frac{f(p_{k-1})}{f'(p_{k-1})} = \frac{p_{k-1}^3 + 3p_{k-1} - 4}{3p_{k-1}^2 - 3},$$

and we obtain the values in Table 2.8.   ∎

Table 2.9 compares the speed of convergence of the various root-finding methods that we have studied so far. The value of the constant A is different for each method.

Program 2.5 (Newton-Raphson Iteration). To approximate a root of $f(x) = 0$ given one initial approximation p_0 and using the iteration

$$p_k = p_{k-1} - \frac{f(p_{k-1})}{f'(p_{k-1})} \quad \text{for } k = 1, 2, \ldots.$$

```
function [p0,err,k,y]=newton(f,df,p0,delta,epsilon,max1)
%Input   - f is the object function input as a string 'f'
%         - df is the derivative of f input as a string 'df'
%         - p0 is the initial approximation to a zero of f
%         - delta is the tolerance for p0
%         - epsilon is the tolerance for the function values y
%         - max1 is the maximum number of iterations
%Output - p0 is the Newton-Raphson approximation to the zero
%         - err is the error estimate for p0
%         - k is the number of iterations
%         - y is the function value f(p0)

for k=1:max1
    p1=p0-feval(f,p0)/feval(df,p0);
    err=abs(p1-p0);
    relerr=2*err/(abs(p1)+delta);
    p0=p1;
    y=feval(f,p0);
    if (err<delta)|(relerr<delta)|(abs(y)<epsilon),break,end
end
```

Program 2.6 (Secant Method). To approximate a root of $f(x) = 0$ given two initial approximations p_0 and p_1 and using the iteration

$$p_{k+1} = p_k - \frac{f(p_k)(p_k - p_{k-1})}{f(p_k) - f(p_{k-1})} \quad \text{for } k = 1, 2, \ldots.$$

```
function [p1,err,k,y]=secant(f,p0,p1,delta,epsilon,max1)
%Input   - f is the object function input as a string 'f'
%         - p0 and p1 are the initial approximations to a zero
%         - delta is the tolerance for p1
%         - epsilon is the tolerance for the function values y
%         - max1 is the maximum number of iterations
%Output - p1 is the secant method approximation to the zero
%         - err is the error estimate for p1
%         - k is the number of iterations
%         - y is the function value f(p1)

for k=1:max1
```

```
p2=p1-feval(f,p1)*(p1-p0)/(feval(f,p1)-feval(f,p0));
err=abs(p2-p1);
relerr=2*err/(abs(p2)+delta);
p0=p1;
p1=p2;
y=feval(f,p1);
if (err<delta)|(relerr<delta)|(abs(y)<epsilon),break,end
end
```

Exercises for Newton-Raphson and Secant Methods

For problems involving calculations, you can use either a calculator or a computer.

1. Let $f(x) = x^2 - x + 2$.
   - **(a)** Find the Newton-Raphson formula $p_k = g(p_{k-1})$.
   - **(b)** Start with $p_0 = -1.5$ and find p_1, p_2, and p_3.

2. Let $f(x) = x^2 - x - 3$.
   - **(a)** Find the Newton-Raphson formula $p_k = g(p_{k-1})$.
   - **(b)** Start with $p_0 = 1.6$ and find p_1, p_2, and p_3.
   - **(c)** Start with $p_0 = 0.0$ and find p_1, p_2, p_3, and p_4. What do you conjecture about this sequence?

3. Let $f(x) = (x - 2)^4$.
   - **(a)** Find the Newton-Raphson formula $p_k = g(p_{k-1})$.
   - **(b)** Start with $p_0 = 2.1$ and find p_1, p_2, p_3, and p_4.
   - **(c)** Is the sequence converging quadratically or linearly?

4. Let $f(x) = x^3 - 3x - 2$.
   - **(a)** Find the Newton-Raphson formula $p_k = g(p_{k-1})$.
   - **(b)** Start with $p_0 = 2.1$ and find p_1, p_2, p_3, and p_4.
   - **(c)** Is the sequence converging quadratically or linearly?

5. Consider the function $f(x) = \cos(x)$.
   - **(a)** Find the Newton-Raphson formula $p_k = g(p_{k-1})$.
   - **(b)** We want to find the root $p = 3\pi/2$. Can we use $p_0 = 3$? Why?
   - **(c)** We want to find the root $p = 3\pi/2$. Can we use $p_0 = 5$? Why?

6. Consider the function $f(x) = \arctan(x)$.
   - **(a)** Find the Newton-Raphson formula $p_k = g(p_{k-1})$.
   - **(b)** If $p_0 = 1.0$, then find p_1, p_2, p_3, and p_4. What is $\lim_{n \to \infty} p_k$?
   - **(c)** If $p_0 = 2.0$, then find p_1, p_2, p_3, and p_4. What is $\lim_{n \to \infty} p_k$?

7. Consider the function $f(x) = xe^{-x}$.
   (a)   Find the Newton-Raphson formula $p_k = g(p_{k-1})$.
   (b)   If $p_0 = 0.2$, then find p_1, p_2, p_3, and p_4. What is $\lim_{n \to \infty} p_k$?
   (c)   If $p_0 = 20$, then find p_1, p_2, p_3, and p_4. What is $\lim_{n \to \infty} p_k$?
   (d)   What is the value of $f(p_4)$ in part (c)?

In Exercises 8 through 10, use the secant method and formula (27) and compute the next two iterates p_2 and p_3.

8. Let $f(x) = x^2 - 2x - 1$. Start with $p_0 = 2.6$ and $p_1 = 2.5$.

9. Let $f(x) = x^2 - x - 3$. Start with $p_0 = 1.7$ and $p_1 = 1.67$.

10. Let $f(x) = x^3 - x + 2$. Start with $p_0 = -1.5$ and $p_1 = -1.52$.

11. *Cube-root algorithm.*   Start with $f(x) = x^3 - A$, where A is any real number, and derive the recursive formula

$$p_k = \frac{2p_{k-1} + A/p_{k-1}^2}{3} \qquad \text{for } k = 1, \ 2, \ \ldots.$$

12. Consider $f(x) = x^N - A$, where N is a positive integer.
    (a)   What real values are the solution to $f(x) = 0$ for the various choices of N and A that can arise?
    (b)   Derive the recursive formula

$$p_k = \frac{(N-1)p_{k-1} + A/p_{k-1}^{N-1}}{N} \qquad \text{for } k = 1, \ 2, \ \ldots.$$

    for finding the Nth root of A.

13. Can Newton-Raphson iteration be used to solve $f(x) = 0$ if $f(x) = x^2 - 14x + 50$? Why?

14. Can Newton-Raphson iteration be used to solve $f(x) = 0$ if $f(x) = x^{1/3}$? Why?

15. Can Newton-Raphson iteration be used to solve $f(x) = 0$ if $f(x) = (x-3)^{1/2}$ and the starting value is $p_0 = 4$? Why?

16. Establish the limit of the sequence in (11).

17. Prove that the sequence $\{p_k\}$ in equation (4) of Theorem 2.5 converges to p. Use the following steps.
    (a)   Show that if p is a fixed point of $g(x)$ in equation (5), then p is a zero of $f(x)$.
    (b)   If p is a zero of $f(x)$ and $f'(p) \neq 0$, show that $g'(p) = 0$. Use part (b) and Theorem 2.3 to show that the sequence $\{p_k\}$ in equation (4) converges to p.

18. Prove equation (23) of Theorem 2.6. Use the following steps. By Theorem 1.11, we can expand $f(x)$ about $x = p_k$ to get

$$f(x) = f(p_k) + f'(p_k)(x - p_k) + \frac{1}{2}f''(c_k)(x - p_k)^2.$$

Since p is a zero of $f(x)$, we set $x = p$ and obtain

$$0 = f(p_k) + f'(p_k)(p - p_k) + \frac{1}{2}f''(c_k)(p - p_k)^2.$$

(a) Now assume that $f'(x) \neq 0$ for all x near the root p. Use the facts given above and $f'(p_k) \neq 0$ to show that

$$p - p_k + \frac{f(p_k)}{f'(p_k)} = \frac{-f''(c_k)}{2f'(p_k)}(p - p_k)^2.$$

(b) Assume that $f'(x)$ and $f''(x)$ do not change too rapidly so that we can use the approximations $f'(p_k) \approx f'(p)$ and $f''(c_k) \approx f''(p)$. Now use part (a) to get

$$E_{k+1} \approx \frac{-f''(p)}{2f'(p)}E_k^2.$$

19. Suppose that A is a positive real number.
   (a) Show that A has the representation $A = q \times 2^{2m}$, where $1/4 \leq q < 1$ and m is an integer.
   (b) Use part (a) to show that the square root is $A^{1/2} = q^{1/2} \times 2^m$. *Remark.* Let $p_0 = (2q + 1)/3$, where $1/4 \leq q < 1$, and use Newton's formula (11). After three iterations, p_3 will be an approximation to $q^{1/2}$ with a precision of 24 binary digits. This is the algorithm that is often used in the computer's hardware to compute square roots.

20. (a) Show that formula (27) for the secant method is algebraically equivalent to

$$p_{k+1} = \frac{p_{k-1}f(p_k) - p_k f(p_{k-1})}{f(p_k) - f(p_{k-1})}.$$

   (b) Explain why loss of significance in subtraction makes this formula inferior for computational purposes to the one given in formula (27).

21. Suppose that p is a root of order $M = 2$ for $f(x) = 0$. Prove that the accelerated Newton-Raphson iteration

$$p_k = p_{k-1} - \frac{2f(p_{k-1})}{f'(p_{k-1})}$$

converges quadratically (see Exercise 18).

22. *Halley's method* is another way to speed up convergence of Newton's method. The Halley iteration formula is

$$g(x) = x - \frac{f(x)}{f'(x)}\left[1 - \frac{f(x)f''(x)}{2(f'(x))^2}\right]^{-1}.$$

The term in brackets is the modification of the Newton-Raphson formula. Halley's method will yield cubic convergence $(R = 3)$ at simple zeros of $f(x)$.
   (a) Start with $f(x) = x^2 - A$ and find Halley's iteration formula $g(x)$ for finding $\sqrt{A}$. Use $p_0 = 2$ to approximate $\sqrt{5}$ and compute p_1, p_2, and p_3.

(b) Start with $f(x) = x^3 - 3x + 2$ and find Halley's iteration formula $g(x)$. Use $p_0 = -2.4$ and compute p_1, p_2, and p_3.

23. *Modified Newton-Raphson method for multiple roots.* If p is a root of multiplicity M, then $f(x) = (x - p)^M q(x)$, where $q(p) \neq 0$.

(a) Show that $h(x) = f(x)/f'(x)$ has a simple root at p.

(b) Show that when the Newton-Raphson method is applied to finding the simple root p of $h(x)$, we get $g(x) = x - h(x)/h'(x)$, which becomes

$$g(x) = x - \frac{f(x)f'(x)}{(f'(x))^2 - f(x)f''(x)}.$$

(c) The iteration using $g(x)$ in part (b) converges quadratically to p. Explain why this happens.

(d) Zero is a root of multiplicity 3 for the function $f(x) = \sin(x^3)$. Start with $p_0 = 1$ and compute p_1, p_2, and p_3 using the modified Newton-Raphson method.

24. Suppose that an iterative method for solving $f(x) = 0$ produces the following four consecutive error terms (see Example 2.14): $E_0 = 0.400000$, $E_1 = 0.043797$, $E_2 = 0.000062$, and $E_3 = 0.000000$. Estimate the asymptotic error constant A and the order of convergence R of the sequence generated by the iterative method.

Algorithms and Programs

1. Modify Programs 2.5 and 2.6 to display an appropriate error message when (a) division by zero occurs in (4) or (27), respectively, or (b) the maximum number of iterations, max1, is exceeded.

2. It is often instructive to display the terms in the sequences generated by (4) and (27) (i.e., the second column of Table 2.4). Modify Programs 2.5 and 2.6 to display the sequences generated by (4) and (27), respectively.

3. Modify Program 2.5 to use Newton's square-root algorithm to approximate each of the following square roots to 10 decimal places.

(a) Start with $p_0 = 3$ and approximate $\sqrt{8}$.

(b) Start with $p_0 = 10$ and approximate $\sqrt{91}$.

(c) Start with $p_0 = -3$ and approximate $-\sqrt{8}$.

4. Modify Program 2.5 to use the cube-root algorithm in Exercise 11 to approximate each of the following cube roots to 10 decimal places.

(a) Start with $p_0 = 2$ and approximate $7^{1/3}$.

(b) Start with $p_0 = 6$ and approximate $200^{1/3}$.

(c) Start with $p_0 = -2$ and approximate $(-7)^{1/3}$.

5. Modify Program 2.5 to use the accelerated Newton-Raphson algorithm in Theorem 2.7 to find the root p of order M of each of the following functions.

   (a) $f(x) = (x - 2)^5$, $M = 5$, $p = 2$; start with $p_0 = 1$.

   (b) $f(x) = \sin(x^3)$, $M = 3$, $p = 0$; start with $p_0 = 1$.

   (c) $f(x) = (x - 1)\ln(x)$, $M = 2$, $p = 1$; start with $p_0 = 2$.

6. Modify Program 2.5 to use Halley's method in Exercise 22 to find the simple zero of $f(x) = x^3 - 3x + 2$, using $p_0 = -2.4$.

7. Suppose that the equations of motion for a projectile are

$$y = f(t) = 9600(1 - e^{-t/15}) - 480t$$
$$x = r(t) = 2400(1 - e^{-t/15}).$$

   (a)   Find the elapsed time until impact accurate to 10 decimal places.

   (b)   Find the range accurate to 10 decimal places.

8. (a)   Find the point on the parabola $y = x^2$ that is closest to the point $(3, 1)$ accurate to 10 decimal places.

   (b)   Find the point on the graph of $y = \sin(x - \sin(x))$ that is closest to the point $(2.1, 0.5)$ accurate to 10 decimal places.

   (c)   Find the value of x at which the minimum vertical distance between the graphs of $f(x) = x^2 + 2$ and $g(x) = (x/5) - \sin(x)$ occurs accurate to 10 decimal places.

9. An open-top box is constructed from a rectangular piece of sheet metal measuring 10 by 16 inches. Squares of what size (accurate to 0.000000001 inch) should be cut from the corners if the volume of the box is to be 100 cubic inches?

10. A catenary is the curve formed by a hanging cable. Assume that the lowest point is $(0, 0)$; then the formula for the catenary is $y = C \cosh(x/C) - C$. To determine the catenary that goes through $(\pm a, b)$ we must solve the equation $b = C \cosh(a/C) - C$ for C.

   (a)   Show that the catenary through $(\pm 10, 6)$ is $y = 9.1889 \cosh(x/9.1889) - 9.1889$.

   (b)   Find the catenary that passes through $(\pm 12, 5)$.

2.5   Aitken's Process and Steffensen's and Muller's Methods (Optional)

In Section 2.4 we saw that Newton's method converged slowly at a multiple root and the sequence of iterates $\{p_k\}$ exhibited linear convergence. Theorem 2.7 showed how to speed up convergence, but it depends on knowing the order of the root in advance.

Aitken's Process

A technique called *Aitken's Δ^2 process* can be used to speed up convergence of any sequence that is linearly convergent. In order to proceed, we will need a definition.

Definition 2.6.   Given the sequence $\{p_n\}_{n=0}^{\infty}$, define the forward difference Δp_n by

$$(1) \qquad\qquad \Delta p_n = p_{n+1} - p_n \quad \text{for } n \geq 0.$$

Higher powers $\Delta^k p_n$ are defined recursively by

$$(2) \qquad\qquad \Delta^k p_n = \Delta^{k-1}(\Delta p_n) \quad \text{for } k \geq 2. \qquad\qquad \blacktriangle$$

Theorem 2.8 (Aitken's Acceleration).   Assume that the sequence $\{p_n\}_{n=0}^{\infty}$ converges linearly to the limit p and that $p - p_n \neq 0$ for all $n \geq 0$. If there exists a real number A with $|A| < 1$ such that

$$(3) \qquad\qquad \lim_{n \to \infty} \frac{p - p_{n+1}}{p - p_n} = A,$$

then the sequence $\{q_n\}_{n=0}^{\infty}$ defined by

$$(4) \qquad\qquad q_n = p_n - \frac{(\Delta p_n)^2}{\Delta^2 p_n} = p_n - \frac{(p_{n+1} - p_n)^2}{p_{n+2} - 2p_{n+1} + p_n}$$

converges to p faster than $\{p_n\}_{n=0}^{\infty}$, in the sense that

$$(5) \qquad\qquad \lim_{n \to \infty} \left| \frac{p - q_n}{p - p_n} \right| = 0.$$

Proof.   We will show how to derive formula (4) and will leave the proof of (5) as an exercise. Since the terms in (3) are approaching a limit, we can write

$$(6) \qquad \frac{p - p_{n+1}}{p - p_n} \approx A \quad \text{and} \quad \frac{p - p_{n+2}}{p - p_{n+1}} \approx A \quad \text{when } n \text{ is large.}$$

The relations in (6) imply that

$$(7) \qquad\qquad (p - p_{n+1})^2 \approx (p - p_{n+2})(p - p_n).$$

Table 2.10   Linearly Convergent Sequence $\{p_n\}$

n	p_n	$E_n = p_n - p$	$A_n = \dfrac{E_n}{E_{n-1}}$
1	0.606530660	0.039387369	−0.586616609
2	0.545239212	−0.021904079	−0.556119357
3	0.579703095	0.012559805	−0.573400269
4	0.560064628	−0.007078663	−0.563596551
5	0.571172149	0.004028859	−0.569155345
6	0.564862947	−0.002280343	−0.566002341

Table 2.11   Derived Sequence $\{q_n\}$ Using Aitken's Process

n	q_n	$q_n - p$
1	0.567298989	0.000155699
2	0.567193142	0.000049852
3	0.567159364	0.000016074
4	0.567148453	0.000005163
5	0.567144952	0.000001662
6	0.567143825	0.000000534

When both sides of (7) are expanded and the terms p^2 are canceled, the result is

(8)
$$p \approx \frac{p_{n+2}p_n - p_{n+1}^2}{p_{n+2} - 2p_{n+1} + p_n} = q_n \quad \text{for } n = 0,\ 1,\ \ldots.$$

The formula in (8) is used to define the term q_n. It can be rearranged algebraically to obtain formula (4), which has less error propagation when computer calculations are made.   ●

Example 2.18.   Show that the sequence $\{p_n\}$ in Example 2.2 exhibits linear convergence, and show that the sequence $\{q_n\}$ obtained by Aitken's Δ^2 process converges faster.

The sequence $\{p_n\}$ was obtained by fixed-point iteration using the function $g(x) = e^{-x}$ and starting with $p_0 = 0.5$. After convergence has been achieved, the limit is $P \approx 0.567143290$. The values p_n and q_n are given in Tables 2.10 and 2.11. For illustration, the value of q_1 is given by the calculation

$$q_1 = p_1 - \frac{(p_2 - p_1)^2}{p_3 - 2p_2 + p_1}$$

$$= 0.606530660 - \frac{(-0.061291448)^2}{0.095755331} = 0.567298989. \quad ■$$

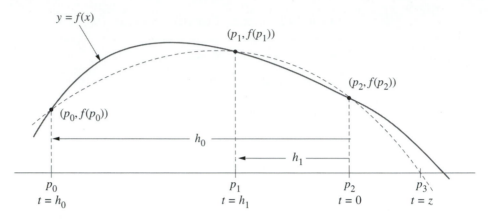

Figure 2.17 The starting approximations p_0, p_1, and p_2 for Muller's method, and the differences h_0 and h_1.

Although the sequence $\{q_n\}$ in Table 2.11 converges linearly, it converges faster than $\{p_n\}$ in the sense of Theorem 2.8, and usually Aitken's method gives a better improvement than this. When Aitken's process is combined with fixed-point iteration, the result is called *Steffensen's acceleration*. The details are given in Program 2.7 and in the exercises.

Muller's Method

Muller's method is a generalization of the secant method, in the sense that it does not require the derivative of the function. It is an iterative method that requires three starting points $(p_0, f(p_0))$, $(p_1, f(p_1))$, and $(p_2, f(p_2))$. A parabola is constructed that passes through the three points; then the quadratic formula is used to find a root of the quadratic for the next approximation. It has been proved that near a simple root Muller's method converges faster than the secant method and almost as fast as Newton's method. The method can be used to find real or complex zeros of a function and can be programmed to use complex arithmetic.

Without loss of generality, we assume that p_2 is the best approximation to the root and consider the parabola through the three starting values, shown in Figure 2.17. Make the change of variable

(9) $$t = x - p_2,$$

and use the differences

(10) $$h_0 = p_0 - p_2 \quad \text{and} \quad h_1 = p_1 - p_2.$$

Consider the quadratic polynomial involving the variable t:

(11) $$y = at^2 + bt + c.$$

Each point is used to obtain an equation involving a, b, and c:

$$
\begin{array}{lll}
\text{At } t = h_0: & ah_0^2 + bh_0 + c = f_0, \\
\text{At } t = h_1: & ah_1^2 + bh_1 + c = f_1, \\
\text{At } t = 0: & a0^2 + b0 + c = f_2.
\end{array}
$$

(12)

From the third equation in (12), we see that

$$
(13) \qquad c = f_2.
$$

Substituting (13) into the first two equations in (12) and using the definition $e_0 = f_0 - c$ and $e_1 = f_1 - c$ results in the linear system

$$
\begin{aligned}
ah_0^2 + bh_0 &= f_0 - c = e_0, \\
ah_1^2 + bh_1 &= f_1 - c = e_1.
\end{aligned}
$$

(14)

Solving the linear system for a and b results in

$$
a = \frac{e_0 h_1 - e_1 h_0}{h_1 h_0^2 - h_0 h_1^2}
$$

(15)

$$
b = \frac{e_1 h_0^2 - e_0 h_1^2}{h_1 h_0^2 - h_0 h_1^2}.
$$

The quadratic formula is used to find the roots $t = z_1, z_2$ of (11):

$$
(16) \qquad z = \frac{-2c}{b \pm \sqrt{b^2 - 4ac}}.
$$

Formula (16) is equivalent to the standard formula for the roots of a quadratic and is better in this case because we know that $c = f_2$.

To ensure the stability of the method, we choose the root in (16) that has the smallest absolute value. If $b > 0$, use the positive sign with the square root, and if $b < 0$, use the negative sign. Then p_3 is shown in Figure 2.17 and is given by

$$
(17) \qquad p_3 = p_2 + z.
$$

To update the iterates, choose the new p_0 and the new p_1 to be the two values selected from among the old $\{p_0, p_1, p_3\}$ that lie closest to p_3 (i.e., throw out the one that is farthest away). Then take new p_2 to be old p_3. Although a lot of auxiliary calculations are done in Muller's method, it only requires one function evaluation per iteration.

If Muller's method is used to find the real roots of $f(x) = 0$, it is possible that one may encounter complex approximations, because the roots of the quadratic in (16) might be complex (nonzero imaginary components). In these cases the imaginary components will have a small magnitude and can be set equal to zero so that the calculations proceed with real numbers.

Table 2.12 Comparison of Convergence near a Simple Root

k	Secant method	Muller's method	Newton's method	Steffensen with Newton
0	−2.600000000	−2.600000000	−2.400000000	−2.400000000
1	−2.400000000	−2.500000000	−2.076190476	−2.076190476
2	−2.106598985	−2.400000000	−2.003596011	−2.003596011
3	−2.022641412	−1.985275287	−2.000008589	−1.982618143
4	−2.001511098	−2.000334062	−2.000000000	−2.000204982
5	−2.000022537	−2.000000218		−2.000000028
6	−2.000000022	−2.000000000		−2.000002389
7	−2.000000000			−2.000000000

Comparison of Methods

Steffensen's method can be used together with the Newton-Raphson fixed-point function $g(x) = x − f(x)/f'(x)$. In the next two examples we look at the roots of the polynomial $f(x) = x^3 − 3x + 2$. The Newton-Raphson function is $g(x) = (2x^3 − 2)/(3x^2 − 3)$. When this function is used in Program 2.7, we get the calculations under the heading Steffensen with Newton in Tables 2.12 and 2.13. For example, starting with $p_0 = −2.4$, we would compute

$$(18) \qquad p_1 = g(p_0) = −2.076190476,$$

and

$$(19) \qquad p_2 = g(p_1) = −2.003596011.$$

Then Aitken's improvement will give $p_3 = −1.982618143$.

Example 2.19 (Convergence near a Simple Root). This is a comparison of methods for the function $f(x) = x^3 − 3x + 2$ near the simple root $p = −2$.

Newton's method and the secant method for this function were given in Examples 2.14 and 2.16, respectively. Table 2.12 provides a summary of calculations for the methods. ∎

Example 2.20 (Convergence near a Double Root). This is a comparison of the methods for the function $f(x) = x^3 − 3x + 2$ near the double root $p = 1$. Table 2.13 provides a summary of calculations. ∎

Newton's method is the best choice for finding a simple root (see Table 2.12). At a double root, either Muller's method or Steffensen's method with the Newton-Raphson formula is a good choice (see Table 2.13). Note in the Aitken's acceleration formula (4) that division by zero can occur as the sequence $\{p_k\}$ converges. In this case, the last calculated approximation to zero should be used as the approximation to the zero of f.

Table 2.13   Comparison of Convergence near a Double Root

k	Secant method	Muller's method	Newton's method	Steffensen with Newton
0	1.400000000	1.400000000	1.200000000	1.200000000
1	1.200000000	1.300000000	1.103030303	1.103030303
2	1.138461538	1.200000000	1.052356417	1.052356417
3	1.083873738	1.003076923	1.026400814	0.996890433
4	1.053093854	1.003838922	1.013257734	0.998446023
5	1.032853156	1.000027140	1.006643418	0.999223213
6	1.020429426	0.999997914	1.003325375	0.999999193
7	1.012648627	0.999999747	1.001663607	0.999999597
8	1.007832124	1.000000000	1.000832034	0.999999798
9	1.004844757		1.000416075	0.999999999
	$\vdots$		$\vdots$	

In the following program the sequence $\{p_k\}$, generated by Steffensen's method with the Newton-Raphson formula, is stored in a matrix Q that has max1 rows and three columns. The first column of Q contains the initial approximation to the root, p_0, and the terms $p_3, p_6, \ldots, p_{3k}, \ldots$ generated by Aitken's acceleration method (4). The second and third columns of Q contain the terms generated by Newton's method. The stopping criteria in the program are based on the difference between consecutive terms from the first column of Q.

Program 2.7 (Steffensen's Acceleration). To quickly find a solution of the fixed-point equation $x = g(x)$ given an initial approximation p_0; where it is assumed that both $g(x)$ and $g'(x)$ are continuous, $|g'(x)| < 1$, and that ordinary fixed-point iteration converges slowly (linearly) to p.

```
function [p,Q]=steff(f,df,p0,delta,epsilon,max1)
%Input   - f is the object function input as a string 'f'
%         - df is the derivative of f input as a string 'df'
%         - p0 is the initial approximation to a zero of f
%         - delta is the tolerance for p0
%         - epsilon is the tolerance for the function values y
%         - max1 is the maximum number of iterations
%Output - p is the Steffensen approximation to the zero
%         - Q is the matrix containing the Steffensen sequence

%Initialize the matrix R
R=zeros(max1,3);
R(1,1)=p0;
```

```
for k=1:max1
    for j=2:3
        %Denominator in Newton-Raphson method is calculated
        nrdenom=feval(df,R(k,j-1));

        %Calculate Newton-Raphson approximations
        if nrdenom==0
            'division by zero in Newton-Raphson method'
            break
        else
            R(k,j)=R(k,j-1)-feval(f,R(k,j-1))/nrdenom;
        end

        %Denominator in Aitken's acceleration process calculated
        aadenom=R(k,3)-2*R(k,2)+R(k,1);

        %Calculate Aitken's acceleration approximations
        if aadenom==0
            'division by zero in Aitken's acceleration'
            break
        else
            R(k+1,1)=R(k,1)-(R(k,2)-R(k,1))^2/aadenom;
        end

    end

    %End program if division by zero occurred
    if (nrdenom==0)|(aadenom==0)
        break
    end

    %Stopping criteria are evaluated
    err=abs(R(k,1)-R(k+1,1));
    relerr=err/(abs(R(k+1,1))+delta);
    y=feval(f,R(k+1,1));
    if (err<delta)|(relerr<delta)|(y<epsilon)
        % p and the matrix Q are determined
        p=R(k+1,1);
        Q=R(1:k+1,:);
        break
    end

end
```

Program 2.8 (Muller's Method).   To find a root of the equation $f(x) = 0$ given three distinct initial approximations p_0, p_1, and p_2.

```
function [p,y,err]=muller(f,p0,p1,p2,delta epsilon,max1)
%Input   - f is the object function input as a string 'f'
%         - p0, p1, and p2 are the initial approximations
%         - delta is the tolerance for p0, p1, and p2
%         - epsilon the the tolerance for the function values y
%         - max1 is the maximum number of iterations
%Output - p is the Muller approximation to the zero of f
%         - y is the function value y = f(p)
%         - err is the error in the approximation of p.
%Initialize the matrices P and Y
P=[p0 p1 p2];
Y=feval(f,P);
%Calculate a and b in formula (15)
for k=1:max1
    h0=P(1)-P(3);h1=P(2)-P(3);e0=Y(1)-Y(3);e1=Y(2)-Y(3);c=Y(3);
    denom=h1*h0^2-h0*h1^2;
    a=(e0*h1-e1*h0)/denom;
    b=(e1*h0^2-e0*h1^2)/denom;
    %Suppress any complex roots
    if b^2-4*a*c > 0
        disc=sqrt(b^2-4*a*c);
    else
        disc=0;
    end
    %Find the smallest root of (17)
    if b < 0
        disc=-disc;
    end
    z=-2*c/(b+disc);
    p=P(3)+z;
    %Sort the entries of P to find the two closest to p
    if abs(p-P(2))<abs(p-P(1))
        Q=[P(2) P(1) P(3)];
        P=Q;
        Y=feval(f,P);
    end
    if abs(p-P(3))<abs(p-P(2))
        R=[P(1) P(3) P(2)];
        P=R;
```

```
        Y=feval(f,P);
    end

    %Replace the entry of P that was farthest from p with p
    P(3)=p;
    Y(3) = feval(f,P(3));
    y=Y(3);

    %Determine stopping criteria
    err=abs(z);
    relerr=err/(abs(p)+delta);
    if (err<delta)|(relerr<delta)|(abs(y)<epsilon)
        break
    end
end
```

Exercises for Aitken's, Steffensen's, and Muller's Methods

1. Find Δp_n, where
   (a) $p_n = 5$ (b) $p_n = 6n + 2$ (c) $p_n = n(n + 1)$

2. Let $p_n = 2n^2 + 1$. Find $\Delta^k p_n$, where
   (a) $k = 2$ (b) $k = 3$ (c) $k = 4$

3. Let $p_n = 1/2^n$. Show that $q_n = 0$ for all n, where q_n is given by formula (4).

4. Let $p_n = 1/n$. Show that $q_n = 1/(2n + 2)$ for all n; hence there is little acceleration of convergence. Does $\{p_n\}$ converge to 0 linearly? Why?

5. Let $p_n = 1/(2^n - 1)$. Show that $q_n = 1/\left(4^{n+1} - 1\right)$ for all n.

6. The sequence $p_n = 1/(4^n + 4^{-n})$ converges linearly to 0. Use Aitken's formula (4) to find q_1, q_2, and q_3, and hence speed up the convergence.

n	p_n	q_n
0	0.5	−0.26437542
1	0.23529412	
2	0.06225681	
3	0.01562119	
4	0.00390619	
5	0.00097656	

7. The sequence $\{p_n\}$ generated by fixed-point iteration starting with $p_0 = 2.5$ and using the function $g(x) = (6 + x)^{1/2}$ converges linearly to $p = 3$. Use Aitken's formula (4) to find q_1, q_2, and q_3, and hence speed up the convergence.

8. The sequence $\{p_n\}$ generated by fixed-point iteration, starting with $p_0 = 3.14$, and using the function $g(x) = \ln(x) + 2$ converges linearly to $p \approx 3.1419322$. Use Aitken's formula (4) to find q_1, q_2, and q_3, and hence speed up the convergence.

9. For the equation $\cos(x) - 1 = 0$, the Newton-Raphson function is $g(x) = x - (1 - \cos(x))/\sin(x) = x - \tan(x/2)$. Use Steffensen's algorithm with $g(x)$ and start with $p_0 = 0.5$, and find p_1, p_2, and p_3; then find p_4, p_5, and p_6.

10. *Convergence of series.* Aitken's method can be used to speed up the convergence of a series. If the nth partial sum of the series is

$$S_n = \sum_{k=1}^{n} A_k,$$

show that the derived series using Aitken's method is

$$T_n = S_n + \frac{A_{n+1}^2}{A_{n+1} - A_{n+2}}.$$

In Exercises 11 through 14, apply Aitken's method and the results of Exercise 10 to speed up the convergence of the series.

11. $S_n = \sum_{k=1}^{n} (0.99)^k$

12. $S_n = \sum_{k=1}^{n} \frac{1}{4^k + 4^{-k}}$

13. $S_n = \sum_{k=1}^{n} \frac{k}{2^{k-1}}$

14. $S_n = \sum_{k=1}^{n} \frac{1}{2^k k}$

15. Use Muller's method to find the root of $f(x) = x^3 - x - 2$. Start with $p_0 = 1.0$, $p_1 = 1.2$, and $p_2 = 1.4$ and find p_3, p_4, and p_5.

16. Use Muller's method to find the root of $f(x) = 4x^2 - e^x$. Start with $p_0 = 4.0$, $p_1 = 4.1$, and $p_2 = 4.2$ and find p_3, p_4, and p_5.

17. Let $\{p_n\}$ and $\{q_n\}$ be any two sequences of real numbers. Show that
    (a) $\Delta(p_n + q_n) = \Delta p_n + \Delta q_n$
    (b) $\Delta(p_n q_n) = p_{n+1} \Delta q_n + q_n \Delta p_n$

18. Start with formula (8), add the terms p_{n+2} and $-p_{n+2}$ to the right side, and show that an equivalent formula is

$$p \approx p_{n+2} - \frac{(p_{n+2} - p_{n+1})^2}{p_{n+2} - 2p_{n+1} + p_n} = q_n.$$

19. Assume that the error in an iteration process satisfies the relation $E_{n+1} = KE_n$ for some constant K and $|K| < 1$.
    (a)   Find an expression for E_n that involves E_0, K, and n.
    (b)   Find an expression for the smallest integer N so that $|E_N| < 10^{-8}$.

Algorithms and Programs

1. Use Steffensen's method with the initial approximation $p_0 = 0.5$ to approximate the zero of $f(x) = x - \sin(x)$ accurate to 10 decimal places.

2. Use Steffensen's method with the initial approximation $p_0 = 0.5$ to approximate the zero of $f(x) = \sin(x^3)$ closest to 0.5 accurate to 10 decimal places.

3. Use Muller's method with the initial approximations $p_0 = 1.5$, $p_1 = 1.4$, and $p_2 = 1.3$ to find a zero of $f(x) = 1 + 2x - \tan(x)$ accurate to 12 decimal places.

4. In Program 2.8 (Muller's method) a 1×3 matrix P is initialized with p_0, p_1, and p_2. Then at the end of the loop, one of the values p_0, p_1, or p_2 is replaced with the new approximation to the zero. This process is continued until the stopping criteria are satisfied, say at $k = K$. Modify Program 2.8 so that, in addition to p and err, a $(K + 1) \times 3$ matrix Q is produced such that the first row of Q contains the 1×3 matrix P with the initial approximations to the zero, and the kth row of Q contains the kth set of three approximations to the zero.

   Use this modification of Program 2.8 with the initial approximations $p_0 = 2.4$, $p_1 = 2.3$, and $p_2 = 2.2$ to find a zero of $f(x) = 3\cos(x) + 2\sin(x)$ accurate to eight decimal places.

3

Solution of Linear Systems $AX = B$

Three planes form the boundary of a solid in the first octant, which is shown in Figure 3.1. Suppose that the equations for these planes are

$$5x + y + z = 5$$
$$x + 4y + z = 4$$
$$x + y + 3z = 3.$$

What are the coordinates of the point of intersection of the three planes? Gaussian elimination can be used to find the solution of the linear system

$$x = 0.76, \quad y = 0.68, \quad \text{and} \quad z = 0.52.$$

In this chapter we develop numerical methods for solving systems of linear equations.

3.1 Introduction to Vectors and Matrices

A real N-dimensional vector X is an ordered set of N real numbers and is usually written in the coordinate form

(1) $$X = (x_1, x_2, \ldots, x_N).$$

Here the numbers x_1, x_2, $\ldots$, and x_N are called the **components or coordinates of** X. The set consisting of all N-dimensional vectors is called N-**dimensional space**. When a vector is used to denote a point or position in space, it is called a **position**

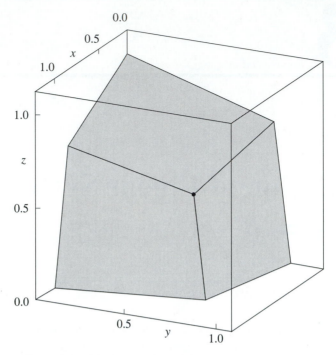

Figure 3.1   The intersection of three planes.

vector. When it is used to denote a movement between two points in space, it is called a *displacement vector*.

Let another vector be $Y = (y_1, y_2, \ldots, y_N)$. The two vectors X and Y are said to be equal if and only if each corresponding coordinate is the same; that is,

(2) $X = Y$ if and only if $x_j = y_j$ for $j = 1, 2, \ldots, N$.

The sum of the vectors X and Y is computed component by component, using the definition

(3) $X + Y = (x_1 + y_1, x_2 + y_2, \ldots, x_N + y_N).$

The negative of the vector X is obtained by replacing each coordinate with its negative:

(4) $-X = (-x_1, -x_2, \ldots, -x_N).$

The difference $Y - X$ is formed by taking the difference in each coordinate:

(5) $Y - X = (y_1 - x_1, y_2 - x_2, \ldots, y_N - x_N).$

Vectors in N-dimensional space obey the algebraic property

$$(6) \qquad\qquad Y - X = Y + (-X).$$

If c is a real number (scalar), we define **scalar multiplication** cX as follows:

$$(7) \qquad\qquad cX = (cx_1, cx_2, \ldots, cx_N).$$

If c and d are scalars, then the weighted sum $cX + dY$ is called a **linear combination** of X and Y, and we write

$$(8) \qquad cX + dY = (cx_1 + dy_1, cx_2 + dy_2, \ldots, cx_N + dy_N).$$

The **dot product** of the two vectors X and Y is a scalar quantity (real number) defined by the equation

$$(9) \qquad\qquad X \cdot Y = x_1 y_1 + x_2 y_2 + \cdots + x_N y_N.$$

The **norm** (or **length**) of the vector X is defined by

$$(10) \qquad\qquad \|X\| = (x_1^2 + x_2^2 + \cdots + x_N^2)^{1/2}.$$

Equation (10) is referred to as the **Euclidean norm** (or **length**) of the vector X.

Scalar multiplication cX stretches the vector X when $|c| > 1$ and shrinks the vector when $|c| < 1$. This is shown by using equation (10):

$$(11) \qquad \begin{aligned} \|cX\| &= (c^2 x_1^2 + c^2 x_2^2 + \cdots + c^2 x_N^2)^{1/2} \\ &= |c|(x_1^2 + x_2^2 + \cdots + x_N^2)^{1/2} = |c| \|X\|. \end{aligned}$$

An important relationship exists between the dot product and norm of a vector. If both sides of equation (10) are squared and equation (9) is used, with Y being replaced with X, we have

$$(12) \qquad \|X\|^2 = x_1^2 + x_2^2 + \cdots + x_N^2 = X \cdot X.$$

If X and Y are position vectors that locate the two points $(x_1, x_2, \ldots, x_N)$ and $(y_1, y_2, \ldots, y_N)$ in N-dimensional space, then the **displacement vector** from X to Y is given by the difference

$$(13) \qquad Y - X \qquad \text{(displacement from position } X \text{ to position } Y\text{).}$$

Notice that if a particle starts at the position X and moves through the displacement $Y - X$, its new position is Y. This can be obtained by the following vector sum:

$$(14) \qquad\qquad Y = X + (Y - X).$$

Using equations (10) and (13), we can write down the formula for the distance between two points in N-space.

$$(15) \qquad \|Y - X\| = \left((y_1 - x_1)^2 + (y_2 - x_2)^2 + \cdots + (y_N - x_N)^2 \right)^{1/2}.$$

When the distance between points is computed using formula (15), we say that the points lie in N-**dimensional Euclidean space**.

Example 3.1.   Let $X = (2, -3, 5, -1)$ and $Y = (6, 1, 2, -4)$. The concepts mentioned above are now illustrated for vectors in 4-space.

Sum	$X + Y = (8, -2, 7, -5)$
Difference	$X - Y = (-4, -4, 3, 3)$
Scalar multiple	$3X = (6, -9, 15, -3)$
Length	$\|X\| = (4 + 9 + 25 + 1)^{1/2} = 39^{1/2}$
Dot product	$X \cdot Y = 12 - 3 + 10 + 4 = 23$
Displacement from X to Y	$Y - X = (4, 4, -3, -3)$
Distance from X to Y	$\|Y - X\| = (16 + 16 + 9 + 9)^{1/2} = 50^{1/2}$ ■

It is sometimes useful to write vectors as columns instead of rows. For example,

$$(16) \qquad X = \begin{bmatrix} x_1 \\ x_2 \\ \vdots \\ x_N \end{bmatrix} \quad \text{and} \quad Y = \begin{bmatrix} y_1 \\ y_2 \\ \vdots \\ y_N \end{bmatrix}.$$

Then the linear combination $cX + dY$ is

$$(17) \qquad cX + dY = \begin{bmatrix} cx_1 + dy_1 \\ cx_2 + dy_2 \\ \vdots \\ cx_N + dy_N \end{bmatrix}.$$

By choosing c and d appropriately in equation (17), we have the sum $1X + 1Y$, the difference $1X - 1Y$, and the scalar multiple $cX + 0Y$. We use the superscript "$'$", for transpose to indicate that a row vector should be converted to a column vector, and vice versa.

$$(18) \qquad (x_1, x_2, \ldots, x_N)' = \begin{bmatrix} x_1 \\ x_2 \\ \vdots \\ x_N \end{bmatrix} \quad \text{and} \quad \begin{bmatrix} x_1 \\ x_2 \\ \vdots \\ x_N \end{bmatrix}' = (x_1, x_2, \ldots, x_N).$$

The set of vectors has a zero element $\mathbf{0}$, which is defined by

$$(19) \qquad \mathbf{0} = (0, 0, \ldots, 0).$$

Theorem 3.1 (Vector Algebra).   Suppose that X, Y, and Z are N-dimensional vectors and a and b are scalars (real numbers). The following properties of vector addition and scalar multiplication hold:

(20)	$Y + X = X + Y$	commutative property
(21)	$\mathbf{0} + X = X + \mathbf{0}$	additive identity

(22) $X - X = X + (-X) = 0$ additive inverse
(23) $(X + Y) + Z = X + (Y + Z)$ associative property
(24) $(a + b)X = aX + bX$ distributive property for scalars
(25) $a(X + Y) = aX + aY$ distributive property for vectors
(26) $a(bX) = (ab)X$ associative property for scalars

Matrices and Two-Dimensional Arrays

A matrix is a rectangular array of numbers that is arranged systematically in rows and columns. A matrix having M rows and N columns is called an $M \times N$ (read "M by N") matrix. The capital letter A denotes a matrix, and the lowercase subscripted letter a_{ij} denotes one of the numbers forming the matrix. We write

(27) $$A = [a_{ij}]_{M \times N} \quad \text{for } 1 \le i \le M, 1 \le j \le N,$$

where a_{ij} is the number in location (i, j) (i.e., stored in the ith row and jth column of the matrix). We refer to a_{ij} as the element in location (i, j). In expanded form we write

(28)
$$
\text{row } i \rightarrow
\begin{bmatrix}
a_{11} & a_{12} & \cdots & a_{1j} & \cdots & a_{1N} \\
a_{21} & a_{22} & \cdots & a_{2j} & \cdots & a_{2N} \\
\vdots & \vdots & & \vdots & & \vdots \\
a_{i1} & a_{i2} & \cdots & a_{ij} & \cdots & a_{iN} \\
\vdots & \vdots & & \vdots & & \vdots \\
a_{M1} & a_{M2} & \cdots & a_{Mj} & \cdots & a_{MN}
\end{bmatrix}
= A.
$$
$$\underset{\text{column } j}{\uparrow}$$

The rows of the $M \times N$ matrix A are N-dimensional vectors:

(29) $$V_i = (a_{i1}, a_{i2}, \ldots, a_{iN}) \quad \text{for } i = 1, 2, \ldots, M.$$

The row vectors in (29) can also be viewed as $1 \times N$ matrices. Here we have sliced the $M \times N$ matrix A into M pieces (submatrices) that are $1 \times N$ matrices.

In this case we could express A as an $M \times 1$ matrix consisting of the $1 \times N$ row matrices V_i; that is,

(30) $$A = \begin{bmatrix} V_1 \\ V_2 \\ \vdots \\ V_i \\ \vdots \\ V_M \end{bmatrix} = \begin{bmatrix} V_1 & V_2 & \cdots & V_i & \cdots & V_M \end{bmatrix}'.$$

Similarly, the columns of the $M \times N$ matrix A are $M \times 1$ matrices:

$$(31) \quad C_1 = \begin{bmatrix} a_{11} \\ a_{21} \\ \vdots \\ a_{i1} \\ \vdots \\ a_{M1} \end{bmatrix}, \quad \cdots, \quad C_j = \begin{bmatrix} a_{1j} \\ a_{2j} \\ \vdots \\ a_{ij} \\ \vdots \\ a_{Mj} \end{bmatrix}, \quad \cdots, \quad C_N = \begin{bmatrix} a_{1N} \\ a_{2N} \\ \vdots \\ a_{iN} \\ \vdots \\ a_{MN} \end{bmatrix}.$$

In this case we could express A as a $1 \times N$ matrix consisting of the $M \times 1$ column matrices C_j:

$$(32) \quad A = \begin{bmatrix} C_1 & C_2 & \cdots & C_j & \cdots & C_N \end{bmatrix}.$$

Example 3.2.   Identify the row and column matrices associated with the 4×3 matrix

$$A = \begin{bmatrix} -2 & 4 & 9 \\ 5 & -7 & 1 \\ 0 & -3 & 8 \\ -4 & 6 & -5 \end{bmatrix}.$$

The four row matrices are $V_1 = \begin{bmatrix} -2 & 4 & 9 \end{bmatrix}$, $V_2 = \begin{bmatrix} 5 & -7 & 1 \end{bmatrix}$, $V_3 = \begin{bmatrix} 0 & -3 & 8 \end{bmatrix}$, and $V_4 = \begin{bmatrix} -4 & 6 & -5 \end{bmatrix}$. The three column matrices are

$$C_1 = \begin{bmatrix} -2 \\ 5 \\ 0 \\ -4 \end{bmatrix}, \quad C_2 = \begin{bmatrix} 4 \\ -7 \\ -3 \\ 6 \end{bmatrix}, \quad \text{and} \quad C_3 = \begin{bmatrix} 9 \\ 1 \\ 8 \\ -5 \end{bmatrix}.$$

Notice how A can be represented with these matrices:

$$A = \begin{bmatrix} V_1 \\ V_2 \\ V_3 \\ V_4 \end{bmatrix} = \begin{bmatrix} C_1 & C_2 & C_3 \end{bmatrix}. \qquad \blacksquare$$

Let $A = [a_{ij}]_{M \times N}$ and $B = [b_{ij}]_{M \times N}$ be two matrices of the same dimension. The two matrices A and B are said to be equal if and only if each corresponding element is the same; that is,

$$(33) \quad A = B \quad \text{if and only if} \quad a_{ij} = b_{ij} \quad \text{for } 1 \le i \le M, \ 1 \le j \le N.$$

The sum of the two $M \times N$ matrices A and B is computed element by element, using the definition

$$(34) \quad A + B = [a_{ij} + b_{ij}]_{M \times N} \quad \text{for } 1 \le i \le M, \ 1 \le j \le N.$$

The negative of the matrix A is obtained by replacing each element with its negative:

(35) $$-A = [-a_{ij}]_{M \times N} \quad \text{for } 1 \le i \le M, \ 1 \le j \le N.$$

The difference $A - B$ is formed by taking the difference of corresponding coordinates:

(36) $$A - B = [a_{ij} - b_{ij}]_{M \times N} \quad \text{for } 1 \le i \le M, \ 1 \le j \le N.$$

If c is a real number (scalar), we define scalar multiplication cA as follows:

(37) $$cA = [ca_{ij}]_{M \times N} \quad \text{for } 1 \le i \le M, \ 1 \le j \le N.$$

If p and q are scalars, the weighted sum $pA + qB$ is called a linear combination of the matrices A and B, and we write

(38) $$pA + qB = [pa_{ij} + qb_{ij}]_{M \times N} \quad \text{for } 1 \le i \le M, \ 1 \le j \le N.$$

The zero matrix of order $M \times N$ consists of all zeros:

(39) $$\mathbf{0} = [0]_{M \times N}.$$

Example 3.3. Find the scalar multiples $2A$ and $3B$ and the linear combination $2A - 3B$ for the matrices

$$A = \begin{bmatrix} -1 & 2 \\ 7 & 5 \\ 3 & -4 \end{bmatrix} \quad \text{and} \quad B = \begin{bmatrix} -2 & 3 \\ 1 & -4 \\ -9 & 7 \end{bmatrix}.$$

Using formula (37), we obtain

$$2A = \begin{bmatrix} -2 & 4 \\ 14 & 10 \\ 6 & -8 \end{bmatrix} \quad \text{and} \quad 3B = \begin{bmatrix} -6 & 9 \\ 3 & -12 \\ -27 & 21 \end{bmatrix}.$$

The linear combination $2A - 3B$ is now found:

$$2A - 3B = \begin{bmatrix} -2+6 & 4-9 \\ 14-3 & 10+12 \\ 6+27 & -8-21 \end{bmatrix} = \begin{bmatrix} 4 & -5 \\ 11 & 22 \\ 33 & -29 \end{bmatrix}. \qquad \blacksquare$$

Theorem 3.2 (Matrix Addition).   Suppose that A, B, and C are $M \times N$ matrices and p and q are scalars. The following properties of matrix addition and scalar multiplication hold:

(40)	$B + A = A + B$	commutative property
(41)	$\mathbf{0} + A = A + \mathbf{0}$	additive identity
(42)	$A - A = A + (-A) = \mathbf{0}$	additive inverse
(43)	$(A + B) + C = A + (B + C)$	associative property
(44)	$(p + q)A = pA + qA$	distributive property for scalars
(45)	$p(A + B) = pA + pB$	distributive property for matrices
(46)	$p(qA) = (pq)A$	associative property for scalars

Exercises for Introduction to Vectors and Matrices

The reader is encouraged to carry out the following exercises by hand and with MATLAB.

1. Given the vectors X and Y, find **(a)** $X + Y$, **(b)** $X - Y$, **(c)** $3X$, **(d)** $\|X\|$, **(e)** $7Y - 4X$, **(f)** $X \cdot Y$, and **(g)** $\|7Y - 4X\|$.
   (i) $X = (3, -4)$ and $Y = (-2, 8)$
   (ii) $X = (-6, 3, 2)$ and $Y = (-8, 5, 1)$
   (iii) $X = (4, -8, 1)$ and $Y = (1, -12, -11)$
   (iv) $X = (1, -2, 4, 2)$ and $Y = (3, -5, -4, 0)$

2. Using the law of cosines, it can be shown that the angle θ between two vectors X and Y is given by the relation

$$\cos(\theta) = \frac{X \cdot Y}{\|X\| \, \|Y\|}.$$

   Find the angle, in radians, between the following vectors:
   (a) $X = (-6, 3, 2)$ and $Y = (2, -2, 1)$
   (b) $X = (4, -8, 1)$ and $Y = (3, 4, 12)$

3. Two vectors X and Y are said to be orthogonal (perpendicular) if the angle between them is $\pi/2$.
   (a)   Prove that X and Y are orthogonal if and only if $X \cdot Y = 0$.

   Use part (a) to determine if the following vectors are orthogonal.
   (b) $X = (-6, 4, 2)$ and $Y = (6, 5, 8)$
   (c) $X = (-4, 8, 3)$ and $Y = (2, 5, 16)$
   (d) $X = (-5, 7, 2)$ and $Y = (4, 1, 6)$
   (e)   Find two different vectors that are orthogonal to $X = (1, 2, -5)$.

4. Find **(a)** $A + B$, **(b)** $A - B$, and **(c)** $3A - 2B$ for the matrices

$$A = \begin{bmatrix} -1 & 9 & 4 \\ 2 & -3 & -6 \\ 0 & 5 & 7 \end{bmatrix}, \qquad B = \begin{bmatrix} -4 & 9 & 2 \\ 3 & -5 & 7 \\ 8 & 1 & -6 \end{bmatrix}.$$

5. The *transpose* of an $M \times N$ matrix A, denoted A', is the $N \times M$ matrix obtained from A by converting the rows of A to columns of A'. That is, if $A = [a_{ij}]_{M \times N}$ and $A' = [b_{ij}]_{N \times M}$, then the elements satisfy the relation

$$b_{ji} = a_{ij} \quad \text{for} \quad 1 \le i \le M, 1 \le j \le N.$$

   Find the transpose of the following matrices.
   (a) $\begin{bmatrix} -2 & 5 & 12 \\ 1 & 4 & -1 \\ 7 & 0 & 6 \\ 11 & -3 & 8 \end{bmatrix}$
   (b) $\begin{bmatrix} 4 & 9 & 2 \\ 3 & 5 & 7 \\ 8 & 1 & 6 \end{bmatrix}$

6. The square matrix A of dimension $N \times N$ is said to be symmetric if $A = A'$ (see Exercise 5 for the definition of A'). Determine whether the following square matrices are symmetric.

(a) $\begin{bmatrix} 1 & -7 & 4 \\ -7 & 2 & 0 \\ 4 & 0 & 3 \end{bmatrix}$
(b) $\begin{bmatrix} 4 & -7 & 1 \\ 0 & 2 & -7 \\ 3 & 0 & 4 \end{bmatrix}$

(c) $A = [a_{ij}]_{N \times N}$, where $a_{ij} = \begin{cases} ij & i = j \\ i - ij + j & i \neq j \end{cases}$

(d) $A = [a_{ij}]_{N \times N}$, where $a_{ij} = \begin{cases} \cos(ij) & i = j \\ i - ij - j & i \neq j \end{cases}$

7. Prove statements (20), (24), and (25) in Theorem 3.1.

3.2   Properties of Vectors and Matrices

A linear combination of the variables $x_1, x_2, \ldots, x_N$ is a sum

$$(1) \qquad\qquad a_1 x_1 + a_2 x_2 + \cdots + a_N x_N$$

where a_k is the coefficient of x_k for $k = 1, 2, \ldots, N$.

A linear equation in $x_1, x_2, \ldots, x_N$ is obtained by requiring the linear combination in (1) to take on a prescribed value b; that is,

$$(2) \qquad\qquad a_1 x_1 + a_2 x_2 + \cdots + a_N x_N = b.$$

Systems of linear equations arise frequently, and if M equations in N unknowns are given, we write

$$
\begin{aligned}
a_{11}x_1 &+ a_{12}x_2 + \cdots + a_{1N}x_N &= b_1 \\
a_{21}x_1 &+ a_{22}x_2 + \cdots + a_{2N}x_N &= b_2 \\
&\quad\vdots \\
a_{k1}x_1 &+ a_{k2}x_2 + \cdots + a_{kN}x_N &= b_k \\
&\quad\vdots \\
a_{M1}x_1 &+ a_{M2}x_2 + \cdots + a_{MN}x_N &= b_M.
\end{aligned}
$$

(3)

To keep track of the different coefficients in each equation, it is necessary to use the two subscripts (k, j). The first subscript locates equation k and the second subscript locates the variable x_j.

A solution to (3) is a set of numerical values $x_1, x_2, \ldots, x_N$ that satisfies all the equations in (3) simultaneously. Hence a solution can be viewed as an N-dimensional vector:

$$(4) \qquad\qquad X = (x_1, x_2, \ldots, x_N).$$

Example 3.4.   Concrete (used for sidewalks, etc.) is a mixture of portland cement, sand, and gravel. A distributor has three batches available for contractors. Batch 1 contains cement, sand, and gravel mixed in the proportions $1/8, 3/8, 4/8$; batch 2 has the proportions $2/10, 5/10, 3/10$; and batch 3 has the proportions $2/5, 3/5, 0/5$.

Let x_1, x_2, and x_3 denote the amount (in cubic yards) to be used from each batch to form a mixture of 10 cubic yards. Also, suppose that the mixture is to contain $b_1 = 2.3$, $b_2 = 4.8$, and $b_3 = 2.9$ cubic yards of portland cement, sand, and gravel, respectively. Then the system of linear equations of the ingredients is

$$
\begin{aligned}
0.125x_1 + 0.200x_2 + 0.400x_3 &= 2.3 \quad \text{(cement)} \\
0.375x_1 + 0.500x_2 + 0.600x_3 &= 4.8 \quad \text{(sand)} \\
0.500x_1 + 0.300x_2 + 0.000x_3 &= 2.9 \quad \text{(gravel)}
\end{aligned}
$$

(5)

The solution to the linear system (5) is $x_1 = 4$, $x_2 = 3$, and $x_3 = 3$, which can be verified by direct substitution into the equations:

$$
\begin{aligned}
(0.125)(4) + (0.200)(3) + (0.400)(3) &= 2.3 \\
(0.375)(4) + (0.500)(3) + (0.600)(3) &= 4.8 \\
(0.500)(4) + (0.300)(3) + (0.000)(3) &= 2.9.
\end{aligned}
$$

■

Matrix Multiplication

Definition 3.1.   If $A = [a_{ik}]_{M \times N}$ and $B = [b_{kj}]_{N \times P}$ are two matrices with the property that A has as many columns as B has rows, then the *matrix product* AB is defined to be the matrix C of dimension $M \times P$:

(6) $$AB = C = [c_{ij}]_{M \times P},$$

where the element c_{ij} of C is given by the dot product of the ith row of A and the jth column of B:

(7) $$c_{ij} = \sum_{k=1}^{N} a_{ik}b_{kj} = a_{i1}b_{1j} + a_{i2}b_{2j} + \cdots + a_{iN}b_{Nj}$$

for $i = 1, 2, \ldots, M$ and $j = 1, 2, \ldots, P$.   ▲

Example 3.5.   Find the product $C = AB$ for the following matrices, and state why BA is not defined.

$$
A = \begin{bmatrix} 2 & 3 \\ -1 & 4 \end{bmatrix}, \qquad B = \begin{bmatrix} 5 & -2 & 1 \\ 3 & 8 & -6 \end{bmatrix}.
$$

The matrix A has two columns and B has two rows, so the matrix product AB is defined. The product of a 2×2 and a 2×3 matrix is a 2×3 matrix. Computation reveals that

$$AB = \begin{bmatrix} 2 & 3 \\ -1 & 4 \end{bmatrix} \begin{bmatrix} 5 & -2 & 1 \\ 3 & 8 & -6 \end{bmatrix}$$

$$= \begin{bmatrix} 10 + 9 & -4 + 24 & 2 - 18 \\ -5 + 12 & 2 + 32 & -1 - 24 \end{bmatrix} = \begin{bmatrix} 19 & 20 & -16 \\ 7 & 34 & -25 \end{bmatrix} = C.$$

When an attempt is made to form the product BA, we discover that the dimensions are not compatible in this order because the rows of B are three-dimensional vectors and the columns of A are two-dimensional vectors. Hence the dot product of the jth row of B and the kth column of A is not defined. ∎

If it happens that $AB = BA$, we say that A and B commute. Most often, even when AB and BA are both defined, the products are not necessarily the same.

We now discuss how to use matrices to represent a linear system of equations. The linear equations in (3) can be written as a matrix product. The coefficients a_{kj} are stored in a matrix A (called the *coefficient matrix*) of dimension $M \times N$, and the unknowns x_j are stored in a matrix X of dimension $N \times 1$. The constants b_k are stored in a matrix B of dimension $M \times 1$. It is conventional to use column matrices for both X and B and write

$$(8) \qquad AX = \begin{bmatrix} a_{11} & a_{12} & \cdots & a_{1j} & \cdots & a_{1N} \\ a_{21} & a_{22} & \cdots & a_{2j} & \cdots & a_{2N} \\ \vdots & \vdots & & \vdots & & \vdots \\ a_{k1} & a_{k2} & \cdots & a_{kj} & \cdots & a_{kN} \\ \vdots & \vdots & & \vdots & & \vdots \\ a_{M1} & a_{M2} & \cdots & a_{Mj} & \cdots & a_{MN} \end{bmatrix} \begin{bmatrix} x_1 \\ x_2 \\ \vdots \\ x_j \\ \vdots \\ x_N \end{bmatrix} = \begin{bmatrix} b_1 \\ b_2 \\ \vdots \\ b_j \\ \vdots \\ b_M \end{bmatrix} = B.$$

The matrix multiplication $AX = B$ in (8) is reminiscent of the dot product for ordinary vectors, because each element b_k in B is the result obtained by taking the dot product of row k in matrix A with the column matrix X.

Example 3.6. Express the system of linear equations (5) in Example 3.4 as a matrix product. Use matrix multiplication to verify that $\begin{bmatrix} 4 & 3 & 3 \end{bmatrix}'$ is the solution of (5):

$$(9) \qquad \begin{bmatrix} 0.125 & 0.200 & 0.400 \\ 0.375 & 0.500 & 0.600 \\ 0.500 & 0.300 & 0.000 \end{bmatrix} \begin{bmatrix} x_1 \\ x_2 \\ x_3 \end{bmatrix} = \begin{bmatrix} 2.3 \\ 4.8 \\ 2.9 \end{bmatrix}.$$

To verify that $\begin{bmatrix} 4 & 3 & 3 \end{bmatrix}'$ is the solution of (5), we must show that $A\begin{bmatrix} 4 & 3 & 3 \end{bmatrix}' = \begin{bmatrix} 2.3 & 4.8 & 2.9 \end{bmatrix}'$:

$$\begin{bmatrix} 0.125 & 0.200 & 0.400 \\ 0.375 & 0.500 & 0.600 \\ 0.500 & 0.300 & 0.000 \end{bmatrix} \begin{bmatrix} 4 \\ 3 \\ 3 \end{bmatrix} = \begin{bmatrix} 0.5 + 0.6 + 1.2 \\ 1.5 + 1.5 + 1.8 \\ 2.0 + 0.9 + 0.0 \end{bmatrix} = \begin{bmatrix} 2.3 \\ 4.8 \\ 2.9 \end{bmatrix}. \qquad ∎$$

Some Special Matrices

The $M \times N$ matrix whose elements are all zero is called the *zero matrix of dimension* $M \times N$ and is denoted by

$$(10) \qquad \mathbf{0} = [0]_{M \times N}.$$

When the dimension is clear, we use $\mathbf{0}$ to denote the zero matrix.

The *identity matrix of order* N is the square matrix given by

$$(11) \qquad \boldsymbol{I}_N = [\delta_{ij}]_{N \times N} \qquad \text{where} \qquad \delta_{ij} = \begin{cases} 1 & \text{when } i = j, \\ 0 & \text{when } i \neq j. \end{cases}$$

It is the multiplicative identity, as illustrated in the next example.

Example 3.7.   Let A be a 2×3 matrix. Then $\boldsymbol{I}_2 A = A \boldsymbol{I}_3 = A$. Multiplication of A on the left by $\boldsymbol{I}_2$ results in

$$\begin{bmatrix} 1 & 0 \\ 0 & 1 \end{bmatrix} \begin{bmatrix} a_{11} & a_{12} & a_{13} \\ a_{21} & a_{22} & a_{23} \end{bmatrix} = \begin{bmatrix} a_{11} + 0 & a_{12} + 0 & a_{13} + 0 \\ a_{21} + 0 & a_{22} + 0 & a_{23} + 0 \end{bmatrix} = A.$$

Multiplication of A on the right by $\boldsymbol{I}_3$ results in

$$\begin{bmatrix} a_{11} & a_{12} & a_{13} \\ a_{21} & a_{22} & a_{23} \end{bmatrix} \begin{bmatrix} 1 & 0 & 0 \\ 0 & 1 & 0 \\ 0 & 0 & 1 \end{bmatrix} = \begin{bmatrix} a_{11} + 0 + 0 & 0 + a_{12} + 0 & 0 + 0 + a_{13} \\ a_{21} + 0 + 0 & 0 + a_{22} + 0 & 0 + 0 + a_{23} \end{bmatrix} = A. \quad \blacksquare$$

Some properties of matrix multiplication are given in the following theorem.

Theorem 3.3 (Matrix Multiplication).   Suppose that c is a scalar and that A, B, and C are matrices such that the indicated sums and products are defined; then

(12)	$(AB)C = A(BC)$	associativity of matrix multiplication
(13)	$IA = AI = A$	identity matrix
(14)	$A(B + C) = AB + AC$	left distributive property
(15)	$(A + B)C = AC + BC$	right distributive property
(16)	$c(AB) = (cA)B = A(cB)$	scalar associative property

Inverse of a Nonsingular Matrix

The concept of an inverse applies to matrices, but special attention must be given. An $N \times N$ matrix A is called *nonsingular* or *invertible* if there exists an $N \times N$ matrix B such that

$$(17) \qquad AB = BA = I.$$

If no such matrix B can be found, A is said to be **singular**. When B can be found and (17) holds, we say that B is the inverse of A and usually write $B = A^{-1}$ and use the familiar relation:

$$(18) \qquad AA^{-1} = A^{-1}A \quad \text{if } A \text{ is nonsingular.}$$

It is easy to show that at most one matrix B can be found that satisfies relation (17). Suppose that C is also an inverse of A (i.e., $AC = CA = I$). Then properties (12) and (13) can be used to obtain

$$C = IC = (BA)C = B(AC) = BI = B.$$

Determinants

The determinant of a square matrix A is a scalar quantity (real number) and is denoted by $\det(A)$ or $|A|$. If A is a $N \times N$ matrix

$$A = \begin{bmatrix} a_{11} & a_{12} & \cdots & a_{1N} \\ a_{21} & a_{22} & \cdots & a_{2N} \\ \vdots & \vdots & & \vdots \\ a_{N1} & a_{N2} & \cdots & a_{NN} \end{bmatrix},$$

then it is customary to write

$$\det(A) = \begin{vmatrix} a_{11} & a_{12} & \cdots & a_{1N} \\ a_{21} & a_{22} & \cdots & a_{2N} \\ \vdots & \vdots & & \vdots \\ a_{N1} & a_{N2} & \cdots & a_{NN} \end{vmatrix}.$$

Although the notation for a determinant may look like a matrix, its properties are completely different. For one, the determinant is a scalar quantity (real number). The definition of $\det(A)$ found in most linear algebra textbooks is not tractable for computation when $N > 3$. We review how to compute determinants using the cofactor expansion method. Evaluation of higher-order determinants is done using Gaussian elimination and is mentioned in the body of Program 3.3.

If $A = [a_{ij}]$ is a 1×1 matrix, we define $\det(A) = a_{11}$. If $A = [a_{ij}]_{N \times N}$, where $N \geq 2$, then let M_{ij} be the determinant of the $N - 1 \times N - 1$ submatrix of A obtained by deleting the ith row and jth column of A. The determinant M_{ij} is said to be the **minor** of a_{ij}. The **cofactor** A_{ij} of a_{ij} is defined as $A_{ij} = (-1)^{i+j} M_{ij}$. Then the determinant of an $N \times N$ matrix A is given by

$$(19) \qquad \det(A) = \sum_{j=1}^{N} a_{ij} A_{ij} \quad (i\text{th row expansion})$$

or

(20) $$\det(A) = \sum_{i=1}^{N} a_{ij} A_{ij} \quad (j\text{th column expansion}).$$

Applying formula (19), with $i = 1$, to the 2×2 matrix

$$A = \begin{bmatrix} a_{11} & a_{12} \\ a_{21} & a_{22} \end{bmatrix},$$

we see that $\det A = a_{11}a_{22} - a_{12}a_{21}$. The following example illustrates how to use formulas (19) and (20) to recursively reduce the calculation of the determinant of an $N \times N$ matrix to the calculation of a number of 2×2 determinants.

Example 3.8.   Use formula (19) with $i = 1$ and formula (20) with $j = 2$ to calculate the determinant of the matrix

$$A = \begin{bmatrix} 2 & 3 & 8 \\ -4 & 5 & -1 \\ 7 & -6 & 9 \end{bmatrix}.$$

Using formula (19) with $i = 1$, we obtain

$$\det A = (2) \begin{vmatrix} 5 & -1 \\ -6 & 9 \end{vmatrix} - (3) \begin{vmatrix} -4 & -1 \\ 7 & 9 \end{vmatrix} + (8) \begin{vmatrix} -4 & 5 \\ 7 & -6 \end{vmatrix}$$
$$= (2)(45 - 6) - (3)(-36 + 7) + (8)(24 - 35)$$
$$= 77.$$

Using formula (20) with $j = 2$, we obtain

$$\det(A) = -(3) \begin{vmatrix} -4 & -1 \\ 7 & 9 \end{vmatrix} + (5) \begin{vmatrix} 2 & 8 \\ 7 & 9 \end{vmatrix} - (-6) \begin{vmatrix} 2 & 8 \\ -4 & -1 \end{vmatrix}$$
$$= 77. \qquad \blacksquare$$

The following theorem gives sufficient conditions for the existence and uniqueness of solutions of the linear system $AX = B$ for square coefficient matrices.

Theorem 3.4.   Assume that A is an $N \times N$ matrix. The following statements are equivalent.

(21) Given any $N \times 1$ matrix B, the linear system $AX = B$ has a unique solution.

(22) The matrix A is nonsingular (i.e., A^{-1} exists).

(23) The system of equations $AX = 0$ has the unique solution $X = 0$.

(24) $\det(A) \neq 0$.

Theorems 3.3 and 3.4 help relate matrix algebra to ordinary algebra. If statement (21) is true, then statement (22) together with properties (12) and (13) give the following line of reasoning:

(25) $AX = B$ implies $A^{-1}AX = A^{-1}B$,   which implies $X = A^{-1}B$.

Example 3.9.   Use the inverse matrix

$$A^{-1} = \frac{1}{5} \begin{bmatrix} 4 & -1 \\ -7 & 3 \end{bmatrix}$$

and the reasoning in (25) to solve the linear system $AX = B$:

$$AX = \begin{bmatrix} 3 & 1 \\ 7 & 4 \end{bmatrix} \begin{bmatrix} x_1 \\ x_2 \end{bmatrix} = \begin{bmatrix} 2 \\ 5 \end{bmatrix} = B.$$

Using (25), we get

$$X = A^{-1}B = \frac{1}{5} \begin{bmatrix} 4 & -1 \\ -7 & 3 \end{bmatrix} \begin{bmatrix} 2 \\ 5 \end{bmatrix} = \frac{1}{5} \begin{bmatrix} 3 \\ 1 \end{bmatrix} = \begin{bmatrix} 0.6 \\ 0.2 \end{bmatrix}. \qquad\blacksquare$$

Remark. In practice we avoid, if possible, the direct numerical calculation of the inverse of a nonsingular matrix or the determinant of a square matrix. These concepts are used as theoretical "tools" to establish the existence and uniqueness of solutions or as a means to express the solution of a linear system algebraically (as in Example 3.9).

Plane Rotations

Suppose that A is a 3×3 matrix and $U = \begin{bmatrix} x & y & z \end{bmatrix}'$ is a 3×1 matrix; then the product $V = AU$ is another 3×1 matrix. This is an example of a linear transformation, and applications are found in the area of computer graphics. The matrix U is equivalent to the positional vector $U = (x, y, z)$, which represents the coordinates of a point in three-dimensional space. Consider three special matrices:

(26)
$$R_x(\alpha) = \begin{bmatrix} 1 & 0 & 0 \\ 0 & \cos(\alpha) & -\sin(\alpha) \\ 0 & \sin(\alpha) & \cos(\alpha) \end{bmatrix},$$

(27)
$$R_y(\beta) = \begin{bmatrix} \cos(\beta) & 0 & \sin(\beta) \\ 0 & 1 & 0 \\ -\sin(\beta) & 0 & \cos(\beta) \end{bmatrix},$$

(28)
$$R_z(\gamma) = \begin{bmatrix} \cos(\gamma) & -\sin(\gamma) & 0 \\ \sin(\gamma) & \cos(\gamma) & 0 \\ 0 & 0 & 1 \end{bmatrix}.$$

Table 3.1   Coordinates of the Vertices of a Cube under Successive Rotations

U	$V = R_z(\pi/4)\,U$	$W = R_y(\pi/6)\,R_z(\pi/4)\,U$
$(0, 0, 0)'$	$(0.000000, 0.000000, 0)'$	$(0.000000, 0.000000, 0.000000)'$
$(1, 0, 0)'$	$(0.707107, 0.707107, 0)'$	$(0.612372, 0.707107, -0.353553)'$
$(0, 1, 0)'$	$(-0.707107, 0.707107, 0)'$	$(-0.612372, 0.707107, 0.353553)'$
$(0, 0, 1)'$	$(0.000000, 0.000000, 1)'$	$(0.500000, 0.000000, 0.866025)'$
$(1, 1, 0)'$	$(0.000000, 1.414214, 0)'$	$(0.000000, 1.414214, 0.000000)'$
$(1, 0, 1)'$	$(0.707107, 0.707107, 1)'$	$(1.112372, 0.707107, 0.512472)'$
$(0, 1, 1)'$	$(-0.707107, 0.707107, 1)'$	$(-0.112372, 0.707107, 1.219579)'$
$(1, 1, 1)'$	$(0.000000, 1.414214, 1)'$	$(0.500000, 1.414214, 0.866025)'$

These matrices $R_x(\alpha)$, $R_y(\beta)$, and $R_z(\gamma)$ are used to rotate points about the x-, y-, and z-axes through the angles α, β, and γ, respectively. The inverses are $R_x(-\alpha)$, $R_y(-\beta)$, and $R_z(-\gamma)$ and they rotate space about the x-, y-, and z-axes through the angles $-\alpha$, $-\beta$, and $-\gamma$, respectively. The next example illustrates the situation, and further investigations are left for the reader.

Example 3.10.   A unit cube is situated in the first octant with one vertex at the origin. First, rotate the cube through an angle $\pi/4$ about the z-axis; then rotate this image through an angle $\pi/6$ about the y-axis. Find the images of all eight vertices of the cube.

The first rotation is given by the transformation

$$
V = R_z\left(\frac{\pi}{4}\right) U = \begin{bmatrix} \cos(\pi/4) & -\sin(\pi/4) & 0 \\ \sin(\pi/4) & \cos(\pi/4) & 0 \\ 0 & 0 & 1 \end{bmatrix} \begin{bmatrix} x \\ y \\ z \end{bmatrix}
$$

$$
= \begin{bmatrix} 0.707107 & -0.707107 & 0.000000 \\ 0.707107 & 0.707107 & 0.000000 \\ 0.000000 & 0.000000 & 1.000000 \end{bmatrix} \begin{bmatrix} x \\ y \\ z \end{bmatrix}.
$$

Then the second rotation is given by

$$
W = R_y\left(\frac{\pi}{6}\right) V = \begin{bmatrix} \cos(\pi/6) & 0 & \sin(\pi/6) \\ 0 & 1 & 0 \\ -\sin(\pi/6) & 0 & \cos(\pi/6) \end{bmatrix} V
$$

$$
= \begin{bmatrix} 0.866025 & 0.000000 & 0.500000 \\ 0.000000 & 1.000000 & 0.000000 \\ -0.500000 & 0.000000 & 0.866025 \end{bmatrix} V.
$$

The composition of the two rotations is

$$
W = R_y\left(\frac{\pi}{6}\right) R_z\left(\frac{\pi}{4}\right) U = \begin{bmatrix} 0.612372 & -0.612372 & 0.500000 \\ 0.707107 & 0.707107 & 0.000000 \\ -0.353553 & 0.353553 & 0.866025 \end{bmatrix} \begin{bmatrix} x \\ y \\ z \end{bmatrix}.
$$

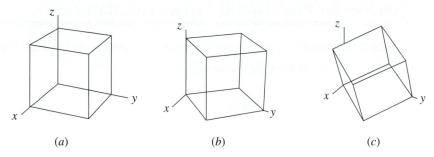

(a) (b) (c)

Figure 3.2   (a) The original starting cube. (b) $V = R_z(\pi/4)U$. Rotation about the z-axis. (c) $W = R_y(\pi/6)V$. Rotation about the y-axis.

Numerical computations for the coordinates of the vertices of the starting cube are given in Table 3.1 (as positional vectors), and the images of these cubes are shown in Figure 3.2(a) through (c).   ∎

MATLAB

The MATLAB functions `det(A)` and `inv(A)` calculate the determinant and inverse (if A is invertible), respectively, of a square matrix A.

Example 3.11.   Use MATLAB to solve the linear system in Example 3.6. Use the inverse matrix method described in (25).

First we verify that A is nonsingular by showing that $\det(A) \neq 0$ (Theorem 3.4).

```
>>A=[0.125 0.200 0.400;0.375 0.500 0.600;0.500 0.300 0.000];
>>det(A)
ans=
    -0.0175
```

Following the reasoning in (25), the solution of $AX = B$ is $X = A^{-1}B$.

```
>>X=inv(A)*[2.3 4.8 2.9]'
X=
    4.0000
    3.0000
    3.0000
```

We can check our solution by verifying that $AX = B$.

```
>>B=A*X
B=
    2.3000
    4.8000
    2.9000
```
∎

Exercises for Properties of Vectors and Matrices

The reader is encouraged to carry out the following exercises by hand and with MATLAB.

1. Find AB and BA for the following matrices:

$$A = \begin{bmatrix} -3 & 2 \\ 1 & 4 \end{bmatrix}, \quad B = \begin{bmatrix} 5 & 0 \\ 2 & -6 \end{bmatrix}.$$

2. Find AB and BA for the following matrices.

$$A = \begin{bmatrix} 1 & -2 & 3 \\ 2 & 0 & 5 \end{bmatrix}, \quad B = \begin{bmatrix} 3 & 0 \\ -1 & 5 \\ 3 & -2 \end{bmatrix}.$$

3. Let A, B, and C be given by

$$A = \begin{bmatrix} 3 & 1 \\ 0 & 4 \end{bmatrix}, \quad B = \begin{bmatrix} 1 & 2 \\ -2 & -6 \end{bmatrix}, \quad C = \begin{bmatrix} 2 & -5 \\ 3 & 4 \end{bmatrix}.$$

   (a)   Find $(AB)C$ and $A(BC)$.
   (b)   Find $A(B + C)$ and $AB + AC$.
   (c)   Find $(A + B)C$ and $AC + BC$.
   (d)   Find $(AB)'$ and $B'A'$.

4. We use the notation $A^2 = AA$. Find A^2 and B^2 for the following matrices:

$$A = \begin{bmatrix} -1 & -7 \\ 5 & 2 \end{bmatrix}, \quad B = \begin{bmatrix} 2 & 0 & 6 \\ -1 & 5 & -4 \\ 3 & -5 & 2 \end{bmatrix}.$$

5. Find the determinant of the following matrices, if it exists.

   (a) $\begin{bmatrix} -1 & -7 \\ 5 & 2 \end{bmatrix}$

   (b) $\begin{bmatrix} 2 & 0 & 6 \\ -1 & 5 & -4 \\ 3 & -5 & 2 \end{bmatrix}$

   (c) $\begin{bmatrix} 1 & 2 \\ 3 & 4 \\ 0 & 0 \end{bmatrix}$

   (d) $\begin{bmatrix} 1 & 2 & 3 & 4 \\ 0 & 2 & 4 & 6 \\ 0 & 0 & 5 & 4 \\ 0 & 0 & 0 & 7 \end{bmatrix}$

6. Show that $R_x(\alpha) R_x(-\alpha) = I$ by direct multiplication of the matrices $R_x(\alpha)$ and $R_x(-\alpha)$ (see formula (26)).

7. (a)   Show that

$$R_x(\alpha) R_y(\beta) = \begin{bmatrix} \cos(\beta) & 0 & \sin(\beta) \\ \sin(\beta)\sin(\alpha) & \cos(\alpha) & -\cos(\beta)\sin(\alpha) \\ -\cos(\alpha)\sin(\beta) & \sin(\alpha) & \cos(\beta)\cos(\alpha) \end{bmatrix}$$

   (see formulas (26) and (27)).

(b)   Show that

$$R_y(\beta)R_x(\alpha) = \begin{bmatrix} \cos(\beta) & \sin(\beta)\sin(\alpha) & \cos(\alpha)\sin(\beta) \\ 0 & \cos(\alpha) & -\sin(\alpha) \\ -\sin(\alpha) & \cos(\beta)\sin(\alpha) & \cos(\beta)\cos(\alpha) \end{bmatrix}.$$

8. If A and B are nonsingular $N \times N$ matrices and $C = AB$, show that $C^{-1} = B^{-1}A^{-1}$. *Hint.* Use the associative property of matrix multiplication.

9. Prove statements (13) and (16) of Theorem 3.3.

10. Let A be an $M \times N$ matrix and X an $N \times 1$ matrix.
    (a)   How many multiplications are needed to calculate AX?
    (b)   How many additions are needed to calculate AX?

11. Let A be an $M \times N$ matrix, and let B and C be $N \times P$ matrices. Prove the left distributive law for matrix multiplication: $A(B + C) = AB + AC$.

12. Let A and B be $M \times N$ matrices, and let C be a $N \times P$ matrix. Prove the right distributive law for matrix multiplication: $(A + B)C = AC + BC$.

13. Find XX' and $X'X$, where $X = \begin{bmatrix} 1 & -1 & 2 \end{bmatrix}$. *Note.* X' is the transpose of X.

14. Let A be a $M \times N$ matrix and B a $N \times P$ matrix. Prove that $(AB)' = B'A'$. *Hint.* Let $C = AB$ and show, using the definition of matrix multiplication, that the (i, j)th entry of C' equals the (i, j)th entry of $B'A'$.

15. Use the result of Exercise 14 and the associative property of matrix multiplication to show that $(ABC)' = C'B'A'$.

Algorithms and Programs

The first column of Table 3.1 contains the coordinates of the vertices of a unit cube situated in the first octant with one vertex at the origin. Note that all eight vertices can be stored in a matrix U of dimension 8×3, where each row represents the coordinates of one of the vertices. It follows from Exercise 14 that the product of U and the transpose of $R_z(\pi/4)$ will produce a matrix of dimension 8×3 (representing the second column of Table 3.1, where each row represents the transformation of the corresponding row in U). Combining this idea with Exercise 15, it follows that the coordinates of the vertices of a cube under any number of successive rotations can be represented by a matrix product.

1. A unit cube is situated in the first octant with one vertex at the origin. First, rotate the cube through an angle of $\pi/6$ about the y-axis; then rotate this image through an angle of $\pi/4$ about the z-axis. Find the images of all eight vertices of the starting cube. Compare this result with the result in Example 3.10.

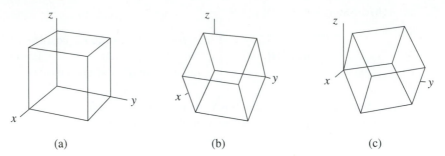

(a)   (b)   (c)

Figure 3.3 (a) The original starting cube. (b) $V = R_y(\pi/6)U$. Rotation about the y-axis. (c) $W = R_z(\pi/4)V$. Rotation about the z-axis.

What is different? Explain your answer using the fact that, in general, matrix multiplication is not commutative (see Figure 3.3(a) to (c)). Use the `plot3` command to plot each of the three cubes.

2. A unit cube is situated in the first octant with one vertex at the origin. First, rotate the cube through an angle of $\pi/12$ about the x-axis; then rotate this image through an angle of $\pi/6$ about the z-axis. Find the images of all eight vertices of the starting cube. Use the `plot3` command to plot each of the three cubes.

3. The tetrahedron with vertices at $(0, 0, 0)$, $(1, 0, 0)$, $(0, 1, 0)$, and $(0, 0, 1)$ is first rotated through an angle of 0.15 radian about the y-axis, then through an angle of -1.5 radians about the z-axis, and finally through an angle of 2.7 radians about the x-axis. Find the images of all four vertices. Use the `plot3` command to plot each of the four images.

3.3 Upper-Triangular Linear Systems

We will now develop the **back-substitution algorithm**, which is useful for solving a linear system of equations that has an upper-triangular coefficient matrix. This algorithm will be incorporated in the algorithm for solving a general linear system in Section 3.4.

Definition 3.2. An $N \times N$ matrix $A = [a_{ij}]$ is called **upper triangular** provided that the elements satisfy $a_{ij} = 0$ whenever $i > j$. The $N \times N$ matrix $A = [a_{ij}]$ is called **lower triangular** provided that $a_{ij} = 0$ whenever $i < j$. ▲

We will develop a method for constructing the solution to upper-triangular linear systems of equations and leave the investigation of lower-triangular systems to the reader. If A is an upper-triangular matrix, then $AX = B$ is said to be an **upper-**

triangular system of linear equations and has the form

$$
\begin{aligned}
a_{11}x_1 + a_{12}x_2 + \ a_{13}x_3 + \cdots + \quad a_{1N-1}x_{N-1} + \quad a_{1N}x_N &= b_1 \\
a_{22}x_2 + \ a_{23}x_3 + \cdots + \quad a_{2N-1}x_{N-1} + \quad a_{2N}x_N &= b_2 \\
a_{33}x_3 + \cdots + \quad a_{3N-1}x_{N-1} + \quad a_{3N}x_N &= b_3
\end{aligned}
$$

(1)

$$
\begin{aligned}
\quad\quad\quad\quad\quad\quad\quad\quad\quad a_{N-1N-1}x_{N-1} + \ a_{N-1N}x_N &= b_{N-1} \\
a_{NN}x_N &= b_N.
\end{aligned}
$$

Theorem 3.5 (Back Substitution).   Suppose that $AX = B$ is an upper-triangular system with the form given in (1). If

(2) $$a_{kk} \neq 0 \quad \text{for } k = 1, 2, \ldots, N,$$

then there exists a unique solution to (1).

Constructive Proof.   The solution is easy to find. The last equation involves only x_N, so we solve it first:

(3) $$x_N = \frac{b_N}{a_{NN}}.$$

Now x_N is known and it can be used in the next-to-last equation:

(4) $$x_{N-1} = \frac{b_{N-1} - a_{N-1N}x_N}{a_{N-1N-1}}.$$

Now x_N and x_{N-1} are used to find x_{N-2}:

(5) $$x_{N-2} = \frac{b_{N-2} - a_{N-2N-1}x_{N-1} - a_{N-2N}x_N}{a_{N-2N-2}}.$$

Once the values $x_N, x_{N-1}, \ldots, x_{k+1}$ are known, the general step is

(6) $$x_k = \frac{b_k - \sum_{j=k+1}^{N} a_{kj}x_j}{a_{kk}} \quad \text{for } k = N - 1, \ N - 2, \ldots, 1.$$

The uniqueness of the solution is easy to see. The Nth equation implies that b_N/a_{NN} is the only possible value of x_N. Then finite induction is used to establish that $x_{N-1}, x_{N-2}, \ldots, x_1$ are unique. •

Example 3.12.   Use back substitution to solve the linear system

$$
\begin{aligned}
4x_1 - x_2 + 2x_3 + 3x_4 &= 20 \\
-2x_2 + 7x_3 - 4x_4 &= -7 \\
6x_3 + 5x_4 &= 4 \\
3x_4 &= 6.
\end{aligned}
$$

Solving for x_4 in the last equation yields

$$x_4 = \frac{6}{3} = 2.$$

Using $x_4 = 2$ in the third equation, we obtain

$$x_3 = \frac{4 - 5(2)}{6} = -1.$$

Now $x_3 = -1$ and $x_4 = 2$ are used to find x_2 in the second equation:

$$x_2 = \frac{-7 - 7(-1) + 4(2)}{-2} = -4.$$

Finally, x_1 is obtained using the first equation:

$$x_1 = \frac{20 + 1(-4) - 2(-1) - 3(2)}{4} = 3. \qquad \blacksquare$$

The condition that $a_{kk} \neq 0$ is essential because equation (6) involves division by a_{kk}. If this requirement is not fulfilled, either no solution exists or infinitely many solutions exist.

Example 3.13. Show that there is no solution to the linear system

$$\begin{aligned}
4x_1 - x_2 + 2x_3 + 3x_4 &= 20 \\
0x_2 + 7x_3 - 4x_4 &= -7 \\
6x_3 + 5x_4 &= 4 \\
3x_4 &= 6.
\end{aligned} \tag{7}$$

Using the last equation in (7), we must have $x_4 = 2$, which is substituted into the second and third equations to obtain

$$\begin{aligned}
7x_3 - \quad 8 &= -7 \\
6x_3 + 10 &= \quad 4.
\end{aligned} \tag{8}$$

The first equation in (8) implies that $x_3 = 1/7$, and the second equation implies that $x_3 = -1$. This contradiction leads to the conclusion that there is no solution to the linear system (7). $\qquad \blacksquare$

Example 3.14. Show that there are infinitely many solutions to

$$\begin{aligned}
4x_1 - x_2 + 2x_3 + 3x_4 &= 20 \\
0x_2 + 7x_3 + 0x_4 &= -7 \\
6x_3 + 5x_4 &= 4 \\
3x_4 &= 6.
\end{aligned} \tag{9}$$

Using the last equation in (9), we must have $x_4 = 2$, which is substituted into the second and third equations to get $x_3 = -1$, which checks out in both equations. But only two values x_3 and x_4 have been obtained from the second through fourth equations, and when they are substituted into the first equation of (9), the result is

$$(10) \qquad\qquad\qquad x_2 = 4x_1 - 16,$$

which has infinitely many solutions; hence (9) has infinitely many solutions. If we choose a value of x_1 in (10), then the value of x_2 is uniquely determined. For example, if we include the equation $x_1 = 2$ in the system (9), then from (10) we compute $x_2 = -8$. $\blacksquare$

Theorem 3.4 states that the linear system $AX = B$, where A is an $N \times N$ matrix, has a unique solution if and only if $\det(A) \neq 0$. The following theorem states that if any entry on the main diagonal of an upper- or lower-triangular matrix is zero, then $\det(A) = 0$. Thus, by inspecting the coefficient matrices in the previous three examples, it is clear that the system in Example 3.12 has a unique solution, and the systems in Examples 3.13 and 3.14 do not have unique solutions. The proof of Theorem 3.6 can be found in most introductory linear algebra textbooks.

Theorem 3.6.   If the $N \times N$ matrix $A = [a_{ij}]$ is either upper or lower triangular, then

$$(11) \qquad\qquad \det(A) = a_{11}a_{22}\cdots a_{NN} = \prod_{i=1}^{N} a_{ii}.$$

The value of the determinant for the coefficient matrix in Example 3.12 is $\det A = 4(-2)(6)(3) = -144$. The values of the determinants of the coefficient matrices in Examples 3.13 and 3.14 are both $4(0)(6)(3) = 0$.

The following program will solve the upper-triangular system (1) by the method of back substitution, provided that $a_{kk} \neq 0$ for $k = 1, 2, \ldots, N$.

Program 3.1 (Back Substitution).   To solve the upper-triangular system $AX = B$ by the method of back substitution. Proceed with the method only if all the diagonal elements are nonzero. First compute $x_N = b_N / a_{NN}$ and then use the rule

$$x_k = \frac{b_k - \sum_{j=k+1}^{N} a_{kj}x_j}{a_{kk}} \qquad \text{for } k = N-1,\ N-2,\ \ldots,\ 1.$$

```
function X=backsub(A,B)
%Input   - A is an n x n upper-triangular nonsingular matrix
%         - B is an n x 1 matrix
%Output  - X is the solution to the linear system AX = B
%Find the dimension of B and initialize X
n=length(B);
X=zeros(n,1);
```

```
X(n)=B(n)/A(n,n);
for k=n-1:-1:1
  X(k)=(B(k)-A(k,k+1:n)*X(k+1:n))/A(k,k);
end
```

Exercises for Upper-Triangular Linear Systems

In Exercises 1 through 3, solve the upper-triangular system and find the value of the determinant of the coefficient matrix.

1. $\begin{aligned} 3x_1 - 2x_2 + x_3 - x_4 &= 8 \\ 4x_2 - x_3 + 2x_4 &= -3 \\ 2x_3 + 3x_4 &= 11 \\ 5x_4 &= 15 \end{aligned}$

2. $\begin{aligned} 5x_1 - 3x_2 - 7x_3 + x_4 &= -14 \\ 11x_2 + 9x_3 + 5x_4 &= 22 \\ 3x_3 - 13x_4 &= -11 \\ 7x_4 &= 14 \end{aligned}$

3. $\begin{aligned} 4x_1 - x_2 + 2x_3 + 2x_4 - x_5 &= 4 \\ -2x_2 + 6x_3 + 2x_4 + 7x_5 &= 0 \\ x_3 - x_4 - 2x_5 &= 3 \\ - 2x_4 - x_5 &= 10 \\ 3x_5 &= 6 \end{aligned}$

4. (a) Consider the two upper-triangular matrices

$$A = \begin{bmatrix} a_{11} & a_{12} & a_{13} \\ 0 & a_{22} & a_{23} \\ 0 & 0 & a_{33} \end{bmatrix} \quad \text{and} \quad B = \begin{bmatrix} b_{11} & b_{12} & b_{13} \\ 0 & b_{22} & b_{23} \\ 0 & 0 & b_{33} \end{bmatrix}.$$

Show that their product $C = AB$ is also upper triangular.

(b) Let A and B be two $N \times N$ upper-triangular matrices. Show that their product is also upper triangular.

5. Solve the lower-triangular system $AX = B$ and find $\det(A)$.

$$\begin{aligned} 2x_1 &= 6 \\ -x_1 + 4x_2 &= 5 \\ 3x_1 - 2x_2 - x_3 &= 4 \\ x_1 - 2x_2 + 6x_3 + 3x_4 &= 2 \end{aligned}$$

6. Solve the lower-triangular system $AX = B$ and find $\det(A)$.

$$\begin{aligned} 5x_1 &= -10 \\ x_1 + 3x_2 &= 4 \\ 3x_1 + 4x_2 + 2x_3 &= 2 \\ -x_1 + 3x_2 - 6x_3 - x_4 &= 5 \end{aligned}$$

7. Show that back substitution requires N divisions, $(N^2 - N)/2$ multiplications, and $(N^2 - N)/2$ additions or subtractions. *Hint.* You can use the formula

$$\sum_{k=1}^{M} k = M(M+1)/2.$$

Algorithms and Programs

1. Use Program 3.1 to solve the system $UX = B$, where

$$U = [u_{ij}]_{10 \times 10} \quad \text{and} \quad u_{ij} = \begin{cases} \cos(ij) & i \le j, \\ 0 & i > j. \end{cases}$$

and $B = [b_{i1}]_{10 \times 1}$ and $b_{i1} = \tan(i)$.

2. *Forward-substitution algorithm.* A linear system $AX = B$ is called lower triangular provided that $a_{ij} = 0$ when $i < j$. Construct a program `forsub`, analogous to Program 3.1, to solve the following lower-triangular system. *Remark.* This program will be used in Section 3.5.

$$
\begin{aligned}
a_{11}x_1 & & & & & = b_1 \\
a_{21}x_1 + & a_{22}x_2 & & & & = b_2 \\
a_{31}x_1 + & a_{32}x_2 + & a_{33}x_3 & & & = b_3 \\
&\vdots & \vdots & \vdots & & \vdots \\
a_{N-11}x_1 + a_{N-12}x_2 + a_{N-13}x_3 + &\cdots + a_{N-1\,N-1}x_{N-1} & & & = b_{N-1} \\
a_{N\,1}x_1 + & a_{N\,2}x_2 + & a_{N\,3}x_3 + \cdots + & a_{N\,N-1}x_{N-1} + a_{NN}x_N & = b_N
\end{aligned}
$$

3. Use `forsub` to solve the system $LX = B$, where

$$L = [l_{ij}]_{20 \times 20} \quad \text{and} \quad l_{ij} = \begin{cases} i + j & i \ge j, \\ 0 & i < j, \end{cases} \quad \text{and } B = [b_{i1}]_{20 \times 1} \text{ and } b_{i1} = i.$$

3.4 Gaussian Elimination and Pivoting

In this section we develop a scheme for solving a general system $AX = B$ of N equations and N unknowns. The goal is to construct an equivalent upper-triangular system $UX = Y$ that can be solved by the method of Section 3.3.

Two linear systems of dimension $N \times N$ are said to be *equivalent* provided that their solution sets are the same. Theorems from linear algebra show that when certain transformations are applied to a given system, the solution sets do not change.

Theorem 3.7 (Elementary Transformations). The following operations applied to a linear system yield an equivalent system:

(1) Interchanges: The order of two equations can be changed.

(2) Scaling: Multiplying an equation by a nonzero constant.

(3) Replacement: An equation can be replaced by the sum of itself and a nonzero multiple of any other equation.

It is common to use (3) by replacing an equation with the difference of that equation and a multiple of another equation. These concepts are illustrated in the next example.

Example 3.15. Find the parabola $y = A + Bx + Cx^2$ that passes through the three points $(1, 1)$, $(2, -1)$, and $(3, 1)$.

For each point we obtain an equation relating the value of x to the value of y. The result is the linear system

$$
\begin{array}{rll}
A + B + C = & 1 & \text{at } (1, 1) \\
A + 2B + 4C = & -1 & \text{at } (2, -1) \\
A + 3B + 9C = & 1 & \text{at } (3, 1).
\end{array}
\tag{4}
$$

The variable A is eliminated from the second and third equations by subtracting the first equation from them. This is an application of the replacement transformation (3), and the resulting equivalent linear system is

$$
\begin{array}{rl}
A + B + C = & 1 \\
B + 3C = & -2 \\
2B + 8C = & 0.
\end{array}
\tag{5}
$$

The variable B is eliminated from the third equation in (5) by subtracting from it two times the second equation. We arrive at the equivalent upper-triangular system:

$$
\begin{array}{rl}
A + B + C = & 1 \\
B + 3C = & -2 \\
2C = & 4.
\end{array}
\tag{6}
$$

The back-substitution algorithm is now used to find the coefficients $C = 4/2 = 2$, $B = -2 - 3(2) = -8$, and $A = 1 - (-8) - 2 = 7$, and the equation of the parabola is $y = 7 - 8x + 2x^2$. ∎

It is efficient to store all the coefficients of the linear system $AX = B$ in an array of dimension $N \times (N + 1)$. The coefficients of B are stored in column $N + 1$ of the array (i.e., $a_{kN+1} = b_k$). Each row contains all the coefficients necessary to represent an equation in the linear system. The **augmented matrix** is denoted $[A|B]$ and the linear system is represented as follows:

$$(7) \qquad [A|B] = \begin{bmatrix} a_{11} & a_{12} & \cdots & a_{1N} & b_1 \\ a_{21} & a_{22} & \cdots & a_{2N} & b_2 \\ \vdots & \vdots & & \vdots & \vdots \\ a_{N1} & a_{N2} & \cdots & a_{NN} & b_N \end{bmatrix}.$$

The system $AX = B$, with augmented matrix given in (7), can be solved by performing row operations on the augmented matrix $[A|B]$. The variables x_k are placeholders for the coefficients and can be omitted until the end of the calculation.

Theorem 3.8 (Elementary Row Operations).   The following operations applied to the augmented matrix (7) yield an equivalent linear system.

(8)   Interchanges: The order of two rows can be changed.

(9)   Scaling: Multiplying a row by a nonzero constant.

(10) Replacement: The row can be replaced by the sum of that row and
a nonzero multiple of any other row; that is:
$$\text{row}_r = \text{row}_r - m_{rp} \times \text{row}_p.$$

It is common to use (10) by replacing a row with the difference of that row and a multiple of another row.

Definition 3.3.   The number a_{rr} in the coefficient matrix A that is used to eliminate a_{kr}, where $k = r + 1, r + 2, \ldots, N$, is called the rth **pivotal element**, and the rth row is called the **pivot row**.   ▲

The following example illustrates how to use the operations in Theorem 3.8 to obtain an equivalent upper-triangular system $UX = Y$ from a linear system $AX = B$, where A is an $N \times N$ matrix.

Example 3.16.   Express the following system in augmented matrix form and find an equivalent upper-triangular system and the solution.

$$\begin{aligned} x_1 + 2x_2 + \ x_3 + 4x_4 &= 13 \\ 2x_1 + 0x_2 + 4x_3 + 3x_4 &= 28 \\ 4x_1 + 2x_2 + 2x_3 + \ x_4 &= 20 \\ -3x_1 + \ x_2 + 3x_3 + 2x_4 &= \ 6. \end{aligned}$$

The augmented matrix is

$$\begin{matrix} \text{pivot} \rightarrow \\ m_{21} = 2 \\ m_{31} = 4 \\ m_{41} = -3 \end{matrix} \begin{bmatrix} \underline{1} & 2 & 1 & 4 & 13 \\ 2 & 0 & 4 & 3 & 28 \\ 4 & 2 & 2 & 1 & 20 \\ -3 & 1 & 3 & 2 & 6 \end{bmatrix}.$$

The first row is used to eliminate elements in the first column below the diagonal. We refer to the first row as the *pivotal row* and the element $a_{11} = 1$ is called the *pivotal element*. The values m_{k1} are the multiples of row 1 that are to be subtracted from row k for $k = 2, 3, 4$. The result after elimination is

$$
\begin{array}{c}
\text{pivot} \rightarrow \\
m_{32} = 1.5 \\
m_{42} = -1.75
\end{array}
\left[
\begin{array}{cccc|c}
1 & 2 & 1 & 4 & 13 \\
0 & \underline{-4} & 2 & -5 & 2 \\
0 & -6 & -2 & -15 & -32 \\
0 & 7 & 6 & 14 & 45
\end{array}
\right].
$$

The second row is used to eliminate elements in the second column that lie below the diagonal. The second row is the pivotal row and the values m_{k2} are the multiples of row 2 that are to be subtracted from row k for $k = 3, 4$. The result after elimination is

$$
\begin{array}{c}
\\
\\
\text{pivot} \rightarrow \\
m_{43} = -1.9
\end{array}
\left[
\begin{array}{cccc|c}
1 & 2 & 1 & 4 & 13 \\
0 & -4 & 2 & -5 & 2 \\
0 & 0 & \underline{-5} & -7.5 & -35 \\
0 & 0 & 9.5 & 5.25 & 48.5
\end{array}
\right].
$$

Finally, the multiple $m_{43} = -1.9$ of the third row is subtracted from the fourth row, and the result is the upper-triangular system

(11)
$$
\left[
\begin{array}{cccc|c}
1 & 2 & 1 & 4 & 13 \\
0 & -4 & 2 & -5 & 2 \\
0 & 0 & -5 & -7.5 & -35 \\
0 & 0 & 0 & -9 & -18
\end{array}
\right].
$$

The back-substitution algorithm can be used to solve (11), and we get

$$
x_4 = 2, \quad x_3 = 4, \quad x_2 = -1, \quad x_1 = 3. \qquad \blacksquare
$$

The process described above is called **Gaussian elimination** and must be modified so that it can be used in most circumstances. If $a_{kk} = 0$, row k cannot be used to eliminate the elements in column k, and row k must be interchanged with some row below the diagonal to obtain a nonzero pivot element. If this cannot be done, then the coefficient matrix of the system of linear equations is singular, and the system does not have a unique solution.

Theorem 3.9 (Gaussian Elimination with Back Substitution).   If A is an $N \times N$ nonsingular matrix, then there exists a system $UX = Y$, equivalent to $AX = B$, where U is an upper-triangular matrix with $u_{kk} \neq 0$. After U and Y are constructed, back substitution can be used to solve $UX = Y$ for X.

Proof.   We will use the augmented matrix with B stored in column $N + 1$:

$$AX = \begin{bmatrix} a_{11}^{(1)} & a_{12}^{(1)} & a_{13}^{(1)} & \cdots & a_{1N}^{(1)} \\ a_{21}^{(1)} & a_{22}^{(1)} & a_{23}^{(1)} & \cdots & a_{2N}^{(1)} \\ a_{31}^{(1)} & a_{32}^{(1)} & a_{33}^{(1)} & \cdots & a_{3N}^{(1)} \\ \vdots & \vdots & \vdots & & \vdots \\ a_{N1}^{(1)} & a_{N2}^{(1)} & a_{N3}^{(1)} & \cdots & a_{NN}^{(1)} \end{bmatrix} \begin{bmatrix} x_1 \\ x_2 \\ x_3 \\ \vdots \\ x_N \end{bmatrix} = \begin{bmatrix} a_{1\,N+1}^{(1)} \\ a_{2\,N+1}^{(1)} \\ a_{3\,N+1}^{(1)} \\ \vdots \\ a_{N\,N+1}^{(1)} \end{bmatrix} = B.$$

Then we will construct an equivalent upper-triangular system $UX = Y$:

$$UX = \begin{bmatrix} a_{11}^{(1)} & a_{12}^{(1)} & a_{13}^{(1)} & \cdots & a_{1N}^{(1)} \\ 0 & a_{22}^{(2)} & a_{23}^{(2)} & \cdots & a_{2N}^{(2)} \\ 0 & 0 & a_{33}^{(3)} & \cdots & a_{3N}^{(3)} \\ \vdots & \vdots & \vdots & & \vdots \\ 0 & 0 & 0 & \cdots & a_{NN}^{(N)} \end{bmatrix} \begin{bmatrix} x_1 \\ x_2 \\ x_3 \\ \vdots \\ x_N \end{bmatrix} = \begin{bmatrix} a_{1\,N+1}^{(1)} \\ a_{2\,N+1}^{(2)} \\ a_{3\,N+1}^{(3)} \\ \vdots \\ a_{N\,N+1}^{(N)} \end{bmatrix} = Y.$$

Step 1.   Store the coefficients in the augmented matrix. The superscript on $a_{rc}^{(1)}$ means that this is the first time that a number is stored in location (r, c):

$$\begin{bmatrix} a_{11}^{(1)} & a_{12}^{(1)} & a_{13}^{(1)} & \cdots & a_{1N}^{(1)} & \bigg| & a_{1\,N+1}^{(1)} \\ a_{21}^{(1)} & a_{22}^{(1)} & a_{23}^{(1)} & \cdots & a_{2N}^{(1)} & \bigg| & a_{2\,N+1}^{(1)} \\ a_{31}^{(1)} & a_{32}^{(1)} & a_{33}^{(1)} & \cdots & a_{3N}^{(1)} & \bigg| & a_{3\,N+1}^{(1)} \\ \vdots & \vdots & \vdots & & \vdots & \bigg| & \vdots \\ a_{N1}^{(1)} & a_{N2}^{(1)} & a_{N3}^{(1)} & \cdots & a_{NN}^{(1)} & \bigg| & a_{N\,N+1}^{(1)} \end{bmatrix}.$$

Step 2.   If necessary, switch rows so that $a_{11}^{(1)} \neq 0$; then eliminate x_1 in rows 2 through N. In this process, m_{r1} is the multiple of row 1 that is subtracted from row r.

$$
\begin{aligned}
&\text{for } r = 2 : N \\
&\quad m_{r1} = a_{r1}^{(1)}/a_{11}^{(1)}; \\
&\quad a_{r1}^{(2)} = 0; \\
&\quad \text{for } c = 2 : N + 1 \\
&\quad\quad a_{rc}^{(2)} = a_{rc}^{(1)} - m_{r1} * a_{1c}^{(1)}; \\
&\quad \text{end} \\
&\text{end}
\end{aligned}
$$

The new elements are written $a_{rc}^{(2)}$ to indicate that this is the second time that a number has been stored in the matrix at location (r, c). The result after step 2 is

$$
\begin{bmatrix}
a_{11}^{(1)} & a_{12}^{(1)} & a_{13}^{(1)} & \cdots & a_{1N}^{(1)} & a_{1\,N+1}^{(1)} \\
0 & a_{22}^{(2)} & a_{23}^{(2)} & \cdots & a_{2N}^{(2)} & a_{2\,N+1}^{(2)} \\
0 & a_{32}^{(2)} & a_{33}^{(2)} & \cdots & a_{3N}^{(2)} & a_{3\,N+1}^{(2)} \\
\vdots & \vdots & \vdots & & \vdots & \vdots \\
0 & a_{N2}^{(2)} & a_{N3}^{(2)} & \cdots & a_{NN}^{(2)} & a_{N\,N+1}^{(2)}
\end{bmatrix}.
$$

Step 3. If necessary, switch the second row with some row below it so that $a_{22}^{(2)} \neq 0$; then eliminate x_2 in rows 3 through N. In this process, m_{r2} is the multiple of row 2 that is subtracted from row r.

$$
\begin{aligned}
&\text{for } r = 3 : N \\
&\quad m_{r2} = a_{r2}^{(2)}/a_{22}^{(2)}; \\
&\quad a_{r2}^{(3)} = 0; \\
&\quad \text{for } c = 3 : N + 1 \\
&\quad\quad a_{rc}^{(3)} = a_{rc}^{(2)} - m_{r2} * a_{2c}^{(2)}; \\
&\quad \text{end} \\
&\text{end}
\end{aligned}
$$

The new elements are written $a_{rc}^{(3)}$ to indicate that this is the third time that a number has been stored in the matrix at location (r, c). The result after step 3 is

$$
\begin{bmatrix}
a_{11}^{(1)} & a_{12}^{(1)} & a_{13}^{(1)} & \cdots & a_{1N}^{(1)} & a_{1\,N+1}^{(1)} \\
0 & a_{22}^{(2)} & a_{23}^{(2)} & \cdots & a_{2N}^{(2)} & a_{2\,N+1}^{(2)} \\
0 & 0 & a_{33}^{(3)} & \cdots & a_{3N}^{(3)} & a_{3\,N+1}^{(3)} \\
\vdots & \vdots & \vdots & & \vdots & \vdots \\
0 & 0 & a_{N3}^{(3)} & \cdots & a_{NN}^{(3)} & a_{N\,N+1}^{(3)}
\end{bmatrix}.
$$

Step $p + 1$. This is the general step. If necessary, switch row p with some row beneath it so that $a_{pp}^{(p)} \neq 0$; then eliminate x_p in rows $p + 1$ through N. Here m_{rp} is the multiple of row p that is subtracted from row r.

$$
\begin{aligned}
&\text{for } r = p + 1 : N \\
&\quad m_{rp} = a_{rp}^{(p)}/a_{pp}^{(p)}; \\
&\quad a_{rp}^{(p+1)} = 0;
\end{aligned}
$$

$$\text{for } c = p + 1 : N + 1$$
$$a_{rc}^{(p+1)} = a_{rc}^{(p)} - m_{rp} * a_{pc}^{(p)};$$
$$\text{end}$$
$$\text{end}$$

The final result after x_{N-1} has been eliminated from row N is

$$\begin{bmatrix} a_{11}^{(1)} & a_{12}^{(1)} & a_{13}^{(1)} & \cdots & a_{1N}^{(1)} & a_{1\,N+1}^{(1)} \\ 0 & a_{22}^{(2)} & a_{23}^{(2)} & \cdots & a_{2N}^{(2)} & a_{2\,N+1}^{(2)} \\ 0 & 0 & a_{33}^{(3)} & \cdots & a_{3N}^{(3)} & a_{3\,N+1}^{(3)} \\ \vdots & \vdots & \vdots & & \vdots & \vdots \\ 0 & 0 & 0 & \cdots & a_{NN}^{(N)} & a_{N\,N+1}^{(N)} \end{bmatrix}.$$

The upper-triangularization process is now complete.

Since A is nonsingular, when row operations are performed the successive matrices are also nonsingular. This guarantees that $a_{kk}^{(k)} \neq 0$ for all k in the construction process. Hence back substitution can be used to solve $UX = Y$ for X, and the theorem is proved.

●

Pivoting to Avoid $a_{pp}^{(p)} = 0$

If $a_{pp}^{(p)} = 0$, row p cannot be used to eliminate the elements in column p below the main diagonal. It is necessary to find row k, where $a_{kp}^{(p)} \neq 0$ and $k > p$, and then interchange row p and row k so that a nonzero pivot element is obtained. This process is called *pivoting*, and the criterion for deciding which row to choose is called a *pivoting strategy*. The **trivial pivoting** strategy is as follows. If $a_{pp}^{(p)} \neq 0$, do not switch rows. If $a_{pp}^{(p)} = 0$, locate the first row below p in which $a_{kp}^{(p)} \neq 0$ and switch rows k and p. This will result in a new element $a_{pp}^{(p)} \neq 0$, which is a nonzero pivot element.

Pivoting to Reduce Error

Because the computer uses fixed-precision arithmetic, it is possible that a small error will be introduced each time that an arithmetic operation is performed. The following example illustrates how use of the trivial pivoting strategy in Gaussian elimination can lead to significant error in the solution of a linear system of equations.

Example 3.17.   The values $x_1 = x_2 = 1.000$ are the solutions to

(12)
$$1.133x_1 + 5.281x_2 = 6.414$$
$$24.14x_1 - 1.210x_2 = 22.93.$$

Use four-digit arithmetic (see Exercises 6 and 7 in Section 1.3) and Gaussian elimination with trivial pivoting to find a computed approximate solution to the system.

The multiple $m_{21} = 24.14/1.133 = 21.31$ of row 1 is to be subtracted from row 2 to obtain the upper-triangular system. Using four digits in the calculations, we obtain the new coefficients

$$a_{22}^{(2)} = -1.210 - 21.31(5.281) = -1.210 - 112.5 = -113.7$$
$$a_{23}^{(2)} = 22.93 - 21.31(6.414) = 22.93 - 136.7 = -113.8.$$

The computed upper-triangular system is

$$1.133x_1 + 5.281x_2 = 6.414$$
$$-113.7x_2 = -113.8.$$

Back substitution is used to compute $x_2 = -113.8/(-113.7) = 1.001$, and $x_1 = (6.414 - 5.281(1.001))/(1.133) = (6.414 - 5.286)/1.133 = 0.9956$.   ∎

The error in the solution of the linear system (12) is due to the magnitude of the multiplier $m_{21} = 21.31$. In the next example the magnitude of the multiplier m_{21} is reduced by first interchanging the first and second equations in the linear system (12) and then using the trivial pivoting strategy in Gaussian elimination to solve the system.

Example 3.18.   Use four-digit arithmetic and Gaussian elimination with trivial pivoting to solve the linear system

$$24.14x_1 - 1.210x_2 = 22.93$$
$$1.133x_1 + 5.281x_2 = 6.414.$$

This time $m_{21} = 1.133/24.14 = 0.04693$ is the multiple of row 1 that is to be subtracted from row 2. The new coefficients are

$$a_{22}^{(2)} = 5.281 - 0.04693(-1.210) = 5.281 + 0.05679 = 5.338$$
$$a_{23}^{(2)} = 6.414 - 0.04693(22.93) = 6.414 - 1.076 = 5.338.$$

The computed upper-triangular system is

$$24.14x_1 - 1.210x_2 = 22.93$$
$$5.338x_2 = 5.338.$$

Back substitution is used to compute $x_2 = 5.338/5.338 = 1.000$, and $x_1 = (22.93 + 1.210(1.000))/24.14 = 1.000$.   ∎

The purpose of a pivoting strategy is to move the entry of greatest magnitude to the main diagonal and then use it to eliminate the remaining entries in the column. If there is more than one nonzero element in column p that lies on or below the main diagonal, then there is a choice to determine which rows to interchange. The ***partial pivoting*** strategy, illustrated in Example 3.18, is the most common one and is used in Program 3.2. To reduce the propagation of error, it is suggested that one check the magnitude of all the elements in column p that lie on or below the main diagonal. Locate row k in which the element that has the largest absolute value lies, that is,

$$|a_{kp}| = \max\{|a_{pp}|, |a_{p+1\,p}|, \ldots, |a_{N-1\,p}|, |a_{Np}|\},$$

and then switch row p with row k if $k > p$. Now, each of the multipliers m_{rp} for $r = p + 1, \ldots, N$ will be less than or equal to 1 in absolute value. This process will usually keep the relative magnitudes of the elements of the matrix U in Theorem 3.9 the same as those in the original coefficient matrix A. Usually, the choice of the larger pivot element in partial pivoting will result in a smaller error being propagated.

In Section 3.5 we will find that it takes a total of $(4N^3 + 9N^2 - 7N)/6$ arithmetic operations to solve an $N \times N$ system. When $N = 20$, the total number of arithmetic operations that must be performed is 5910, and the propagation of error in the computations could result in an erroneous answer. The technique of ***scaled partial pivoting*** or equilibrating can be used to further reduce the effect of error propagation. In scaled partial pivoting we search all the elements in column p that lie on or below the main diagonal for the one that is largest relative to the entries in its row. First search rows p through N for the largest element in magnitude in each row, say s_r:

(13) $s_r = \max\{|a_{rp}|, |a_{rp+1}|, \ldots, |a_{rN}|\}$ for $r = p, \ p + 1, \ \ldots, \ N.$

The pivotal row k is determined by finding

(14) $$\frac{|a_{kp}|}{s_k} = \max\left\{\frac{|a_{pp}|}{s_p}, \frac{|a_{p+1\,p}|}{s_{p+1}}, \ldots, \frac{|a_{Np}|}{s_N}\right\}.$$

Now interchange row p and k, unless $p = k$. Again, this pivoting process is designed to keep the relative magnitudes of the elements in the matrix U in Theorem 3.9 the same as those in the original coefficient matrix A.

Ill Conditioning

A matrix A is called ***ill conditioned*** if there exists a matrix B for which small perturbations in the coefficients of A or B will produce large changes in $X = A^{-1}B$. The system $AX = B$ is said to be ill conditioned when A is ill conditioned. In this case, numerical methods for computing an approximate solution are prone to have more error.

One circumstance involving ill conditioning occurs when A is "nearly singular" and the determinant of A is close to zero. Ill conditioning can also occur in systems

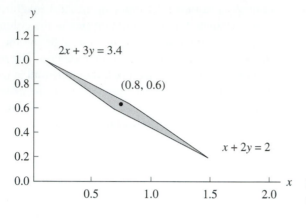

Figure 3.4 A region where two equations are "almost satisfied."

of two equations when two lines are nearly parallel (or in three equations when three planes are nearly parallel). A consequence of ill conditioning is that substitution of erroneous values may appear to be genuine solutions. For example, consider the two equations

$$(15) \qquad \begin{aligned} x + 2y - 2.00 &= 0 \\ 2x + 3y - 3.40 &= 0. \end{aligned}$$

Substitution of $x_0 = 1.00$ and $y_0 = 0.48$ into these equations "almost produces zeros":

$$1 + 2(0.48) - 2.00 = 1.96 - 2.00 = -0.04 \approx 0$$
$$2 + 3(0.48) - 3.40 = 3.44 - 3.40 = 0.04 \approx 0.$$

Here the discrepancy from 0 is only ± 0.04. However, the true solution to this linear system is $x = 0.8$ and $y = 0.6$, so the errors in the approximate solution are $x - x_0 = 0.80 - 1.00 = -0.20$ and $y - y_0 = 0.60 - 0.48 = 0.12$. Thus, merely substituting values into a set of equations is not a reliable test for accuracy. The rhombus-shaped region in Figure 3.4 represents a set where both equations in (15) are "almost satisfied":

$$R = \{(x, y) : |x + 2y - 2.00| < 0.1 \quad \text{and} \quad |2x + 3y - 3.40| < 0.2\}.$$

There are points in R that are far away from the solution point $(0.8, 0.6)$ and yet produce small values when substituted into the equations in (15). If it is suspected that a linear system is ill conditioned, computations should be carried out in multiple-precision arithmetic. The interested reader should research the topic of condition number of a matrix to get more information on this phenomenon.

Ill conditioning has more drastic consequences when several equations are involved. Consider the problem of finding the cubic polynomial $y = c_1x^3 + c_2x^2 + c_3x + c_4$ that passes through the four points $(2, 8)$, $(3, 27)$, $(4, 64)$, and $(5, 125)$ (clearly,

$y = x^3$ is the desired cubic polynomial). In Chapter 5 we will introduce the method of least squares. Applying the method of least squares to find the coefficients requires that the following linear system be solved:

$$\begin{bmatrix} 20{,}514 & 4{,}424 & 978 & 224 \\ 4{,}424 & 978 & 224 & 54 \\ 978 & 224 & 54 & 14 \\ 224 & 54 & 14 & 4 \end{bmatrix} \begin{bmatrix} c_1 \\ c_2 \\ c_3 \\ c_4 \end{bmatrix} = \begin{bmatrix} 20{,}514 \\ 4{,}424 \\ 978 \\ 224 \end{bmatrix}.$$

A computer that carried nine digits of precision was used to compute the coefficients and obtained

$$c_1 = 1.000004, \quad c_2 = -0.000038, \quad c_3 = 0.000126, \quad \text{and} \quad c_4 = -0.000131.$$

Although this computation is close to the true solution, $c_1 = 1$ and $c_2 = c_3 = c_4 = 0$, it shows how easy it is for error to creep into the solution. Furthermore, suppose that the coefficient $a_{11} = 20{,}514$ in the upper-left corner of the coefficient matrix is changed to the value $20{,}515$ and the perturbed system is solved. Values obtained with the same computer were

$$c_1 = 0.642857, \quad c_2 = 3.75000, \quad c_3 = -12.3928, \quad \text{and} \quad c_4 = 12.7500,$$

which is a worthless answer. Ill conditioning is not easy to detect. If the system is solved a second time with slightly perturbed coefficients and an answer that differs significantly from the first one is discovered, then it is realized that ill conditioning is present. Sensitivity analysis is a topic normally introduced in advanced numerical analysis texts.

MATLAB

In Program 3.2 the MATLAB statement [A B] is used to construct the augmented matrix for the linear system $AX = B$, and the max command is used to determine the pivot element in partial pivoting. Once the equivalent triangulated matrix $[U|Y]$ is obtained it is separated into U and Y, and Program 3.1 is used to carry out back substitution (backsub(U,Y)). The use of these commands and processes is illustrated in the following example.

Example 3.19.   (a) Use MATLAB to construct the augmented matrix for the linear system in Example 3.16; (b) use the max command to find the element of greatest magnitude in the first column of the coefficient matrix A; and (c) break the augmented matrix in (11) into the coefficient matrix U and constant matrix Y of the upper-triangular system $UX = Y$.
(a)
```
>> A=[1 2 1 4;2 0 4 3;4 2 2 1;-3 1 3 2];
>> B=[13 28 20 6]';
>> Aug=[A B]
```

```
Aug=
    1 2 1 4 13
    2 0 4 3 28
    4 2 2 1 20
   -3 1 3 2 6
```

(b) In the following MATLAB display, a is the element of greatest magnitude in the first column of A and j is the row number.

```
>>[a,j]=max{abs(A(1:4,1))}
a=
    4
j=
    3
```

(c) Let Augup $= [U|Y]$ be the upper-triangular matrix in (11).

```
>> Augup=[1 2 1 4 13;0 -4 2 -5 2;0 0 -5 -7.5 -35;0 0 0 -9 -18];
>> U=Augup(1:4,1:4)
U=
   1.0000 2.0000 1.0000  4.0000
       0   -4.0000 2.0000 -5.0000
       0      0    -5.0000 -7.5000
       0      0       0    -9.0000
>> Y=Augup(1:4,5)
Y=
      13
       2
     -35
     -18
```

■

Program 3.2 (Upper Triangularization Followed by Back Substitution). To construct the solution to $AX = B$, by first reducing the augmented matrix $[A|B]$ to upper-triangular form and then performing back substitution.

```
function X = uptrbk(A,B)

%Input   - A is an N x N nonsingular matrix
%         - B is an N x 1 matrix
%Output - X is an N x 1 matrix containing the solution to AX=B.
%Initialize X and the temporary storage matrix C
      [N N]=size(A);
      X=zeros(N,1);
      C=zeros(1,N+1);
%Form the augmented matrix:Aug=[A|B]
      Aug=[A B];
```

```
for p=1:N-1
   %Partial pivoting for column p
   [Y,j]=max(abs(Aug(p:N,p)));
   %Interchange row p and j
   C=Aug(p,:);
   Aug(p,:)=Aug(j+p-1,:);
   Aug(j+p-1,:)=C;
if Aug(p,p)==0
   'A was singular.  No unique solution'
   break
end

%Elimination process for column p
   for k=p+1:N
      m=Aug(k,p)/Aug(p,p);
      Aug(k,p:N+1)=Aug(k,p:N+1)-m*Aug(p,p:N+1);
   end
end

%Back Substitution on [U|Y] using Program 3.1
X=backsub(Aug(1:N,1:N),Aug(1:N,N+1));
```

Exercises for Gaussian Elimination and Pivoting

In Exercises 1 through 4, show that $AX = B$ is equivalent to the upper-triangular system $UX = Y$ and find the solution.

1.

$$2x_1 + 4x_2 - 6x_3 = -4$$
$$x_1 + 5x_2 + 3x_3 = 10$$
$$x_1 + 3x_2 + 2x_3 = 5$$

$$2x_1 + 4x_2 - 6x_3 = -4$$
$$3x_2 + 6x_3 = 12$$
$$3x_3 = 3$$

2.

$$x_1 + x_2 + 6x_3 = 7$$
$$-x_1 + 2x_2 + 9x_3 = 2$$
$$x_1 - 2x_2 + 3x_3 = 10$$

$$x_1 + x_2 + 6x_3 = 7$$
$$3x_2 + 15x_3 = 9$$
$$12x_3 = 12$$

3.

$$2x_1 - 2x_2 + 5x_3 = 6$$
$$2x_1 + 3x_2 + x_3 = 13$$
$$-x_1 + 4x_2 - 4x_3 = 3$$

$$2x_1 - 2x_2 + 5x_3 = 6$$
$$5x_2 - 4x_3 = 7$$
$$0.9x_3 = 1.8$$

4.

$$-5x_1 + 2x_2 - x_3 = -1$$
$$x_1 + 0x_2 + 3x_3 = 5$$
$$3x_1 + x_2 + 6x_3 = 17$$

$$-5x_1 + 2x_2 - x_3 = -1$$
$$0.4x_2 + 2.8x_3 = 4.8$$
$$-10x_3 = -10$$

5. Find the parabola $y = A + Bx + Cx^2$ that passes through $(1, 4)$, $(2, 7)$, and $(3, 14)$.

6. Find the parabola $y = A + Bx + Cx^2$ that passes through $(1, 6)$, $(2, 5)$, and $(3, 2)$.

7. Find the cubic $y = A + Bx + Cx^2 + Dx^3$ that passes through $(0, 0)$, $(1, 1)$, $(2, 2)$, and $(3, 2)$.

In Exercises 8 through 10, show that $AX = B$ is equivalent to the upper-triangular system $UX = Y$ and find the solution.

8. $\begin{aligned} 4x_1 + 8x_2 + 4x_3 + 0x_4 &= 8 \\ x_1 + 5x_2 + 4x_3 - 3x_4 &= -4 \\ x_1 + 4x_2 + 7x_3 + 2x_4 &= 10 \\ x_1 + 3x_2 + 0x_3 - 2x_4 &= -4 \end{aligned}$ $\qquad$ $\begin{aligned} 4x_1 + 8x_2 + 4x_3 + 0x_4 &= 8 \\ 3x_2 + 3x_3 - 3x_4 &= -6 \\ 4x_3 + 4x_4 &= 12 \\ x_4 &= 2 \end{aligned}$

9. $\begin{aligned} 2x_1 + 4x_2 - 4x_3 + 0x_4 &= 12 \\ x_1 + 5x_2 - 5x_3 - 3x_4 &= 18 \\ 2x_1 + 3x_2 + x_3 + 3x_4 &= 8 \\ x_1 + 4x_2 - 2x_3 + 2x_4 &= 8 \end{aligned}$ $\qquad$ $\begin{aligned} 2x_1 + 4x_2 - 4x_3 + 0x_4 &= 12 \\ 3x_2 - 3x_3 - 3x_4 &= 12 \\ 4x_3 + 2x_4 &= 0 \\ 3x_4 &= -6 \end{aligned}$

10. $\begin{aligned} x_1 + 2x_2 + 0x_3 - x_4 &= 9 \\ 2x_1 + 3x_2 - x_3 + 0x_4 &= 9 \\ 0x_1 + 4x_2 + 2x_3 - 5x_4 &= 26 \\ 5x_1 + 5x_2 + 2x_3 - 4x_4 &= 32 \end{aligned}$ $\qquad$ $\begin{aligned} x_1 + 2x_2 + 0x_3 - x_4 &= 9 \\ -x_2 - x_3 + 2x_4 &= -9 \\ -2x_3 + 3x_4 &= -10 \\ 1.5x_4 &= -3 \end{aligned}$

11. Find the solution to the following linear system.

$$\begin{aligned} x_1 + 2x_2 \qquad\qquad &= 7 \\ 2x_1 + 3x_2 - x_3 \qquad &= 9 \\ 4x_2 + 2x_3 + 3x_4 &= 10 \\ 2x_3 - 4x_4 &= 12 \end{aligned}$$

12. Find the solution to the following linear system.

$$\begin{aligned} x_1 + x_2 \qquad\qquad &= 5 \\ 2x_1 - x_2 + 5x_3 \qquad &= -9 \\ 3x_2 - 4x_3 + 2x_4 &= 19 \\ 2x_3 + 6x_4 &= 2 \end{aligned}$$

13. The Rockmore Corp. is considering the purchase of a new computer and will choose either the DoGood 174 or the MightDo 11. They test both computers' ability to solve the linear system

$$34x + 55y - 21 = 0$$
$$55x + 89y - 34 = 0.$$

The DoGood 174 computer gives $x = -0.11$ and $y = 0.45$, and its check for accuracy is found by substitution:

$$34(-0.11) + 55(0.45) - 21 = 0.01$$
$$55(-0.11) + 89(0.45) - 34 = 0.00.$$

The MightDo 11 computer gives $x = -0.99$ and $y = 1.01$, and its check for accuracy is found by substitution:

$$34(-0.99) + 55(1.01) - 21 = 0.89$$
$$55(-0.99) + 89(1.01) - 34 = 1.44.$$

Which computer gave the better answer? Why?

14. Solve, using four-digit rounding arithmetic, the following linear systems using (i) Gaussian elimination with partial pivoting, and (ii) Gaussian elimination with scaled partial pivoting.

(a)
$$2x_1 - \quad 3x_2 + \quad 100x_3 = 1$$
$$x_1 + \quad 10x_2 - 0.001x_3 = 0$$
$$3x_1 - 100x_2 + \quad 0.01x_3 = 0$$

(b)
$$x_1 + \quad 20x_2 - \quad x_3 + 0.001x_4 = 0$$
$$2x_1 - \quad 5x_2 + \quad 30x_3 - \quad 0.1x_4 = 1$$
$$5x_1 + \quad x_2 - 100x_3 - \quad 10x_4 = 0$$
$$2x_1 - 100x_2 - \quad x_3 + \quad x_4 = 0$$

15. The Hilbert matrix is a classical ill-conditioned matrix and small changes in its coefficients will produce a large change in the solution to the perturbed system.

(a)   Find the exact solution of $AX = B$ (leave all numbers as fractions and do exact arithmetic) using the Hilbert matrix of dimension 4×4:

$$A = \begin{bmatrix} 1 & \frac{1}{2} & \frac{1}{3} & \frac{1}{4} \\ \frac{1}{2} & \frac{1}{3} & \frac{1}{4} & \frac{1}{5} \\ \frac{1}{3} & \frac{1}{4} & \frac{1}{5} & \frac{1}{6} \\ \frac{1}{4} & \frac{1}{5} & \frac{1}{6} & \frac{1}{7} \end{bmatrix}, \qquad B = \begin{bmatrix} 1 \\ 0 \\ 0 \\ 0 \end{bmatrix}.$$

(b)   Now solve $AX = B$ using four-digit rounding arithmetic:

$$A = \begin{bmatrix} 1.0000 & 0.5000 & 0.3333 & 0.2500 \\ 0.5000 & 0.3333 & 0.2500 & 0.2000 \\ 0.3333 & 0.2500 & 0.2000 & 0.1667 \\ 0.2500 & 0.2000 & 0.1667 & 0.1429 \end{bmatrix}, \qquad B = \begin{bmatrix} 1 \\ 0 \\ 0 \\ 0 \end{bmatrix}.$$

Note. The coefficient matrix in part (b) is an approximation to the coefficient matrix in part (a).

Algorithms and Programs

1. Many applications involve matrices with many zeros. Of practical importance are *tridiagonal systems* (see Exercises 11 and 12) of the form

$$
\begin{aligned}
d_1 x_1 + c_1 x_2 &= b_1 \\
a_1 x_1 + d_2 x_2 + c_2 x_3 &= b_2 \\
a_2 x_2 + d_3 x_3 + c_3 x_4 &= b_3 \\
&\ \ \vdots \\
a_{N-2} x_{N-2} + d_{N-1} x_{N-1} + c_{N-1} x_N &= b_{N-1} \\
a_{N-1} x_{N-1} + d_N x_N &= b_N.
\end{aligned}
$$

   Construct a program that will solve a tridiagonal system. You may assume that row interchanges are not needed and that row k can be used to eliminate x_k in row $k + 1$.

2. Use Program 3.2 to find the sixth-degree polynomial $y = a_1 + a_2 x + a_3 x^2 + a_4 x^3 + a_5 x^4 + a_6 x^5 + a_7 x^6$ that passes through $(0, 1)$, $(1, 3)$, $(2, 2)$, $(3, 1)$, $(4, 3)$, $(5, 2)$, and $(6, 1)$. Use the `plot` command to plot the polynomial and the given points on the same graph. Explain any discrepancies in your graph.

3. Use Program 3.2 to solve the linear system $AX = B$, where $A = [a_{ij}]_{N \times N}$ and $a_{ij} = i^{j-1}$, and $B = [b_{ij}]_{N \times 1}$, where $b_{11} = N$ and $b_{i1} = (i^N - 1)/(i - 1)$ for $i \geq 2$. Use $N = 3, 7$, and 11. The exact solution is $X = \begin{bmatrix} 1 & 1 & \cdots & 1 & 1 \end{bmatrix}'$. Explain any deviations from the exact solution.

4. Construct a program that changes the pivoting strategy in Program 3.2 to scaled partial pivoting.

5. Use your scaled partial pivoting program from Problem 4 to solve the system given in Problem 3 for $N = 11$. Explain any improvements in the solutions.

6. Modify Program 3.2 so that it will efficiently solve M linear systems with the same coefficient matrix A but different column matrices B. The M linear systems look like

$$
AX_1 = B_1, \qquad AX_2 = B_2, \qquad \ldots, \qquad AX_M = B_M.
$$

7. The following discussion is presented for matrices of dimension 3×3, but the concepts apply to matrices of dimension $N \times N$. If A is nonsingular, then A^{-1} exists and $AA^{-1} = I$. Let C_1, C_2, and C_3 be the columns of A^{-1} and E_1, E_2, and E_3 be the columns of I. The equation $AA^{-1} = I$ can be represented as

$$
A \begin{bmatrix} C_1 & C_2 & C_3 \end{bmatrix} = \begin{bmatrix} E_1 & E_2 & E_3 \end{bmatrix}.
$$

   This matrix product is equivalent to the three linear systems

$$
AC_1 = E_1, \qquad AC_2 = E_2, \qquad \text{and} \qquad AC_3 = E_3.
$$

Thus finding A^{-1} is equivalent to solving the three linear systems.

Using Program 3.2 or your program from Problem 6, find the inverse of each of the following matrices. Check your answer by computing the product AA^{-1} and also by using the command inv(A). Explain any differences.

(a) $\begin{bmatrix} 2 & 0 & 1 \\ 3 & 2 & 5 \\ 1 & -1 & 0 \end{bmatrix}$

(b) $\begin{bmatrix} 16 & -120 & 240 & -140 \\ -120 & 1200 & -2700 & 1680 \\ 240 & -2700 & 6480 & -4200 \\ -140 & 1680 & -4200 & 2800 \end{bmatrix}$

3.5 Triangular Factorization

In Section 3.3 we saw how easy it is to solve an upper-triangular system. Now we introduce the concept of factorization of a given matrix A into the product of a lower-triangular matrix L that has 1's along the main diagonal and an upper-triangular matrix U with nonzero diagonal elements. For ease of notation we illustrate the concepts with matrices of dimension 4×4, but they apply to an arbitrary system of dimension $N \times N$.

Definition 3.4. The nonsingular matrix A has a ***triangular factorization*** if it can be expressed as the product of a lower-triangular matrix L and an upper-triangular matrix U:

(1) $$A = LU.$$

In matrix form, this is written as

$$\begin{bmatrix} a_{11} & a_{12} & a_{13} & a_{14} \\ a_{21} & a_{22} & a_{23} & a_{24} \\ a_{31} & a_{32} & a_{33} & a_{34} \\ a_{41} & a_{42} & a_{43} & a_{44} \end{bmatrix} = \begin{bmatrix} 1 & 0 & 0 & 0 \\ m_{21} & 1 & 0 & 0 \\ m_{31} & m_{32} & 1 & 0 \\ m_{41} & m_{42} & m_{43} & 1 \end{bmatrix} \begin{bmatrix} u_{11} & u_{12} & u_{13} & u_{14} \\ 0 & u_{22} & u_{23} & u_{24} \\ 0 & 0 & u_{33} & u_{34} \\ 0 & 0 & 0 & u_{44} \end{bmatrix}. \quad \blacktriangle$$

The condition that A is nonsingular implies that $u_{kk} \neq 0$ for all k. The notation for the entries in L is m_{ij}, and the reason for the choice of m_{ij} instead of l_{ij} will be pointed out soon.

Solution of a Linear System

Suppose that the coefficient matrix A for the linear system $AX = B$ has a triangular factorization (1); then the solution to

(2) $$LUX = B$$

can be obtained by defining $Y = UX$ and then solving two systems:

(3)   first solve $LY = B$ for Y;   then solve $UX = Y$ for X.

In equation form, we must first solve the lower-triangular system

(4)
$$
\begin{aligned}
y_1 &&&&= b_1 \\
m_{21}y_1 &+ y_2 &&&= b_2 \\
m_{31}y_1 &+ m_{32}y_2 &+ y_3 &&= b_3 \\
m_{41}y_1 &+ m_{42}y_2 &+ m_{43}y_3 &+ y_4 &= b_4
\end{aligned}
$$

to obtain y_1, y_2, y_3, and y_4 and use them in solving the upper-triangular system

(5)
$$
\begin{aligned}
u_{11}x_1 + u_{12}x_2 + u_{13}x_3 + u_{14}x_4 &= y_1 \\
u_{22}x_2 + u_{23}x_3 + u_{24}x_4 &= y_2 \\
u_{33}x_3 + u_{34}x_4 &= y_3 \\
u_{44}x_4 &= y_4.
\end{aligned}
$$

Example 3.20.   Solve

$$
\begin{aligned}
x_1 + 2x_2 + 4x_3 + x_4 &= 21 \\
2x_1 + 8x_2 + 6x_3 + 4x_4 &= 52 \\
3x_1 + 10x_2 + 8x_3 + 8x_4 &= 79 \\
4x_1 + 12x_2 + 10x_3 + 6x_4 &= 82.
\end{aligned}
$$

Use the triangular factorization method and the fact that

$$
A = \begin{bmatrix} 1 & 2 & 4 & 1 \\ 2 & 8 & 6 & 4 \\ 3 & 10 & 8 & 8 \\ 4 & 12 & 10 & 6 \end{bmatrix} = \begin{bmatrix} 1 & 0 & 0 & 0 \\ 2 & 1 & 0 & 0 \\ 3 & 1 & 1 & 0 \\ 4 & 1 & 2 & 1 \end{bmatrix} \begin{bmatrix} 1 & 2 & 4 & 1 \\ 0 & 4 & -2 & 2 \\ 0 & 0 & -2 & 3 \\ 0 & 0 & 0 & -6 \end{bmatrix} = LU.
$$

Use the forward-substitution method to solve $LY = B$:

(6)
$$
\begin{aligned}
y_1 &&&= 21 \\
2y_1 &+ y_2 &&= 52 \\
3y_1 &+ y_2 &+ y_3 &= 79 \\
4y_1 &+ y_2 &+ 2y_3 + y_4 &= 82.
\end{aligned}
$$

Compute the values $y_1 = 21$, $y_2 = 52 - 2(21) = 10$, $y_3 = 79 - 3(21) - 10 = 6$, and $y_4 = 82 - 4(21) - 10 - 2(6) = -24$, or $Y = \begin{bmatrix} 21 & 10 & 6 & -24 \end{bmatrix}'$. Next write the system $UX = Y$:

(7)
$$
\begin{aligned}
x_1 + 2x_2 + 4x_3 + x_4 &= 21 \\
4x_2 - 2x_3 + 2x_4 &= 10 \\
-2x_3 + 3x_4 &= 6 \\
-6x_4 &= -24.
\end{aligned}
$$

Now use back substitution and compute the solution $x_4 = -24/(-6) = 4$, $x_3 = (6 - 3(4))/(-2) = 3$, $x_2 = (10 - 2(4) + 2(3))/4 = 2$, and $x_1 = 21 - 4 - 4(3) - 2(2) = 1$, or $X = \begin{bmatrix} 1 & 2 & 3 & 4 \end{bmatrix}'$. ∎

Triangular Factorization

We now discuss how to obtain the triangular factorization. If row interchanges are not necessary when using Gaussian elimination, the multipliers m_{ij} are the subdiagonal entries in L.

Example 3.21.   Use Gaussian elimination to construct the triangular factorization of the matrix

$$A = \begin{bmatrix} 4 & 3 & -1 \\ -2 & -4 & 5 \\ 1 & 2 & 6 \end{bmatrix}.$$

The matrix L will be constructed from an identity matrix placed at the left. For each row operation used to construct the upper-triangular matrix, the multipliers m_{ij} will be put in their proper places at the left. Start with

$$A = \begin{bmatrix} 1 & 0 & 0 \\ 0 & 1 & 0 \\ 0 & 0 & 1 \end{bmatrix} \begin{bmatrix} 4 & 3 & -1 \\ -2 & -4 & 5 \\ 1 & 2 & 6 \end{bmatrix}.$$

Row 1 is used to eliminate the elements of A in column 1 below a_{11}. The multiples $m_{21} = -0.5$ and $m_{31} = 0.25$ of row 1 are subtracted from rows 2 and 3, respectively. These multipliers are put in the matrix at the left and the result is

$$A = \begin{bmatrix} 1 & 0 & 0 \\ -0.5 & 1 & 0 \\ 0.25 & 0 & 1 \end{bmatrix} \begin{bmatrix} 4 & 3 & -1 \\ 0 & -2.5 & 4.5 \\ 0 & 1.25 & 6.25 \end{bmatrix}.$$

Row 2 is used to eliminate the elements in column 2 below the diagonal of the second factor of A in the above product. The multiple $m_{32} = -0.5$ of the second row is subtracted from row 3, and the multiplier is entered in the matrix at the left and we have the desired triangular factorization of A.

(8)
$$A = \begin{bmatrix} 1 & 0 & 0 \\ -0.5 & 1 & 0 \\ 0.25 & -0.5 & 1 \end{bmatrix} \begin{bmatrix} 4 & 3 & -1 \\ 0 & -2.5 & 4.5 \\ 0 & 0 & 8.5 \end{bmatrix}.$$ ∎

Theorem 3.10 (Direct Factorization $A = LU$: No Row Interchanges).   Suppose that Gaussian elimination, without row interchanges, can be performed successfully to solve the general linear system $AX = B$. Then the matrix A can be factored as the product of a lower-triangular matrix L and an upper-triangular matrix U:

$$A = LU.$$

Furthermore, L can be constructed to have 1's on its diagonal and U will have nonzero diagonal elements. After finding L and U, the solution X is computed in two steps:

1. Solve $LY = B$ for Y using forward substitution.
2. Solve $UX = Y$ for X using back substitution.

Proof. We will show that, when the Gaussian elimination process is followed and B is stored in column $N + 1$ of the augmented matrix, the result after the upper-triangularization step is the equivalent upper-triangular system $UX = Y$. The matrices $L, U, B,$ and Y will have the form

$$
L = \begin{bmatrix}
1 & 0 & 0 & & 0 \\
m_{21} & 1 & 0 & \cdots & 0 \\
m_{31} & m_{32} & 1 & \cdots & 0 \\
\vdots & \vdots & \vdots & & \vdots \\
m_{N1} & m_{N2} & m_{N3} & \cdots & 1
\end{bmatrix}, \qquad
B = \begin{bmatrix}
a_{1\,N+1}^{(1)} \\
a_{2\,N+1}^{(2)} \\
a_{3\,N+1}^{(3)} \\
\vdots \\
a_{N\,N+1}^{(N)}
\end{bmatrix}
$$

$$
U = \begin{bmatrix}
a_{11}^{(1)} & a_{12}^{(1)} & a_{13}^{(1)} & \cdots & a_{1N}^{(1)} \\
0 & a_{22}^{(2)} & a_{23}^{(2)} & \cdots & a_{2N}^{(2)} \\
0 & 0 & a_{33}^{(3)} & \cdots & a_{3N}^{(3)} \\
\vdots & \vdots & \vdots & & \vdots \\
0 & 0 & 0 & \cdots & a_{NN}^{(N)}
\end{bmatrix}, \qquad
Y = \begin{bmatrix}
a_{1\,N+1}^{(1)} \\
a_{2\,N+1}^{(2)} \\
a_{3\,N+1}^{(3)} \\
\vdots \\
a_{N\,N+1}^{(N)}
\end{bmatrix}.
$$

Remark. To find just L and U, the $(N + 1)$st column is not needed.

Step 1. Store the coefficients in the augmented matrix. The superscript on $a_{rc}^{(1)}$ means that this is the first time that a number is stored in location (r, c).

$$
\begin{bmatrix}
a_{11}^{(1)} & a_{12}^{(1)} & a_{13}^{(1)} & \cdots & a_{1N}^{(1)} & a_{1\,N+1}^{(1)} \\
a_{21}^{(1)} & a_{22}^{(1)} & a_{23}^{(1)} & \cdots & a_{2N}^{(1)} & a_{2\,N+1}^{(1)} \\
a_{31}^{(1)} & a_{32}^{(1)} & a_{33}^{(1)} & \cdots & a_{3N}^{(1)} & a_{3\,N+1}^{(1)} \\
\vdots & \vdots & \vdots & & \vdots & \vdots \\
a_{N1}^{(1)} & a_{N2}^{(1)} & a_{N3}^{(1)} & \cdots & a_{NN}^{(1)} & a_{N\,N+1}^{(1)}
\end{bmatrix}
$$

Step 2. Eliminate x_1 in rows 2 through N and store the multiplier m_{r1}, used to eliminate x_1 in row r, in the matrix at location $(r, 1)$.

$$\text{for } r = 2 : N$$
$$\quad m_{r1} = a_{r1}^{(1)}/a_{11}^{(1)};$$
$$\quad a_{r1} = m_{r1};$$
$$\quad \text{for } c = 2 : N + 1$$
$$\qquad a_{rc}^{(2)} = a_{rc}^{(1)} - m_{r1} * a_{1c}^{(1)};$$
$$\quad \text{end}$$
$$\text{end}$$

The new elements are written $a_{rc}^{(2)}$ to indicate that this is the second time that a number has been stored in the matrix at location (r, c). The result after step 2 is

$$
\left[
\begin{array}{ccccc|c}
a_{11}^{(1)} & a_{12}^{(1)} & a_{13}^{(1)} & \cdots & a_{1N}^{(1)} & a_{1\,N+1}^{(1)} \\
m_{21} & a_{22}^{(2)} & a_{23}^{(2)} & \cdots & a_{2N}^{(2)} & a_{2\,N+1}^{(2)} \\
m_{31} & a_{32}^{(2)} & a_{33}^{(2)} & \cdots & a_{3N}^{(2)} & a_{3\,N+1}^{(2)} \\
\vdots & \vdots & \vdots & & \vdots & \vdots \\
m_{N1} & a_{N2}^{(2)} & a_{N3}^{(2)} & \cdots & a_{NN}^{(2)} & a_{N\,N+1}^{(2)}
\end{array}
\right]
$$

Step 3.   Eliminate x_2 in rows 3 through N and store the multiplier m_{r2}, used to eliminate x_2 in row r, in the matrix at location $(r, 2)$.

$$\text{for } r = 3 : N$$
$$\quad m_{r2} = a_{r2}^{(2)}/a_{22}^{(2)};$$
$$\quad a_{r2} = m_{r2};$$
$$\quad \text{for } c = 3 : N + 1$$
$$\qquad a_{rc}^{(3)} = a_{rc}^{(2)} - m_{r2} * a_{2c}^{(2)};$$
$$\quad \text{end}$$
$$\text{end}$$

The new elements are written $a_{rc}^{(3)}$ to indicate that this is the third time that a number has been stored in the matrix at the location (r, c).

$$
\left[
\begin{array}{ccccc|c}
a_{11}^{(1)} & a_{12}^{(1)} & a_{13}^{(1)} & \cdots & a_{1N}^{(1)} & a_{1\,N+1}^{(1)} \\
m_{21} & a_{22}^{(2)} & a_{23}^{(2)} & \cdots & a_{2N}^{(2)} & a_{2\,N+1}^{(2)} \\
m_{31} & m_{32} & a_{33}^{(3)} & \cdots & a_{3N}^{(3)} & a_{3\,N+1}^{(3)} \\
\vdots & \vdots & \vdots & & \vdots & \vdots \\
m_{N1} & m_{N2} & a_{N3}^{(3)} & \cdots & a_{NN}^{(3)} & a_{N\,N+1}^{(3)}
\end{array}
\right]
$$

Step $p + 1$.   This is the general step. Eliminate x_p in rows $p + 1$ through N and store the multipliers at the location (r, p).

$$\text{for } r = p + 1 : N$$
$$m_{rp} = a_{rp}^{(p)} / a_{pp}^{(p)};$$
$$a_{rp} = m_{rp};$$
$$\text{for } c = p + 1 : N + 1$$
$$a_{rc}^{(p+1)} = a_{rc}^{(p)} - m_{rp} * a_{pc}^{(p)};$$
$$\text{end}$$
$$\text{end}$$

The final result after x_{N-1} has been eliminated from row N is

$$\begin{bmatrix} a_{11}^{(1)} & a_{12}^{(1)} & a_{13}^{(1)} & \cdots & a_{1N}^{(1)} & a_{1\,N+1}^{(1)} \\ m_{21} & a_{22}^{(2)} & a_{23}^{(2)} & \cdots & a_{2N}^{(2)} & a_{2\,N+1}^{(2)} \\ m_{31} & m_{32} & a_{33}^{(3)} & \cdots & a_{3N}^{(3)} & a_{3\,N+1}^{(3)} \\ \vdots & \vdots & \vdots & & \vdots & \vdots \\ m_{N1} & m_{N2} & m_{N3} & \cdots & a_{NN}^{(N)} & a_{N\,N+1}^{(N)} \end{bmatrix}$$

The upper-triangular process is now complete. Notice that one array is used to store the elements of both L and U. The 1's of L are not stored, nor are the 0's of L and U that lie above and below the diagonal, respectively. Only the essential coefficients needed to reconstruct L and U are stored!

We must now verify that the product $LU = A$. Suppose that $D = LU$ and consider the case when $r \leq c$. Then d_{rc} is

$$(9) \qquad d_{rc} = m_{r1} a_{1c}^{(1)} + m_{r2} a_{2c}^{(2)} + \cdots + m_{rr-1} a_{r-1c}^{(r-1)} + a_{rc}^{(r)}.$$

Using the replacement equations in steps 1 through $p + 1 = r$, we obtain the following substitutions:

$$m_{r1} a_{1c}^{(1)} = a_{rc}^{(1)} - a_{rc}^{(2)},$$
$$m_{r2} a_{2c}^{(2)} = a_{rc}^{(2)} - a_{rc}^{(3)},$$
$$(10) \qquad \qquad \vdots$$
$$m_{rr-1} a_{r-1c}^{(r-1)} = a_{rc}^{(r-1)} - a_{rc}^{(r)}.$$

When the substitutions in (10) are used in (9), the result is

$$d_{rc} = a_{rc}^{(1)} - a_{rc}^{(2)} + a_{rc}^{(2)} - a_{rc}^{(3)} + \cdots + a_{rc}^{(r-1)} - a_{rc}^{(r)} + a_{rc}^{(r)} = a_{rc}^{(1)}.$$

The other case, $r > c$, is similar to prove.   ●

Computational Complexity

The process for triangularizing is the same for both the Gaussian elimination and triangular factorization methods. We can count the operations if we look at the first N columns of the augmented matrix in Theorem 3.10. The outer loop of step $p + 1$ requires $N - p = N - (p + 1) + 1$ divisions to compute the multipliers m_{rp}. Inside the loops, but for the first N columns only, a total of $(N - p)(N - p)$ multiplications and the same number of subtractions are required to compute the new row elements $a_{rc}^{(p+1)}$. This process is carried out for $p = 1, 2, \ldots, N - 1$. Thus the triangular factorization portion of $A = LU$ requires

(11) $$\sum_{p=1}^{N-1} (N - p)(N - p + 1) = \frac{N^3 - N}{3} \qquad \text{multiplications and divisions}$$

and

(12) $$\sum_{p=1}^{N-1} (N - p)(N - p) = \frac{2N^3 - 3N^2 + N}{6} \qquad \text{subtractions.}$$

To establish (11), we use the summation formulas

$$\sum_{k=1}^{M} k = \frac{M(M + 1)}{2} \qquad \text{and} \qquad \sum_{k=1}^{M} k^2 = \frac{M(M + 1)(2M + 1)}{6}.$$

Using the change of variables $k = N - p$, we rewrite (11) as

$$\sum_{p=1}^{N-1} (N - p)(N - p + 1) = \sum_{p=1}^{N-1} (N - p) + \sum_{p=1}^{N-1} (N - p)^2$$

$$= \sum_{k=1}^{N-1} k + \sum_{k=1}^{N-1} k^2$$

$$= \frac{(N - 1)N}{2} + \frac{(N - 1)(N)(2N - 1)}{6}$$

$$= \frac{N^3 - N}{3}.$$

Once the triangular factorization $A = LU$ has been obtained, the solution to the lower-triangular system $LY = B$ will require $0 + 1 + \cdots + N - 1 = (N^2 - N)/2$ multiplications and subtractions; no divisions are required because the diagonal elements of L are 1's. Then the solution of the upper-triangular system $UX = Y$ requires $1 + 2 + \cdots + N = (N^2 + N)/2$ multiplications and divisions and $(N^2 - N)/2$ subtractions. Therefore, finding the solution to $LUX = B$ requires

$$N^2 \text{ multiplications and divisions, and } N^2 - N \text{ subtractions.}$$

We see that the bulk of the calculations lies in the triangularization portion of the solution. If the linear system is to be solved many times, with the same coefficient matrix A but with different column matrices B, it is not necessary to triangularize the matrix each time if the factors are saved. This is the reason the triangular factorization method is usually chosen over the elimination method. However, if only one linear system is solved, the two methods are the same, except that the triangular factorization method stores the multipliers.

Permutation Matrices

The $A = LU$ factorization in Theorem 3.10 assumes that there are no row interchanges. It is possible that a nonsingular matrix A cannot be factored directly as $A = LU$.

Example 3.22. Show that the following matrix cannot be factored directly as $A = LU$:

$$A = \begin{bmatrix} 1 & 2 & 6 \\ 4 & 8 & -1 \\ -2 & 3 & 5 \end{bmatrix}.$$

Suppose that A has a direct factorization LU; then

(13)
$$\begin{bmatrix} 1 & 2 & 6 \\ 4 & 8 & -1 \\ -2 & 3 & 5 \end{bmatrix} = \begin{bmatrix} 1 & 0 & 0 \\ m_{21} & 1 & 0 \\ m_{31} & m_{32} & 1 \end{bmatrix} \begin{bmatrix} u_{11} & u_{12} & u_{13} \\ 0 & u_{22} & u_{23} \\ 0 & 0 & u_{33} \end{bmatrix}.$$

The matrices L and U on the right-hand side of (13) can be multiplied and each element of the product compared with the corresponding element of the matrix A. In the first column, $1 = 1u_{11}$, then $4 = m_{21}u_{11} = m_{21}$, and finally, $-2 = m_{31}u_{11} = m_{31}$. In the second column, $2 = 1u_{12}$, then $8 = m_{21}u_{12} = (4)(2) + u_{22}$ implies that $u_{22} = 0$; and finally, $3 = m_{31}u_{12} + m_{32}u_{22} = (-2)(2) + m_{32}(0) = -4$, which is a contradiction. Therefore, A does not have a LU factorization. ∎

A permutation of the first N positive integers $1, 2, \ldots, N$ is an arrangement $k_1, k_2, \ldots, k_N$ of these integers in a definite order. For example, $1, 4, 2, 3, 5$ is a permutation of the five integers $1, 2, 3, 4, 5$. The standard base vectors $E_i = [0\ 0\ \cdots\ 0\ 1_i\ 0\ \cdots\ 0]$, for $i = 1, 2, \ldots, N$, are used in the next definition.

Definition 3.5. An $N \times N$ **permutation matrix** P is a matrix with precisely one entry whose value is 1 in each column and row, and all of whose other entries are 0. The rows of P are a permutation of the rows of the identity matrix and can be written as

(14)
$$P = \begin{bmatrix} E'_{k_1} & E'_{k_2} & \cdots & E'_{k_N} \end{bmatrix}'.$$

The elements of $P = [p_{ij}]$ have the form

$$p_{ij} = \begin{cases} 1 & j = k_i, \\ 0 & \text{otherwise.} \end{cases}$$

For example, the following 4×4 matrix is a permutation matrix,

(15)
$$P = \begin{bmatrix} 0 & 1 & 0 & 0 \\ 1 & 0 & 0 & 0 \\ 0 & 0 & 0 & 1 \\ 0 & 0 & 1 & 0 \end{bmatrix} = \begin{bmatrix} E_2' & E_1' & E_4' & E_3' \end{bmatrix}'. \qquad \blacktriangle$$

Theorem 3.11.   Suppose that $P = \begin{bmatrix} E_{k_1}' & E_{k_2}' & \cdots & E_{k_N}' \end{bmatrix}'$ is a permutation matrix. The product PA is a new matrix whose rows consist of the rows of A rearranged in the order $\text{row}_{k_1} A$, $\text{row}_{k_2} A$, ..., $\text{row}_{k_N} A$.

Example 3.23.   Let A be a 4×4 matrix and let P be the permutation matrix given in (15); then PA is the matrix whose rows consist of the rows of A rearranged in the order $\text{row}_2 A$, $\text{row}_1 A$, $\text{row}_4 A$, $\text{row}_3 A$.

Computing the product, we have

$$\begin{bmatrix} 0 & 1 & 0 & 0 \\ 1 & 0 & 0 & 0 \\ 0 & 0 & 0 & 1 \\ 0 & 0 & 1 & 0 \end{bmatrix} \begin{bmatrix} a_{11} & a_{12} & a_{13} & a_{14} \\ a_{21} & a_{22} & a_{23} & a_{24} \\ a_{31} & a_{32} & a_{33} & a_{34} \\ a_{41} & a_{42} & a_{43} & a_{44} \end{bmatrix} = \begin{bmatrix} a_{21} & a_{22} & a_{23} & a_{24} \\ a_{11} & a_{12} & a_{13} & a_{14} \\ a_{41} & a_{42} & a_{43} & a_{44} \\ a_{31} & a_{32} & a_{33} & a_{34} \end{bmatrix}. \qquad \blacksquare$$

Theorem 3.12.   If P is a permutation matrix, then it is nonsingular and $P^{-1} = P'$.

Theorem 3.13.   If A is a nonsingular matrix, then there exists a permutation matrix P so that PA has a triangular factorization

(16)
$$PA = LU.$$

The proofs can be found in advanced linear algebra texts.

Example 3.24.   If rows 2 and 3 of the matrix in Example 3.22 are interchanged, then the resulting matrix PA has a triangular factorization.

The permutation matrix that switches rows 2 and 3 is $P = \begin{bmatrix} E_1' & E_3' & E_2' \end{bmatrix}'$. Computing the product PA, we obtain

$$PA = \begin{bmatrix} 1 & 0 & 0 \\ 0 & 0 & 1 \\ 0 & 1 & 0 \end{bmatrix} \begin{bmatrix} 1 & 2 & 6 \\ 4 & 8 & -1 \\ -2 & 3 & 5 \end{bmatrix} = \begin{bmatrix} 1 & 2 & 6 \\ -2 & 3 & 5 \\ 4 & 8 & -1 \end{bmatrix}.$$

Now Gaussian elimination without row interchanges can be used:

$$
\begin{array}{c}
\text{pivot} \rightarrow \\
m_{21} = -2 \\
m_{31} = 4
\end{array}
\left[
\begin{array}{ccc}
\underline{1} & 2 & 6 \\
-2 & 3 & 5 \\
4 & 8 & -1
\end{array}
\right].
$$

After x_2 has been eliminated from column 2, row 3, we have

$$
\begin{array}{c}
\\
\text{pivot} \rightarrow \\
m_{32} = 0
\end{array}
\left[
\begin{array}{ccc}
1 & 2 & 6 \\
0 & \underline{7} & 17 \\
0 & 0 & -25
\end{array}
\right] = U.
\qquad \blacksquare
$$

Extending the Gaussian Elimination Process

The following theorem is an extension of Theorem 3.10, which includes the cases when row interchanges are required. Thus triangular factorization can be used to find the solution to any linear system $AX = B$, where A is nonsingular.

Theorem 3.14 (Indirect Factorization: $PA = LU$).   Let A be a given $N \times N$ matrix. Assume that Gaussian elimination can be performed successfully to solve the general linear system $AX = B$, but that row interchanges are required. Then there exists a permutation matrix P so that the product PA can be factored as the product of a lower-triangular matrix L and an upper-triangular matrix U:

$$
PA = LU.
$$

Furthermore, L can be constructed to have 1's on its main diagonal and U will have nonzero diagonal elements. The solution X is found in four steps:

1. Construct the matrices L, U, and P.

2. Compute the column vector PB.

3. Solve $LY = PB$ for Y using forward substitution.

4. Solve $UX = Y$ for X using back substitution.

Remark. Suppose that $AX = B$ is to be solved for a fixed matrix A and several different column matrices B. Then step 1 is performed only once and steps 2 through 4 are used to find the solution X that corresponds to B. Steps 2 through 4 are a computationally efficient way to construct the solution X and require $O(N^2)$ operations instead of the $O(N^3)$ operations required by Gaussian elimination.

MATLAB

The MATLAB command [L,U,P]=lu(A) creates the lower-triangular matrix L, the upper-triangular matrix U (from the triangular factorization of A), and the permutation matrix P from Theorem 3.14.

Example 3.25.   Use the MATLAB command [L,U,P]=lu(A) on the matrix A in Example 3.22. Verify that $A = P^{-1}LU$ (equivalent to showing that $PA = LU$).

```
>>A=[1 2 6 ;4 8 -1;-2 3 -5];
>>[L,U,P]=lu(A)


L=
    1.0000  0        0
   -0.5000  1.0000  0
    0.2500  0        1.0000


U=
    4.0000  8.0000  -1.0000
    0       7.0000  4.5000
    0       0        6.2500


P=
    0 1 0
    0 0 1
    1 0 0
>>inv(P)*L*U
    1  2 6
    4  8 -1
   -2  3 5
```
■

As indicated previously, the triangular factorization method is often chosen over the elimination method. In addition, it is used in the inv(A) and det(A) commands in MATLAB. For example, from the study of linear algebra we know that the determinant of a nonsingular matrix A equals $(-1)^q \det U$, where U is the upper-triangular matrix from the triangular factorization of A and q is the number of row interchanges required to obtain P from the identity matrix I. Since U is an upper-triangular matrix, we know that the determinant of U is just the product of the elements on its main diagonal (Theorem 3.6). The reader should verify in Example 3.25 that

$$\det(A) = 175 = (-1)^2(175) = (-1)^2 \det(U).$$

The following program implements the process described in the proof of Theorem 3.10. It is an extension of Program 3.2 and uses partial pivoting. The interchanging of rows due to partial pivoting is recorded in the matrix R. The matrix R is then used in the forward substitution step to find the matrix Y.

Program 3.3 ($PA = LU$: **Factorization with Pivoting**). To construct the solution to the linear system $AX = B$, where A is a nonsingular matrix.

```
function X = lufact(A,B)

%Input   - A is an N x N matrix
%         - B is an N x 1 matrix
%Output - X is an N x 1 matrix containing the solution to AX = B.

%Initialize X, Y, the temporary storage matrix C, and the row
% permutation information matrix R
    [N,N]=size(A);
    X=zeros(N,1);
    Y=zeros(N,1);
    C=zeros(1,N);
    R=1:N;

for p=1:N-1
%Find the pivot row for column p
    [max1,j]=max(abs(A(p:N,p)));
%Interchange row p and j
    C=A(p,:);
    A(p,:)=A(j+p-1,:);
    A(j+p-1,:)=C;
    d=R(p);
    R(p)=R(j+p-1);
    R(j+p-1)=d;
if A(p,p)==0
    'A is singular.  No unique solution'
    break
end
%Calculate multiplier and place in subdiagonal portion of A
    for k=p+1:N
        mult=A(k,p)/A(p,p);
        A(k,p) = mult;
        A(k,p+1:N)=A(k,p+1:N)-mult*A(p,p+1:N);
    end
end

%Solve for Y
Y(1) = B(R(1));
for k=2:N
    Y(k)= B(R(k))-A(k,1:k-1)*Y(1:k-1);
end

%Solve for X
X(N)=Y(N)/A(N,N);
```

```
for k=N-1:-1:1
   X(k)=(Y(k)-A(k,k+1:N)*X(k+1:N))/A(k,k);
end
```

Exercises for Triangular Factorization

1. Solve $LY = B$, $UX = Y$, and verify that $B = AX$ for **(a)** $B = \begin{bmatrix} -4 & 10 & 5 \end{bmatrix}'$ and
(b) $B = \begin{bmatrix} 20 & 49 & 32 \end{bmatrix}'$, where $A = LU$ is

$$\begin{bmatrix} 2 & 4 & -6 \\ 1 & 5 & 3 \\ 1 & 3 & 2 \end{bmatrix} = \begin{bmatrix} 1 & 0 & 0 \\ 1/2 & 1 & 0 \\ 1/2 & 1/3 & 1 \end{bmatrix} \begin{bmatrix} 2 & 4 & -6 \\ 0 & 3 & 6 \\ 0 & 0 & 3 \end{bmatrix}.$$

2. Solve $LY = B$, $UX = Y$, and verify that $B = AX$ for **(a)** $B = \begin{bmatrix} 7 & 2 & 10 \end{bmatrix}'$ and
(b) $B = \begin{bmatrix} 23 & 35 & 7 \end{bmatrix}'$, where $A = LU$ is

$$\begin{bmatrix} 1 & 1 & 6 \\ -1 & 2 & 9 \\ 1 & -2 & 3 \end{bmatrix} = \begin{bmatrix} 1 & 0 & 0 \\ -1 & 1 & 0 \\ 1 & -1 & 1 \end{bmatrix} \begin{bmatrix} 1 & 1 & 6 \\ 0 & 3 & 15 \\ 0 & 0 & 12 \end{bmatrix}.$$

3. Find the triangular factorization $A = LU$ for the matrices

(a) $\begin{bmatrix} -5 & 2 & -1 \\ 1 & 0 & 3 \\ 3 & 1 & 6 \end{bmatrix}$ **(b)** $\begin{bmatrix} 1 & 0 & 3 \\ 3 & 1 & 6 \\ -5 & 2 & -1 \end{bmatrix}$

4. Find the triangular factorization $A = LU$ for the matrices

(a) $\begin{bmatrix} 4 & 2 & 1 \\ 2 & 5 & -2 \\ 1 & -2 & 7 \end{bmatrix}$ **(b)** $\begin{bmatrix} 1 & -2 & 7 \\ 4 & 2 & 1 \\ 2 & 5 & -2 \end{bmatrix}$

5. Solve $LY = B$, $UX = Y$, and verify that $B = AX$ for **(a)** $B = \begin{bmatrix} 8 & -4 & 10 & -4 \end{bmatrix}'$
and **(b)** $B = \begin{bmatrix} 28 & 13 & 23 & 4 \end{bmatrix}'$, where $A = LU$ is

$$\begin{bmatrix} 4 & 8 & 4 & 0 \\ 1 & 5 & 4 & -3 \\ 1 & 4 & 7 & 2 \\ 1 & 3 & 0 & -2 \end{bmatrix} = \begin{bmatrix} 1 & 0 & 0 & 0 \\ \frac{1}{4} & 1 & 0 & 0 \\ \frac{1}{4} & \frac{2}{3} & 1 & 0 \\ \frac{1}{4} & \frac{1}{3} & -\frac{1}{2} & 1 \end{bmatrix} \begin{bmatrix} 4 & 8 & 4 & 0 \\ 0 & 3 & 3 & -3 \\ 0 & 0 & 4 & 4 \\ 0 & 0 & 0 & 1 \end{bmatrix}.$$

6. Find the triangular factorization $A = LU$ for the matrix

$$\begin{bmatrix} 1 & 1 & 0 & 4 \\ 2 & -1 & 5 & 0 \\ 5 & 2 & 1 & 2 \\ -3 & 0 & 2 & 6 \end{bmatrix}.$$

7. Establish the formula in (12).

8. Show that a triangular factorization is unique in the following sense: If A is nonsingular and $L_1 U_1 = A = L_2 U_2$, then $L_1 = L_2$ and $U_1 = U_2$.

9. Prove the case $r > c$ at the end of Theorem 3.10.

10. (a)   Verify Theorem 3.12 by showing that $PP' = I = P'P$ for the permutation matrix

$$P = \begin{bmatrix} 0 & 1 & 0 & 0 \\ 1 & 0 & 0 & 0 \\ 0 & 0 & 0 & 1 \\ 0 & 0 & 1 & 0 \end{bmatrix}.$$

   (b)   Prove Theorem 3.12. *Hint.* Use the definition of matrix multiplication and the fact that each row and column of P and P' contains exactly one 1.

11. Prove that the inverse of a nonsingular $N \times N$ upper-triangular matrix is an upper-triangular matrix.

Algorithms and Programs

1. Use Program 3.3 to solve the system $AX = B$, where

$$A = \begin{bmatrix} 1 & 3 & 5 & 7 \\ 2 & -1 & 3 & 5 \\ 0 & 0 & 2 & 5 \\ -2 & -6 & -3 & 1 \end{bmatrix} \quad \text{and} \quad B = \begin{bmatrix} 1 \\ 2 \\ 3 \\ 4 \end{bmatrix}.$$

   Use the [L,U,P]=lu(A) command in MATLAB to check your answer.

2. Use Program 3.3 to solve the linear system $AX = B$, where $A = [a_{ij}]_{N \times N}$ and $a_{ij} = i^{j-1}$, and $B = [b_{ij}]_{N \times 1}$, where $b_{11} = N$ and $b_{i1} = (i^N - 1)/(i - 1)$ for $i \geq 2$. Use $N = 3, 7$, and 11. The exact solution is $X = \begin{bmatrix} 1 & 1 & \cdots & 1 & 1 \end{bmatrix}'$. Explain any deviations from the exact solution.

3. Modify Program 3.3 so that it will compute A^{-1} by repeatedly solving N linear systems

$$AC_J = E_J \quad \text{for } J = 1, 2, \ldots, N.$$

Then

$$A \begin{bmatrix} C_1 & C_2 & \cdots & C_N \end{bmatrix} = \begin{bmatrix} E_1 & E_2 & \cdots & E_N \end{bmatrix}$$

and

$$A^{-1} = \begin{bmatrix} C_1 & C_2 & \cdots & C_N \end{bmatrix}.$$

Make sure that you compute the LU factorization only once!

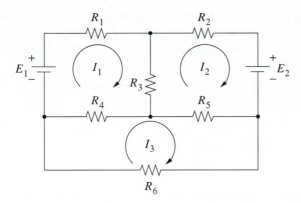

Figure 3.5   The electrical network for Exercise 4.

4. Kirchhoff's voltage law says that the sum of the voltage drops around any closed path in the network in a given direction is zero. When this principle is applied to the circuit shown in Figure 3.5, we obtain the following linear system of equations:

(1)
$$
\begin{aligned}
(R_1 + R_3 + R_4)I_1 + & & R_3 I_2 + & & R_4 I_3 = E_1 \\
R_3 I_1 + & (R_2 + R_3 + R_5)I_2 - & & R_5 I_3 = E_2 \\
R_4 I_1 - & & R_5 I_2 + (R_4 + R_5 + R_6)I_3 = 0.
\end{aligned}
$$

Use Program 3.3 to solve for the current I_1, I_2, and I_3 if

(a) $R_1 = 1$, $R_2 = 1$, $R_3 = 2$, $R_4 = 1$, $R_5 = 2$, $R_6 = 4$, and $E_1 = 23$, $E_2 = 29$
(b) $R_1 = 1$, $R_2 = 0.75$, $R_3 = 1$, $R_4 = 2$, $R_5 = 1$, $R_6 = 4$, and $E_1 = 12$, $E_2 = 21.5$
(c) $R_1 = 1$, $R_2 = 2$, $R_3 = 4$, $R_4 = 3$, $R_5 = 1$, $R_6 = 5$, and $E_1 = 41$, $E_2 = 38$

5. In calculus the following integral would be found by the technique of partial fractions:

$$
\int \frac{x^2 + x + 1}{(x - 1)(x - 2)(x - 3)^2(x^2 + 1)} \, dx.
$$

This would require finding the coefficients A_i, for $i = 1, 2, \ldots, 6$, in the expression

$$
\frac{x^2 + x + 1}{(x - 1)(x - 2)(x - 3)^2(x^2 + 1)}
$$
$$
= \frac{A_1}{x - 1} + \frac{A_2}{x - 2} + \frac{A_3}{(x - 3)^2} + \frac{A_4}{x - 3} + \frac{A_5 x + A_6}{x^2 + 1}.
$$

Use Program 3.3 to find the partial fraction coefficients.

6. Use Program 3.3 to solve the linear system $AX = B$, where A is generated using the MATLAB command A=rand(10,10) and B=[1 2 3 ... 10]'. Remember to verify that A is nonsingular ($\det(A) \neq 0$) before using Program 3.3. Check the accuracy of your answer by forming the matrix difference $AX - B$ and examining how close

the elements are to zero (an accurate answer would produce $AX - B = \mathbf{0}$). Repeat this process using a coefficient matrix A generated by the command A=rand(20,20) and B=[1 2 3 ... 20]'. Explain any apparent differences in the accuracy of Program 3.3 on these two systems.

7. In (8) of Section 3.1 we defined the concept of linear combination in N-dimensional space. For example, the vector $(4, -3)$, which is equivalent to the matrix $\begin{bmatrix} 4 & -3 \end{bmatrix}'$, could be written as a linear combination of $\begin{bmatrix} 1 & 0 \end{bmatrix}'$ and $\begin{bmatrix} 0 & 1 \end{bmatrix}'$:

$$\begin{bmatrix} 4 \\ -3 \end{bmatrix} = 4 \begin{bmatrix} 1 \\ 0 \end{bmatrix} + (-3) \begin{bmatrix} 0 \\ 1 \end{bmatrix}.$$

Use Program 3.3 to show that the matrix $\begin{bmatrix} 1 & 3 & 5 & 7 & 9 \end{bmatrix}'$ can be written as a linear combination of

$$\begin{bmatrix} 0 \\ 4 \\ -2 \\ 3 \\ -1 \end{bmatrix}, \quad \begin{bmatrix} 2 \\ 0 \\ 0 \\ 4 \\ 4 \end{bmatrix}, \quad \begin{bmatrix} 3 \\ 2 \\ 0 \\ 5 \\ 1 \end{bmatrix}, \quad \begin{bmatrix} 5 \\ 6 \\ -3 \\ 0 \\ 2 \end{bmatrix}, \quad \text{and} \quad \begin{bmatrix} 1 \\ 4 \\ -2 \\ 7 \\ 0 \end{bmatrix}.$$

Explain why any matrix $\begin{bmatrix} x_1 & x_2 & x_3 & x_4 & x_5 \end{bmatrix}'$ can be written as a linear combination of these matrices.

3.6   Iterative Methods for Linear Systems

The goal of this section is to extend some of the iterative methods introduced in Chapter 2 to higher dimensions. We consider an extension of fixed-point iteration that applies to systems of linear equations.

Jacobi Iteration

Example 3.26.   Consider the system of equations

(1)
$$\begin{aligned} 4x - y + z &= 7 \\ 4x - 8y + z &= -21 \\ -2x + y + 5z &= 15. \end{aligned}$$

These equations can be written in the form

(2)
$$\begin{aligned} x &= \frac{7 + y - z}{4} \\ y &= \frac{21 + 4x + z}{8} \\ z &= \frac{15 + 2x - y}{5}. \end{aligned}$$

Table 3.2   Convergent Jacobi Iteration for the Linear System (1)

k	x_k	y_k	z_k
0	1.0	2.0	2.0
1	1.75	3.375	3.0
2	1.84375	3.875	3.025
3	1.9625	3.925	2.9625
4	1.99062500	3.97656250	3.00000000
5	1.99414063	3.99531250	3.00093750
⋮	⋮	⋮	⋮
15	1.99999993	3.99999985	2.99999993
⋮	⋮	⋮	⋮
19	2.00000000	4.00000000	3.00000000

This suggests the following Jacobi iterative process:

$$x_{k+1} = \frac{7 + y_k - z_k}{4}$$

(3)
$$y_{k+1} = \frac{21 + 4x_k + z_k}{8}$$

$$z_{k+1} = \frac{15 + 2x_k - y_k}{5}.$$

Let us show that if we start with $\boldsymbol{P}_0 = (x_0, y_0, z_0) = (1, 2, 2)$, then the iteration in (3) appears to converge to the solution $(2, 4, 3)$.

Substitute $x_0 = 1$, $y_0 = 2$, and $z_0 = 2$ into the right-hand side of each equation in (3) to obtain the new values

$$x_1 = \frac{7 + 2 - 2}{4} = 1.75$$

$$y_1 = \frac{21 + 4 + 2}{8} = 3.375$$

$$z_1 = \frac{15 + 2 - 2}{5} = 3.00.$$

The new point $\boldsymbol{P}_1 = (1.75, 3.375, 3.00)$ is closer to $(2, 4, 3)$ than $\boldsymbol{P}_0$. Iteration using (3) generates a sequence of points $\{\boldsymbol{P}_k\}$ that converges to the solution $(2, 4, 3)$ (see Table 3.2). ■

This process is called *Jacobi iteration* and can be used to solve certain types of linear systems. After 19 steps, the iteration has converged to the nine-digit machine approximation $(2.00000000, 4.00000000, 3.00000000)$.

Linear systems with as many as 100,000 variables often arise in the solution of partial differential equations. The coefficient matrices for these systems are sparse;

that is, a large percentage of the entries of the coefficient matrix are zero. If there is a pattern to the nonzero entries (i.e., tridiagonal systems), then an iterative process provides an efficient method for solving these large systems.

Sometimes the Jacobi method does not work. Let us experiment and see that a rearrangement of the original linear system can result in a system of iteration equations that will produce a divergent sequence of points.

Example 3.27. Let the linear system (1) be rearranged as follows:

(4)
$$-2x + y + 5z = 15$$
$$4x - 8y + z = -21$$
$$4x - y + z = 7.$$

These equations can be written in the form

(5)
$$x = \frac{-15 + y + 5z}{3}$$
$$y = \frac{21 + 4x + z}{8}$$
$$z = 7 - 4x + y.$$

This suggests the following Jacobi iterative process:

(6)
$$x_{k+1} = \frac{-15 + y_k + 5z_k}{3}$$
$$y_{k+1} = \frac{21 + 4x_k + z_k}{8}$$
$$z_{k+1} = 7 - 4x_k + y_k.$$

See that if we start with $\boldsymbol{P}_0 = (x_0, y_0, z_0) = (1, 2, 2)$, then the iteration using (6) will diverge away from the solution $(2, 4, 3)$.

Substitute $x_0 = 1$, $y_0 = 2$, and $z_0 = 2$ into the right-hand side of each equation in (6) to obtain the new values x_1, y_1, and z_1:

$$x_1 = \frac{-15 + 2 + 10}{2} = -1.5$$
$$y_1 = \frac{21 + 4 + 2}{8} = 3.375$$
$$z_1 = 7 - 4 + 2 = 5.00.$$

The new point $\boldsymbol{P}_1 = (-1.5, 3.375, 5.00)$ is farther away from the solution $(2, 4, 3)$ than $\boldsymbol{P}_0$. Iteration using the equations in (6) produces a divergent sequence (see Table 3.3). ∎

Table 3.3   Divergent Jacobi Iteration for the Linear System (4)

k	x_k	y_k	z_k
0	1.0	2.0	2.0
1	−1.5	3.375	5.0
2	6.6875	2.5	16.375
3	34.6875	8.015625	−17.25
4	−46.617188	17.8125	−123.73438
5	−307.929688	−36.150391	211.28125
6	502.62793	−124.929688	1202.56836
⋮	⋮	⋮	⋮

Gauss-Seidel Iteration

Sometimes the convergence can be speeded up. Observe that the Jacobi iterative process (3) yields three sequences $\{x_k\}$, $\{y_k\}$, and $\{z_k\}$ that converge to 2, 4, and 3, respectively (see Table 3.2). Since x_{k+1} is expected to be a better approximation to x than x_k, it seems reasonable that x_{k+1} could be used in place of x_k in the computation of y_{k+1}. Similarly, x_{k+1} and y_{k+1} might be used in the computation of z_{k+1}. The next example shows what happens when this is applied to the equations in Example 3.26.

Example 3.28.   Consider the system of equations given in (1) and the Gauss-Seidel iterative process suggested by (2):

(7)
$$x_{k+1} = \frac{7 + y_k - z_k}{4}$$
$$y_{k+1} = \frac{21 + 4x_{k+1} + z_k}{8}$$
$$z_{k+1} = \frac{15 + 2x_{k+1} - y_{k+1}}{5}.$$

See that if we start with $\boldsymbol{P}_0 = (x_0, y_0, z_0) = (1, 2, 2)$, then iteration using (7) will converge to the solution $(2, 4, 3)$.

Substitute $y_0 = 2$ and $z_0 = 2$ into the first equation of (7) and obtain

$$x_1 = \frac{7 + 2 - 2}{4} = 1.75.$$

Then substitute $x_1 = 1.75$ and $z_0 = 2$ into the second equation and get

$$y_1 = \frac{21 + 4(1.75) + 2}{8} = 3.75.$$

Finally, substitute $x_1 = 1.75$ and $y_1 = 3.75$ into the third equation to get

$$z_1 = \frac{15 + 2(1.75) - 3.75}{5} = 2.95.$$

Table 3.4   Convergent Gauss-Seidel Iteration for the System (1)

k	x_k	y_k	z_k
0	1.0	2.0	2.0
1	1.75	3.75	2.95
2	1.95	3.96875	2.98625
3	1.995625	3.99609375	2.99903125
⋮	⋮	⋮	⋮
8	1.99999983	3.99999988	2.99999996
9	1.99999998	3.99999999	3.00000000
10	2.00000000	4.00000000	3.00000000

The new point $P_1 = (1.75, 3.75, 2.95)$ is closer to $(2, 4, 3)$ than P_0 and is better than the value given in Example 3.26. Iteration using (7) generates a sequence $\{P_k\}$ that converges to $(2, 4, 3)$ (see Table 3.4). ∎

In view of Examples 3.26 and 3.27, it is necessary to have some criterion to determine whether the Jacobi iteration will converge. Hence we make the following definition.

Definition 3.6.   A matrix A of dimension $N \times N$ is said to be **strictly diagonally dominant** provided that

(8)
$$|a_{kk}| > \sum_{\substack{j=1 \\ j \neq k}}^{N} |a_{kj}| \quad \text{for } k = 1, 2, \ldots, N. \qquad \blacktriangle$$

This means that in each row of the matrix the magnitude of the element on the main diagonal must exceed the sum of the magnitudes of all other elements in the row. The coefficient matrix of the linear system (1) in Example 3.26 is strictly diagonally dominant because

$$\text{In row 1:} \quad |4| > |-1| + |1|$$
$$\text{In row 2:} \quad |-8| > |4| + |1|$$
$$\text{In row 3:} \quad |5| > |-2| + |1|.$$

All the rows satisfy relation (8) in Definition 3.6; therefore, the coefficient matrix A for the linear system (1) is strictly diagonally dominant.

The coefficient matrix A of the linear system (4) in Example 3.27 is not strictly diagonally dominant because

In row 1:	$\|-2\| < \|1\| + \|5\|$
In row 2:	$\|-8\| > \|4\| + \|1\|$
In row 3:	$\|1\| < \|4\| + \|-1\|$.

Rows 1 and 3 do not satisfy relation (8) in Definition 3.6; therefore, the coefficient matrix A for the linear system (4) is not strictly diagonally dominant.

We now generalize the Jacobi and Gauss-Seidel iteration processes. Suppose that the given linear system is

$$
\begin{aligned}
a_{11}x_1 + a_{12}x_2 &+ \cdots + a_{1j}x_j + \cdots + \ a_{1N}x_N &= b_1 \\
a_{21}x_1 + a_{22}x_2 &+ \cdots + a_{2j}x_j + \cdots + \ a_{2N}x_N &= b_2 \\
&\ \ \vdots \\
a_{j1}x_1 + a_{j2}x_2 &+ \cdots + a_{jj}x_j + \cdots + \ a_{jN}x_N &= b_j \\
&\ \ \vdots \\
a_{N1}x_1 + a_{N2}x_2 &+ \cdots + a_{Nj}x_j + \cdots + \ a_{NN}x_N &= b_N.
\end{aligned}
$$

(9)

Let the kth point be $P_k = (x_1^{(k)}, x_2^{(k)}, \ldots, x_j^{(k)}, \ldots, x_N^{(k)})$; then the next point is $P_{k+1} = (x_1^{(k+1)}, x_2^{(k+1)}, \ldots, x_j^{(k+1)}, \ldots, x_N^{(k+1)})$. The superscript (k) on the coordinates of P_k enables us to identify the coordinates that belong to this point. The iteration formulas use row j of (9) to solve for $x_j^{(k+1)}$ in terms of a linear combination of the previous values $x_1^{(k)}, x_2^{(k)}, \ldots, x_j^{(k)}, \ldots, x_N^{(k)}$:

Jacobi iteration:

$$
(10) \quad x_j^{(k+1)} = \frac{b_j - a_{j1}x_1^{(k)} - \cdots - a_{jj-1}x_{j-1}^{(k)} - a_{jj+1}x_{j+1}^{(k)} - \cdots - a_{jN}x_N^{(k)}}{a_{jj}}
$$

for $j = 1, 2, \ldots, N$.

Jacobi iteration uses all old coordinates to generate all new coordinates, whereas Gauss-Seidel iteration uses the new coordinates as they become available:

Gauss-Seidel iteration:

$$
(11) \quad x_j^{(k+1)} = \frac{b_j - a_{j1}x_1^{(k+1)} - \cdots - a_{jj-1}x_{j-1}^{(k+1)} - a_{jj+1}x_{j+1}^{(k)} - \cdots - a_{jN}x_N^{(k)}}{a_{jj}}
$$

for $j = 1, 2, \ldots, N$.

The following theorem gives a sufficient condition for Jacobi iteration to converge.

Theorem 3.15 (Jacobi Iteration).   Suppose that A is a strictly diagonally dominant matrix. Then $AX = B$ has a unique solution $X = P$. Iteration using formula (10) will produce a sequence of vectors $\{P_k\}$ that will converge to P for any choice of the starting vector P_0.

Proof.   The proof can be found in advanced texts on numerical analysis.   ●

It can be proved that the Gauss-Seidel method will also converge when the matrix A is strictly diagonally dominant. In many cases the Gauss-Seidel method will converge faster than the Jacobi method; hence it is usually preferred (compare Examples 3.26 and 3.28). It is important to understand the slight modification of formula (10) that has been made to obtain formula (11). In some cases the Jacobi method will converge even though the Gauss-Seidel method will not.

Convergence

A measure of the closeness between vectors is needed so that we can determine if $\{P_k\}$ is converging to P. The Euclidean distance (see Section 3.1) between $P = (x_1, x_2, \ldots, x_N)$ and $Q = (y_1, y_2, \ldots, y_N)$ is

$$(12) \qquad \|P - Q\| = \left(\sum_{j=1}^{N} (x_j - y_j)^2 \right)^{1/2}.$$

Its disadvantage is that it requires considerable computing effort. Hence we introduce a different norm, $\|X\|_1$:

$$(13) \qquad \|X\|_1 = \sum_{j=1}^{N} |x_j|.$$

The following result ensures that $\|X\|_1$ has the mathematical structure of a metric and hence is suitable to use as a generalized "distance formula." From the study of linear algebra we know that on a finite-dimensional vector space all norms are equivalent; that is, if two vectors are close in the $\|*\|_1$ norm, then they are also close in the Euclidean norm $\|*\|$.

Theorem 3.16.   Let X and Y be N-dimensional vectors and c be a scalar. Then the function $\|X\|_1$ has the following properties:

$$(14) \qquad \|X\|_1 \geq 0,$$

$$(15) \qquad \|X\|_1 = 0 \quad \text{if and only if} \quad X = 0,$$

$$(16) \qquad \|cX\|_1 = |c|\,\|X\|_1,$$

$$(17) \qquad \|X + Y\|_1 \leq \|X\|_1 + \|Y\|_1.$$

Proof. We prove (17) and leave the others as exercises. For each j, the triangle inequality for real numbers states that $|x_j + y_j| \le |x_j| + |y_j|$. Summing these yields inequality (17):

$$\|X + Y\|_1 = \sum_{j=1}^{N} |x_j + y_j| \le \sum_{j=1}^{N} |x_j| + \sum_{j=1}^{N} |y_j| = \|X\|_1 + \|Y\|_1 .$$

The norm given by (13) can be used to define the distance between points.   ●

Definition 3.7.   Suppose that X and Y are two points in N-dimensional space. We define the distance between X and Y in the $\|*\|_1$ norm as

$$\|X - Y\|_1 = \sum_{j=1}^{N} |x_j - y_j|.$$ ▲

Example 3.29.   Determine the Euclidean distance and $\|*\|_1$ distance between the points $P = (2, 4, 3)$ and $Q = (1.75, 3.75, 2.95)$.

The Euclidean distance is

$$\|P - Q\| = ((2 - 1.75)^2 + (4 - 3.75)^2 + (3 - 2.95)^2)^{1/2} = 0.3570.$$

The $\|*\|_1$ distance is

$$\|P - Q\|_1 = |2 - 1.75| + |4 - 3.75| + |3 - 2.95| = 0.55.$$

The $\|*\|_1$ is easier to compute and use for determining convergence in N-dimensional space.   ■

The MATLAB command `A(j,[1:j-1,j+1:N])` is used in Program 3.4. This effectively selects all elements in the jth row of A, except the element in the jth column (i.e., `A(j,j)`). This notation is used to simplify the Jacobi iteration (10) step in Program 3.4.

In both Programs 3.4 and 3.5 we have used the MATLAB command `norm`, which is the Euclidean norm. The $\|*\|_1$ can also be used and the reader is encouraged to check the Help menu in MATLAB or one of the reference works for information on the `norm` command.

Program 3.4 (Jacobi Iteration).   To solve the linear system $AX = B$ by starting with an initial guess $X = P_0$ and generating a sequence $\{P_k\}$ that converges to the solution. A sufficient condition for the method to be applicable is that A is strictly diagonally dominant.

```
function X=jacobi(A,B,P,delta, max1)
% Input   - A is an N x N nonsingular matrix
```

```
%          - B is an N x 1 matrix
%          - P is an N x 1 matrix; the initial guess
%          - delta is the tolerance for P
%          - max1 is the maximum number of iterations
% Output  - X is an N x 1 matrix: the Jacobi approximation to
%            the solution of AX = B
N = length(B);

for k=1:max1
    for j=1:N
        X(j)=(B(j)-A(j,[1:j-1,j+1:N])*P([1:j-1,j+1:N]))/A(j,j);
    end
    err=abs(norm(X'-P));
    relerr=err/(norm(X)+eps);
    P=X';
        if(err<delta)|(relerr<delta)
        break
    end
end
X=X';
```

Program 3.5 (Gauss-Seidel Iteration).   To solve the linear system $AX = B$ by starting with the initial guess $X = P_0$ and generating a sequence $\{P_k\}$ that converges to the solution. A sufficient condition for the method to be applicable is that A is strictly diagonally dominant.

```
function X=gseid(A,B,P,delta, max1)

% Input  - A is an N x N nonsingular matrix
%          - B is an N x 1 matrix
%          - P is an N x 1 matrix; the initial guess
%          - delta is the tolerance for P
%          - max1 is the maximum number of iterations
% Output - X is an N x 1 matrix: the Gauss-Seidel
%            approximation to the solution of AX = B
N = length(B);

for k=1:max1
    for j=1:N
        if j==1
            X(1)=(B(1)-A(1,2:N)*P(2:N))/A(1,1);
        elseif j==N
            X(N)=(B(N)-A(N,1:N-1)*(X(1:N-1))')/A(N,N);
        else
            %X contains the kth approximations and P the (k-1)st
```

```
        X(j)=(B(j)-A(j,1:j-1)*X(1:j-1)'
             -A(j,j+1:N)*P(j+1:N))/A(j,j);
    end
 end
 err=abs(norm(X'-P));
 relerr=err/(norm(X)+eps);
 P=X';
    if(err<delta)|(relerr<delta)
        break
    end
end
X=X';
```

Exercises for Iterative Methods for Linear Systems

In Exercises 1 through 8:

(a) Start with $P_0 = 0$ and use Jacobi iteration to find P_k for $k = 1, 2, 3$. Will Jacobi iteration converge to the solution?

(b) Start with $P_0 = 0$ and use Gauss-Seidel iteration to find P_k for $k = 1, 2, 3$. Will Gauss-Seidel iteration converge to the solution?

1.
$$4x - y = 15$$
$$x + 5y = 9$$

2.
$$8x - 3y = 10$$
$$-x + 4y = 6$$

3.
$$-x + 3y = 1$$
$$6x - 2y = 2$$

4.
$$2x + 3y = 1$$
$$7x - 2y = 1$$

5.
$$5x - y + z = 10$$
$$2x + 8y - z = 11$$
$$-x + y + 4z = 3$$

6.
$$2x + 8y - z = 11$$
$$5x - y + z = 10$$
$$-x + y + 4z = 3$$

7.
$$x - 5y - z = -8$$
$$4x + y - z = 13$$
$$2x - y - 6z = -2$$

8.
$$4x + y - z = 13$$
$$x - 5y - z = -8$$
$$2x - y - 6z = -2$$

9. Let $X = (x_1, x_2, \ldots, x_N)$. Prove that the $\|*\|_1$ norm

$$\|X\|_1 = \sum_{k=1}^{N} |x_k|$$

satisfies the three properties (14)–(16).

10. Let $X = (x_1, x_2, \ldots, x_N)$. Prove that the Euclidean norm

$$\|X\| = \left(\sum_{k=1}^{N} (x_k)^2 \right)^{1/2}.$$

satisfies the four properties given in (14)–(17).

11. Let $X = (x_1, x_2, \ldots, x_N)$. Prove that the $\|*\|_\infty$ norm

$$\|X\|_\infty = \max_{1 \le k \le N} |x_k|$$

satisfies the four properties given in (14)–(17).

Algorithms and Programs

1. Use both Programs 3.4 and 3.5 to solve the linear systems in Exercises 1 through 8. Use the `format long` command and `delta` $= 10^{-9}$.

2. In Theorem 3.14 the condition that A be strictly diagonally dominant is a sufficient but not necessary condition. Use both Programs 3.4 and 3.5 and several different initial guesses for P_0 on the following linear system. *Note.* The Jacobi iteration appears to converge, while the Gauss-Seidel iteration diverges.

$$
\begin{array}{rcrcrcl}
x & & & + & z & = & 2 \\
-x & + & y & & & = & 0 \\
x & + & 2y & - & 3z & = & 0
\end{array}
$$

3. Consider the following tridiagonal linear system, and assume that the coefficient matrix is strictly diagonally dominant.

$$
\begin{array}{ll}
d_1 x_1 + c_1 x_2 & = b_1 \\
a_1 x_1 + d_2 x_2 + c_2 x_3 & = b_2 \\
\quad\quad a_2 x_2 + d_3 x_3 + c_3 x_4 & = b_3 \\
\quad\quad\quad \cdot \quad\quad\quad \cdot \quad\quad\quad \cdot & \quad \cdot \\
\quad\quad\quad\quad \cdot \quad\quad\quad \cdot \quad\quad\quad \cdot & \\
\quad\quad\quad\quad\quad \cdot \quad\quad\quad \cdot \quad\quad\quad \cdot & \\
a_{N-2} x_{N-2} + d_{N-1} x_{N-1} + c_{N-1} x_N & = b_{N-1} \\
\quad\quad\quad\quad a_{N-1} x_{N-1} + d_N x_N & = b_N.
\end{array}
$$

(i) Write an iterative algorithm, following (9)–(11), that will solve this system. Your algorithm should efficiently use the "sparseness" of the coefficient matrix.
(ii) Construct a MATLAB program based on your algorithm in and solve the following tridiagonal systems.

(a)

$$\begin{aligned}
4m_1 + m_2 &= 3 \\
m_1 + 4m_2 + m_3 &= 3 \\
m_2 + 4m_3 + m_4 &= 3 \\
m_3 + 4m_4 + m_5 &= 3 \\
&\;\;\vdots \\
m_{48} + 4m_{49} + m_{50} &= 3 \\
m_{49} + 4m_{50} &= 3
\end{aligned}$$

(b)

$$\begin{aligned}
4m_1 + m_2 &= 1 \\
m_1 + 4m_2 + m_3 &= 2 \\
m_2 + 4m_3 + m_4 &= 1 \\
m_3 + 4m_4 + m_5 &= 2 \\
&\;\;\vdots \\
m_{48} + 4m_{49} + m_{50} &= 1 \\
m_{49} + 4m_{50} &= 2
\end{aligned}$$

4. Use Gauss-Seidel iteration to solve the following band system.

$$\begin{aligned}
12x_1 - 2x_2 + x_3 &= 5 \\
-2x_1 + 12x_2 - 2x_3 + x_4 &= 5 \\
x_1 - 2x_2 + 12x_3 - 2x_4 + x_5 &= 5 \\
x_2 - 2x_3 + 12x_4 - 2x_5 + x_6 &= 5 \\
&\;\;\vdots \\
x_{46} - 2x_{47} + 12x_{48} - 2x_{49} + x_{50} &= 5 \\
x_{47} - 2x_{48} + 12x_{49} - 2x_{50} &= 5 \\
x_{48} - 2x_{49} + 12x_{50} &= 5
\end{aligned}$$

5. In Programs 3.4 and 3.5 the relative error between consecutive iterates is used as a stopping criterion. The problems with using this criterion exclusively were discussed in Section 2.3. The linear system $AX = B$ can be rewritten as $AX - B = 0$. If X_k is the kth iterate from a Jacobi or Gauss-Seidel iteration procedure, then the norm of the *residual* $AX_k - B$ is, in general, a more appropriate stopping criterion.

Modify Programs 3.4 and 3.5 to use the residual as a stopping criterion. Use the modified programs to solve the band system in Problem 4.

3.7 Iteration for Nonlinear Systems: Seidel and Newton's Methods (Optional)

Iterative techniques will now be discussed that extend the methods of Chapter 2 and Section 3.6 to the case of systems of nonlinear functions. Consider the functions

(1)
$$\begin{aligned}
f_1(x, y) &= x^2 - 2x - y + 0.5 \\
f_2(x, y) &= x^2 + 4y^2 - 4.
\end{aligned}$$

We seek a method of solution for the system of nonlinear equations

(2) $$f_1(x, y) = 0 \quad \text{and} \quad f_2(x, y) = 0.$$

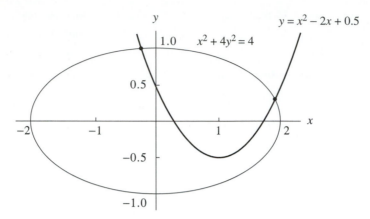

Figure 3.6   The graphs for the nonlinear system $y = x^2 - 2x + 0.5$ and $x^2 + 4y^2 = 4$.

The equations $f_1(x, y) = 0$ and $f_2(x, y) = 0$ implicitly define curves in the xy-plane. Hence a solution of the system (2) is a point (p, q) where the two curves cross (i.e., both $f_1(p, q) = 0$ and $f_2(p, q) = 0$). The curves for the system in (1) are well known:

(3)
$$x^2 - 2x + 0.5 = 0 \quad \text{is the graph of a parabola,}$$
$$x^2 + 4y^2 - 4 = 0 \quad \text{is the graph of an ellipse.}$$

The graphs in Figure 3.6 show that there are two solution points and that they are in the vicinity of $(-0.2, 1.0)$ and $(1.9, 0.3)$.

The first technique is fixed-point iteration. A method must be devised for generating a sequence $\{(p_k, q_k)\}$ that converges to the solution (p, q). The first equation in (3) can be used to solve directly for x. However, a multiple of y can be added to each side of the second equation to get $x^2 + 4y^2 - 8y - 4 = -8y$. The choice of adding $-8y$ is crucial and will be explained later. We now have an equivalent system of equations:

(4)
$$x = \frac{x^2 - y + 0.5}{2}$$
$$y = \frac{-x^2 - 4y^2 + 8y + 4}{8}.$$

These two equations are used to write the recursive formulas. Start with an initial point (p_0, q_0), and then compute the sequence $\{(p_{k+1}, q_{k+1})\}$ using

(5)
$$p_{k+1} = g_1(p_k, q_k) = \frac{p_k^2 - q_k + 0.5}{2}$$
$$q_{k+1} = g_2(p_k, q_k) = \frac{-p_k^2 - 4q_k^2 + 8q_k + 4}{8}.$$

Table 3.5 Fixed-Point Iteration Using the Formulas in (5)

	Case (i): Start with (0, 1)			Case (ii): Start with (2, 0)	
k	p_k	q_k	k	p_k	q_k
0	0.00	1.00	0	2.00	0.00
1	−0.25	1.00	1	2.25	0.00
2	−0.21875	0.9921875	2	2.78125	−0.1328125
3	−0.2221680	0.9939880	3	4.184082	−0.6085510
4	−0.2223147	0.9938121	4	9.307547	−2.4820360
5	−0.2221941	0.9938029	5	44.80623	−15.891091
6	−0.2222163	0.9938095	6	1,011.995	−392.60426
7	−0.2222147	0.9938083	7	512,263.2	−205,477.82
8	−0.2222145	0.9938084		This sequence is diverging.	
9	−0.2222146	0.9938084			

Case (i): If we use the starting value $(p_0, q_0) = (0, 1)$, then

$$p_1 = \frac{0^2 - 1 + 0.5}{2} = -0.25 \quad \text{and} \quad q_1 = \frac{-0^2 - 4(1)^2 + 8(1) + 4}{8} = 1.0.$$

Iteration will generate the sequence in case (i) of Table 3.5. In this case the sequence converges to the solution that lies near the starting value $(0, 1)$.

Case (ii): If we use the starting value $(p_0, q_0) = (2, 0)$, then

$$p_1 = \frac{2^2 - 0 + 0.5}{2} = 2.25 \quad \text{and} \quad q_1 = \frac{-2^2 - 4(0)^2 + 8(0) + 4}{8} = 0.0.$$

Iteration will generate the sequence in case (ii) of Table 3.5. In this case the sequence diverges away from the solution.

Iteration using formulas (5) cannot be used to find the second solution (1.900677, 0.3112186). To find this point, a different pair of iteration formulas are needed. Start with equation (3) and add $-2x$ to the first equation and $-11y$ to the second equation and get

$$x^2 - 4x - y + 0.5 = -2x \quad \text{and} \quad x^2 + 4y^2 - 11y - 4 = -11y.$$

These equations can then be used to obtain the iteration formulas

(6)
$$p_{k+1} = g_1(p_k, q_k) = \frac{-p_k^2 + 4p_k + q_k - 0.5}{2}$$

$$q_{k+1} = g_2(p_k, q_k) = \frac{-p_k^2 - 4q_k^2 + 11q_k + 4}{11}.$$

Table 3.6 shows how to use (6) to find the second solution.

Table 3.6 Fixed-Point Iteration Using the Formulas in (6)

k	p_k	q_k
0	2.00	0.00
1	1.75	0.0
2	1.71875	0.0852273
3	1.753063	0.1776676
4	1.808345	0.2504410
8	1.903595	0.3160782
12	1.900924	0.3112267
16	1.900652	0.3111994
20	1.900677	0.3112196
24	1.900677	0.3112186

Theory

We want to determine why equations (6) were suitable for finding the solution near $(1.9, 0.3)$ and equations (5) were not. In Section 2.1 the size of the derivative at the fixed point was the necessary idea. When functions of several variables are used, the partial derivatives must be used. The generalization of "the derivative" for systems of functions of several variables is the Jacobian matrix. We will consider only a few introductory ideas regarding this topic. More details can be found in any textbook on advanced calculus.

Definition 3.8. Assume that $f_1(x, y)$ and $f_2(x, y)$ are functions of the independent variables x and y; then their ***Jacobian matrix*** $J(x, y)$ is

$$(7) \qquad \begin{bmatrix} \dfrac{\partial f_1}{\partial x} & \dfrac{\partial f_1}{\partial y} \\[2mm] \dfrac{\partial f_2}{\partial x} & \dfrac{\partial f_2}{\partial y} \end{bmatrix}.$$

Similarly, if $f_1(x, y, z)$, $f_2(x, y, z)$, and $f_3(x, y, z)$ are functions of the independent variables x, y, and z, then their 3×3 Jacobian matrix $J(x, y, z)$ is defined as follows:

$$(8) \qquad \begin{bmatrix} \dfrac{\partial f_1}{\partial x} & \dfrac{\partial f_1}{\partial y} & \dfrac{\partial f_1}{\partial z} \\[2mm] \dfrac{\partial f_2}{\partial x} & \dfrac{\partial f_2}{\partial y} & \dfrac{\partial f_2}{\partial z} \\[2mm] \dfrac{\partial f_3}{\partial x} & \dfrac{\partial f_3}{\partial y} & \dfrac{\partial f_3}{\partial z} \end{bmatrix}. \qquad \blacktriangle$$

Example 3.30.   Find the Jacobian matrix $J(x, y, z)$ of order 3×3 at the point $(1, 3, 2)$ for the three functions

$$f_1(x, y, z) = x^3 - y^2 + y - z^4 + z^2$$
$$f_2(x, y, z) = xy + yz + xz$$
$$f_3(x, y, z) = \frac{y}{xz}.$$

The Jacobian matrix is

$$J(x, y, z) = \begin{bmatrix} \dfrac{\partial f_1}{\partial x} & \dfrac{\partial f_1}{\partial y} & \dfrac{\partial f_1}{\partial z} \\[2mm] \dfrac{\partial f_2}{\partial x} & \dfrac{\partial f_2}{\partial y} & \dfrac{\partial f_2}{\partial z} \\[2mm] \dfrac{\partial f_3}{\partial x} & \dfrac{\partial f_3}{\partial y} & \dfrac{\partial f_3}{\partial z} \end{bmatrix} = \begin{bmatrix} 3x^2 & -2y+1 & -4z^3+2z \\[2mm] y+z & x+z & y+x \\[2mm] \dfrac{-y}{x^2 z} & \dfrac{1}{xz} & \dfrac{-y}{xz^2} \end{bmatrix}.$$

Thus the Jacobian evaluated at the point $(1, 3, 2)$ is the 3×3 matrix

$$J(1, 3, 2) = \begin{bmatrix} 3 & -5 & -28 \\[1mm] 5 & 3 & 4 \\[1mm] -\frac{3}{2} & \frac{1}{2} & -\frac{3}{4} \end{bmatrix}. \qquad \blacksquare$$

Generalized Differential

For a function of several variables, the differential is used to show how changes of the independent variables affect the change in the dependent variables. Suppose that we have

$$(9) \qquad u = f_1(x, y, z), \qquad v = f_2(x, y, z), \qquad \text{and} \qquad w = f_3(x, y, z).$$

Suppose that the values of the functions in (9) are known at the point (x_0, y_0, z_0) and we wish to predict their value at a nearby point (x, y, z). Let du, dv, and dw denote differential changes in the dependent variables and dx, dy, and dz denote differential changes in the independent variables. These changes obey the relationships

$$du = \frac{\partial f_1}{\partial x}(x_0, y_0, z_0)\, dx + \frac{\partial f_1}{\partial y}(x_0, y_0, z_0)\, dy + \frac{\partial f_1}{\partial z}(x_0, y_0, z_0)\, dz,$$

$$(10) \qquad dv = \frac{\partial f_2}{\partial x}(x_0, y_0, z_0)\, dx + \frac{\partial f_2}{\partial y}(x_0, y_0, z_0)\, dy + \frac{\partial f_2}{\partial z}(x_0, y_0, z_0)\, dz,$$

$$dw = \frac{\partial f_3}{\partial x}(x_0, y_0, z_0)\, dx + \frac{\partial f_3}{\partial y}(x_0, y_0, z_0)\, dy + \frac{\partial f_3}{\partial z}(x_0, y_0, z_0)\, dz.$$

If vector notation is used, (10) can be compactly written by using the Jacobian matrix. The function changes are dF and the changes in the variables are denoted dX.

$$(11) \qquad dF = \begin{bmatrix} du \\ dv \\ dw \end{bmatrix} = J(x_0, y_0, z_0) \begin{bmatrix} dx \\ dy \\ dz \end{bmatrix} = J(x_0, y_0, z_0)\, dX.$$

Example 3.31.   Use the Jacobian matrix to find the differential changes (du, dv, dw) when the independent variables change from $(1, 3, 2)$ to $(1.02, 2.97, 2.01)$ for the system of functions

$$u = f_1(x, y, z) = x^3 - y^2 + y - z^4 + z^2$$
$$v = f_2(x, y, z) = xy + yz + xz$$
$$w = f_3(x, y, z) = \frac{y}{xz}.$$

Use equation (11) with $J(1, 3, 2)$ of Example 3.30 and the differential changes $(dx, dy, dz) = (0.02, -0.03, 0.01)$ to obtain

$$\begin{bmatrix} du \\ dv \\ dw \end{bmatrix} = \begin{bmatrix} 3 & -5 & -28 \\ 5 & 3 & 4 \\ -\frac{3}{2} & \frac{1}{2} & -\frac{3}{4} \end{bmatrix} \begin{bmatrix} 0.02 \\ -0.03 \\ 0.01 \end{bmatrix} = \begin{bmatrix} -0.07 \\ 0.05 \\ -0.0525 \end{bmatrix}.$$

Notice that the function values at $(1.02, 2.97, 2.01)$ are close to the linear approximations obtained by adding the differentials $du = -0.07$, $dv = 0.05$, and $dw = -0.0525$ to the corresponding function values $f_1(1, 3, 2) = -17$, $f_2(1, 3, 2) = 11$, and $f_3(1, 3, 2) = 1.5$; that is,

$$f_1(1.02, 2.97, 2.01) = -17.072 \approx -17.07 = f_1(1, 3, 2) + du$$
$$f_2(1.02, 2.97, 2.01) = 11.0493 \approx 11.05 = f_2(1, 3, 2) + dv \qquad\blacksquare$$
$$f_3(1.02, 2.97, 2.01) = 1.44864 \approx 1.4475 = f_3(1, 3, 2) + dw.$$

Convergence near Fixed Points

The extensions of the definitions and theorems in Section 2.1 to the case of two and three dimensions are now given. The notation for N-dimensional functions has not been used. The reader can easily find these extensions in many books on numerical analysis.

Definition 3.9.   A *fixed point* for the system of two equations

$$(12) \qquad x = g_1(x, y) \quad \text{and} \quad y = g_2(x, y)$$

is a point (p, q) such that $p = g_1(p, q)$ and $q = g_2(p, q)$. Similarly, in three dimensions a fixed point for the system

$$(13) \qquad x = g_1(x, y, z), \quad y = g_2(x, y, z), \quad \text{and} \quad z = g_3(x, y, z)$$

is a point (p, q, r) such that $p = g_1(p, q, r)$, $q = g_2(p, q, r)$, and $r = g_3(p, q, r)$. ▲

Definition 3.10. For the functions (12), *fixed-point iteration* is

(14) $$p_{k+1} = g_1(p_k, q_k) \quad \text{and} \quad q_{k+1} = g_2(p_k, q_k)$$

for $k = 0, 1, \ldots$. Similarly, for the functions (13), *fixed-point iteration* is

(15)
$$
\begin{aligned}
p_{k+1} &= g_1(p_k, q_k, r_k) \\
q_{k+1} &= g_2(p_k, q_k, r_k) \\
r_{k+1} &= g_3(p_k, q_k, r_k)
\end{aligned}
$$

for $k = 0, 1, \ldots$. ▲

Theorem 3.17 (Fixed-Point Iteration). Assume that the functions in (12) and (13) and their first partial derivatives are continuous on a region that contains the fixed point (p, q) or (p, q, r), respectively. If the starting point is chosen sufficiently close to the fixed point, then one of the following cases applies.

Case (i): Two dimensions. If (p_0, q_0) is sufficiently close to (p, q) and if

(16)
$$
\begin{aligned}
\left| \frac{\partial g_1}{\partial x}(p, q) \right| + \left| \frac{\partial g_1}{\partial y}(p, q) \right| &< 1, \\
\left| \frac{\partial g_2}{\partial x}(p, q) \right| + \left| \frac{\partial g_2}{\partial y}(p, q) \right| &< 1,
\end{aligned}
$$

then the iteration in (14) converges to the fixed point (p, q).

Case (ii): Three dimensions. If (p_0, q_0, r_0) is sufficiently close to (p, q, r) and if

(17)
$$
\begin{aligned}
\left| \frac{\partial g_1}{\partial x}(p, q, r) \right| + \left| \frac{\partial g_1}{\partial y}(p, q, r) \right| + \left| \frac{\partial g_1}{\partial z}(p, q, r) \right| &< 1, \\
\left| \frac{\partial g_2}{\partial x}(p, q, r) \right| + \left| \frac{\partial g_2}{\partial y}(p, q, r) \right| + \left| \frac{\partial g_2}{\partial z}(p, q, r) \right| &< 1, \\
\left| \frac{\partial g_3}{\partial x}(p, q, r) \right| + \left| \frac{\partial g_3}{\partial y}(p, q, r) \right| + \left| \frac{\partial g_3}{\partial z}(p, q, r) \right| &< 1,
\end{aligned}
$$

then the iteration in (15) converges to the fixed point (p, q, r).

If conditions (16) or (17) are not met, the iteration might diverge. This will usually be the case if the sum of the magnitudes of the partial derivatives is much larger than 1. Theorem 3.17 can be used to show why the iteration (5) converged to the fixed point near $(-0.2, 1.0)$. The partial derivatives are

$$
\begin{aligned}
\frac{\partial}{\partial x} g_1(x, y) &= x, & \frac{\partial}{\partial y} g_1(x, y) &= -\frac{1}{2}, \\
\frac{\partial}{\partial x} g_2(x, y) &= -\frac{x}{4}, & \frac{\partial}{\partial y} g_2(x, y) &= -y + 1.
\end{aligned}
$$

Indeed, for all (x, y) satisfying $-0.5 < x < 0.5$ and $0.5 < y < 1.5$, the partial derivatives satisfy

$$\left| \frac{\partial}{\partial x} g_1(x, y) \right| + \left| \frac{\partial}{\partial y} g_1(x, y) \right| = |x| + |-0.5| < 1,$$

$$\left| \frac{\partial}{\partial x} g_2(x, y) \right| + \left| \frac{\partial}{\partial y} g_2(x, y) \right| = \frac{|-x|}{4} + |-y + 1| < 0.625 < 1.$$

Therefore, the partial derivative conditions in (16) are met and Theorem 3.17 implies that fixed-point iteration will converge to $(p, q) \approx (-0.2222146, 0.9938084)$. Notice that near the other fixed point $(1.90068, 0.31122)$ the partial derivatives do not meet the conditions in (16); hence convergence is not guaranteed. That is,

$$\left| \frac{\partial}{\partial x} g_1(1.90068, 0.31122) \right| + \left| \frac{\partial}{\partial y} g_1(1.90068, 0.31122) \right| = 2.40068 > 1,$$

$$\left| \frac{\partial}{\partial x} g_2(1.90068, 0.31122) \right| + \left| \frac{\partial}{\partial y} g_2(1.90068, 0.31122) \right| = 1.16395 > 1.$$

Seidel Iteration

An improvement, analogous to the Gauss-Seidel method for linear systems, of fixed-point iteration can be made. Suppose that p_{k+1} is used in the calculation of q_{k+1} (in three dimensions both p_{k+1} and q_{k+1} are used to compute r_{k+1}). When these modifications are incorporated in formulas (14) and (15), the method is called *Seidel iteration*:

(18) $$p_{k+1} = g_1(p_k, q_k) \quad \text{and} \quad q_{k+1} = g_2(p_{k+1}, q_k)$$

and

(19) $$\begin{aligned} p_{k+1} &= g_1(p_k, q_k, r_k) \\ q_{k+1} &= g_2(p_{k+1}, q_k, r_k) \\ r_{k+1} &= g_3(p_{k+1}, q_{k+1}, r_k). \end{aligned}$$

Program 3.6 will implement Seidel iteration for nonlinear systems. Implementation of fixed-point iteration is left for the reader.

Newton's Method for Nonlinear Systems

We now outline the derivation of Newton's method in two dimensions. Newton's method can easily be extended to higher dimensions.

Consider the system

(20) $$\begin{aligned} u &= f_1(x, y) \\ v &= f_2(x, y), \end{aligned}$$

which can be considered a transformation from the xy-plane to the uv-plane. We are interested in the behavior of this transformation near the point (x_0, y_0) whose image is the point (u_0, v_0). If the two functions have continuous partial derivatives, then the differential can be used to write a system of linear approximations that is valid near the point (x_0, y_0):

(21)
$$u - u_0 \approx \frac{\partial}{\partial x} f_1(x_0, y_0)(x - x_0) + \frac{\partial}{\partial y} f_1(x_0, y_0)(y - y_0),$$

$$v - v_0 \approx \frac{\partial}{\partial x} f_2(x_0, y_0)(x - x_0) + \frac{\partial}{\partial y} f_2(x_0, y_0)(y - y_0).$$

The system (21) is a local linear transformation that relates small changes in the independent variables to small changes in the dependent variable. When the Jacobian matrix $J(x_0, y_0)$ is used, this relationship is easier to visualize:

(22)
$$\begin{bmatrix} u - u_0 \\ v - v_0 \end{bmatrix} = \begin{bmatrix} \dfrac{\partial}{\partial x} f_1(x_0, y_0) & \dfrac{\partial}{\partial y} f_1(x_0, y_0) \\ \dfrac{\partial}{\partial x} f_2(x_0, y_0) & \dfrac{\partial}{\partial y} f_2(x_0, y_0) \end{bmatrix} \begin{bmatrix} x - x_0 \\ y - y_0 \end{bmatrix}.$$

If the system in (20) is written as a vector function $V = F(X)$, the Jacobian $J(x, y)$ is the two-dimensional analog of the derivative, because (22) can be written as

(23)
$$\Delta F \approx J(x_0, y_0) \, \Delta X.$$

We now use (23) to derive Newton's method in two dimensions.

Consider the system (20) with u and v set equal to zero:

(24)
$$0 = f_1(x, y)$$
$$0 = f_2(x, y).$$

Suppose that (p, q) is a solution of (24); that is,

(25)
$$0 = f_1(p, q)$$
$$0 = f_2(p, q).$$

To develop Newton's method for solving (24), we need to consider small changes in the functions near the point (p_0, q_0):

(26)
$$\Delta u = u - u_0, \qquad \Delta p = x - p_0.$$
$$\Delta v = v - v_0, \qquad \Delta q = y - q_0.$$

Set $(x, y) = (p, q)$ in (20) and use (25) to see that $(u, v) = (0, 0)$. Hence the changes in the dependent variables are

(27)
$$u - u_0 = f_1(p, q) - f_1(p_0, q_0) = 0 - f_1(p_0, q_0)$$
$$v - v_0 = f_2(p, q) - f_2(p_0, q_0) = 0 - f_2(p_0, q_0).$$

Use the result of (27) in (22) to get the linear transformation

(28)
$$\begin{bmatrix} \dfrac{\partial}{\partial x} f_1(p_0, q_0) & \dfrac{\partial}{\partial y} f_1(p_0, q_0) \\[2ex] \dfrac{\partial}{\partial x} f_2(p_0, q_0) & \dfrac{\partial}{\partial y} f_2(p_0, q_0) \end{bmatrix} \begin{bmatrix} \Delta p \\ \Delta q \end{bmatrix} \approx - \begin{bmatrix} f_1(p_0, q_0) \\ f_2(p_0, q_0) \end{bmatrix}.$$

If the Jacobian $J(p_0, q_0)$ in (28) is nonsingular, we can solve for $\Delta P = \begin{bmatrix} \Delta p & \Delta q \end{bmatrix}' = \begin{bmatrix} p & q \end{bmatrix}' - \begin{bmatrix} p_0 & q_0 \end{bmatrix}'$ as follows:

(29)
$$\Delta P \approx - J(p_0, q_0)^{-1} F(p_0, q_0).$$

Then the next approximation P_1 to the solution $P = \begin{bmatrix} p & q \end{bmatrix}'$ is

(30)
$$P_1 = P_0 + \Delta P = P_0 - J(p_0, q_0)^{-1} F(p_0, q_0).$$

Notice that (30) is the generalization of Newton's method for the one-variable case; that is, $p_1 = p_0 - f(p_0)/f'(p_0)$.

Outline of Newton's Method

Suppose that P_k has been obtained.

    Step 1. Evaluate the function

$$F(P_k) = \begin{bmatrix} f_1(p_k, q_k) \\ f_2(p_k, q_k) \end{bmatrix}.$$

    Step 2. Evaluate the Jacobian

$$J(P_k) = \begin{bmatrix} \dfrac{\partial}{\partial x} f_1(p_k, q_k) & \dfrac{\partial}{\partial y} f_1(p_k, q_k) \\[2ex] \dfrac{\partial}{\partial x} f_2(p_k, q_k) & \dfrac{\partial}{\partial y} f_2(p_k, q_k) \end{bmatrix}.$$

    Step 3. Solve the linear system

$$J(P_k)\Delta P = -F(P_k) \quad \text{for } \Delta P.$$

    Step 4. Compute the next point:

$$P_{k+1} = P_k + \Delta P.$$

Now, repeat the process.

Example 3.32.   Consider the nonlinear system

$$0 = x^2 - 2x - y + 0.5$$
$$0 = x^2 + 4y^2 - 4.$$

Use Newton's method with the starting value $(p_0, q_0) = (2.00, 0.25)$ and compute (p_1, q_1), (p_2, q_2), and (p_3, q_3).

The function vector and Jacobian matrix are

$$F(x, y) = \begin{bmatrix} x^2 - 2x - y + 0.5 \\ x^2 + 4y^2 - 4 \end{bmatrix}, \quad J(x, y) = \begin{bmatrix} 2x - 2 & -1 \\ 2x & 8y \end{bmatrix}.$$

At the point $(2.00, 0.25)$ they take on the values

$$F(2.00, 0.25) = \begin{bmatrix} 0.25 \\ 0.25 \end{bmatrix}, \quad J(2.00, 0.25) = \begin{bmatrix} 2.0 & -1.0 \\ 4.0 & 2.0 \end{bmatrix}.$$

The differentials Δp and Δq are solutions of the linear system

$$\begin{bmatrix} 2.0 & -1.0 \\ 4.0 & 2.0 \end{bmatrix} \begin{bmatrix} \Delta p \\ \Delta q \end{bmatrix} = - \begin{bmatrix} 0.25 \\ 0.25 \end{bmatrix}.$$

A straightforward calculation reveals that

$$\Delta P = \begin{bmatrix} \Delta p \\ \Delta q \end{bmatrix} = \begin{bmatrix} -0.09375 \\ 0.0625 \end{bmatrix}.$$

The next point in the iteration is

$$P_1 = P_0 + \Delta P = \begin{bmatrix} 2.00 \\ 0.25 \end{bmatrix} + \begin{bmatrix} -0.09375 \\ 0.0625 \end{bmatrix} = \begin{bmatrix} 1.90625 \\ 0.3125 \end{bmatrix}.$$

Similarly, the next two points are

$$P_2 = \begin{bmatrix} 1.900691 \\ 0.311213 \end{bmatrix} \quad \text{and} \quad P_3 = \begin{bmatrix} 1.900677 \\ 0.311219 \end{bmatrix}.$$

The coordinates of P_3 are accurate to six decimal places. Calculations for finding P_2 and P_3 are summarized in Table 3.7.   ■

Table 3.7   Function Values, Jacobian Matrices, and Differentials Required for Each Iteration in Newton's Solution to Example 3.32

P_k	Solution of the linear system $J(P_k)\Delta P = -F(P_k)$	$P_k + \Delta P$
$\begin{bmatrix} 2.00 \\ 0.25 \end{bmatrix}$	$\begin{bmatrix} 2.0 & -1.0 \\ 4.0 & 2.0 \end{bmatrix} \begin{bmatrix} -0.09375 \\ 0.0625 \end{bmatrix} = -\begin{bmatrix} 0.25 \\ 0.25 \end{bmatrix}$	$\begin{bmatrix} 1.90625 \\ 0.3125 \end{bmatrix}$
$\begin{bmatrix} 1.90625 \\ 0.3125 \end{bmatrix}$	$\begin{bmatrix} 1.8125 & -1.0 \\ 3.8125 & 2.5 \end{bmatrix} \begin{bmatrix} -0.005559 \\ -0.001287 \end{bmatrix} = -\begin{bmatrix} 0.008789 \\ 0.024414 \end{bmatrix}$	$\begin{bmatrix} 1.900691 \\ 0.311213 \end{bmatrix}$
$\begin{bmatrix} 1.900691 \\ 0.311213 \end{bmatrix}$	$\begin{bmatrix} 1.801381 & -1.000000 \\ 3.801381 & 2.489700 \end{bmatrix} \begin{bmatrix} -0.000014 \\ 0.000006 \end{bmatrix} = -\begin{bmatrix} 0.000031 \\ 0.000038 \end{bmatrix}$	$\begin{bmatrix} 1.900677 \\ 0.311219 \end{bmatrix}$

Implementation of Newton's method can require the determination of several partial derivatives. It is permissible to use numerical approximations for the values of these partial derivatives, but care must be taken to determine the proper step size. In higher dimensions it is necessary to use the methods for solving linear systems introduced earlier in this chapter to solve for ΔP.

MATLAB

Programs 3.6 (Nonlinear Seidel Iteration) and 3.7 (Newton-Raphson Method) will require saving the nonlinear system $X = G(X)$, and the nonlinear system $F(X) = 0$ and its Jacobian matrix, JF, respectively, as M-files. As an example, consider saving the nonlinear system in Example 3.32 and the related Jacobian matrix as the M-files F.m and JF.m, respectively.

```
function Z=F(X)                function W=JF(X)
x=X(1);y=X(2);                 x=X(1);y=X(2);
Z=zeros(1,2);                  W=[2*x-2 -1;2*x 8*y];
Z(1)=x^2-2*x-y+0.5;
Z(2)=x^2+4y^2-4;
```

The functions may be evaluated using the standard MATLAB commands.

```
>>A=feval('F',[2.00 0.25])
A=
   0.2500 0.2500
>>V=JF([2.00 0.25])
B=
   2 -1
   4 2
```

> **Program 3.6 (Nonlinear Seidel Iteration).**   To solve the nonlinear fixed-point system $X = G(X)$, given one initial approximation P_0, and generating a sequence $\{P_k\}$ that converges to the solution P.

```
function [P,iter] = seidel(G,P,delta, max1)

%Input   - G is the nonlinear system saved in the M-file G.m
%          - P is the initial guess at the solution
%          - delta is the error bound
%          - max1 is the number of iterations
%Output - P is the Seidel approximation to the solution
%          - iter is the number of iterations required
N=length(P);

for k=1:max1
    X=P;
    % X is the kth approximation to the solution
    for j=1:N
        A=feval('G',X);
        % Update the terms of X as they are calculated
        X(j)=A(j);
    end
    err=abs(norm(X-P));
    relerr=err/(norm(X)+eps);
    P=X;
    iter=k;
    if(err<delta)|(relerr<delta)
        break
    end
end
```

In the following program the MATLAB command A\B is used to solve the linear system $AX = B$ (see Q=P-(J\Y')'). Programs developed earlier in this chapter could be used in place of this MATLAB command. The choice of an appropriate program to solve the linear system would depend on the size and characteristics of the Jacobian matrix.

> **Program 3.7 (Newton-Raphson Method).**   To solve the nonlinear system $F(X) = 0$, given one initial approximation P_0 and generating a sequence $\{P_k\}$ that converges to the solution P.

```
function [P,iter,err]=newdim(F,JF,P,delta,epsilon,max1)

%Input   - F is the system saved as the M-file F.m
%          - JF is the Jacobian of F saved as the M-file JF.M
%          - P is the initial approximation to the solution
```

```
%           - delta is the tolerance for P
%           - epsilon is the tolerance for F(P)
%           - max1 is the maximum number of iterations
%Output - P is the approximation to the solution
%           - iter is the number of iterations required
%           - err is the error estimate for P
Y=feval(F,P);

for k=1:max1
   J=feval(JF,P);
   Q=P-(J\Y')';
   Z=feval(F,Q);
   err=norm(Q-P);
   relerr=err/(norm(Q)+eps);
   P=Q;
   Y=Z;
   iter=k;
   if (err<delta)|(relerr<delta)|(abs(Y)<epsilon)
      break
   end
end
```

Exercises for Iteration for Nonlinear Systems

1. Find (analytically) the fixed point(s) for each of the following systems.
   (a) $x = g_1(x, y) = x - y^2$
         $y = g_2(x, y) = -x + 6y$
   (b) $x = g_1(x, y) = (x^2 - y^2 - x - 3)/3$
         $y = g_2(x, y) = (-x + y - 1)/3$
   (c) $x = g_1(x, y) = \sin(y)$
         $y = g_2(x, y) = -6x + y$
   (d) $x = g_1(x, y, z) = 9 - 3y - 2z$
         $y = g_2(x, y, z) = 2 - x + z$
         $z = g_3(x, y, z) = -9 + 3x + 4y - z$

2. Find (analytically) the zero(s) for each of the following systems. Evaluate the Jacobian of each system at each zero.
   (a) $0 = f_1(x, y) = 2x + y - 6$
         $0 = f_2(x, y) = x + 2y$
   (b) $0 = f_1(x, y) = 3x^2 + 2y - 4$
         $0 = f_2(x, y) = 2x + 2y - 3$

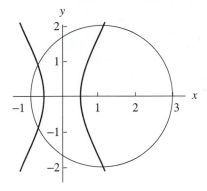

Figure 3.7   The hyperbola and circle for Exercise 5.

(c) $0 = f_1(x, y) = 2x - 4\cos(y)$
      $0 = f_2(x, y) = 4x\sin(y)$

(d) $0 = f_1(x, y, z) = x^2 + y^2 - z$
      $0 = f_2(x, y, z) = x^2 + y^2 + z^2 - 1$
      $0 = f_3(x, y, z) = x + y$

3. Find a region in the xy-plane such that if (p_0, q_0) is in the region then fixed-point iteration is guaranteed to converge (use an argument similar to the one that followed Theorem 3.17) for the system:

$$x = g_1(x, y) = (x^2 - y^2 - x - 3)/3$$
$$y = g_2(x, y) = (x + y + 1)/3.$$

4. Rewrite the following linear system in fixed-point form. Find bounds on x, y, and z such that fixed-point iteration is sure to converge for any initial guess (p_0, q_0, r_0) that satisfies the boundary conditions.

$$6x + y + z = 1$$
$$x + 4y + z = 2$$
$$x + y + 5z = 0$$

5. For the given nonlinear system (see Figure 3.7), use the initial approximation $(p_0, q_0) = (1.1, 2.0)$, and compute the next three approximations to the fixed point using **(a)** fixed-point iteration and equations (14) and **(b)** Seidel iteration using equations (18).

$$x = g_1(x, y) = \frac{8x - 4x^2 + y^2 + 1}{8} \qquad \text{(hyperbola)}$$

$$y = g_2(x, y) = \frac{2x - x^2 + 4y - y^2 + 3}{4} \qquad \text{(circle)}.$$

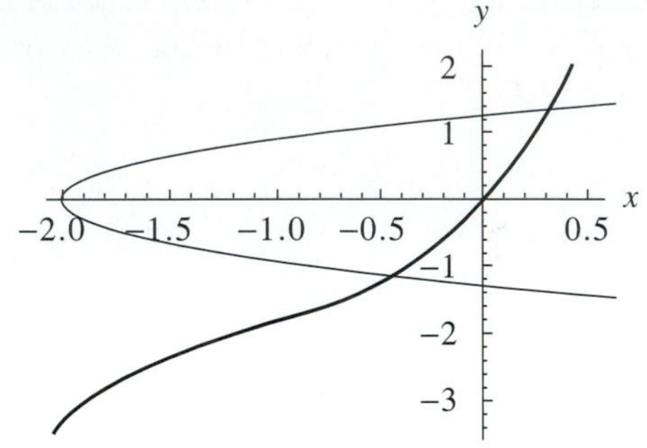

Figure 3.8 The cubic and parabola for Exercise 6.

6. For the following nonlinear system (see Figure 3.8), use the initial approximation $(p_0, q_0) = (-0.3, -1.3)$, and compute the next three approximations to the fixed point using **(a)** fixed-point iteration and equations (14) and **(b)** Seidel iteration using equations (18).

$$x = g_1(x, y) = \frac{y - x^3 + 3x^2 + 3x}{7} \qquad \text{(cubic)}$$

$$y = g_2(x, y) = \frac{y^2 + 2y - x - 2}{2} \qquad \text{(parabola)}.$$

7. Consider the nonlinear system

$$0 = f_1(x, y) = x^2 - y - 0.2$$
$$0 = f_2(x, y) = y^2 - x - 0.3.$$

These parabolas intersect in two points as shown in Figure 3.9.

(a) Start with $(p_0, q_0) = (1.2, 1.2)$ and apply Newton's method to compute (p_1, q_1) and (p_2, q_2).

(b) Start with $(p_0, q_0) = (-0.2, -0.2)$ and apply Newton's method to compute (p_1, q_1) and (p_2, q_2).

8. Consider the nonlinear system shown in Figure 3.10.

$$0 = f_1(x, y) = x^2 + y^2 - 2$$
$$0 = f_2(x, y) = xy - 1.$$

(a) Verify that the solutions are $(1, 1)$ and $(-1, -1)$.

(b) What difficulties might arise if we try to use Newton's method to find the solutions?

9. Show that Jacobi iteration for a 3×3 linear system is a special case of fixed-point iteration (15). Furthermore, verify that if the coefficient matrix from a 3×3 linear system is strictly diagonally dominant, then condition (17) is satisfied.

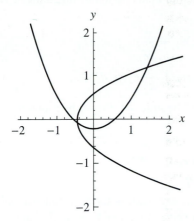

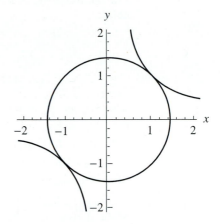

Figure 3.9   The parabolas for
Exercise 7.

Figure 3.10   The circle and hyperbola for Exercise 8.

10. Show that Newton's method for two equations can be written in fixed-point iteration
    form

    $$x = g_1(x, y), \quad y = g_2(x, y),$$

    where $g_1(x, y)$ and $g_2(x, y)$ are given by

    $$g_1(x, y) = x - \frac{f_1(x, y)\dfrac{\partial}{\partial y} f_2(x, y) - f_2(x, y)\dfrac{\partial}{\partial y} f_1(x, y)}{\det(J(x, y))}$$

    $$g_2(x, y) = y - \frac{f_2(x, y)\dfrac{\partial}{\partial x} f_1(x, y) - f_1(x, y)\dfrac{\partial}{\partial x} f_2(x, y)}{\det(J(x, y))}.$$

11. Fixed-point iteration is used to solve the nonlinear system (12). Use the following
    steps to prove that conditions in (16) are sufficient to guarantee that $\{(p_k, q_k)\}$ con-
    verges to (p, q). Assume that there is a constant K with $0 < K < 1$ so that

    $$\left|\frac{\partial}{\partial x} g_1(x, y)\right| + \left|\frac{\partial}{\partial y} g_1(x, y)\right| < K$$

    and

    $$\left|\frac{\partial}{\partial x} g_2(x, y)\right| + \left|\frac{\partial}{\partial y} g_2(x, y)\right| < K$$

    for all (x, y) in the rectangle $R = \{(x, y) : a < x < b, c < y < d\}$. Also assume
    that $a < p_0 < b$ and $c < q_0 < d$. Define

    $$e_k = p - p_k, \quad E_k = q - q_k, \quad \text{and} \quad r_k = \max\{|e_k|, |E_k|\}.$$

Use the following form of the mean value theorem applied to functions of two variables:

$$e_{k+1} = \frac{\partial}{\partial x} g_1(a_k^*, q_k) e_k + \frac{\partial}{\partial y} g_1(p, c_k^*) E_k$$

$$E_{k+1} = \frac{\partial}{\partial x} g_2(b_k^*, q_k) e_k + \frac{\partial}{\partial y} g_2(p, d_k^*) E_k,$$

where a_k^* and b_k^* lie in $[a, b]$ and c_k^* and d_k^* lie in $[c, d]$. Prove the following:

(a) $|e_1| \le K r_0$ and $|E_1| \le K r_0$

(b) $|e_2| \le K r_1 \le K^2 r_0$ and $|E_2| \le K r_1 \le K^2 r_0$

(c) $|e_k| \le K r_{k-1} \le K^k r_0$ and $|E_k| \le K r_{k-1} \le K^k r_0$

(d) $\lim_{n \to \infty} p_k = p$ and $\lim_{n \to \infty} q_k = q$

12. As noted earlier, the Jacobian matrix of system (20) is the two-dimensional analog of the derivative. Write system (20) as a vector function $V = F(X)$, and let $J(F)$ be the Jacobian matrix of this system. Given two nonlinear systems $V = F(X)$ and $V = G(X)$ and the real number c, prove:

(a) $J(cF(X)) = cJ(F(X))$

(b) $J(F(X) + G(X)) = J(F(X)) + J(G(X))$

Algorithms and Programs

1. Use Program 3.6 to approximate the fixed points of the systems in Exercises 5 and 6. Answers should be accurate to 10 decimal places.

2. Use Program 3.7 to approximate the zeros of the systems in Exercises 7 and 8. Answers should be accurate to 10 decimal places.

3. Construct a program to find the fixed points of a system using fixed-point iteration. Use the program to approximate the fixed points of the systems in Exercises 5 and 6. Answers should be accurate to eight decimal places.

4. Use Program 3.7 to approximate the zeros of the following systems. Answers should be accurate to 10 decimal places.

(a) $0 = x^2 - x + y^2 + z^2 - 5$

$0 = x^2 + y^2 - y + z^2 - 4$

$0 = x^2 + y^2 + z^2 + z - 6$

(b) $0 = x^2 - x + 2y^2 + yz - 10$

$0 = 5x - 6y + z$

$0 = z - x^2 - y^2$

(c) $0 = (x + 1)^2 + (y + 1)^2 - z$

$0 = (x - 1)^2 + y^2 - z$

$0 = 4x^2 + 2y^2 + z^2 - 16$

(d) $0 = 9x^2 + 36y^2 + 4z^2 - 36$

$0 = x^2 - 2y^2 - 20z$

$0 = 16x - x^3 - 2y^2 - 16z^2$

5. We wish to solve the nonlinear system

$$0 = 7x^3 - 10x - y - 1$$
$$0 = 8y^3 - 11y + x - 1.$$

Use MATLAB to sketch the graphs of both curves on the same coordinate system. Use the graph to verify that there are nine points where the graphs intersect. Using the graph, estimate the points of intersection. Use these estimates and Program 3.7 to approximate the points of intersection to nine decimal places.

6. The system in Problem 5 can be rewritten in fixed-point form:

$$x = \frac{7x^3 - y - 1}{10}$$
$$y = \frac{8y^3 + x - 1}{11}.$$

Do some computer experimentation. Discover that, no matter what starting value is used, only one of the nine solutions can be found using fixed-point iteration (on this particular fixed-point form). Are there other fixed-point forms of the system in Problem 5 that could be used to find other solutions of the system?

4

Interpolation and Polynomial Approximation

The computational procedures used in computer software for the evaluation of a library function, such as $\sin(x)$, $\cos(x)$, or e^x, involve polynomial appproximation. The state-of-the-art methods use rational functions (which are the quotients of polynomials). However, the theory of polynomial approximation is suitable for a first course in numerical analysis, and we consider them in this chapter. Suppose that the function $f(x) = e^x$ is to be approximated by a polynomial of degree $n = 2$ over the interval $[-1, 1]$. The Taylor polynomial is shown in Figure 4.1(a) and can be contrasted with

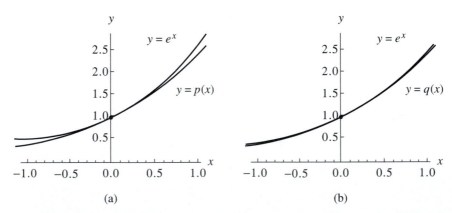

(a)   (b)

Figure 4.1   (a) The Taylor polynomial $p(x) = 1.000000 + 1.000000x + 0.500000x^2$, which approximates $f(x) = e^x$ over $[-1, 1]$. (b) The Chebyshev approximation $q(x) = 1.000000 + 1.129772x + 0.532042x^2$ for $f(x) = e^x$ over $[-1, 1]$.

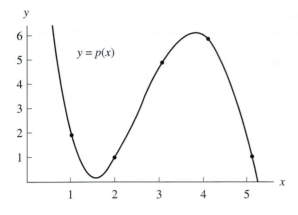

Figure 4.2   The graph of the collocation polynomial that passes through $(1, 2)$, $(2, 1)$, $(3, 5)$, $(4, 6)$, and $(5, 1)$.

the Chebyshev approximation in Figure 4.1(b). The maximum error for the Taylor approximation is 0.218282, whereas the maximum error for the Chebyshev polynomial is 0.056468. In this chapter we develop the basic theory needed to investigate these matters.

An associated problem involves construction of the collocation polynomial. Given $n + 1$ points in the plane (no two of which are aligned vertically), the collocation polynomial is the unique polynomial of degree $\leq n$ that passes through the points. In cases where data are known to a high degree of precision, the collocation polynomial is sometimes used to find a polynomial that passes through the given data points. A variety of methods can be used to construct the collocation polynomial: solving a linear system for its coefficients, the use of Lagrange coefficient polynomials, and the construction of a divided differences table and the coefficients of the Newton polynomial. All three techniques are important for a practitioner of numerical analysis to know. For example, the collocation polynomial of degree $n = 4$ that passes through the five points $(1, 2)$, $(2, 1)$, $(3, 5)$, $(4, 6)$, and $(5, 1)$ is

$$P(x) = \frac{5x^4 - 82x^3 + 427x^2 - 806x + 504}{24},$$

and a graph showing both the points and the polynomial is given in Figure 4.2.

4.1   Taylor Series and Calculation of Functions

Limit processes are the basis of calculus. For example, the derivative

$$f'(x) = \lim_{h \to 0} \frac{f(x + h) - f(x)}{h}$$

is the limit of the difference quotient where both the numerator and the denominator go to zero. A Taylor series illustrates another type of limit process. In this case an

Table 4.1   Taylor Series Expansions for Some Common Functions

$$\sin(x) = x - \frac{x^3}{3!} + \frac{x^5}{5!} - \frac{x^7}{7!} + \cdots \qquad \text{for all } x$$

$$\cos(x) = 1 - \frac{x^2}{2!} + \frac{x^4}{4!} - \frac{x^6}{6!} + \cdots \qquad \text{for all } x$$

$$e^x = 1 + x + \frac{x^2}{2!} + \frac{x^3}{3!} + \frac{x^4}{4!} + \cdots \qquad \text{for all } x$$

$$\ln(1+x) = x - \frac{x^2}{2} + \frac{x^3}{3} - \frac{x^4}{4} + \cdots \qquad -1 \le x \le 1$$

$$\arctan(x) = x - \frac{x^3}{3} + \frac{x^5}{5} - \frac{x^7}{7} + \cdots \qquad -1 \le x \le 1$$

$$(1+x)^p = 1 + px + \frac{p(p-1)}{2!} x^2 + \frac{p(p-1)(p-2)}{3!} x^3 + \cdots \qquad \text{for } |x| < 1$$

infinite number of terms is added together by taking the limit of certain partial sums. An important application is their use to represent the elementary functions: $\sin(x)$, $\cos(x)$, e^x, $\ln(x)$, etc. Table 4.1 gives several of the common Taylor series expansions. The partial sums can be accumulated until an approximation to the function is obtained that has the accuracy specified. Series solutions are used in the areas of engineering and physics.

We want to learn how a finite sum can be used to obtain a good approximation to an infinite sum. For illustration we shall use the exponential series in Table 4.1 to compute the number $e = e^1$, which is the base of the natural logarithm and exponential functions. Here we choose $x = 1$ and use the series

$$e^1 = 1 + \frac{1}{1!} + \frac{1^2}{2!} + \frac{1^3}{3!} + \frac{1^4}{4!} + \cdots + \frac{1^k}{k!} + \cdots .$$

The definition for the sum of an infinite series in Section 1.1 requires that the partial sums S_N tend to a limit. The values of these sums are given in Table 4.2.

A natural way to think about the power series representation of a function is to view the expansion as the limiting case of polynomials of increasing degree. If enough terms are added, then an accurate approximation will be obtained. This needs to be made precise. What degree should be chosen for the polynomial, and how do we calculate the coefficients for the powers of x in the polynomial? Theorem 4.1 answers these questions.

Table 4.2 Partial Sums S_n Used to Determine e

n	$S_n = 1 + \frac{1}{1!} + \frac{1}{2!} + \cdots + \frac{1}{n!}$
0	1.0
1	2.0
2	2.5
3	2.666666666666...
4	2.708333333333...
5	2.716666666666...
6	2.718055555555...
7	2.718253968254...
8	2.718278769841...
9	2.718281525573...
10	2.718281801146...
11	2.718281826199...
12	2.718281828286...
13	2.718281828447...
14	2.718281828458...
15	2.718281828459...

Theorem 4.1 (Taylor Polynomial Approximation). Assume that $f \in C^{N+1}[a, b]$ and $x_0 \in [a, b]$ is a fixed value. If $x \in [a, b]$, then

$$(1) \qquad f(x) = P_N(x) + E_N(x),$$

where $P_N(x)$ is a polynomial that can be used to approximate $f(x)$:

$$(2) \qquad f(x) \approx P_N(x) = \sum_{k=0}^{N} \frac{f^{(k)}(x_0)}{k!}(x - x_0)^k.$$

The error term $E_N(x)$ has the form

$$(3) \qquad E_N(x) = \frac{f^{(N+1)}(c)}{(N+1)!}(x - x_0)^{N+1}$$

for some value $c = c(x)$ that lies between x and x_0.

Proof. The proof is left as an exercise. ●

Relation (2) indicates how the coefficients of the Taylor polynomial are calculated. Although the error term (3) involves a similar expression, notice that $f^{(N+1)}(c)$ is to be evaluated at an undetermined number c that depends on the value of x. For this reason we do not try to evaluate $E_N(x)$: it is used to determine a bound for the accuracy of the approximation.

Example 4.1. Show why 15 terms are all that are needed to obtain the 13-digit approximation $e = 2.718281828459$ in Table 4.2.

Expand $f(x) = e^x$ in a Taylor polynomial of degree 15 using the fixed value $x_0 = 0$ and involving the powers $(x - 0)^k = x^k$. The derivatives required are $f'(x) = f''(x) = \cdots = f^{(16)} = e^x$. The first 15 derivatives are used to calculate the coefficients $a_k = e^0/k!$ and are used to write

$$(4) \qquad P_{15}(x) = 1 + x + \frac{x^2}{2!} + \frac{x^3}{3!} + \cdots + \frac{x^{15}}{15!}.$$

Setting $x = 1$ in (4) gives the partial sum $S_{15} = P_{15}(1)$. The remainder term is needed to show the accuracy of the approximation:

$$(5) \qquad E_{15}(x) = \frac{f^{(16)}(c)x^{16}}{16!}.$$

Since we chose $x_0 = 0$ and $x = 1$, the value c lies between them (i.e., $0 < c < 1$), which implies that $e^c < e^1$. Notice that the partial sums in Table 4.2 are bounded above by 3. Combining these two inequalities yields $e^c < 3$, which is used in the following calculation

$$|E_{15}(1)| = \frac{|f^{(16)}(c)|}{16!} \le \frac{e^c}{16!} < \frac{3}{16!} < 1.433844 \times 10^{-13}.$$

Therefore, all the digits in the approximation $e \approx 2.718281828459$ are correct, because the actual error (whatever it is) must be less than 2 in the thirteenth decimal place. ∎

Instead of giving a rigorous proof of Theorem 4.1, we shall discuss some of the features of the approximation; the reader can look in any standard reference text on calculus for more details. For illustration, we again use the function $f(x) = e^x$ and the value $x_0 = 0$. From elementary calculus we know that the slope of the curve $y = e^x$ at the point (x, e^x) is $f'(x) = e^x$. Hence the slope at the point $(0, 1)$ is $f'(0) = 1$. Therefore, the tangent line to the curve at the point $(0, 1)$ is $y = 1 + x$. This is the same formula that would be obtained if we used $N = 1$ in Theorem 4.1; that is, $P_1(x) = f(0) + f'(0)x/1! = 1 + x$. Therefore, $P_1(x)$ is the equation of the tangent line to the curve. The graphs are shown in Figure 4.3.

Observe that the approximation $e^x \approx 1 + x$ is good near the center $x_0 = 0$ and that the distance between the curves grows as x moves away from 0. Notice that the slopes of the curves agree at $(0, 1)$. In calculus we learned that the second derivative indicates whether a curve is concave up or down. The study of curvature[1] shows that if two curves $y = f(x)$ and $y = g(x)$ have the property that $f(x_0) = g(x_0)$, $f'(x_0) = g'(x_0)$, and $f''(x_0) = g''(x_0)$ then they have the same curvature at x_0. This property would be desirable for a polynomial function that approximates $f(x)$. Corollary 4.1 shows that the Taylor polynomial has this property for $N \ge 2$.

---

[1]The curvature K of a graph $y = f(x)$ at (x_0, y_0) is defined by $K = |f''(x_0)|/(1 + [f'(x_0)]^2)^{3/2}$.

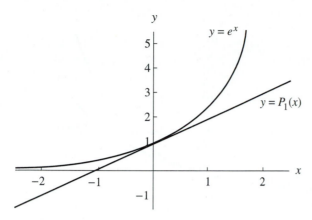

Figure 4.3 The graphs of $y = e^x$
and $y = P_1(x) = 1 + x$.

Corollary 4.1. If $P_N(x)$ is the Taylor polynomial of degree N given in Theorem 4.1, then

$$(6) \qquad\qquad P_N^{(k)}(x_0) = f^{(k)}(x_0) \qquad \text{for } k = 0, \ 1, \ \ldots, \ N.$$

Proof. Set $x = x_0$ in equations (2) and (3), and the result is $P_N(x_0) = f(x_0)$. Thus statement (6) is true for $k = 0$. Now differentiate the right-hand side of (2) and get

$$(7) \qquad P_N'(x) = \sum_{k=1}^{N} \frac{f^{(k)}(x_0)}{(k-1)!}(x - x_0)^{k-1} = \sum_{k=0}^{N-1} \frac{f^{(k+1)}(x_0)}{k!}(x - x_0)^k.$$

Set $x = x_0$ in (7) to obtain $P_N'(x_0) = f'(x_0)$. Thus statement (6) is true for $k = 1$. Successive differentiations of (7) will establish the other identities in (6). The details are left as an exercise.   •

Applying Corollary 4.1, we see that $y = P_2(x)$ has the properties $f(x_0) = P_2(x_0)$, $f'(x_0) = P_2'(x_0)$, and $f''(x_0) = P_2''(x_0)$; hence the graphs have the same curvature at x_0. For example, consider $f(x) = e^x$ and $P_2(x) = 1 + x + x^2/2$. The graphs are shown in Figure 4.4 and it is seen that they curve up in the same fashion at $(0, 1)$.

In the theory of approximation, one seeks to find an accurate polynomial approximation to the analytic function[2] $f(x)$ over $[a, b]$. This is one technique used in developing computer software. The accuracy of a Taylor polynomial is increased when we choose N large. The accuracy of any given polynomial will generally decrease as the value of x moves away from the center x_0. Hence we must choose N large enough and restrict the maximum value of $|x - x_0|$ so that the error does not exceed a specified bound. If we choose the interval width to be $2R$ and x_0 in the center (i.e., $|x - x_0| < R$),

---

[2]The function $f(x)$ is analytic at x_0 if it has continuous derivatives of all orders and can be represented as a Taylor series in an interval about x_0.

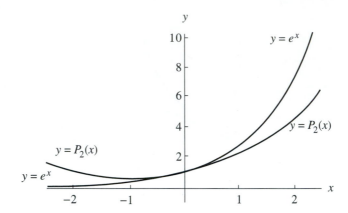

Figure 4.4   The graphs of $y = e^x$ and $y = P_2(x) = 1 + x + x^2/2$.

Table 4.3   Values for the Error Bound $|error| < e^R R^{N+1}/(N+1)!$ Using the Approximation $e^x \approx P_N(x)$ for $|x| \le R$

	$R = 2.0$, $\lvert x \rvert \le 2.0$	$R = 1.5$, $\lvert x \rvert \le 1.5$	$R = 1.0$, $\lvert x \rvert \le 1.0$	$R = 0.5$, $\lvert x \rvert \le 0.5$
$e^x \approx P_5(x)$	0.65680499	0.07090172	0.00377539	0.00003578
$e^x \approx P_6(x)$	0.18765857	0.01519323	0.00053934	0.00000256
$e^x \approx P_7(x)$	0.04691464	0.00284873	0.00006742	0.00000016
$e^x \approx P_8(x)$	0.01042548	0.00047479	0.00000749	0.00000001

the absolute value of the error satisfies the relation

$$\text{(8)} \qquad |error| = |E_N(x)| \le \frac{M R^{N+1}}{(N+1)!},$$

where $M \le \max\{|f^{(N+1)}(z)| : x_0 - R \le z \le x_0 + R\}$. If the derivatives are uniformly bounded, the error bound in (8) is proportional to $R^{N+1}/(N+1)!$ and decreases for fixed R, when N gets large or, for fixed N, when R goes to 0. Table 4.3 shows how the choices of these two parameters affect the accuracy of the approximation $e^x \approx P_N(x)$ over the interval $|x| \le R$. The error is smallest when N is largest and R smallest. Graphs for P_2, P_3, and P_4 are given in Figure 4.5.

Example 4.2.   Establish the error bounds for the approximation $e^x \approx P_8(x)$ on each of the intervals $|x| \le 1.0$ and $|x| \le 0.5$.

If $|x| \le 1.0$, then letting $R = 1.0$ and $|f^{(9)}(c)| = |e^c| \le e^{1.0} = M$ in (8) implies that

$$|error| = |E_8(x)| \le \frac{e^{1.0}(1.0)^9}{9!} \approx 0.00000749.$$

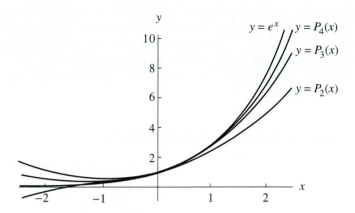

Figure 4.5   The graphs of $y = e^x$, $y = P_2(x)$, $y = P_3(x)$, and $y = P_4(x)$.

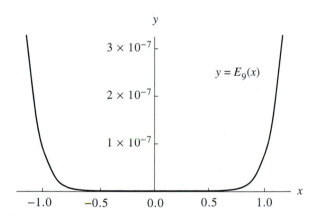

Figure 4.6   The graph of the error $y = E_9(x) = e^x - P_9(x)$.

If $|x| \leq 0.5$, then letting $R = 0.5$ and $|f^{(9)}(c)| = |e^c| \leq e^{0.5} = M$ in (8) implies that

$$|\text{error}| = |E_8(x)| \leq \frac{e^{0.5}(0.5)^9}{9!} \approx 0.00000001. \qquad \blacksquare$$

Example 4.3.   If $f(x) = e^x$, show that $N = 9$ is the smallest integer, so that the $|\text{error}| = |E_N(x)| \leq 0.0000005$ for x in $[-1, 1]$. Hence $P_9(x)$ can be used to compute approximate values of e^x that will be accurate in the sixth decimal place.

We need to find the smallest integer N so that

$$|\text{error}| = |E_N(x)| \leq \frac{e^c(1)^{N+1}}{(N+1)!} < 0.0000005.$$

In Example 4.2 we saw that $N = 8$ was too small, so we try $N = 9$ and discover that $|E_N(x)| \leq e^1(1)^{9+1}/(9+1)! \leq 0.000000749$. This value is slightly larger than desired; hence we would be likely to choose $N = 10$. But we used $e^c \leq e^1$ as a crude estimate in finding the error bound. Hence 0.000000749 is a little larger than the actual error. Figure 4.6 shows a graph of $E_9(x) = e^x - P_9(x)$. Notice that the maximum vertical range is about 3×10^{-7} and occurs at the right endpoint $(1, E_9(1))$. Indeed, the maximum error on the interval is $E_9(1) = 2.718281828 - 2.718281526 \approx 3.024 \times 10^{-7}$. Therefore, $N = 9$ is justified. ∎

Methods for Evaluating a Polynomial

There are several mathematically equivalent ways to evaluate a polynomial. Consider, for example, the function

$$(9) \qquad f(x) = (x - 1)^8.$$

The evaluation of f will require the use of an exponential function. Or the binomial formula can be used to expand $f(x)$ in powers of x:

$$(10) \qquad f(x) = \sum_{k=0}^{8} \binom{8}{k} x^{8-k}(-1)^k$$

$$= x^8 - 8x^7 + 28x^6 - 56x^5 + 70x^4 - 56x^3 + 28x^2 - 8x + 1.$$

Horner's method (see Section 1.1), which is also called ***nested multiplication***, can now be used to evaluate the polynomial in (10). When applied to formula (10), nested multiplication permits us to write

$$(11) \qquad f(x) = (((((((x - 8)x + 28)x - 56)x + 70)x - 56)x + 28)x - 8)x + 1.$$

To evaluate $f(x)$ now requires seven multiplications and eight additions or subtractions. The necessity of using an exponential function to evaluate the polynomial has now been eliminated.

We end this section with the theorem that relates the Taylor series in Table 4.1 and the Taylor polynomials of Theorem 4.1.

Theorem 4.2 (Taylor Series). Assume that $f(x)$ is analytic on an interval (a, b) containing x_0. Suppose that the Taylor polynomials (2) tend to a limit

$$(12) \qquad S(x) = \lim_{N \to \infty} P_N(x) = \lim_{N \to \infty} \sum_{k=0}^{N} \frac{f^{(k)}(x_0)}{k!} (x - x_0)^k;$$

then $f(x)$ has the Taylor series expansion

$$(13) \qquad f(x) = \sum_{k=0}^{\infty} \frac{f^{(k)}(x_0)}{k!} (x - x_0)^k.$$

Proof. This follows directly from the definition of convergence of series in Section 1.1. The limit condition is often stated by saying that the error term must go to zero as N goes to infinity. Therefore, a necessary and sufficient condition for (13) to hold is that

$$(14) \qquad \lim_{N \to \infty} E_N(x) = \lim_{N \to \infty} \frac{f^{(N+1)}(c)(x - x_0)^{N+1}}{(N+1)!} = 0,$$

where c depends on N and x.   •

Exercises for Taylor Series and Calculation of Functions

1. Let $f(x) = \sin(x)$ and apply Theorem 4.1.
   (a) Use $x_0 = 0$ and find $P_5(x)$, $P_7(x)$, and $P_9(x)$.
   (b) Show that if $|x| \le 1$, then the approximation

   $$\sin(x) \approx x - \frac{x^3}{3!} + \frac{x^5}{5!} - \frac{x^7}{7!} + \frac{x^9}{9!}$$

   has the error bound $|E_9(x)| < 1/10! \le 2.75574 \times 10^{-7}$.
   (c) Use $x_0 = \pi/4$ and find $P_5(x)$, which involves powers of $(x - \pi/4)$.

2. Let $f(x) = \cos(x)$ and apply Theorem 4.1.
   (a) Use $x_0 = 0$ and find $P_4(x)$, $P_6(x)$, and $P_8(x)$.
   (b) Show that if $|x| \le 1$, then the approximation

   $$\cos(x) \approx 1 - \frac{x^2}{2!} + \frac{x^4}{4!} - \frac{x^6}{6!} + \frac{x^8}{8!}$$

   has the error bound $|E_8(x)| < 1/9! \le 2.75574 \times 10^{-6}$.
   (c) Use $x_0 = \pi/4$ and find $P_4(x)$, which involves powers of $(x - \pi/4)$.

3. Does $f(x) = x^{1/2}$ have a Taylor series expansion about $x_0 = 0$? Justify your answer. Does the function $f(x) = x^{1/2}$ have a Taylor series expansion about $x_0 = 1$? Justify your answer.

4. (a) Find a Taylor polynomial of degree $N = 5$ for $f(x) = 1/(1 + x)$ expanded about $x_0 = 0$.
   (b) Find the error term $E_5(x)$ for the polynomial in part (a).

5. Find the Taylor polynomial of degree $N = 3$ for $f(x) = e^{-x^2/2}$ expanded about $x_0 = 0$.

6. Find the Taylor polynomial of degree $N = 3$, $P_3(x)$, for $f(x) = x^3 - 2x^2 + 2x$ expanded about $x_0 = 1$. Show that $f(x) = P_3(x)$.

7. **(a)** Find the Taylor polynomial of degree $N = 5$ for $f(x) = x^{1/2}$ expanded about $x_0 = 4$.

   (b) Find the Taylor polynomial of degree $N = 5$ for $f(x) = x^{1/2}$ expanded about $x_0 = 9$.

   (c) Determine which of the polynomials in parts (a) and (b) best approximates $(6.5)^{1/2}$.

8. Use $f(x) = (2 + x)^{1/2}$ and apply Theorem 4.1.

   (a) Find the Taylor polynomial $P_3(x)$ expanded about $x_0 = 2$.

   (b) Use $P_3(x)$ to find an approximation to $3^{1/2}$.

   (c) Find the maximum value of $|f^{(4)}(c)|$ on the interval $1 \leq c \leq 3$ and find a bound for $|E_3(x)|$.

9. Determine the degree of the Taylor polynomial $P_N(x)$ expanded about $x_0 = 0$ that should be used to approximate $e^{0.1}$ so that the error is less than 10^{-6}.

10. Determine the degree of the Taylor polynomial $P_N(x)$ expanded about $x_0 = \pi$ that should be used to approximate $\cos(33\pi/32)$ so that the error is less than 10^{-6}.

11. **(a)** Find the Taylor polynomial of degree $N = 4$ for $F(x) = \int_{-1}^{x} \cos(t^2) \, dt$ expanded about $x_0 = 0$.

    (b) Use the Taylor polynomial to approximate $F(0.1)$.

    (c) Find a bound on the error to the approximation in part (b).

12. **(a)** Use the geometric series

$$\frac{1}{1 + x^2} = 1 - x^2 + x^4 - x^6 + x^8 - \cdots \qquad \text{for } |x| < 1,$$

and integrate both sides term by term to obtain

$$\arctan(x) = x - \frac{x^3}{3} + \frac{x^5}{5} - \frac{x^7}{7} + \cdots \qquad \text{for } |x| < 1.$$

   (b) Use $\pi/6 = \arctan(3^{-1/2})$ and the series in part (a) to show that

$$\pi = 3^{1/2} \times 2 \left(1 - \frac{3^{-1}}{3} + \frac{3^{-2}}{5} - \frac{3^{-3}}{7} + \frac{3^{-4}}{9} - \cdots \right).$$

   (c) Use the series in part (b) to compute π accurate to eight digits.
       Fact. $\pi \approx 3.141592653589793284 \ldots$.

13. Use $f(x) = \ln(1 + x)$ and $x_0 = 0$, and apply Theorem 4.1.

    (a) Show that $f^{(k)}(x) = (-1)^{k-1}((k-1)!)/(1+x)^k$.

    (b) Show that the Taylor polynomial of degree N is

$$P_N(x) = x - \frac{x^2}{2} + \frac{x^3}{3} - \frac{x^4}{4} + \cdots + \frac{(-1)^{N-1}x^N}{N}.$$

(c)   Show that the error term for $P_N(x)$ is

$$E_N(x) = \frac{(-1)^N x^{N+1}}{(N+1)(1+c)^{N+1}}.$$

(d)   Evaluate $P_3(0.5)$, $P_6(0.5)$, and $P_9(0.5)$. Compare with $\ln(1.5)$.

(e)   Show that if $0.0 \le x \le 0.5$, then the approximation

$$\ln(x) \approx x - \frac{x^2}{2} + \frac{x^3}{3} - \cdots + \frac{x^7}{7} - \frac{x^8}{8} + \frac{x^9}{9}$$

has the error bound $|E_9| \le 0.00009765\ldots$.

14. *Binomial series.* Let $f(x) = (1+x)^p$ and $x_0 = 0$.

(a)   Show that $f^{(k)}(x) = p(p-1)\cdots(p-k+1)(1+x)^{p-k}$.

(b)   Show that the Taylor polynomial of degree N is

$$P_N(x) = 1 + px + \frac{p(p-1)x^2}{2!} + \cdots + \frac{p(p-1)\cdots(p-N+1)x^N}{N!}.$$

(c)   Show that

$$E_N(x) = p(p-1)\cdots(p-N)x^{N+1}/((1+c)^{N+1-p}(N+1)!).$$

(d)   Set $p = 1/2$ and compute $P_2(0.5)$, $P_4(0.5)$, and $P_6(0.5)$. Compare with $(1.5)^{1/2}$.

(e)   Show that if $0.0 \le x \le 0.5$, then the approximation

$$(1+x)^{1/2} \approx 1 + \frac{x}{2} - \frac{x^2}{8} + \frac{x^3}{16} - \frac{5x^4}{128} + \frac{7x^5}{256}$$

has the error bound $|E_5| \le (0.5)^6(21/1024) = 0.0003204\ldots$.

(f)   Show that if $p = N$ is a positive integer, then

$$P_N(x) = 1 + Nx + \frac{N(N-1)x^2}{2!} + \cdots + Nx^{N-1} + x^N.$$

Notice that this is the familiar binomial expansion.

15. Find c such that $|E_4| < 10^{-6}$ whenever $|x - x_0| < c$.

(a)   Let $f(x) = \cos(x)$ and $x_0 = 0$.

(b)   Let $f(x) = \sin(x)$ and $x_0 = \pi/2$.

(c)   Let $f(x) = e^x$ and $x_0 = 0$.

16. (a) Suppose that $y = f(x)$ is an even function (i.e., $f(-x) = f(x)$ for all x in the domain of f). What can be said about $P_N(x)$?

(b)   Suppose that $y = f(x)$ is an odd function (i.e., $f(-x) = -f(x)$ for all x in the domain of f). What can be said about $P_N(x)$?

17. Let $y = f(x)$ be a polynomial of degree N. If $f(x_0) > 0$ and $f'(x_0), \ldots, f^{(N)}(x_0) \geq 0$, show that all the real roots of f are less than x_0. *Hint.* Expand f in a Taylor polynomial of degree N about x_0.

18. Let $f(x) = e^x$. Use Theorem 4.1 to find $P_N(x)$, for $N = 1, 2, 3, \ldots$, expanded about $x_0 = 0$. Show that every real root of $P_N(x)$ has multiplicity less than or equal to 1. *Note.* If p is a root of multiplicity M of the polynomial $P(x)$, then p is a root of multiplicity $M - 1$ of $P'(x)$.

19. Finish the proof of Corollary 4.1 by writing down the expression for $P_N^{(k)}(x)$ and showing that

$$P_N^{(k)}(x_0) = f^{(k)}(x_0) \quad \text{for } k = 2, 3, \ldots, N.$$

Exercises 20 and 21 form a proof of Taylor's theorem.

20. Let $g(t)$ and its derivatives $g^{(k)}(t)$, for $k = 1, 2, \ldots, N + 1$, be continuous on the interval (a, b), which contains x_0. Suppose that there exist two distinct points x and x_0 such that $g(x) = 0$, and $g(x_0) = g'(x_0) = \ldots g^{(N)}(x_0) = 0$. Prove that there exists a value c that lies between x_0 and x such that $g^{(N+1)}(c) = 0$.

    Remark. Note that $g(t)$ is a function of t, and the values x and x_0 are to be treated as constants with respect to the variable t.

    Hint. Use Rolle's theorem (Theorem 1.5, Section 1.1) on the interval with endpoints x_0 and x to find the number c_1 such that $g'(c_1) = 0$. Then use Rolle's theorem applied to the function $g'(t)$ on the interval with end points x_0 and c_1 to find the number c_2 such that $g''(c_2) = 0$. Inductively repeat the process until the number c_{N+1} is found such that $g^{(N+1)}(c_{N+1}) = 0$.

21. Use the result of Exercise 20 and the special function

$$g(t) = f(t) - P_N(t) - E_N(x) \frac{(t - x_0)^{N+1}}{(x - x_0)^{N+1}},$$

where $P_N(x)$ is the Taylor polynomial of degree N, to prove that the error term $E_N(x) = f(x) - P_N(x)$ has the form

$$E_N(x) = f^{(N+1)}(c) \frac{(x - x_0)^{N+1}}{(N + 1)!}.$$

Hint. Find $g^{(N+1)}(t)$ and evaluate it at $t = c$.

Algorithms and Programs

The matrix nature of MATLAB allows us quickly to evaluate functions at a large number of values. If X=[-1 0 1], then sin(X) will produce [sin(-1) sin(0) sin(1)]. Similarly, if X=-1:0.1:1, then Y=sin(X) will produce a matrix Y of the same dimension as X with the appropriate values of sine. These two row matrices can be displayed in the form of a table by defining the matrix D = [X' Y'] (*Note*. The matrices X and Y must be of the same length.)

1. **(a)** Use the `plot` command to plot $\sin(x)$, $P_5(x)$, $P_7(x)$, and $P_9(x)$ from Exercise 1 on the same graph using the interval $-1 \leq x \leq 1$.

   (b) Create a table with columns that consist of $\sin(x)$, $P_5(x)$, $P_7(x)$, and $P_9(x)$ evaluated at 10 equally spaced values of x from the interval $[-1, 1]$.

2. **(a)** Use the `plot` command to plot $\cos(x)$, $P_4(x)$, $P_6(x)$, and $P_8(x)$ from Exercise 2 on the same graph using the interval $-1 \leq x \leq 1$.

   (b) Create a table with columns that consist of $\cos(x)$, $P_4(x)$, $P_6(x)$, and $P_8(x)$ evaluated at 19 equally spaced values of x from the interval $[-1, 1]$.

4.2 Introduction to Interpolation

In Section 4.1 we saw how a Taylor polynomial can be used to approximate the function $f(x)$. The information needed to construct the Taylor polynomial is the value of f and its derivatives at x_0. A shortcoming is that the higher-order derivatives must be known, and often they are either not available or they are hard to compute.

Suppose that the function $y = f(x)$ is known at the $N + 1$ points $(x_0, y_0), \ldots, (x_N, y_N)$, where the values x_k are spread out over the interval $[a, b]$ and satisfy

$$a \leq x_0 < x_1 < \cdots < x_N \leq b \quad \text{and} \quad y_k = f(x_k).$$

A polynomial $P(x)$ of degree N will be constructed that passes through these $N + 1$ points. In the construction, only the numerical values x_k and y_k are needed. Hence the higher-order derivatives are not necessary. The polynomial $P(x)$ can be used to approximate $f(x)$ over the entire interval $[a, b]$. However, if the error function $E(x) = f(x) - P(x)$ is required, then we will need to know $f^{(N+1)}(x)$ and a bound for its magnitude, that is,

$$M = \max\{|f^{(N+1)}(x)| : a \leq x \leq b\}.$$

Situations in statistical and scientific analysis arise where the function $y = f(x)$ is available only at $N + 1$ tabulated points (x_k, y_k), and a method is needed to approximate $f(x)$ at nontabulated abscissas. If there is a significant amount of error in the tabulated values, then the methods of curve fitting in Chapter 5 should be considered. On the other hand, if the points (x_k, y_k) are known to a high degree of accuracy, then the polynomial curve $y = P(x)$ that passes through them can be considered. When $x_0 < x < x_N$, the approximation $P(x)$ is called an ***interpolated value***. If either $x < x_0$ or $x_N < x$, then $P(x)$ is called an ***extrapolated value***. Polynomials are used to design software algorithms to approximate functions, for numerical differentiation, for numerical integration, and for making computer-drawn curves that must pass through specified points.

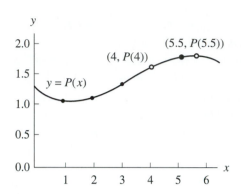

Figure 4.7 (a) The approximating polynomial $P(x)$ can be used for interpolation at the point $(4, P(4))$ and extrapolation at the point $(5.5, P(5.5))$.

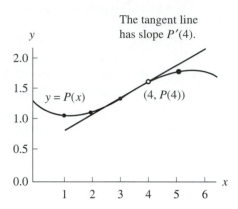

Figure 4.7 (b) The approximating polynomial $P(x)$ is differentiated and $P'(x)$ is used to find the slope at the interpolation point $(4, P(4))$.

Let us briefly mention how to evaluate the polynomial $P(x)$:

$$(1) \qquad P(x) = a_N x^N + a_{N-1} x^{N-1} + \cdots + a_2 x^2 + a_1 x + a_0.$$

Horner's method of synthetic division is an efficient way to evaluate $P(x)$. The derivative $P'(x)$ is

$$(2) \qquad P'(x) = N a_N x^{N-1} + (N-1) a_{N-1} x^{N-2} + \cdots + 2 a_2 x + a_1$$

and the indefinite integral $I(x) = \int P(x)\,dx$, which satisfies $I'(x) = P(x)$, is

$$(3) \qquad I(x) = \frac{a_N x^{N+1}}{N+1} + \frac{a_{N-1} x^N}{N} + \cdots + \frac{a_2 x^3}{3} + \frac{a_1 x^2}{2} + a_0 x + C,$$

where C is the constant of integration. Algorithm 4.1 (end of Section 4.2) shows how to adapt Horner's method to $P'(x)$ and $I(x)$.

Example 4.4. The polynomial $P(x) = -0.02x^3 + 0.2x^2 - 0.4x + 1.28$ passes through the four points $(1, 1.06)$, $(2, 1.12)$, $(3, 1.34)$, and $(5, 1.78)$. Find **(a)** $P(4)$, **(b)** $P'(4)$, **(c)** $\int_1^4 P(x)dx$, and **(d)** $P(5.5)$. Finally, **(e)** show how to find the coefficients of $P(x)$.
Use Algorithm 4.1(i)–(iii) (this is equivalent to the process in Table 1.2) with $x = 4$.

(a)
$$b_3 = a_3 = -0.02$$
$$b_2 = a_2 + b_3 x = 0.2 + (-0.02)(4) = 0.12$$
$$b_1 = a_1 + b_2 x = -0.4 + (0.12)(4) = 0.08$$
$$b_0 = a_0 + b_1 x = 1.28 + (0.08)(4) = 1.60.$$

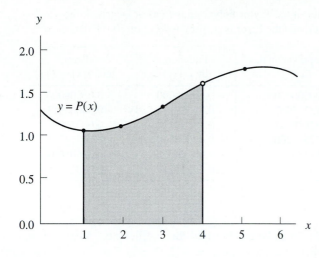

Figure 4.8   The approximating polynomial $P(x)$ is integrated and its antiderivative is used to find the area under the curve for $1 \leq x \leq 4$.

The interpolated value is $P(4) = 1.60$ (see Figure 4.7(a)).

(b)
$$d_2 = 3a_3 = -0.06$$
$$d_1 = 2a_2 + d_2x = 0.4 + (-0.06)(4) = 0.16$$
$$d_0 = a_1 + d_1x = -0.4 + (0.16)(4) = 0.24.$$

The numerical derivative is $P'(4) = 0.24$ (see Figure 4.7(b)).

(c)
$$i_4 = \frac{a_3}{4} = -0.005$$
$$i_3 = \frac{a_2}{3} + i_4x = 0.06666667 + (-0.005)(4) = 0.04666667$$
$$i_2 = \frac{a_1}{2} + i_3x = -0.2 + (0.04666667)(4) = -0.01333333$$
$$i_1 = a_0 + i_2x = 1.28 + (-0.01333333)(4) = 1.22666667$$
$$i_0 = 0 + i_1x = 0 + (1.22666667)(4) = 4.90666667.$$

Hence $I(4) = 4.90666667$. Similarly, $I(1) = 1.14166667$. Therefore, $\int_1^4 P(x)\,dx = I(4) - I(1) = 3.765$ (see Figure 4.8).
(d) Use Algorithm 4.1(i) with $x = 5.5$.

$$b_3 = a_3 = -0.02$$
$$b_2 = a_2 + b_3x = 0.2 + (-0.02)(5.5) = 0.09$$
$$b_1 = a_1 + b_2x = -0.4 + (0.09)(5.5) = 0.095$$
$$b_0 = a_0 + b_1x = 1.28 + (0.095)(5.5) = 1.8025.$$

The extrapolated value is $P(5.5) = 1.8025$ (see Figure 4.7(a)).

Table 4.4 Values of the Taylor Polynomial $T(x)$ of Degree 5, the
Function $\ln(1 + x)$, and the Error $\ln(1 + x) - T(x)$ on $[0, 1]$

x	Taylor polynomial, $T(x)$	Function, $\ln(1 + x)$	Error, $\ln(1 + x) - T(x)$
0.0	0.00000000	0.00000000	0.00000000
0.2	0.18233067	0.18232156	−0.00000911
0.4	0.33698133	0.33647224	−0.00050909
0.6	0.47515200	0.47000363	−0.00514837
0.8	0.61380267	0.58778666	−0.02601601
1.0	0.78333333	0.69314718	−0.09018615

(e) The methods of Chapter 3 can be used to find the coefficients. Assume that $P(x) = A + Bx + Cx^2 + Dx^3$; then at each value $x = 1, 2, 3,$ and 5 we get a linear equation involving $A, B, C,$ and D.

$$
\begin{aligned}
&At\ x = 1 : A + 1B + \ \ 1C + \ \ \ \ 1D = 1.06 \\
&At\ x = 2 : A + 2B + \ \ 4C + \ \ \ \ 8D = 1.12 \\
&At\ x = 3 : A + 3B + \ \ 9C + \ \ 27D = 1.34 \\
&At\ x = 5 : A + 5B + 25C + 125D = 1.78
\end{aligned}
$$

(4)

The solution to (4) is $A = 1.28$, $B = -0.4$, $C = 0.2$, and $D = -0.2$. ∎

This method for finding the coefficients is mathematically sound, but sometimes the matrix is difficult to solve accurately. In this chapter we design algorithms specifically for polynomials.

Let us return to the topic of using a polynomial to calculate approximations to a known function. In Section 4.1 we saw that the fifth-degree Taylor polynomial for $f(x) = \ln(1 + x)$ is

(5)
$$
T(x) = x - \frac{x^2}{2} + \frac{x^3}{3} - \frac{x^4}{4} + \frac{x^5}{5}.
$$

If $T(x)$ is used to approximate $\ln(1 + x)$ on the interval $[0, 1]$, then the error is 0 at $x = 0$ and is largest when $x = 1$ (see Table 4.4). Indeed, the error between $T(1)$ and the correct value $\ln(2)$ is 13%. We seek a polynomial of degree 5 that will approximate $\ln(1 + x)$ better over the interval $[0, 1]$. The polynomial $P(x)$ in Example 4.5 is an interpolating polynomial and will approximate $\ln(1 + x)$ with an error no bigger than 0.00002385 over the interval $[0, 1]$.

Example 4.5. Consider the function $f(x) = \ln(1 + x)$ and the polynomial

$$
P(x) = 0.02957206x^5 - 0.12895295x^4 + 0.28249626x^3
$$
$$
- 0.48907554x^2 + 0.99910735x
$$

Table 4.5   Values of the Approximating Polynomial $P(x)$ of Example 4.5, the Function $f(x) = \ln(1 + x)$, and the Error $E(x)$ on $[-0.1, 1.1]$

x	Approximating polynomial, $P(x)$	Function, $f(x) = \ln(1 + x)$	Error, $E(x) = f(x) - P(x)$
-0.1	-0.10509718	-0.10536052	-0.00026334
0.0	0.00000000	0.00000000	0.00000000
0.1	0.09528988	0.09531018	0.00002030
0.2	0.18232156	0.18232156	0.00000000
0.3	0.26237015	0.26236426	-0.00000589
0.4	0.33647224	0.33647224	0.00000000
0.5	0.40546139	0.40546511	0.00000372
0.6	0.47000363	0.47000363	0.00000000
0.7	0.53063292	0.53062825	-0.00000467
0.8	0.58778666	0.58778666	0.00000000
0.9	0.64184118	0.64185389	0.00001271
1.0	0.69314718	0.69314718	0.00000000
1.1	0.74206529	0.74193734	-0.00012795

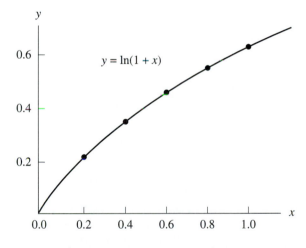

Figure 4.9   The graph of $y = P(x)$, which "lies on top" of the graph $y = \ln(1 + x)$.

based on the six nodes $x_k = k/5$ for $k = 0, 1, 2, 3, 4$, and 5. The following are empirical descriptions of the approximation $P(x) \approx \ln(1 + x)$.

1. $P(x_k) = f(x_k)$ at each node (see Table 4.5).

2. The maximum error on the interval $[-0.1, 1.1]$ occurs at $x = -0.1$ and $|\text{error}| \leq 0.00026334$ for $-0.1 \leq x \leq 1.1$ (see Figure 4.10). Hence the graph of $y = P(x)$ would appear identical to that of $y = \ln(1 + x)$ (see Figure 4.9).

3. The maximum error on the interval $[0, 1]$ occurs at $x = 0.06472456$ and $|\text{error}| \leq 0.00002385$ for $0 \leq x \leq 1$ (see Figure 4.10).

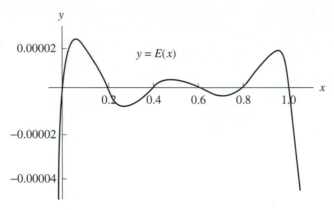

Figure 4.10 The graph of the error $y = E(x) =$ $\ln(1 + x) - P(x)$.

Remark. At a node x_k we have $f(x_k) = P(x_k)$. Hence $E(x_k) = 0$ at a node. The graph of $E(x) = f(x) - P(x)$ looks like a vibrating string, with the nodes being the abscissa, where there is no displacement. ∎

Algorithm 4.1 (Polynomial Calculus). To evaluate the polynomial $P(x)$, its derivative $P'(x)$, and its integral $\int P(x)\, dx$ by performing synthetic division.

INPUT N {Degree of $P(x)$}
INPUT $A(0), A(1), \ldots, A(N)$ {Coefficients of $P(x)$}
INPUT C {Constant of integration}
INPUT X {Independent variable}

(i) Algorithm to Evaluate $P(x)$	Space-saving version:
$B(N) := A(N)$	Poly $:= A(N)$
FOR $K = N - 1$ DOWNTO 0 DO	FOR $K = N - 1$ DOWNTO 0 DO
$B(K) := A(K) + B(K + 1) * X$	Poly $:= A(K) + $ Poly $* X$
PRINT "The value $P(x)$ is", $B(0)$	PRINT "The value $P(x)$ is", Poly
(ii) Algorithm to Evaluate $P'(x)$	Space-saving version:
$D(N - 1) := N * A(N)$	Deriv $:= N * A(N)$
FOR $K = N - 1$ DOWNTO 1 DO	FOR $K = N - 1$ DOWNTO 1 DO
$D(K - 1) := K * A(K) + D(K) * X$	Deriv $:= K * A(K) + $ Deriv $* X$
PRINT "The value $P'(x)$ is", $D(0)$	PRINT "The value $P'(x)$ is", Deriv
(iii) Algorithm to Evaluate $I(x)$	Space-saving version:
$I(N + 1) := A(N)/(N + 1)$	Integ $:= A(N)/(N + 1)$
FOR $K = N$ DOWNTO 1 DO	FOR $K = N$ DOWNTO 1 DO
$I(K) := A(K - 1)/K + I(K + 1) * X$	Integ $:= A(K - 1)/K + $ Integ $* X$
$I(0) := C + I(1) * X$	Integ $:= C + $ Integ $* X$
PRINT "The value $I(x)$ is", $I(0)$	PRINT "The value $I(x)$ is", Integ

Exercises for Introduction to Interpolation

1. Consider $P(x) = -0.02x^3 + 0.1x^2 - 0.2x + 1.66$, which passes through the four points $(1, 1.54)$, $(2, 1.5)$, $(3, 1.42)$, and $(5, 0.66)$.
   (a) Find $P(4)$.
   (b) Find $P'(4)$.
   (c) Find the definite integral of $P(x)$ taken over $[1, 4]$.
   (d) Find the extrapolated value $P(5.5)$.
   (e) Show how to find the coefficients of $P(x)$.

2. Consider $P(x) = -0.04x^3 + 0.14x^2 - 0.16x + 2.08$, which passes through the four points $(0, 2.08)$, $(1, 2.02)$, $(2, 2.00)$, and $(4, 1.12)$.
   (a) Find $P(3)$.
   (b) Find $P'(3)$.
   (c) Find the definite integral of $P(x)$ taken over $[0, 3]$.
   (d) Find the extrapolated value $P(4.5)$.
   (e) Show how to find the coefficients of $P(x)$.

3. Consider $P(x) = -0.0292166667x^3 + 0.275x^2 - 0.570833333x + 1.375$, which passes through the four points $(1, 1.05)$, $(2, 1.10)$, $(3, 1.35)$, and $(5, 1.75)$.
   (a) Show that the ordinates 1.05, 1.10, 1.35, and 1.75 differ from those of Example 4.4 by less than 1.8%, yet the coefficients of x^3 and x differ by more than 42%.
   (b) Find $P(4)$ and compare with Example 4.4.
   (c) Find $P'(4)$ and compare with Example 4.4.
   (d) Find the definite integral of $P(x)$ taken over $[1, 4]$ and compare with Example 4.4.
   (e) Find the extrapolated value $P(5.5)$ and compare with Example 4.4.

   Remark. Part (a) shows that the computation of the coefficients of an interpolating polynomial is an ill-conditioned problem.

Algorithms and Programs

1. Write a program in MATLAB that will implement Algorithm 4.1. The program should accept the coefficients of the polynomial $P(x) = a_N x^N + a_{N-1} x^{N-1} + \cdots + a_2 x^2 + a_1 x + a_0$ as an $1 \times N$ matrix: $P = \begin{bmatrix} a_N & a_{N-1} & \cdots & a_2 & a_1 & a_0 \end{bmatrix}$.

2. For each of the given functions, the fifth-degree polynomial $P(x)$ passes through the six points $(0, f(0))$, $(0.2, f(0.2))$, $(0.4, f(0.4))$, $(0.6, f(0.6))$, $(0.8, f(0.8))$, $(1, f(1))$. The six coefficients of $P(x)$ are $a_0, a_1, \ldots, a_5$, where

$$P(x) = a_5 x^5 + a_4 x^4 + a_3 x^3 + a_2 x^2 + a_1 x + a_0.$$

(i) Find the coefficients of $P(x)$ by solving the 6×6 system of linear equations

$$a_0 + a_1 x + a_2 x^2 + a_3 x^3 + a_4 x^4 + a_5 x^5 = f(x_j)$$

using $x_j = (j - 1)/5$ and $j = 1, 2, 3, 4, 5, 6$ for the six unknowns $\{a_k\}_{k=0}^{5}$.

(ii) Use your MATLAB program from Problem 1 to compute the interpolated values $P(0.3)$, $P(0.4)$, and $P(0.5)$ and compare with $f(0.3)$, $f(0.4)$, and $f(0.5)$, respectively.

(iii) Use your MATLAB program to compute the extrapolated values $P(-0.1)$ and $P(1.1)$ and compare with $f(-0.1)$ and $f(1.1)$, respectively.

(iv) Use your MATLAB program to find the integral of $P(x)$ taken over $[0, 1]$ and compare with the integral of $f(x)$ taken over $[0, 1]$. Plot $f(x)$ and $P(x)$ over $[0, 1]$ on the same graph.

(v) Make a table of values for $P(x_k)$, $f(x_k)$, and $E(x_k) = f(x_k) - P(x_k)$, where $x_k = k/100$ for $k = 0, 1, \ldots, 100$.

  (a) $f(x) = e^x$

  (b) $f(x) = \sin(x)$

  (c) $f(x) = (x + 1)^{(x+1)}$

3. A portion of an amusement park ride is to be modeled using three polynomials. The first section is to be a first-degree polynomial, $P_1(x)$, that covers a horizontal distance of 100 feet, starts at a height of 110 feet, and ends at a height of 60 feet. The third section is also to be a first-degree polynomial, $Q_1(x)$, that covers a horizontal distance of 50 feet, starts at a height of 65 feet, and ends at a height of 70 feet. The middle section is to be a polynomial, $P(x)$ (of smallest possible degree), that covers a horizontal distance of 150 feet.

  (a) Find expressions for $P(x)$, $P_1(x)$, and $Q_1(x)$ such that $P(100) = P_1(100)$, $P'(100) = P_1'(100)$, $P(250) = Q_1(250)$, and $P'(250) = Q_1'(250)$ and the curvature of $P(x)$ equals the curvature of $P_1(x)$ at $x = 100$ and equals the curvature of $Q_1(x)$ at $x = 250$.

  (b) Plot the graphs of $P_1(x)$, $P(x)$, and $Q_1(x)$ on the same coordinate system.

  (c) Use Algorithm 4.1(iii) to find the average height of the ride over the given horizontal distance.

4.3   Lagrange Approximation

Interpolation means to estimate a missing function value by taking a weighted average of known function values at neighboring points. Linear interpolation uses a line segment that passes through two points. The slope between (x_0, y_0) and (x_1, y_1) is $m = (y_1 - y_0)/(x_1 - x_0)$, and the point-slope formula for the line $y = m(x - x_0) + y_0$ can be rearranged as

(1)
$$y = P(x) = y_0 + (y_1 - y_0)\frac{x - x_0}{x_1 - x_0}.$$

When formula (1) is expanded, the result is a polynomial of degree ≤ 1. Evaluation of $P(x)$ at x_0 and x_1 produces y_0 and y_1, respectively:

(2)
$$P(x_0) = y_0 + (y_1 - y_0)(0) = y_0,$$
$$P(x_1) = y_0 + (y_1 - y_0)(1) = y_1.$$

The French mathematician Joseph Louis Lagrange used a slightly different method to find this polynomial. He noticed that it could be written as

(3)
$$y = P_1(x) = y_0 \frac{x - x_1}{x_0 - x_1} + y_1 \frac{x - x_0}{x_1 - x_0}.$$

Each term on the right side of (3) involves a linear factor; hence the sum is a polynomial of degree ≤ 1. The quotients in (3) are denoted by

(4)
$$L_{1,0}(x) = \frac{x - x_1}{x_0 - x_1} \quad \text{and} \quad L_{1,1}(x) = \frac{x - x_0}{x_1 - x_0}.$$

Computation reveals that $L_{1,0}(x_0) = 1$, $L_{1,0}(x_1) = 0$, $L_{1,1}(x_0) = 0$, and $L_{1,1}(x_1) = 1$ so that the polynomial $P_1(x)$ in (3) also passes through the two given points:

(5)
$$P_1(x_0) = y_0 + y_1(0) = y_0 \quad \text{and} \quad P_1(x_1) = y_0(0) + y_1 = y_1.$$

The terms $L_{1,0}(x)$ and $L_{1,1}(x)$ in (4) are called **Lagrange coefficient polynomials** based on the nodes x_0 and x_1. Using this notation, (3) can be written in summation form

(6)
$$P_1(x) = \sum_{k=0}^{1} y_k L_{1,k}(x).$$

Suppose that the ordinates y_k are computed with the formula $y_k = f(x_k)$. If $P_1(x)$ is used to approximate $f(x)$ over the interval $[x_0, x_1]$, we call the process **interpolation**. If $x < x_0$ (or $x_1 < x$), then using $P_1(x)$ is called **extrapolation**. The next example illustrates these concepts.

Example 4.6.   Consider the graph $y = f(x) = \cos(x)$ over $[0.0, 1.2]$.

(a) Use the nodes $x_0 = 0.0$ and $x_1 = 1.2$ to construct a linear interpolation polynomial $P_1(x)$.

(b) Use the nodes $x_0 = 0.2$ and $x_1 = 1.0$ to construct a linear approximating polynomial $Q_1(x)$.

(a) Using (3) with the abscissas $x_0 = 0.0$ and $x_1 = 1.2$ and the ordinates $y_0 = \cos(0.0) = 1.000000$ and $y_1 = \cos(1.2) = 0.362358$ produces

$$P_1(x) = 1.000000 \frac{x - 1.2}{0.0 - 1.2} + 0.362358 \frac{x - 0.0}{1.2 - 0.0}$$
$$= -0.833333(x - 1.2) + 0.301965(x - 0.0).$$

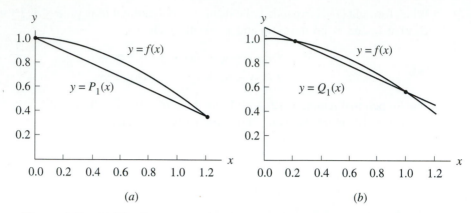

Figure 4.11   (a) The linear approximation $y = P_1(x)$ where the nodes $x_0 = 0.0$ and $x_1 = 1.2$ are the endpoints of the interval $[a, b]$. (b) The linear approximation $y = Q_1(x)$ where the nodes $x_0 = 0.2$ and $x_1 = 1.0$ lie inside the interval $[a, b]$.

(b) When the nodes $x_0 = 0.2$ and $x_1 = 1.0$ with $y_0 = \cos(0.2) = 0.980067$ and $y_1 = \cos(1.0) = 0.540302$ are used, the result is

$$Q_1(x) = 0.980067\frac{x - 1.0}{0.2 - 1.0} + 0.540302\frac{x - 0.2}{1.0 - 0.2}$$
$$= -1.225083(x - 1.0) + 0.675378(x - 0.2).$$

Figure 4.11(a) and (b) show the graph of $y = \cos(x)$ and compare it with $y = P_1(x)$ and $y = Q_1(x)$, respectively. Numerical computations are given in Table 4.6 and reveal that $Q_1(x)$ has less error at the points x_k that satisfy $0.1 \leq x_k \leq 1.1$. The largest tabulated error, $f(0.6) - P_1(0.6) = 0.144157$, is reduced to $f(0.6) - Q_1(0.6) = 0.065151$ by using $Q_1(x)$. ∎

The generalization of (6) is the construction of a polynomial $P_N(x)$ of degree at most N that passes through the $N + 1$ points $(x_0, y_0), (x_1, y_1), \ldots, (x_N, y_N)$ and has the form

(7)
$$P_N(x) = \sum_{k=0}^{N} y_k L_{N,k}(x),$$

where $L_{N,k}$ is the Lagrange coefficient polynomial based on these nodes:

(8)
$$L_{N,k}(x) = \frac{(x - x_0) \cdots (x - x_{k-1})(x - x_{k+1}) \cdots (x - x_N)}{(x_k - x_0) \cdots (x_k - x_{k-1})(x_k - x_{k+1}) \cdots (x_k - x_N)}.$$

It is understood that the terms $(x - x_k)$ and $(x_k - x_k)$ do not appear on the right side of

Table 4.6   Comparison of $f(x) = \cos(x)$ and the Linear Approximations $P_1(x)$ and $Q_1(x)$

x_k	$f(x_k) = \cos(x_k)$	$P_1(x_k)$	$f(x_k) - P_1(x_k)$	$Q_1(x_k)$	$f(x_k) - Q_1(x_k)$
0.0	1.000000	1.000000	0.000000	1.090008	−0.090008
0.1	0.995004	0.946863	0.048141	1.035037	−0.040033
0.2	0.980067	0.893726	0.086340	0.980067	0.000000
0.3	0.955336	0.840589	0.114747	0.925096	0.030240
0.4	0.921061	0.787453	0.133608	0.870126	0.050935
0.5	0.877583	0.734316	0.143267	0.815155	0.062428
0.6	0.825336	0.681179	0.144157	0.760184	0.065151
0.7	0.764842	0.628042	0.136800	0.705214	0.059628
0.8	0.696707	0.574905	0.121802	0.650243	0.046463
0.9	0.621610	0.521768	0.099842	0.595273	0.026337
1.0	0.540302	0.468631	0.071671	0.540302	0.000000
1.1	0.453596	0.415495	0.038102	0.485332	−0.031736
1.2	0.362358	0.362358	0.000000	0.430361	−0.068003

equation (8). It is appropriate to introduce the product notation for (8), and we write

(9)
$$L_{N,k}(x) = \frac{\prod_{\substack{j=0 \\ j \neq k}}^{N}(x - x_j)}{\prod_{\substack{j=0 \\ j \neq k}}^{N}(x_k - x_j)}.$$

Here the notation in (9) indicates that in the numerator the product of the linear factors $(x - x_j)$ is to be formed, but the factor $(x - x_k)$ is to be left out (or skipped). A similar construction occurs in the denominator.

A straightforward calculation shows that for each fixed k, the Lagrange coefficient polynomial $L_{N,k}(x)$ has the property

(10) $L_{N,k}(x_j) = 1$ when $j = k$ and $L_{N,k}(x_j) = 0$ when $j \neq k$.

Then direct substitution of these values into (7) is used to show that the polynomial curve $y = P_N(x)$ goes through (x_j, y_j):

(11)
$$\begin{aligned} P_N(x_j) &= y_0 L_{N,0}(x_j) + \cdots + y_j L_{N,j}(x_j) + \cdots + y_N L_{N,N}(x_j) \\ &= y_0(0) + \cdots + y_j(1) + \cdots + y_N(0) = y_j. \end{aligned}$$

To show that $P_N(x)$ is unique, we invoke the fundamental theorem of algebra, which states that a nonzero polynomial $T(x)$ of degree $\leq N$ has at most N roots. In other words, if $T(x)$ is zero at $N + 1$ distinct abscissas, it is identically zero. Suppose that $P_N(x)$ is not unique and that there exists another polynomial $Q_N(x)$ of degree $\leq N$ that also passes through the $N+1$ points. Form the difference polynomial $T(x) =$

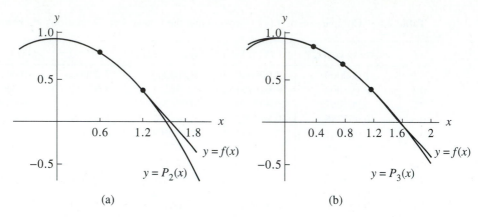

Figure 4.12 (a) The quadratic approximation polynomial $y = P_2(x)$ based on the nodes $x_0 = 0.0$, $x_1 = 0.6$, and $x_2 = 1.2$. (b) The cubic approximation polynomial $y = P_3(x)$ based on the nodes $x_0 = 0.0$, $x_1 = 0.4$, $x_2 = 0.8$, and $x_3 = 1.2$.

$P_N(x) - Q_N(x)$. Observe that the polynomial $T(x)$ has degree $\leq N$ and that $T(x_j) = P_N(x_j) - Q_N(x_j) = y_j - y_j = 0$, for $j = 0, 1, \ldots, N$. Therefore, $T(x) \equiv 0$ and it follows that $Q_N(x) = P_N(x)$.

When (7) is expanded, the result is similar to (3). The Lagrange quadratic interpolating polynomial through the three points (x_0, y_0), (x_1, y_1), and (x_2, y_2) is

$$(12) \quad P_2(x) = y_0 \frac{(x - x_1)(x - x_2)}{(x_0 - x_1)(x_0 - x_2)} + y_1 \frac{(x - x_0)(x - x_2)}{(x_1 - x_0)(x_1 - x_2)} + y_2 \frac{(x - x_0)(x - x_1)}{(x_2 - x_0)(x_2 - x_1)}.$$

The Lagrange cubic interpolating polynomial through the four points (x_0, y_0), (x_1, y_1), (x_2, y_2), and (x_3, y_3) is

$$(13) \quad \begin{aligned} P_3(x) = {} & y_0 \frac{(x - x_1)(x - x_2)(x - x_3)}{(x_0 - x_1)(x_0 - x_2)(x_0 - x_3)} + y_1 \frac{(x - x_0)(x - x_2)(x - x_3)}{(x_1 - x_0)(x_1 - x_2)(x_1 - x_3)} \\ & + y_2 \frac{(x - x_0)(x - x_1)(x - x_3)}{(x_2 - x_0)(x_2 - x_1)(x_2 - x_3)} + y_3 \frac{(x - x_0)(x - x_1)(x - x_2)}{(x_3 - x_0)(x_3 - x_1)(x_3 - x_2)}. \end{aligned}$$

Example 4.7. Consider $y = f(x) = \cos(x)$ over $[0.0, 1.2]$.

(a) Use the three nodes $x_0 = 0.0$, $x_1 = 0.6$, and $x_2 = 1.2$ to construct a quadratic interpolation polynomial $P_2(x)$.

(b) Use the four nodes $x_0 = 0.0$, $x_1 = 0.4$, $x_2 = 0.8$, and $x_3 = 1.2$ to construct a cubic interpolation polynomial $P_3(x)$.

(a) Using $x_0 = 0.0$, $x_1 = 0.6$, $x_2 = 1.2$ and $y_0 = \cos(0.0) = 1$, $y_1 = \cos(0.6) =$

0.825336, and $y_2 = \cos(1.2) = 0.362358$ in equation (12) produces

$$P_2(x) = 1.0\frac{(x - 0.6)(x - 1.2)}{(0.0 - 0.6)(0.0 - 1.2)} + 0.825336\frac{(x - 0.0)(x - 1.2)}{(0.6 - 0.0)(0.6 - 1.2)}$$
$$+ 0.362358\frac{(x - 0.0)(x - 0.6)}{(1.2 - 0.0)(1.2 - 0.6)}$$
$$= 1.388889(x - 0.6)(x - 1.2) - 2.292599(x - 0.0)(x - 1.2)$$
$$+ 0.503275(x - 0.0)(x - 0.6).$$

(b) Using $x_0 = 0.0$, $x_1 = 0.4$, $x_2 = 0.8$, $x_3 = 1.2$ and $y_0 = \cos(0.0) = 1.0$, $y_1 = \cos(0.4) = 0.921061$, $y_2 = \cos(0.8) = 0.696707$, and $y_3 = \cos(1.2) = 0.362358$ in equation (13) produces

$$P_3(x) = 1.000000\frac{(x - 0.4)(x - 0.8)(x - 1.2)}{(0.0 - 0.4)(0.0 - 0.8)(0.0 - 1.2)}$$
$$+ 0.921061\frac{(x - 0.0)(x - 0.8)(x - 1.2)}{(0.4 - 0.0)(0.4 - 0.8)(0.4 - 1.2)}$$
$$+ 0.696707\frac{(x - 0.0)(x - 0.4)(x - 1.2)}{(0.8 - 0.0)(0.8 - 0.4)(0.8 - 1.2)}$$
$$+ 0.362358\frac{(x - 0.0)(x - 0.4)(x - 0.8)}{(1.2 - 0.0)(1.2 - 0.4)(1.2 - 0.8)}$$
$$= -2.604167(x - 0.4)(x - 0.8)(x - 1.2)$$
$$+ 7.195789(x - 0.0)(x - 0.8)(x - 1.2)$$
$$- 5.443021(x - 0.0)(x - 0.4)(x - 1.2)$$
$$+ 0.943641(x - 0.0)(x - 0.4)(x - 0.8).$$

The graphs of $y = \cos(x)$ and the polynomials $y = P_2(x)$ and $y = P_3(x)$ are shown in Figure 4.12(a) and (b), respectively.   ∎

Error Terms and Error Bounds

It is important to understand the nature of the error term when the Lagrange polynomial is used to approximate a continuous function $f(x)$. It is similar to the error term for the Taylor polynomial, except that the factor $(x - x_0)^{N+1}$ is replaced with the product $(x - x_0)(x - x_1) \cdots (x - x_N)$. This is expected because interpolation is exact at each of the $N + 1$ nodes x_k, where we have $E_N(x_k) = f(x_k) - P_N(x_k) = y_k - y_k = 0$ for $k = 0, 1, 2, \ldots, N$.

Theorem 4.3 (Lagrange Polynomial Approximation). Assume that $f \in C^{N+1}[a, b]$ and that $x_0, x_1, \ldots, x_N \in [a, b]$ are $N + 1$ nodes. If $x \in [a, b]$, then

(14) $$f(x) = P_N(x) + E_N(x),$$

where $P_N(x)$ is a polynomial that can be used to approximate $f(x)$:

$$(15) \qquad f(x) \approx P_N(x) = \sum_{k=0}^{N} f(x_k) L_{N,k}(x).$$

The error term $E_N(x)$ has the form

$$(16) \qquad E_N(x) = \frac{(x - x_0)(x - x_1) \cdots (x - x_N) f^{(N+1)}(c)}{(N + 1)!}$$

for some value $c = c(x)$ that lies in the interval $[a, b]$.

Proof.   As an example of the general method, we establish (16) when $N = 1$. The general case is discussed in the exercises. Start by defining the special function $g(t)$ as follows:

$$(17) \qquad g(t) = f(t) - P_1(t) - E_1(x) \frac{(t - x_0)(t - x_1)}{(x - x_0)(x - x_1)}.$$

Notice that x, x_0, and x_1 are constants with respect to the variable t and that $g(t)$ evaluates to be zero at these three values; that is,

$$g(x) = f(x) - P_1(x) - E_1(x) \frac{(x - x_0)(x - x_1)}{(x - x_0)(x - x_1)} = f(x) - P_1(x) - E_1(x) = 0,$$

$$g(x_0) = f(x_0) - P_1(x_0) - E_1(x) \frac{(x_0 - x_0)(x_0 - x_1)}{(x - x_0)(x - x_1)} = f(x_0) - P_1(x_0) = 0,$$

$$g(x_1) = f(x_1) - P_1(x_1) - E_1(x) \frac{(x_1 - x_0)(x_1 - x_1)}{(x - x_0)(x - x_1)} = f(x_1) - P_1(x_1) = 0.$$

Suppose that x lies in the open interval (x_0, x_1). Applying Rolle's theorem to $g(t)$ on the interval $[x_0, x]$ produces a value d_0, with $x_0 < d_0 < x$, such that

$$(18) \qquad g'(d_0) = 0.$$

A second application of Rolle's theorem to $g(t)$ on $[x, x_1]$ will produce a value d_1, with $x < d_1 < x_1$, such that

$$(19) \qquad g'(d_1) = 0.$$

Equations (18) and (19) show that the function $g'(t)$ is zero at $t = d_0$ and $t = d_1$. A third use of Rolle's theorem, but this time applied to $g'(t)$ over $[d_0, d_1]$, produces a value c for which

$$(20) \qquad g^{(2)}(c) = 0.$$

Now go back to (17) and compute the derivatives $g'(t)$ and $g''(t)$:

$$(21) \qquad g'(t) = f'(t) - P_1'(t) - E_1(x)\frac{(t-x_0) + (t-x_1)}{(x-x_0)(x-x_1)},$$

$$(22) \qquad g''(t) = f''(t) - 0 - E_1(x)\frac{2}{(x-x_0)(x-x_1)}.$$

In (22) we have used the fact the $P_1(t)$ is a polynomial of degree $N = 1$; hence its second derivative is $P_1''(t) \equiv 0$. Evaluation of (22) at the point $t = c$ and using (20) yields

$$(23) \qquad 0 = f''(c) - E_1(x)\frac{2}{(x-x_0)(x-x_1)}.$$

Solving (23) for $E_1(x)$ results in the desired form (16) for the remainder:

$$(24) \qquad E_1(x) = \frac{(x-x_0)(x-x_1)f^{(2)}(c)}{2!},$$

and the proof is complete.   ●

The next result addresses the special case when the nodes for the Lagrange polynomial are equally spaced $x_k = x_0 + hk$, for $k = 0, 1, \ldots, N$, and the polynomial $P_N(x)$ is used only for interpolation inside the interval $[x_0, x_N]$.

Theorem 4.4 (Error Bounds for Lagrange Interpolation, Equally Spaced Nodes).
Assume that $f(x)$ is defined on $[a, b]$, which contains equally spaced nodes $x_k = x_0 + hk$. Additionally, assume that $f(x)$ and the derivatives of $f(x)$, up to the order $N + 1$, are continuous and bounded on the special subintervals $[x_0, x_1]$, $[x_0, x_2]$, and $[x_0, x_3]$, respectively; that is,

$$(25) \qquad |f^{(N+1)}(x)| \le M_{N+1} \qquad \text{for } x_0 \le x \le x_N,$$

for $N = 1, 2, 3$. The error terms (16) corresponding to the cases $N = 1, 2$, and 3 have the following useful bounds on their magnitude:

$$(26) \qquad |E_1(x)| \le \frac{h^2 M_2}{8} \qquad \text{valid for } x \in [x_0, x_1],$$

$$(27) \qquad |E_2(x)| \le \frac{h^3 M_3}{9\sqrt{3}} \qquad \text{valid for } x \in [x_0, x_2],$$

$$(28) \qquad |E_3(x)| \le \frac{h^4 M_4}{24} \qquad \text{valid for } x \in [x_0, x_3].$$

Proof. We establish (26) and leave the others for the reader. Using the change of variables $x - x_0 = t$ and $x - x_1 = t - h$, the error term $E_1(x)$ can be written as

$$(29) \qquad E_1(x) = E_1(x_0 + t) = \frac{(t^2 - ht)f^{(2)}(c)}{2!} \qquad \text{for } 0 \le t \le h.$$

The bound for the derivative for this case is

$$(30) \qquad |f^{(2)}(c)| \leq M_2 \qquad \text{for } x_0 \leq c \leq x_1.$$

Now determine a bound for the expression $(t^2 - ht)$ in the numerator of (29); call this term $\Phi(t) = t^2 - ht$. Since $\Phi'(t) = 2t - h$, there is one critical point $t = h/2$ that is the solution to $\Phi'(t) = 0$. The extreme values of $\Phi(t)$ over $[0, h]$ occur either at an end point $\Phi(0) = 0$, $\Phi(h) = 0$ or at the critical point $\Phi(h/2) = -h^2/4$. Since the latter value is the largest, we have established the bound

$$(31) \qquad |\Phi(t)| = |t^2 - ht| \leq \frac{|-h^2|}{4} = \frac{h^2}{4} \qquad \text{for } 0 \leq t \leq h.$$

Using (30) and (31) to estimate the magnitude of the product in the numerator in (29) results in

$$(32) \qquad |E_1(x)| = \frac{|\Phi(t)||f^{(2)}(c)|}{2!} \leq \frac{h^2 M_2}{8},$$

and formula (26) is established. ●

Comparison of Accuracy and $O(h^{N+1})$

The significance of Theorem 4.4 is to understand a simple relationship between the size of the error terms for linear, quadratic, and cubic interpolation. In each case the error bound $|E_N(x)|$ depends on h in two ways. First, h^{N+1} is explicitly present so that $|E_N(x)|$ is proportional to h^{N+1}. Second, the values M_{N+1} generally depend on h and tend to $|f^{(N+1)}(x_0)|$ as h goes to zero. Therefore, as h goes to zero, $|E_N(x)|$ converges to zero with the same rapidity that h^{N+1} converges to zero. The notation $O(h^{N+1})$ is used when discussing this behavior. For example, the error bound (26) can be expressed as

$$|E_1(x)| = O(h^2) \qquad \text{valid for } x \in [x_0, x_1].$$

The notation $O(h^2)$ stands in place of $h^2 M_2/8$ in relation (26) and is meant to convey the idea that the bound for the error term is approximately a multiple of h^2; that is,

$$|E_1(x)| \leq Ch^2 \approx O(h^2).$$

As a consequence, if the derivatives of $f(x)$ are uniformly bounded on the interval $[a, b]$ and $|h| < 1$, then choosing N large will make h^{N+1} small, and the higher-degree approximating polynomial will have less error.

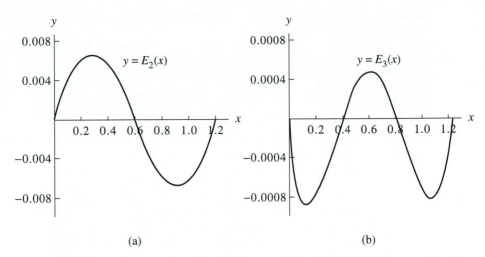

Figure 4.13   (a) The error function $E_2(x) = \cos(x) - P_2(x)$. (b) The error function $E_3(x) = \cos(x) - P_3(x)$.

Example 4.8.   Consider $y = f(x) = \cos(x)$ over [0.0, 1.2]. Use formulas (26) through (28) and determine the error bounds for the Lagrange polynomials $P_1(x)$, $P_2(x)$, and $P_3(x)$ that were constructed in Examples 4.6 and 4.7.

First, determine the bounds M_2, M_3, and M_4 for the derivatives $|f^{(2)}(x)|$, $|f^{(3)}(x)|$, and $|f^{(4)}(x)|$, respectively, taken over the interval [0.0, 1.2]:

$$|f^{(2)}(x)| = |-\cos(x)| \le |-\cos(0.0)| = 1.000000 = M_2,$$
$$|f^{(3)}(x)| = |\sin(x)| \le |\sin(1.2)| = 0.932039 = M_3,$$
$$|f^{(4)}(x)| = |\cos(x)| \le |\cos(0.0)| = 1.000000 = M_4.$$

For $P_1(x)$ the spacing of the nodes is $h = 1.2$, and its error bound is

$$(33) \qquad |E_1(x)| \le \frac{h^2 M_2}{8} \le \frac{(1.2)^2(1.000000)}{8} = 0.180000.$$

For $P_2(x)$ the spacing of the nodes is $h = 0.6$, and its error bound is

$$(34) \qquad |E_2(x)| \le \frac{h^3 M_3}{9\sqrt{3}} \le \frac{(0.6)^3(0.932039)}{9\sqrt{3}} = 0.012915.$$

For $P_3(x)$ the spacing of the nodes is $h = 0.4$, and its error bound is

$$(35) \qquad |E_3(x)| \le \frac{h^4 M_4}{24} \le \frac{(0.4)^4(1.000000)}{24} = 0.001067. \qquad\blacksquare$$

From Example 4.6 we saw that $|E_1(0.6)| = |\cos(0.6) - P_1(0.6)| = 0.144157$, so the bound 0.180000 in (33) is reasonable. The graphs of the error functions $E_2(x) = \cos(x) - P_2(x)$ and $E_3(x) = \cos(x) - P_3(x)$ are shown in Figure 4.13(a) and (b),

Table 4.7 Comparison of $f(x) = \cos(x)$ and the Quadratic and Cubic Polynomial Approximations $P_2(x)$ and $P_3(x)$

x_k	$f(x_k) = \cos(x_k)$	$P_2(x_k)$	$E_2(x_k)$	$P_3(x_k)$	$E_3(x_k)$
0.0	1.000000	1.000000	0.0	1.000000	0.0
0.1	0.995004	0.990911	0.004093	0.995835	−0.000831
0.2	0.980067	0.973813	0.006253	0.980921	−0.000855
0.3	0.955336	0.948707	0.006629	0.955812	−0.000476
0.4	0.921061	0.915592	0.005469	0.921061	0.0
0.5	0.877583	0.874468	0.003114	0.877221	0.000361
0.6	0.825336	0.825336	0.0	0.824847	0.00089
0.7	0.764842	0.768194	−0.003352	0.764491	0.000351
0.8	0.696707	0.703044	−0.006338	0.696707	0.0
0.9	0.621610	0.629886	−0.008276	0.622048	−0.000438
1.0	0.540302	0.548719	−0.008416	0.541068	−0.000765
1.1	0.453596	0.459542	−0.005946	0.454320	−0.000724
1.2	0.362358	0.362358	0.0	0.362358	0.0

respectively, and numerical computations are given in Table 4.7. Using values in the table, we find that $|E_2(1.0)| = |\cos(1.0) - P_2(1.0)| = 0.008416$ and $|E_3(0.2)| = |\cos(0.2) - P_3(0.2)| = 0.000855$, which is in reasonable agreement with the bounds 0.012915 and 0.001607 given in (34) and (35), respectively.

MATLAB

The following program finds the collocation polynomial through a given set of points by constructing a vector whose entries are the coefficients of the Lagrange interpolatory polynomial. The program uses the commands poly and conv. The poly command creates a vector whose entries are the coefficients of a polynomial with specified roots. The conv commands produces a vector whose entries are the coefficients of a polynomial that is the product of two other polynomials.

Example 4.9. Find the product of two first-degree polynomials, $P(x)$ and $Q(x)$, with roots 2 and 3, respectively.

```
>>P=poly(2)
P=
    1 -2
>>Q=poly(3)
Q=
    1 -3
>>conv(P,Q)
ans=
    1 -5 6
```

Thus the product of $P(x)$ and $Q(x)$ is $x^2 - 5x + 6$. ∎

Program 4.1 (Lagrange Approximation). To evaluate the Lagrange polynomial $P(x) = \sum_{k=0}^{N} y_k L_{N,k}(x)$ based on $N+1$ points (x_k, y_k) for $k = 0, 1, \ldots, N$.

```
function [C,L]=lagran(X,Y)

%Input   - X is a vector that contains a list of abscissas
%         - Y is a vector that contains a list of ordinates
%Output - C is a matrix that contains the coefficients of
%           the Lagrange interpolatory polynomial
%         - L is a matrix that contains the Lagrange
%           coefficient polynomials
w=length(X);
n=w-1;
L=zeros(w,w);
%Form the Lagrange coefficient polynomials
for k=1:n+1
    V=1;
    for j=1:n+1
    if k~=j
    V=conv(V,poly(X(j)))/(X(k)-X(j));
    end
end
    L(k,:)=V;
end
%Determine the coefficients of the Lagrange interpolating
%polynomial
C=Y*L;
```

Exercises for Lagrange Approximation

1. Find Lagrange polynomials that approximate $f(x) = x^3$.
    (a) Find the linear interpolation polynomial $P_1(x)$ using the nodes $x_0 = -1$ and $x_1 = 0$.
    (b) Find the quadratic interpolation polynomial $P_2(x)$ using the nodes $x_0 = -1$, $x_1 = 0$, and $x_2 = 1$.
    (c) Find the cubic interpolation polynomial $P_3(x)$ using the nodes $x_0 = -1$, $x_1 = 0$, $x_2 = 1$, and $x_3 = 2$.
    (d) Find the linear interpolation polynomial $P_1(x)$ using the nodes $x_0 = 1$ and $x_1 = 2$.
    (e) Find the quadratic interpolation polynomial $P_2(x)$ using the nodes $x_0 = 0$, $x_1 = 1$, and $x_2 = 2$.

2. Let $f(x) = x + 2/x$.

(a) Use quadratic Lagrange interpolation based on the nodes $x_0 = 1$, $x_1 = 2$, and $x_2 = 2.5$ to approximate $f(1.5)$ and $f(1.2)$.

(b) Use cubic Lagrange interpolation based on the nodes $x_0 = 0.5$, $x_1 = 1$, $x_2 = 2$, and $x_3 = 2.5$ to approximate $f(1.5)$ and $f(1.2)$.

3. Let $f(x) = 2\sin(\pi x/6)$, where x is in radians.

(a) Use quadratic Lagrange interpolation based on the nodes $x_0 = 0$, $x_1 = 1$, and $x_2 = 3$ to approximate $f(2)$ and $f(2.4)$.

(b) Use cubic Lagrange interpolation based on the nodes $x_0 = 0$, $x_1 = 1$, $x_2 = 3$, and $x_3 = 5$ to approximate $f(2)$ and $f(2.4)$.

4. Let $f(x) = 2\sin(\pi x/6)$, where x is in radians.

(a) Use quadratic Lagrange interpolation based on the nodes $x_0 = 0$, $x_1 = 1$, and $x_2 = 3$ to approximate $f(4)$ and $f(3.5)$.

(b) Use cubic Lagrange interpolation based on the nodes $x_0 = 0$, $x_1 = 1$, $x_2 = 3$, and $x_3 = 5$ to approximate $f(4)$ and $f(3.5)$.

5. Write down the error term $E_3(x)$ for cubic Lagrange interpolation to $f(x)$, where interpolation is to be exact at the four nodes $x_0 = -1$, $x_1 = 0$, $x_2 = 3$, and $x_4 = 4$ and $f(x)$ is given by

(a) $f(x) = 4x^3 - 3x + 2$

(b) $f(x) = x^4 - 2x^3$

(c) $f(x) = x^5 - 5x^4$

6. Let $f(x) = x^x$.

(a) Find the quadratic Lagrange polynomial $P_2(x)$ using the nodes $x_0 = 1$, $x_1 = 1.25$, and $x_2 = 1.5$.

(b) Use the polynomial from part (a) to estimate the average value of $f(x)$ over the interval $[1, 1.5]$.

(c) Use expression (27) of Theorem 4.4 to obtain a bound on the error in approximating $f(x)$ with $P_2(x)$.

7. Consider the Lagrange coefficient polynomials $L_{2,k}(x)$ that are used for quadratic interpolation at the nodes x_0, x_1, and x_2. Define $g(x) = L_{2,0}(x) + L_{2,1}(x) + L_{2,2}(x) - 1$.

(a) Show that g is a polynomial of degree ≤ 2.

(b) Show that $g(x_k) = 0$ for $k = 0, 1, 2$.

(c) Show that $g(x) = 0$ for all x. *Hint.* Use the fundamental theorem of algebra.

8. Let $L_{N,0}(x)$, $L_{N,1}(x)$, ..., and $L_{N,N}(x)$ be the Lagrange coefficient polynomials based on the $N + 1$ nodes $x_0, x_1, \ldots$, and x_N. Show that $\sum_{k=0}^{N} L_{N,k}(x) = 1$ for any real number x.

9. Let $f(x)$ be a polynomial of degree $\leq N$. Let $P_N(x)$ be the Lagrange polynomial of degree $\leq N$ based on the $N + 1$ nodes $x_0, x_1, \ldots, x_N$. Show that $f(x) = P_N(x)$ for all x. *Hint.* Show that the error term $E_N(x)$ is identically zero.

10. Consider the function $f(x) = \sin(x)$ on the interval $[0, 1]$. Use Theorem 4.4 to determine the step size h so that

   (a) linear Lagrange interpolation has an accuracy of 10^{-6} (i.e., find h such that $|E_1(x)| < 5 \times 10^{-7}$).

   (b) quadratic Lagrange interpolation has an accuracy of 10^{-6} (i.e., find h such that $|E_2(x)| < 5 \times 10^{-7}$).

   (c) cubic Lagrange interpolation has an accuracy of 10^{-6} (i.e., find h such that $|E_3(x)| < 5 \times 10^{-7}$).

11. Start with equation (16) and $N = 2$, and prove inequality (27). Let $x_1 = x_0 + h$, $x_2 = x_0 + 2h$. Prove that if $x_0 \le x \le x_2$, then

$$|x - x_0||x - x_1||x - x_2| \le \frac{2h^3}{3 \times 3^{1/2}}.$$

   Hint. Use the substitutions $t = x - x_1$, $t + h = x - x_0$, and $t - h = x - x_2$ and the function $v(t) = t^3 - th^2$ on the interval $-h \le t \le h$. Set $v'(t) = 0$ and solve for t in terms of h.

12. *Linear interpolation in two dimensions.* Consider the polynomial $z = P(x, y) = A + Bx + Cy$ that passes through the three points (x_0, y_0, z_0), (x_1, y_1, z_1), and (x_2, y_2, z_2). Then A, B, and C are the solution values for the linear system of equations

$$A + Bx_0 + Cy_0 = z_0$$
$$A + Bx_1 + Cy_1 = z_1$$
$$A + Bx_2 + Cy_2 = z_2.$$

   (a) Find A, B, and C so that $z = P(x, y)$ passes through the points $(1, 1, 5)$, $(2, 1, 3)$, and $(1, 2, 9)$.

   (b) Find A, B, and C so that $z = P(x, y)$ passes through the points $(1, 1, 2.5)$, $(2, 1, 0)$, and $(1, 2, 4)$.

   (c) Find A, B, and C so that $z = P(x, y)$ passes through the points $(2, 1, 5)$, $(1, 3, 7)$, and $(3, 2, 4)$.

   (d) Can values A, B, and C be found so that $z = P(x, y)$ passes through the points $(1, 2, 5)$, $(3, 2, 7)$, and $(1, 2, 0)$? Why?

13. Use Theorem 1.7, the generalized Rolle's theorem, and the special function

$$g(t) = f(t) - P_N(t) - E_n(x)\frac{(t - x_0)(t - x_1)\cdots(t - x_N)}{(x - x_0)(x - x_1)\cdots(x - x_N)},$$

   where $P_N(x)$ is the Lagrange polynomial of degree N, to prove that the error term $E_N(x) = f(x) - P_N(x)$ has the form

$$E_N(x) = (x - x_0)(x - x_1)\cdots(x - x_N)\frac{f^{(N+1)}(c)}{(N + 1)!}.$$

   Hint. Find $g^{(N+1)}(t)$ and then evaluate it at $t = c$.

Algorithms and Programs

1. Use Program 4.1 to find the coefficients of the interpolatory polynomials in Problem 2(i) (a), (b), and (c) in the Algorithms and Programs in Section 4.2. Plot the graphs of each function and the associated interpolatory polynomial on the same coordinate system.

2. The measured temperatures during a 5-hour period in a suburb of Los Angeles on November 8 are given in the following table.

   (a) Use Program 4.1 to construct a Lagrange interpolatory polynomial for the data in the table.

   (b) Use Algorithm 4.1(iii) to estimate the average temperature during the given 5-hour period.

   (c) Graph the data in the table and the polynomial from part (a) on the same coordinate system. Discuss the possible error that can result from using the polynomial in part (a) to estimate the average temperature.

Time, P.M.	Degrees Fahrenheit
1	66
2	66
3	65
4	64
5	63
6	63

4.4 Newton Polynomials

It is sometimes useful to find several approximating polynomials $P_1(x)$, $P_2(x)$, ..., $P_N(x)$ and then choose the one that suits our needs. If the Lagrange polynomials are used, there is no constructive relationship between $P_{N-1}(x)$ and $P_N(x)$. Each polynomial has to be constructed individually, and the work required to compute the higher-degree polynomials involves many computations. We take a new approach and construct Newton polynomials that have the recursive pattern

(1) $$P_1(x) = a_0 + a_1(x - x_0),$$

(2) $$P_2(x) = a_0 + a_1(x - x_0) + a_2(x - x_0)(x - x_1),$$

(3)
$$P_3(x) = a_0 + a_1(x - x_0) + a_2(x - x_0)(x - x_1)$$
$$+ a_3(x - x_0)(x - x_1)(x - x_2),$$

$$\vdots$$

(4)
$$P_N(x) = a_0 + a_1(x - x_0) + a_2(x - x_0)(x - x_1)$$
$$+ a_3(x - x_0)(x - x_1)(x - x_2)$$
$$+ a_4(x - x_0)(x - x_1)(x - x_2)(x - x_3) + \cdots$$
$$+ a_N(x - x_0) \cdots (x - x_{N-1}).$$

Here the polynomial $P_N(x)$ is obtained from $P_{N-1}(x)$ using the recursive relationship

(5) $$P_N(x) = P_{N-1}(x) + a_N(x - x_0)(x - x_1)(x - x_2) \cdots (x - x_{N-1}).$$

The polynomial (4) is said to be a Newton polynomial with N **centers** x_0, x_1, $\ldots$, x_{N-1}. It involves sums of products of linear factors up to

$$a_N(x - x_0)(x - x_1)(x - x_2) \cdots (x - x_{N-1}),$$

so $P_N(x)$ will simply be an ordinary polynomial of degree $\leq N$.

Example 4.10.   Given the centers $x_0 = 1$, $x_1 = 3$, $x_2 = 4$, and $x_3 = 4.5$ and the coefficients $a_0 = 5$, $a_1 = -2$, $a_2 = 0.5$, $a_3 = -0.1$, and $a_4 = 0.003$, find $P_1(x)$, $P_2(x)$, $P_3(x)$, and $P_4(x)$ and evaluate $P_k(2.5)$ for $k = 1, 2, 3, 4$.

Using formulas (1) through (4), we have

$$P_1(x) = 5 - 2(x - 1),$$
$$P_2(x) = 5 - 2(x - 1) + 0.5(x - 1)(x - 3),$$
$$P_3(x) = P_2(x) - 0.1(x - 1)(x - 3)(x - 4),$$
$$P_4(x) = P_3(x) + 0.003(x - 1)(x - 3)(x - 4)(x - 4.5).$$

Evaluating the polynomials at $x = 2.5$ results in

$$P_1(2.5) = 5 - 2(1.5) = 2,$$
$$P_2(2.5) = P_1(2.5) + 0.5(1.5)(-0.5) = 1.625,$$
$$P_3(2.5) = P_2(2.5) - 0.1(1.5)(-0.5)(-1.5) = 1.5125,$$
$$P_4(2.5) = P_3(2.5) + 0.003(1.5)(-0.5)(-1.5)(-2.0) = 1.50575. \qquad \blacksquare$$

Nested Multiplication

If N is fixed and the polynomial $P_N(x)$ is evaluated many times, then nested multiplication should be used. The process is similar to nested multiplication for ordinary polynomials, except that the centers x_k must be subtracted from the independent variable x. The nested multiplication form for $P_3(x)$ is

(6) $$P_3(x) = ((a_3(x - x_2) + a_2)(x - x_1) + a_1)(x - x_0) + a_0.$$

To evaluate $P_3(x)$ for a given value of x, start with the innermost grouping and form successively the quantities

(7)
$$
\begin{aligned}
S_3 &= a_3, \\
S_2 &= S_3(x - x_2) + a_2, \\
S_1 &= S_2(x - x_1) + a_1, \\
S_0 &= S_1(x - x_0) + a_0.
\end{aligned}
$$

The quantity S_0 is now $P_3(x)$.

Example 4.11. Compute $P_3(2.5)$ in Example 4.10 using nested multiplication.
Using (6), we write

$$P_3(x) = ((-0.1(x - 4) + 0.5)(x - 3) - 2)(x - 1) + 5.$$

The values in (7) are

$$
\begin{aligned}
S_3 &= -0.1, \\
S_2 &= -0.1(2.5 - 4) + 0.5 = 0.65, \\
S_1 &= 0.65(2.5 - 3) - 2 = -2.325, \\
S_0 &= -2.325(2.5 - 1) + 5 = 1.5125.
\end{aligned}
$$

Therefore, $P_3(2.5) = 1.5125.$ ∎

Polynomial Approximation, Nodes, and Centers

Suppose that we want to find the coefficients a_k for all the polynomials $P_1(x), \ldots, P_N(x)$ that approximate a given function $f(x)$. Then $P_k(x)$ will be based on the centers $x_0, x_1, \ldots, x_k$ and have the nodes $x_0, x_1, \ldots, x_{k+1}$. For the polynomial $P_1(x)$ the coefficients a_0 and a_1 have a familiar meaning. In this case

(8)
$$P_1(x_0) = f(x_0) \quad \text{and} \quad P_1(x_1) = f(x_1).$$

Using (1) and (8) to solve for a_0, we find that

(9)
$$f(x_0) = P_1(x_0) = a_0 + a_1(x_0 - x_0) = a_0.$$

Hence $a_0 = f(x_0)$. Next, using (1), (8), and (9), we have

$$f(x_1) = P_1(x_1) = a_0 + a_1(x_1 - x_0) = f(x_0) + a_1(x_1 - x_0),$$

which can be solved for a_1, and we get

(10)
$$a_1 = \frac{f(x_1) - f(x_0)}{x_1 - x_0}.$$

Hence a_1 is the slope of the secant line passing through the two points $(x_0, f(x_0))$ and $(x_1, f(x_1))$.

The coefficients a_0 and a_1 are the same for both $P_1(x)$ and $P_2(x)$. Evaluating (2) at the node x_2, we find that

(11) $f(x_2) = P_2(x_2) = a_0 + a_1(x_2 - x_0) + a_2(x_2 - x_0)(x_2 - x_1).$

The values for a_0 and a_1 in (9) and (10) can be used in (11) to obtain

$$a_2 = \frac{f(x_2) - a_0 - a_1(x_2 - x_0)}{(x_2 - x_0)(x_2 - x_1)}$$

$$= \left(\frac{f(x_2) - f(x_0)}{x_2 - x_0} - \frac{f(x_1) - f(x_0)}{x_1 - x_0} \right) \Big/ (x_2 - x_1).$$

For computational purposes we prefer to write this last quantity as

(12) $$a_2 = \left(\frac{f(x_2) - f(x_1)}{x_2 - x_1} - \frac{f(x_1) - f(x_0)}{x_1 - x_0} \right) \Big/ (x_2 - x_0).$$

The two formulas for a_2 can be shown to be equivalent by writing the quotients over the common denominator $(x_2 - x_1)(x_2 - x_0)(x_1 - x_0)$. The details are left for the reader. The numerator in (12) is the difference between the first-order divided differences. In order to proceed, we need to introduce the idea of divided differences.

Definition 4.1.   The *divided differences* for a function $f(x)$ are defined as follows:

$$f[x_k] = f(x_k),$$

$$f[x_{k-1}, x_k] = \frac{f[x_k] - f[x_{k-1}]}{x_k - x_{k-1}},$$

(13)

$$f[x_{k-2}, x_{k-1}, x_k] = \frac{f[x_{k-1}, x_k] - f[x_{k-2}, x_{k-1}]}{x_k - x_{k-2}},$$

$$f[x_{k-3}, x_{k-2}, x_{k-1}, x_k] = \frac{f[x_{k-2}, x_{k-1}, x_k] - f[x_{k-3}, x_{k-2}, x_{k-1}]}{x_k - x_{k-3}}.$$

The recursive rule for constructing higher-order divided differences is

(14) $$f[x_{k-j}, x_{k-j+1}, \ldots, x_k] = \frac{f[x_{k-j+1}, \ldots, x_k] - f[x_{k-j}, \ldots, x_{k-1}]}{x_k - x_{k-j}}$$

and is used to construct the divided differences in Table 4.8.   ▲

The coefficients a_k of $P_N(x)$ depend on the values $f(x_j)$, for $j = 0, 1, \ldots, k$. The next theorem shows that a_k can be computed using divided differences:

(15) $a_k = f[x_0, x_1, \ldots, x_k].$

Table 4.8   Divided-Difference Table for $y = f(x)$

x_k	$f[x_k]$	$f[\ ,\ ]$	$f[\ ,\ ,\ ]$	$f[\ ,\ ,\ ,\ ]$	$f[\ ,\ ,\ ,\ ,\ ]$
x_0	$f[x_0]$				
x_1	$f[x_1]$	$f[x_0, x_1]$			
x_2	$f[x_2]$	$f[x_1, x_2]$	$f[x_0, x_1, x_2]$		
x_3	$f[x_3]$	$f[x_2, x_3]$	$f[x_1, x_2, x_3]$	$f[x_0, x_1, x_2, x_3]$	
x_4	$f[x_4]$	$f[x_3, x_4]$	$f[x_2, x_3, x_4]$	$f[x_1, x_2, x_3, x_4$	$f[x_0, x_1, x_2, x_3, x_4]$

Theorem 4.5 (Newton Polynomial).   Suppose that $x_0, x_1, \ldots, x_N$ are $N+1$ distinct numbers in $[a, b]$. There exists a unique polynomial $P_N(x)$ of degree at most N with the property that

$$f(x_j) = P_N(x_j) \quad \text{for } j = 0, 1, \ldots, N.$$

The Newton form of this polynomial is

(16) $\qquad P_N(x) = a_0 + a_1(x - x_0) + \cdots + a_N(x - x_0)(x - x_1) \cdots (x - x_{N-1}),$

where $a_k = f[x_0, x_1, \ldots, x_k]$, for $k = 0, 1, \ldots, N$.

Remark. If $\{(x_j, y_j)\}_{j=0}^{N}$ is a set of points whose abscissas are distinct, the values $f(x_j) = y_j$ can be used to construct the unique polynomial of degree $\leq N$ that passes through the $N + 1$ points.

Corollary 4.2 (Newton Approximation).   Assume that $P_N(x)$ is the Newton polynomial given in Theorem 4.5 and is used to approximate the function $f(x)$, that is,

(17) $\qquad\qquad\qquad\qquad f(x) = P_N(x) + E_N(x).$

If $f \in C^{N+1}[a, b]$, then for each $x \in [a, b]$ there corresponds a number $c = c(x)$ in (a, b), so that the error term has the form

(18) $\qquad\qquad E_N(x) = \dfrac{(x - x_0)(x - x_1) \cdots (x - x_N) f^{(N+1)}(c)}{(N + 1)!}.$

Remark. The error term $E_N(x)$ is the same as the one for Lagrange interpolation, which was introduced in equation (16) of Section 4.3.

It is of interest to start with a known function $f(x)$ that is a polynomial of degree N and compute its divided-difference table. In this case we know that $f^{(N+1)}(x) = 0$ for all x, and calculation will reveal that the $(N + 1)$st divided difference is zero. This will happen because the divided difference (14) is proportional to a numerical approximation for the jth derivative.

Table 4.9   Divided-Difference Table Used for Constructing the Newton Polynomial $P_3(x)$ in Example 4.12.

x_k	$f[x_k]$	First divided difference	Second divided difference	Third divided difference	Fourth divided difference	Fifth divided difference
$x_0 = 1$	-3					
$x_1 = 2$	0	3				
$x_2 = 3$	15	15	6			
$x_3 = 4$	48	33	9	1		
$x_4 = 5$	105	57	12	1	0	
$x_5 = 6$	192	87	15	1	0	0

Table 4.10   Divided-Difference Table Used for Constructing the Newton Polynomials $P_k(x)$ in Example 4.13

x_k	$f[x_k]$	$f[\ ,\ ]$	$f[\ ,\ ,\ ]$	$f[\ ,\ ,\ ,\ ]$	$f[\ ,\ ,\ ,\ ,\ ]$
$x_0 = 0.0$	1.0000000				
$x_1 = 1.0$	0.5403023	-0.4596977			
$x_2 = 2.0$	-0.4161468	-0.9564491	-0.2483757		
$x_3 = 3.0$	-0.9899925	-0.5738457	0.1913017	0.1465592	
$x_4 = 4.0$	-0.6536436	0.3363499	0.4550973	0.0879318	-0.0146568

Example 4.12.   Let $f(x) = x^3 - 4x$. Construct the divided-difference table based on the nodes $x_0 = 1, x_1 = 2, \ldots, x_5 = 6$, and find the Newton polynomial $P_3(x)$ based on x_0, x_1, x_2, and x_3.

See Table 4.9. $\blacksquare$

The coefficients $a_0 = -3$, $a_1 = 3$, $a_2 = 6$, and $a_3 = 1$ of $P_3(x)$ appear on the diagonal of the divided-difference table. The centers $x_0 = 1$, $x_1 = 2$, and $x_2 = 3$ are the values in the first column. Using formula (3), we write

$$P_3(x) = -3 + 3(x - 1) + 6(x - 1)(x - 2) + (x - 1)(x - 2)(x - 3).$$

Example 4.13.   Construct a divided-difference table for $f(x) = \cos(x)$ based on the five points $(k, \cos(k))$, for $k = 0, 1, 2, 3, 4$. Use it to find the coefficients a_k and the four Newton interpolating polynomials $P_k(x)$, for $k = 1, 2, 3, 4$.

For simplicity we round off the values to seven decimal places, which are displayed in Table 4.10. The nodes x_0, x_1, x_2, x_3 and the diagonal elements a_0, a_1, a_2, a_3, a_4 in

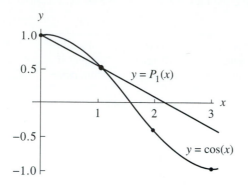

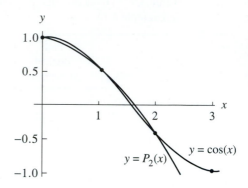

Figure 4.14 (a) The graphs of $y = \cos(x)$ and the linear Newton polynomial $y = P_1(x)$ based on the nodes $x_0 = 0.0$ and $x_1 = 1.0$.

Figure 4.14 (b) The graphs of $y = \cos(x)$ and the quadratic Newton polynomial $y = P_2(x)$ based on the nodes $x_0 = 0.0$, $x_1 = 1.0$, and $x_2 = 2.0$.

Table 4.10 are used in formula (16), and we write down the first four Newton polynomials:

$$P_1(x) = 1.0000000 - 0.4596977(x - 0.0),$$
$$P_2(x) = 1.0000000 - 0.4596977(x - 0.0) - 0.2483757(x - 0.0)(x - 1.0),$$
$$P_3(x) = 1.0000000 - 0.4596977(x - 0.0) - 0.2483757(x - 0.0)(x - 1.0)$$
$$+ 0.1465592(x - 0.0)(x - 1.0)(x - 2.0),$$
$$P_4(x) = 1.0000000 - 0.4596977(x - 0.0) - 0.2483757(x - 0.0)(x - 1.0)$$
$$+ 0.1465592(x - 0.0)(x - 1.0)(x - 2.0)$$
$$- 0.0146568(x - 0.0)(x - 1.0)(x - 2.0)(x - 3.0).$$

The following sample calculation shows how to find the coefficient a_2.

$$f[x_0, x_1] = \frac{f[x_1] - f[x_0]}{x_1 - x_0} = \frac{0.5403023 - 10000000}{1.0 - 0.0} = -0.4596977,$$
$$f[x_1, x_2] = \frac{f[x_2] - f[x_1]}{x_2 - x_1} = \frac{-0.4161468 - 0.5403023}{2.0 - 1.0} = -0.9564491,$$
$$a_2 = f[x_0, x_1, x_2] = \frac{f[x_1, x_2] - f[x_0, x_1]}{x_2 - x_0} = \frac{-0.9564491 + 0.4596977}{2.0 - 0.0} = -0.2483757.$$

The graphs of $y = \cos(x)$ and $y = P_1(x)$, $y = P_2(x)$, and $y = P_3(x)$ are shown in Figure 4.14(a), (b), and (c), respectively.

For computational purposes the divided differences in Table 4.8 need to be stored in an array which is chosen to be $D(k, j)$, so that

(19) $$D(k, j) = f[x_{k-j}, x_{k-j+1}, \ldots, x_k] \quad \text{for } j \leq k.$$

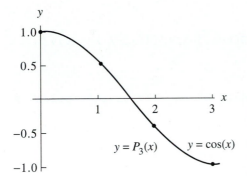

Figure 4.14 (c) The graphs of $y = \cos(x)$ and the cubic Newton polynomial $y = P_2(x)$ based on the nodes $x_0 = 0.0$, $x_1 = 1.0$, $x_2 = 2.0$, and $x_3 = 3.0$.

Relation (14) is used to obtain the formula to recursively compute the entries in the array:

$$(20) \qquad D(k, j) = \frac{D(k, j-1) - D(k-1, j-1)}{x_k - x_{k-j}}.$$

Notice that the value a_k in (15) is the diagonal element $a_k = D(k, k)$. The algorithm for computing the divided differences and evaluating $P_N(x)$ is now given. We remark that Problem 2 in Algorithms and Programs investigates how to modify the algorithm so that the values $\{a_k\}$ are computed using a one-dimensional array. ∎

Program 4.2 (Newton Interpolation Polynomial). To construct and evaluate the Newton polynomial of degree $\leq N$ that passes through $(x_k, y_k) = (x_k, f(x_k))$ for $k = 0, 1, \ldots, N$:

$$(21) \qquad \begin{aligned} P(x) = {}& d_{0,0} + d_{1,1}(x - x_0) + d_{2,2}(x - x_0)(x - x_1) \\ & + \cdots + d_{N,N}(x - x_0)(x - x_1) \cdots (x - x_{N-1}), \end{aligned}$$

where

$$d_{k,0} = y_k \quad \text{and} \quad d_{k,j} = \frac{d_{k,j-1} - d_{k-1,j-1}}{x_k - x_{k-j}}.$$

```
function [C,D]=newpoly(X,Y)
%Input   - X is a vector that contains a list of abscissas
%         - Y is a vector that contains a list of ordinates
%Output - C is a vector that contains the coefficients
%           of the Newton intepolatory polynomial
%         - D is the divided-difference table
n=length(X);
D=zeros(n,n);
D(:,1)=Y';
% Use formula (20) to form the divided-difference table
```

```
for j=2:n
    for k=j:n
        D(k,j)=(D(k,j-1)-D(k-1,j-1))/(X(k)-X(k-j+1));
    end
end

%Determine the coefficients of the Newton interpolating
%polynomial
C=D(n,n);
for k=(n-1):-1:1
    C=conv(C,poly(X(k)));
    m=length(C);
    C(m)=C(m)+D(k,k);
end
```

Exercises for Newton Polynomials

In Exercises 1 through 4, use the centers x_0, x_1, x_2, and x_3 and the coefficients a_0, a_1, a_2, a_3, and a_4 to find the Newton polynomials $P_1(x)$, $P_2(x)$, $P_3(x)$, and $P_4(x)$, and evaluate them at the value $x = c$. *Hint.* Use equations (1) through (4) and the techniques of Example 4.9.

1. $a_0 = 4$ $a_1 = -1$ $a_2 = 0.4$ $a_3 = 0.01$ $a_4 = -0.002$
   $x_0 = 1$ $x_1 = 3$ $x_2 = 4$ $x_3 = 4.5$ $c = 2.5$

2. $a_0 = 5$ $a_1 = -2$ $a_2 = 0.5$ $a_3 = -0.1$ $a_4 = 0.003$
   $x_0 = 0$ $x_1 = 1$ $x_2 = 2$ $x_3 = 3$ $c = 2.5$

3. $a_0 = 7$ $a_1 = 3$ $a_2 = 0.1$ $a_3 = 0.05$ $a_4 = -0.04$
   $x_0 = -1$ $x_1 = 0$ $x_2 = 1$ $x_3 = 4$ $c = 3$

4. $a_0 = -2$ $a_1 = 4$ $a_2 = -0.04$ $a_3 = 0.06$ $a_4 = 0.005$
   $x_0 = -3$ $x_1 = -1$ $x_2 = 1$ $x_3 = 4$ $c = 2$

In Exercises 5 through 8:

(a) Compute the divided-difference table for the tabulated function.

(b) Write down the Newton polynomials $P_1(x)$, $P_2(x)$, $P_3(x)$, and $P_4(x)$.

(c) Evaluate the Newton polynomials in part (b) at the given values of x.

(d) Compare the values in part (c) with the actual function value $f(x)$.

5. $f(x) = x^{1/2}$

  $x = 4.5, 7.5$

k	x_k	$f(x_k)$
0	4.0	2.00000
1	5.0	2.23607
2	6.0	2.44949
3	7.0	2.64575
4	8.0	2.82843

6. $f(x) = 3.6/x$

  $x = 2.5, 3.5$

k	x_k	$f(x_k)$
0	1.0	3.60
1	2.0	1.80
2	3.0	1.20
3	4.0	0.90
4	5.0	0.72

7. $f(x) = 3 \sin^2(\pi x/6)$

  $x = 1.5, 3.5$

k	x_k	$f(x_k)$
0	0.0	0.00
1	1.0	0.75
2	2.0	2.25
3	3.0	3.00
4	4.0	2.25

8. $f(x) = e^{-x}$

  $x = 0.5, 1.5$

k	x_k	$f(x_k)$
0	0.0	1.00000
1	1.0	0.36788
2	2.0	0.13534
3	3.0	0.04979
4	4.0	0.01832

9. Consider the $M + 1$ points $(x_0, y_0), \ldots, (x_M, y_M)$.

  (a) If the $(N + 1)$st divided differences are zero, then show that the $(N + 2)$nd up to the Mth divided differences are zero.

  (b) If the $(N + 1)$st divided differences are zero, then show that there exists a polynomial $P_N(x)$ of degree N such that

$$P_N(x_k) = y_k \quad \text{for } k = 0, 1, \ldots, M.$$

In Exercises 10 through 12, use the result of Exercise 9 to find the polynomial $P_N(x)$ that goes through the $M + 1$ points ($N < M$).

10.

x_k	y_k
0	−2
1	2
2	4
3	4
4	2
5	−2

11.

x_k	y_k
1	8
2	17
3	24
4	29
5	32
6	33

12.

x_k	y_k
0	5
1	5
2	3
3	5
4	17
5	45
6	95

13. Use Corollary 4.2 to find a bound on the maximum error ($|E_2(x)|$) on the interval $[0, \pi]$, when the Newton interpolatory polynomial $P_2(x)$ is used to approximate $f(x) = \cos(\pi x)$ at the centers $x_0 = 0$, $x_1 = \pi/2$, and $x_2 = \pi$.

Algorithms and Programs

1. Use Program 4.2 and repeat Problem 2 in Algorithms and Programs from Section 4.3.

2. In Program 4.2 the matrix D is used to store the divided-difference table.

   (a) Verify that the following modification of Program 4.2 is an equivalent way to compute the Newton interpolatory polynomial.

```
for k=0:N
    A(k)=Y(k);
end
for j=1:N
    for k=N:-1:j
        A(k)=(A(k)-A(k-1))/(X(k)-X(k-j));
    end
end
```

   (b) Repeat Problem 1 using this modification of Program 4.2

4.5 Chebyshev Polynomials (Optional)

We now turn our attention to polynomial interpolation for $f(x)$ over $[-1, 1]$ based on the nodes $-1 \le x_0 < x_1 < \cdots < x_N \le 1$. Both the Lagrange and Newton polynomials satisfy

$$f(x) = P_N(x) + E_N(x),$$

where

(1) $$E_N(x) = Q(x)\frac{f^{(N+1)}(c)}{(N+1)!}$$

and $Q(x)$ is the polynomial of degree $N + 1$:

(2) $$Q(x) = (x - x_0)(x - x_1) \cdots (x - x_N).$$

Using the relationship

$$|E_N(x)| \le |Q(x)|\frac{\max_{-1 \le x \le 1}\{|f^{(N+1)}(x)|\}}{(N+1)!},$$

our task is to follow Chebyshev's derivation on how to select the set of nodes $\{x_k\}_{k=0}^{N}$ that minimizes $\max_{-1 \le x \le 1}\{|Q(x)|\}$. This leads us to a discussion of Chebyshev polynomials and some of their properties. To begin, the first eight Chebyshev polynomials are listed in Table 4.11.

Table 4.11   Chebyshev Polynomials
$T_0(x)$ through $T_7(x)$

$$T_0(x) = 1$$
$$T_1(x) = x$$
$$T_2(x) = 2x^2 - 1$$
$$T_3(x) = 4x^3 - 3x$$
$$T_4(x) = 8x^4 - 8x^2 + 1$$
$$T_5(x) = 16x^5 - 20x^3 + 5x$$
$$T_6(x) = 32x^6 - 48x^4 + 18x^2 - 1$$
$$T_7(x) = 64x^7 - 112x^5 + 56x^3 - 7x$$

Properties of Chebyshev Polynomials

Property 1. Recurrence Relation

Chebyshev polynomials can be generated in the following way. Set $T_0(x) = 1$ and $T_1(x) = x$ and use the recurrence relation

$$(3) \qquad T_k(x) = 2x T_{k-1}(x) - T_{k-2}(x) \qquad \text{for } k = 2, 3, \ldots.$$

Property 2. Leading Coefficient

The coefficient of x^N in $T_N(x)$ is 2^{N-1} when $N \geq 1$.

Property 3. Symmetry

When $N = 2M$, $T_{2M}(x)$ is an even function, that is,

$$(4) \qquad\qquad\qquad T_{2M}(-x) = T_{2M}(x).$$

When $N = 2M + 1$, $T_{2M+1}(x)$ is an odd function, that is,

$$(5) \qquad\qquad\qquad T_{2M+1}(-x) = -T_{2M+1}(x).$$

Property 4. Trigonometric Representation on $[-1, 1]$

$$(6) \qquad\qquad T_N(x) = \cos(N \arccos(x)) \qquad \text{for } -1 \leq x \leq 1.$$

Property 5. Distinct Zeros in $[-1, 1]$

$T_N(x)$ has N distinct zeros x_k that lie in the interval $[-1, 1]$ (see Figure 4.15):

$$(7) \qquad\qquad x_k = \cos\left(\frac{(2k + 1)\pi}{2N}\right) \qquad \text{for } k = 0, 1, \ldots, N - 1.$$

These values are called the **Chebyshev abscissas (nodes)**.

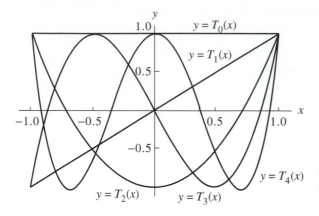

Figure 4.15 The graphs of the Chebyshev polynomials $T_0(x)$, $T_1(x)$, ..., $T_4(x)$ over $[-1, 1]$.

Property 6. Extreme Values

$$(8) \qquad\qquad |T_N(x)| \le 1 \qquad \text{for } -1 \le x \le 1.$$

Property 1 is often used as the definition for higher-order Chebyshev polynomials. Let us show that $T_3(x) = 2x T_2(x) - T_1(x)$. Using the expressions for $T_1(x)$ and $T_2(x)$ in Table 4.11, we obtain

$$2x T_2(x) - T_1(x) = 2x(2x^2 - 1) - x = 4x^3 - 3x = T_3(x).$$

Property 2 is proved by observing that the recurrence relation doubles the leading coefficient of $T_{N-1}(x)$ to get the leading coefficient of $T_N(x)$.

Property 3 is established by showing that $T_{2M}(x)$ involves only even powers of x and $T_{2M+1}(x)$ involves only odd powers of x. The details are left for the reader.

The proof of property 4 uses the trigonometric identity

$$\cos(k\theta) = \cos(2\theta)\cos((k-2)\theta) - \sin(2\theta)\sin((k-2)\theta).$$

Substitute $\cos(2\theta) = 2\cos^2(\theta) - 1$ and $\sin(2\theta) = 2\sin(\theta)\cos(\theta)$ and get

$$\cos(k\theta) = 2\cos(\theta)(\cos(\theta)\cos((k-2)\theta) - \sin(\theta)\sin((k-2)\theta)) - \cos((k-2)\theta),$$

which is simplified as

$$\cos(k\theta) = 2\cos(\theta)\cos((k-1)\theta) - \cos((k-2)\theta).$$

Finally, substitute $\theta = \arccos(x)$ and obtain

$$(9) \quad 2x\cos((k-1)\arccos(x)) - \cos((k-2)\arccos(x))$$
$$= \cos(k\arccos(x)) \qquad \text{for } -1 \le x \le 1.$$

The first two Chebyshev polynomials are $T_0(x) = \cos(0 \arccos(x)) = 1$ and $T_1(x) = \cos(1 \arccos(x)) = x$. Now assume that $T_k(x) = \cos(k \arccos(x))$ for $k = 2$, $3, \ldots, N - 1$. Formula (3) is used with (9) to establish the general case:

$$
\begin{aligned}
T_N(x) &= 2x T_{N-1}(x) - T_{N-2}(x) \\
&= 2x \cos((N-1) \arccos(x)) - \cos((N-2) \arccos(x)) \\
&= \cos(N \arccos(x)) \quad \text{for } -1 \le x \le 1.
\end{aligned}
$$

Properties 5 and 6 are consequences of property 4.

Minimax

The Russian mathematician Chebyshev studied how to minimize the upper bound for $|E_N(x)|$. One upper bound can be formed by taking the product of the maximum value of $|Q(x)|$ over all x in $[-1, 1]$ and the maximum value $|f^{(N+1)}(x)/(N+1)!|$ over all x in $[-1, 1]$. To minimize the factor $\max\{|Q(x)|\}$, Chebyshev discovered that x_0, $x_1, \ldots, x_N$ should be chosen so that $Q(x) = (1/2^N) T_{N+1}(x)$.

Theorem 4.6. Assume that N is fixed. Among all possible choices for $Q(x)$ in equation (2), and thus among all possible choices for the distinct nodes $\{x_k\}_{k=0}^{N}$ in $[-1, 1]$, the polynomial $T(x) = T_{N+1}(x)/2^N$ is the unique choice that has the property

$$
\max_{-1 \le x \le 1} \{|T(x)|\} \le \max_{-1 \le x \le 1} \{|Q(x)|\}.
$$

Moreover,

(10)
$$
\max_{-1 \le x \le 1} \{|T(x)|\} = \frac{1}{2^N}.
$$

The consequence of this result can be stated by saying that for Lagrange interpolation $f(x) = P_N(x) + E_N(x)$ on $[-1, 1]$, the minimum value of the error bound

$$
(\max\{|Q(x)|\})(\max\{|f^{(N+1)}(x)/(N+1)!|\})
$$

is achieved when the nodes $\{x_k\}$ are the Chebyshev abscissas of $T_{N+1}(x)$. As an illustration, we look at the Lagrange coefficient polynomials that are used in forming $P_3(x)$. First we use equally spaced nodes and then the Chebyshev nodes. Recall that the Lagrange polynomial of degree $N = 3$ has the form

(11) $P_3(x) = f(x_0)L_{3,0}(x) + f(x_1)L_{3,1}(x) + f(x_2)L_{3,2}(x) + f(x_3)L_{3,3}(x)$.

Equally Spaced Nodes

If $f(x)$ is approximated by a polynomial of degree at most $N = 3$ on $[-1, 1]$, the equally spaced nodes $x_0 = -1$, $x_1 = -1/3$, $x_2 = 1/3$, and $x_3 = 1$ are easy to use for calculations. Substitution of these values into formula (8) of Section 4.3 and simplifying will produce the coefficient polynomials $L_{3,k}(x)$ in Table 4.12.

Table 4.12   Lagrange Coefficient Polynomials Used to Form $P_3(x)$ Based on Equally Spaced Nodes $x_k = -1 + 2k/3$

$$L_{3,0}(x) = -0.06250000 + 0.06250000x + 0.56250000x^2 - 0.56250000x^3$$
$$L_{3,1}(x) = 0.56250000 - 1.68750000x - 0.56250000x^2 + 1.68750000x^3$$
$$L_{3,2}(x) = 0.56250000 + 1.68750000x - 0.56250000x^2 - 1.68750000x^3$$
$$L_{3,3}(x) = -0.06250000 - 0.06250000x + 0.56250000x^2 + 0.56250000x^3$$

Table 4.13   Coefficient Polynomials Used to Form $P_3(x)$ Based on the Chebyshev Nodes $x_k = \cos((7 - 2k)\pi/8)$

$$C_0(x) = -0.10355339 + 0.11208538x + 0.70710678x^2 - 0.76536686x^3$$
$$C_1(x) = 0.60355339 - 1.57716102x - 0.70710678x^2 + 1.84775906x^3$$
$$C_2(x) = 0.60355339 + 1.57716102x - 0.70710678x^2 - 1.84775906x^3$$
$$C_3(x) = -0.10355339 - 0.11208538x + 0.70710678x^2 + 0.76536686x^3$$

Chebyshev Nodes

When $f(x)$ is to be approximated by a polynomial of degree at most $N = 3$, using the Chebyshev nodes $x_0 = \cos(7\pi/8)$, $x_1 = \cos(5\pi/8)$, $x_2 = \cos(3\pi/8)$, and $x_3 = \cos(\pi/8)$, the coefficient polynomials are tedious to find (but this can be done by a computer). The results after simplification are shown in Table 4.13.

Example 4.14.   Compare the Lagrange polynomials of degree $N = 3$ for $f(x) = e^x$ that are obtained by using the coefficient polynomials in Tables 4.12 and 4.13, respectively.
Using equally spaced nodes, we get the polynomial

$$P(x) = 0.99519577 + 0.99904923x + 0.54788486x^2 + 0.17615196x^3.$$

This is obtained by finding the function values

$$f(x_0) = e^{(-1)} = 0.36787944, \qquad f(x_1) = e^{(-1/3)} = 0.71653131,$$
$$f(x_2) = e^{(1/3)} = 1.39561243, \qquad f(x_3) = e^{(1)} = 2.71828183,$$

and using the coefficient polynomials $L_{3,k}(x)$ in Table 4.12, and forming the linear combination

$$P(x) = 0.36787944L_{3,0}(x) + 0.71653131L_{3,1}(x) + 1.39561243L_{3,2}(x)$$
$$+ 2.71828183L_{3,3}(x).$$

Similarly, when the Chebyshev nodes are used, we obtain

$$V(x) = 0.99461532 + 0.99893323x + 0.54290072x^2 + 0.17517569x^3.$$

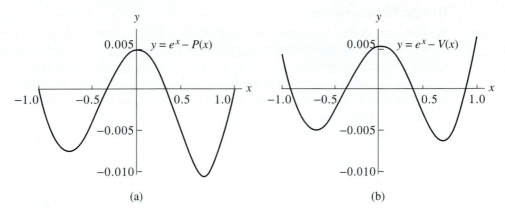

(a)   (b)

Figure 4.16   (a) The error function $y = e^x - P(x)$ for Lagrange approximation over $[-1, 1]$. (b) The error function $y = e^x - V(x)$ for Lagrange approximation over $[-1, 1]$.

Notice that the coefficients are different from those of $P(x)$. This is a consequence of using different nodes and function values:

$$f(x_0) = e^{-0.92387953} = 0.39697597,$$
$$f(x_1) = e^{-0.38268343} = 0.68202877,$$
$$f(x_2) = e^{0.38268343} = 1.46621380,$$
$$f(x_3) = e^{0.92387953} = 2.51904417.$$

Then the alternative set of coefficient polynomials $C_k(x)$ in Table 4.13 is used to form the linear combination

$$V(x) = 0.39697597 C_0(x) + 0.68202877 C_1(x) + 1.46621380 C_2(x) + 2.51904417 C_3(x).$$

For a comparison of the accuracy of $P(x)$ and $V(x)$, the error functions are graphed in Figure 4.16(a) and (b), respectively. The maximum error $|e^x - P(x)|$ occurs at $x = 0.75490129$, and

$$|e^x - P(x)| \leq 0.00998481 \quad \text{for } -1 \leq x \leq 1.$$

The maximum error $|e^x - V(x)|$ occurs at $x = 1$, and we get

$$|e^x - V(x)| \leq 0.00665687 \quad \text{for } -1 \leq x \leq 1.$$

Notice that the maximum error in $V(x)$ is about two-thirds the maximum error in $P(x)$. Also, the error is spread out more evenly over the interval.   ∎

Runge Phenomenon

We now look deeper to see the advantage of using the Chebyshev interpolation nodes. Consider Lagrange interpolating to $f(x)$ over the interval $[-1, 1]$ based on equally spaced nodes. Does the error $E_N(x) = f(x) - P_N(x)$ tend to zero as N increases? For functions like $\sin(x)$ or e^x, where all the derivatives are bounded by the same constant M, the answer is yes. In general, the answer to this question is no, and it is easy to find functions for which the sequence $\{P_N(x)\}$ does not converge. If $f(x) = 1/(1+12x^2)$, the maximum of the error term $E_N(x)$ grows when $N \to \infty$. This nonconvergence is called the **Runge phenomenon**. The Lagrange polynomial of degree 10 based on 11 equally spaced nodes for this function is shown in Figure 4.17(a). Wild oscillations occur near the end of the interval. If the number of nodes is increased, then the oscillations become larger. This problem occurs because the nodes are equally spaced!

If the Chebyshev nodes are used to construct an interpolating polynomial of degree 10 to $f(x) = 1/(1 + 12x^2)$, the error is much smaller, as seen in Figure 14.17(b). Under the condition that Chebyshev nodes be used, the error $E_N(x)$ will go to zero as $N \to \infty$. In general, if $f(x)$ and $f'(x)$ are continuous on $[-1, 1]$, then it can be proved that Chebyshev interpolation will produce a sequence of polynomials $\{P_N(x)\}$ that converges uniformly to $f(x)$ over $[-1, 1]$.

Transforming the Interval

Sometimes it is necessary to take a problem stated on an interval $[a, b]$ and reformulate the problem on the interval $[c, d]$ where the solution is known. If the approximation $P_N(x)$ to $f(x)$ is to be obtained on the interval $[a, b]$, then we change the variable so that the problem is reformulated on $[-1, 1]$:

$$(12) \qquad x = \left(\frac{b-a}{2}\right)t + \frac{a+b}{2} \qquad \text{or} \qquad t = 2\frac{x-a}{b-a} - 1,$$

where $a \le x \le b$ and $-1 \le t \le 1$.

The required Chebyshev nodes of $T_{N+1}(t)$ on $[-1, 1]$ are

$$(13) \qquad t_k = \cos\left((2N + 1 - 2k)\frac{\pi}{2N+2}\right) \qquad \text{for } k = 0, 1, \ldots, N$$

and the interpolating nodes on $[a, b]$ are obtained by using (12):

$$(14) \qquad x_k = t_k\frac{b-a}{2} + \frac{a+b}{2} \qquad \text{for } k = 0, 1, \ldots, N.$$

Theorem 4.7 (Lagrange-Chebyshev Approximation Polynomial).   Assume that $P_N(x)$ is the Lagrange polynomial that is based on the Chebyshev nodes given in (14). If $f \in C^{N+1}[a, b]$, then

$$(15) \qquad |f(x) - P_N(x)| \le \frac{2(b-a)^{N+1}}{4^{N+1}(N+1)!} \max_{a \le x \le b}\{|f^{(N+1)}(x)|\}.$$

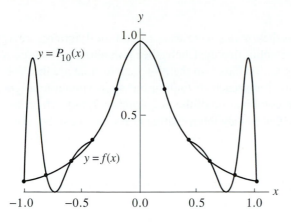

Figure 4.17 (a) The polynomial approximation to $y = 1/(1 + 12x^2)$ based on 11 equally spaced nodes over $[-1, 1]$.

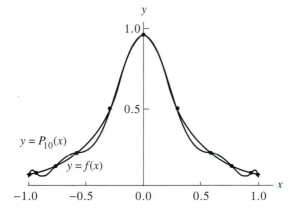

Figure 4.17 (b) The polynomial approximation to $y = 1/(1 + 12x^2)$ based on 11 Chebyshev nodes over $[-1, 1]$.

Example 4.15. For $f(x) = \sin(x)$ on $[0, \pi/4]$, find the Chebyshev nodes and the error bound (15) for the Lagrange polynomial $P_5(x)$.

Formulas (12), (13), and (14) are used to find the nodes;

$$ x_k = \cos\left(\frac{(11 - 2k)\pi}{12}\right)\frac{\pi}{8} + \frac{\pi}{8} \quad \text{for } k = 0, 1, \ldots, 5. $$

Using the bound $|f^{(6)}(x)| \le |-\sin(\pi/4)| = 2^{-1/2} = M$ in (15), we get

$$ |f(x) - P_N(x)| \le \left(\frac{\pi}{8}\right)^6\left(\frac{2}{6!}\right)2^{-1/2} \le 0.00000720. \qquad \blacksquare $$

Orthogonal Property

In Example 4.14, the Chebyshev nodes were used to find the Lagrange interpolating polynomial. In general, this implies that the Chebyshev polynomial of degree N can be obtained by Lagrange interpolation based on the $N + 1$ nodes that are the $N + 1$ zeros of $T_{N+1}(x)$. However, a direct approach to finding the approximation polynomial is to express $P_N(x)$ as a linear combination of the polynomials $T_k(x)$, which were given in Table 4.11 Therefore, the Chebyshev interpolating polynomial can be written in the form

$$(16) \qquad P_N(x) = \sum_{k=0}^{N} c_k T_k(x) = c_0 T_0(x) + c_1 T_1(x) + \cdots + c_N T_N(x).$$

The coefficients $\{c_k\}$ in (16) are easy to find. The technical proof requires the use of the following orthogonality properties. Let

$$(17) \qquad x_k = \cos\left(\pi \frac{2k+1}{2N+2}\right) \qquad \text{for } k = 0, 1, \ldots, N;$$

$$(18) \qquad \sum_{k=0}^{N} T_i(x_k)T_j(x_k) = 0 \qquad \text{when } i \neq j,$$

$$(19) \qquad \sum_{k=0}^{N} T_i(x_k)T_j(x_k) = \frac{N+1}{2} \qquad \text{when } i = j \neq 0,$$

$$(20) \qquad \sum_{k=0}^{N} T_0(x_k)T_0(x_k) = N + 1.$$

Property 4 and the identities (18) and (20) can be used to prove the following theorem.

Theorem 4.8 (Chebyshev Approximation).   The Chebyshev approximation polynomial $P_N(x)$ of degree $\leq N$ for $f(x)$ over $[-1, 1]$ can be written as a sum of $\{T_j(x)\}$:

$$(21) \qquad f(x) \approx P_N(x) = \sum_{j=1}^{N} c_j T_j(x).$$

The coefficients $\{c_j\}$ are computed with the formulas

$$(22) \qquad c_0 = \frac{1}{N+1} \sum_{k=0}^{N} f(x_k) T_0(x_k) = \frac{1}{N+1} \sum_{k=0}^{N} f(x_k)$$

and

$$c_j = \frac{2}{N+1} \sum_{k=0}^{N} f(x_k) T_j(x_k)$$

(23)

$$= \frac{2}{N+1} \sum_{k=0}^{N} f(x_k) \cos\left(\frac{j\pi(2k+1)}{2N+2}\right) \quad \text{for } j = 1, 2, \ldots, N.$$

Example 4.16. Find the Chebyshev polynomial $P_3(x)$ that approximates the function $f(x) = e^x$ over $[-1, 1]$.

The coefficients are calculated using formulas (22) and (23), and the nodes $x_k = \cos(\pi(2k+1)/8)$ for $k = 0, 1, 2, 3$.

$$c_0 = \frac{1}{4} \sum_{k=0}^{3} e^{x_k} T_0(x_k) = \frac{1}{4} \sum_{k=0}^{3} e^{x_k} = 1.26606568,$$

$$c_1 = \frac{1}{2} \sum_{k=0}^{3} e^{x_k} T_1(x_k) = \frac{1}{2} \sum_{k=0}^{3} e^{x_k} x_k = 1.13031500,$$

$$c_2 = \frac{1}{2} \sum_{k=0}^{3} e^{x_k} T_2(x_k) = \frac{1}{2} \sum_{k=0}^{3} e^{x_k} \cos\left(2\pi \frac{2k+1}{8}\right) = 0.27145036,$$

$$c_3 = \frac{1}{2} \sum_{k=0}^{3} e^{x_k} T_3(x_k) = \frac{1}{2} \sum_{k=0}^{3} e^{x_k} \cos\left(3\pi \frac{2k+1}{8}\right) = 0.04379392.$$

Therefore, the Chebyshev polynomial $P_3(x)$ for e^x is

(24)
$$P_3(x) = 1.26606568 T_0(x) + 1.13031500 T_1(x)$$
$$+ 0.27145036 T_2(x) + 0.04379392 T_3(x).$$

If the Chebyshev polynomial (24) is expanded in powers of x, the result is

$$P_3(x) = 0.99461532 + 0.99893324x + 0.54290072x^2 + 0.17517568x^3,$$

which is the same as the polynomial $V(x)$ in Example 4.14. If the goal is to find the Chebyshev polynomial, formulas (22) and (23) are preferred. ∎

MATLAB

The following program uses the `eval` command instead of the `feval` command used in earlier programs. The `eval` command interprets a MATLAB text string as an expression or statement. For example, the following commands will quickly evaluate cosine at the values $x = k/10$ for $k = 0, 1, \ldots, 5$:

```
>> x=0:.1:.5;
>> eval('cos(x)')
ans =
    1.0000 0.9950 0.9801 0.9553 0.9211 0.8776
```

Program 4.3 (Chebyshev Approximation). To construct and evaluate the Chebyshev interpolating polynomial of degree N over the interval $[-1, 1]$, where

$$P(x) = \sum_{j=0}^{N} c_j T_j(x)$$

is based on the nodes

$$x_k = \cos\left(\frac{(2k+1)\pi}{2N+2}\right).$$

```
function [C,X,Y]=cheby(fun,n,a,b)
%Input   - fun is the string function to be approximated
%         - N is the degree of the Chebyshev interpolating
%           polynomial
%         - a is the left endpoint
%         - b is the right endpoint
%Output  - C is the coefficient list for the polynomial
%         - X contains the abscissas
%         - Y contains the ordinates
if nargin==2, a=-1;b=1;end
d=pi/(2*n+2);
C=zeros(1,n+1);

for k=1:n+1
    X(k)=cos((2*k-1)*d);
end

X=(b-a)*X/2+(a+b)/2;
x=X;
Y=eval(fun);

for k =1:n+1
    z=(2*k-1)*d;
    for j=1:n+1
        C(j)=C(j)+Y(k)*cos((j-1)*z);
    end
end
C=2*C/(n+1);
C(1)=C(1)/2;
```

Exercises for Chebyshev Polynomials

1. Use property 1 and
   (a)   construct $T_4(x)$ from $T_3(x)$ and $T_2(x)$.
   (b)   construct $T_5(x)$ from $T_4(x)$ and $T_3(x)$.

2. Use property 1 and
   (a)   construct $T_6(x)$ from $T_5(x)$ and $T_4(x)$.
   (b)   construct $T_7(x)$ from $T_6(x)$ and $T_5(x)$.

3. Use mathematical induction to prove property 2.

4. Use mathematical induction to prove property 3.

5. Find the maximum and minimum values of $T_2(x)$ over the interval $[-1, 1]$.

6. Find the maximum and minimum values of $T_3(x)$ over the interval $[-1, 1]$.
   Hint. $T_3'(1/2) = 0$ and $T_3'(-1/2) = 0$.

7. Find the maximum and minimum values of $T_4(x)$ over the interval $[-1, 1]$.
   Hint. $T_4'(0) = 0$, $T_4'(2^{-1/2}) = 0$, and $T_4'(-2^{-1/2}) = 0$.

8. Let $f(x) = \sin(x)$ on $[-1, 1]$.
   (a)   Use the coefficient polynomials in Table 4.13 to obtain the Lagrange-Chebyshev polynomial approximation $P_3(x)$.
   (b)   Find the error bound for $|\sin(x) - P_3(x)|$.

9. Let $f(x) = \ln(x + 2)$ on $[-1, 1]$.
   (a)   Use the coefficient polynomials in Table 4.13 to obtain the Lagrange-Chebyshev polynomial approximation $P_3(x)$.
   (b)   Find the error bound for $|\ln(x + 2) - P_3(x)|$.

10. The Lagrange polynomial of degree $N = 2$ has the form

$$f(x) = f(x_0)L_{2,0}(x) + f(x_1)L_{2,1}(x) + f(x_2)L_{2,2}(x).$$

   If the Chebyshev nodes $x_0 = \cos(5\pi/6)$, $x_1 = 0$, and $x_2 = \cos(\pi/6)$ are used, show that the coefficient polynomials are

$$L_{2,0}(x) = -\frac{x}{\sqrt{3}} + \frac{2x^2}{3},$$

$$L_{2,1}(x) = 1 - \frac{4x^2}{3},$$

$$L_{2,2}(x) = \frac{x}{\sqrt{3}} + \frac{2x^2}{3}.$$

11. Let $f(x) = \cos(x)$ on $[-1, 1]$.
   (a)   Use the coefficient polynomials in Exercise 10 to get the Lagrange-Chebyshev polynomial approximation $P_2(x)$.
   (b)   Find the error bound for $|\cos(x) - P_2(x)|$.

12. Let $f(x) = e^x$ on $[-1, 1]$.

    (a) Use the coefficient polynomials in Exercise 10 to get the Lagrange-Chebyshev polynomial approximation $P_2(x)$.

    (b) Find the error bound for $|e^x - P_2(x)|$.

In Exercises 13 through 15, compare the Taylor polynomial and the Lagrange-Chebyshev approximates to $f(x)$ on $[-1, 1]$. Find their error bounds.

13. $f(x) = \sin(x)$ and $N = 7$; the Lagrange-Chebyshev polynomial is

$$\sin(x) \approx 0.99999998x - 0.16666599x^2 + 0.00832995x^5 - 0.00019297x^7.$$

14. $f(x) = \cos(x)$ and $N = 6$; the Lagrange-Chebyshev polynomial is

$$\cos(x) \approx 1 - 0.49999734x^2 + 0.04164535x^4 - 0.00134608x^6.$$

15. $f(x) = e^x$ and $N = 7$; the Lagrange-Chebyshev polynomial is

$$e^x \approx 0.99999980 + 0.99999998x + 0.50000634x^2$$
$$+ 0.16666737x^3 + 0.04163504x^4 + 0.00832984x^5$$
$$+ 0.00143925x^6 + 0.00020399x^7.$$

16. Prove equation (18).

17. Prove equation (19).

Algorithms and Programs

In Problems 1 through 6, use Program 4.3 to compute the coefficients $\{c_k\}$ for the Chebyshev polynomial approximation $P_N(x)$ to $f(x)$ over $[-1, 1]$, when **(a)** $N = 4$, **(b)** $N = 5$, **(c)** $N = 6$, and **(d)** $N = 7$. In each case, plot $f(x)$ and $P_N(x)$ on the same coordinate system.

    1. $f(x) = e^x$ **2.** $f(x) = \sin(x)$

    3. $f(x) = \cos(x)$ **4.** $f(x) = \ln(x + 2)$

    5. $f(x) = (x + 2)^{1/2}$ **6.** $f(x) = (x + 2)^{(x+2)}$

7. Use Program 4.3 ($N = 5$) to obtain an approximation for $\int_0^1 \cos(x^2)\,dx$.

4.6   Padé Approximations

In this section we introduce the notion of rational approximations for functions. The function $f(x)$ will be approximated over a small portion of its domain. For example, if $f(x) = \cos(x)$, it is sufficient to have a formula to generate approximations on the interval $[0, \pi/2]$. Then trigonometric identities can be used to compute $\cos(x)$ for any value x that lies outside $[0, \pi/2]$.

A rational approximation to $f(x)$ on $[a, b]$ is the quotient of two polynomials $P_N(x)$ and $Q_M(x)$ of degrees N and M, respectively. We use the notation $R_{N,M}(x)$ to denote this quotient:

$$(1) \qquad\qquad R_{N,M}(x) = \frac{P_N(x)}{Q_M(x)} \quad \text{ for } a \le x \le b.$$

Our goal is to make the maximum error as small as possible. For a given amount of computational effort, one can usually construct a rational approximation that has a smaller overall error on $[a, b]$ than a polynomial approximation. Our development is an introduction and will be limited to Padé approximations.

The *method of Padé* requires that $f(x)$ and its derivative be continuous at $x = 0$. There are two reasons for the arbitrary choice of $x = 0$. First, it makes the manipulations simpler. Second, a change of variable can be used to shift the calculations over to an interval that contains zero. The polynomials used in (1) are

$$(2) \qquad\qquad P_N(x) = p_0 + p_1 x + p_2 x^2 + \cdots + p_N x^N$$

and

$$(3) \qquad\qquad Q_M(x) = 1 + q_1 x + q_2 x^2 + \cdots + q_M x^M.$$

The polynomials in (2) and (3) are constructed so that $f(x)$ and $R_{N,M}(x)$ agree at $x = 0$ and their derivatives up to $N + M$ agree at $x = 0$. In the case $Q_0(x) = 1$, the approximation is just the Maclaurin expansion for $f(x)$. For a fixed value of $N + M$ the error is smallest when $P_N(x)$ and $Q_M(x)$ have the same degree or when $P_N(x)$ has degree one higher than $Q_M(x)$.

Notice that the constant coefficient of Q_M is $q_0 = 1$. This is permissible, because it cannot be 0 and $R_{N,M}(x)$ is not changed when both $P_N(x)$ and $Q_M(x)$ are divided by the same constant. Hence the rational function $R_{N,M}(x)$ has $N + M + 1$ unknown coefficients. Assume that $f(x)$ is analytic and has the Maclaurin expansion

$$(4) \qquad\qquad f(x) = a_0 + a_1 x + a_2 x^2 + \cdots + a_k x^k + \cdots,$$

and form the difference $f(x)Q_M(x) - P_N(x) = Z(x)$:

$$(5) \qquad \left(\sum_{j=0}^{\infty} a_j x^j \right) \left(\sum_{j=0}^{M} q_j x^j \right) - \sum_{j=0}^{N} p_j x^j = \sum_{j=N+M+1}^{\infty} c_j x^j.$$

The lower index $j = M + N + 1$ in the summation on the right side of (5) is chosen because the first $N + M$ derivatives of $f(x)$ and $R_{N,M}(x)$ are to agree at $x = 0$.

When the left side of (5) is multiplied out and the coefficients of the powers of x^j are set equal to zero for $k = 0, 1, \ldots, N + M$, the result is a system of $N + M + 1$ linear equations:

(6)
$$
\begin{aligned}
a_0 - p_0 &= 0 \\
q_1 a_0 + a_1 - p_1 &= 0 \\
q_2 a_0 + q_1 a_1 + a_2 - p_2 &= 0 \\
q_3 a_0 + q_2 a_1 + q_1 a_2 + a_3 - p_3 &= 0 \\
q_M a_{N-M} + q_{M-1} a_{N-M+1} + \cdots + a_N - p_N &= 0
\end{aligned}
$$

and

(7)
$$
\begin{aligned}
q_M a_{N-M+1} + q_{M-1} a_{N-M+2} + \cdots + q_1 a_N \quad &+ a_{N+1} = 0 \\
q_M a_{N-M+2} + q_{M-1} a_{N-M+3} + \cdots + q_1 a_{N+1} \quad &+ a_{N+2} = 0 \\
\vdots \qquad\qquad\qquad\qquad &\qquad\quad \vdots \\
q_M a_N \quad + q_{M-1} a_{N+1} \quad + \cdots + q_1 a_{N+M-1} + a_{N+M} &= 0.
\end{aligned}
$$

Notice that in each equation the sum of the subscripts on the factors of each product is the same, and this sum increases consecutively from 0 to $N + M$. The M equations in (7) involve only the unknowns $q_1, q_2, \ldots, q_M$ and must be solved first. Then the equations in (6) are used successively to find $p_0, p_1, \ldots, p_N$.

Example 4.17.   Establish the Padé approximation

(8)
$$
\cos(x) \approx R_{4,4}(x) = \frac{15{,}120 - 6900x^2 + 313x^4}{15{,}120 + 660x^2 + 13x^4}.
$$

See Figure 4.18 for the graphs of $\cos(x)$ and $R_{4,4}(x)$ over $[-5, 5]$.

If the Maclaurin expansion for $\cos(x)$ is used, we will obtain nine equations in nine unknowns. Instead, notice that both $\cos(x)$ and $R_{4,4}(x)$ are even functions and involve powers of x^2. We can simplify the computations if we start with $f(x) = \cos(x^{1/2})$:

(9)
$$
f(x) = 1 - \frac{1}{2}x + \frac{1}{24}x^2 - \frac{1}{720}x^3 + \frac{1}{40{,}320}x^4 - \cdots .
$$

In this case, equation (5) becomes

$$
\left(1 - \frac{1}{2}x + \frac{1}{24}x^2 - \frac{1}{720}x^3 + \frac{1}{40{,}320}x^4 - \cdots \right)\left(1 + q_1 x + q_2 x^2\right) - p_0 - p_1 x - p_2 x^2
$$
$$
= 0 + 0x + 0x^2 + 0x^3 + 0x^4 + c_5 x^5 + c_6 x^6 + \cdots .
$$

When the coefficients of the first five powers of x are compared, we get the following

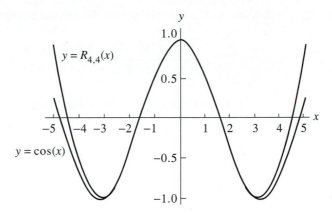

Figure 4.18   The graph of $y = \cos(x)$ and its Padé approximation $R_{4,4}(x)$.

system of linear equations:

$$1 - p_0 = 0$$

$$-\frac{1}{2} + q_1 - p_1 = 0$$

(10)
$$\frac{1}{24} - \frac{1}{2}q_1 + q_2 - p_2 = 0$$

$$-\frac{1}{720} + \frac{1}{24}q_1 - \frac{1}{2}q_2 = 0$$

$$\frac{1}{40,320} - \frac{1}{720}q_1 + \frac{1}{24}q_2 = 0.$$

The last two equations in (10) must be solved first. They can be rewritten in a form that is easy to solve:

$$q_1 - 12q_2 = \frac{1}{30} \quad \text{and} \quad -q_1 + 30q_2 = \frac{-1}{56}.$$

First find q_2 by adding the equations; then find q_1:

$$q_2 = \frac{1}{18}\left(\frac{1}{30} - \frac{1}{56}\right) = \frac{13}{15,120},$$

(11)
$$q_1 = \frac{1}{30} + \frac{156}{15,120} = \frac{11}{252}.$$

Now the first three equations of (10) are used. It is obvious that $p_0 = 1$, and we can use q_1 and q_2 in (11) to solve for p_1 and p_2:

$$p_1 = -\frac{1}{2} + \frac{11}{252} = -\frac{115}{252},$$

(12)
$$p_2 = \frac{1}{24} - \frac{11}{504} + \frac{13}{15,120} = \frac{313}{15,120}.$$

Now use the coefficients in (11) and (12) to form the rational approximation to $f(x)$:

$$(13) \qquad f(x) \approx \frac{1 - 115x/252 + 313x^2/15,120}{1 + 11x/252 + 13x^2/15,120}.$$

Since $\cos(x) = f(x^2)$, we can substitute x^2 for x in equation (13) and the result is the formula for $R_{4,4}(x)$ in (8). ∎

Continued Fraction Form

The Padé approximation $R_{4,4}(x)$ in Example 4.17 requires a minimum of 12 arithmetic operations to perform an evaluation. It is possible to reduce this number to seven by the use of continued fractions. This is accomplished by starting with (8) and finding the quotient and its polynomial remainder.

$$R_{4,4}(x) = \frac{15,120/313 - (6900/313)x^2 + x^4}{15,120/13 + (660/13)x^2 + x^4}$$

$$= \frac{313}{13} - \left(\frac{296,280}{169}\right)\left(\frac{12,600/823 + x^2}{15,120/13 + (600/13)x^2 + x^4}\right).$$

The process is carried out once more using the term in the previous remainder. The result is

$$R_{4,4}(x) = \frac{313}{13} - \cfrac{296,280/169}{\cfrac{15,120/13 + (660/13)x^2 + x^4}{12,600/823 + x^2}}$$

$$= \frac{313}{13} - \cfrac{296,280/169}{\cfrac{379,380}{10,699} + x^2 + \cfrac{420,078,960/677,329}{12,600/823 + x^2}}.$$

The fractions are converted to decimal form for computational purposes and we obtain

$$(14) \quad R_{4,4}(x) = 24.07692308$$

$$- \frac{1753.13609467}{35.45938873 + x^2 + 620.19928277/(15.30984204 + x^2)}.$$

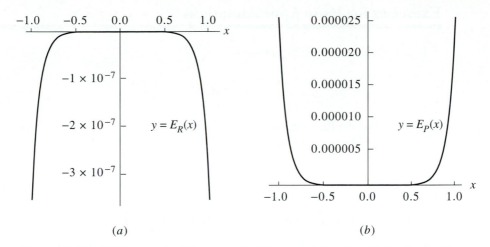

(a)   (b)

Figure 4.19   (a) The graph of the error $E_R(x) = \cos(x) - R_{4,4}(x)$ for the Padé approximation $R_{4,4}(x)$. (b) The graph of the error $E_P(x) = \cos(x) - P_6(x)$ for the Taylor approximation $P_6(x)$.

To evaluate (14), first compute and store x^2, then proceed from the bottom right term in the denominator and tally the operations: addition, division, addition, addition, division, and subtraction. Hence it takes a total of seven arithmetic operations to evaluate $R_{4,4}(x)$ in continued fraction form in (14).

We can compare $R_{4,4}(x)$ with the Taylor polynomial $P_6(x)$ of degree $N = 6$, which requires seven arithmetic operations to evaluate when it is written in the nested form

$$P_6(x) = 1 + x^2 \left(-\frac{1}{2} + x^2 \left(\frac{1}{24} - \frac{1}{720} x^2 \right) \right)$$

(15)

$$= 1 + x^2(-0.5 + x^2(0.0416666667 - 0.0013888889x^2)).$$

The graphs of $E_R(x) = \cos(x) - R_{4,4}(x)$ and $E_P(x) = \cos(x) - P_6(x)$ over $[-1, 1]$ are shown in Figure 4.19(a) and (b), respectively. The largest errors occur at the endpoints and are $E_R(1) = -0.0000003599$ and $E_P(1) = 0.0000245281$, respectively. The magnitude of the largest error for $R_{4,4}(x)$ is about 1.467% of the error for $P_6(x)$. The Padé approximation outperforms the Taylor approximation better on smaller intervals, and over $[-0.1, 0.1]$ we find that $E_R(0.1) = -0.0000000004$ and $E_P(0.1) = 0.0000000966$, so the magnitude of the error for $R_{4,4}(x)$ is about 0.384% of the magnitude of the error for $P_6(x)$.

Exercises for Padé Approximations

1. Establish the Padé approximation:

$$e^x \approx R_{1,1}(x) = \frac{2+x}{2-x}.$$

2. **(a)** Find the Padé approximation $R_{1,1}(x)$ for $f(x) = \ln(1+x)/x$. *Hint.* Start with the Maclaurin expansion:

$$f(x) = 1 - \frac{x}{2} + \frac{x^2}{3} - \cdots .$$

   (b) Use the result in part (a) to establish the approximation

$$\ln(1+x) \approx R_{2,1}(x) = \frac{6x + x^2}{6 + 4x}.$$

3. **(a)** Find $R_{1,1}(x)$ for $f(x) = \tan(x^{1/2})/x^{1/2}$. *Hint.* Start with the Maclaurin expansion:

$$f(x) = 1 + \frac{x}{3} + \frac{2x^2}{15} + \cdots .$$

   (b) Use the result in part (a) to establish the approximation

$$\tan(x) \approx R_{3,2}(x) = \frac{15x - x^3}{15 - 6x^2}.$$

4. **(a)** Find $R_{1,1}(x)$ for $f(x) = \arctan(x^{1/2})/x^{1/2}$. *Hint.* Start with the Maclaurin expansion:

$$f(x) = 1 - \frac{x}{3} + \frac{x^2}{5} - \cdots .$$

   (b) Use the result in part (a) to establish the approximation

$$\arctan(x) \approx R_{3,2}(x) = \frac{15x + 4x^3}{15 + 9x^2}.$$

   (c) Express the rational function $R_{3,2}(x)$ in part (b) in continued fraction form.

5. **(a)** Establish the Padé approximation:

$$e^x \approx R_{2,2}(x) = \frac{12 + 6x + x^2}{12 - 6x + x^2}.$$

   (b) Express the rational function $R_{2,2}(x)$ in part (a) in continued fraction form.

6. (a)   Find the Padé approximation $R_{2,2}(x)$ for $f(x) = \ln(1+x)/x$. *Hint.* Start with the Maclaurin expansion:

$$f(x) = 1 - \frac{x}{2} + \frac{x^2}{3} - \frac{x^3}{4} + \frac{x^4}{5} - \cdots .$$

(b)   Use the result in part (a) to establish

$$\ln(1+x) \approx R_{3,2}(x) = \frac{30x + 21x^2 + x^3}{30 + 36x + 9x^2}.$$

(c)   Express the rational function $R_{3,2}(x)$ in part (b) in continued fraction form.

7. (a)   Find $R_{2,2}(x)$ for $f(x) = \tan(x^{1/2})/x^{1/2}$. *Hint.* Start with the Maclaurin expansion:

$$f(x) = 1 + \frac{x}{3} + \frac{2x^2}{15} + \frac{17x^3}{315} + \frac{62x^4}{2835} + \cdots .$$

(b)   Use the result in part (a) to establish

$$\tan(x) \approx R_{5,4}(x) = \frac{945x - 105x^3 + x^5}{945 - 420x^2 + 15x^4}.$$

(c)   Express the rational function $R_{5,4}(x)$ in part (b) in continued fraction form.

8. (a)   Find $R_{2,2}(x)$ for $f(x) = \arctan(x^{1/2})/x^{1/2}$. *Hint.* Start with the Maclaurin expansion:

$$f(x) = 1 - \frac{x}{3} + \frac{x^2}{5} - \frac{x^3}{7} + \frac{x^4}{9} - \cdots .$$

(b)   Use the result in part (a) to establish

$$\arctan(x) \approx R_{5,4}(x) = \frac{945x + 735x^3 + 64x^5}{945 + 1050x^2 + 225x^4}.$$

(c)   Express the rational function $R_{5,4}(x)$ in part (b) in continued fraction form.

9. Establish the Padé approximation:

$$e^x \approx R_{3,3}(x) = \frac{120 + 60x + 12x^2 + x^3}{120 - 60x + 12x^2 - x^3}.$$

10. Establish the Padé approximation:

$$e^x \approx R_{4,4}(x) = \frac{1680 + 840x + 180x^2 + 20x^3 + x^4}{1680 - 840x + 180x^2 - 20x^3 + x^4}.$$

Algorithms and Programs

1. Compare the following approximations to $f(x) = e^x$.

   Taylor: $T_4(x) = 1 + x + \dfrac{x^2}{2} + \dfrac{x^3}{6} + \dfrac{x^4}{24}$

   Padé: $R_{2,2}(x) = \dfrac{12 + 6x + x^2}{12 - 6x + x^2}$

   (a) Plot $f(x)$, $T_4(x)$, and $R_{2,2}(x)$ on the same coordinate system.
   (b) Determine the maximum error that occurs when $f(x)$ is approximated with $T_4(x)$ and $R_{2,2}(x)$, respectively, over the interval $[-1, 1]$.

2. Compare the following approximations to $f(x) = \ln(1 + x)$.

   Taylor: $T_5(x) = x - \dfrac{x^2}{2} + \dfrac{x^3}{3} - \dfrac{x^4}{4} + \dfrac{x^5}{5}$

   Padé: $R_{3,2}(x) = \dfrac{30x + 21x^2 + x^3}{30 + 36x + 9x^2}$

   (a) Plot $f(x)$, $T_5(x)$, and $R_{3,2}(x)$ on the same coordinate system.
   (b) Determine the maximum error that occurs when $f(x)$ is approximated with $T_5(x)$ and $R_{3,2}(x)$, respectively, over the interval $[-1, 1]$.

3. Compare the following approximations to $f(x) = \tan(x)$.

   Taylor: $T_9(x) = x + \dfrac{x^3}{3} + \dfrac{2x^5}{15} + \dfrac{17x^7}{315} + \dfrac{62x^9}{2835}$

   Padé: $R_{5,4}(x) = \dfrac{945x - 105x^3 + x^5}{945 - 420x^2 + 15x^4}$

   (a) Plot $f(x)$, $T_9(x)$, and $R_{5,4}(x)$ on the same coordinate system.
   (b) Determine the maximum error that occurs when $f(x)$ is approximated with $T_9(x)$ and $R_{5,4}(x)$, respectively, over the interval $[-1, 1]$.

4. Compare the following Padé approximations to $f(x) = \sin(x)$ over the interval $[-1.2, 1.2]$.

   $$R_{5,4}(x) = \dfrac{166{,}320x - 22{,}260x^3 + 551x^5}{15(11{,}088 + 364x^2 + 5x^4)}$$

   $$R_{7,6}(x) = \dfrac{11{,}511{,}339{,}840x - 1{,}640{,}635{,}920x^2 + 52{,}785{,}432x^5 - 479{,}249x^7}{7(1{,}644{,}477{,}120 + 39{,}702{,}960x^2 + 453{,}960x^4 + 2623x^6)}$$

   (a) Plot $f(x)$, $R_{5,4}(x)$, and $R_{7,6}(x)$ on the same coordinate system.
   (b) Determine the maximum error that occurs when $f(x)$ is approximated with $R_{5,4}(x)$ and $R_{7,6}(x)$, respectively, over the interval $[-1.2, 1.2]$.

5. (a) Use equations (6) and (7) to derive $R_{6,6}(x)$ and $R_{8,8}(x)$ for $f(x) = \cos(x)$ over the interval $[-1.2, 1.2]$.

(b) Plot $f(x)$, $R_{6,6}(x)$, and $R_{8,8}(x)$ on the same coordinate system.

(c) Determine the maximum error that occurs when $f(x)$ is approximated with $R_{6,6}(x)$ and $R_{8,8}(x)$, respectively, over the interval $[-1.2, 1.2]$.

5

Curve Fitting

Applications of numerical techniques in science and engineering often involve curve fitting of experimental data. For example, in 1601 the German astronomer Johannes Kepler formulated the third law of planetary motion, $T = Cx^{3/2}$, where x is the distance to the sun measured in millions of kilometers, T is the orbital period measured in days, and C is a constant. The observed data pairs (x, T) for the first four planets, Mercury, Venus, Earth, and Mars, are $(58, 88)$, $(108, 225)$, $(150, 365)$, and $(228, 687)$, and the coefficient C obtained from the method of least squares is $C = 0.199769$. The curve $T = 0.199769x^{3/2}$ and the data points are shown in Figure 5.1.

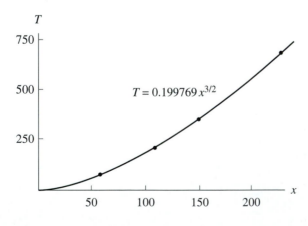

Figure 5.1 The least-squares fit $T = 0.199769x^{3/2}$ for the first four planets using Kepler's third law of planetary motion.

5.1   Least-Squares Line

In science and engineering it is often the case that an experiment produces a set of data points $(x_1, y_1), \ldots, (x_N, y_N)$, where the abscissas $\{x_k\}$ are distinct. One goal of numerical methods is to determine a formula $y = f(x)$ that relates these variables. Usually, a class of allowable formulas is chosen and then coefficients must be determined. There are many different possibilities for the type of function that can be used. Often there is an underlying mathematical model, based on the physical situation, that will determine the form of the function. In this section we emphasize the class of linear functions of the form

$$(1) \qquad\qquad\qquad y = f(x) = Ax + B.$$

In Chapter 4 we saw how to construct a polynomial that passes through a set of points. If all the numerical values $\{x_k\}$, $\{y_k\}$ are known to several significant digits of accuracy, then polynomial interpolation can be used successfully; otherwise, it cannot. Some experiments are devised using specialized equipment so that the data points will have at least five digits of accuracy. However, many experiments are done with equipment that is reliable only to three or fewer digits of accuracy. Often, there is an experimental error in the measurements, and although three digits are recorded for the values $\{x_k\}$ and $\{y_k\}$, it is realized that the true value $f(x_k)$ satisfies

$$(2) \qquad\qquad\qquad f(x_k) = y_k + e_k,$$

where e_k is the measurement error.

How do we find the best linear approximation of the form (1) that goes near (not always through) the points? To answer this question, we need to discuss the **errors** (also called **deviations** or **residuals**):

$$(3) \qquad\qquad\qquad e_k = f(x_k) - y_k \qquad \text{for } 1 \le k \le N.$$

There are several norms that can be used with the residuals in (3) to measure how far the curve $y = f(x)$ lies from the data.

$$(4) \qquad \text{Maximum error:} \qquad E_\infty(f) = \max_{1 \le k \le N}\{|f(x_k) - y_k|\},$$

$$(5) \qquad \text{Average error:} \qquad E_1(f) = \frac{1}{N}\sum_{k=1}^{N}|f(x_k) - y_k|,$$

$$(6) \qquad \begin{array}{l}\text{Root-mean-square}\\ \text{error:}\end{array} \qquad E_2(f) = \left(\frac{1}{N}\sum_{k=1}^{N}|f(x_k) - y_k|^2\right)^{1/2}.$$

The next example shows how to apply these norms when a function and a set of points are given.

Table 5.1 Calculations for Finding $E_1(f)$ and $E_2(f)$ for Example 5.1

x_k	y_k	$f(x_k) = 8.6 - 1.6x_k$	$|e_k|$	e_k^2
-1	10.0	10.2	0.2	0.04
0	9.0	8.6	0.4	0.16
1	7.0	7.0	0.0	0.00
2	5.0	5.4	0.4	0.16
3	4.0	3.8	0.2	0.04
4	3.0	2.2	0.8	0.64
5	0.0	0.6	0.6	0.36
6	-1.0	-1.0	0.0	0.00
			2.6	1.40

Example 5.1. Compare the maximum error, average error, and rms error for the linear approximation $y = f(x) = 8.6 - 1.6x$ to the data points $(-1, 10)$, $(0, 9)$, $(1, 7)$, $(2, 5)$, $(3, 4)$, $(4, 3)$, $(5, 0)$, and $(6, -1)$.

The errors are found using the values for $f(x_k)$ and e_k given in Table 5.1.

(7) $$E_\infty(f) = \max\{0.2, 0.4, 0.0, 0.4, 0.2, 0.8, 0.6, 0.0\} = 0.8,$$

(8) $$E_1(f) = \frac{1}{8}(2.6) = 0.325,$$

(9) $$E_2(f) = \left(\frac{1.4}{8}\right)^{1/2} \approx 0.41833.$$

We can see that the maximum error is largest, and if one point is badly in error, its value determines $E_\infty(f)$. The average error $E_1(f)$ simply averages the absolute value of the error at the various points. It is often used because it is easy to compute. The error $E_2(f)$ is often used when the statistical nature of the errors is considered.

A best-fitting line is found by minimizing one of the quantities in equations (4) through (6). Hence there are three best-fitting lines that we could find. The third norm $E_2(f)$ is the traditional choice because it is much easier to minimize computationally. ∎

Finding the Least-Squares Line

Let $\{(x_k, y_k)\}_{k=1}^N$ be a set of N points, where the abscissas $\{x_k\}$ are distinct. The **least-squares line** $y = f(x) = Ax + B$ is the line that minimizes the root-mean-square error $E_2(f)$.

The quantity $E_2(f)$ will be a minimum if and only if the quantity $N(E_2(f))^2 = \sum_{k=1}^N (Ax_k + B - y_k)^2$ is a minimum. The latter is visualized geometrically by minimizing the sum of the squares of the vertical distances from the points to the line. The next result explains this process.

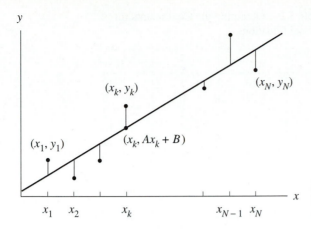

y

(x_k, y_k)

(x_N, y_N)

(x_1, y_1)

$(x_k, Ax_k + B)$

x_1 x_2 x_k x_{N-1} x_N x

Figure 5.2   The vertical distances between the points $\{(x_k, y_k)\}$ and the least-squares line $y = Ax + B$.

Theorem 5.1 (Least-Squares Line).   Suppose that $\{(x_k, y_k)\}_{k=1}^{N}$ are N points, where the abscissas $\{x_k\}_{k=1}^{N}$ are distinct. The coefficients of the least-squares line

$$y = Ax + B$$

are the solution to the following linear system, known as the *normal equations*:

(10)
$$\left(\sum_{k=1}^{N} x_k^2\right) A + \left(\sum_{k=1}^{N} x_k\right) B = \sum_{k=1}^{N} x_k y_k,$$
$$\left(\sum_{k=1}^{N} x_k\right) A + NB = \sum_{k=1}^{N} y_k.$$

Proof.   Geometrically, we start with the line $y = Ax + B$. The vertical distance d_k from the point (x_k, y_k) to the point $(x_k, Ax_k + B)$ on the line is $d_k = |Ax_k + B - y_k|$ (see Figure 5.2). We must minimize the sum of the squares of the vertical distances d_k:

(11)
$$E(A, B) = \sum_{k=1}^{N} (Ax_k + B - y_k)^2 = \sum_{k=1}^{N} d_k^2.$$

The minimum value of $E(A, B)$ is determined by setting the partial derivatives $\partial E/\partial A$ and $\partial E/\partial B$ equal to zero and solving these equations for A and B. Notice that $\{x_k\}$ and $\{y_k\}$ are constants in equation (11) and that A and B are the variables! Hold B fixed, differentiate $E(A, B)$ with respect to A, and get

(12)
$$\frac{\partial E(A, B)}{\partial A} = \sum_{k=1}^{N} 2(Ax_k + B - y_k)(x_k) = 2 \sum_{k=1}^{N} (Ax_k^2 + Bx_k - x_k y_k).$$

Table 5.2   Obtaining the Coefficients for
Normal Equations

x_k	y_k	x_k^2	$x_k y_k$
-1	10	1	-10
0	9	0	0
1	7	1	7
2	5	4	10
3	4	9	12
4	3	16	12
5	0	25	0
6	-1	36	-6
20	37	92	25

Now hold A fixed and differentiate $E(A, B)$ with respect to B and get

$$(13) \qquad \frac{\partial E(A, B)}{\partial B} = \sum_{k=1}^{N} 2(Ax_k + B - y_k) = 2\sum_{k=1}^{N}(Ax_k + B - y_k).$$

Setting the partial derivatives equal to zero in (12) and (13), use the distributive properties of summation to obtain

$$(14) \qquad 0 = \sum_{k=1}^{N}(Ax_k^2 + Bx_k - x_k y_k) = A\sum_{k=1}^{N}x_k^2 + B\sum_{k=1}^{N}x_k - \sum_{k=1}^{N}x_k y_k,$$

$$(15) \qquad 0 = \sum_{k=1}^{N}(Ax_k + B - y_k) = A\sum_{k=1}^{N}x_k + NB - \sum_{k=1}^{N}y_k.$$

Equations (14) and (15) can be rearranged in the standard form for a system and result in the normal equations (10). The solution to this system can be obtained by one of the techniques for solving a linear system from Chapter 3. However, the method employed in Program 5.1 translates the data points so that a well-conditioned matrix is employed (see the Exercises).   ●

Example 5.2.   Find the least-squares line for the data points given in Example 5.1.
    The sums required for the normal equations (10) are easily obtained using the values in Table 5.2. The linear system involving A and B is

$$92A + 20B = 25$$
$$20A + \ 8B = 37.$$

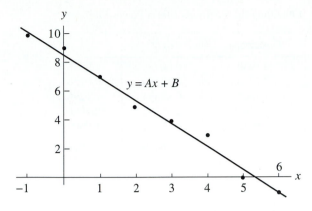

Figure 5.3 The least-squares line $y = -1.6071429x + 8.6428571$.

The solution of the linear system is $A \approx -1.6071429$ and $B \approx 8.6428571$. Therefore, the least-squares line is (see Figure 5.3)

$$y = -1.6071429x + 8.6428571 \qquad \blacksquare$$

Power Fit $y = Ax^M$

Some situations involve $f(x) = Ax^M$, where M is a known constant. The example of planetary motion given in Figure 5.1 is an example. In these cases there is only one parameter A to be determined.

Theorem 5.2 (Power Fit). Suppose that $\{(x_k, y_k)\}_{k=1}^{N}$ are N points, where the abscissas are distinct. The coefficient A of the least-squares power curve $y = Ax^M$ is given by

$$(16) \qquad A = \left(\sum_{k=1}^{N} x_k^M y_k \right) \bigg/ \left(\sum_{k=1}^{N} x_k^{2M} \right).$$

Using the least-squares technique, we seek a minimum of the function $E(A)$:

$$(17) \qquad E(A) = \sum_{k=1}^{N} (Ax_k^M - y_k)^2.$$

In this case it will suffice to solve $E'(A) = 0$. The derivative is

$$(18) \qquad E'(A) = 2 \sum_{k=1}^{N} (Ax_k^M - y_k)(x_k^M) = 2 \sum_{k=1}^{N} (Ax_k^{2M} - x_k^M y_k).$$

Table 5.3 Obtaining the Coefficient for a Power Fit

Time, t_k	Distance, d_k	$d_k t_k^2$	t_k^4
0.200	0.1960	0.00784	0.0016
0.400	0.7850	0.12560	0.0256
0.600	1.7665	0.63594	0.1296
0.800	3.1405	2.00992	0.4096
1.000	4.9075	4.90750	1.0000
		7.68680	1.5664

Hence the coefficient A is the solution of the equation

$$(19) \qquad 0 = A \sum_{k=1}^{N} x_k^{2M} - \sum_{k=1}^{N} x_k^M y_k,$$

which reduces to the formula in equation (16).

Example 5.3. Students collected the experimental data in Table 5.3. The relation is $d = \frac{1}{2}gt^2$, where d is distance in meters and t is time in seconds. Find the gravitational constant g.

The values in Table 5.3 are used to find the summations required in formula (16), where the power used is $M = 2$.

The coefficient is $A = 7.68680/1.5664 = 4.9073$, and we get $d = 4.9073t^2$ and $g = 2A = 9.7146$ m/sec^2. ∎

The following program for constructing a least-squares line is computationally stable: it gives reliable results in cases when the normal equations (10) are ill conditioned. The reader is asked to develop the algorithm for this program in Exercises 4 through 7.

Program 5.1 (Least-Squares Line). To construct the least-squares line $y = Ax + B$ that fits the N data points $(x_1, y_1), \ldots, (x_N, y_N)$.

```
function [A,B]=lsline(X,Y)

%Input   - X is the 1xn abscissa vector
%         - Y is the 1xn ordinate vector
%Output  - A is the coefficient of x in Ax + B
%         - B is the constant coefficient in Ax + B
xmean=mean(X);
ymean=mean(Y);
sumx2=(X-xmean)*(X-xmean)';
sumxy=(Y-ymean)*(X-xmean)';
```

```
A=sumxy/sumx2;
B=ymean-A*xmean;
```

Exercises for Least-Squares Line

In Exercises 1 and 2, find the least-squares line $y = f(x) = Ax + B$ for the data and calculate $E_2(f)$

1. (a)

x_k	y_k	$f(x_k)$
-2	1	1.2
-1	2	1.9
0	3	2.6
1	3	3.3
2	4	4.0

(b)

x_k	y_k	$f(x_k)$
-6	7	7.0
-2	5	4.6
0	3	3.4
2	2	2.2
6	0	-0.2

(c)

x_k	y_k	$f(x_k)$
-4	-3	-3.0
-1	-1	-0.9
0	0	-0.2
2	1	1.2
3	2	1.9

2. (a)

x_k	y_k	$f(x_k)$
-4	1.2	0.44
-2	2.8	3.34
0	6.2	6.24
2	7.8	9.14
4	13.2	12.04

(b)

x_k	y_k	$f(x_k)$
-6	-5.3	-6.00
-2	-3.5	-2.84
0	-1.7	-1.26
2	0.2	0.32
6	4.0	3.48

(c)

x_k	y_k	$f(x_k)$
-8	6.8	7.32
-2	5.0	3.81
0	2.2	2.64
4	0.5	0.30
6	-1.3	-0.87

3. Find the power fit $y = Ax$, where $M = 1$, which is a line through the origin, for the data and calculate $E_2(f)$.

(a)

x_k	y_k	$f(x_k)$
-4	-3	-2.8
-1	-1	-0.7
0	0	0.0
2	1	1.4
3	2	2.1

(b)

x_k	y_k	$f(x_k)$
3	1.6	1.722
4	2.4	2.296
5	2.9	2.870
6	3.4	3.444
8	4.6	4.592

(c)

x_k	y_k	$f(x_k)$
1	1.6	1.58
2	2.8	3.16
3	4.7	4.74
4	6.4	6.32
5	8.0	7.90

4. Define the means $\bar{x}$ and $\bar{y}$ for the points $\{(x_k, y_k)\}_{k=1}^{N}$ by

$$\bar{x} = \frac{1}{N} \sum_{k=1}^{N} x_k \quad \text{and} \quad \bar{y} = \frac{1}{N} \sum_{k=1}^{N} y_k.$$

Show that the point $(\bar{x}, \bar{y})$ lies on the least-squares line determined by the given set of points.

5. Show that the solution of the system in (10) is given by

$$A = \frac{1}{D} \left(N \sum_{k=1}^{N} x_k y_k - \sum_{k=1}^{N} x_k \sum_{k=1}^{N} y_k \right),$$

$$B = \frac{1}{D} \left(\sum_{k=1}^{N} x_k^2 \sum_{k=1}^{N} y_k - \sum_{k=1}^{N} x_k \sum_{k=1}^{N} x_k y_k \right),$$

where

$$D = N \sum_{k=1}^{N} x_k^2 - \left(\sum_{k=1}^{N} x_k \right)^2.$$

Hint. Use Gaussian elimination on the system in (10).

6. Show that the value of D in Exercise 5 is nonzero.
Hint. Show that $D = N \sum_{k=1}^{N} (x_k - \bar{x})^2$.

7. Show that the coefficients A and B for the least-squares line can be computed as follows. First compute the means $\bar{x}$ and $\bar{y}$ in Exercise 4, and then perform the calculations:

$$C = \sum_{k=1}^{N} (x_k - \bar{x})^2, \quad A = \frac{1}{C} \sum_{k=1}^{N} (x_k - \bar{x})(y_k - \bar{y}), \quad B = \bar{y} - A\bar{x}.$$

Hint. Use $X_k = x_k - \bar{x}$, $Y_k = y_k - \bar{y}$ and first find the line $Y = AX$.

8. Find the power fits $y = Ax^2$ and $y = Bx^3$ for the following data and use $E_2(f)$ to determine which curve fits best.

(a)

x_k	y_k
2.0	5.1
2.3	7.5
2.6	10.6
2.9	14.4
3.2	19.0

(b)

x_k	y_k
2.0	5.9
2.3	8.3
2.6	10.7
2.9	13.7
3.2	17.0

9. Find the power fits $y = A/x$ and $y = B/x^2$ for the following data and use $E_2(f)$ to determine which curve fits best.

(a)

x_k	y_k
0.5	7.1
0.8	4.4
1.1	3.2
1.8	1.9
4.0	0.9

(b)

x_k	y_k
0.7	8.1
0.9	4.9
1.1	3.3
1.6	1.6
3.0	0.5

10. (a)   Derive the normal equation for finding the least-squares linear fit through the origin $y = Ax$.

   (b)   Derive the normal equation for finding the least-squares power fit $y = Ax^2$.

   (c)   Derive the normal equations for finding the least-squares parabola $y = Ax^2 + B$.

11. Consider the construction of a least-squares line for each of the sets of data points determined by $S_N = \{(k/N, (k/N)^2)\}_{k=1}^{N}$, where $N = 2, 3, 4, \ldots$. Note that for each value of N, the points in S_N all lie on the graph of $f(x) = x^2$ over the closed interval $[0, 1]$. Let $\bar{x}_N$ and $\bar{y}_N$ be the means for the given data points (see Exercise 4). Let $\hat{x}$ be the mean of the values of x in the interval $[0, 1]$, and let $\hat{y}$ be the mean (average) value of $f(x) = x^2$ over the interval $[0, 1]$.

   (a)   Show $\lim_{N \to \infty} \bar{x}_N = \hat{x}$.

   (b)   Show $\lim_{N \to \infty} \bar{y}_N = \hat{y}$.

12. Consider the construction of a least-squares line for each of the sets of data points:

$$S_N = \left\{ \left((b-a)\frac{k}{N} + a, \; f((b-a)\frac{k}{N} + a) \right) \right\}_{k=1}^{N}$$

for $N = 2, 3, 4, \ldots$. Assume that $y = f(x)$ is an integrable function over the closed interval $[a, b]$. Repeat parts (a) and (b) from Exercise 11.

Algorithms and Programs

1. Hooke's law states that $F = kx$, where F is the force (in ounces) used to stretch a spring and x is the increase in its length (in inches). Use Program 5.1 to find an approximation to the spring constant k for the following data.

   (a)

x_k	F_k
0.2	3.6
0.4	7.3
0.6	10.9
0.8	14.5
1.0	18.2

   (b)

x_k	F_k
0.2	5.3
0.4	10.6
0.6	15.9
0.8	21.2
1.0	26.4

2. Write a program to find the gravitational constant g for the following sets of data. Use the power fit that was shown in Example 5.3.

   (a)

Time, t_k	Distance, d_k
0.200	0.1960
0.400	0.7835
0.600	1.7630
0.800	3.1345
1.000	4.8975

   (b)

Time, t_k	Distance, d_k
0.200	0.1965
0.400	0.7855
0.600	1.7675
0.800	3.1420
1.000	4.9095

3. The following data give the distances of the nine planets from the sun and their sidereal period in days.

Planet	Distance from sun (km $\times 10^6$)	Sidereal period (days)
Mercury	57.59	87.99
Venus	108.11	224.70
Earth	149.57	365.26
Mars	227.84	686.98
Jupiter	778.14	4,332.4
Saturn	1427.0	10,759
Uranus	2870.3	30,684
Neptune	4499.9	60,188
Pluto	5909.0	90,710

   Modify your program from Problem 2 to calculate $E_2(f)$. Use it to find the power fit of the form $y = Cx^{3/2}$ for (a) the first four planets and (b) all nine planets.

4. (a) Find the least-squares line for the data points $\{(x_k, y_k)\}_{k=1}^{50}$, where $x_k = (0.1)k$ and $y_k = x_k + \cos(k^{1/2})$.

   (b) Calculate $E_2(f)$.

   (c) Plot the set of data points and the least-squares line on the same coordinate system.

5.2   Methods of Curve Fitting

Data Linearization Method for $y = Ce^{Ax}$

Suppose that we are given the points $(x_1, y_1), (x_2, y_2), \ldots, (x_N, y_N)$ and want to fit an exponential curve of the form

$$(1) \qquad\qquad\qquad\qquad y = Ce^{Ax}.$$

The first step is to take the logarithm of both sides:

$$(2) \qquad\qquad\qquad\qquad \ln(y) = Ax + \ln(C).$$

Then introduce the change of variables:

$$(3) \qquad\qquad Y = \ln(y), \qquad X = x, \qquad \text{and} \qquad B = \ln(C).$$

This results in a linear relation between the new variables X and Y:

$$(4) \qquad\qquad\qquad\qquad Y = AX + B.$$

The original points (x_k, y_k) in the xy-plane are transformed into the points $(X_k, Y_k) = (x_k, \ln(y_k))$ in the XY-plane. This process is called **data linearization**. Then the least-squares line (4) is fit to the points $\{(X_k, Y_k)\}$. The normal equations for finding A and B are

$$(5) \qquad
\begin{aligned}
\left(\sum_{k=1}^{N} X_k^2 \right) A + \left(\sum_{k=1}^{N} X_k \right) B &= \sum_{k=1}^{N} X_k Y_k, \\[2mm]
\left(\sum_{k=1}^{N} X_k \right) A + \quad N B \quad &= \sum_{k=1}^{N} Y_k.
\end{aligned}$$

After A and B have been found, the parameter C in equation (1) is computed:

$$(6) \qquad\qquad\qquad\qquad C = e^{B}.$$

Example 5.4.   Use the data linearization method and find the exponential fit $y = Ce^{Ax}$ for the five data points $(0, 1.5)$, $(1, 2.5)$, $(2, 3.5)$, $(3, 5.0)$, and $(4, 7.5)$.
   Apply the transformation (3) to the original points and obtain

$$(7) \quad
\begin{aligned}
\{(X_k, Y_k)\} &= \{(0, \ln(1.5), (1, \ln(2.5)), (2, \ln(3.5)), (3, \ln(5.0)), (4, \ln(7.5))\} \\
&= \{(0, 0.40547), (1, 0.91629), (2, 1.25276), (3, 1.60944), (4, 2.01490)\}.
\end{aligned}$$

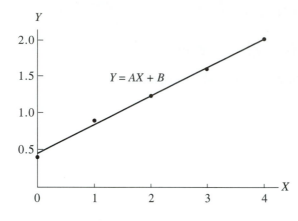

Figure 5.4 The transformed data points $\{(X_k, Y_k)\}$.

Table 5.4 Obtaining Coefficients of the Normal Equations for the Transformed Data Points $\{(X_k, Y_k)\}$

x_k	y_k	X_k	$Y_k = \ln(y_k)$	X_k^2	$X_k Y_k$
0.0	1.5	0.0	0.405465	0.0	0.000000
1.0	2.5	1.0	0.916291	1.0	0.916291
2.0	3.5	2.0	1.252763	4.0	2.505526
3.0	5.0	3.0	1.609438	9.0	4.828314
4.0	7.5	4.0	2.014903	16.0	8.059612
		10.0	6.198860	30.0	16.309743
		$= \sum X_k$	$= \sum Y_k$	$= \sum X_k^2$	$= \sum X_k Y_k$

These transformed points are shown in Figure 5.4 and exhibit a linearized form. The equation of the least-squares line $Y = AX + B$ for the points (7) in Figure 5.4 is

$$(8) \qquad\qquad Y = 0.391202X + 0.457367.$$

Calculation of the coefficients for the normal equations in (5) is shown in Table 5.4.
The resulting linear system (5) for determining A and B is

$$(9) \qquad\qquad \begin{aligned} 30A + 10B &= 16.309742 \\ 10A + 5B &= 6.198860. \end{aligned}$$

The solution is $A = 0.3912023$ and $B = 0.457367$. Then C is obtained with the calculation $C = e^{0.457367} = 1.579910$, and these values for A and C are substituted into equation (1) to obtain the exponential fit (see Figure 5.5):

$$(10) \qquad\qquad y = 1.579910e^{0.3912023x} \qquad \text{(fit by data linearization).} \qquad\blacksquare$$

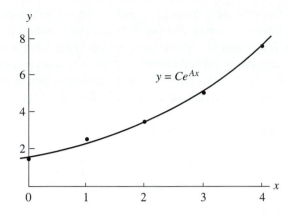

Figure 5.5   The exponential fit $y = 1.579910e^{0.3912023x}$ obtained by using the data linearization method.

Nonlinear Least-Squares Method for $y = Ce^{Ax}$

Suppose that we are given the points $(x_1, y_1), (x_2, y_2), \ldots, (x_N, y_N)$ and want to fit an exponential curve:

$$(11) \qquad\qquad y = Ce^{Ax}.$$

The nonlinear least-squares procedure requires that we find a minimum of

$$(12) \qquad E(A, C) = \sum_{k=1}^{N} (Ce^{Ax_k} - y_k)^2.$$

The partial derivatives of $E(A, C)$ with respect to A and C are

$$(13) \qquad \frac{\partial E}{\partial A} = 2 \sum_{k=1}^{N} (Ce^{Ax_k} - y_k)(Cx_k e^{Ax_k})$$

and

$$(14) \qquad \frac{\partial E}{\partial C} = 2 \sum_{k=1}^{N} (Ce^{Ax_k} - y_k)(e^{Ax_k}).$$

When the partial derivatives in (13) and (14) are set equal to zero and then simplified, the resulting normal equations are

$$(15) \qquad \begin{aligned} C \sum_{k=1}^{N} x_k e^{2Ax_k} - \sum_{k=1}^{N} x_k y_k e^{Ax_k} &= 0, \\ C \sum_{k=1}^{N} e^{Ax_k} - \sum_{k=1}^{N} y_k e^{Ax_k} &= 0. \end{aligned}$$

The equations in (15) are nonlinear in the unknowns A and C and can be solved using Newton's method. This is a time-consuming computation and the iteration involved requires good starting values for A and C. Many software packages have a built-in minimization subroutine for functions of several variables that can be used to minimize $E(A, C)$ directly, For example, the Nelder-Mead simplex algorithm can be used to minimize (12) directly and bypass the need for equations (13) through (15).

Example 5.5.   Use the least-squares method and determine the exponential fit $y = Ce^{Ax}$ for the five data points $(0, 1.5)$, $(1, 2.5)$, $(2, 3.5)$, $(3, 5.0)$, and $(4, 7.5)$.

For this solution we must minimize the quantity $E(A, C)$, which is

$$
(16) \qquad
\begin{aligned}
E(A, C) &= (C - 1.5)^2 + (Ce^A - 2.5)^2 + (Ce^{2A} - 3.5)^2 \\
&\quad + (Ce^{3A} - 5.0)^2 + (Ce^{4A} - 7.5)^2.
\end{aligned}
$$

We use the `fmins` command in MATLAB to approximate the values of A and C that minimize $E(A, C)$. First we define $E(A, C)$ as an M-file in MATLAB.

```
function z=E(u)
A=u(1);
C=u(2);
z=(C-1.5).^2+(C.*exp(A)-2.5).^2+(C.*exp(2*A)-3.5).^2+...
    (C.*exp(3*A)-5.0).^2+(C.*exp(4*A)-7.5).^2;
```

Using the `fmins` command in the MATLAB Command Window and the initial values $A = 1.0$ and $C = 1.0$, we find

```
>>fmins('E',[1 1])
ans =
   0.38357046980073 1.61089952247928
```

Thus the exponential fit to the five data points is

$$
(17) \qquad y = 1.6108995 e^{0.3835705} \qquad \text{(fit by nonlinear least squares)}.
$$

A comparison of the solutions using data linearization and nonlinear least squares is given in Table 5.5. There is a slight difference in the coefficients. For the purpose of interpolation it can be seen that the approximations differ by no more than 2% over the interval $[0, 4]$ (see Table 5.5 and Figure 5.6). If there is a normal distribution of the errors in the data, (17) is usually the preferred choice. When extrapolation is made beyond the range of the data, the two solutions will diverge and the discrepancy increases to about 6% when $x = 10$.   ∎

Transformations for Data Linearization

The technique of data linearization has been used by scientists to fit curves such as $y = Ce^{(Ax)}$, $y = A \ln(x) + B$, and $y = A/x + B$. Once the curve has been chosen, a suitable transformation of the variables must be found so that a linear relation is

Table 5.5 Comparison of the Two Exponential Fits

x_k	y_k	$1.5799e^{0.39120x}$	$1.6109e^{0.38357x}$
0.0	1.5	1.5799	1.6109
1.0	2.5	2.3363	2.3640
2.0	3.5	3.4548	3.4692
3.0	5.0	5.1088	5.0911
4.0	7.5	7.5548	7.4713
5.0		11.1716	10.9644
6.0		16.5202	16.0904
7.0		24.4293	23.6130
8.0		36.1250	34.6527
9.0		53.4202	50.8535
10.0		78.9955	74.6287

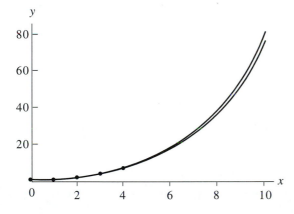

Figure 5.6 A graphical comparison of the two exponential curves.

obtained. For example, the reader can verify that $y = D/(x + C)$ is transformed into a linear problem $Y = AX + B$ by using the change of variables (and constants) $X = xy$, $Y = y$, $C = -1/A$, and $D = -B/A$. Graphs of several cases of the possibilities for the curves are shown in Figure 5.7, and other useful transformations are given in Table 5.6.

Linear Least Squares

The linear least-squares problem is stated as follows. Suppose that N data points $\{(x_k, y_k)\}$ and a set of M linear independent functions $\{f_j(x)\}$ are given. We want

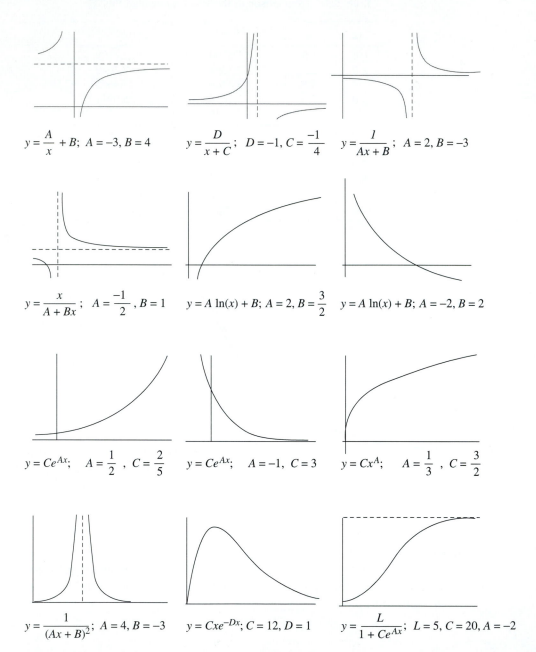

Figure 5.7 Possibilities for the curves used in "data linearization."

Table 5.6   Change of Variable(s) for Data Linearization

Function, $y = f(x)$	Linearized form, $Y = AX + B$	Change of variable(s) and constants
$y = \dfrac{A}{x} + B$	$y = A\dfrac{1}{x} + B$	$X = \dfrac{1}{x},\, Y = y$
$y = \dfrac{D}{x + C}$	$y + \dfrac{-1}{C}(xy) + \dfrac{D}{C}$	$X = xy,\, Y = y$
		$C = \dfrac{-1}{A},\, D = \dfrac{-B}{A}$
$y = \dfrac{1}{Ax + B}$	$\dfrac{1}{y} = Ax + B$	$X = x,\, Y = \dfrac{1}{y}$
$y = \dfrac{x}{Ax + B}$	$\dfrac{1}{y} = A\dfrac{1}{x} + B$	$X = \dfrac{1}{x},\, Y = \dfrac{1}{y}$
$y = A\ln(x) + B$	$y = A\ln(x) + B$	$X = \ln(x),\, Y = y$
$y = Ce^{Ax}$	$\ln(y) = Ax + \ln(C)$	$X = x,\, Y = \ln(y)$
		$C = e^{B}$
$y = Cx^{A}$	$\ln(y) = A\ln(x) + \ln(C)$	$X = \ln(x),\, Y = \ln(y)$
		$C = e^{B}$
$y = (Ax + B)^{-2}$	$y^{-1/2} = Ax + B$	$X = x,\, Y = y^{-1/2}$
$y = Cxe^{-Dx}$	$\ln\left(\dfrac{y}{x}\right) = -Dx + \ln(C)$	$X = x,\, Y = \ln\left(\dfrac{y}{x}\right)$
		$C = e^{B},\, D = -A$
$y = \dfrac{L}{1 + Ce^{Ax}}$	$\ln\left(\dfrac{L}{y} - 1\right) = Ax + \ln(C)$	$X = x,\, Y = \ln\left(\dfrac{L}{y} - 1\right)$
		$C = e^{B}$ and L is a constant that must be given

to find M coefficients $\{c_j\}$ so that the function $f(x)$ given by the linear combination

$$(18) \qquad f(x) = \sum_{j=1}^{M} c_j f_j(x)$$

will minimize the sum of the squares of the errors:

$$(19) \quad E(c_1, c_2, \ldots, c_M) = \sum_{k=1}^{N}(f(x_k) - y_k)^2 = \sum_{k=1}^{N}\left(\left(\sum_{j=1}^{M} c_j f_j(x_k)\right) - y_k\right)^2.$$

For E to be minimized it is necessary that each partial derivative be zero (i.e., $\partial E/\partial c_i = 0$ for $i = 1, 2, \ldots, M$), and this results in the system of equations

(20) $$\sum_{k=1}^{N} \left(\left(\sum_{j=1}^{M} c_j f_j(x_k) \right) - y_k \right) (f_i(x_k)) = 0 \quad \text{for } i = 1, 2, \ldots, M.$$

Interchanging the order of the summations in (20) will produce an $M \times M$ system of linear equations where the unknowns are the coefficients $\{c_j\}$. They are called the normal equations:

(21) $$\sum_{j=1}^{M} \left(\sum_{k=1}^{N} f_i(x_k) f_j(x_k) \right) c_j = \sum_{k=1}^{N} f_i(x_k) y_k \quad \text{for } i = 1, 2, \ldots, M.$$

Matrix Formulation

Although (21) is easily recognized as a system of M linear equations in M unknowns, one must be clever so that wasted computations are not performed when writing the system in matrix notation. The key is to write down the matrices $\boldsymbol{F}$ and $\boldsymbol{F}'$ as follows:

$$\boldsymbol{F} = \begin{bmatrix} f_1(x_1) & f_2(x_1) & \cdots & f_M(x_1) \\ f_1(x_2) & f_2(x_2) & \cdots & f_M(x_2) \\ f_1(x_3) & f_2(x_3) & \cdots & f_M(x_3) \\ \vdots & \vdots & & \vdots \\ f_1(x_N) & f_2(x_N) & \cdots & f_M(x_N) \end{bmatrix},$$

$$\boldsymbol{F}' = \begin{bmatrix} f_1(x_1) & f_1(x_2) & f_1(x_3) & \cdots & f_1(x_N) \\ f_2(x_1) & f_2(x_2) & f_2(x_3) & \cdots & f_2(x_N) \\ \vdots & \vdots & \vdots & & \vdots \\ f_M(x_1) & f_M(x_2) & f_M(x_3) & \cdots & f_M(x_N) \end{bmatrix}.$$

Consider the product of $\boldsymbol{F}'$ and the column matrix $\boldsymbol{Y}$:

(22) $$\boldsymbol{F}'\boldsymbol{Y} = \begin{bmatrix} f_1(x_1) & f_1(x_2) & f_1(x_3) & \cdots & f_1(x_N) \\ f_2(x_1) & f_2(x_2) & f_2(x_3) & \cdots & f_2(x_N) \\ \vdots & \vdots & \vdots & & \vdots \\ f_M(x_1) & f_M(x_2) & f_M(x_3) & \cdots & f_M(x_N) \end{bmatrix} \begin{bmatrix} y_1 \\ y_2 \\ \vdots \\ y_N \end{bmatrix}.$$

The element in the ith row of the product $\boldsymbol{F}'\boldsymbol{Y}$ in (22) is the same as the ith element in the column matrix in equation (21); that is,

(23) $$\sum_{k=1}^{N} f_i(x_k) y_k = \text{row}_i\, \boldsymbol{F}' \cdot [y_1 \quad y_2 \quad \cdots \quad y_N]'.$$

Now consider the product $F'F$, which is an $M \times M$ matrix:

$$F'F$$

$$= \begin{bmatrix} f_1(x_1) & f_1(x_2) & f_1(x_3) & \cdots & f_1(x_N) \\ f_2(x_1) & f_2(x_2) & f_2(x_3) & \cdots & f_2(x_N) \\ \vdots & \vdots & \vdots & & \vdots \\ f_M(x_1) & f_M(x_2) & f_M(x_3) & \cdots & f_M(x_N) \end{bmatrix} \begin{bmatrix} f_1(x_1) & f_2(x_1) & \cdots & f_M(x_1) \\ f_1(x_2) & f_2(x_2) & \cdots & f_M(x_2) \\ f_1(x_3) & f_2(x_3) & \cdots & f_M(x_3) \\ \vdots & \vdots & & \vdots \\ f_1(x_N) & f_2(x_N) & \cdots & f_M(x_N) \end{bmatrix}.$$

The element in the ith row and jth column of $F'F$ is the coefficient of c_j in the ith row in equation (21); that is,

$$(24) \qquad \sum_{k=1}^{N} f_i(x_k) f_j(x_k) = f_i(x_1) f_j(x_1) + f_i(x_2) f_j(x_2) + \cdots + f_i(x_N) f_j(x_N).$$

When M is small, a computationally efficient way to calculate the linear least-squares coefficients for (18) is to store the matrix F, compute $F'F$, and $F'Y$ and then solve the linear system

$$(25) \qquad\qquad F'FC = F'Y \qquad \text{for the coefficient matrix } C.$$

Polynomial Fitting

When the foregoing method is adapted to using the functions $\{f_j(x) = x^{j-1}\}$ and the index of summation ranges from $j = 1$ to $j = M + 1$, the function $f(x)$ will be a polynomial of degree M:

$$(26) \qquad\qquad f(x) = c_1 + c_2 x + c_3 x^2 + \cdots + c_{M+1} x^M.$$

We now show how to find the **least-squares parabola**, and the extension to a polynomial of higher degree is easily made and is left for the reader.

Theorem 5.3 (Least-Squares Parabola). Suppose that $\{(x_k, y_k)\}_{k=1}^{N}$ are N points, where the abscissas are distinct. The coefficients of the least-squares parabola

$$(27) \qquad\qquad y = f(x) = Ax^2 + Bx + C$$

are the solution values A, B, and C of the linear system

$$\left(\sum_{k=1}^{N} x_k^4 \right) A + \left(\sum_{k=1}^{N} x_k^3 \right) B + \left(\sum_{k=1}^{N} x_k^2 \right) C = \sum_{k=1}^{N} y_k x_k^2,$$

$$(28) \qquad \left(\sum_{k=1}^{N} x_k^3 \right) A + \left(\sum_{k=1}^{N} x_k^2 \right) B + \left(\sum_{k=1}^{N} x_k \right) C = \sum_{k=1}^{N} y_k x_k,$$

$$\left(\sum_{k=1}^{N} x_k^2 \right) A + \left(\sum_{k=1}^{N} x_k \right) B + NC = \sum_{k=1}^{N} y_k.$$

Table 5.7   Obtaining the Coefficients for the Least-Squares Parabola of Example 5.6

x_k	y_k	x_k^2	x_k^3	x_k^4	$x_k y_k$	$x_k^2 y_k$
-3	3	9	-27	81	-9	27
0	1	0	0	0	0	0
2	1	4	8	16	2	4
4	3	16	64	256	12	48
3	8	29	45	353	5	79

Proof.   The coefficients A, B, and C will minimize the quantity:

$$(29) \qquad E(A, B, C) = \sum_{k=1}^{N}(Ax_k^2 + Bx_k + C - y_k)^2.$$

The partial derivatives $\partial E / \partial A$, $\partial E / \partial B$, and $\partial E / \partial C$ must all be zero. This results in

$$0 = \frac{\partial E(A, B, C)}{\partial A} = 2\sum_{k=1}^{N}(Ax_k^2 + Bx_k + C - y_k)^1(x_k^2),$$

$$(30) \qquad 0 = \frac{\partial E(A, B, C)}{\partial B} = 2\sum_{k=1}^{N}(Ax_k^2 + Bx_k + C - y_k)^1(x_k),$$

$$0 = \frac{\partial E(A, B, C)}{\partial C} = 2\sum_{k=1}^{N}(Ax_k^2 + Bx_k + C - y_k)^1(1).$$

Using the distributive property of addition, we can move the values A, B, and C outside the summations in (30) to obtain the normal equations that are given in (28).   ●

Example 5.6.   Find the least-squares parabola for the four points $(-3, 3)$, $(0, 1)$, $(2, 1)$, and $(4, 3)$.

The entries in Table 5.7 are used to compute the summations required in the linear system (28).

The linear system (28) for finding A, B, and C becomes

$$353A + 45B + 29C = 79$$
$$45A + 29B + 3C = 5$$
$$29A + 3B + 4C = 8.$$

The solution to the linear system is $A = 585/3278$, $B = -631/3278$, and $C = 1394/1639$, and the desired parabola is (see Figure 5.8)

$$y = \frac{585}{3278}x^2 - \frac{631}{3278}x + \frac{1394}{1639} = 0.178462x^2 - 0.192495x + 0.850519. \qquad ■$$

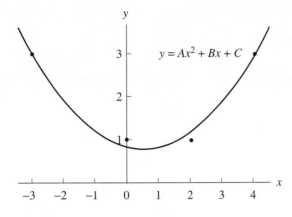

Figure 5.8 The least-squares parabola for Example 5.6.

Polynomial Wiggle

It is tempting to use a least-squares polynomial to fit data that are nonlinear. But if the data do not exhibit a polynomial nature, the resulting curve may exhibit large oscillations. This phenomenon, called ***polynomial wiggle***, becomes more pronounced with higher-degree polynomials. For this reason we seldom use a polynomial of degree 6 or above unless it is known that the true function we are working with is a polynomial.

For example, let $f(x) = 1.44/x^2 + 0.24x$ be used to generate the six data points $(0.25, 23.1)$, $(1.0, 1.68)$, $(1.5, 1.0)$, $(2.0, 0.84)$, $(2.4, 0.826)$, and $(5.0, 1.2576)$. The result of curve fitting with the least-squares polynomials

$$P_2(x) = 22.93 - 16.96x + 2.553x^2,$$

$$P_3(x) = 33.04 - 46.51x + 19.51x^2 - 2.296x^3,$$

$$P_4(x) = 39.92 - 80.93x + 58.39x^2 - 17.15x^3 + 1.680x^4,$$

and

$$P_5(x) = 46.02 - 118.1x + 119.4x^2 - 57.51x^3 + 13.03x^4 - 1.085x^5$$

is shown in Figure 5.9(a) through (d). Notice that $P_3(x)$, $P_4(x)$, and $P_5(x)$ exhibit a large wiggle in the interval $[2, 5]$. Even though $P_5(x)$ goes through the six points, it produces the worst fit. If we must fit a polynomial to these data, $P_2(x)$ should be the choice.

The following program uses the matrix F with entries $f_j(x) = x_k^{j-1}$ from equation (18).

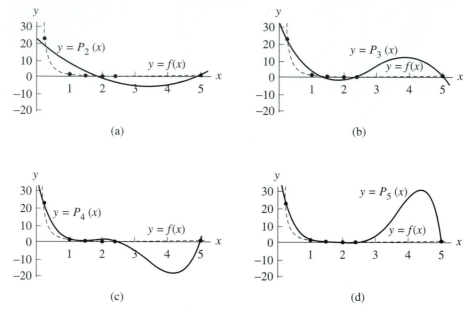

Figure 5.9 (a) Using $P_2(x)$ to fit data. (b) Using $P_3(x)$ to fit data. (c) Using $P_4(x)$ to fit data. (d) Using $P_5(x)$ to fit data.

Program 5.2 (Least-Squares Polynomial). To construct the least-squares polynomial of degree M of the form

$$P_M(x) = c_1 + c_2 x + c_3 x^2 + \cdots + c_M x^{M-1} + c_{M+1} x^M$$

that fits the N data points $\{(x_k, y_k)\}_{k=1}^{N}$.

```
function C = lspoly(X,Y,M)
%Input    - X is the 1xn abscissa vector
%         - Y is the 1xn ordinate vector
%         - M is the degree of the least-squares polynomial
% Output  - C is the coefficient list for the polynomial
n=length(X);
B=zeros(1:M+1);
F=zeros(n,M+1);
%Fill the columns of F with the powers of X
for k=1:M+1
    F(:,k)=X'.^(k-1);
end
%Solve the linear system from (25)
```

```
A=F'*F;
B=F'*Y';
C=A\B;
C=flipud(C);
```

Exercises for Methods of Curve Fitting

1. Find the least-squares parabola $f(x) = Ax^2 + Bx + C$ for each set of data.

(a)

x_k	y_k
-3	15
-1	5
1	1
3	5

(b)

x_k	y_k
-3	-1
-1	25
1	25
3	1

2. Find the least-squares parabola $f(x) = Ax^2 + Bx + C$ for each set of data.

(a)

x_k	y_k
-2	-5.8
-1	1.1
0	3.8
1	3.3
2	-1.5

(b)

x_k	y_k
-2	2.8
-1	2.1
0	3.25
1	6.0
2	11.5

(c)

x_k	y_k
-2	10
-1	1
0	0
1	2
2	9

3. For the given set of data, find the least-squares curve:

(a) $f(x) = Ce^{Ax}$, by using the change of variables $X = x$, $Y = \ln(y)$, and $C = e^B$, from Table 5.6, to linearize the data points.

(b) $f(x) = Cx^A$, by using the change of variables $X = \ln(x)$, $Y = \ln(y)$, and $C = e^B$, from Table 5.6, to linearize the data points.

(c) Use $E_2(f)$ to determine which curve gives the best fit.

x_k	y_k
1	0.6
2	1.9
3	4.3
4	7.6
5	12.6

4. For the given set of data, find the least-squares curve:

   (a) $f(x) = Ce^{Ax}$, by using the change of variables $X = x$, $Y = \ln(y)$, and $C = e^B$, from Table 5.6, to linearize the data points.

   (b) $f(x) = 1/(Ax + B)$, by using the change of variables $X = x$ and $Y = 1/y$, from Table 5.6, to linearize the data points.

   (c)   Use $E_2(f)$ to determine which curve gives the best fit.

x_k	y_k
-1	6.62
0	3.94
1	2.17
2	1.35
3	0.89

5. For each set of data, find the least-squares curve:

   (a) $f(x) = Ce^{Ax}$, by using the change of variables $X = x$, $Y = \ln(y)$, and $C = e^B$, from Table 5.6, to linearize the data points.

   (b) $f(x) = (Ax + B)^{-2}$, by using the change of variables $X = x$ and $Y = y^{-1/2}$, from Table 5.6, to linearize the data points.

   (c)   Use $E_2(f)$ to determine which curve gives the best fit.

(i)

x_k	y_k
-1	13.45
0	3.01
1	0.67
2	0.15

(ii)

x_k	y_k
-1	13.65
0	1.38
1	0.49
3	0.15

6. *Logistic population growth.* When the population $P(t)$ is bounded by the limiting value L, it follows a logistic curve and has the form $P(t) = L/(1 + Ce^{At})$. Find A and C for the following data, where L is a known value.

   (a) $(0, 200)$, $(1, 400)$, $(2, 650)$, $(3, 850)$, $(4, 950)$, and $L = 1000$.

   (b) $(0, 500)$, $(1, 1000)$, $(2, 1800)$, $(3, 2800)$, $(4, 3700)$, and $L = 5000$.

7. Use the data for the U.S. population and find the logistic curve $P(t)$. Estimate the population in the year 2000.

(a)   Assume that $L = 8 \times 10^8$.

Year	t_k	P_k
1800	-10	5.3
1850	-5	23.2
1900	0	76.1
1950	5	152.3

(b)   Assume that $L = 8 \times 10^8$.

Year	t_k	P_k
1900	0	76.1
1920	2	106.5
1940	4	132.6
1960	6	180.7
1980	8	226.5

In Exercises 8 through 15, carry out the indicated change of variables in Table 5.6, and derive the linearized form for each of the following functions.

8. $y = \dfrac{A}{x} + B$

9. $y = \dfrac{D}{x + C}$

10. $y = \dfrac{1}{Ax + B}$

11. $y = \dfrac{x}{A + Bx}$

12. $y = A \ln(x) + B$

13. $y = Cx^A$

14. $y = (Ax + B)^{-2}$

15. $y = Cxe^{-Dx}$

16. (a)   Follow the procedure outlined in the proof of Theorem 5.3 and derive the normal equations for the least-squares curve $f(x) = A\cos(x) + B\sin(x)$.

(b)   Use the results from part (a) to find the least-squares curve $f(x) = A\cos(x) + B\sin(x)$ for the following data:

x_k	y_k
-3.0	-0.1385
-1.5	-2.1587
0.0	0.8330
1.5	2.2774
3.0	-0.5110

17. The least-squares plane $z = Ax + By + C$ for the N points $(x_1, y_1, z_1), \ldots,$ (x_N, y_N, z_N) is obtained by minimizing

$$E(A, B, C) = \sum_{k=1}^{N}(Ax_k + By_k + C - z_k)^2.$$

Derive the normal equations:

$$\left(\sum_{k=1}^{N} x_k^2\right) A + \left(\sum_{k=1}^{N} x_k y_k\right) B + \left(\sum_{k=1}^{N} x_k\right) C = \sum_{k=1}^{N} z_k x_k,$$

$$\left(\sum_{k=1}^{N} x_k y_k\right) A + \left(\sum_{k=1}^{N} y_k^2\right) B + \left(\sum_{k=1}^{N} y_k\right) C = \sum_{k=1}^{N} z_k y_k,$$

$$\left(\sum_{k=1}^{N} x_k\right) A + \left(\sum_{k=1}^{N} y_k\right) B + NC = \sum_{k=1}^{N} z_k.$$

18. Find the least-squares planes for the following data.
    (a) $(1, 1, 7), (1, 2, 9), (2, 1, 10), (2, 2, 11), (2, 3, 12)$
    (b) $(1, 2, 6), (2, 3, 7), (1, 1, 8), (2, 2, 8), (2, 1, 9)$
    (c) $(3, 1, -3), (2, 1, -1), (2, 2, 0), (1, 1, 1), (1, 2, 3)$

19. Consider the following table of data:

x_k	y_k
1.0	2.0
2.0	5.0
3.0	10.0
4.0	17.0
5.0	26.0

When the change of variables $X = xy$ and $Y = 1/y$ are used with the function $y = D/(x + C)$, the transformed least-squares fit is

$$y = \frac{-17.719403}{x - 5.476617}.$$

When the change of variables $X = x$ and $Y = 1/y$ are used with the function $y = 1/(Ax + B)$, the transformed least-squares fit is

$$y = \frac{1}{-0.1064253x + 0.4987330}.$$

Determine which fit is best and why one of the solutions is completely absurd.

Algorithms and Programs

1. The temperature cycle in a suburb of Los Angeles on November 8 is given in the accompanying table. There are 24 data points.
   (a) Follow the procedure outlined in Example 5.5 (use the `fmins` command) to find the least-squares curve of the form $f(x) = A\cos(Bx) + C\sin(Dx) + E$ for the given set of data.

(b)   Determine $E_2(f)$.

(c)   Plot the data and the least-squares curve from part (a) on the same coordinate system.

Time, p.m.	Degrees	Time, a.m.	Degrees
1	66	1	58
2	66	2	58
3	65	3	58
4	64	4	58
5	63	5	57
6	63	6	57
7	62	7	57
8	61	8	58
9	60	9	60
10	60	10	64
11	59	11	67
Midnight	58	Noon	68

5.3   Interpolation by Spline Functions

Polynomial interpolation for a set of $N + 1$ points $\{(x_k, y_k)\}_{k=0}^{N}$ is frequently unsatisfactory. As discussed in Section 5.2, a polynomial of degree N can have $N - 1$ relative maxima and minima, and the graph can wiggle in order to pass through the points. Another method is to piece together the graphs of lower-degree polynomials $S_k(x)$ and interpolate between the successive nodes (x_k, y_k) and (x_{k+1}, y_{k+1}) (see Figure 5.10).

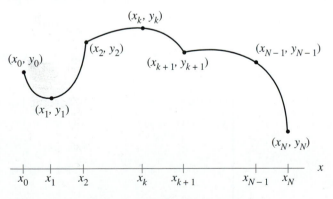

Figure 5.10   Piecewise polynomial interpolation.

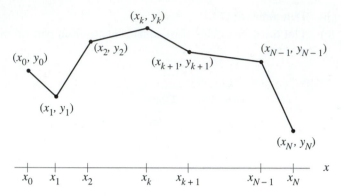

Figure 5.11 Piecewise linear interpolation (a linear spline).

The two adjacent portions of the curve $y = S_k(x)$ and $y = S_{k+1}(x)$, which lie above $[x_k, x_{k+1}]$ and $[x_{k+1}, x_{k+2}]$, respectively, pass through the common **knot** (x_{k+1}, y_{k+1}). The two portions of the graph are tied together at the knot (x_{k+1}, y_{k+1}), and the set of functions $\{S_k(x)\}$ forms a piecewise polynomial curve, which is denoted by $S(x)$.

Piecewise Linear Interpolation

The simplest polynomial to use, a polynomial of degree 1, produces a polygonal path that consists of line segments that pass through the points. The Lagrange polynomial from Section 4.3 is used to represent this piecewise linear curve:

$$(1) \qquad S_k(x) = y_k \frac{x - x_{k+1}}{x_k - x_{k+1}} + y_{k+1} \frac{x - x_k}{x_{k+1} - x_k} \qquad \text{for } x_k \leq x \leq x_{k+1}.$$

The resulting curve looks like a broken line (see Figure 5.11).

An equivalent expression can be obtained if we use the point-slope formula for a line segment:

$$S_k(x) = y_k + d_k(x - x_k),$$

where $d_k = (y_{k+1} - y_k)/(x_{k+1} - x_k)$. The resulting **linear spline** function can be written in the form

$$(2) \qquad S(x) = \begin{cases} y_0 + d_0(x - x_0) & \text{for } x \text{ in } [x_0, x_1], \\ y_1 + d_1(x - x_1) & \text{for } x \text{ in } [x_1, x_2], \\ \quad \vdots & \quad \vdots \\ y_k + d_k(x - x_k) & \text{for } x \text{ in } [x_k, x_{k+1}], \\ \quad \vdots & \quad \vdots \\ y_{N-1} + d_{N-1}(x - x_{N-1}) & \text{for } x \text{ in } [x_{N-1}, x_N]. \end{cases}$$

The form of equation (2) is better than equation (1) for the explicit calculation of $S(x)$. It is assumed that the abscissas are ordered $x_0 < x_1 < \cdots < x_{N-1} < x_N$. For a fixed value of x, the interval $[x_k, x_{k+1}]$ containing x can be found by successively computing the differences $x - x_1, \ldots, x - x_k, x - x_{k+1}$ until $k + 1$ is the smallest integer such that $x - x_{k+1} < 0$. Hence we have found k so that $x_k \leq x \leq x_{k+1}$, and the value of the spline function $S(x)$ is

$$(3) \qquad S(x) = S_k(x) = y_k + d_k(x - x_k) \qquad \text{for } x_k \leq x \leq x_{k+1}.$$

These techniques can be extended to higher-order polynomials. For example, if an odd number of nodes $x_0, x_1, \ldots, x_{2M}$ is given, then a piecewise quadratic polynomial can be constructed on each subinterval $[x_{2k}, x_{2k+2}]$, for $k = 0, 1, \ldots, M - 1$. A shortcoming of the resulting quadratic spline is that the curvature at the even nodes x_{2k} changes abruptly, and this can cause an undesired bend or distortion in the graph. The second derivative of a quadratic spline is discontinuous at the even nodes. If we use piecewise cubic polynomials, then both the first and second derivatives can be made continuous.

Piecewise Cubic Splines

The fitting of a polynomial curve to a set of data points has applications in CAD (computer-assisted design), CAM (computer-assisted manufacturing), and computer graphics systems. An operator wants to draw a smooth curve through data points that are not subject to error. Traditionally, it was common to use a french curve or an architect's spline and subjectively draw a curve that looks smooth when viewed by the eye. Mathematically, it is possible to construct cubic functions $S_k(x)$ on each interval $[x_k, x_{k+1}]$ so that the resulting piecewise curve $y = S(x)$ and its first and second derivatives are all continuous on the larger interval $[x_0, x_N]$. The continuity of $S'(x)$ means that the graph $y = S(x)$ will not have sharp corners. The continuity of $S''(x)$ means that the *radius of curvature* is defined at each point.

Definition 5.1. Suppose that $\{(x_k, y_k)\}_{k=0}^{N}$ are $N + 1$ points, where $a = x_0 < x_1 < \cdots < x_N = b$. The function $S(x)$ is called a **cubic spline** if there exist N cubic polynomials $S_k(x)$ with coefficients $s_{k,0}$, $s_{k,1}$, $s_{k,2}$, and $s_{k,3}$ that satisfy the following properties:

   I. $S(x) = S_k(x) = s_{k,0} + s_{k,1}(x - x_k) + s_{k,2}(x - x_k)^2 + s_{k,3}(x - x_k)^3$
       for $x \in [x_k, x_{k+1}]$ and $k = 0, 1, \ldots, N - 1$.

  II. $S(x_k) = y_k$ for $k = 0, 1, \ldots, N$.

 III. $S_k(x_{k+1}) = S_{k+1}(x_{k+1})$ for $k = 0, 1, \ldots, N - 2$.

 IV. $S_k'(x_{k+1}) = S_{k+1}'(x_{k+1})$ for $k = 0, 1, \ldots, N - 2$.

  V. $S_k''(x_{k+1}) = S_{k+1}''(x_{k+1})$ for $k = 0, 1, \ldots, N - 2$.   ▲

Property I states that $S(x)$ consists of piecewise cubics. Property II states that the piecewise cubics interpolate the given set of data points. Properties III and IV require that the piecewise cubics represent a smooth continuous function. Property V states that the second derivative of the resulting function is also continuous.

Existence of Cubic Splines

Let us try to determine if it is possible to construct a cubic spline that satisfies properties I through V. Each cubic polynomial $S_k(x)$ has four unknown constants ($s_{k,0}$, $s_{k,1}$, $s_{k,2}$, and $s_{k,3}$); hence there are $4N$ coefficients to be determined. Loosely speaking, we have $4N$ degrees of freedom or conditions that must be specified. The data points supply $N + 1$ conditions, and properties III, IV, and V each supply $N - 1$ conditions. Hence, $N + 1 + 3(N - 1) = 4N - 2$ conditions are specified. This leaves us two additional degrees of freedom. We will call them ***endpoint constraints***: they will involve either $S'(x)$ or $S''(x)$ at x_0 and x_N and will be discussed later. We now proceed with the construction.

Since $S(x)$ is piecewise cubic, its second derivative $S''(x)$ is piecewise linear on $[x_0, x_N]$. The linear Lagrange interpolation formula gives the following representation for $S''(x) = S_k''(x)$:

$$(4) \qquad S_k''(x) = S''(x_k)\frac{x - x_{k+1}}{x_k - x_{k+1}} + S''(x_{k+1})\frac{x - x_k}{x_{k+1} - x_k}.$$

Use $m_k = S''(x_k)$, $m_{k+1} = S''(x_{k+1})$, and $h_k = x_{k+1} - x_k$ in (4) to get

$$(5) \qquad S_k''(x) = \frac{m_k}{h_k}(x_{k+1} - x) + \frac{m_{k+1}}{h_k}(x - x_k)$$

for $x_k \leq x \leq x_{k+1}$ and $k = 0, 1, \ldots, N - 1$. Integrating (5) twice will introduce two constants of integration, and the result can be manipulated so that it has the form

$$(6) \quad S_k(x) = \frac{m_k}{6h_k}(x_{k+1} - x)^3 + \frac{m_{k+1}}{6h_k}(x - x_k)^3 + p_k(x_{k+1} - x) + q_k(x - x_k).$$

Substituting x_k and x_{k+1} into equation (6) and using the values $y_k = S_k(x_k)$ and $y_{k+1} = S_k(x_{k+1})$ yields the following equations that involve p_k and q_k, respectively:

$$(7) \qquad y_k = \frac{m_k}{6}h_k^2 + p_k h_k \quad \text{and} \quad y_{k+1} = \frac{m_{k+1}}{6}h_k^2 + q_k h_k.$$

These two equations are easily solved for p_k and q_k, and when these values are substituted into equation (6), the result is the following expression for the cubic function $S_k(x)$:

$$\begin{aligned}(8) \qquad S_k(x) = & -\frac{m_k}{6h_k}(x_{k+1} - x)^3 + \frac{m_{k+1}}{6h_k}(x - x_k)^3 \\ & + \left(\frac{y_k}{h_k} - \frac{m_k h_k}{6}\right)(x_{k+1} - x) + \left(\frac{y_{k+1}}{h_k} - \frac{m_{k+1}h_k}{6}\right)(x - x_k).\end{aligned}$$

Notice that the representation (8) has been reduced to a form that involves only the unknown coefficients $\{m_k\}$. To find these values, we must use the derivative of (8), which is

(9)
$$S_k'(x) = -\frac{m_k}{2h_k}(x_{k+1} - x)^2 + \frac{m_{k+1}}{2h_k}(x - x_k)^2$$
$$-\left(\frac{y_k}{h_k} - \frac{m_k h_k}{6}\right) + \frac{y_{k+1}}{h_k} - \frac{m_{k+1}h_k}{h_k}.$$

Evaluating (9) at x_k and simplifying the result yield

(10) $\qquad S_k'(x_k) = -\dfrac{m_k}{3}h_k - \dfrac{m_{k+1}}{6}h_k + d_k, \qquad \text{where } d_k = \dfrac{y_{k+1} - y_k}{h_k}.$

Similarly, we can replace k by $k - 1$ in (9) to get the expression for $S_{k-1}'(x)$ and evaluate it at x_k to obtain

(11) $\qquad S_{k-1}'(x_k) = \dfrac{m_k}{3}h_{k-1} + \dfrac{m_{k-1}}{6}h_{k-1} + d_{k-1}.$

Now use property IV and equations (10) and (11) to obtain an important relation involving m_{k-1}, m_k, and m_{k+1}:

(12) $\qquad h_{k-1}m_{k-1} + 2(h_{k-1} + h_k)m_k + h_k m_{k+1} = u_k,$

where $u_k = 6\,(d_k - d_{k-1})$ for $k = 1, 2, \ldots, N - 1$.

Construction of Cubic Splines

Observe that the unknowns in (12) are the desired values $\{m_k\}$, and the other terms are constants obtained by performing simple arithmetic with the data points $\{(x_k, y_k)\}$. Therefore, in reality, system (12) is an underdetermined system of $N - 1$ linear equations involving $N + 1$ unknowns. Hence two additional equations must be supplied. They are used to eliminate m_0 from the first equation and m_N from the $(N - 1)$st equation in system (12). The standard strategies for the endpoint constraints are summarized in Table 5.8.

Consider strategy (v) in Table 5.8. If m_0 is given, then $h_0 m_0$ can be computed, and the first equation (when $k = 1$) of (12) is

(13) $\qquad 2(h_0 + h_1)m_1 + h_1 m_2 = u_1 - h_0 m_0.$

Table 5.8 Endpoint Constraints for a Cubic Spline

	Description of the strategy	Equations involving m_0 and m_N
(i)	*Clamped cubic spline:* specify $S'(x_0)$, $S'(x_n)$ (the "best choice" if the derivatives are known)	$m_0 = \dfrac{3}{h_0}(d_0 - S'(x_0)) - \dfrac{m_1}{2}$ $m_N = \dfrac{3}{h_{N-1}}(S'(x_N) - d_{N-1}) - \dfrac{m_{N-1}}{2}$
(ii)	*Natural cubic spline* (a "relaxed curve")	$m_0 = 0, m_N = 0$
(iii)	Extrapolate $S''(x)$ to the endpoints	$m_0 = m_1 - \dfrac{h_0(m_2 - m_1)}{h_1},$ $m_N = m_{N-1} + \dfrac{h_{N-1}(m_{N-1} - m_{N-2})}{h_{N-2}}$
(iv)	$S''(x)$ is constant near the endpoints	$m_0 = m_1, m_N = m_{N-1}$
(v)	Specify $S''(X)$ at each endpoint	$m_0 = S''(x_0), m_N = S''(x_N)$

Similarly, if m_N is given, then $h_{N-1}m_N$ can be computed, and the last equation (when $k = N - 1$) of (12) is

$$(14) \qquad h_{N-2}m_{N-2} + 2(h_{N-2} + h_{N-1})m_{N-1} = u_{N-1} - h_{N-1}m_N.$$

Equations (13) and (14) with (12) used for $k = 2, 3, \ldots, N - 2$ form $N - 1$ linear equations involving the coefficients $m_1, m_2, \ldots, m_{N-1}$.

Regardless of the particular strategy chosen in Table 5.8, we can rewrite equations 1 and $N - 1$ in (12) and obtain a tridiagonal linear system of the form $HM = V$, which involves $m_1, m_2, \ldots, m_{N-1}$:

$$(15) \qquad \begin{bmatrix} b_1 & c_1 & & & & \\ a_1 & b_2 & c_2 & & & \\ & & \ddots & & & \\ & & & a_{N-3} & b_{N-2} & c_{N-2} \\ & & & & a_{N-2} & b_{N-1} \end{bmatrix} \begin{bmatrix} m_1 \\ m_2 \\ \vdots \\ m_{N-2} \\ m_{N-1} \end{bmatrix} = \begin{bmatrix} v_1 \\ v_2 \\ \vdots \\ v_{N-2} \\ v_{N-1} \end{bmatrix}.$$

The linear system in (15) is strictly diagonally dominant and has a unique solution (see Chapter 3 for details). After the coefficients $\{m_k\}$ are determined, the spline coefficients $\{s_{k,j}\}$ for $S_k(x)$ are computed using the formulas

(16)
$$s_{k,0} = y_k, \qquad s_{k,1} = d_k - \frac{h_k(2m_k + m_{k+1})}{6},$$

$$s_{k,2} = \frac{m_k}{2}, \qquad s_{k,3} = \frac{m_{k+1} - m_k}{6h_k}.$$

Each cubic polynomial $S_k(x)$ can be written in nested multiplication form for efficient computation:

(17) $\qquad S_k(x) = ((s_{k,3}w + s_{k,2})w + s_{k,1})w + y_k, \qquad$ where $w = x - x_k$

and $S_k(x)$ is used on the interval $x_k \le x \le x_{k+1}$.

Equations (12) together with a strategy from Table 5.8 can be used to construct a cubic spline with distinctive properties at the endpoints. Specifically, the values for m_0 and m_N in Table 5.8 are used to customize the first and last equations in (12) and form the system of $N - 1$ equations given in (15). Then the tridiagonal system is solved for the remaining coefficients $m_1, m_2, \ldots, m_{N-1}$. Finally, the formulas in (16) are used to determine the spline coefficients. For reference, we now state how the equations must be prepared for each different type of spline.

Endpoint Constraints

The following five lemmas show the form of the tridiagonal linear system that must be solved for each of the different endpoint constraints in Table 5.8.

Lemma 5.1 (Clamped Spline).   There exists a unique cubic spline with the first derivative boundary conditions $S'(a) = d_0$ and $S'(b) = d_N$.

Proof.   Solve the linear system

$$\left(\frac{3}{2}h_0 + 2h_1\right)m_1 + h_1m_2 = u_1 - 3(d_0 - S'(x_0))$$

$$h_{k-1}m_{k-1} + 2(h_{k-1} + h_k)m_k + h_km_{k+1} = u_k \qquad \text{for } k = 2, 3, \ldots, N-2$$

$$h_{N-2}m_{N-2} + \left(2h_{N-2} + \frac{3}{2}h_{N-1}\right)m_{N-1} = u_{N-1} - 3(S'(x_N) - d_{N-1}). \qquad \bullet$$

Remark. The clamped spline involves slope at the ends. This spline can be visualized as the curve obtained when a flexible elastic rod is forced to pass through the data points, and the rod is clamped at each end with a fixed slope. This spline would be useful to a draftsman for drawing a smooth curve through several points.

Lemma 5.2 (Natural Spline).   There exists a unique cubic spline with the free boundary conditions $S''(a) = 0$ and $S''(b) = 0$.

Proof.   Solve the linear system

$$2(h_0 + h_1)m_1 + h_1 m_2 = u_1$$
$$h_{k-1}m_{k-1} + 2(h_{k-1} + h_k)m_k + h_k m_{k+1} = u_k \qquad \text{for } k = 2, 3, \ldots, N - 2.$$
$$h_{N-2}m_{N-2} + 2(h_{N-2} + h_{N-1})m_{N-1} = u_{N-1}.$$

    ●

Remark. The natural spline is the curve obtained by forcing a flexible elastic rod through the data points but letting the slope at the ends be free to equilibrate to the position that minimizes the oscillatory behavior of the curve. It is useful for fitting a curve to experimental data that are significant to several significant digits.

Lemma 5.3 (Extrapolated Spline).   There exists a unique cubic spline that uses extrapolation from the interior nodes at x_1 and x_2 to determine $S''(a)$ and extrapolation from the nodes at x_{N-1} and x_{N-2} to determine $S''(b)$.

Proof.   Solve the linear system

$$\left(3h_0 + 2h_1 + \frac{h_0^2}{h_1}\right)m_1 + \left(h_1 - \frac{h_0^2}{h_1}\right)m_2 = u_1$$
$$h_{k-1}m_{k-1} + 2(h_{k-1} + h_k)m_k + h_k m_{k+1} = u_k \qquad \text{for } k = 2, 3, \ldots, N - 2$$
$$\left(h_{N-2} - \frac{h_{N-1}^2}{h_{N-2}}\right)m_{N-2} + \left(2h_{N-2} + 3h_{N-1} + \frac{h_{N-1}^2}{h_{N-2}}\right)m_{N-1} = u_{N-1}.$$

    ●

Remark. The extrapolated spline is equivalent to assuming that the end cubic is an extension of the adjacent cubic; that is, the spline forms a single cubic curve over the interval $[x_0, x_2]$ and another single cubic over the interval $[x_{N-2}, x_N]$.

Lemma 5.4 (Parabolically Terminated Spline).   There exists a unique cubic spline that uses $S'''(x) \equiv 0$ on the interval $[x_0, x_1]$ and $S'''(x) \equiv 0$ on $[x_{N-1}, x_N]$.

Proof.   Solve the linear system

$$(3h_0 + 2h_1)m_1 + h_1 m_2 = u_1$$
$$h_{k-1}m_{k-1} + 2(h_{k-1} + h_k)m_k + h_k m_{k+1} = u_k \qquad \text{for } k = 2, 3, \ldots, N - 2$$
$$h_{N-2}m_{N-2} + (2h_{N-2} + 3h_{N-1})m_{N-1} = u_{N-1}.$$

    ●

Remark. The assumption that $S''(x) \equiv 0$ on the interval $[x_0, x_1]$ forces the cubic to degenerate to a quadratic over $[x_0, x_1]$, and a similar situation occurs over $[x_{N-1}, x_N]$.

Lemma 5.5 (Endpoint Curvature-Adjusted Spline).   There exists a unique cubic spline with the second derivative boundary conditions $S''(a)$ and $S''(b)$ specified.

Proof.   Solve the linear system

$$2(h_0 + h_1)m_1 + h_1 m_2 = u_1 - h_0 S''(x_0)$$

$$h_{k-1} m_{k-1} + 2(h_{k-1} + h_k)m_k + h_k m_{k+1} = u_k \quad \text{for } k = 2, 3, \ldots, N - 2$$

$$h_{N-2} m_{N-2} + 2(h_{N-2} + h_{N-1})m_{N-1} = u_{N-1} - h_{N-1} S''(x_N). \qquad \bullet$$

Remark. Imposing values for $S''(a)$ and $S''(b)$ permits the practitioner to adjust the curvature at each endpoint.

The next five examples illustrate the behavior of the various splines. It is possible to mix the end conditions to obtain an even wider variety of possibilities, but we leave these variations to the reader to investigate.

Example 5.7.   Find the clamped cubic spline that passes through $(0, 0)$, $(1, 0.5)$, $(2, 2.0)$, and $(3, 1.5)$ with the first derivative boundary conditions $S'(0) = 0.2$ and $S'(3) = -1$.
First, compute the quantities

$$h_0 = h_1 = h_2 = 1$$
$$d_0 = (y_1 - y_0)/h_0 = (0.5 - 0.0)/1 = 0.5$$
$$d_1 = (y_2 - y_1)/h_1 = (2.0 - 0.5)/1 = 1.5$$
$$d_2 = (y_3 - y_2)/h_2 = (1.5 - 2.0)/1 = -0.5$$
$$u_1 = 6(d_1 - d_0) = 6(1.5 - 0.5) = 6.0$$
$$u_2 = 6(d_2 - d_1) = 6(-0.5 - 1.5) = -12.0.$$

Then use Lemma 5.1 and obtain the equations

$$\left(\frac{3}{2} + 2\right)m_1 + m_2 = 6.0 - 3(0.5 - 0.2) = 5.1,$$

$$m_1 + \left(2 + \frac{3}{2}\right)m_2 = -12.0 - 3(-1.0 - (-0.5)) = -10.5.$$

When these equations are simplified and put in matrix notation, we have

$$\begin{bmatrix} 3.5 & 1.0 \\ 1.0 & 3.5 \end{bmatrix} \begin{bmatrix} m_1 \\ m_2 \end{bmatrix} = \begin{bmatrix} 5.1 \\ -10.5 \end{bmatrix}.$$

It is a straightforward task to compute the solution $m_1 = 2.25$ and $m_2 = -3.72$. Now apply the equations in (i) of Table 5.8 to determine the coefficients m_0 and m_3:

$$m_0 = 3(0.5 - 0.2) - \frac{2.52}{2} = -0.36,$$

$$m_3 = 3(-1.0 + 0.5) - \frac{-3.72}{2} = 0.36.$$

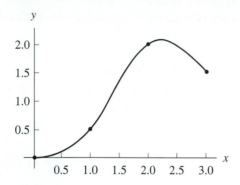

Figure 5.12   The clamped cubic spline with derivative boundary conditions: $S'(0) = 0.2$ and $S'(3) = -1$.

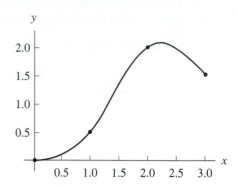

Figure 5.13   The natural cubic spline with $S''(0) = 0$ and $S''(3) = 0$.

Next, the values $m_0 = -0.36$, $m_1 = 2.25$, $m_2 = -3.72$, and $m_3 = 0.36$ are substituted into equations (16) to find the spline coefficients. The solution is

$$
\begin{aligned}
S_0(x) &= 0.48x^3 - 0.18x^2 + 0.2x && \text{for } 0 \le x \le 1, \\
S_1(x) &= -1.04(x-1)^3 + 1.26(x-1)^2 \\
&\quad + 1.28(x-1) + 0.5 && \text{for } 1 \le x \le 2, \\
S_2(x) &= 0.68(x-2)^3 - 1.86(x-2)^2 \\
&\quad + 0.68(x-2) + 2.0 && \text{for } 2 \le x \le 3.
\end{aligned}
$$

(18)

This clamped cubic spline is shown in Figure 5.12.   ∎

Example 5.8.   Find the natural cubic spline that passes through $(0, 0.0)$, $(1, 0.5)$, $(2, 2.0)$, and $(3, 1.5)$ with the free boundary conditions $S''(x) = 0$ and $S''(3) = 0$.
   Use the same values $\{h_k\}$, $\{d_k\}$, and $\{u_k\}$ that were computed in Example 5.7. Then use Lemma 5.2 and obtain the equations

$$
\begin{aligned}
2(1+1)m_1 + m_2 &= 6.0, \\
m_1 + 2(1+1)m_2 &= -12.0.
\end{aligned}
$$

The matrix form of this linear system is

$$
\begin{bmatrix} 4.0 & 1.0 \\ 1.0 & 4.0 \end{bmatrix} \begin{bmatrix} m_1 \\ m_2 \end{bmatrix} = \begin{bmatrix} 6.0 \\ -12.0 \end{bmatrix}.
$$

It is easy to find the solution $m_1 = 2.4$ and $m_2 = -3.6$. Since $m_0 = S''(0) = 0$ and

$m_3 = S''(3) = 0$, when equations (16) are used to find the spline coefficients, the result is

$$S_0(x) = 0.4x^3 + 0.1x \qquad\qquad \text{for } 0 \le x \le 1,$$

$$S_1(x) = -(x-1)^3 + 1.2(x-1)^2$$

(19)
$$\qquad\qquad + 1.3(x-1) + 0.5 \qquad\qquad \text{for } 1 \le x \le 2,$$

$$S_2(x) = 0.6(x-2)^3 - 1.8(x-2)^2$$

$$\qquad\qquad + 0.7(x-2) + 2.0 \qquad\qquad \text{for } 2 \le x \le 3.$$

This natural cubic spline is shown in Figure 5.13. ∎

Example 5.9.   Find the extrapolated cubic spline through $(0, 0.0)$, $(1, 0.5)$, $(2, 2.0)$, and $(3, 1.5)$.

Use the values $\{h_k\}$, $\{d_k\}$, and $\{u_k\}$ from Example 5.7 with Lemma 5.3 and obtain the linear system

$$(3 + 2 + 1)m_1 + (1 - 1)m_2 = 6.0,$$

$$(1 - 1)m_1 + (2 + 3 + 1)m_2 = -12.0.$$

The matrix form is

$$\begin{bmatrix} 6.0 & 0.0 \\ 0.0 & 6.0 \end{bmatrix} \begin{bmatrix} m_1 \\ m_2 \end{bmatrix} = \begin{bmatrix} 6.0 \\ -12.0 \end{bmatrix},$$

and it is trivial to obtain $m_1 = 1.0$ and $m_2 = -2.0$. Now apply the equations in (iii) of Table 5.8 to compute m_0 and m_3:

$$m_0 = 1.0 - (-2.0 - 1.0) = 4.0,$$

$$m_3 = -2.0 + (-2.0 - 1.0) = -5.0.$$

Finally, the values for $\{m_k\}$ are substituted in equations (16) to find the spline coefficients. The solution is

$$S_0(x) = -0.5x^3 + 2.0x^2 - x \qquad\qquad \text{for } 0 \le x \le 1,$$

$$S_1(x) = -0.5(x-1)^3 + 0.5(x-1)^2$$

(20)
$$\qquad\qquad + 1.5(x-1) + 0.5 \qquad\qquad \text{for } 1 \le x \le 2,$$

$$S_2(x) = -0.5(x-2)^3 - (x-2)^2$$

$$\qquad\qquad + (x-2) + 2.0 \qquad\qquad \text{for } 2 \le x \le 3.$$

The extrapolated cubic spline is shown in Figure 5.14. ∎

Example 5.10.   Find the parabolically terminated cubic spline through $(0, 0.0)$, $(1, 0.5)$, $(2, 2.0)$, and $(3, 1.5)$.

Use $\{h_k\}$, $\{d_k\}$, and $\{u_k\}$ from Example 5.7 and then apply Lemma 5.4 to obtain

$$(3 + 2)m_1 + m_2 = 6.0,$$

$$m_1 + (2 + 3)m_2 = -12.0.$$

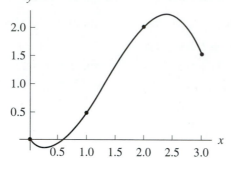

Figure 5.14 The extrapolated cubic spline.

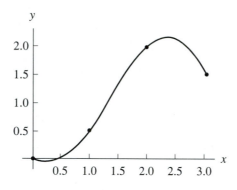

Figure 5.15 The parabolically terminated cubic spline.

The matrix form is

$$\begin{bmatrix} 5.0 & 1.0 \\ 1.0 & 5.0 \end{bmatrix} \begin{bmatrix} m_1 \\ m_2 \end{bmatrix} = \begin{bmatrix} 6.0 \\ -12.0 \end{bmatrix},$$

and the solution is $m_1 = 1.75$ and $m_2 = -2.75$. Since $S''(x) \equiv 0$ on the subinterval at each end, formulas (iv) in Table 5.8 imply that we have $m_0 = m_1 = 1.75$ and $m_3 = m_2 = -2.75$. Then the values for $\{m_k\}$ are substituted in equations (16) to get the solution

$$
\begin{aligned}
S_0(x) &= 0.875x^2 - 0.375x & \text{for } 0 \leq x \leq 1, \\
S_1(x) &= -0.75(x-1)^3 + 0.875(x-1)^2 \\
&\quad + 1.375(x-1) + 0.5 & \text{for } 1 \leq x \leq 2, \\
S_2(x) &= -1.375(x-2)^2 + 0.875(x-2) + 2.0 & \text{for } 2 \leq x \leq 3.
\end{aligned}
$$

(21)

This parabolically terminated cubic spline is shown in Figure 5.15.   ∎

Example 5.11. Find the curvature-adjusted cubic spline through $(0, 0.0)$, $(1, 0.5)$, $(2, 2.0)$, and $(3, 1.5)$ with the second derivative boundary conditions $S''(0) = -0.3$ and $S''(3) = 3.3$.

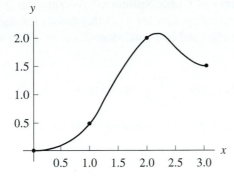

Figure 5.16   The curvature adjusted cubic spline with $S''(0) = -0.3$ and $S''(3) = 3.3$.

Use $\{h_k\}$, $\{d_k\}$, and $\{u_k\}$ from Example 5.7 and then apply Lemma 5.5 to obtain

$$2(1 + 1)m_1 + m_2 = 6.0 - (-0.3) = 6.3,$$
$$m_1 + 2(1 + 1)m_2 = -12.0 - (3.3) = -15.3.$$

The matrix form is

$$\begin{bmatrix} 4.0 & 1.0 \\ 1.0 & 4.0 \end{bmatrix} \begin{bmatrix} m_1 \\ m_2 \end{bmatrix} = \begin{bmatrix} 6.3 \\ -15.3 \end{bmatrix},$$

and the solution is $m_1 = 2.7$ and $m_2 = -4.5$. The given boundary conditions are used to determine $m_0 = S''(0) = -0.3$ and $m_3 = S''(3) = 3.3$. Substitution of $\{m_k\}$ in equations (16) produces the solution

$$
\begin{aligned}
S_0(x) &= 0.5x^3 - 0.15x^2 + 0.15x && \text{for } 0 \le x \le 1, \\
S_1(x) &= -1.2(x - 1)^3 + 1.35(x - 1)^2 \\
&\quad + 1.35(x - 1) + 0.5 && \text{for } 1 \le x \le 2, \\
S_2(x) &= 1.3(x - 2)^3 - 2.25(x - 2)^2 \\
&\quad + 0.45(x - 2) + 2.0 && \text{for } 2 \le x \le 3.
\end{aligned}
$$

(22)

This curvature-adjusted cubic spline is shown in Figure 5.16.   ∎

Suitability of Cubic Splines

A practical feature of splines is the minimum of the oscillatory behavior that they possess. Consequently, among all functions $f(x)$ that are twice continuously differentiable on $[a, b]$ and interpolate a given set of data points $\{(x_k, y_k)\}_{k=0}^{N}$, the cubic spline has less wiggle. The next result explains this phenomenon.

Theorem 5.4 (Minimum Property of Cubic Splines). Assume that $f \in C^2[a, b]$ and $S(x)$ is the unique cubic spline interpolant for $f(x)$ that passes through the points $\{(x_k, f(x_k))\}_{k=0}^N$ and satisfies the clamped end conditions $S'(a) = f'(a)$ and $S'(b) = f'(b)$. Then

$$(23) \qquad \int_a^b (S''(x))^2 \, dx \le \int_a^b (f''(x))^2 \, dx.$$

Proof. Use integration by parts and the end conditions to obtain

$$\int_a^b S''(x)(f''(x) - S''(x)) \, dx$$

$$= S''(x)(f'(x) - S'(x)) \Big|_{x=a}^{x=b} - \int_a^b S'''(x)(f'(x) - S'(x)) \, dx$$

$$= 0 - 0 - \int_a^b S'''(x)(f'(x) - S'(x)) \, dx.$$

Since $S'''(x) = 6s_{k,3}$ on the subinterval $[x_k, x_{k+1}]$, it follows that

$$\int_{x_k}^{x_{k+1}} S'''(x)(f'(x) - S'(x)) \, dx = 6s_{k,3}(f(x) - S(x)) \Big|_{x=x_k}^{x=x_{k+1}} = 0$$

for $k = 0, 1, \ldots, N - 1$. Hence $\int_a^b S''(x)(f''(x) - S''(x)) \, dx = 0$, and it follows that

$$(24) \qquad \int_a^b S''(x) f''(x) \, dx = \int_a^b (S''(x))^2 \, dx.$$

Since $0 \le (f''(x) - S''(x))^2$, we get the integral relationship

$$(25) \qquad \begin{aligned} 0 &\le \int_a^b (f''(x) - S''(x))^2 \, dx \\ &= \int_a^b (f''(x))^2 \, dx - 2 \int_a^b f''(x)S''(x) \, dx + \int_a^b (S''(x))^2 \, dx. \end{aligned}$$

Now the result in (24) is substituted into (25) and the result is

$$0 \le \int_a^b (f''(x))^2 \, dx - \int_a^b (S''(x))^2 \, dx.$$

This is easily rewritten to obtain the relation (23), and the result is proved. ●

The following program constructs a clamped cubic spline interpolant for the data points $\{(x_k, y_k)\}_{k=0}^N$. The coefficients, in descending order, of $S_k(x)$, for $k = 0, 1, \ldots, N - 1$, are found in the $(k - 1)$st row of the output matrix S. In the exercises the reader will be asked to modify the program for the other endpoint constraints listed in Table 5.8 and described in Lemmas 5.2 through 5.5.

Program 5.3 (Clamped Cubic Spline). To construct and evaluate a clamped cubic spline interpolant $S(x)$ for the $N + 1$ data points $\{(x_k, y_k)\}_{k=0}^{N}$.

```
function S=csfit(X,Y,dx0,dxn)

%Input   - X is the 1xn abscissa vector
%         - Y is the 1xn ordinate vector
%         - dx0 = S'(x0) first derivative boundary condition
%         - dxn = S'(xn) first derivative boundary condition
%Output - S: rows of S are the coefficients, in descending
%            order, for the cubic interpolants
N=length(X)-1;
H=diff(X);
D=diff(Y)./H;
A=H(2:N-1);
B=2*(H(1:N-1)+H(2:N));
C=H(2:N);
U=6*diff(D);

%Clamped spline endpoint constraints
B(1)=B(1)-H(1)/2;
U(1)=U(1)-3*(D(1)-dx0);
B(N-1)=B(N-1)-H(N)/2;
U(N-1)=U(N-1)-3*(dxn-D(N));

for k=2:N-1
    temp=A(k-1)/B(k-1);
    B(k)=B(k)-temp*C(k-1);
    U(k)=U(k)-temp*U(k-1);
end

M(N)=U(N-1)/B(N-1);

for k=N-2:-1:1
    M(k+1)=(U(k)-C(k)*M(k+2))/B(k);
end

M(1)=3*(D(1)-dx0)/H(1)-M(2)/2;
M(N+1)=3*(dxn-D(N))/H(N)-M(N)/2;

for k=0:N-1
    S(k+1,1)=(M(k+2)-M(k+1))/(6*H(k+1));
    S(k+1,2)=M(k+1)/2;
    S(k+1,3)=D(k+1)-H(k+1)*(2*M(k+1)+M(k+2))/6;
    S(k+1,4)=Y(k+1);
end
```

Example 5.12.   Find the clamped cubic spline that passes through $(0, 0.0)$, $(1, 0.5)$, $(2, 2.0)$, and $(3, 1.5)$ with the first derivative boundary conditions $S'(0) = 0.2$ and $S'(3) = -1$.

In MATLAB:

```
>>X=[0 1 2 3]; Y=[0 0.5 2.0 1.5];dx0=0.2; dxn=-1;
>>S=csfit(X,Y,dx0,dxn)
S =
   0.4800 -0.1800 0.2000 0
  -1.0400  1.2600 1.2800 0.5000
   0.6800 -1.8600 0.6800 2.0000
```

Notice that the rows of S are precisely the coefficients of the cubic spline interpolants in equation (18) in Example 5.7. The following commands show how to plot the cubic spline interpolant using the `polyval` command. The resulting graph is the same as Figure 5.12.

```
>>x1=0:.01:1; y1=polyval(S(1,:),x1-X(1));
>>x2=1:.01:2; y2=polyval(S(2,:),x2-X(2));
>>x3=2:.01:3; y3=polyval(S(3,:),x3-X(3));
>>plot(x1,y1,x2,y2,x3,y3,X,Y,'.')
```

■

Exercises for Interpolation by Spline Functions

1. Consider the polynomial $S(x) = a_0 + a_1 x + a_2 x^2 + a_3 x^3$.
   (a)   Show that the conditions $S(1) = 1$, $S'(1) = 0$, $S(2) = 2$, and $S'(2) = 0$ produce the system of equations

$$
\begin{aligned}
a_0 + a_1 + a_2 + a_3 &= 1 \\
a_1 + 2a_2 + 3a_3 &= 0 \\
a_0 + 2a_1 + 4a_2 + 8a_3 &= 2 \\
a_1 + 4a_2 + 12a_3 &= 0.
\end{aligned}
$$

   (b)   Solve the system in part (a) and graph the resulting cubic polynomial.

2. Consider the polynomial $S(x) = a_0 + a_1 x + a_2 x^2 + a_3 x^3$.
   (a)   Show that the conditions $S(1) = 3$, $S'(1) = -4$, $S(2) = 1$, and $S'(2) = 2$ produce the system of equations

$$
\begin{aligned}
a_0 + a_1 + a_2 + a_3 &= 3 \\
a_1 + 2a_2 + 3a_3 &= -4 \\
a_0 + 2a_1 + 4a_2 + 8a_3 &= 1 \\
a_1 + 4a_2 + 12a_3 &= 2.
\end{aligned}
$$

   (b)   Solve the system in part (a) and graph the resulting cubic polynomial.

3. Determine which of the following functions are cubic splines. *Hint.* Which, if any, of the five parts of Definition 5.1 does a given function $f(x)$ not satisfy?

(a) $f(x) = \begin{cases} \frac{19}{2} - \frac{81}{4}x + 15x^2 - \frac{13}{4}x^3 & \text{for } 1 \le x \le 2 \\ \frac{-77}{2} + \frac{207}{4}x - 21x^2 + \frac{11}{4}x^3 & \text{for } 2 \le x \le 3 \end{cases}$

(b) $f(x) = \begin{cases} 11 - 24x + 18x^2 - 4x^3 & \text{for } 1 \le x \le 2 \\ -54 + 72x - 30x^2 + 4x^3 & \text{for } 2 \le x \le 3 \end{cases}$

(c) $f(x) = \begin{cases} 18 - \frac{75}{2}x + 26x^2 - \frac{11}{2}x^3 & \text{for } 1 \le x \le 2 \\ -70 + \frac{189}{2}x - 40x^2 + \frac{11}{2}x^3 & \text{for } 2 \le x \le 3 \end{cases}$

(d) $f(x) = \begin{cases} 13 - 31x + 23x^2 - 5x^3 & \text{for } 1 \le x \le 2 \\ -35 + 51x - 22x^2 + 3x^3 & \text{for } 2 \le x \le 3 \end{cases}$

4. Find the clamped cubic spline that passes through the points $(-3, 2)$, $(-2, 0)$, $(1, 3)$, and $(4, 1)$ with the first derivative boundary conditions $S'(-3) = -1$ and $S'(4) = 1$.

5. Find the natural cubic spline that passes through the points $(-3, 2)$, $(-2, 0)$, $(1, 3)$, and $(4, 1)$ with the free boundary conditions $S''(-3) = 0$ and $S''(4) = 0$.

6. Find the extrapolated cubic spline that passes through the points $(-3, 2)$, $(-2, 0)$, $(1, 3)$, and $(4, 1)$.

7. Find the parabolically terminated cubic spline that passes through the points $(-3, 2)$, $(-2, 0)$, $(1, 3)$, and $(4, 1)$.

8. Find the curvature-adjusted cubic spline that passes through the points $(-3, 2)$, $(-2, 0)$, $(1, 3)$, and $(4, 1)$ with the second derivative boundary conditions $S''(-3) = -1$ and $S''(4) = 2$.

9. (a) Find the clamped cubic spline that passes through the points $\{(x_k, f(x_k))\}_{k=0}^3$, on the graph of $f(x) = x + 2/x$, using the nodes $x_0 = 1/2$, $x_1 = 1$, $x_2 = 3/2$, and $x_3 = 2$. Use the first derivative boundary conditions $S'(x_0) = f'(x_0)$ and $S'(x_3) = f'(x_3)$. Graph f and the clamped cubic spline interpolant on the same coordinate system.

(b) Find the natural cubic spline that passes through the points $\{(x_k, f(x_k))\}_{k=0}^3$, on the graph of $f(x) = x + 2/x$, using the nodes $x_0 = 1/2$, $x_1 = 1$, $x_2 = 3/2$, and $x_3 = 2$. Use the free boundary conditions $S''(x_0) = 0$ and $S''(x_3) = 0$. Graph f and the natural cubic spline interpolant on the same coordinate system.

10. (a) Find the clamped cubic spline that passes through the points $\{(x_k, f(x_k))\}_{k=0}^3$, on the graph of $f(x) = \cos(x^2)$, using the nodes $x_0 = 0$, $x_1 = \sqrt{\pi/2}$, $x_2 = \sqrt{3\pi/2}$, and $x_3 = \sqrt{5\pi/2}$. Use the first derivative boundary conditions $S'(x_0) = f'(x_0)$ and $S'(x_3) = f'(x_3)$. Graph f and the clamped cubic spline interpolant on the same coordinate system.

(b) Find the natural cubic spline that passes through the points $\{(x_k, f(x_k))\}_{k=0}^3$, on the graph of $f(x) = \cos(x^2)$, using the nodes $x_0 = 0$, $x_1 = \sqrt{\pi/2}$, $x_2 = \sqrt{3\pi/2}$, and $x_3 = \sqrt{5\pi/2}$. Use the free boundary conditions $S''(x_0) = 0$ and

$S''(x_3) = 0$. Graph f and the natural cubic spline interpolant on the same coordinate system.

11. Use the substitutions

$$x_{k+1} - x = h_k + (x_k - x)$$

and

$$(x_{k+1} - x)^3 = h_k^3 + 3h_k^2(x_k - x) + 3h_k(x_k - x)^2 + (x_k - x)^3$$

to show that when equation (8) is expanded into powers of $(x_k - x)$, the coefficients are those given in equations (16).

12. Consider each cubic function $S_k(x)$ over the interval $[x_k, x_{k+1}]$.
    (a)   Give a formula for $\int_{x_k}^{x_{k+1}} S_k(x)\,dx$.
    Then evaluate $\int_{x_0}^{x_3} S(x)\,dx$ in part (a) of
    (b)   Exercise 9   (c)   Exercise 10

13. Show how strategy (i) in Table 5.8 and system (12) are combined to obtain the equations in Lemma 5.1.

14. Show how strategy (iii) in Table 5.8 and system (12) are combined to obtain the equation in Lemma 5.3.

15. (a)   Using the nodes $x_0 = -2$ and $x_1 = 0$, show that $f(x) = x^3 - x$ is its own clamped cubic spline on the interval $[-2, 0]$.
    (b)   Using the nodes $x_0 = -2$, $x_1 = 0$, and $x_2 = 2$, show that $f(x) = x^3 - x$ is its own clamped cubic spline on the interval $[-2, 2]$. *Note.* f has an inflection point at x_1.
    (c)   Use the results from parts (a) and (b) to show that any third-degree polynomial, $f(x) = a_0 + a_1 x + a_2 x^2 + a_3 x^3$, is its own clamped cubic spline on any closed interval $[a, b]$.
    (d)   What, if anything, can be said about the other four types of cubic splines described in Lemmas 5.2 through 5.5?

Algorithms and Programs

1. The distance d_k that a car traveled at time t_k is given in the follwoing table. Use Program 5.3 with the first derivative boundary conditions $S'(0) = 0$ and $S'(8) = 98$, and find the clamped cubic spline for the points.

Time, t_k	0	2	4	6	8
Distance, d_k	0	40	160	300	480

2. Modify Program 5.3 to find the (a) natural, (b) extrapolated, (c) parabolically terminated, or (d) endpoint curvature-adjusted cubic splines for a given set of points.

3. Use your programs from Problem 2 to find the five different cubic splines for the points $(0, 1)$, $(1, 0)$, $(2, 0)$, $(3, 1)$, $(4, 2)$, $(5, 2)$, and $(6, 1)$, where $S'(0) = -0.6$, $S'(6) = -1.8$, $S''(0) = 1$, and $S''(6) = -1$. Plot the five cubic splines and the points on the same coordinate system.

4. Use your programs from Problem 2 to find the five different cubic splines for the points $(0, 0)$, $(1, 4)$, $(2, 8)$, $(3, 9)$, $(4, 9)$, $(5, 8)$, and $(6, 6)$, where $S'(0) = 1$, $S'(6) = -2$, $S''(0) = 1$, and $S''(6) = -1$. Plot the five cubic splines and the points on the same coordinate system.

5. The accompanying table gives the hourly temperature readings (Fahrenheit) during a 12-hour period in a suburb of Los Angeles. Find the natural cubic spline for the data. Graph the natural cubic spline and the data on the same coordinate system. Use the natural cubic spline and the results of part (a) of Exercise 12 to approximate the average temperature during the 12-hour period.

Time, a.m.	Degrees	Time, a.m.	Degrees
1	58	7	57
2	58	8	58
3	58	9	60
4	58	10	64
5	57	11	67
6	57	Noon	68

6. Approximate the graph of $f(x) = x - \cos(x^3)$ over the interval $[-3, 3]$ using a clamped cubic spline.

5.4   Fourier Series and Trigonometric Polynomials

Scientists and engineers often study physical phenomena, such as light and sound, that have a periodic character. They are described by functions $g(x)$ that are periodic,

$$(1) \qquad\qquad g(x + P) = g(x) \qquad \text{for all } x.$$

The number P is called a **period** of the function.

It will suffice to consider functions that have period 2π. If $g(x)$ has period P, then $f(x) = g(Px/2\pi)$ will be periodic with period 2π. This is verified by the observation that

$$(2) \qquad\qquad f(x + 2\pi) = g\left(\frac{Px}{2\pi} + P\right) = g\left(\frac{Px}{2\pi}\right) = f(x).$$

Henceforth in this section we shall assume that $f(x)$ is a function that is periodic with period 2π, that is,

$$(3) \qquad\qquad f(x + 2\pi) = f(x) \qquad \text{for all } x.$$

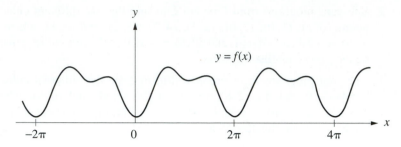

Figure 5.17 A continuous function $f(x)$ with period 2π.

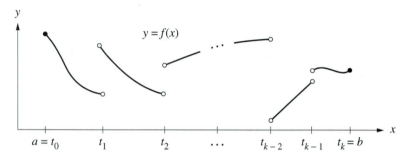

Figure 5.18 A piecewise continuous function over $[a, b]$.

The graph $y = f(x)$ is obtained by repeating the portion of the graph in any interval of length 2π, as shown in Figure 5.17.

Examples of functions with period 2π are $\sin(jx)$ and $\cos(jx)$, where j is an integer. This raises the following question: Can a periodic function be represented by the sum of terms involving $a_j \cos(jx)$ and $b_j \sin(jx)$? We will soon see that the answer is yes in all interesting cases.

Definition 5.2. The function $f(x)$ is said to be **piecewise continuous** on $[a, b]$ if there exist values $t_0, t_1, \ldots, t_K$ with $a = t_0 < t_1 < \cdots < t_K = b$ such that $f(x)$ is continuous on each open interval $t_{i-1} < x < t_i$ for $i = 1, 2, \ldots, K$, and $f(x)$ has left- and right-hand limits at each of the points t_i. The situation is illustrated in Figure 5.18.

▲

Definition 5.3. Assume that $f(x)$ is periodic with period 2π and that $f(x)$ is piecewise continuous on $[-\pi, \pi]$. The **Fourier series** $S(x)$ for $f(x)$ is

(4)
$$S(x) = \frac{a_0}{2} + \sum_{j=1}^{\infty}(a_j \cos(jx) + b_j \sin(jx)),$$

where the coefficients a_j and b_j are computed with Euler's formulas:

(5)
$$a_j = \frac{1}{\pi} \int_{-\pi}^{\pi} f(x) \cos(jx) \, dx \quad \text{for } j = 0, 1, \ldots$$

and

(6)
$$b_j = \frac{1}{\pi} \int_{-\pi}^{\pi} f(x) \sin(jx) \, dx \quad \text{for } j = 1, 2, \ldots . \qquad \blacktriangle$$

The factor $\frac{1}{2}$ in the constant term $a_0/2$ in the Fourier series (4) has been introduced for convenience so that a_0 could be obtained from the general formula (5) by setting $j = 0$. Convergence of the Fourier series is discussed in the next result.

Theorem 5.5 (Fourier Expansion).   Assume that $S(x)$ is the Fourier series for $f(x)$ over $[-\pi, \pi]$. If $f'(x)$ is piecewise continuous on $[-\pi, \pi]$ and has both a left- and right-hand derivative at each point in this interval, then $S(x)$ is convergent for all $x \in [-\pi, \pi]$. The relation

$$S(x) = f(x)$$

holds at all points $x \in [-\pi, \pi]$, where $f(x)$ is continuous. If $x = a$ is a point of discontinuity of f, then

$$S(a) = \frac{f(a^-) + f(a^+)}{2},$$

where $f(a^-)$ and $f(a^+)$ denote the left- and right-hand limits, respectively. With this understanding, we obtain the Fourier expansion:

(7)
$$f(x) = \frac{a_0}{2} + \sum_{j=1}^{\infty} (a_j \cos(jx) + b_j \sin(jx)).$$

A brief outline of the derivation of formulas (5) and (6) is given at the end of the subsection.

Example 5.13.   Show that the function $f(x) = x/2$ for $-\pi < x < \pi$, extended periodically by the equation $f(x + 2\pi) = f(x)$, has the Fourier series representation

$$f(x) = \sum_{j=1}^{\infty} \frac{(-1)^{j+1}}{j} \sin(jx) = \sin(x) - \frac{\sin(2x)}{2} + \frac{\sin(3x)}{3} - \cdots .$$

Using Euler's formulas and integration by parts, we get

$$a_j = \frac{1}{\pi} \int_{-\pi}^{\pi} \frac{x}{2} \cos(jx) \, dx = \frac{x \sin(jx)}{2\pi j} + \frac{\cos(jx)}{2\pi j^2} \bigg|_{-\pi}^{\pi} = 0$$

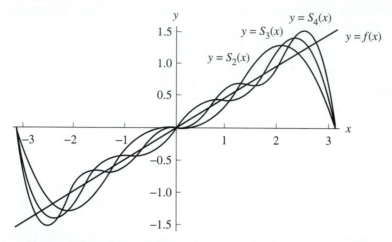

Figure 5.19   The function $f(x) = x/2$ over $[-\pi, \pi]$ and its trigonometric approximations $S_2(x)$, $S_3(x)$, and $S_4(x)$.

for $j = 1, 2, 3, \ldots$, and

$$b_j = \frac{1}{\pi} \int_{-\pi}^{\pi} \frac{x}{2} \sin(jx)\, dx = \frac{-x\cos(jx)}{2\pi j} + \frac{\sin(jx)}{2\pi j^2}\Big|_{-\pi}^{\pi} = \frac{(-1)^{j+1}}{j}$$

for $j = 1, 2, 3, \ldots$. The coefficient a_0 is obtained by a separate calculation:

$$a_0 = \frac{1}{\pi} \int_{-\pi}^{\pi} \frac{x}{2}\, dx = \frac{x^2}{4\pi}\Big|_{-\pi}^{\pi} = 0.$$

These calculations show that all the coefficients of the cosine functions are zero. The
graph of $f(x)$ and the partial sums

$$S_2(x) = \sin(x) - \frac{\sin(2x)}{2},$$

$$S_3(x) = \sin(x) - \frac{\sin(2x)}{2} + \frac{\sin(3x)}{3},$$

and

$$S_4(x) = \sin(x) - \frac{\sin(2x)}{2} + \frac{\sin(3x)}{3} - \frac{\sin(4x)}{4}$$

are shown in Figure 5.19.   ∎

We now state some general properties of Fourier series. The proofs are left as
exercises.

Theorem 5.6 (Cosine Series).   Suppose that $f(x)$ is an even function; that is, suppose that $f(-x) = f(x)$ holds for all x. If $f(x)$ has period 2π and if $f(x)$ and $f'(x)$ are piecewise continuous, then the Fourier series for $f(x)$ involves only cosine terms:

(8) $$f(x) = \frac{a_0}{2} + \sum_{j=1}^{\infty} a_j \cos(jx),$$

where

(9) $$a_j = \frac{2}{\pi} \int_0^{\pi} f(x) \cos(jx)\, dx \quad \text{for } j = 0,\ 1,\ \dots.$$

Theorem 5.7 (Sine Series).   Suppose that $f(x)$ is an odd function; that is, $f(-x) = -f(x)$ holds for all x. If $f(x)$ has period 2π and if $f(x)$ and $f'(x)$ are piecewise continuous, then the Fourier series for $f(x)$ involves only the sine terms:

(10) $$f(x) = \sum_{j=1}^{\infty} b_j \sin(jx),$$

where

(11) $$b_j = \frac{2}{\pi} \int_0^{\pi} f(x) \sin(jx)\, dx \quad \text{for } j = 1,\ 2,\ \dots.$$

Example 5.14.   Show that the function $f(x) = |x|$ for $-\pi < x < \pi$, extended periodically by the equation $f(x + 2\pi) = f(x)$, has the Fourier cosine representation

(12)
$$f(x) = \frac{\pi}{2} - \frac{4}{\pi} \sum_{j=1}^{\infty} \frac{\cos((2j-1)x)}{(2j-1)^2}$$
$$= \frac{\pi}{2} - \frac{4}{\pi} \left(\cos(x) + \frac{\cos(3x)}{3^2} + \frac{\cos(5x)}{5^2} + \cdots \right).$$

The function $f(x)$ is an even function, so we can use Theorem 5.6 and need only to compute the coefficients $\{a_j\}$:

$$a_j = \frac{2}{\pi} \int_0^{\pi} x \cos(jx)\, dx = \frac{2x \sin(jx)}{\pi j} + \frac{2 \cos(jx)}{\pi j^2} \Big|_0^{\pi}$$
$$= \frac{2 \cos(j\pi) - 2}{\pi j^2} = \frac{2((-1)^j - 1)}{\pi j^2} \quad \text{for } j = 1,\ 2,\ 3,\ \dots.$$

Since $((-1)^j - 1) = 0$ when j is even, the cosine series will involve only the odd terms. The odd coefficients have the pattern

$$a_1 = \frac{-4}{\pi}, \qquad a_3 = \frac{-4}{\pi 3^2}, \qquad a_5 = \frac{-4}{\pi 5^2}, \qquad \dots.$$

The coefficient a_0 is obtained by the separate calculation

$$a_0 = \frac{2}{\pi} \int_0^\pi x \, dx = \frac{x^2}{\pi} \Big|_0^\pi = \pi.$$

Therefore, we have found the desired coefficients in (12). ■

Proof of Euler's Formulas for Theorem 5.5.   The following heuristic argument assumes the existence and convergence of the Fourier series representation. To determine a_0, we can integrate both sides of (7) and get

$$
\begin{aligned}
\int_{-\pi}^\pi f(x) \, dx &= \int_{-\pi}^\pi \left(\frac{a_0}{2} + \sum_{j=1}^\infty (a_j \cos(jx) + b_j \sin(jx)) \right) dx \\
&= \int_{-\pi}^\pi \frac{a_0}{2} \, dx + \sum_{j=1}^\infty a_j \int_{-\pi}^\pi \cos(jx) \, dx + \sum_{j=1}^\infty b_j \int_{-\pi}^\pi \sin(jx) \, dx \\
&= \pi a_0 + 0 + 0.
\end{aligned}
$$
(13)

Justification for switching the order of integration and summation requires a detailed treatment of uniform convergence and can be found in advanced texts. Hence we have shown that

$$a_0 = \frac{1}{\pi} \int_{-\pi}^\pi f(x) \, dx. \tag{14}$$

To determine a_m, we let $m > 0$ be a fixed integer, multiply both sides of (7) by $\cos(mx)$, and integrate both sides to obtain

(15)

$$
\begin{aligned}
\int_{-\pi}^\pi f(x) \cos(mx) \, dx &= \frac{a_0}{2} \int_{-\pi}^\pi \cos(mx) \, dx + \sum_{j=1}^\infty a_j \int_{-\pi}^\pi \cos(jx) \cos(mx) \, dx \\
&\quad + \sum_{j=1}^\infty b_j \int_{-\pi}^\pi \sin(jx) \cos(mx) \, dx.
\end{aligned}
$$

Equation (15) can be simplified by using the orthogonal properties of the trigonometric functions, which are now stated. The value of the first term on the right-hand side of (15) is

$$\frac{a_0}{2} \int_{-\pi}^\pi \cos(mx) \, dx = \frac{a_0 \sin(mx)}{2m} \Big|_{-\pi}^\pi = 0. \tag{16}$$

The value of the term involving $\cos(jx) \cos(mx)$ is found by using the trigonometric identity

$$\cos(jx) \cos(mx) = \frac{1}{2} \cos((j+m)x) + \frac{1}{2} \cos((j-m)x). \tag{17}$$

When $j \neq m$, then (17) is used to get

(18)
$$a_j \int_{-\pi}^{\pi} \cos(jx) \cos(mx)\,dx = \frac{1}{2} a_j \int_{-\pi}^{\pi} \cos((j+m)x)\,dx$$
$$+ \frac{1}{2} a_j \int_{-\pi}^{\pi} \cos((j-m)x)\,dx = 0 + 0 = 0.$$

When $j = m$, the value of the integral is

(19)
$$a_m \int_{-\pi}^{\pi} \cos(jx) \cos(mx)\,dx = a_m \pi.$$

The value of the term on the right side of (15) involving $\sin(jx) \cos(mx)$ is found by using the trigonometric identity

(20)
$$\sin(jx) \cos(mx) = \frac{1}{2} \sin((j+m)x) + \frac{1}{2} \sin((j-m)x).$$

For all values of j and m in (20), we obtain

(21)
$$b_j \int_{-\pi}^{\pi} \sin(jx) \cos(mx)\,dx = \frac{1}{2} b_j \int_{-\pi}^{\pi} \sin((j+m)x)\,dx$$
$$+ \frac{1}{2} b_j \int_{-\pi}^{\pi} \sin((j-m)x)\,dx = 0 + 0 = 0.$$

Therefore, using the results of (16), (18), (19), and (21) in equation (15), we conclude that

(22)
$$\pi a_m = \int_{-\pi}^{\pi} f(x) \cos(mx)\,dx, \quad \text{for } m = 1,\, 2,\, \ldots.$$

Therefore, Euler's formula (5) is established.   Euler's formula (6) is proved similarly.   ●

Trigonometric Polynomial Approximation

Definition 5.4.   A series of the form

(23)
$$T_M(x) = \frac{a_0}{2} + \sum_{j=1}^{M} (a_j \cos(jx) + b_j \sin(jx))$$

is called a ***trigonometric polynomial*** of order M.   ▲

Theorem 5.8 (Discrete Fourier Series).   Suppose that $\{(x_j, y_j)\}_{j=0}^{N}$ are $N+1$ points, where $y_j = f(x_j)$, and the abscissas are equally spaced:

$$(24) \qquad x_j = -\pi + \frac{2j\pi}{N} \qquad \text{for } j = 0, 1, \ldots, N.$$

If $f(x)$ is periodic with period 2π and $2M < N$, then there exists a trigonometric polynomial $T_M(x)$ of the form (23) that minimizes the quantity

$$(25) \qquad \sum_{k=1}^{N} (f(x_k) - T_M(x_k))^2.$$

The coefficients a_j and b_j of this polynomial are computed with the formulas

$$(26) \qquad a_j = \frac{2}{N} \sum_{k=1}^{N} f(x_k) \cos(jx_k) \qquad \text{for } j = 0, 1, \ldots, M,$$

and

$$(27) \qquad b_j = \frac{2}{N} \sum_{k=1}^{N} f(x_k) \sin(jx_k) \qquad \text{for } j = 1, 2, \ldots, M.$$

Although formulas (26) and (27) are defined with the least-squares procedure, they can also be viewed as numerical approximations to the integrals in Euler's formulas (5) and (6). Euler's formulas give the coefficients for the Fourier series of a continuous function, whereas formulas (26) and (27) give the trigonometric polynomial coefficients for curve fitting to data points. The next example uses data points generated by the function $f(x) = x/2$ at discrete points. When more points are used, the trigonometric polynomial coefficients get closer to the Fourier series coefficients.

Example 5.15.   Use the 12 equally spaced points $x_k = -\pi + k\pi/6$, for $k = 1, 2, \ldots, 12$, and find the trigonometric polynomial approximation for $M = 5$ to the 12 data points $\{(x_k, f(x_k))\}_{k=1}^{12}$, where $f(x) = x/2$. Also compare the results when 60 and 360 points are used and with the first five terms of the Fourier series expansion for $f(x)$ that is given in Example 5.13.

Since the periodic extension is assumed, at a point of discontinuity, the function value $f(\pi)$ must be computed using the formula

$$(28) \qquad f(\pi) = \frac{f(\pi^-) + f(\pi^+)}{2} = \frac{\pi/2 - \pi/2}{2} = 0.$$

The function $f(x)$ is an odd function; hence the coefficients for the cosine terms are all zero (i.e., $a_j = 0$ for all j). The trigonometric polynomial of degree $M = 5$ involves only the sine terms, and when formula (27) is used with (28), we get

$$(29) \qquad \begin{aligned} T_5(x) &= 0.9770486 \sin(x) - 0.4534498 \sin(2x) + 0.26179938 \sin(3x) \\ &\quad - 0.1511499 \sin(4x) + 0.0701489 \sin(5x). \end{aligned}$$

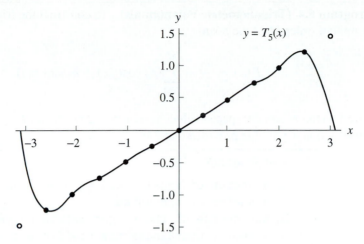

Figure 5.20 The trigonometric polynomial $T_5(x)$ of degree $M = 5$, based on 12 data points that lie on the line $y = x/2$.

Table 5.9 Comparison of Trigonometric Polynomial Coefficients for Approximations to $f(x) = x/2$ over $[-\pi, \pi]$

	Trigonometric polynomial coefficients			Fourier series coefficients
	12 points	60 points	360 points	
b_1	0.97704862	0.99908598	0.99997462	1.0
b_2	−0.45344984	−0.49817096	−0.49994923	−0.5
b_3	0.26179939	0.33058726	0.33325718	0.33333333
b_4	−0.15114995	−0.24633386	−0.24989845	−0.25
b_5	0.07014893	0.19540972	0.19987306	0.2

The graph of $T_5(x)$ is shown in Figure 5.20.

The coefficients of the fifth-degree trigonometric polynomial change slightly when the number of interpolation points increases to 60 and 360. As the number of points increases, they get closer to the coefficients of the Fourier series expansion of $f(x)$. The results are compared in Table 5.9. ∎

The following program constructs matrices A and B that contain the coefficients a_j and b_j, respectively, of the trigonometric polynomial (23) of order M.

Program 5.4 (Trigonometric Polynomials). To construct the trigonometric polynomial of order M of the form

$$P(x) = \frac{a_0}{2} + \sum_{j=1}^{M} (a_j \cos(jx) + b_j \sin(jx))$$

based on the N equally spaced values $x_k = -\pi + 2\pi k/N$, for $k = 1, 2, \ldots, N$. The construction is possible provided that $2M + 1 \le N$.

```
function [A,B]=tpcoeff(X,Y,M)

%Input   - X is a vector of equally spaced abscissas in [-pi,pi]
%         - Y is a vector of ordinates
%         - M is the degree of the trigonometric polynomial
%Output  - A is a vector containing the coefficients of cos(jx)
%         - B is a vector containing the coefficients of sin(jx)

N=length(X)-1;
max1=fix((N-1)/2);

if M>max1
    M=max1;
end

A=zeros(1,M+1);
B=zeros(1,M+1);
Yends=(Y(1)+Y(N+1))/2;
Y(1)=Yends;
Y(N+1)=Yends;
A(1)=sum(Y);

for j=1:M
    A(j+1)=cos(j*X)*Y';
    B(j+1)=sin(j*X)*Y';
end

A=2*A/N;
B=2*B/N;
A(1)=A(1)/2;
```

The following short program will evaluate the trigonometric polynomial $P(x)$ of order M from Program 5.4 at a particular value of x.

```
function z=tp(A,B,x,M)

z=A(1);
for j= 1:M
    z=z+A(j+1)*cos(j*x)+B(j+1)*sin(j*x);
end
```

For example, the following sequence of commands in the MATLAB command window will produce a graph analogous to Figure 5.20.

```
>>x=-pi:.01:pi;
>>y=tp(A,B,x,M);
>>plot(x,y,X,Y,'o')
```

Exercises for Fourier Series and Trigonometric Polynomials

In Exercises 1 through 5, find the Fourier series representation of the given function. *Hint.* Follow the procedures outlined in Examples 5.13 and 5.14. Graph each function and the partial sums $S_2(x)$, $S_3(x)$, and $S_4(x)$ of its Fourier series representation on the same coordinate system (see Figure 5.19).

1. $f(x) = \begin{cases} -1 & \text{for } -\pi < x < 0 \\ 1 & \text{for } 0 < x < \pi \end{cases}$

2. $f(x) = \begin{cases} \dfrac{\pi}{2} + x & \text{for } -\pi \le x < 0 \\ \dfrac{\pi}{2} - x & \text{for } 0 \le x < \pi \end{cases}$

3. $f(x) = \begin{cases} 0 & \text{for } -\pi \le x < 0 \\ x & \text{for } 0 \le x < \pi \end{cases}$

4. $f(x) = \begin{cases} -1 & \text{for } \frac{\pi}{2} < x < \pi \\ 1 & \text{for } \frac{-\pi}{2} < x < \frac{\pi}{2} \\ -1 & \text{for } -\pi < x < \frac{-\pi}{2} \end{cases}$

5. $f(x) = \begin{cases} -\pi - x & \text{for } -\pi \le x < -\pi/2 \\ x & \text{for } -\pi/2 \le x < \pi/2 \\ \pi - x & \text{for } \pi/2 \le x < \pi \end{cases}$

6. In Exercise 1, set $x = \pi/2$ and show that

$$\frac{\pi}{4} = 1 - \frac{1}{3} + \frac{1}{5} - \frac{1}{7} + \cdots .$$

7. In Exercise 2, set $x = 0$ and show that

$$\frac{\pi^2}{8} = 1 + \frac{1}{3^2} + \frac{1}{5^2} + \frac{1}{7^2} + \cdots .$$

8. Find the Fourier cosine series representation for the periodic function whose definition on one period is $f(x) = x^2/4$ where $-\pi \le x < \pi$.

9. Suppose that $f(x)$ is a periodic function with period $2P$; that is, $f(x + 2P) = f(x)$ for all x. By making an appropriate substitution, show that Euler's formulas (5) and

(6) for f are

$$a_0 = \frac{1}{P} \int_{-P}^{P} f(x)\, dx$$

$$a_j = \frac{1}{P} \int_{-P}^{P} f(x) \cos\left(\frac{j\pi x}{P}\right) dx \quad \text{for } j = 1, 2, \ldots$$

$$b_j = \frac{1}{P} \int_{-P}^{P} f(x) \sin\left(\frac{j\pi x}{P}\right) dx \quad \text{for } j = 1, 2, \ldots.$$

In Exercises 10 through 12, use the results of Exercise 9 to find the Fourier series representation of the given function. Graph $f(x)$, $S_4(x)$, and $S_6(x)$ on the same coordinate system.

10. $f(x) = \begin{cases} 0 & \text{for } -2 \le x < 0 \\ 1 & \text{for } 0 \le x < 2 \end{cases}$

11. $f(x) = \begin{cases} -1 & \text{for } -3 \le x < -1 \\ x & \text{for } -1 \le x < 1 \\ 1 & \text{for } 1 \le x < 3 \end{cases}$

12. $f(x) = -x^2 + 9 \quad \text{for } -3 \le x < 3$

13. Prove Theorem 5.6.

14. Prove Theorem 5.7.

Algorithms and Programs

1. Use Program 5.4 with $N = 12$ points and follow Example 5.15 to find the trigonometric polynomial of degree $M = 5$ for the equally spaced points $\{(x_k, f(x_k))\}_{k=1}^{12}$, where $f(x)$ is the function in (**a**) Exercise 1, (**b**) Exercise 2, (**c**) Exercise 3, and (**d**) Exercise 4. In each case, produce a graph of $f(x)$, $T_5(x)$, and $\{(x_k, f(x_k))\}_{k=1}^{12}$ on the same coordinate system.

2. Use Program 5.4 to find the coefficients of $T_5(x)$ in Example 5.15 when first 60 and then 360 equally spaced points are used.

3. Modify Program 5.4 so that it will find the trigonometric polynomial of period $2P = b - a$ when the data points are equally spaced over the interval $[a, b]$.

4. Use your modification of Program 5.4 to find $T_5(x)$ for (**a**) $f(x)$ in Exercise 10, using 12 equally spaced data points, and (**b**) $f(x)$ in Exercise 12, using 60 equally spaced data points. In each case, graph $T_5(x)$ and the data points on the same coordinate system.

5. The temperature cycle (Fahrenheit) in a suburb of Los Angeles on November 8 is given in Table 5.10. There are 24 data points.
   (**a**) Find the trigonometric polynomial $T_7(x)$.
   (**b**) Graph $T_7(x)$ and the 24 data points on the same coordinate system.
   (**c**) Repeat parts (a) and (b) using temperatures from your locale.

Table 5.10   Data for Problem 5

Time, p.m.	Degrees	Time, a.m.	Degrees
1	66	1	58
2	66	2	58
3	65	3	58
4	64	4	58
5	63	5	57
6	63	6	57
7	62	7	57
8	61	8	58
9	60	9	60
10	60	10	64
11	59	11	67
Midnight	58	Noon	68

Table 5.11   Data for Problem 6

Calendar date	Average degrees
Jan. 1	−14
Jan. 29	−9
Feb. 26	2
Mar. 26	15
Apr. 23	35
May 21	52
June 18	62
July 16	63
Aug. 13	58
Sept. 10	50
Oct. 8	34
Nov. 5	12
Dec. 3	−5

6. The yearly temperature cycle (Fahrenheit) for Fairbanks, Alaska, is given in Table 5.11. There are 13 equally spaced data points, which correspond to a measurement every 28 days.

   (a)   Find the trigonometric polynomial $T_6(x)$.

   (b)   Graph $T_6(x)$ and the 13 data points on the same coordinate system.

5.5 Bézier Curves

Pierre Bézier at Renault and Paul de Casteljau at Citroën independently developed the *Bézier curve* for CAD/CAM operations, in the 1970s. These parametrically defined polynomials are a class of approximating splines. Bézier curves are the basis of the entire Adobe PostScript drawing model that is used in the software products Adobe Illustrator, Macromedia Freehand, and Fontographer. Bézier curves continue to be the primary method of representing curves and surfaces in computer graphics (CAD/CAM, computer-aided geometric design).

In Casteljau's original development, Bézier curves were defined implicitly by a recursive algorithm (see Property 1 below). The development of the properties of Bézier curves will be facilitated by defining them explicitly in terms of *Bernstein polynomials*.

Definition 5.5. *Bernstein polynomials* of degree N are defined by

$$B_{i,N}(t) = \binom{N}{i} t^i (1-t)^{N-i},$$

for $i = 0, 1, 2, \ldots, N$, where $\binom{N}{i} = \dfrac{N!}{i! \, (N-i)!}.$ ▲

In general, there are $N + 1$ Bernstein polynomials of degree N. For example, the Bernstein polynomials of degrees 1, 2, and 3 are

(1) $\qquad\qquad\qquad B_{0,1}(t) = 1 - t, \; B_{1,1}(t) = t;$

(2) $\qquad B_{0,2}(t) = (1-t)^2, \; B_{1,2}(t) = 2t(1-t), \; B_{2,2}(t) = t^2; \qquad$ and

(3) $\quad B_{0,3}(t) = (1-t)^3, \; B_{1,3}(t) = 3t(1-t)^2, \; B_{2,3}(t) = 3t^2(1-t), \; B_{3,3}(t) = t^3;$

respectively.

Properties of Bernstein Polynomials

Property 1. Recurrence Relation

Bernstein polynomials can be generated in the following way. Set $B_{0,0}(t) = 1$ and $B_{i,N}(t) = 0$ for $i < 0$ or $i > N$, and use the recurrence relation

(4) $\quad B_{i,N}(t) = (1-t)B_{i,N-1}(t) + t B_{i-1,N-1}(t) \qquad$ for $i = 1, 2, 3, \ldots, N-1.$

Property 2. Nonnegative on [0, 1]

The Bernstein polynomials are nonnegative over the interval [0, 1] (see Figure 5.21).

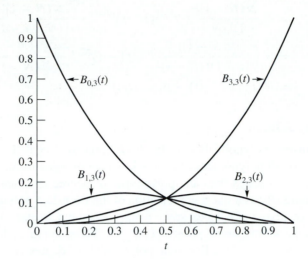

Figure 5.21   Bernstein polynomials of degree three.

Property 3. The Bernstein polynomials form a partition of unity

$$(5) \qquad \sum_{i=0}^{N} B_{i,N}(t) = 1$$

Substituting $x = t$ and $y = 1 - t$ into the binomial theorem

$$(x + y)^N = \sum_{i=0}^{N} \binom{N}{i} x^i y^{N-i}$$

yields

$$\sum_{i=0}^{N} \binom{N}{i} x^i y^{N-i} = (t + (1 - t))^N = 1^N = 1.$$

Property 4. Derivatives

$$(6) \qquad \frac{d}{dt} B_{i,N}(t) = N(B_{i-1,N-1}(t) - B_{i,N-1}(t))$$

Formula (6) is established by taking the derivative of the Bernstein polynomial in Definition 5.5.

$$\frac{d}{dt} B_{i,N}(t) = \frac{d}{dt} \binom{N}{i} t^i (1 - t)^{N-i}$$

$$= \frac{i N!}{i! (N-i)!} t^{i-1} (1 - t)^{N-i} - \frac{(N-i)N!}{i! (N-i)!} t^i (1 - t)^{N-i-1}$$

$$
\begin{aligned}
&= \frac{N(N-1)!}{(i-1)!\,(N-i)!}t^{i-1}(1-t)^{N-i} - \frac{N(N-1)!}{i!\,(N-i-1)!}t^{i}(1-t)^{N-i-1} \\
&= N\left(\frac{(N-1)!}{(i-1)!\,(N-i)!}t^{i-1}(1-t)^{N-i} - \frac{(N-1)!}{i!\,(N-i-1)!}t^{i}(1-t)^{N-i-1}\right) \\
&= N\big(B_{i-1,N-1}(t) - B_{i,N-1}(t)\big)
\end{aligned}
$$

Property 5. Basis

The Bernstein polynomials of order N ($B_{i,N}(t)$ for $i = 0, 1, \ldots, N$) form a basis of the space of all polynomials of degree less than or equal to N.

Property 5 states than any polynomial of degree less than or equal to N can be written uniquely as a linear combination of the Bernstein polynomials of order N. The concept of a basis of a vector space is introduced in Chapter 11.

Given a set of *control points*, $\{\mathbf{P}_i\}_{i=0}^{N}$, a Bézier curve of degree N is now defined as a weighted sum of the Bernstein polynomials of degree N.

Definition 5.6. Given a set of control points $\{\mathbf{P}_i\}_{i=0}^{N}$, where $\mathbf{P}_i = (x_i, y_i)$, a *Bézier curve of degree* N is

$$
(7) \qquad\qquad \mathbf{P}(t) = \sum_{i=0}^{N} \mathbf{P}_i B_{i,N}(t),
$$

where $B_{i,N}(t)$, for $i = 0, 1, \ldots, N$, are the Bernstein polynomials of degree N, and $t \in [0, 1]$. ▲

In formula (7) the control points are ordered pairs representing x- and y-coordinates in the plane. Without ambiguity the control points can be treated as vectors and the corresponding Bernstein polynomials as scalars. Thus formula (7) can be represented parametrically as $\mathbf{P}(t) = (x(t), y(t))$, where

$$
(8) \qquad\qquad x(t) = \sum_{i=0}^{N} x_i B_{i,N}(t) \quad \text{and} \quad y(t) = \sum_{i=0}^{N} y_i B_{i,N}(t),
$$

and $0 \leq t \leq 1$. The function $\mathbf{P}(t)$ is said to be a vector-valued function, or equivalently, the range of the function is a set of points in the xy-plane.

Example 5.16. Find the Bézier curve which has the control points $(2, 2)$, $(1, 1.5)$, $(3.5, 0)$, and $(4, 1)$.

Substituting the x- and y-coordinates of the control points and $N = 3$ into formula (8) yields

$$
(9) \qquad\qquad x(t) = 2B_{0,3}(t) + 1B_{1,3}(t) + 3.5B_{2,3}(t) + 4B_{3,3}(t)
$$

$$
(10) \qquad\qquad y(t) = 2B_{0,3}(t) + 1.5B_{1,3}(t) + 0B_{2,3}(t) + 1B_{3,3}(t).
$$

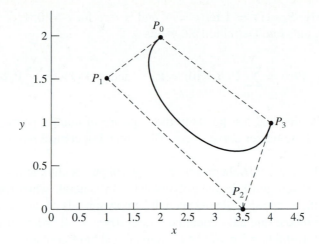

Figure 5.22   Bézier curve of degree three and convex hull of control points.

Substituting the Bernstein polynomials of degree three, found in formula (3), into formulas (9) and (10) yields

(11) $x(t) = 2(1 - t)^3 + 3t(1 - t)^2 + 10.5t^2(1 - t) + 4t^3$

(12) $y(t) = 2(1 - t)^3 + 4.5t(1 - t)^2 + t^3.$

Simplifying formulas (11) and (12) yields

$$\mathbf{P}(t) = (2 - 3t + 10.5t^2 - 5.5t^3,\ 2 - 1.5t - 3t^2 + 3.5t^3),$$

where $0 \le t \le 1$.   ∎

The functions $x(t)$ and $y(t)$ in formulas (11) and (12) are polynomials and are continuous and differentiable over the interval $0 \le t \le 1$. Thus the graph of the Bézier curve $\mathbf{P}(t)$ is a continuous and differentiable curve in the xy-plane (see Figure 5.22), where $0 \le t \le 1$. *Note.* $\mathbf{P}(0) = (2, 2)$ and $\mathbf{P}(1) = (4, 1)$. The graph of the curve starts at the first control point $(2, 2)$ and ends at the last control point $(4, 1)$.

Properties of Bézier Curves

Property 1. The points $\mathbf{P}_0$ and $\mathbf{P}_1$ are on the curve $P(t)$

Substituting $t = 0$ into Definition 5.5 yields

$$B_{i,N}(0) = \begin{cases} 1 & \text{for } i = 0 \\ 0 & \text{for } i \ne 0. \end{cases}$$

Similarly, $B_{i,N}(1) = 1$ for $i = N$ and is zero for $i = 0, 1, \ldots, N - 1$. Substituting these results into Definition 5.6 yields

$$\mathbf{P}(0) = \sum_{i=0}^{N} \mathbf{P}_i B_{i,N}(0) = \mathbf{P}_0 \quad \text{and} \quad \mathbf{P}(1) = \sum_{i=0}^{N} \mathbf{P}_i B_{i,N}(1) = \mathbf{P}_N.$$

Thus the first and last points in the sequence of control points, $\{\mathbf{P}_i\}_{i=0}^{N}$, are the endpoints of the Bézier curve. *Note*. The remaining control points are not necessarily on the curve.

   In Example 5.16 there were four control points and the resulting components $x(t)$ and $y(t)$ were third-degree polynomials. In general, when there are $N + 1$ control points the resulting components will be polynomials of degree N. Since polynomials are continuous and have continuous derivatives of all orders, it follows that the Bézier curve in Definition 5.6 will be continuous and have derivatives of all orders.

Property 2. $\mathbf{P}(t)$ is continuous and has derivatives of all orders on the interval [0, 1]

The derivative of $\mathbf{P}(t)$, with respect to t, is

$$\mathbf{P}'(t) = \frac{d}{dt} \sum_{i=0}^{N} \mathbf{P}_i B_{i,N}(t)$$

$$= \sum_{i=0}^{N} \mathbf{P}_i \frac{d}{dt} B_{i,N}(t)$$

$$= \sum_{i=0}^{N} \mathbf{P}_i N(B_{i-1,N-1}(t) - B_{i,N-1}(t))$$

(Property 4 of Bernstein polynomials). Setting $t = 0$ and substituting $B_{i,N}(0) = 1$ for $i = 0$ and $B_{i,N}(0) = 0$ for $i \geq 1$ (Definition 5.5) into the right-hand side of the expression for $P'(t)$ and simplifying yields

$$\mathbf{P}'(0) = \sum_{i=0}^{N} \mathbf{P}_i N(B_{i-1,N-1}(0) - B_{i,N-1}(0)) = N(\mathbf{P}_1 - \mathbf{P}_0).$$

Similarly, $\mathbf{P}'(1) = N(\mathbf{P}_N - \mathbf{P}_{N-1})$. In other words, the tangent lines to a Bézier curve at the endpoints are parallel to the lines through the endpoints and the adjacent control points. The property is illustrated in Figure 5.23.

Property 3. $\mathbf{P}'(0) = N(\mathbf{P}_1 - \mathbf{P}_0)$ and $\mathbf{P}'(1) = N(\mathbf{P}_N - \mathbf{P}_{N-1})$

The final property is based on the concept of a ***convex set***. A subset C of the xy-plane is said to be a convex set, provided that all the points on the line segment joining any two points in C are also elements of the set C. For example, a line segment or a circle and its interior are convex sets, while a circle without its interior is not a convex set. The convex set concept extends naturally to higher-dimension spaces.

Definition 5.7.   The *convex hull* of a set C is the intersection of all convex sets containing C.   ▲

Figure 5.22 shows the convex hull (the indicated quadrilateral and its interior) of the control points for the Bézier curve from Example 5.16. In the xy-plane the convex hull of a set of points, $\{P_i\}_{i=0}^{N}$, may be *visualized* by placing pins at each point and placing a rubber band around the resulting configuration.

A sum $\sum_{i=0}^{N} m_i P_i$ is said to be a *convex combination* of the points $\{P_i\}_{i=0}^{N}$, provided that the set of coefficients $m_0, m_1, \ldots, m_N$ are nonnegative and $\sum_{i=0}^{N} m_i = 1$. A convex combination of points must necessarily be a subset of the convex hull of the set of points. It follows from properties 2 and 3 of the Bernstein polynomials that the Bézier curve in formula (7) is a convex combination of the control points. Therefore, the graph of the curve must lie in the convex hull of the control points.

Property 4. The Bézier curve lies in the convex hull of its set of control points

The properties indicate that the graph of a Bézier curve of degree N is a continuous curve, bounded by the convex hull of the set of control points, $\{P_i\}_{i=0}^{N}$, and that the curve begins and ends at points P_0 and P_N, respectively. Bézier observed that the graph is sequentially *pulled* toward each of the remaining control points $P_1, P_2, \ldots, P_{N-1}$. For example, if the control points P_1 and P_{N-1} are replaced by the control points Q_1 and Q_{N-1}, which are farther away (but in the same direction) from the respective endpoints, then the resulting Bézier curve will more closely approximate the tangent line near the endpoints. Figure 5.23 illustrates the pulling and tangent effects using the Bézier curve $P(t)$ from Example 5.16 and the curve $Q(t)$ with control points $(2, 2)$, $(0, 1)$, $(3, -1)$, and $(4, 1)$. Clearly, Q_1, P_1, and $P_0 = Q_0$, and Q_2, P_2, and $P_3 = Q_3$ are collinear, respectively.

The effectiveness of Bézier curves lies in the ease with which the shape of the curve can be modified (mouse, keyboard, or other graphical interface) by making small adjustments to the control points. Figure 5.24 shows four Bézier curves, of different degrees, with the corresponding sets of control points sequentially connected to form polygonal paths. The reader should observe that the polygonal paths provide a rough *sketch* of the resulting Bézier curves. Changing the coordinates of any one control point, say P_k, will change the shape of the entire curve over the parameter interval $0 \le t \le 1$. The changes in the shape of the curve will be somewhat localized, since the Bernstein polynomial $B_{k,N}$, corresponding to the control point P_k (formula (7)) , has a maximum at the parameter value $t = k/N$. Thus the majority of the change in the shape of the graph of the Bézier curve will occur near the point $P(k/N)$. Consequently, creating a curve of a specified shaped requires a relatively small number of changes to the original set of control points.

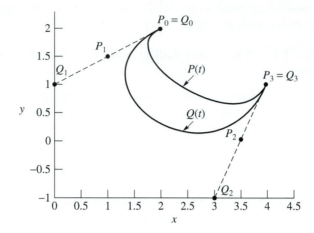

Figure 5.23 $P(t)$, $Q(t)$ and control points.

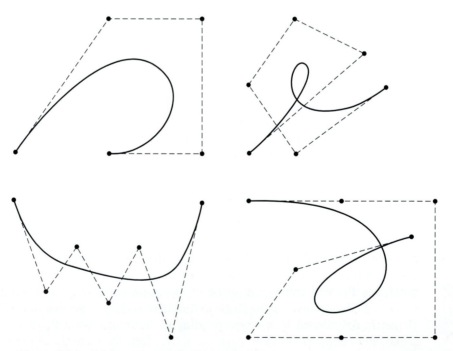

Figure 5.24 Bézier curves and polygonal paths.

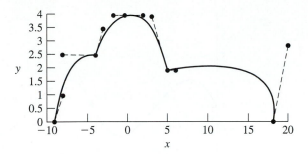

Figure 5.25   Composite Bźier curves.

In practice, curves are produced using a sequence of Bézier curves sharing common endpoints. This process is analogous to that used in the creation of cubic splines. In that case it was necessary to use a sequence of cubic polynomials to avoid the oscillatory behavior of polynomials of high degree. Property 4 shows that the oscillatory behavior of higher-degree polynomials is not a problem with Bézier curves. Since changing one control point changes the shape of a Bézier curve, it is simpler to break the process into a series of Bézier curves and minimize the number of changes in the control points.

Example 5.17.   Find the composite Bézier curve for the four sets of control points

$$\{(-9, 0), (-8, 1), (-8, 2.5), (-4, 2.5)\}, \qquad \{(-4, 2.5), (-3, 3.5), (-1, 4), (0, 4)\}$$
$$\{(0, 4), (2, 4), (3, 4), (5, 2)\}, \qquad \{(5, 2), (6, 2), (20, 3), (18, 0)\}$$

Following the process outlined in Example 5.16 yields

$$\mathbf{P}_1(t) = (-9 + 3t - 3t^2 + 5t^3, 3t + 1.5t^2 - 2t^3)$$
$$\mathbf{P}_2(t) = (-4 + 3t + 3t^2 - 2t^3, 2.5 + 3t - 1.5t^2)$$
$$\mathbf{P}_3(t) = (6t - 3t^2 + 2t^3, 4 - 2t^3)$$
$$\mathbf{P}_4(t) = (5 + 3t + 39t^2 - 29t^3, 2 + 3t^2 - 5t^3).$$

The graph of the composite Bézier curve and corresponding control points is shown in Figure 5.25. ∎

The Bézier curves in Example 5.17 do not meet *smoothly* at the common endpoints. To have two Bézier curves $\mathbf{P}(t)$ and $\mathbf{Q}(t)$ meet smoothly would require that $\mathbf{P}_N = \mathbf{Q}_0$ and $\mathbf{P}'(\mathbf{P}_N) = \mathbf{Q}'(\mathbf{Q}_0)$. Property 3 indicates that it is sufficient to require that the control points $\mathbf{P}_{N-1}$, $\mathbf{P}_N = \mathbf{Q}_0$, and $\mathbf{Q}_1$ be collinear. To illustrate, consider the Bézier curves $\mathbf{P}(t)$ and $\mathbf{Q}(t)$ of degree three with the control point sets

$$\{(0, 3), (1, 5), (2, 1), (3, 3)\} \quad \text{and} \quad \{(3, 3), (4, 5), (5, 1), (6, 3)\},$$

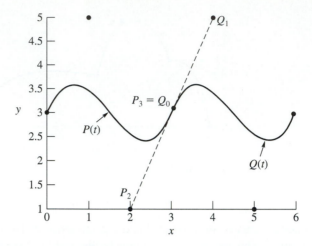

Figure 5.26 Matching derivatives at Bézier curves at common endpoints.

respectively. Clearly, the control points $(2, 1)$, $(3, 3)$, and $(4, 5)$ are collinear. Again, following the process outlined in Example 5.16:

(13) $$\mathbf{P}(t) = (3t, 3 + 6t - 18t^2 + 12t^3)$$

(14) $$\mathbf{Q}(t) = (3 + 3t, 3 + 6t - 18t^2 + 12t^3)$$

and

$$\mathbf{P}'(t) = (3, 6 - 36t + 36t^2) \quad \text{and} \quad \mathbf{Q}'(t) = (3, 6 - 36t + 36t^2).$$

Substituting $t = 1$ and $t = 0$ into $\mathbf{P}'(t)$ and $\mathbf{Q}'(t)$, respectively, yields

$$\mathbf{P}'(1) = (3, 6) = \mathbf{Q}'(0)$$

The graphs of $\mathbf{P}(t)$ and $\mathbf{Q}(t)$ and the smoothness at the common endpoint are shown in Figure 5.26.

The `plot` command is used to graph parametric curves in MATLAB. The Bézier curve in Example 5.16 can be plotted as follows:

```
t=0:.01:1;
x=2-3*t+10.5*t.^2-5.5*t.^3;
y=2-1.5*t-3*t.^2+3.5*t.^3;
plot(x,y)
```

Exercises for Bézier Curves

1. Expand completely the Bernstein polynomials $B_{2,4}(t)$, $B_{3,5}(t)$, and $B_{5,7}(t)$.

2. Use Definition 5.5 to prove formula (4).

3. Show that the Bernstein polynomials are nonnegative over the interval $[0, 1]$.

4. Verify formula (5) for the case $N = 3$ by carrying out the sum $\sum_{i=0}^{3} B_{i,3}(t)$.

5. Use formula (6) to evaluate $\dfrac{d}{dt} B_{3,5}(t)$ at $t = 1/3$ and $t = 2/3$.

6. Prove that $B_{i,N}(t)$ takes on its maximum value, over the interval $[0, 1]$, at $t = i/N$.

7. Use Definition 5.5 to establish the formula $t B_{i,N}(t) = \dfrac{i+1}{N+1} B_{i+1,N+1}(t)$.

8. Find the Bézier curve of degree N for each set of control points.
   (a) $N = 3$; $\{(1, 3), (3, -1), (2, 4), (3, 0)\}$
   (b) $N = 4$; $\{(-2, 3), (-1, 3), (3, 5), (3, 4), (2, 3)\}$
   (c) $N = 5$; $\{(1, 1), (2, 2), (3, 4), (4, 4), (5, 2), (6, 1)\}$

9. Find the Bézier curve of degree three with the control points $(1, 1)$, $(2, 3)$, $(3, 5)$, and $(4, 7)$. Explain why, in general, $N + 1$ collinear control points will produce a linear Bézier curve.

10. Show $\mathbf{P}'(1) = N(\mathbf{P}_N - \mathbf{P}_{N-1})$.

11. Show that
   (a) $\mathbf{P}''(0) = N(N - 1)(\mathbf{P}_2 - 2\mathbf{P}_1 + \mathbf{P}_0)$
   (b) $\mathbf{P}''(1) = N(N - 1)(\mathbf{P}_N - 2\mathbf{P}_{N-1} + \mathbf{P}_{N-2})$

12. Determine the convex hull of each set of points.
   (a) $\{(1, 1), (3, 0), (5, -1), (7, -2)\}$
   (b) $\{(-4, 2), (0, 2), (-3, 5), (2, 5), (1, 2)\}$
   (c) $\{(0, 0), (0, 1), (1/4, 1/4), (0, 1/2)\}$

Algorithms and Programs

1. Write a MATLAB program to generate and plot a Bézier curve. Construct the program so that it accepts sets of control points as $N \times 2$ matrices. The first and second columns of the matrix should correspond to the x- and y-coordinates of the control points. The program should be able to handle the cases $N = 3$, 4, and 5.

2. Use the program in Problem 1 to plot the Bézier curves from Exercise 8.

3. Write a MATLAB program to generate and plot a composite Bézier curve. Use the program to generate and plot the composite Bézier curve for the three sets of control points: $\{(0, 0), (1, 2), (1, 1), (3, 0)\}$,
   $\{(3, 0), (4, -1), (5, -2), (6, 1), (7, 0)\}$, and $\{(7, 0), (4, -3), (2, -1), (0, 0)\}$.

4. Use the programs from Problem 1 and 3 to create
   (a)   an infinity symbol: ∞.
   (b)   a lowercase beta: β.

6

Numerical Differentiation

Formulas for numerical derivatives are important in developing algorithms for solving boundary value problems for ordinary differential equations and partial differential equations (see Chapters 9 and 10). Standard examples of numerical differentiation often use known functions so that the numerical approximation can be compared with the exact answer. For illustration, we use the Bessel function $J_1(x)$, whose tabulated values can be found in standard reference books. Eight equally spaced points over $[0, 7]$ are $(0, 0.0000)$, $(1, 0.4400)$, $(2, 0.5767)$, $(3, 0.3391)$, $(4, -0.0660)$,

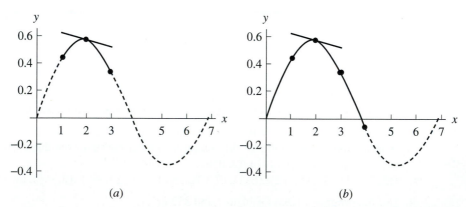

(a) (b)

Figure 6.1 (a) The tangent to $p_2(x)$ at $(2, 0.5767)$ with slope $p'_2(2) = -0.0505$. (b) The tangent to $p_4(x)$ at $(2, 0.5767)$ with slope $p'_4(2) = -0.0618$.

$(5, -0.3276)$, $(6, -0.2767)$, and $(7, -0.004)$. The underlying principle is differentiation of an interpolation polynomial. Let us focus our attention on finding $J_1'(2)$. The interpolation polynomial $p_2(x) = -0.0710 + 0.6982x - 0.1872x^2$ passes through the three points $(1, 0.4400)$, $(2, 0.5767)$, and $(3, 0.3391)$ and is used to obtain $J_1'(2) \approx p_2'(2) = -0.0505$. This quadratic polynomial $p_2(x)$ and its tangent line at $(2, J_1(2))$ are shown in Figure 6.1(a). If five interpolation points are used, a better approximation can be determined. The polynomial $p_4(x) = 0.4986x + 0.011x^2 - 0.0813x^3 + 0.0116x^4$ passes through $(0, 0.0000)$, $(1, 0.4400)$, $(2, 0.5767)$, $(3, 0.3391)$, and $(4, -0.0660)$ and is used to obtain $J_1'(2) \approx p_4'(2) = -0.0618$. The quartic polynomial $p_4(x)$ and its tangent line at $(2, J_1(2))$ are shown in Figure 6.1(b). The true value for the derivative is $J_1'(2) = -0.0645$, and the errors in $p_2(x)$ and $p_4(x)$ are -0.0140 and -0.0026, respectively. In this chapter we develop the introductory theory needed to investigate the accuracy of numerical differentiation.

6.1   Approximating the Derivative

Limit of the Difference Quotient

We now turn our attention to the numerical process for approximating the derivative of $f(x)$:

$$(1) \qquad f'(x) = \lim_{h \to 0} \frac{f(x+h) - f(x)}{h}.$$

The method seems straightforward; choose a sequence $\{h_k\}$ so that $h_k \to 0$ and compute the limit of the sequence

$$(2) \qquad D_k = \frac{f(x + h_k) - f(x)}{h_k} \qquad \text{for } k = 1, 2, \ldots, n, \ldots.$$

The reader may notice that we will only compute a finite number of terms $D_1, D_2, \ldots$, D_N in the sequence (2), and it appears that we should use D_N for our answer. The following question is often posed: Why compute $D_1, D_2, \ldots, D_{N-1}$? Equivalently, we could ask: What value h_N should be chosen so that D_N is a good approximation to the derivative $f'(x)$? To answer this question, we must look at an example to see why there is no simple solution.

For example, consider the function $f(x) = e^x$ and use the step sizes $h = 1$, $1/2$, and $1/4$ to construct the secant lines between the points $(0, 1)$ and $(h, f(h))$, respectively. As h gets small, the secant line approaches the tangent line as shown in Figure 6.2. Although Figure 6.2 gives a good visualization of the process described in (1), we must make numerical computations with $h = 0.00001$ to get an acceptable numerical answer, and for this value of h the graphs of the tangent line and secant line would be indistinguishable.

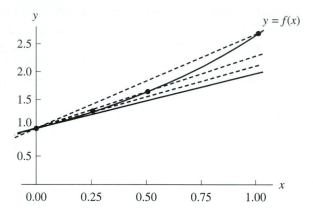

Figure 6.2   Several secant lines for $y = e^x$.

Table 6.1   Finding the Difference Quotients $D_k = (e^{1+h_k} - e)/h_k$

h_k	$f_k = f(1 + h_k)$	$f_k - e$	$D_k = (f_k - e)/h_k$
$h_1 = 0.1$	3.004166024	0.285884196	2.858841960
$h_2 = 0.01$	2.745601015	0.027319187	2.731918700
$h_3 = 0.001$	2.721001470	0.002719642	2.719642000
$h_4 = 0.0001$	2.718553670	0.000271842	2.718420000
$h_5 = 0.00001$	2.718309011	0.000027183	2.718300000
$h_6 = 10^{-6}$	2.718284547	0.000002719	2.719000000
$h_7 = 10^{-7}$	2.718282100	0.000000272	2.720000000
$h_8 = 10^{-8}$	2.718281856	0.000000028	2.800000000
$h_9 = 10^{-9}$	2.718281831	0.000000003	3.000000000
$h_{10} = 10^{-10}$	2.718281828	0.000000000	0.000000000

Example 6.1.   Let $f(x) = e^x$ and $x = 1$. Compute the difference quotients D_k using the step sizes $h_k = 10^{-k}$ for $k = 1, 2, \ldots, 10$. Carry out nine decimal places in all calculations.

A table of the values $f(1 + h_k)$ and $(f(1 + h_k) - f(1))/h_k$ that are used in the computation of D_k is shown in Table 6.1.   ■

The largest value $h_1 = 0.1$ does not produce a good approximation $D_1 \approx f'(1)$, because the step size h_1 is too large and the difference quotient is the slope of the secant line through two points that are not close enough to each other. When formula (2) is used with a fixed precision of nine decimal places, h_9 produced the approximation $D_9 = 3$ and h_{10} produced $D_{10} = 0$. If h_k is too small, then the computed function values $f(x + h_k)$ and $f(x)$ are very close together. The difference $f(x + h_k) - f(x)$ can exhibit the problem of loss of significance due to the subtraction of quantities that are nearly equal. The value $h_{10} = 10^{-10}$ is so small that the stored values of $f(x + h_{10})$ and $f(x)$ are the same, and hence the computed difference quotient is zero.

In Example 6.1 the mathematical value for the limit is $f'(1) \approx 2.718281828$. Observe that the value $h_5 = 10^{-5}$ gives the best approximation, $D_5 = 2.7183$.

    Example 6.1 shows that it is not easy to find numerically the limit in equation (2). The sequence starts to converge to e, and D_5 is the closest; then the terms move away from e. In Program 6.1 it is suggested that terms in the sequence $\{D_k\}$ should be computed until $|D_{N+1} - D_N| \geq |D_N - D_{N-1}|$. This is an attempt to determine the best approximation before the terms start to move away from the limit. When this criterion is applied to Example 6.1, we have $0.0007 = |D_6 - D_5| > |D_5 - D_4| = 0.00012$; hence D_5 is the answer we choose. We now proceed to develop formulas that give a reasonable amount of accuracy for larger values of h.

Central-Difference Formulas

If the function $f(x)$ can be evaluated at values that lie to the left and right of x, then the best two-point formula will involve abscissas that are chosen symmetrically on both sides of x.

Theorem 6.1 (Centered Formula of Order $O(h^2)$).   Assume that $f \in C^3[a, b]$ and that $x - h, x, x + h \in [a, b]$. Then

$$(3) \qquad\qquad f'(x) \approx \frac{f(x + h) - f(x - h)}{2h}.$$

Furthermore, there exists a number $c = c(x) \in [a, b]$ such that

$$(4) \qquad\qquad f'(x) = \frac{f(x + h) - f(x - h)}{2h} + E_{\text{trunc}}(f, h),$$

where

$$E_{\text{trunc}}(f, h) = -\frac{h^2 f^{(3)}(c)}{6} = O(h^2).$$

The term $E(f, h)$ is called the ***truncation error***.

Proof.   Start with the second-degree Taylor expansions $f(x) = P_2(x) + E_2(x)$, about x, for $f(x + h)$ and $f(x - h)$:

$$(5) \qquad\qquad f(x + h) = f(x) + f'(x)h + \frac{f^{(2)}(x)h^2}{2!} + \frac{f^{(3)}(c_1)h^3}{3!}$$

and

$$(6) \qquad\qquad f(x - h) = f(x) - f'(x)h + \frac{f^{(2)}(x)h^2}{2!} - \frac{f^{(3)}(c_2)h^3}{3!}.$$

After (6) is subtracted from (5), the result is

$$(7) \qquad f(x + h) - f(x - h) = 2f'(x)h + \frac{((f^{(3)}(c_1) + f^{(3)}(c_2))h^3}{3!}.$$

Since $f^{(3)}(x)$ is continuous, the intermediate value theorem can be used to find a value c so that

(8)
$$\frac{f^{(3)}(c_1) + f^{(3)}(c_2)}{2} = f^{(3)}(c).$$

This can be substituted into (7) and the terms rearranged to yield

(9)
$$f'(x) = \frac{f(x+h) - f(x-h)}{2h} - \frac{f^{(3)}(c)h^2}{3!}.$$

The first term on the right side of (9) is the central-difference formula (3), the second term is the truncation error, and the proof is complete.   ●

Suppose that the value of the third derivative $f^{(3)}(c)$ does not change too rapidly; then the truncation error in (4) goes to zero in the same manner as h^2, which is expressed by using the notation $O(h^2)$. When computer calculations are used, it is not desirable to choose h too small. For this reason it is useful to have a formula for approximating $f'(x)$ that has a truncation error term of the order $O(h^4)$.

Theorem 6.2 (Centered Formula of Order $O(h^4)$).   Assume that $f \in C^5[a, b]$ and that $x - 2h, x - h, x, x + h, x + 2h \in [a, b]$. Then

(10)
$$f'(x) \approx \frac{-f(x+2h) + 8f(x+h) - 8f(x-h) + f(x-2h)}{12h}.$$

Furthermore, there exists a number $c = c(x) \in [a, b]$ such that

(11) $$f'(x) = \frac{-f(x+2h) + 8f(x+h) - 8f(x-h) + f(x-2h)}{12h} + E_{\text{trunc}}(f, h),$$

where

$$E_{\text{trunc}}(f, h) = \frac{h^4 f^{(5)}(c)}{30} = O(h^4).$$

Proof.   One way to derive formula (10) is as follows. Start with the difference between the fourth-degree Taylor expansions $f(x) = P_4(x) + E_4(x)$, about x, of $f(x+h)$ and $f(x-h)$:

(12)
$$f(x+h) - f(x-h) = 2f'(x)h + \frac{2f^{(3)}(x)h^3}{3!} + \frac{2f^{(5)}(c_1)h^5}{5!}.$$

Then use the step size $2h$, instead of h, and write down the following approximation:

(13)
$$f(x+2h) - f(x-2h) = 4f'(x)h + \frac{16f^{(3)}(x)h^3}{3!} + \frac{64f^{(5)}(c_2)h^5}{5!}.$$

Next multiply the terms in equation (12) by 8 and subtract (13) from it. The terms involving $f^{(3)}(x)$ will be eliminated and we get

(14)
$$-f(x+2h) + 8f(x+h) - 8f(x-h) + f(x-2h)$$
$$= 12f'(x)h + \frac{(16f^{(5)}(c_1) - 64f^{(5)}(c_2))h^5}{120}.$$

If $f^{(5)}(x)$ has one sign and if its magnitude does not change rapidly, we can find a value c that lies in $[x - 2h, x + 2h]$ so that

(15)
$$16f^{(5)}(c_1) - 64f^{(5)}(c_2) = -48f^{(5)}(c).$$

After (15) is substituted into (14) and the result is solved for $f'(x)$, we obtain

(16) $$f'(x) = \frac{-f(x+2h) + 8f(x+h) - 8f(x-h) + f(x-2h)}{12h} + \frac{f^{(5)}(c)h^4}{30}.$$

The first term on the right side of (16) is the central-difference formula (10) and the second term is the truncation error; the theorem is proved.   ●

Suppose that $|f^{(5)}(c)|$ is bounded for $c \in [a, b]$; then the truncation error in (11) goes to zero in the same manner as h^4, which is expressed with the notation $O(h^4)$. Now we can make a comparison of the two formulas (3) and (10). Suppose that $f(x)$ has five continuous derivatives and that $|f^{(3)}(c)|$ and $|f^{(5)}(c)|$ are about the same. Then the truncation error for the fourth-order formula (10) is $O(h^4)$ and will go to zero faster than the truncation error $O(h^2)$ for the second-order formula (3). This permits the use of a larger step size.

Example 6.2.   Let $f(x) = \cos(x)$.

(a) Use formulas (3) and (10) with step sizes $h = 0.1, 0.01, 0.001$, and 0.0001, and calculate approximations for $f'(0.8)$. Carry nine decimal places in all the calculations.

(b) Compare with the true value $f'(0.8) = -\sin(0.8)$.

(a) Using formula (3) with $h = 0.01$, we get

$$f'(0.8) \approx \frac{f(0.81) - f(0.79)}{0.02} \approx \frac{0.689498433 - 0.703845316}{0.02} \approx -0.717344150.$$

Using formula (10) with $h = 0.01$, we get

$$f'(0.8) \approx \frac{-f(0.82) + 8f(0.81) - 8f(0.79) + f(0.78)}{0.12}$$
$$\approx \frac{-0.682221207 + 8(0.689498433) - 8(0.703845316) + 0.710913538}{0.12}$$
$$\approx -0.717356108.$$

(b) The error in approximation for formulas (3) and (10) turns out to be -0.000011941 and 0.000000017, respectively. In this example, formula (10) gives a better approximation to $f'(0.8)$ than formula (3) when $h = 0.01$. The error analysis will illuminate this example and show why this happened . The other calculations are summarized in Table 6.2.   ■

Table 6.2 Numerical Differentiation Using Formulas (3) and (10)

Step size	Approximation by formula (3)	Error using formula (3)	Approximation by formula (10)	Error using formula (10)
0.1	−0.716161095	−0.001194996	−0.717353703	−0.000002389
0.01	−0.717344150	−0.000011941	−0.717356108	0.000000017
0.001	−0.717356000	−0.000000091	−0.717356167	0.000000076
0.0001	−0.717360000	−0.000003909	−0.717360833	0.000004742

Error Analysis and Optimum Step Size

An important topic in the study of numerical differentiation is the effect of the computer's round-off error. Let us examine the formulas more closely. Assume that a computer is used to make numerical computations and that

$$f(x_0 - h) = y_{-1} + e_{-1} \quad \text{and} \quad f(x_0 + h) = y_1 + e_1,$$

where $f(x_0 - h)$ and $f(x_0 + h)$ are approximated by the numerical values y_{-1} and y_1, and e_{-1} and e_1 are the associated round-off errors, respectively. The following result indicates the complex nature of error analysis for numerical differentiation.

Corollary 6.1(a). Assume that f satisfies the hypotheses of Theorem 6.1 and use the *computational formula*

(17)
$$f'(x_0) \approx \frac{y_1 - y_{-1}}{2h}.$$

The error analysis is explained by the following equations:

(18)
$$f'(x_0) = \frac{y_1 - y_{-1}}{2h} + E(f, h),$$

where

(19)
$$E(f, h) = E_{\text{round}}(f, h) + E_{\text{trunc}}(f, h)$$
$$= \frac{e_1 - e_{-1}}{2h} - \frac{h^2 f^{(3)}(c)}{6},$$

where the *total error term* $E(f, h)$ has a part due to round-off error plus a part due to truncation error.

Corollary 6.1(b). Assume that f satisfies the hypotheses of Theorem 6.1 and that numerical computations are made. If $|e_{-1}| \le \epsilon$, $|e_1| \le \epsilon$, and $M = \max_{a \le x \le b}\{|f^{(3)}(x)|\}$, then

(20)
$$|E(f, h)| \le \frac{\epsilon}{h} + \frac{Mh^2}{6},$$

and the value of h that minimizes the right-hand side of (20) is

$$(21) \qquad\qquad h = \left(\frac{3\epsilon}{M}\right)^{1/3}.$$

When h is small, the portion of (19) involving $(e_1 - e_{-1})/2h$ can be relatively large. In Example 6.2, when $h = 0.0001$, this difficulty was encountered. The round-off errors are

$$f(0.8001) = 0.696634970 + e_1 \qquad \text{where } e_1 \approx -0.0000000003$$
$$f(0.7999) = 0.696778442 + e_{-1} \qquad \text{where } e_{-1} \approx 0.0000000005.$$

The truncation error term is

$$\frac{-h^2 f^{(3)}(c)}{6} \approx -(0.0001)^2 \left(\frac{\sin(0.8)}{6}\right) \approx 0.000000001.$$

The error term $E(f, h)$ in (19) can now be estimated:

$$E(f, h) \approx \frac{-0.0000000003 - 0.0000000005}{0.0002} - 0.000000001$$
$$= -0.000004001.$$

Indeed, the computed numerical approximation for the derivative using $h = 0.0001$ is found by the calculation

$$f'(0.8) \approx \frac{f(0.8001) - f(0.7999)}{0.0002} = \frac{0.696634970 - 0.696778442}{0.0002}$$
$$= -0.717360000,$$

and a loss of about four significant digits is evident. The error is -0.000003909 and this is close to the predicted error, -0.000004001.

When formula (21) is applied to Example 6.2, we can use the bound $|f^{(3)}(x)| \leq |\sin(x)| \leq 1 = M$ and the value $\epsilon = 0.5 \times 10^{-9}$ for the magnitude of the round-off error. The optimal value for h is easily calculated: $h = (1.5 \times 10^{-9}/1)^{1/3} = 0.001144714$. The step size $h = 0.001$ was closest to the optimal value 0.001144714 and it gave the best approximation to $f'(0.8)$ among the four choices involving formula (3) (see Table 6.2 and Figure 6.3).

An error analysis of formula (10) is similar. Assume that a computer is used to make numerical computations and that $f(x_0 + kh) = y_k + e_k$.

Corollary 6.2(a). Assume that f satisfies the hypotheses of Theorem 6.2 and use the *computational formula*

$$(22) \qquad\qquad f'(x_0) \approx \frac{-y_2 + 8y_1 - 8y_{-1} + y_{-2}}{12h}.$$

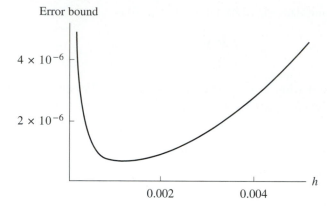

Figure 6.3 Finding the optimal step size $h = 0.001144714$ when formula (21) is applied to $f(x) = \cos(x)$ in Example 6.2.

The error analysis is explained by the following equations:

$$(23) \qquad f'(x_0) = \frac{-y_2 + 8y_1 - 8y_{-1} + y_{-2}}{12h} + E(f, h),$$

where

$$(24) \qquad \begin{aligned} E(f, h) &= E_{\text{round}}(f, h) + E_{\text{trunc}}(f, h) \\ &= \frac{-e_2 + 8e_1 - 8e_{-1} + e_{-2}}{12h} + \frac{h^4 f^{(5)}(c)}{30}, \end{aligned}$$

where the total error term $E(f, h)$ has a part due to round-off error plus a part due to truncation error.

Corollary 6.2(b). Assume that f satisfies the hypotheses of Theorem 6.2 and that numerical computations are made. If $|e_k| \leq \epsilon$ and $M = \max_{a \leq x \leq b}\{|f^{(5)}(x)|\}$, then

$$(25) \qquad |E(f, h)| \leq \frac{3\epsilon}{2h} + \frac{Mh^4}{30},$$

and the value of h that minimizes the right-hand side of (25) is

$$(26) \qquad h = \left(\frac{45\epsilon}{4M}\right)^{1/5}.$$

When formula (25) is applied to Example 6.2, we can use the bound $|f^{(5)}(x)| \leq |\sin(x)| \leq 1 = M$ and the value $\epsilon = 0.5 \times 10^{-9}$ for the magnitude of the round-off error. The optimal value for h is easily calculated: $h = (22.5 \times 10^{-9}/4)^{1/5} = 0.022388475$. The step size $h = 0.01$ was closest to the optimal value 0.022388475, and it gave the best approximation to $f'(0.8)$ among the four choices involving formula (10) (see Table 6.2 and Figure 6.4).

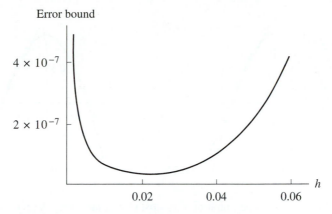

Figure 6.4   Finding the optimal step size
$h = 0.022388475$ when formula (26) is applied to
$f(x) = \cos(x)$ in Example 6.2.

We should not end the discussion of Example 6.2 without mentioning that numerical differentiation formulas can be obtained by an alternative derivation. They can be derived by differentiation of an interpolation polynomial. For example, the Lagrange form of the quadratic polynomial $p_2(x)$ that passes through the three points $(0.7, \cos(0.7))$, $(0.8, \cos(0.8))$, and $(0.9, \cos(0.9))$ is

$$p_2(x) = 38.2421094(x - 0.8)(x - 0.9) - 69.6706709(x - 0.7)(x - 0.9)$$
$$+ 31.0804984(x - 0.7)(x - 0.8).$$

This polynomial can be expanded to obtain the usual form:

$$p_2(x) = 1.046875165 - 0.159260044x - 0.348063157x^2.$$

A similar computation can be used to obtain the quartic polynomial $p_4(x)$ that passes through the points $(0.6, \cos(0.6))$, $(0.7, \cos(0.7))$, $(0.8, \cos(0.8))$, $(0.9, \cos(0.9))$, and $(1.0, \cos(1.0))$:

$$p_4(x) = 0.998452927 + 0.009638391x - 0.523291341x^2$$
$$+ 0.026521229x^3 + 0.028981100x^4.$$

When these polynomials are differentiated, they produce $p_2'(0.8) = -0.716161095$ and $p_4'(0.8) = -0.717353703$, which agree with the values listed under $h = 0.1$ in Table 6.2. The graphs of $p_2(x)$ and $p_4(x)$ and their tangent lines at $(0.8, \cos(0.8))$ are shown in Figure 6.5(a) and (b), respectively.

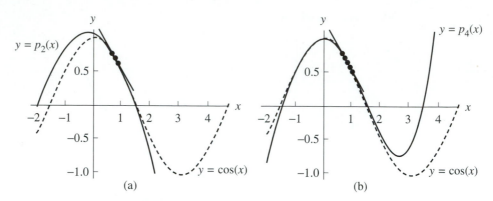

Figure 6.5 (a) The graph of $y = \cos(x)$ and the interpolating polynomial $p_2(x)$ used to estimate $f'(0.8) \approx p_2'(0.8) = -0.716161095$. (b) The graph of $y = \cos(x)$ and the interpolating polynomial $p_4(x)$ used to estimate $f'(0.8) \approx p_4'(0.8) = -0.717353703$.

Richardson's Extrapolation

In this section we emphasize the relationship between formulas (3) and (10). Let $f_k = f(x_k) = f(x_0 + kh)$, and use the notation $D_0(h)$ and $D_0(2h)$ to denote the approximations to $f'(x_0)$ that are obtained from (3) with step sizes h and $2h$, respectively:

$$(27) \qquad\qquad f'(x_0) \approx D_0(h) + Ch^2$$

and

$$(28) \qquad\qquad f'(x_0) \approx D_0(2h) + 4Ch^2.$$

If we multiply relation (27) by 4 and subtract relation (28) from this product, then the terms involving C cancel and the result is

$$(29) \qquad 3f'(x_0) \approx 4D_0(h) - D_0(2h) = \frac{4(f_1 - f_{-1})}{2h} - \frac{f_2 - f_{-2}}{4h}.$$

Next solve for $f'(x_0)$ in (29) and get

$$(30) \qquad f'(x_0) \approx \frac{4D_0(h) - D_0(2h)}{3} = \frac{-f_2 + 8f_1 - 8f_{-1} + f_{-2}}{12h}.$$

The last expression in (30) is the central-difference formula (10).

Example 6.3. Let $f(x) = \cos(x)$. Use (27) and (28) with $h = 0.01$, and show how the linear combination $(4D_0(h) - D_0(2h))/3$ in (30) can be used to obtain the approximation to $f'(0.8)$ given in (10). Carry nine decimal places in all the calculations.

Use (27) and (28) with $h = 0.01$ to get

$$D_0(h) \approx \frac{f(0.81) - f(0.79)}{0.02} \approx \frac{0.689498433 - 0.703845316}{0.02}$$
$$\approx -0.717344150$$

and

$$D_0(2h) \approx \frac{f(0.82) - f(0.78)}{0.04} \approx \frac{0.682221207 - 0.710913538}{0.04}$$
$$\approx -0.717308275.$$

Now the linear combination in (30) is computed:

$$f'(0.8) \approx \frac{4D_0(h) - D_0(2h)}{3} \approx \frac{4(-0.717344150) - (-0.717308275)}{3}$$
$$\approx -0.717356108.$$

This is exactly the same as the solution in Example 6.2 that used (10) directly to approximate $f'(0.8)$. ∎

The method of obtaining a formula for $f'(x_0)$ of higher order from a formula of lower order is called **extrapolation**. The proof requires that the error term for (3) can be expanded in a series containing only even powers of h. We have already seen how to use step sizes h and $2h$ to remove the term involving h^2. To see how h^4 is removed, let $D_1(h)$ and $D_1(2h)$ denote the approximations to $f'(x_0)$ of order $O(h^4)$ obtained with formula (16) using step sizes h and $2h$, respectively. Then

$$(31) \qquad f'(x_0) = \frac{-f_2 + 8f_1 - 8f_{-1} + f_{-2}}{24h} + \frac{h^4 f^{(5)}(c_1)}{30} \approx D_1(h) + Ch^4$$

and

$$(32) \qquad f'(x_0) = \frac{-f_4 + 8f_2 - 8f_{-2} + f_{-4}}{12h} + \frac{16h^4 f^{(5)}(c_2)}{30} \approx D_1(2h) + 16Ch^4.$$

Suppose that $f^{(5)}(x)$ has one sign and does not change too rapidly; then the assumption that $f^{(5)}(c_1) \approx f^{(5)}(c_2)$ can be used to eliminate the terms involving h^4 in (31) and (32), and the result is

$$(33) \qquad\qquad f'(x_0) \approx \frac{16D_1(h) - D_1(2h)}{15}.$$

The general pattern for improving calculations is stated in the next result.

Theorem 6.3 (Richardson's Extrapolation).   Suppose that two approximations of order $O(h^{2k})$ for $f'(x_0)$ are $D_{k-1}(h)$ and $D_{k-1}(2h)$ and that they satisfy

$$(34) \qquad f'(x_0) = D_{k-1}(h) + c_1 h^{2k} + c_2 h^{2k+2} + \cdots$$

and

$$(35) \qquad f'(x_0) = D_{k-1}(2h) + 4^k c_1 h^{2k} + 4^{k+1} c_2 h^{2k+2} + \cdots .$$

Then an improved approximation has the form

$$(36) \qquad f'(x_0) = D_k(h) + O(h^{2k+2}) = \frac{4^k D_{k-1}(h) - D_{k-1}(2h)}{4^k - 1} + O(h^{2k+2}).$$

The following program implements the centered formula of order $O(h^2)$, equation (3), to approximate the derivative of a function at a given point. A sequence of approximations $\{D_k\}$ is generated, where the centered interval for D_{k+1} is one-tenth as long as the centered interval for D_k. The output is a matrix L=[H' D' E'], where H is a vector containing the step sizes, D is a vector containing the approximations to the derivative, and E is a vector containing the error bounds. *Note.* The function f needs to be input as a string; that is, 'f'.

Program 6.1 (Differentiation Using Limits).   To approximate $f'(x)$ numerically by generating the sequence

$$f'(x) \approx D_k = \frac{f(x + 10^{-k}h) - f(x - 10^{-k}h)}{2(10^{-k}h)} \qquad \text{for } k = 0, \ldots, n$$

until $|D_{n+1} - D_n| \geq |D_n - D_{n-1}|$ or $|D_n - D_{n-1}| <$ tolerance, which is an attempt to find the best approximation $f'(x) \approx D_n$.

```
function [L,n]=difflim(f,x,toler)
%Input  - f is the function input as a string 'f'
%        - x is the differentiation point
%        - toler is the tolerance for the error
%Output-L=[H' D' E']:
%            H is the vector of step sizes
%            D is the vector of approximate derivatives
%            E is the vector of error bounds
%        - n is the coordinate of the ''best approximation''
max1=15;
h=1;
H(1)=h;
D(1)=(feval(f,x+h)-feval(f,x-h))/(2*h);
```

```
E(1)=0;
R(1)=0;
for n=1:2
    h=h/10;
    H(n+1)=h;
    D(n+1)=(feval(f,x+h)-feval(f,x-h))/(2*h);
    E(n+1)=abs(D(n+1)-D(n));
    R(n+1)=2*E(n+1)/(abs(D(n+1))+abs(D(n))+eps);
end
n=2;
while((E(n)>E(n+1))&(R(n)>toler))&n<max1
    h=h/10;
    H(n+2)=h;
    D(n+2)=(feval(f,x+h)-feval(f,x-h))/(2*h);
    E(n+2)=abs(D(n+2)-D(n+1));
    R(n+2)=2*E(n+2)/(abs(D(n+2))+abs(D(n+1))+eps);
    n=n+1;
end
n=length(D)-1;
L=[H' D' E'];
```

Program 6.2 implements Theorem 6.3 (Richardson's extrapolation). Note that the expression for the elements in row j is algebraically equivalent to formula (36).

Program 6.2 (Differentiation Using Extrapolation). To approximate $f'(x)$ numerically by generating a table of approximations $D(j, k)$ for $k \leq j$, and using $f'(x) \approx D(n, n)$ as the final answer. The approximations $D(j, k)$ are stored in a lower-triangular matrix. The first column is

$$D(j, 0) = \frac{f(x + 2^{-j}h) - f(x - 2^{-j}h)}{2^{-j+1}h}$$

and the elements in row j are

$$D(j, k) = D(j, k - 1) + \frac{D(j, k - 1) - D(j - 1, k - 1)}{4^k - 1} \quad \text{for } 1 \leq k \leq j.$$

```
function [D,err,relerr,n]=diffext(f,x,delta,toler)
%Input   -f is the function input as a string 'f'
%        - delta is the tolerance for the error
%        - toler is the tolerance for the relative error
%Output - D is the matrix of approximate derivatives
%        - err is the error bound
```

```
%           - relerr is the relative error bound
%           - n is the coordinate of the ''best approximation''
err=1;
relerr=1;
h=1;
j=1;
D(1,1)=(feval(f,x+h)-feval(f,x-h))/(2*h);
while relerr>toler & err>delta &j<12
    h=h/2;
    D(j+1,1)=(feval(f,x+h)-feval(f,x-h))/(2*h);
    for k=1:j
        D(j+1,k+1)=D(j+1,k)+(D(j+1,k)-D(j,k))/((4^k)-1);
    end
    err=abs(D(j+1,j+1)-D(j,j));
    relerr=2*err/(abs(D(j+1,j+1))+abs(D(j,j))+eps);
    j=j+1;
end
[n,n]=size(D);
```

Exercises for Approximating the Derivative

1. Let $f(x) = \sin(x)$, where x is measured in radians.
   (a) Calculate approximations to $f'(0.8)$ using formula (3) with $h = 0.1$, $h = 0.01$, and $h = 0.001$. Carry eight or nine decimal places.
   (b) Compare with the value $f'(0.8) = \cos(0.8)$.
   (c) Compute bounds for the truncation error (4). Use

   $$|f^{(3)}(c)| \leq \cos(0.7) \approx 0.764842187$$

   for all cases.

2. Let $f(x) = e^x$.
   (a) Calculate approximations to $f'(2.3)$ using formula (3) with $h = 0.1$, $h = 0.01$, and $h = 0.001$. Carry eight or nine decimal places.
   (b) Compare with the value $f'(2.3) = e^{2.3}$.
   (c) Compute bounds for the truncation error (4). Use

   $$|f^{(3)}(c)| \leq e^{2.4} \approx 11.02317638$$

   for all cases.

3. Let $f(x) = \sin(x)$, where x is measured in radians.
  (a) Calculate approximations to $f'(0.8)$ using formula (10) with $h = 0.1$ and $h = 0.01$, and compare with $f'(0.8) = \cos(0.8)$.
  (b) Use the extrapolation formula in (29) to compute the approximations to $f'(0.8)$ in part (a).
  (c) Compute bounds for the truncation error (11). Use

$$|f^{(5)}(c)| \le \cos(0.6) \approx 0.825335615$$

  for both cases.

4. Let $f(x) = e^x$.
  (a) Calculate approximations to $f'(2.3)$ using formula (10) with $h = 0.1$ and $h = 0.01$, and compare with $f'(2.3) = e^{2.3}$.
  (b) Use the extrapolation formula in (29) to compute the approximations to $f'(2.3)$ in part (a).
  (c) Compute bounds for the truncation error (11). Use

$$|f^{(5)}(c)| \le e^{2.5} \approx 12.18249396$$

  for both cases.

5. Compare the numerical differentiation formulas (3) and (10). Let $f(x) = x^3$ and find approximations for $f'(2)$.
  (a) Use formula (3) with $h = 0.05$.
  (b) Use formula (10) with $h = 0.05$.
  (c) Compute bounds for the truncation errors (4) and (11).

6. (a) Use Taylor's theorem to show that

$$f(x + h) = f(x) + hf'(x) + \frac{h^2 f^{(2)}(c)}{2}, \qquad \text{where } |c - x| < h.$$

  (b) Use part (a) to show that the difference quotient in equation (2) has error of order $O(h) = -hf^{(2)}(c)/2$.
  (c) Why is formula (3) better to use than formula (2)?

7. *Partial differentiation formulas.*   The partial derivative $f_x(x, y)$ of $f(x, y)$ with respect to x is obtained by holding y fixed and differentiating with respect to x. Similarly, $f_y(x, y)$ is found by holding x fixed and differentiating with respect to y. Formula (3) can be adapted to partial derivatives

(1)
$$f_x(x, y) = \frac{f(x + h, y) - f(x - h, y)}{2h} + O(h^2),$$

$$f_y(x, y) = \frac{f(x, y + h) - f(x, y - h)}{2h} + O(h^2).$$

  (a) Let $f(x, y) = xy/(x + y)$. Calculate approximations to $f_x(2, 3)$ and $f_y(2, 3)$ using the formulas in (1) with $h = 0.1$, 0.01, and 0.001. Compare with the values obtained by differentiating $f(x, y)$ partially.

(b) Let $z = f(x, y) = \arctan(y/x)$, where z is in radians. Calculate approximations to $f_x(3, 4)$ and $f_y(3, 4)$ using the formulas in (1) with $h = 0.1, 0.01$, and 0.001. Compare with the values obtained by differentiating $f(x, y)$ partially.

8. Complete the details that show how (33) is obtained from equations (31) and (32).

9. (a) Show that (21) is the value of h that minimizes the right-hand side of (20).

(b) Show that (26) is the value of h that minimizes the right-hand side of (25).

10. The voltage $E = E(t)$ in an electrical circuit obeys the equation $E(t) = L(dI/dt) + RI(t)$, where R is resistance and L is inductance. Use $L = 0.05$ and $R = 2$ and values for $I(t)$ in the table following.

t	$I(t)$
1.0	8.2277
1.1	7.2428
1.2	5.9908
1.3	4.5260
1.4	2.9122

(a) Find $I'(1.2)$ by numerical differentiation, and use it to compute $E(1.2)$.

(b) Compare your answer with $I(t) = 10e^{-t/10} \sin(2t)$.

11. The distance $D = D(t)$ traveled by an object is given in the table following.

t	$D(t)$
8.0	17.453
9.0	21.460
10.0	25.752
11.0	30.301
12.0	35.084

(a) Find the velocity $V(10)$ by numerical differentiation.

(b) Compare your answer with $D(t) = -70 + 7t + 70e^{-t/10}$.

12. Let $f(x)$ be given by the table following. The inherent round-off error has the bound $|e_k| \le 5 \times 10^{-6}$. Use the rounded values in your calculations.

x	$f(x) = \cos(x)$
1.100	0.45360
1.190	0.37166
1.199	0.36329
1.200	0.36236
1.201	0.36143
1.210	0.35302
1.300	0.26750

(a)   Find approximations for $f'(1.2)$ using formula (17) with $h = 0.1$, $h = 0.01$, and $h = 0.001$.

(b)   Compare with $f'(1.2) = -\sin(1.2) \approx -0.93204$.

(c)   Find the total error bound (19) for the three cases in part (a).

13. Let $f(x)$ be given by the table following. The inherent round-off error has the bound $|e_k| \leq 5 \times 10^{-6}$. Use the rounded values in your calculations.

x	$f(x) = \ln(x)$
2.900	1.06471
2.990	1.09527
2.999	1.09828
3.000	1.09861
3.001	1.09895
3.010	1.10194
3.100	1.13140

(a)   Find approximations for $f'(3.0)$ using formula (17) with $h = 0.1$, $h = 0.01$, and $h = 0.001$.

(b)   Compare with $f'(3.0) = \frac{1}{3} \approx 0.33333$.

(c)   Find the total error bound (19) for the three cases in part (a).

14. Suppose that a table of the function $f(x_k)$ is computed where the values are rounded off to three decimal places and the inherent round-off error is 5×10^{-4}. Also, assume that $|f^{(3)}(c)| \leq 1.5$ and $|f^{(5)}(c)| \leq 1.5$.

(a)   Find the best step size h for formula (17).

(b)   Find the best step size h for formula (22).

15. Let $f(x)$ be given by the table following. The inherent round-off error has the bound $|e_k| \leq 5 \times 10^{-6}$. Use the rounded values in your calculations.

x	$f(x) = \cos(x)$
1.000	0.54030
1.100	0.45360
1.198	0.36422
1.199	0.36329
1.200	0.36236
1.201	0.36143
1.202	0.36049
1.300	0.26750
1.400	0.16997

(a)   Approximate $f'(1.2)$ using (22) with $h = 0.1$ and $h = 0.001$.

(b)   Find the total error bound (24) for the two cases in part (a).

16. Let $f(x)$ be given by the table following. The inherent round-off error has the bound $|e_k| \leq 5 \times 10^{-6}$. Use the rounded values in your calculations.

x	$f(x) = \ln(x)$
2.800	1.02962
2.900	1.06471
2.998	1.09795
2.999	1.09828
3.000	1.09861
3.001	1.09895
3.002	1.09928
3.100	1.13140
3.200	1.16315

   (a) Approximate $f'(3.0)$ using (22) with $h = 0.1$ and $h = 0.001$.

   (b) Find the total error bound (24) for the two cases in part (a).

Algorithms and Programs

1. Use Program 6.1 to approximate the derivatives of each of the following functions at the given value of x. Approximations should be accurate to 13 decimal places. *Note.* It may be necessary to change the values of max1 and the initial value of h in the program.

   (a) $f(x) = 60x^{45} - 32x^{33} + 233x^5 - 47x^2 - 77$; $x = 1/\sqrt{3}$

   (b) $f(x) = \tan\left(\cos\left(\dfrac{\sqrt{5} + \sin(x)}{1 + x^2}\right)\right)$; $x = \dfrac{1 + \sqrt{5}}{3}$

   (c) $f(x) = \sin(\cos(1/x))$; $x = 1/\sqrt{2}$

   (d) $f(x) = \sin(x^3 - 7x^2 + 6x + 8)$; $x = \dfrac{1 - \sqrt{5}}{2}$

   (e) $f(x) = x^{x^x}$; $x = 0.0001$

2. Modify Program 6.1 to implement the centered formula (10) of order $O(h^4)$. Use this program to approximate the derivatives of the functions given in Problem 1. Again, approximations should be accurate to 13 decimal places.

3. Use Program 6.2 to approximate the derivatives of the functions given in Problem 1. Again, approximations should be accurate to 13 decimal places. *Note.* It may be necessary to change the initial values of err, relerr, and h.

6.2   Numerical Differentiation Formulas

More Central-Difference Formulas

The formulas for $f'(x_0)$ in the preceding section required that the function can be computed at abscissas that lie on both sides of x, and they were referred to as central-difference formulas. Taylor series can be used to obtain central-difference formulas for the higher derivatives. The popular choices are those of order $O(h^2)$ and $O(h^4)$ and are given in Tables 6.3 and 6.4. In these tables we use the convention that $f_k = f(x_0 + kh)$ for $k = -3, -2, -1, 0, 1, 2, 3$.

For illustration, we will derive the formula for $f''(x)$ of order $O(h^2)$ in Table 6.3. Start with the Taylor expansions

$$(1) \quad f(x + h) = f(x) + hf'(x) + \frac{h^2 f''(x)}{2} + \frac{h^3 f^{(3)}(x)}{6} + \frac{h^4 f^{(4)}(x)}{24} + \cdots$$

Table 6.3   Central-Difference Formulas of Order $O(h^2)$

$$f'(x_0) \approx \frac{f_1 - f_{-1}}{2h}$$

$$f''(x_0) \approx \frac{f_1 - 2f_0 + f_{-1}}{h^2}$$

$$f^{(3)}(x_0) \approx \frac{f_2 - 2f_1 + 2f_{-1} - f_{-2}}{2h^3}$$

$$f^{(4)}(x_0) \approx \frac{f_2 - 4f_1 + 6f_0 - 4f_{-1} + f_{-2}}{h^4}$$

Table 6.4   Central-Difference Formulas of Order $O(h^4)$

$$f'(x_0) \approx \frac{-f_2 + 8f_1 - 8f_{-1} + f_{-2}}{12h}$$

$$f''(x_0) \approx \frac{-f_2 + 16f_1 - 30f_0 + 16f_{-1} - f_{-2}}{12h^2}$$

$$f^{(3)}(x_0) \approx \frac{-f_3 + 8f_2 - 13f_1 + 13f_{-1} - 8f_{-2} + f_{-3}}{8h^3}$$

$$f^{(4)}(x_0) \approx \frac{-f_3 + 12f_2 - 39f_1 + 56f_0 - 39f_{-1} + 12f_{-2} - f_{-3}}{6h^4}$$

and

$$(2) \quad f(x - h) = f(x) - hf'(x) + \frac{h^2 f''(x)}{2} - \frac{h^3 f^{(3)}(x)}{6} + \frac{h^4 f^{(4)}(x)}{24} - \cdots .$$

Adding equations (1) and (2) will eliminate the terms involving the odd derivatives $f'(x)$, $f^{(3)}(x)$, $f^{(5)}(x)$, ...:

$$(3) \quad f(x + h) + f(x - h) = 2f(x) + \frac{2h^2 f''(x)}{2} + \frac{2h^4 f^{(4)}(x)}{24} + \cdots .$$

Solving equation (3) for $f''(x)$ yields

$$(4) \quad \begin{aligned} f''(x) = {} & \frac{f(x + h) - 2f(x) + f(x - h)}{h^2} - \frac{2h^2 f^{(4)}(x)}{4!} \\ & - \frac{2h^4 f^{(6)}(x)}{6!} - \cdots - \frac{2h^{2k-2} f^{(2k)}(x)}{(2k)!} - \cdots . \end{aligned}$$

If the series in (4) is truncated at the fourth derivative, there exists a value c that lies in $[x - h, x + h]$, so that

$$(5) \quad f''(x_0) = \frac{f_1 - 2f_0 + f_{-1}}{h^2} - \frac{h^2 f^{(4)}(c)}{12}.$$

This gives us the desired formula for approximating $f''(x)$:

$$(6) \quad f''(x_0) \approx \frac{f_1 - 2f_0 + f_{-1}}{h^2}.$$

Example 6.4. Let $f(x) = \cos(x)$.

(a) Use formula (6) with $h = 0.1, 0.01$, and 0.001 and find approximations to $f''(0.8)$. Carry nine decimal places in all calculations.

(b) Compare with the true value $f''(0.8) = -\cos(0.8)$.

(a) The calculation for $h = 0.01$ is

$$\begin{aligned} f''(0.8) &\approx \frac{f(0.81) - 2f(0.80) + f(0.79)}{0.0001} \\ &\approx \frac{0.689498433 - 2(0.696706709) + 0.703845316}{0.0001} \\ &\approx -0.696690000. \end{aligned}$$

(b) The error in this approximation is -0.000016709. The other calculations are summarized in Table 6.5. The error analysis will illuminate this example and show why $h = 0.01$ was best. ∎

Table 6.5   Numerical Approximations to $f''(x)$ for Example 6.4

Step size	Approximation by formula (6)	Error using formula (6)
$h = 0.1$	-0.696126300	-0.000580409
$h = 0.01$	-0.696690000	-0.000016709
$h = 0.001$	-0.696000000	-0.000706709

Error Analysis

Let $f_k = y_k + e_k$, where e_k is the error in computing $f(x_k)$, including noise in measurement and round-off error. Then formula (6) can be written

$$(7) \qquad f''(x_0) = \frac{y_1 - 2y_0 + y_{-1}}{h^2} + E(f, h).$$

The error term $E(h, f)$ for the numerical derivative (7) will have a part due to round-off error and a part due to truncation error:

$$(8) \qquad E(f, h) = \frac{e_1 - 2e_0 + e_{-1}}{h^2} - \frac{h^2 f^{(4)}(c)}{12}.$$

If it is assumed that each error e_k is of the magnitude ϵ, with signs that accumulate errors, and that $|f^{(4)}(x)| \leq M$, then we get the following error bound:

$$(9) \qquad |E(f, h)| \leq \frac{4\epsilon}{h^2} + \frac{Mh^2}{12}.$$

If h is small, then the contribution $4\epsilon/h^2$ due to round-off error is large. When h is large, the contribution $Mh^2/12$ is large. The optimal step size will minimize the quantity

$$(10) \qquad g(h) = \frac{4\epsilon}{h^2} + \frac{Mh^2}{12}.$$

Setting $g'(h) = 0$ results in $-8\epsilon/h^3 + Mh/6 = 0$, which yields the equation $h^4 = 48\epsilon/M$, from which we obtain the optimal value:

$$(11) \qquad h = \left(\frac{48\epsilon}{M}\right)^{1/4}.$$

When formula (11) is applied to Example 6.4, use the bound $|f^{(4)}(x)| \leq |\cos(x)| \leq 1 = M$ and the value $\epsilon = 0.5 \times 10^{-9}$. The optimal step size is $h = (24 \times 10^{-9}/1)^{1/4} = 0.01244666$, and we see that $h = 0.01$ was closest to the optimal value.

Since the portion of the error due to round off is inversely proportional to the square of h, this term grows when h gets small. This is sometimes referred to as the **step-size dilemma**. One partial solution to this problem is to use a formula of higher order so that a larger value of h will produce the desired accuracy. The formula for $f''(x_0)$ of order $O(h^4)$ in Table 6.4 is

$$(12) \qquad f''(x_0) = \frac{-f_2 + 16f_1 - 30f_0 + 16f_{-1} - f_{-2}}{12h^2} + E(f, h).$$

The error term for (12) has the form

$$(13) \qquad E(f, h) = \frac{16\epsilon}{3h^2} + \frac{h^4 f^{(6)}(c)}{90},$$

where c lies in the interval $[x - 2h, x + 2h]$. A bound for $|E(f, h)|$ is

$$(14) \qquad |E(f, h)| \le \frac{16\epsilon}{3h^2} + \frac{h^4 M}{90},$$

where $|f^{(6)}(x)| \le M$. The optimal value for h is given by the formula

$$(15) \qquad h = \left(\frac{240\epsilon}{M}\right)^{1/6}.$$

Example 6.5. Let $f(x) = \cos(x)$.

  (a) Use formula (12) with $h = 1.0, 0.1$, and 0.01 and find approximations to $f''(0.8)$. Carry nine decimal places in all the calculations.

  (b) Compare with the true value $f''(0.8) = -\cos(0.8)$.

  (c) Determine the optimal step size.

(a) The calculation for $h = 0.1$ is

$$f''(0.8)$$
$$\approx \frac{-f(1.0) + 16f(0.9) - 30f(0.8) + 16f(0.7) - f(0.6)}{0.12}$$
$$\approx \frac{-0.540302306 + 9.945759488 - 20.90120127 + 12.23747499 - 0.825335615}{0.12}$$
$$\approx -0.696705958.$$

(b) The error in this approximation is -0.000000751. The other calculations are summarized in Table 6.6.

(c) When formula (15) is applied, we can use the bound $|f^{(6)}(x)| \le |\cos(x)| \le 1 = M$ and the value $\epsilon = 0.5 \times 10^{-9}$. These values give the optimal step size $h = (120 \times 10^{-9}/1)^{1/6} = 0.070231219$. ∎

Table 6.6   Numerical Approximations to $f''(x)$ for Example 6.5

Step size	Approximation by formula (12)	Error using formula (12)
$h = 1.0$	-0.689625413	-0.007081296
$h = 0.1$	-0.696705958	-0.000000751
$h = 0.01$	-0.696690000	-0.000016709

Table 6.7   Forward- and Backward-Difference Formulas of Order $O(h^2)$

$$f'(x_0) \approx \frac{-3f_0 + 4f_1 - f_2}{2h} \qquad \left(\begin{array}{c} \text{forward} \\ \text{difference} \end{array}\right)$$

$$f'(x_0) \approx \frac{3f_0 - 4f_{-1} + f_{-2}}{2h} \qquad \left(\begin{array}{c} \text{backward} \\ \text{difference} \end{array}\right)$$

$$f''(x_0) \approx \frac{2f_0 - 5f_1 + 4f_2 - f_3}{h^2} \qquad \left(\begin{array}{c} \text{forward} \\ \text{difference} \end{array}\right)$$

$$f''(x_0) \approx \frac{2f_0 - 5f_{-1} + 4f_{-2} - f_{-3}}{h^2} \qquad \left(\begin{array}{c} \text{backward} \\ \text{difference} \end{array}\right)$$

$$f^{(3)}(x_0) \approx \frac{-5f_0 + 18f_1 - 24f_2 + 14f_3 - 3f_4}{2h^3}$$

$$f^{(3)}(x_0) \approx \frac{5f_0 - 18f_{-1} + 24f_{-2} - 14f_{-3} + 3f_{-4}}{2h^3}$$

$$f^{(4)}(x_0) \approx \frac{3f_0 - 14f_1 + 26f_2 - 24f_3 + 11f_4 - 2f_5}{h^4}$$

$$f^{(4)}(x_0) \approx \frac{3f_0 - 14f_{-1} + 26f_{-2} - 24f_{-3} + 11f_{-4} - 2f_{-5}}{h^4}$$

Generally, if numerical differentiation is performed, only about half the accuracy of which the computer is capable is obtained. This severe loss of significant digits will almost always occur unless we are fortunate to find a step size that is optimal. Hence we must always proceed with caution when numerical differentiation is performed. The difficulties are more pronounced when working with experimental data, where the function values have been rounded to only a few digits. If a numerical derivative must be obtained from data, we should consider curve fitting, by using least-squares techniques, and differentiate the formula for the curve.

Differentiation of the Lagrange Polynomial

If the function must be evaluated at abscissas that lie on one side of x_0, the central-difference formulas cannot be used. Formulas for equally spaced abscissas that lie to the right (or left) of x_0 are called forward (or backward) -difference formulas. These formulas can be derived by differentiation of the Lagrange interpolation polynomial. Some of the common forward- and backward-difference formulas are given in Table 6.7.

Example 6.6. Derive the formula

$$f''(x_0) \approx \frac{2f_0 - 5f_1 + 4f_2 - f_3}{h^2}.$$

Start with the Lagrange interpolation polynomial for $f(t)$ based on the four points x_0, x_1, x_2, and x_3.

$$f(t) \approx f_0 \frac{(t - x_1)(t - x_2)(t - x_3)}{(x_0 - x_1)(x_0 - x_2)(x_0 - x_3)} + f_1 \frac{(t - x_0)(t - x_2)(t - x_3)}{(x_1 - x_0)(x_1 - x_2)(x_1 - x_3)}$$
$$+ f_2 \frac{(t - x_0)(t - x_1)(t - x_3)}{(x_2 - x_0)(x_2 - x_1)(x_2 - x_3)} + f_3 \frac{(t - x_0)(t - x_1)(t - x_2)}{(x_3 - x_0)(x_3 - x_1)(x_3 - x_2)}.$$

Differentiate the products in the numerators twice and get

$$f''(t) \approx f_0 \frac{2((t - x_1) + (t - x_2) + (t - x_3))}{(x_0 - x_1)(x_0 - x_2)(x_0 - x_3)} + f_1 \frac{2((t - x_0) + (t - x_2) + (t - x_3))}{(x_1 - x_0)(x_1 - x_2)(x_1 - x_3)}$$
$$+ f_2 \frac{2((t - x_0) + (t - x_1) + (t - x_3))}{(x_2 - x_0)(x_2 - x_1)(x_2 - x_3)} + f_3 \frac{2((t - x_0) + (t - x_1) + (t - x_2))}{(x_3 - x_0)(x_3 - x_1)(x_3 - x_2)}.$$

Then substitution of $t = x_0$ and the fact that $x_i - x_j = (i - j)h$ produces

$$f''(x_0) \approx f_0 \frac{2((x_0 - x_1) + (x_0 - x_2) + (x_0 - x_3))}{(x_0 - x_1)(x_0 - x_2)(x_0 - x_3)}$$
$$+ f_1 \frac{2((x_0 - x_0) + (x_0 - x_2) + (x_0 - x_3))}{(x_1 - x_0)(x_1 - x_2)(x_1 - x_3)}$$
$$+ f_2 \frac{2((x_0 - x_0) + (x_0 - x_1) + (x_0 - x_3))}{(x_2 - x_0)(x_2 - x_1)(x_2 - x_3)}$$
$$+ f_3 \frac{2((x_0 - x_0) + (x_0 - x_1) + (x_0 - x_2))}{(x_3 - x_0)(x_3 - x_1)(x_3 - x_2)}$$
$$= f_0 \frac{2((-h) + (-2h) + (-3h))}{(-h)(-2h)(-3h)} + f_1 \frac{2((0) + (-2h) + (-3h))}{(h)(-h)(-2h)}$$
$$+ f_2 \frac{2((0) + (-h) + (-3h))}{(2h)(h)(-h)} + f_3 \frac{2((0) + (-h) + (-2h))}{(3h)(2h)(h)}$$
$$= f_0 \frac{-12h}{-6h^3} + f_1 \frac{-10h}{2h^3} + f_2 \frac{-8h}{-2h^3} + f_3 \frac{-6h}{6h^3} = \frac{2f_0 - 5f_1 + 4f_2 - f_3}{h^2},$$

and the formula is established. ■

Example 6.7.   Derive the formula

$$f'''(x_0) \approx \frac{-5f_0 + 18f_1 - 24f_2 + 14f_3 - 3f_4}{2h^3}.$$

Start with the Lagrange interpolation polynomial for $f(t)$ based on the five points x_0, x_1, x_2, x_3, and x_4.

$$f(t) \approx f_0 \frac{(t - x_1)(t - x_2)(t - x_3)(t - x_4)}{(x_0 - x_1)(x_0 - x_2)(x_0 - x_3)(x_0 - x_4)}$$

$$+ f_1 \frac{(t - x_0)(t - x_2)(t - x_3)(t - x_4)}{(x_1 - x_0)(x_1 - x_2)(x_1 - x_3)(x_1 - x_4)}$$

$$+ f_2 \frac{(t - x_0)(t - x_1)(t - x_3)(t - x_4)}{(x_2 - x_0)(x_2 - x_1)(x_2 - x_3)(x_2 - x_4)}$$

$$+ f_3 \frac{(t - x_0)(t - x_1)(t - x_2)(t - x_4)}{(x_3 - x_0)(x_3 - x_1)(x_3 - x_2)(x_3 - x_4)}$$

$$+ f_4 \frac{(t - x_0)(t - x_1)(t - x_2)(t - x_3)}{(x_4 - x_0)(x_4 - x_1)(x_4 - x_2)(x_4 - x_3)}$$

Differentiate the numerators three times, then use the substitution $x_i - x_j = (i - j)h$ in the denominators and get

$$f'''(t) \approx f_0 \frac{6((t - x_1) + (t - x_2) + (t - x_3) + (t - x_4))}{(-h)(-2h)(-3h)(-4h)}$$

$$+ f_1 \frac{6((t - x_0) + (t - x_2) + (t - x_3) + (t - x_4))}{(h)(-h)(-2h)(-3h)}$$

$$+ f_2 \frac{6((t - x_0) + (t - x_1) + (t - x_3) + (t - x_4))}{(2h)(h)(-h)(2h)}$$

$$+ f_3 \frac{6((t - x_0) + (t - x_1) + (t - x_2) + (t - x_4))}{(3h)(2h)(h)(-h)}$$

$$+ f_4 \frac{6((t - x_0) + (t - x_1) + (t - x_2) + (t - x_3))}{(4h)(3h)(2h)(h)}.$$

Then substitution of $t = x_0$ in the form $t - x_j = x_0 - x_j = -jh$ produces

$$f'''(x_0) \approx f_0 \frac{6((-h) + (-2h) + (-3h) + (-4h))}{24h^4} + f_1 \frac{6((0) + (-2h) + (-3h) + (-4h))}{-6h^4}$$

$$+ f_2 \frac{6((0) + (-h) + (-3h) + (-4h))}{4h^4} + f_3 \frac{6((0) + (-h) + (-2h) + (-4h))}{-6h^4}$$

$$+ f_4 \frac{6((0) + (-h) + (-2h) + (-3h))}{24h^4}$$

$$= f_0 \frac{-60h}{24h^4} + f_1 \frac{54h}{6h^4} + f_2 \frac{-48h}{4h^4} + f_3 \frac{42h}{6h^4} + f_4 \frac{-36h}{24h^4}$$

$$= \frac{-5f_0 + 18f_1 - 24f_2 + 14f_3 - 3f_4}{2h^3},$$

and the formula is established.   ∎

Differentiation of the Newton Polynomial

In this section we show the relationship between the three formulas of order $O(h^2)$ for approximating $f'(x_0)$, and a general algorithm is given for computing the numerical derivative. In Section 4.3 we saw that the Newton polynomial $P(t)$ of degree $N = 2$ that approximates $f(t)$ using the nodes t_0, t_1, and t_2 is

$$(16) \qquad P(t) = a_0 + a_1(t - t_0) + a_2(t - t_0)(t - t_1),$$

where $a_0 = f(t_0)$, $a_1 = (f(t_1) - f(t_0))/(t_1 - t_0)$, and

$$a_2 = \frac{\dfrac{f(t_2) - f(t_1)}{t_2 - t_1} - \dfrac{f(t_1) - f(t_0)}{t_1 - t_0}}{t_2 - t_0}.$$

The derivative of $P(t)$ is

$$(17) \qquad P'(t) = a_1 + a_2((t - t_0) + (t - t_1)),$$

and when it is evaluated at $t = t_0$, the result is

$$(18) \qquad P'(t_0) = a_1 + a_2(t_0 - t_1) \approx f'(t_0).$$

Observe that the nodes $\{t_k\}$ do not need to be equally spaced for formulas (16) through (18) to hold. Choosing the abscissas in different orders will produce different formulas for approximating $f'(x)$.

Case (i): If $t_0 = x$, $t_1 = x + h$, and $t_2 = x + 2h$, then

$$a_1 = \frac{f(x + h) - f(x)}{h},$$

$$a_2 = \frac{f(x) - 2f(x + h) + f(x + 2h)}{2h^2}.$$

When these values are substituted into (18), we get

$$P'(x) = \frac{f(x + h) - f(x)}{h} + \frac{-f(x) + 2f(x + h) - f(x + 2h)}{2h}.$$

This is simplified to obtain

$$(19) \qquad P'(x) = \frac{-3f(x) + 4f(x + h) - f(x + 2h)}{2h} \approx f'(x),$$

which is the second-order forward-difference formula for $f'(x)$.

Case (ii): If $t_0 = x$, $t_1 = x + h$, and $t_2 = x - h$, then

$$a_1 = \frac{f(x + h) - f(x)}{h},$$

$$a_2 = \frac{f(x + h) - 2f(x) + f(x - h)}{2h^2}.$$

When these values are substituted into (18), we get

$$P'(x) = \frac{f(x+h) - f(x)}{h} + \frac{-f(x+h) + 2f(x) - f(x-h)}{2h}.$$

This is simplified to obtain

(20) $$P'(x) = \frac{f(x+h) - f(x-h)}{2h} \approx f'(x),$$

which is the second-order central-difference formula for $f'(x)$.

   Case (iii): If $t_0 = x$, $t_1 = x - h$, and $t_2 = x - 2h$, then

$$a_1 = \frac{f(x) - f(x-h)}{h},$$

$$a_2 = \frac{f(x) - 2f(x-h) + f(x-2h)}{2h^2}.$$

These values are substituted into (18) and simplified to get

(21) $$P'(x) = \frac{3f(x) - 4f(x-h) + f(x-2h)}{2h} \approx f'(x),$$

which is the second-order backward-difference formula for $f'(x)$.

   The Newton polynomial $P(t)$ of degree N that approximates $f(t)$ using the nodes $t_0, t_1, \ldots, t_N$ is

(22)
$$\begin{aligned}
P(t) = {} & a_0 + a_1(t - t_0) + a_2(t - t_0)(t - t_1) \\
& + a_3(t - t_0)(t - t_1)(t - t_2) + \cdots + a_N(t - t_0) \cdots (t - t_{N-1}).
\end{aligned}$$

The derivative of $P(t)$ is

(23)
$$\begin{aligned}
P'(t) = {} & a_1 + a_2((t - t_0) + (t - t_1)) \\
& + a_3((t - t_0)(t - t_1) + (t - t_0)(t - t_2) + (t - t_1)(t - t_2)) \\
& + \cdots + a_N \sum_{k=0}^{N-1} \prod_{\substack{j=0 \\ j \neq k}}^{N-1} (t - t_j).
\end{aligned}$$

   When $P'(t)$ is evaluated at $t = t_0$, several of the terms in the summation are zero, and $P'(t_0)$ has the simpler form

(24)
$$\begin{aligned}
P'(t_0) = {} & a_1 + a_2(t_0 - t_1) + a_3(t_0 - t_1)(t_0 - t_2) + \cdots \\
& + a_N(t_0 - t_1)(t_0 - t_2)(t_0 - t_3) \cdots (t_0 - t_{N-1}).
\end{aligned}$$

   The kth partial sum on the right side of equation (24) is the derivative of the Newton polynomial of degree k based on the first k nodes. If

$$|t_0 - t_1| \leq |t_0 - t_2| \leq \cdots \leq |t_0 - t_N|, \quad \text{and if} \quad \{(t_j, 0)\}_{j=0}^{N}$$

forms a set of $N + 1$ equally spaced points on the real axis, the kth partial sum is an approximation to $f'(t_0)$ of order $O(h^{k-1})$.

Suppose that $N = 5$. If the five nodes are $t_k = x + hk$ for $k = 0, 1, 2, 3$, and 4, then (24) is an equivalent way to compute the forward-difference formula for $f'(x)$ of order $O(h^4)$. If the five nodes $\{t_k\}$ are chosen to be $t_0 = x$, $t_1 = x + h$, $t_2 = x - h$, $t_3 = x + 2h$, and $t_4 = x - 2h$, then (24) is the central-difference formula for $f'(x)$ of order $O(h^4)$. When the five nodes are $t_k = x - kh$, then (24) is the backward-difference formula for $f'(x)$ of order $O(h^4)$.

The following program is an extension of Program 4.2 and can be used to implement formula (24). Note that the nodes do not need to be equally spaced. Also, it computes the derivative at only one point $f'(x_0)$.

Program 6.3 (Differentiation Based on $N + 1$ Nodes). To approximate $f'(x)$ numerically by constructing the Nth-degree Newton polynomial

$$P(x) = a_0 + a_1(x - x_0) + a_2(x - x_0)(x - x_1)$$
$$+ a_3(x - x_0)(x - x_1)(x - x_2) + \cdots + a_N(x - x_0) \cdots (x - x_{N-1})$$

and using $f'(x_0) \approx P'(x_0)$ as the final answer. The method must be used at x_0. The points can be rearranged $\{x_k, x_0, \ldots, x_{k-1}, x_{k+1}, \ldots, x_N\}$ to compute $f'(x_k) \approx P'(x_k)$.

```
function [A,df]=diffnew(X,Y)

%Input   - X is the 1xn abscissa vector
%         - Y is the 1xn ordinate vector
%Output - A is the 1xn vector containing the coefficients of
%           the Nth-degree Newton polynomial
%         - df is the approximate derivative

A=Y;
N=length(X);

for j=2:N
   for k=N:-1:j
       A(k)=(A(k)-A(k-1))/(X(k)-X(k-j+1));
   end
end

x0=X(1);
df=A(2);
prod=1;
n1=length(A)-1;

for k=2:n1
   prod=prod*(x0-X(k));
   df=df+prod*A(k+1);
end
```

Exercises for Numerical Differentiation Formulas

1. Let $f(x) = \ln(x)$ and carry eight or nine decimal places.
   - **(a)**   Use formula (6) with $h = 0.05$ to approximate $f''(5)$.
   - **(b)**   Use formula (6) with $h = 0.01$ to approximate $f''(5)$.
   - **(c)**   Use formula (12) with $h = 0.1$ to approximate $f''(5)$.
   - **(d)**   Which answer, (a), (b), or (c), is most accurate?

2. Let $f(x) = \cos(x)$ and carry eight or nine decimal places.
   - **(a)**   Use formula (6) with $h = 0.05$ to approximate $f''(1)$.
   - **(b)**   Use formula (6) with $h = 0.01$ to approximate $f''(1)$.
   - **(c)**   Use formula (12) with $h = 0.1$ to approximate $f''(1)$.
   - **(d)**   Which answer, (a), (b), or (c), is most accurate?

3. Consider the table for $f(x) = \ln(x)$ rounded to four decimal places.

x	$f(x) = \ln(x)$
4.90	1.5892
4.95	1.5994
5.00	1.6094
5.05	1.6194
5.10	1.6292

   - **(a)**   Use formula (6) with $h = 0.05$ to approximate $f''(5)$.
   - **(b)**   Use formula (6) with $h = 0.01$ to approximate $f''(5)$.
   - **(c)**   Use formula (12) with $h = 0.05$ to approximate $f''(5)$.
   - **(d)**   Which answer, (a), (b), or (c), is most accurate?

4. Consider the table for $f(x) = \cos(x)$ rounded to four decimal places.

x	$f(x) = \cos(x)$
0.90	0.6216
0.95	0.5817
1.00	0.5403
1.05	0.4976
1.10	0.4536

   - **(a)**   Use formula (6) with $h = 0.05$ to approximate $f''(1)$.
   - **(b)**   Use formula (6) with $h = 0.01$ to approximate $f''(1)$.
   - **(c)**   Use formula (12) with $h = 0.05$ to approximate $f''(1)$.
   - **(d)**   Which answer, (a), (b), or (c), is most accurate?

5. Use the numerical differentiation formula (6) and $h = 0.01$ to approximate $f''(1)$ for the functions
   - **(a)** $f(x) = x^2$ **(b)** $f(x) = x^4$

6. Use the numerical differentiation formula (12) and $h = 0.1$ to approximate $f''(1)$ for the functions
   (a) $f(x) = x^4$ **(b)** $f(x) = x^6$

7. Use the Taylor expansions for $f(x + h)$, $f(x - h)$, $f(x + 2h)$, and $f(x - 2h)$ and derive the central-difference formula:

$$f^{(3)}(x) \approx \frac{f(x + 2h) - 2f(x + h) + 2f(x - h) - f(x - 2h)}{2h^3}.$$

8. Use the Taylor expansions for $f(x + h)$, $f(x - h)$, $f(x + 2h)$, and $f(x - 2h)$ and derive the central-difference formula:

$$f^{(4)}(x) \approx \frac{f(x + 2h) - 4f(x + h) + 6f(x) - 4f(x - h) + f(x - 2h)}{h^4}.$$

9. Find the approximations to $f'(x_k)$ of order $\boldsymbol{O}(h^2)$ at each of the four points in the tables.

(a)

x	$f(x)$
0.0	0.989992
0.1	0.999135
0.2	0.998295
0.3	0.987480

(b)

x	$f(x)$
0.0	0.141120
0.1	0.041581
0.2	−0.058374
0.3	−0.157746

10. Use the approximations

$$f'\left(x + \frac{h}{2}\right) \approx \frac{f_1 - f_0}{h} \quad \text{and} \quad f'\left(x - \frac{h}{2}\right) \approx \frac{f_0 - f_{-1}}{h}$$

and derive the approximation

$$f''(x) \approx \frac{f_1 - 2f_0 + f_{-1}}{h^2}.$$

11. Use formulas (16) through (18) and derive a formula for $f'(x)$ based on the abscissas $t_0 = x$, $t_1 = x + h$, and $t_2 = x + 3h$.

12. Use formulas (16) through (18) and derive a formula for $f'(x)$ based on the abscissas $t_0 = x$, $t_1 = x - h$, and $t_2 = x + 2h$.

13. The numerical solution of a certain differential equation requires an approximation to $f''(x) + f'(x)$ of order $\boldsymbol{O}(h^2)$.
   (a) Find the central-difference formula for $f''(x) + f'(x)$ by adding the formulas for $f'(x)$ and $f''(x)$ of order $\boldsymbol{O}(h^2)$.
   (b) Find the forward-difference formula for $f''(x) + f'(x)$ by adding the formulas for $f'(x)$ and $f''(x)$ of order $\boldsymbol{O}(h^2)$.
   (c) What would happen if a formula for $f'(x)$ of order $\boldsymbol{O}(h^4)$ were added to a formula for $f''(x)$ of order $\boldsymbol{O}(h^2)$?

14. Critique the following argument. Taylor's formula can be used to get the representations

$$f(x + h) = f(x) + hf'(x) + \frac{h^2 f''(x)}{2} + \frac{h^3 f^{(3)}(c)}{6}$$

and

$$f(x - h) = f(x) - hf'(x) + \frac{h^2 f''(x)}{2} - \frac{h^3 f^{(3)}(c)}{6}.$$

Adding these quantities results in

$$f(x + h) + f(x - h) = 2f(x) + h^2 f''(x),$$

which can be solved to obtain an exact formula for $f''(x)$:

$$f''(x) = \frac{f(x + h) - 2f(x) + f(x - h)}{h^2}.$$

Algorithms and Programs

1. Modify Program 6.3 so that it will calculate $P'(x_M)$ for $M = 1, 2, \ldots, N + 1$.

7

Numerical Integration

Numerical integration is a primary tool used by engineers and scientists to obtain approximate answers for definite integrals that cannot be solved analytically. In the area of statistical thermodynamics, the Debye model for calculating the heat capacity of a solid involves the following function;

$$\Phi(x) = \int_0^x \frac{t^3}{e^t - 1} \, dt.$$

Since there is no analytic expression for $\Phi(x)$, numerical integration must be used to obtain approximate values. For example, the value $\Phi(5)$ is the area under the curve

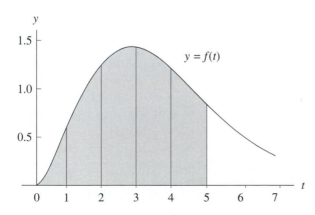

Figure 7.1 The area under the curve $y = f(t)$ for $0 \le t \le 5$.

Table 7.1   Values of $\Phi(x)$

x	$\Phi(x)$
1.0	0.2248052
2.0	1.1763426
3.0	2.5522185
4.0	3.8770542
5.0	4.8998922
6.0	5.5858554
7.0	6.0031690
8.0	6.2396238
9.0	6.3665739
10.0	6.4319219

$y = f(t) = t^3/(e^t - 1)$ for $0 \leq t \leq 5$ (see Figure 7.1). The numerical approximation for $\Phi(5)$ is

$$\Phi(5) = \int_0^5 \frac{t^3}{e^t - 1}\, dt \approx 4.8998922.$$

Each additional value of $\Phi(x)$ must be determined by another numerical integration. Table 7.1 lists several of these approximations over the interval $[1, 10]$.

The purpose of this chapter is to develop the basic principles of numerical integration. In Chapter 9, numerical integration formulas are used to derive the predictor-corrector methods for solving differential equations.

7.1   Introduction to Quadrature

We now approach the subject of numerical integration. The goal is to approximate the definite integral of $f(x)$ over the interval $[a, b]$ by evaluating $f(x)$ at a finite number of sample points.

Definition 7.1.   Suppose that $a = x_0 < x_1 < \cdots < x_M = b$. A formula of the form

$$(1) \qquad Q[f] = \sum_{k=0}^{M} w_k f(x_k) = w_0 f(x_0) + w_1 f(x_1) + \cdots + w_M f(x_M)$$

with the property that

$$(2) \qquad \int_a^b f(x)\, dx = Q[f] + E[f]$$

is called a numerical integration or *quadrature* formula. The term $E[f]$ is called the *truncation error* for integration. The values $\{x_k\}_{k=0}^{M}$ are called the *quadrature nodes*, and $\{w_k\}_{k=0}^{M}$ are called the *weights*.   ▲

Depending on the application, the nodes $\{x_k\}$ are chosen in various ways. For the trapezoidal rule, Simpson's rule, and Boole's rule, the nodes are chosen to be equally spaced. For Gauss-Legendre quadrature, the nodes are chosen to be zeros of certain Legendre polynomials. When the integration formula is used to develop a predictor formula for differential equations, all the nodes are chosen less than b. For all applications, it is necessary to know something about the accuracy of the numerical solution.

Definition 7.2.   The *degree of precision* of a quadrature formula is the positive integer n such that $E[P_i] = 0$ for all polynomials $P_i(x)$ of degree $i \leq n$, but for which $E[P_{n+1}] \neq 0$ for some polynomial $P_{n+1}(x)$ of degree $n + 1$.   ▲

The form of $E[P_i]$ can be anticipated by studying what happens when $f(x)$ is a polynomial. Consider the arbitrary polynomial

$$P_i(x) = a_i x^i + a_{i-1} x^{i-1} + \cdots + a_1 x + a_0$$

of degree i. If $i \leq n$, then $P_i^{(n+1)}(x) \equiv 0$ for all x, and $P_{n+1}^{(n+1)}(x) = (n+1)! a_{n-1}$ for all x. Thus it is not surprising that the general form for the truncation error term is

(3)
$$E[f] = K f^{(n+1)}(c),$$

where K is a suitably chosen constant and n is the degree of precision. The proof of this general result can be found in advanced books on numerical integration.

The derivation of quadrature formulas is sometimes based on polynomial interpolation. Recall that there exists a unique polynomial $P_M(x)$ of degree $\leq M$ passing through the $M + 1$ equally spaced points $\{(x_k, f(x_k))\}_{k=0}^{M}$. When this polynomial is used to approximate $f(x)$ over $[a, b]$, and then the integral of $f(x)$ is approximated by the integral of $P_M(x)$, the resulting formula is called a *Newton-Cotes quadrature formula* (see Figure 7.2). When the sample points $x_0 = a$ and $x_M = b$ are used, it is called a *closed* Newton-Cotes formula. The next result gives the formulas when approximating polynomials of degree $M = 1, 2, 3$, and 4 are used.

Theorem 7.1 (Closed Newton-Cotes Quadrature Formula).   Assume that $x_k = x_0 + kh$ are equally spaced nodes and $f_k = f(x_k)$. The first four closed Newton-Cotes

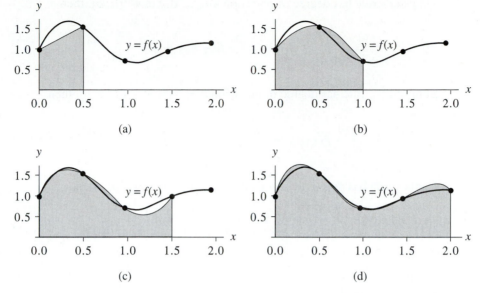

Figure 7.2 (a) The trapezoidal rule integrates $y = P_1(x)$ over $[x_0, x_1] = [0.0, 0.5]$.
(b) Simpson's rule integrates $y = P_2(x)$ over $[x_0, x_1] = [0.0, 1.0]$. (c) Simpson's $\frac{3}{8}$ rule
integrates $y = P_3(x)$ over $[x_0, x_3] = [0.0, 1.5]$. (d) Boole's rule integrates $y = P_4(x)$
over $[x_0, x_4] = [0.0, 2.0]$.

quadrature formulas are

$$(4) \qquad \int_{x_0}^{x_1} f(x)\, dx \approx \frac{h}{2}(f_0 + f_1) \qquad\qquad \text{(trapezoidal rule)},$$

$$(5) \qquad \int_{x_0}^{x_2} f(x)\, dx \approx \frac{h}{3}(f_0 + 4f_1 + f_2) \qquad\quad \text{(Simpson's rule)},$$

$$(6) \qquad \int_{x_0}^{x_3} f(x)\, dx \approx \frac{3h}{8}(f_0 + 3f_1 + 3f_2 + f_3) \quad \text{(Simpson's } \tfrac{3}{8} \text{ rule)},$$

$$(7) \qquad \int_{x_0}^{x_4} f(x)\, dx \approx \frac{2h}{45}(7f_0 + 32f_1 + 12f_2 + 32f_3 + 7f_4)$$

$$\text{(Boole's rule)}.$$

Corollary 7.1 (Newton-Cotes Precision).   Assume that $f(x)$ is sufficiently differentiable; then $E[f]$ for Newton-Cotes quadrature involves an appropriate higher derivative. The trapezoidal rule has degree of precision $n = 1$. If $f \in C^2[a, b]$, then

$$(8) \qquad \int_{x_0}^{x_1} f(x)\, dx = \frac{h}{2}(f_0 + f_1) - \frac{h^3}{12} f^{(2)}(c).$$

Simpson's rule has degree of precision $n = 3$. If $f \in C^4[a, b]$, then

(9)
$$\int_{x_0}^{x_2} f(x)\, dx = \frac{h}{3}(f_0 + 4f_1 + f_2) - \frac{h^5}{90} f^{(4)}(c).$$

Simpson's $\frac{3}{8}$ rule has degree of precision $n = 3$. If $f \in C^4[a, b]$, then

(10)
$$\int_{x_0}^{x_3} f(x)\, dx = \frac{3h}{8}(f_0 + 3f_1 + 3f_2 + f_3) - \frac{3h^5}{80} f^{(4)}(c).$$

Boole's rule has degree of precision $n = 5$. If $f \in C^6[a, b]$, then

(11)
$$\int_{x_0}^{x_4} f(x)\, dx = \frac{2h}{45}(7f_0 + 32f_1 + 12f_2 + 32f_3 + 7f_4) - \frac{8h^7}{945} f^{(6)}(c).$$

Proof of Theorem 7.1.   Start with the Lagrange polynomial $P_M(x)$ based on x_0, x_1, ..., x_M that can be used to approximate $f(x)$:

(12)
$$f(x) \approx P_M(x) = \sum_{k=0}^{M} f_k L_{M,k}(x),$$

where $f_k = f(x_k)$ for $k = 0, 1, \ldots, M$. An approximation for the integral is obtained by replacing the integrand $f(x)$ with the polynomial $P_M(x)$. This is the general method for obtaining a Newton-Cotes integration formula:

$$\int_{x_0}^{x_M} f(x)\, dx \approx \int_{x_0}^{x_M} P_M(x)\, dx$$

(13)
$$= \int_{x_0}^{x_M} \left(\sum_{k=0}^{M} f_k L_{M,k}(x) \right) dx = \sum_{k=0}^{M} \left(\int_{x_0}^{x_M} f_k L_{M,k}(x)\, dx \right)$$

$$= \sum_{k=0}^{M} \left(\int_{x_0}^{x_M} L_{M,k}(x)\, dx \right) f_k = \sum_{k=0}^{M} w_k f_k.$$

The details for the general computations of the coefficients of w_k in (13) are tedious. We shall give a sample proof of Simpson's rule, which is the case $M = 2$. This case involves the approximating polynomial
(14)
$$P_2(x) = f_0 \frac{(x - x_1)(x - x_2)}{(x_0 - x_1)(x_0 - x_2)} + f_1 \frac{(x - x_0)(x - x_2)}{(x_1 - x_0)(x_1 - x_2)} + f_2 \frac{(x - x_0)(x - x_1)}{(x_2 - x_0)(x_2 - x_1)}.$$

Since f_0, f_1, and f_2 are constants with respect to integration, the relations in (13) lead to

(15)
$$\int_{x_0}^{x_2} f(x)\,dx \approx f_0 \int_{x_0}^{x_2} \frac{(x-x_1)(x-x_2)}{(x_0-x_1)(x_0-x_2)}\,dx + f_1 \int_{x_0}^{x_2} \frac{(x-x_0)(x-x_2)}{(x_1-x_0)(x_1-x_2)}\,dx$$
$$+ f_2 \int_{x_0}^{x_2} \frac{(x-x_0)(x-x_1)}{(x_2-x_0)(x_2-x_1)}\,dx.$$

We introduce the change of variable $x = x_0 + ht$ with $dx = h\,dt$ to assist with the evaluation of the integrals in (15). The new limits of integration are from $t = 0$ to $t = 2$. The equal spacing of the nodes $x_k = x_0 + kh$ leads to $x_k - x_j = (k-j)h$ and $x - x_k = h(t-k)$, which are used to simplify (15) and get

(16)
$$\int_{x_0}^{x_2} f(x)\,dx \approx f_0 \int_0^2 \frac{h(t-1)h(t-2)}{(-h)(-2h)}h\,dt + f_1 \int_0^2 \frac{h(t-0)h(t-2)}{(h)(-h)}h\,dt$$
$$+ f_2 \int_0^2 \frac{h(t-0)h(t-1)}{(2h)(h)}h\,dt$$
$$= f_0\frac{h}{2}\int_0^2 (t^2 - 3t + 2)\,dt - f_1 h\int_0^2 (t^2 - 2t)\,dt + f_2\frac{h}{2}\int_0^2 (t^2 - t)\,dt$$
$$= f_0\frac{h}{2}\left(\frac{t^3}{3} - \frac{3t^2}{2} + 2t\right)\bigg|_{t=0}^{t=2} - f_1 h\left(\frac{t^3}{3} - t^2\right)\bigg|_{t=0}^{t=2}$$
$$+ f_2\frac{h}{2}\left(\frac{t^3}{3} - \frac{t^2}{2}\right)\bigg|_{t=0}^{t=2}$$
$$= f_0\frac{h}{2}\left(\frac{2}{3}\right) - f_1 h\left(\frac{-4}{3}\right) + f_2\frac{h}{2}\left(\frac{2}{3}\right)$$
$$= \frac{h}{3}(f_0 + 4f_1 + f_2),$$

and the proof is complete. We postpone a sample proof of Corollary 7.1 until Section 7.2. •

Example 7.1. Consider the function $f(x) = 1 + e^{-x}\sin(4x)$, the equally spaced quadrature nodes $x_0 = 0.0$, $x_1 = 0.5$, $x_2 = 1.0$, $x_3 = 1.5$, and $x_4 = 2.0$, and the corresponding function values $f_0 = 1.00000$, $f_1 = 1.55152$, $f_2 = 0.72159$, $f_3 = 0.93765$, and $f_4 = 1.13390$. Apply the various quadrature formulas (4) through (7).

The step size is $h = 0.5$, and the computations are

$$\int_0^{0.5} f(x)\,dx \approx \frac{0.5}{2}(1.00000 + 1.55152) = 0.63788$$

$$\int_0^{1.0} f(x)\,dx \approx \frac{0.5}{3}(1.00000 + 4(1.55152) + 0.72159) = 1.32128$$

$$\int_0^{1.5} f(x)\,dx \approx \frac{3(0.5)}{8}(1.00000 + 3(1.55152) + 3(0.72159) + 0.93765)$$
$$= 1.64193$$

$$\int_0^{2.0} f(x)\,dx \approx \frac{2(0.5)}{45}(7(1.00000) + 32(1.55152) + 12(0.72159)$$
$$+ 32(0.93765) + 7(1.13390)) = 2.29444. \qquad \blacksquare$$

It is important to realize that the quadrature formulas (4) through (7) applied in the illustration above give approximations for definite integrals over different intervals. The graph of the curve $y = f(x)$ and the areas under the Lagrange polynomials $y = P_1(x)$, $y = P_2(x)$, $y = P_3(x)$, and $y = P_4(x)$ are shown in Figure 7.2(a) through (d), respectively.

In Example 7.1 we applied the quadrature rules with $h = 0.5$. If the endpoints of the interval $[a, b]$ are held fixed, the step size must be adjusted for each rule. The step sizes are $h = b - a$, $h = (b - a)/2$, $h = (b - a)/3$, and $h = (b - a)/4$ for the trapezoidal rule, Simpson's rule, Simpson's $\frac{3}{8}$ rule, and Boole's rule, respectively. The next example illustrates this point.

Example 7.2.   Consider the integration of the function $f(x) = 1 + e^{-x}\sin(4x)$ over the fixed interval $[a, b] = [0, 1]$. Apply the various formulas (4) through (7).

For the trapezoidal rule, $h = 1$ and

$$\int_0^1 f(x)\,dx \approx \frac{1}{2}(f(0) + f(1))$$

$$= \frac{1}{2}(1.00000 + 0.72159) = 0.86079.$$

For Simpson's rule, $h = 1/2$, and we get

$$\int_0^1 f(x)\,dx \approx \frac{1/2}{3}(f(0) + 4f(\tfrac{1}{2}) + f(1))$$

$$= \frac{1}{6}(1.00000 + 4(1.55152) + 0.72159) = 1.32128.$$

For Simpson's $\frac{3}{8}$ rule, $h = 1/3$, and we obtain

$$\int_0^1 f(x)\,dx \approx \frac{3(1/3)}{8}(f(0) + 3f(\tfrac{1}{3}) + 3f(\tfrac{2}{3}) + f(1))$$

$$= \frac{1}{8}(1.00000 + 3(1.69642) + 3(1.23447) + 0.72159) = 1.31440.$$

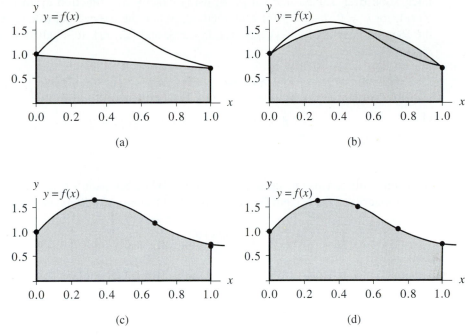

Figure 7.3   (a) The trapezoidal rule used over [0, 1] yields the approximation 0.86079. (b) Simpson's rule used over [0, 1] yields the approximation 1.32128. (c) Simpson's $\frac{3}{8}$ rule used over [0, 1] yields the approximation 1.31440. (d) Boole's rule used over [0, 1] yields the approximation 1.30859.

For Boole's rule, $h = 1/4$, and the result is

$$\int_0^1 f(x)\,dx \approx \frac{2(1/4)}{45}\left(7f(0) + 32f\left(\tfrac{1}{4}\right) + 12f\left(\tfrac{1}{2}\right) + 32f\left(\tfrac{3}{4}\right) + 7f(1)\right)$$

$$= \frac{1}{90}(7(1.00000) + 32(1.65534) + 12(1.55152)$$

$$+ 32(1.06666) + 7(0.72159)) = 1.30859.$$

The true value of the definite integral is

$$\int_0^1 f(x)\,dx = \frac{21e - 4\cos(4) - \sin(4)}{17e} = 1.3082506046426\ldots,$$

and the approximation 1.30859 from Boole's rule is best. The area under each of the Lagrange polynomials $P_1(x)$, $P_2(x)$, $P_3(x)$, and $P_4(x)$ is shown in Figure 7.3(a) through (d), respectively.   ■

To make a fair comparison of quadrature methods, we must use the same number of function evaluations in each method. Our final example is concerned with comparing integration over a fixed interval $[a, b]$ using exactly five function evaluations $f_k = f(x_k)$, for $k = 0, 1, \ldots, 4$ for each method. When the trapezoidal rule is applied on the four subintervals $[x_0, x_1]$, $[x_1, x_2]$, $[x_2, x_3]$, and $[x_3, x_4]$, it is called a *composite trapezoidal rule*:

$$
\int_{x_0}^{x_4} f(x)\,dx = \int_{x_0}^{x_1} f(x)\,dx + \int_{x_1}^{x_2} f(x)\,dx + \int_{x_2}^{x_3} f(x)\,dx + \int_{x_3}^{x_4} f(x)\,dx
$$

(17)
$$
\approx \frac{h}{2}(f_0 + f_1) + \frac{h}{2}(f_1 + f_2) + \frac{h}{2}(f_2 + f_3) + \frac{h}{2}(f_3 + f_4)
$$

$$
= \frac{h}{2}(f_0 + 2f_1 + 2f_2 + 2f_3 + f_4).
$$

Simpson's rule can also be used in this manner. When Simpson's rule is applied on the two subintervals $[x_0, x_2]$ and $[x_2, x_4]$, it is called a *composite Simpson's rule*:

$$
\int_{x_0}^{x_4} f(x)\,dx = \int_{x_0}^{x_2} f(x)\,dx + \int_{x_2}^{x_4} f(x)\,dx
$$

(18)
$$
\approx \frac{h}{3}(f_0 + 4f_1 + f_2) + \frac{h}{3}(f_2 + 4f_3 + f_4)
$$

$$
= \frac{h}{3}(f_0 + 4f_1 + 2f_2 + 4f_3 + f_4).
$$

The next example compares the values obtained with (17), (18), and (7).

Example 7.3. Consider the integration of the function $f(x) = 1 + e^{-x}\sin(4x)$ over $[a, b] = [0, 1]$. Use exactly five function evaluations and compare the results from the composite trapezoidal rule, composite Simpson rule, and Boole's rule.

The uniform step size is $h = 1/4$. The composite trapezoidal rule (17) produces

$$
\int_0^1 f(x)\,dx \approx \frac{1/4}{2}(f(0) + 2f(\tfrac{1}{4}) + 2f(\tfrac{1}{2}) + 2f(\tfrac{3}{4}) + f(1))
$$

$$
= \frac{1}{8}(1.00000 + 2(1.65534) + 2(1.55152) + 2(1.06666) + 0.72159)
$$

$$
= 1.28358.
$$

Using the composite Simpson's rule (18), we get

$$
\int_0^1 f(x)\,dx \approx \frac{1/4}{3}(f(0) + 4f(\tfrac{1}{4}) + 2f(\tfrac{1}{2}) + 4f(\tfrac{3}{4}) + f(1))
$$

$$
= \frac{1}{12}(1.00000 + 4(1.65534) + 2(1.55152) + 4(1.06666) + 0.72159)
$$

$$
= 1.30938.
$$

We have already seen the result of Boole's rule in Example 7.2:

$$
\int_0^1 f(x)\,dx \approx \frac{2(1/4)}{45}(7f(0) + 32f(\tfrac{1}{4}) + 12f(\tfrac{1}{2}) + 32f(\tfrac{3}{4}) + 7f(1))
$$

$$
= 1.30859.
$$

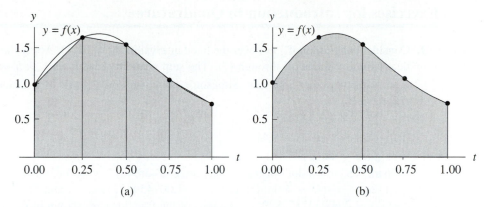

Figure 7.4 (a) The composite trapezoidal rule yields the approximation 1.28358. (b) The composite Simpson rule yields the approximation 1.30938.

The true value of the integral is

$$\int_0^1 f(x)\,dx = \frac{21e - 4\cos(4) - \sin(4)}{17e} = 1.3082506046426\ldots,$$

and the approximation 1.30938 from Simpson's rule is much better than the value 1.28358 obtained from the trapezoidal rule. Again, the approximation 1.30859 from Boole's rule is closest. Graphs for the areas under the trapezoids and parabolas are shown in Figure 7.4(a) and (b), respectively. ∎

Example 7.4. Determine the degree of precision of Simpson's $\frac{3}{8}$ rule.

It will suffice to apply Simpson's $\frac{3}{8}$ rule over the interval $[0, 3]$ with the five test functions $f(x) = 1, x, x^2, x^3$, and x^4. For the first four functions, Simpson's $\frac{3}{8}$ rule is exact.

$$\int_0^3 1\,dx = 3 = \frac{3}{8}(1 + 3(1) + 3(1) + 1)$$

$$\int_0^3 x\,dx = \frac{9}{2} = \frac{3}{8}(0 + 3(1) + 3(2) + 3)$$

$$\int_0^3 x^2\,dx = 9 = \frac{3}{8}(0 + 3(1) + 3(4) + 9)$$

$$\int_0^3 x^3\,dx = \frac{81}{4} = \frac{3}{8}(0 + 3(1) + 3(8) + 27).$$

The function $f(x) = x^4$ is the lowest power of x for which the rule is not exact.

$$\int_0^3 x^4\,dx = \frac{243}{5} \approx \frac{99}{2} = \frac{3}{8}(0 + 3(1) + 3(16) + 81).$$

Therefore, the degree of precision of Simpson's $\frac{3}{8}$ rule is $n = 3$. ∎

Exercises for Introduction to Quadrature

1. Consider integration of $f(x)$ over the fixed interval $[a, b] = [0, 1]$. Apply the various quadrature formulas (4) through (7). The step sizes are $h = 1$, $h = \frac{1}{2}$, $h = \frac{1}{3}$, and $h = \frac{1}{4}$ for the trapezoidal rule, Simpson's rule, Simpson's $\frac{3}{8}$ rule, and Boole's rule, respectively.

   (a) $f(x) = \sin(\pi x)$
   (b) $f(x) = 1 + e^{-x}\cos(4x)$
   (c) $f(x) = \sin(\sqrt{x})$

   Remark. The true values of the definite integrals are (a) $2/\pi = 0.636619772367\ldots$, (b) $(18e - \cos(4) + 4\sin(4))/(17e) = 1.007459631397\ldots$, and (c) $2(\sin(1) - \cos(1)) = 0.602337357879\ldots$. Graphs of the functions are shown in Figure 7.5(a) through (c), respectively.

2. Consider integration of $f(x)$ over the fixed interval $[a, b] = [0, 1]$. Apply the various quadrature formulas: the composite trapezoidal rule (17), the composite Simpson rule (18), and Boole's rule (7). Use five function evaluations at equally spaced nodes. The uniform step size is $h = \frac{1}{4}$.

   (a) $f(x) = \sin(\pi x)$
   (b) $f(x) = 1 + e^{-x}\cos(4x)$
   (c) $f(x) = \sin(\sqrt{x})$

3. Consider a general interval $[a, b]$. Show that Simpson's rule produces exact results for the functions $f(x) = x^2$ and $f(x) = x^3$; that is,

   (a) $\int_a^b x^2\,dx = \dfrac{b^3}{3} - \dfrac{a^3}{3}$
   (b) $\int_a^b x^3\,dx = \dfrac{b^4}{4} - \dfrac{a^4}{4}$

4. Integrate the Lagrange interpolation polynomial

$$P_1(x) = f_0\frac{x - x_1}{x_0 - x_1} + f_1\frac{x - x_0}{x_1 - x_0}$$

   over the interval $[x_0, x_1]$ and establish the trapezoidal rule.

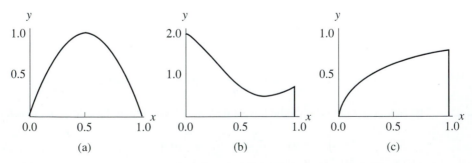

Figure 7.5 (a) $y = \sin(\pi x)$, (b) $y = 1 + e^{-x}\cos(4x)$, (c) $y = \sin(\sqrt{x})$.

5. Determine the degree of precision of the trapezoidal rule. It will suffice to apply the trapezoidal rule over $[0, 1]$ with the three test functions $f(x) = 1, x$, and x^2.

6. Determine the degree of precision of Simpson's rule. It will suffice to apply Simpson's rule over $[0, 2]$ with the five test functions $f(x) = 1, x, x^2, x^3$, and x^4. Contrast your result with the degree of precision of Simpson's $\frac{3}{8}$ rule.

7. Determine the degree of precision of Boole's rule. It will suffice to apply Boole's rule over $[0, 4]$ with the seven test functions $f(x) = 1, x, x^2, x^3, x^4, x^5$, and x^6.

8. The intervals in Exercises 5, 6, and 7 and Example 7.4 were selected to simplify the calculation of the quadrature nodes. But on any closed interval $[a, b]$ over which the function f is integrable, each of the four quadrature rules (4) through (7) has the degree of precision determined in Exercises 5, 6, and 7 and Example 7.4, respectively. A quadrature formula on the interval $[a, b]$ can be obtained from a quadrature formula on the interval $[c, d]$ by making a change of variables with the linear function

$$x = g(t) = \frac{b-a}{d-c}t + \frac{ad - bc}{d-c},$$

where $dx = \dfrac{b-a}{d-c} dt$.

(a) Verify that $x = g(t)$ is the line passing through the points (c, a) and (d, b).

(b) Verify that the trapezoidal rule has the same degree of precision on the interval $[a, b]$ as on the interval $[0, 1]$.

(c) Verify that Simpson's rule has the same degree of precision on the interval $[a, b]$ as on the interval $[0, 2]$.

(d) Verify that Boole's rule has the same degree of precision on the interval $[a, b]$ as on the interval $[0, 4]$.

9. Derive Simpson's $\frac{3}{8}$ rule using Lagrange polynomial interpolation. *Hint.* After changing the variable, integrals similar to those in (16) are obtained:

$$\int_{x_0}^{x_3} f(x)\, dx \approx -f_0 \frac{h}{6} \int_0^3 (t-1)(t-2)(t-3)\, dt + f_1 \frac{h}{2} \int_0^3 (t-0)(t-2)(t-3)\, dt$$

$$-f_2 \frac{h}{2} \int_0^3 (t-0)(t-1)(t-3)\, dt + f_3 \frac{h}{6} \int_0^3 (t-0)(t-1)(t-2)\, dt$$

$$= f_0 \frac{h}{6} \left(\frac{-t^4}{4} + 2t^3 - \frac{11t^2}{2} + 6t \right) \Bigg|_{t=0}^{t=3} + f_1 \frac{h}{2} \left(\frac{t^4}{4} - \frac{5t^3}{3} + 3t^2 \right) \Bigg|_{t=0}^{t=3}$$

$$+ f_2 \frac{h}{2} \left(\frac{-t^4}{4} + \frac{4t^3}{3} - \frac{3t^2}{2} \right) \Bigg|_{t=0}^{t=3} + f_3 \frac{h}{6} \left(\frac{t^4}{4} - t^3 + t^2 \right) \Bigg|_{t=0}^{t=3}.$$

10. Derive the closed Newton-Cotes quadrature formula, based on a Lagrange approximating polynomial of degree 5, using the six equally spaced nodes $x_k = x_0 + kh$, where $k = 0, 1, \ldots, 5$.

11. In the proof of Theorem 7.1, Simpson's rule was derived by integrating the second-degree Lagrange polynomial based on the three equally spaced nodes x_0, x_1, and x_2. Derive Simpson's rule by integrating the second-degree Newton polynomial based on the three equally spaced nodes x_0, x_1, and x_2.

7.2   Composite Trapezoidal and Simpson's Rule

An intuitive method of finding the area under the curve $y = f(x)$ over $[a, b]$ is by approximating that area with a series of trapezoids that lie above the intervals $\{[x_k, x_{k+1}]\}$.

Theorem 7.2 (Composite Trapezoidal Rule).   Suppose that the interval $[a, b]$ is subdivided into M subintervals $[x_k, x_{k+1}]$ of width $h = (b-a)/M$ by using the equally spaced nodes $x_k = a + kh$, for $k = 0, 1, \ldots, M$. The *composite trapezoidal rule for M subintervals* can be expressed in any of three equivalent ways:

(1a)
$$T(f, h) = \frac{h}{2} \sum_{k=1}^{M} (f(x_{k-1}) + f(x_k))$$

or

(1b)
$$T(f, h) = \frac{h}{2}(f_0 + 2f_1 + 2f_2 + 2f_3 + \cdots + 2f_{M-2} + 2f_{M-1} + f_M)$$

or

(1c)
$$T(f, h) = \frac{h}{2}(f(a) + f(b)) + h \sum_{k=1}^{M-1} f(x_k).$$

This is an approximation to the integral of $f(x)$ over $[a, b]$, and we write

(2)
$$\int_a^b f(x)\, dx \approx T(f, h).$$

Proof.   Apply the trapezoidal rule over each subinterval $[x_{k-1}, x_k]$ (see Figure 7.6). Use the additive property of the integral for subintervals:

(3)
$$\int_a^b f(x)\, dx = \sum_{k=1}^{M} \int_{x_{k-1}}^{x_k} f(x)\, dx \approx \sum_{k=1}^{M} \frac{h}{2}(f(x_{k-1}) + f(x_k)).$$

Since $h/2$ is a constant, the distributive law of addition can be applied to obtain (1a). Formula (1b) is the expanded version of (1a). Formula (1c) shows how to group all the intermediate terms in (1b) that are multiplied by 2.   •

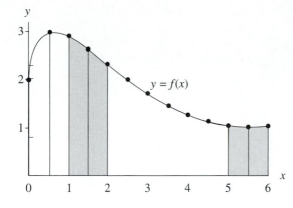

Figure 7.6   Approximating the area under the curve $y = 2 + \sin(2\sqrt{x})$ with the composite trapezoidal rule.

Approximating $f(x) = 2 + \sin(2\sqrt{x})$ with piecewise linear polynomials results in places where the approximation is close and places where it is not. To achieve accuracy, the composite trapezoidal rule must be applied with many subintervals. In the next example we have chosen to integrate this function numerically over the interval $[1, 6]$. Investigation of the integral over $[0, 1]$ is left as an exercise.

Example 7.5.   Consider $f(x) = 2 + \sin(2\sqrt{x})$. Use the composite trapezoidal rule with 11 sample points to compute an approximation to the integral of $f(x)$ taken over $[1, 6]$.

To generate 11 sample points, we use $M = 10$ and $h = (6 - 1)/10 = 1/2$. Using formula (1c), the computation is

$$
\begin{aligned}
T(f, \tfrac{1}{2}) = {} & \frac{1/2}{2}(f(1) + f(6)) \\
& + \frac{1}{2}(f(\tfrac{3}{2}) + f(2) + f(\tfrac{5}{2}) + f(3) + f(\tfrac{7}{2}) + f(4) + f(\tfrac{9}{2}) + f(5) + f(\tfrac{11}{2})) \\
= {} & \frac{1}{4}(2.90929743 + 1.01735756) \\
& + \frac{1}{2}(2.63815764 + 2.30807174 + 1.97931647 + 1.68305284 + 1.43530410 \\
& + 1.24319750 + 1.10831775 + 1.02872220 + 1.00024140) \\
= {} & \frac{1}{4}(3.92665499) + \frac{1}{2}(14.42438165) \\
= {} & 0.98166375 + 7.21219083 = 8.19385457. \qquad \blacksquare
\end{aligned}
$$

Theorem 7.3 (Composite Simpson Rule).   Suppose that $[a, b]$ is subdivided into $2M$ subintervals $[x_k, x_{k+1}]$ of equal width $h = (b - a)/(2M)$ by using $x_k = a + kh$ for $k = 0, 1, \ldots, 2M$. The *composite Simpson rule for 2M subintervals* can be expressed in any of three equivalent ways:

(4a)
$$S(f, h) = \frac{h}{3} \sum_{k=1}^{M} (f(x_{2k-2}) + 4f(x_{2k-1}) + f(x_{2k}))$$

or

(4b)
$$S(f, h) = \frac{h}{3}(f_0 + 4f_1 + 2f_2 + 4f_3$$
$$+ \cdots + 2f_{2M-2} + 4f_{2M-1} + f_{2M})$$

or

(4c)
$$S(f, h) = \frac{h}{3}(f(a) + f(b)) + \frac{2h}{3} \sum_{k=1}^{M-1} f(x_{2k}) + \frac{4h}{3} \sum_{k=1}^{M} f(x_{2k-1}).$$

This is an approximation to the integral of $f(x)$ over $[a, b]$, and we write

(5)
$$\int_a^b f(x)\, dx \approx S(f, h).$$

Proof. Apply Simpson's rule over each subinterval $[x_{2k-2}, x_{2k}]$ (see Figure 7.7). Use the additive property of the integral for subintervals:

(6)
$$\int_a^b f(x)\, dx = \sum_{k=1}^{M} \int_{x_{2k-2}}^{x_{2k}} f(x)\, dx$$
$$\approx \sum_{k=1}^{M} \frac{h}{3}(f(x_{2k-2}) + 4f(x_{2k-1}) + f(x_{2k})).$$

Since $h/3$ is a constant, the distributive law of addition can be applied to obtain (4a). Formula (4b) is the expanded version of (4a). Formula (4c) groups all the intermediate terms in (4b) that are multiplied by 2 and those that are multiplied by 4. •

Approximating $f(x) = 2 + \sin(2\sqrt{x})$ with piecewise quadratic polynomials produces places where the approximation is close and places where it is not. To achieve accuracy the composite Simpson rule must be applied with several subintervals. In the next example we have chosen to integrate this function numerically over $[1, 6]$ and leave investigation of the integral over $[0, 1]$ as an exercise.

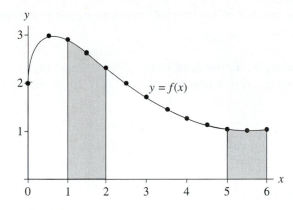

Figure 7.7   Approximating the area under the curve $y = 2 + \sin(2\sqrt{x})$ with the composite Simpson rule.

Example 7.6.   Consider $f(x) = 2 + \sin(2\sqrt{x})$. Use the composite Simpson rule with 11 sample points to compute an approximation to the integral of $f(x)$ taken over $[1, 6]$.

To generate 11 sample points, we must use $M = 5$ and $h = (6 - 1)/10 = 1/2$. Using formula (4c), the computation is

$$S(f, \tfrac{1}{2}) = \frac{1}{6}(f(1) + f(6)) + \frac{1}{3}(f(2) + f(3) + f(4) + f(5))$$

$$+ \frac{2}{3}(f(\tfrac{3}{2}) + f(\tfrac{5}{2}) + f(\tfrac{7}{2}) + f(\tfrac{9}{2}) + f(\tfrac{11}{2}))$$

$$= \frac{1}{6}(2.90929743 + 1.01735756)$$

$$+ \frac{1}{3}(2.30807174 + 1.68305284 + 1.24319750 + 1.02872220)$$

$$+ \frac{2}{3}(2.63815764 + 1.97931647 + 1.43530410 + 1.10831775 + 1.00024140)$$

$$= \frac{1}{6}(3.92665499) + \frac{1}{3}(6.26304429) + \frac{2}{3}(8.16133735)$$

$$= 0.65444250 + 2.08768143 + 5.44089157 = 8.18301550. \qquad \blacksquare$$

Error Analysis

The significance of the next two results is to understand that the error terms $E_T(f, h)$ and $E_S(f, h)$ for the composite trapezoidal rule and composite Simpson rule are of the order $O(h^2)$ and $O(h^4)$, respectively. This shows that the error for Simpson's rule converges to zero faster than the error for the trapezoidal rule as the step size h decreases to zero. In cases where the derivatives of $f(x)$ are known, the formulas

$$E_T(f, h) = \frac{-(b - a) f^{(2)}(c) h^2}{12} \quad \text{and} \quad E_S(f, h) = \frac{-(b - a) f^{(4)}(c) h^4}{180}$$

can be used to estimate the number of subintervals required to achieve a specified accuracy.

Corollary 7.2 (Trapezoidal Rule: Error Analysis). Suppose that $[a, b]$ is subdivided into M subintervals $[x_k, x_{k+1}]$ of width $h = (b - a)/M$. The composite trapezoidal rule

$$(7) \qquad T(f, h) = \frac{h}{2}(f(a) + f(b)) + h \sum_{k=1}^{M-1} f(x_k)$$

is an approximation to the integral

$$(8) \qquad \int_a^b f(x)\, dx = T(f, h) + E_T(f, h).$$

Furthermore, if $f \in C^2[a, b]$, there exists a value c with $a < c < b$ so that the error term $E_T(f, h)$ has the form

$$(9) \qquad E_T(f, h) = \frac{-(b - a) f^{(2)}(c)h^2}{12} = O(h^2).$$

Proof. We first determine the error term when the rule is applied over $[x_0, x_1]$. Integrating the Lagrange polynomial $P_1(x)$ and its remainder yields

$$(10) \qquad \int_{x_0}^{x_1} f(x)\, dx = \int_{x_0}^{x_1} P_1(x)\, dx + \int_{x_0}^{x_1} \frac{(x - x_0)(x - x_1) f^{(2)}(c(x))}{2!}\, dx.$$

The term $(x - x_0)(x - x_1)$ does not change sign on $[x_0, x_1]$, and $f^{(2)}(c(x))$ is continuous. Hence the second mean value theorem for integrals implies that there exists a value c_1 so that

$$(11) \qquad \int_{x_0}^{x_1} f(x)\, dx = \frac{h}{2}(f_0 + f_1) + f^{(2)}(c_1) \int_{x_0}^{x_1} \frac{(x - x_0)(x - x_1)}{2!}\, dx.$$

Use the change of variable $x = x_0 + ht$ in the integral on the right side of (11):

$$(12) \qquad \begin{aligned} \int_{x_0}^{x_1} f(x)\, dx &= \frac{h}{2}(f_0 + f_1) + \frac{f^{(2)}(c_1)}{2} \int_0^1 h(t - 0)h(t - 1)h\, dt \\ &= \frac{h}{2}(f_0 + f_1) + \frac{f^{(2)}(c_1)h^3}{2} \int_0^1 (t^2 - t)\, dt \\ &= \frac{h}{2}(f_0 + f_1) - \frac{f^{(2)}(c_1)h^3}{12}. \end{aligned}$$

Now we are ready to add up the error terms for all of the intervals $[x_k, x_{k+1}]$:

(13)
$$\int_a^b f(x)\,dx = \sum_{k=1}^M \int_{x_{k-1}}^{x_k} f(x)\,dx$$

$$= \sum_{k=1}^M \frac{h}{2}(f(x_{k-1}) + f(x_k)) - \frac{h^3}{12}\sum_{k=1}^M f^{(2)}(c_k).$$

The first sum is the composite trapezoidal rule $T(f, h)$. In the second term, one factor of h is replaced with its equivalent $h = (b - a)/M$, and the result is

$$\int_a^b f(x)\,dx = T(f, h) - \frac{(b-a)h^2}{12}\left(\frac{1}{M}\sum_{k=1}^M f^{(2)}(c_k)\right).$$

The term in parentheses can be recognized as an average of values for the second derivative and hence is replaced by $f^{(2)}(c)$. Therefore, we have established that

$$\int_a^b f(x)\,dx = T(f, h) - \frac{(b-a)f^{(2)}(c)h^2}{12},$$

and the proof of Corollary 7.2 is complete.   ●

Corollary 7.3 (Simpson's Rule: Error Analysis).   Suppose that $[a, b]$ is subdivided into $2M$ subintervals $[x_k, x_{k+1}]$ of equal width $h = (b - a)/(2M)$. The composite Simpson rule

(14) $$S(f, h) = \frac{h}{3}(f(a) + f(b)) + \frac{2h}{3}\sum_{k=1}^{M-1} f(x_{2k}) + \frac{4h}{3}\sum_{k=1}^M f(x_{2k-1})$$

is an approximation to the integral

(15) $$\int_a^b f(x)\,dx = S(f, h) + E_S(f, h).$$

Furthermore, if $f \in C^4[a, b]$, there exists a value c with $a < c < b$ so that the error term $E_S(f, h)$ has the form

(16) $$E_S(f, h) = \frac{-(b-a)f^{(4)}(c)h^4}{180} = O(h^4).$$

Example 7.7.   Consider $f(x) = 2 + \sin(2\sqrt{x})$. Investigate the error when the composite trapezoidal rule is used over $[1, 6]$ and the number of subintervals is 10, 20, 40, 80, and 160.

Table 7.2   Composite Trapezoidal Rule for
$f(x) = 2 + \sin(2\sqrt{x})$ over $[1, 6]$

M	h	$T(f, h)$	$E_T(f, h) = O(h^2)$
10	0.5	8.19385457	−0.01037540
20	0.25	8.18604926	−0.00257006
40	0.125	8.18412019	−0.00064098
80	0.0625	8.18363936	−0.00016015
160	0.03125	8.18351924	−0.00004003

Table 7.2 shows the approximations $T(f, h)$. The antiderivative of $f(x)$ is

$$F(x) = 2x - \sqrt{x}\cos(2\sqrt{x}) + \frac{\sin(2\sqrt{x})}{2},$$

and the true value of the definite integral is

$$\int_1^6 f(x)\, dx = F(x)\Big|_{x=1}^{x=6} = 8.1834792077.$$

This value was used to compute the values $E_T(f, h) = 8.1834792077 - T(f, h)$ in Table 7.2. It is important to observe that when h is reduced by a factor of $\frac{1}{2}$ the successive errors $E_T(f, h)$ are diminished by approximately $\frac{1}{4}$. This confirms that the order is $O(h^2)$.   ∎

Example 7.8.   Consider $f(x) = 2 + \sin(2\sqrt{x})$. Investigate the error when the composite Simpson rule is used over $[1, 6]$ and the number of subintervals is 10, 20, 40, 80, and 160.

Table 7.3 shows the approximations $S(f, h)$. The true value of the integral is 8.1834792077, which was used to compute the values $E_S(f, h) = 8.1834792077 - S(f, h)$ in Table 7.3. It is important to observe that when h is reduced by a factor of $\frac{1}{2}$, the successive errors $E_S(f, h)$ are diminished by approximately $\frac{1}{16}$. This confirms that the order is $O(h^4)$.   ∎

Example 7.9.   Find the number M and the step size h so that the error $E_T(f, h)$ for the composite trapezoidal rule is less than 5×10^{-9} for the approximation $\int_2^7 dx/x \approx T(f, h)$.

The integrand is $f(x) = 1/x$ and its first two derivatives are $f'(x) = -1/x^2$ and $f^{(2)}(x) = 2/x^3$. The maximum value of $|f^{(2)}(x)|$ taken over $[2, 7]$ occurs at the endpoint $x = 2$, and thus we have the bound $|f^{(2)}(c)| \leq |f^{(2)}(2)| = \frac{1}{4}$, for $2 \leq c \leq 7$. This is used with formula (9) to obtain

(17)
$$|E_T(f, h)| = \frac{|-(b-a)f^{(2)}(c)h^2|}{12} \leq \frac{(7-2)\frac{1}{4}h^2}{12} = \frac{5h^2}{48}.$$

Table 7.3   Composite Simpson Rule for
$f(x) = 2 + \sin(2\sqrt{x})$ over $[1, 6]$

M	h	$S(f, h)$	$E_S(f, h) = O(h^4)$
5	0.5	8.18301549	0.00046371
10	0.25	8.18344750	0.00003171
20	0.125	8.18347717	0.00000204
40	0.0625	8.18347908	0.00000013
80	0.03125	8.18347920	0.00000001

The step size h and number M satisfy the relation $h = 5/M$, and this is used in (17) to get the relation

$$(18) \qquad\qquad |E_T(f, h)| \leq \frac{125}{48M^2} \leq 5 \times 10^{-9}.$$

Now rewrite (18) so that it is easier to solve for M:

$$(19) \qquad\qquad \frac{25}{48} \times 10^9 \leq M^2.$$

Solving (19), we find that $22821.77 \leq M$. Since M must be an integer, we choose $M = 22{,}822$, and the corresponding step size is $h = 5/22{,}822 = 0.000219086846$. When the composite trapezoidal rule is implemented with this many function evaluations, there is a possibility that the rounded-off function evaluations will produce a significant amount of error. When the computation was performed, the result was

$$T\left(f, \frac{5}{22{,}822}\right) = 1.252762969,$$

which compares favorably with the true value $\int_2^7 dx/x = \ln(x)|_{x=2}^{x=7} = 1.252762968$. The error is smaller than predicted because the bound $\frac{1}{4}$ for $|f^{(2)}(c)|$ was used. Experimentation shows that it takes about 10,001 function evaluations to achieve the desired accuracy of 5×10^{-9}, and when the calculation is performed with $M = 10{,}000$, the result is

$$T\left(f, \frac{5}{10{,}000}\right) = 1.252762973. \qquad\qquad ■$$

The composite trapezoidal rule usually requires a large number of function evaluations to achieve an accurate answer. This is contrasted in the next example with Simpson's rule, which will require significantly fewer evaluations.

Example 7.10.   Find the number M and the step size h so that the error $E_S(f, h)$ for the composite Simpson rule is less than 5×10^{-9} for the approximation $\int_2^7 dx/x \approx S(f, h)$.

The integrand is $f(x) = 1/x$, and $f^{(4)}(x) = 24/x^5$. The maximum value of $|f^{(4)}(c)|$ taken over $[2, 7]$ occurs at the endpoint $x = 2$, and thus we have the bound

$$|f^{(4)}(c)| \le |f^{(4)}(2)| = \frac{3}{4}$$

for $2 \le c \le 7$. This is used with formula (16) to obtain

$$(20) \qquad |E_S(f, h)| = \frac{|-(b-a)f^{(4)}(c)h^4|}{180} \le \frac{(7-2)\frac{3}{4}h^4}{180} = \frac{h^4}{48}.$$

The step size h and number M satisfy the relation $h = 5/(2M)$, and this is used in (20) to get the relation

$$(21) \qquad |E_S(f, h)| \le \frac{625}{768M^4} \le 5 \times 10^{-9}.$$

Now rewrite (21) so that it is easier to solve for M:

$$(22) \qquad \frac{125}{768} \times 10^9 \le M^4.$$

Solving (22), we find that $112.95 \le M$. Since M must be an integer, we chose $M = 113$, and the corresponding step size is $h = 5/226 = 0.02212389381$. When the composite Simpson rule was performed, the result was

$$S\left(f, \frac{5}{226}\right) = 1.252762969,$$

which agrees with $\int_2^7 dx/x = \ln(x)|_{x=2}^{x=7} = 1.252762968$. Experimentation shows that it takes about 129 function evaluations to achieve the desired accuracy of 5×10^{-9}, and when the calculation is performed with $M = 64$, the result is

$$S\left(f, \frac{5}{128}\right) = 1.252762973. \qquad \blacksquare$$

So we see that the composite Simpson rule using 229 evaluations of $f(x)$ and the composite trapezoidal rule using 22,823 evaluations of $f(x)$ achieve the same accuracy. In Example 7.10, Simpson's rule required about $\frac{1}{100}$ the number of function evaluations.

Program 7.1 (Composite Trapezoidal Rule). To approximate the integral

$$\int_a^b f(x)\, dx \approx \frac{h}{2}(f(a) + f(b)) + h \sum_{k=1}^{M-1} f(x_k)$$

by sampling $f(x)$ at the $M + 1$ equally spaced points $x_k = a + kh$, for $k = 0, 1, 2, \ldots, M$. Notice that $x_0 = a$ and $x_M = b$.

```
function s=traprl(f,a,b,M)

%Input   - f is the integrand input as a string 'f'
%         - a and b are upper and lower limits of integration
%         - M is the number of subintervals
%Output - s is the trapezoidal rule sum
h=(b-a)/M;
s=0;

for k=1:(M-1)
   x=a+h*k;
   s=s+feval(f,x);
end

s=h*(feval(f,a)+feval(f,b))/2+h*s;
```

Program 7.2 (Composite Simpson Rule). To approximate the integral

$$\int_a^b f(x)\, dx \approx \frac{h}{3}(f(a) + f(b)) + \frac{2h}{3} \sum_{k=1}^{M-1} f(x_{2k}) + \frac{4h}{3} \sum_{k=1}^{M} f(x_{2k-1})$$

by sampling $f(x)$ at the $2M + 1$ equally spaced points $x_k = a + kh$, for $k = 0, 1, 2, \ldots, 2M$. Notice that $x_0 = a$ and $x_{2M} = b$.

```
function s=simprl(f,a,b,M)

%Input   - f is the integrand input as a string 'f'
%         - a and b are upper and lower limits of integration
%         - M is the number of subintervals
% Output - s is the Simpson rule sum
h=(b-a)/(2*M);
s1=0;
s2=0;

for k=1:M
   x=a+h*(2*k-1);
   s1=s1+feval(f,x);
end
for k=1:(M-1)
```

```
   x=a+h*2*k;
   s2=s2+feval(f,x);
end
s=h*(feval(f,a)+feval(f,b)+4*s1+2*s2)/3;
```

Exercises for Composite Trapezoidal and Simpson's Rule

1. **(i)** Approximate each integral using the composite trapezoidal rule with $M = 10$.

   (ii) Approximate each integral using the composite Simpson rule with $M = 5$.

   (a) $\int_{-1}^{1} (1 + x^2)^{-1} dx$ **(b)** $\int_{0}^{1} (2 + \sin(2\sqrt{x})) dx$ **(c)** $\int_{0.25}^{4} dx/\sqrt{x}$

   (d) $\int_{0}^{4} x^2 e^{-x} dx$ **(e)** $\int_{0}^{2} 2x \cos(x) dx$ **(f)** $\int_{0}^{\pi} \sin(2x)e^{-x} dx$

2. *Length of a curve.* The arc length of the curve $y = f(x)$ over the interval $a \le x \le b$ is

$$\text{length} = \int_{a}^{b} \sqrt{1 + (f'(x)^2)} \, dx.$$

   (i) Approximate the arc length of each function using the composite trapezoidal rule with $M = 10$.

   (ii) Approximate the arc length of each function using the composite Simpson rule with $M = 5$.

   (a) $f(x) = x^3$ for $0 \le x \le 1$

   (b) $f(x) = \sin(x)$ for $0 \le x \le \pi/4$

   (c) $f(x) = e^{-x}$ for $0 \le x \le 1$

3. *Surface area.* The solid of revolution obtained by rotating the region under the curve $y = f(x)$, where $a \le x \le b$, about the x-axis has surface area given by

$$\text{area} = 2\pi \int_{a}^{b} f(x)\sqrt{1 + (f'(x))^2} \, dx.$$

   (i) Approximate the surface area using the composite trapezoidal rule with $M = 10$.

   (ii) Approximate the surface area using the composite Simpson rule with $M = 5$.

   (a) $f(x) = x^3$ for $0 \le x \le 1$

   (b) $f(x) = \sin(x)$ for $0 \le x \le \pi/4$

   (c) $f(x) = e^{-x}$ for $0 \le x \le 1$

4. (a) Verify that the trapezoidal rule ($M = 1$, $h = 1$) is exact for polynomials of degree ≤ 1 of the form $f(x) = c_1 x + c_0$ over $[0, 1]$.

   (b) Use the integrand $f(x) = c_2 x^2$ and verify that the error term for the trapezoidal rule ($M = 1$, $h = 1$) over the interval $[0, 1]$ is

$$E_T(f, h) = \frac{-(b - a) f^{(2)}(c) h^2}{12}.$$

5. (a) Verify that Simpson's rule ($M = 1$, $h = 1$) is exact for polynomials of degree ≤ 3 of the form $f(x) = c_3 x^3 + c_2 x^2 + c_1 x + c_0$ over $[0, 2]$.

   (b) Use the integrand $f(x) = c_4 x^4$ and verify that the error term for Simpson's rule ($M = 1$, $h = 1$) over the interval $[0, 2]$ is

$$E_S(f, h) = \frac{-(b - a) f^{(4)}(c) h^4}{180}.$$

6. Derive the trapezoidal rule ($M = 1$, $h = 1$) by using the method of undetermined coefficients.

   (a) Find the constants w_0 and w_1 so that $\int_0^1 g(t) \, dt = w_0 g(0) + w_1 g(1)$ is exact for the two functions $g(t) = 1$ and $g(t) = t$.

   (b) Use the relation $f(x_0 + ht) = g(t)$ and the change of variable $x = x_0 + ht$ and $dx = h \, dt$ to translate the trapezoidal rule over $[0, 1]$ to the interval $[x_0, x_1]$.

   Hint for part (a). You will get a linear system involving the two unknowns w_0 and w_1.

7. Derive Simpson's rule ($M = 1$, $h = 1$) by using the method of undetermined coefficients.

   (a) Find the constants w_0, w_1, and w_2 so that $\int_0^2 g(t) \, dt = w_0 g(0) + w_1 g(1) + w_2 g(2)$ is exact for the three functions $g(t) = 1$, $g(t) = t$, and $g(t) = t^2$.

   (b) Use the relation $f(x_0 + ht) = g(t)$ and the change of variable $x = x_0 + ht$ and $dx = h \, dt$ to translate the trapezoidal rule over $[0, 2]$ to the interval $[x_0, x_2]$.

   Hint for part (a). You will get a linear system involving the three unknowns w_0, w_1, and w_2.

8. Determine the number M and the interval width h so that the composite trapezoidal rule for M subintervals can be used to compute the given integral with an accuracy of 5×10^{-9}.

   (a) $\displaystyle\int_{-\pi/6}^{\pi/6} \cos(x) \, dx$ **(b)** $\displaystyle\int_2^3 \frac{1}{5 - x} \, dx$ **(c)** $\displaystyle\int_0^2 x e^{-x} \, dx$

   Hint for part (c). $f^{(2)}(x) = (x - 2)e^{-x}$.

9. Determine the number M and the interval width h so that the composite Simpson rule for $2M$ subintervals can be used to compute the given integral with an accuracy of 5×10^{-9}.

   (a) $\displaystyle\int_{-\pi/6}^{\pi/6} \cos(x) \, dx$ **(b)** $\displaystyle\int_2^3 \frac{1}{5 - x} \, dx$ **(c)** $\displaystyle\int_0^2 x e^{-x} \, dx$

   Hint for part (c). $f^{(4)}(x) = (x - 4)e^{-x}$.

10. Consider the definite integral $\int_{-0.1}^{0.1} \cos(x)\,dx = 2\sin(0.1) = 0.1996668333$. The following table gives approximations using the composite trapezoidal rule. Calculate $E_T(f, h) = 0.199668 - T(f, h)$ and confirm that the order is $O(h^2)$.

M	h	$S(f, h)$	$E_T(f, h) = O(h^2)$
1	0.2	0.1990008	
2	0.1	0.1995004	
4	0.05	0.1996252	
8	0.025	0.1996564	
16	0.0125	0.1996642	

11. Consider the definite integral $\int_{-0.75}^{0.75} \cos(x)\,dx = 2\sin(0.75) = 1.363277520$. The following table gives approximations using the composite Simpson rule. Calculate $E_S(f, h) = 1.3632775 - S(f, h)$ and confirm that the order is $O(h^4)$.

M	h	$S(f, h)$	$E_S(f, h) = O(h^4)$
1	0.75	1.3658444	
2	0.375	1.3634298	
4	0.1875	1.3632869	
8	0.09375	1.3632781	

12. *Midpoint rule.* The midpoint rule on $[x_0, x_1]$ is

$$\int_{x_0}^{x_1} f(x)\,dx = 2hf(x_0 + h) + \frac{h^3}{3} f''(c), \qquad \text{where } h = \frac{x_1 - x_0}{2}.$$

(a) Expand $F(x)$, the antiderivative of $f(x)$, in a Taylor series about $x_0 + h$ and establish the midpoint rule on $[x_0, x_1]$.

(b) Use part (a) and show that the composite midpoint rule for approximating the integral of $f(x)$ over $[a, b]$ is

$$M(f, h) = h \sum_{k=1}^{N} f\left(a + \left(k - \frac{1}{2}\right)h\right), \qquad \text{where } h = \frac{b - a}{N}.$$

This is an approximation to the integral of $f(x)$ over $[a, b]$, and we write

$$\int_a^b f(x)\,dx \approx M(f, h).$$

(c) Show that the error term $E_M(f, h)$ for part (b) is

$$E_M(f, h) = \frac{h^3}{3} \sum_{k=1}^{N} f^{(2)}(c_k) = \frac{(b - a)f^{(2)}(c)h^2}{3} = O(h^2).$$

13. Use the midpoint rule with $M = 10$ to approximate the integrals in Exercise 1.

14. Prove Corollary 7.3.

Algorithms and Programs

1. **(a)** For each integral in Exercise 1, compute M and the interval width h so that the composite trapezoidal rule can be used to compute the given integral with an accuracy of nine decimal places. Use Program 7.1 to approximate each integral.

   (b) For each integral in Exercise 1, compute M and the interval width h so that the composite Simpson's rule can be used to compute the given integral with an accuracy of nine decimal places. Use Program 7.2 to approximate each integral.

2. Use Program 7.2 to approximate the definite integrals in Exercise 2 with an accuracy of 11 decimal places.

3. The composite trapezoidal rule can be adapted to integrate a function known only at a set of points. Adapt Program 7.1 to approximate the integral of a function over an interval $[a, b]$ that passes through M given points. (*Note.* The nodes need not be equally spaced.) Use this program to approximate the integral of a function that passes through the points $\left\{\left(\sqrt{k^2+1}, k^{1/3}\right)\right\}_{k=0}^{13}$.

4. The composite Simpson's rule can be adapted to integrate a function known only at a set of points. Adapt Program 7.2 to approximate the integral of a function over an interval $[a, b]$ that passes through M given points. (*Note.* The nodes need not be equally spaced.) Use this program to approximate the integral of a function that passes through the points $\left\{\left(\sqrt{k^2+1}, k^{1/3}\right)\right\}_{k=0}^{13}$.

5. Modify Program 7.1 so that it uses the composite midpoint rule (Exercise 12) to approximate the integral of $f(x)$ over $[a, b]$. Use this program to approximate the definite integrals in Exercise 1 with an accuracy of 11 decimal places.

6. Obtain approximations to each of the following definite integrals with an accuracy of ten decimal places. Use any of the programs from this section.

   (a) $\displaystyle \int_{1/7\pi}^{1/4\pi} \sin(1/x)\, dx$

   (b) $\displaystyle \int_{1/5\pi+10^{-5}}^{1/4\pi-10^{-5}} \frac{1}{\sin(1/x)}\, dx$

7. The following example shows how Simpson's rule can be used to approximate the solution of an integral equation. The equation $v(x) = x^2 + 0.1 \int_0^1 (x^2+t)v(t)\, dt$ is to be solved using Simpson's rule with $h = 1/2$. Let $t_0 = 0$, $t_1 = 1/2$, and $t_2 = 1$; then

$$\int_0^1 (x^2+t)v(t)\, dt \approx \frac{1/2}{3}\left((x_n^2+0)v_0 + 4\left(x_n^2+\frac{1}{2}\right)v_1 + (x_n^2+1)v_2\right).$$

Let

$$(1) \qquad v(x_n) = x_n^2 + 0.1\left(\frac{1}{6}((x_n^2+0)v_0 + 4\left(x_n^2+\frac{1}{2}\right)v_1 + (x_n^2+1)v_2)\right).$$

Substituting $x_0 = 0$, $x_1 = 1/2$, and $x_2 = 1$ into equation (1) yields the system of linear equations

$$v_0 = 0 + \frac{1}{60}((0)v_0 + 2v_1 + v_2)$$

(2) $$v_1 = \frac{1}{4} + \frac{1}{60}\left(\frac{1}{4}v_0 + 3v_1 + \frac{5}{4}v_2\right)$$

$$v_2 = 1 + \frac{1}{60}(v_0 + 6v_1 + 2v_2)$$

Substituting the solution of system (2) ($v_0 = 0.0273$, $v_1 = 0.2866$, $v_2 = 1.0646$) into equation (1) and simplifying yields the approximation

(3) $$v(x) \approx 1.037305x^2 + 0.027297.$$

(a) As a check, substitute the solution into the right-hand side of the integral equation, integrate and simplify the right-hand side, and compare the result with the approximation in (3).

(b) Use the composite Simpson rule with $h = 0.5$ to approximate the solution of the integral equation

$$v(x) = x^2 + 0.1 \int_0^1 (x^2 + t)v(t)\,dt.$$

Use the procedure outlined in part (a) to check your solution.

7.3 Recursive Rules and Romberg Integration

In this section we show how to compute Simpson approximations with a special linear combination of trapezoidal rules. The approximation will have greater accuracy if one uses a larger number of subintervals. How many should we choose? The sequential process helps answer this question by trying two subintervals, four subintervals, and so on, until the desired accuracy is obtained. First, a sequence $\{T(J)\}$ of trapezoidal rule approximations must be generated. As the number of subintervals is doubled, the number of function values is roughly doubled, because the function must be evaluated at all the previous points and at the midpoints of the previous subintervals (see Figure 7.8). Theorem 7.4 explains how to eliminate redundant function evaluations and additions.

Theorem 7.4 (Successive Trapezoidal Rules). Suppose that $J \geq 1$ and the points $\{x_k = a + kh\}$ subdivide $[a, b]$ into $2^J = 2M$ subintervals of equal width $h = (b - a)/2^J$. The trapezoidal rules $T(f, h)$ and $T(f, 2h)$ obey the relationship

(1) $$T(f, h) = \frac{T(f, 2h)}{2} + h\sum_{k=1}^{M} f(x_{2k-1}).$$

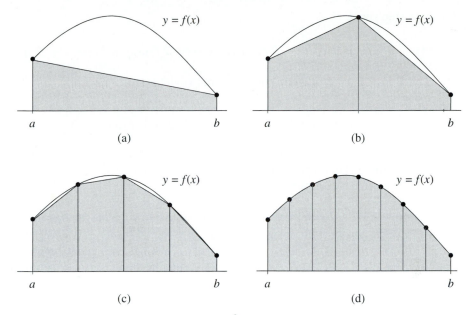

Figure 7.8 (a) $T(0)$ is the area under $2^0 = 1$ trapezoid. (b) $T(1)$ is the area under $2^1 = 2$ trapezoids. (c) $T(2)$ is the area under $2^2 = 4$ trapezoids. (d) $T(3)$ is the area under $2^3 = 8$ trapezoids.

Definition 7.3 (Sequence of Trapezoidal Rules). Define $T(0) = (h/2)(f(a) + f(b))$, which is the trapezoidal rule with step size $h = b - a$. Then for each $J \geq 1$ define $T(J) = T(f, h)$, where $T(f, h)$ is the trapezoidal rule with step size $h = (b - a)/2^J$. ▲

Corollary 7.4 (Recursive Trapezoidal Rule). Start with $T(0) = (h/2)(f(a) + f(b))$. Then a sequence of trapezoidal rules $\{T(J)\}$ is generated by the recursive formula

$$(2) \qquad T(J) = \frac{T(J-1)}{2} + h \sum_{k=1}^{M} f(x_{2k-1}) \qquad \text{for } J = 1,\ 2,\ \ldots,$$

where $h = (b - a)/2^J$ and $\{x_k = a + kh\}$.

Proof. For the even nodes $x_0 < x_2 < \cdots < x_{2M-2} < x_{2M}$, we use the trapezoidal rule with step size $2h$:

$$(3) \qquad T(J-1) = \frac{2h}{2}(f_0 + 2f_2 + 2f_4 + \cdots + 2f_{2M-4} + 2f_{2M-2} + f_{2M}).$$

For all of the nodes $x_0 < x_1 < x_2 < \cdots < x_{2M-1} < x_{2M}$, we use the trapezoidal rule with step size h:

(4) $$T(J) = \frac{h}{2}(f_0 + 2f_1 + 2f_2 + \cdots + 2f_{2M-2} + 2f_{2M-1} + f_{2M}).$$

Collecting the even and odd subscripts in (4) yields

(5) $$T(J) = \frac{h}{2}(f_0 + 2f_2 + \cdots + 2f_{2M-2} + f_{2M}) + h\sum_{k=1}^{M} f_{2k-1}.$$

Substituting (3) into (5) results in $T(J) = T(J-1)/2 + h\sum_{k=1}^{M} f_{2k-1}$, and the proof of the theorem is complete. ●

Example 7.11. Use the sequential trapezoidal rule to compute the approximations $T(0)$, $T(1)$, $T(2)$, and $T(3)$ for the integral $\int_1^5 dx/x = \ln(5) - \ln(1) = 1.609437912$.

Table 7.4 shows the nine values required to compute $T(3)$ and the midpoints required to compute $T(1)$, $T(2)$, and $T(3)$. Details for obtaining the results are as follows:

When $h = 4$: $\quad T(0) = \frac{4}{2}(1.000000 + 0.200000) = 2.400000.$

When $h = 2$: $\quad T(1) = \frac{T(0)}{2} + 2(0.333333)$

$$= 1.200000 + 0.666666 = 1.866666.$$

When $h = 1$: $\quad T(2) = \frac{T(1)}{2} + 1(0.500000 + 0.250000)$

$$= 0.933333 + 0.750000 = 1.683333.$$

When $h = \frac{1}{2}$: $\quad T(3) = \frac{T(2)}{2} + \frac{1}{2}(0.666667 + 0.400000$

$$+ 0.285714 + 0.222222)$$

$$= 0.841667 + 0.787302 = 1.628968. \quad ∎$$

Our next result shows an important relationship between the trapezoidal rule and Simpson's rule. When the trapezoidal rule is computed using step sizes $2h$ and h, the result is $T(f, 2h)$ and $T(f, h)$, respectively. These values are combined to obtain Simpson's rule:

(6) $$S(f, h) = \frac{4T(f, h) - T(f, 2h)}{3}.$$

Theorem 7.5 (Recursive Simpson Rules). Suppose that $\{T(J)\}$ is the sequence of trapezoidal rules generated by Corollary 7.4. If $J \geq 1$ and $S(J)$ is Simpson's rule for 2^J subintervals of $[a, b]$, then $S(J)$ and the trapezoidal rules $T(J-1)$ and $T(J)$ obey the relationship

(7) $$S(J) = \frac{4T(J) - T(J-1)}{3} \quad \text{for } J = 1, 2, \ldots.$$

Table 7.4   The Nine Points Used to Compute $T(3)$ and the Midpoints Required to Compute $T(1)$, $T(2)$, and $T(3)$

x	$f(x) = \dfrac{1}{x}$	Endpoints for computing $T(0)$	Midpoints for computing $T(1)$	Midpoints for computing $T(2)$	Midpoints for computing $T(3)$
1.0	1.000000	1.000000			
1.5	0.666667				0.666667
2.0	0.500000			0.500000	
2.5	0.400000				0.400000
3.0	0.333333		0.333333		
3.5	0.285714				0.285714
4.0	0.250000			0.250000	
4.5	0.222222				0.222222
5.0	0.200000	0.200000			

Proof.   The trapezoidal rule $T(J)$ with step size h yields the approximation

$$
(8) \qquad \int_a^b f(x)\,dx \approx \frac{h}{2}(f_0 + 2f_1 + 2f_2 + \cdots + 2f_{2M-2} + 2f_{2M-1} + f_{2M})
$$
$$
= T(J).
$$

The trapezoidal rule $T(J-1)$ with step size $2h$ produces

$$
(9) \qquad \int_a^b f(x)\,dx \approx h(f_0 + 2f_2 + \cdots + 2f_{2M-2} + f_{2M}) = T(J-1).
$$

Multiplying relation (8) by 4 yields

$$
(10) \qquad 4\int_a^b f(x)\,dx \approx h(2f_0 + 4f_1 + 4f_2 + \cdots + 4f_{2M-2} + 4f_{2M-1} + 2f_M)
$$
$$
= 4T(J).
$$

Now subtract (9) from (10) and the result is

$$
(11) \qquad 3\int_a^b f(x)\,dx \approx h(f_0 + 4f_1 + 2f_2 + \cdots + 2f_{2M-2} + 4f_{2M-1} + f_{2M})
$$
$$
= 4T(J) - T(J-1).
$$

This can be rearranged to obtain

$$
(12) \qquad \int_a^b f(x)\,dx \approx \frac{h}{3}(f_0 + 4f_1 + 2f_2 + \cdots + 2f_{2M-2} + 4f_{2M-1} + f_{2M})
$$
$$
= \frac{4T(J) - T(J-1)}{3}.
$$

The middle term in (12) is Simpson's rule $S(J) = S(f, h)$ and hence the theorem is proved.   ●

Example 7.12. Use the sequential Simpson rule to compute the approximations $S(1)$, $S(2)$, and $S(3)$ for the integral of Example 7.11.

Using the results of Example 7.11 and formula (7) with $J = 1, 2$, and 3, we compute

$$S(1) = \frac{4T(1) - T(0)}{3} = \frac{4(1.866666) - 2.400000}{3} = 1.688888,$$

$$S(2) = \frac{4T(2) - T(1)}{3} = \frac{4(1.683333) - 1.866666}{3} = 1.622222,$$

$$S(3) = \frac{4T(3) - T(2)}{3} = \frac{4(1.628968) - 1.683333}{3} = 1.610846. \qquad \blacksquare$$

In Section 7.1 the formula for Boole's rule was given in Theorem 7.1. It was obtained by integrating the Lagrange polynomial of degree 4 based on the nodes x_0, x_1, x_2, x_3, and x_4. An alternative method for establishing Boole's rule is mentioned in the exercises. When it is applied M times over $4M$ equally spaced subintervals of $[a, b]$ of step size $h = (b - a)/(4M)$, we call it the **composite Boole rule**:

$$(13) \qquad B(f, h) = \frac{2h}{45} \sum_{k=1}^{M} (7 f_{4k-4} + 32 f_{4k-3} + 12 f_{4k-2} + 32 f_{4k-1} + 7 f_{4k}).$$

The next result gives the relationship between the sequential Boole and Simpson rules.

Theorem 7.6 (Recursive Boole Rules). Suppose that $\{S(J)\}$ is the sequence of Simpson's rules generated by Theorem 7.5. If $J \geq 2$ and $B(J)$ is Boole's rule for 2^J subintervals of $[a, b]$, then $B(J)$ and Simpson's rules $S(J - 1)$ and $S(J)$ obey the relationship

$$(14) \qquad B(J) = \frac{16S(J) - S(J - 1)}{15} \qquad \text{for } J = 2, 3, \ldots.$$

Proof. The proof is left as an exercise for the reader. $\qquad \bullet$

Example 7.13. Use the sequential Boole rule to compute the approximations $B(2)$ and $B(3)$ for the integral of Example 7.11.

Using the results of Example 7.12 and formula (14) with $J = 2$ and 3, we compute

$$B(2) = \frac{16S(2) - S(1)}{15} = \frac{16(1.622222) - 1.688888}{15} = 1.617778,$$

$$B(3) = \frac{16S(3) - S(2)}{15} = \frac{16(1.610846) - 1.622222}{15} = 1.610088. \qquad \blacksquare$$

The reader may wonder what we are leading up to. We will now show that formulas (7) and (14) are special cases of the process of Romberg integration. Let us announce that the next level of approximation for the integral of Example 7.11 is

$$\frac{64B(3) - B(2)}{63} = \frac{64(1.610088) - 1.617778}{63} = 1.609490,$$

and this answer gives an accuracy of five decimal places.

Romberg Integration

In Section 7.2 we saw that the error terms $E_T(f, h)$ and $E_S(f, h)$ for the composite trapezoidal rule and composite Simpson rule are of order $O(h^2)$ and $O(h^4)$, respectively. It is not difficult to show that the error term $E_B(f, h)$ for the composite Boole rule is of the order $O(h^6)$. Thus we have the pattern

$$(15) \qquad \int_a^b f(x)\,dx = T(f, h) + O(h^2),$$

$$(16) \qquad \int_a^b f(x)\,dx = S(f, h) + O(h^4),$$

$$(17) \qquad \int_a^b f(x)\,dx = B(f, h) + O(h^6).$$

The pattern for the remainders in (15) through (17) is extended in the following sense. Suppose that an approximation rule is used with step sizes h and $2h$; then an algebraic manipulation of the two answers is used to produce an improved answer. Each successive level of improvement increases the order of the error term from $O(h^{2N})$ to $O(h^{2N+2})$. This process, called ***Romberg integration***, has its strengths and weaknesses.

The Newton-Cotes rules are seldom used past Boole's rule. This is because the nine-point Newton-Cotes quadrature rule involves negative weights, and all the rules past the 10-point rule involve negative weights. This could introduce loss of significance error due to round off. The Romberg method has the advantages that all the weights are positive and the equally spaced abscissas are easy to compute.

A computational weakness of Romberg integration is that twice as many function evaluations are needed to decrease the error from $O(h^{2N})$ to $O(h^{2N+2})$. The use of the sequential rules will help keep the number of computations down. The development of Romberg integration relies on the theoretical assumption that, if $f \in C^N[a, b]$ for all N, then the error term for the trapezoidal rule can be represented in a series involving only even powers of h; that is,

$$(18) \qquad \int_a^b f(x)\,dx = T(f, h) + E_T(f, h),$$

where

$$(19) \qquad E_T(f, h) = a_1 h^2 + a_2 h^4 + a_3 h^6 + \cdots.$$

Since only even powers of h can occur in (19), the Richardson improvement process is used successively first to eliminate a_1, next to eliminate a_2, then to eliminate a_3, and so on. This process generates quadrature formulas whose error terms have even orders $O(h^4)$, $O(h^6)$, $O(h^8)$, and so on. We shall show that the first improvement is Simpson's rule for $2M$ intervals. Start with $T(f, 2h)$ and $T(f, h)$ and the equations

$$(20) \qquad \int_a^b f(x)\,dx = T(f, 2h) + a_1 4h^2 + a_2 16h^4 + a_3 64h^6 + \cdots$$

and

(21)
$$\int_a^b f(x)\,dx = T(f, h) + a_1 h^2 + a_2 h^4 + a_3 h^6 + \cdots .$$

Multiply equation (21) by 4 and obtain

(22)
$$4\int_a^b f(x)\,dx = 4T(f, h) + a_1 4h^2 + a_2 4h^4 + a_3 4h^6 + \cdots .$$

Eliminate a_1 by subtracting (20) from (22). The result is

(23)
$$3\int_a^b f(x)\,dx = 4T(f, h) - T(f, 2h) - a_2 12h^4 - a_3 60h^6 - \cdots .$$

Now divide equation (23) by 3 and rename the coefficients in the series:

(24)
$$\int_a^b f(x)\,dx = \frac{4T(f, h) - T(f, 2h)}{3} + b_1 h^4 + b_2 h^6 + \cdots .$$

As noted in (6), the first quantity on the right side of (24) is Simpson's rule $S(f, h)$. This shows that $E_S(f, h)$ involves only even powers of h:

(25)
$$\int_a^b f(x)\,dx = S(f, h) + b_1 h^4 + b_2 h^6 + b_3 h^8 + \cdots .$$

To show that the second improvement is Boole's rule, start with (25) and write down the formula involving $S(f, 2h)$:

(26)
$$\int_a^b f(x)\,dx = S(f, 2h) + b_1 16h^4 + b_2 64h^6 + b_3 256h^8 + \cdots .$$

When b_1 is eliminated from (25) and (26), the result involves Boole's rule:

(27)
$$\int_a^b f(x)\,dx = \frac{16S(f, h) - S(f, 2h)}{15} - \frac{b_2 48h^6}{15} - \frac{b_3 240h^8}{15} - \cdots$$
$$= B(f, h) - \frac{b_2 48h^6}{15} - \frac{b_3 240h^8}{15} - \cdots .$$

The general pattern for Romberg integration relies on Lemma 7.1.

Lemma 7.1 (Richardson's Improvement for Romberg Integration).   Given two approximations $R(2h, K - 1)$ and $R(h, K - 1)$ for the quantity Q that satisfy

$$(28) \qquad Q = R(h, K - 1) + c_1 h^{2K} + c_2 h^{2K+2} + \cdots$$

and

$$(29) \qquad Q = R(2h, K - 1) + c_1 4^K h^{2K} + c_2 4^{K+1} h^{2K+2} + \cdots,$$

an improved approximation has the form

$$(30) \qquad Q = \frac{4^K R(h, K - 1) - R(2h, K - 1)}{4^K - 1} + O(h^{2K+2}).$$

Proof.   The proof is straightforward and is left for the reader.   ●

Definition 7.4.   Define the sequence $\{R(J, K) : J \geq K\}_{J=0}^{\infty}$ of quadrature formulas for $f(x)$ over $[a, b]$ as follows:

$$(31) \qquad
\begin{aligned}
R(J, 0) &= T(J) &\qquad &\text{for } J \geq 0, \text{ is the sequential trapezoidal rule.} \\
R(J, 1) &= S(J) &\qquad &\text{for } J \geq 1, \text{ is the sequential Simpson rule.} \\
R(J, 2) &= B(J) &\qquad &\text{for } J \geq 2, \text{ is the sequential Boole's rule.}
\end{aligned}
\qquad ▲$$

The starting rules, $\{R(J, 0)\}$, are used to generate the first improvement, $\{R(J, 1)\}$, which in turn is used to generate the second improvement, $\{R(J, 2)\}$. We have already seen the patterns

$$(32) \qquad
\begin{aligned}
R(J, 1) &= \frac{4^1 R(J, 0) - R(J - 1, 0)}{4^1 - 1} &\qquad &\text{for } J \geq 1 \\
R(J, 2) &= \frac{4^2 R(J, 1) - R(J - 1, 1)}{4^2 - 1} &\qquad &\text{for } J \geq 2,
\end{aligned}$$

which are the rules in (24) and (27) stated using the notation in (31). The general rule for constructing improvements is

$$(33) \qquad R(J, K) = \frac{4^K R(J, K - 1) - R(J - 1, K - 1)}{4^K - 1} \qquad \text{for } J \geq K.$$

Table 7.5 Romberg Integration Tableau

J	$R(J, 0)$ Trapezoidal rule	$R(J, 1)$ Simpson's rule	$R(J, 2)$ Boole's rule	$R(J, 3)$ Third improvement	$R(J, 4)$ Fourth improvement
0	$R(0, 0)$				
1	$R(1, 0)$	$R(1, 1)$			
2	$R(2, 0)$	$R(2, 1)$	$R(2, 2)$		
3	$R(3, 0)$	$R(3, 1)$	$R(3, 2)$	$R(3, 3)$	
4	$R(4, 0)$	$R(4, 1)$	$R(4, 2)$	$R(4, 3)$	$R(4, 4)$

Table 7.6 Romberg Integration Tableau for Example 7.14

J	$R(J, 0)$ Trapezoidal rule	$R(J, 1)$ Simpson's rule	$R(J, 2)$ Boole's rule	$R(J, 3)$ Third improvement
0	0.785398163397			
1	1.726812656758	2.040617487878		
2	1.960534166564	2.038441336499	2.038296259740	
3	2.018793948078	2.038213875249	2.038198711166	2.038197162776
4	2.033347341805	2.038198473047	2.038197446234	2.038197426156
5	2.036984954990	2.038197492719	2.038197427363	2.038197427064

For computational purposes, the values $R(J, K)$ are arranged in the Romberg integration tableau given in Table 7.5.

Example 7.14. Use Romberg integration to find approximations for the definite integral

$$\int_0^{\pi/2} (x^2 + x + 1) \cos(x) \, dx = -2 + \frac{\pi}{2} + \frac{\pi^2}{4} = 2.038197427067 \ldots .$$

The computations are given in Table 7.6. In each column the numbers are converging to the value $2.038197427067 \ldots$. The values in the Simpson's rule column converge faster than the values in the trapezoidal rule column. For this example, convergence in columns to the right is faster than the adjacent column to the left.

Convergence of the Romberg values in Table 7.6 is easier to see if we look at the error terms $E(J, K) = -2 + \pi/2 + \pi^2/4 - R(J, K)$. Suppose that the interval width is $h = b - a$ and that the higher derivatives of $f(x)$ are of the same magnitude. The error in column K of the Romberg table diminishes by about a factor of $1/2^{2K+2} = 1/4^{K+1}$ as one progresses down its rows. The errors $E(J, 0)$ diminish by a factor of $1/4$, the errors $E(J, 1)$ diminish by a factor of $1/16$, and so on. This can be observed by inspecting the entries $\{E(J, K)\}$ in Table 7.7. ∎

Table 7.7 Romberg Error Tableau for Example 7.14

J	h	$E(J, 0) = O(h^2)$	$E(J, 1) = O(h^4)$	$E(J, 2) = O(h^6)$	$E(J, 3) = O(h^8)$
0	$b - a$	-1.252799263670			
1	$\dfrac{b-a}{2}$	-0.311384770309	0.002420060811		
2	$\dfrac{b-a}{4}$	-0.077663260503	0.000243909432	0.000098832673	
3	$\dfrac{b-a}{8}$	-0.019403478989	0.000016448182	0.000001284099	-0.000000264291
4	$\dfrac{b-a}{16}$	-0.004850085262	0.000001045980	0.000000019167	-0.000000000912
5	$\dfrac{b-a}{32}$	-0.001212472077	0.000000065651	0.000000000296	-0.000000000003

Theorem 7.7 (Precision of Romberg Integration). Assume that $f \in C^{2K+2}[a, b]$. Then the truncation error term for the Romberg approximation is given in the formula

$$(34) \qquad \int_a^b f(x)\, dx = R(J, K) + b_K h^{2K+2} f^{(2K+2)}(c_{J,K})$$

$$= R(J, K) + O(h^{2K+2}),$$

where $h = (b - a)/2^J$, b_K is a constant that depends on K, and $c_{J,K} \in [a, b]$.

Example 7.15. Apply Theorem 7.7 and show that

$$\int_0^2 10x^9\, dx = 1024 \equiv R(4, 4).$$

The integrand is $f(x) = 10x^9$, and $f^{(10)}(x) \equiv 0$. Thus the value $K = 4$ will make the error term identically zero. A numerical computation will produce $R(4, 4) = 1024$. ∎

Program 7.3 (Recursive Trapezoidal Rule). To approximate

$$\int_a^b f(x)\, dx \approx \frac{h}{2} \sum_{k=1}^{2^J} (f(x_{k-1}) + f(x_k))$$

by using the trapezoidal rule and successively increasing the number of subintervals of $[a, b]$. The Jth iteration samples $f(x)$ at $2^J + 1$ equally spaced points.

```
function T=rctrap(f,a,b,n)
%Input   - f is the integrand input as a string 'f'
%         - a and b are upper and lower limits of integration
%         - n is the number of times for recursion
```

```
%Output - T is the recursive trapezoidal rule list
M=1;
h=b-a;
T=zeros(1,n+1);
T(1)=h*(feval(f,a)+feval(f,b))/2;
for j=1:n
   M=2*M;
   h=h/2;
   s=0;
   for k=1:M/2
      x=a+h*(2*k-1);
      s=s+feval(f,x);
   end
   T(j+1)=T(j)/2+h*s;
end
```

Program 7.4 (Romberg Integration). To approximate the integral

$$\int_a^b f(x)\,dx \approx R(J, J)$$

by generating a table of approximations $R(J, K)$ for $J \geq K$ and using $R(J + 1, J + 1)$ as the final answer. The approximations $R(J, K)$ are stored in a special lower-triangular matrix. The elements $R(J, 0)$ of column 0 are computed using the sequential trapezoidal rule based on 2^J subintervals of $[a, b]$; then $R(J, K)$ is computed using Romberg's rule. The elements of row J are

$$R(J, K) = R(J, K - 1) + \frac{R(J, K - 1) - R(J - 1, K - 1)}{4^K - 1},$$

for $1 \leq K \leq J$. The program is terminated in the $(J + 1)$st row when $|R(J, J) - R(J + 1, J + 1)| < \text{tol}$.

```
function [R,quad,err,h]=romber(f,a,b,n,tol)

%Input  - f is the integrand input as a string 'f'
%         - a and b are upper and lower limits of integration
%         - n is the maximum number of rows in the table
%         - tol is the tolerance
%Output - R is the Romberg table
%         - quad is the quadrature value
%         - err is the error estimate
%         - h is the smallest step size used

M=1;
```

```
h=b-a;
err=1;
J=0;
R=zeros(4,4);
R(1,1)=h*(feval(f,a)+feval(f,b))/2;
while((err>tol)&(J<n))|(J<4)
    J=J+1;
    h=h/2;
    s=0;
    for p=1:M
        x=a+h*(2*p-1);
        s=s+feval(f,x);
    end
    R(J+1,1)=R(J,1)/2+h*s;
    M=2*M;
    for K=1:J
        R(J+1,K+1)=R(J+1,K)+(R(J+1,K)-R(J,K))/(4^K-1);
    end
    err=abs(R(J,J)-R(J+1,K+1));
end
quad=R(J+1,J+1);
```

Exercises for Recursive Rules and Romberg Integration

1. For each of the following definite integrals, construct (by hand) a Romberg table (Table 7.5) with three rows.

   (a) $\displaystyle\int_0^3 \frac{\sin(2x)}{1+x^2}\, dx = 0.4761463020\ldots$

   (b) $\displaystyle\int_0^3 \sin(4x)e^{-2x}\, dx = 0.1997146621\ldots$

   (c) $\displaystyle\int_{0.04}^1 \frac{1}{\sqrt{x}}\, dx = 1.6$

   (d) $\displaystyle\int_0^2 \frac{1}{x^2 + \frac{1}{10}}\, dx = 4.4713993943\ldots$

   (e) $\displaystyle\int_{1/(2\pi)}^2 \sin\left(\frac{1}{x}\right)\, dx = 1.1140744942\ldots$

   (f) $\displaystyle\int_0^2 \sqrt{4-x^2}\, dx = \pi = 3.1415926535\ldots$

2. Assume that the sequential trapezoidal rule converges to L (i.e., $\lim_{J \to \infty} T(J) = L$).
   (a) Show that the sequential Simpson rule converges to L (i.e., $\lim_{J \to \infty} S(J) = L$).
   (b) Show that the sequential Boole rule converges to L (i.e., $\lim_{J \to \infty} B(J) = L$).

3. (a) Verify that Boole's rule ($M = 1, h = 1$) is exact for polynomials of degree ≤ 5 of the form $f(x) = c_5 x^5 + c_4 x^4 + \cdots + c_1 x + c_0$ over $[0, 4]$.
   (b) Use the integrand $f(x) = c_6 x^6$ and verify that the error term for Boole's rule ($M = 1, h = 1$) over the interval $[0, 4]$ is

$$E_B(f, h) = \frac{-2(b - a) f^{(6)}(c) h^6}{945}.$$

4. Derive Boole's rule ($M = 1, h = 1$) by using the method of undetermined coefficients: Find the constants w_0, w_1, w_2, w_3, and w_4 so that

$$\int_0^4 g(t) \, dt = w_0 g(0) + w_1 g(1) + w_2 g(2) + w_3 g(3) + w_4 g(4)$$

is exact for the five functions $g(t) = 1, t, t^2, t^3$, and t^4. *Hint.* You will get the linear system

$$
\begin{aligned}
w_0 + w_1 + w_2 + w_3 + w_4 &= 4 \\
w_1 + 2w_2 + 3w_3 + 4w_4 &= 8 \\
w_1 + 4w_2 + 9w_3 + 16w_4 &= \frac{64}{3} \\
w_1 + 8w_2 + 27w_3 + 64w_4 &= 64 \\
w_1 + 16w_2 + 81w_3 + 256w_4 &= \frac{1024}{5}.
\end{aligned}
$$

5. Establish the relation $B(J) = (16S(J) - S(J - 1))/15$ for the case $J = 2$. Use the following information:

$$S(1) = \frac{2h}{3}(f_0 + 4f_2 + f_4)$$

and

$$S(2) = \frac{h}{3}(f_0 + 4f_1 + 2f_2 + 4f_3 + f_4).$$

6. *Simpson's $\frac{3}{8}$ rule.* Consider the trapezoidal rules over the closed interval $[x_0, x_3]$: $T(f, 3h) = (3h/2)(f_0 + f_3)$ with step size $3h$, and $T(f, h) = (h/2)(f_0 + 2f_1 + 2f_2 + f_3)$ with step size h. Show that the linear combination $(9T(f, h) - T(f, 3h))/8$ produces Simpson's-$\frac{3}{8}$ rule.

7. Use equations (25) and (26) to establish equation (27).

8. Use equations (28) and (29) to establish equation (30).

9. Determine the smallest integer K for which

    (a) $\int_0^2 8x^7 \, dx = 256 \equiv R(K, K)$.

    (b) $\int_0^2 11x^{10} \, dx = 2048 \equiv R(K, K)$.

10. Romberg integration was used to approximate the integrals **(i)** $\int_0^1 \sqrt{x} \, dx$ and **(ii)** $\int_0^1 2t^2 \, dt$, and the results are given in the following table:

Approximations for (i)	Approximations for (ii)
$R(0, 0) = 0.5000000$	$R(0, 0) = 1.0000000$
$R(1, 1) = 0.6380712$	$R(1, 1) = 0.6666667$
$R(2, 2) = 0.6577566$	$R(2, 2) = 0.6666667$
$R(3, 3) = 0.6636076$	$R(3, 3) = 0.6666667$
$R(4, 4) = 0.6655929$	$R(4, 4) = 0.6666667$

    (a)   Use the change of variable $x = t^2$ and $dx = 2t \, dt$ and show that the two integrals have the same numerical value.

    (b)   Discuss why convergence of the Romberg sequence is slower for integral (i) and faster for integral (ii).

11. *Romberg integration based on the midpoint rule.* The composite midpoint rule is competitive with the composite trapezoidal rule with respect to efficiency and the speed of convergence. Use the following facts about the midpoint rule: $\int_a^b f(x) \, dx = M(f, h) + E_M(f, h)$. The rule $M(f, h)$ and the error term $E_M(f, h)$ are given by

$$M(f, h) = h \sum_{k=1}^{N} f\left(a + \left(k - \frac{1}{2}\right)h\right), \qquad \text{where } h = \frac{b - a}{N},$$

and

$$E_M(f, h) = a_1 h^2 + a_2 h^4 + a_3 h^6 + \cdots .$$

    (a)   Start with

$$M(0) = (b - a) f\left(\frac{a + b}{2}\right).$$

    Develop the sequential midpoint rule for computing

$$M(J) = M(f, h_J) = h_J \sum_{k=1}^{2^J} f\left(a + \left(k - \frac{1}{2}\right)h_J\right),$$

    where $h_J = \dfrac{b - a}{2^J}$.

    (b)   Show how the sequential midpoint rule can be used in place of the sequential trapezoidal rule in Romberg integration.

Algorithms and Programs

1. Use Program 7.4 to approximate the definite integrals in Exercise 1 with an accuracy of 11 decimal places.

2. Use Program 7.4 to approximate the following two definite integrals with an accuracy of 10 decimal places. The exact value of each definite integral is π. Explain any apparent differences in the rates of convergence of the two Romberg sequences.

   (a) $\displaystyle\int_0^2 \sqrt{4x - x^2}\, dx$

   (b) $\displaystyle\int_0^1 \frac{4}{1 + x^2}\, dx$

3. The normal probability density function is $f(t) = (1/\sqrt{2\pi})e^{-t^2/2}$, and the cumulative distribution is a function defined by $\Phi(x) = \frac{1}{2} + (1/\sqrt{2\pi}) \int_0^x e^{-t^2/2}\, dt$. Compute values for $\Phi(0.5)$, $\Phi(1.0)$, $\Phi(1.5)$, $\Phi(2.0)$, $\Phi(2.5)$, $\Phi(3.0)$, $\Phi(3.5)$, and $\Phi(4.0)$ that have eight digits of accuracy.

4. Modify Program 7.3 so that it will stop when consecutive values $T(K-1)$ and $T(K)$ for the sequential trapezoidal rule differ by less than 5×10^{-6}.

5. Modify Program 7.3 so that it will also compute values for the sequential Simpson and Boole rules.

6. Modify Program 7.4 so that it uses the sequential midpoint rule to perform Romberg integration (use the results of Exercise 11). Use your program to approximate the following integrals with an accuracy of 10 decimal places.

   (a) $\displaystyle\int_0^1 \frac{\sin(x)}{x}\, dx$

   (b) $\displaystyle\int_{-1}^1 \sqrt{1 - x^2}\, dx$

7. In Program 7.4 the approximations to a given definite integral are stored on the main diagonal of a lower-triangular matrix. Modify Program 7.4 so that the rows of the Romberg integration tableau are sequentially computed and stored in a $n \times 1$ matrix R; hence it saves space. Test your program on the integrals in Exercise 1.

7.4   Adaptive Quadrature

The composite quadrature rules necessitate the use of equally spaced points. Typically, a small step size h was used uniformly across the entire interval of integration to ensure the overall accuracy. This does not take into account that some portions of the curve may have large functional variations that require more attention than other portions of the curve. It is useful to introduce a method that adjusts the step size to be smaller over portions of the curve where a larger functional variation occurs. This technique is called **adaptive quadrature**. The method is based on Simpson's rule.

Simpson's rule uses two subintervals over $[a_k, b_k]$:

(1)
$$S(a_k, b_k) = \frac{h}{3}(f(a_k) + 4f(c_k) + f(b_k)),$$

where $c_k = \frac{1}{2}(a_k + b_k)$ is the center of $[a_k, b_k]$ and $h = (b_k - a_k)/2$. Furthermore, if $f \in C^4[a_k, b_k]$, then there exists a value $d_1 \in [a_k, b_k]$ so that

$$(2) \qquad \int_{a_k}^{b_k} f(x)\, dx = S(a_k, b_k) - h^5 \frac{f^{(4)}(d_1)}{90}.$$

Refinement

A composite Simpson rule using four subintervals of $[a_k, b_k]$ can be performed by bisecting this interval into two equal subintervals $[a_{k1}, b_{k1}]$ and $[a_{k2}, b_{k2}]$ and applying formula (1) recursively over each piece. Only two additional evaluations of $f(x)$ are needed, and the result is

$$(3) \qquad
\begin{aligned}
S(a_{k1}, b_{k1}) + S(a_{k2}, b_{k2}) &= \frac{h}{6}(f(a_{k1}) + 4f(c_{k1}) + f(b_{k1})) \\
&\quad + \frac{h}{6}(f(a_{k2}) + 4f(c_{k2}) + f(b_{k2})),
\end{aligned}$$

where $a_{k1} = a_k$, $b_{k1} = a_{k2} = c_k$, $b_{k2} = b_k$, c_{k1} is the midpoint of $[a_{k1}, b_{k1}]$, and c_{k2} is the midpoint of $[a_{k2}, b_{k2}]$. In formula (3) the step size is $h/2$, which accounts for the factors $h/6$ on the right side of the equation. Furthermore, if $f \in C^4[a, b]$, there exists a value $d_2 \in [a_k, b_k]$ so that

$$(4) \qquad \int_{a_k}^{b_k} f(x)\, dx = S(a_{k1}, b_{k1}) + S(a_{k2}, b_{k2}) - \frac{h^5}{16}\frac{f^{(4)}(d_2)}{90}.$$

Assume that $f^{(4)}(d_1) \approx f^{(4)}(d_2)$; then the right sides of equations (2) and (4) are used to obtain the relation

$$(5) \qquad S(a_k, b_k) - h^5 \frac{f^{(4)}(d_2)}{90} \approx S(a_{k1}, b_{k1}) + S(a_{k2}, b_{k2}) - \frac{h^5}{16}\frac{f^{(4)}(d_2)}{90},$$

which can be written as

$$(6) \qquad -h^5 \frac{f^{(4)}(d_2)}{90} \approx \frac{16}{15}(S(a_{k1}, b_{k1}) + S(a_{k2}, b_{k2}) - S(a_k, b_k)).$$

Then (6) is substituted in (4) to obtain the error estimate:

$$(7) \qquad
\begin{aligned}
&\left| \int_{a_k}^{b_k} f(x)\, dx - S(a_{k1}, b_{k1}) - S(a_{k2}, b_{k2}) \right| \\
&\qquad \approx \frac{1}{15}|S(a_{k1}, b_{k1}) + S(a_{k2}, b_{k2}) - S(a_k, b_k)|.
\end{aligned}$$

Because of the assumption $f^{(4)}(d_1) \approx f^{(4)}(d_2)$, the fraction $\frac{1}{15}$ is replaced with $\frac{1}{10}$ on the right side of (7) when implementing the method. This justifies the following test.

Accuracy Test

Assume that the tolerance $\epsilon_k > 0$ is specified for the interval $[a_k, b_k]$. If

$$(8) \qquad \frac{1}{10} |S(a_{k1}, b_{k1}) + S(a_{k2}, b_{k2}) - S(a_k, b_k)| < \epsilon_k,$$

we infer that

$$(9) \qquad \left| \int_{a_k}^{b_k} f(x)\, dx - S(a_{k1}, b_{k1}) - S(a_{k2}, b_{k2}) \right| < \epsilon_k.$$

Thus the composite Simpson rule (3) is used to approximate the integral

$$(10) \qquad \int_{a_k}^{b_k} f(x)\, dx \approx S(a_{k1}, b_{k1}) + S(a_{k2}, b_{k2}),$$

and the error bound for this approximation over $[a_k, b_k]$ is ϵ_k.

Adaptive quadrature is implemented by applying Simpson's rules (1) and (3). Start with $\{[a_0, b_0], \epsilon_0\}$, where ϵ_0 is the tolerance for numerical quadrature over $[a_0, b_0]$. The interval is refined into subintervals labeled $[a_{01}, b_{01}]$ and $[a_{02}, b_{02}]$. If the accuracy test (8) is passed, quadrature formula (3) is applied to $[a_0, b_0]$ and we are done. If the test in (8) fails, the two subintervals are relabeled $[a_1, b_1]$ and $[a_2, b_2]$, over which we use the tolerances $\epsilon_1 = \frac{1}{2}\epsilon_0$ and $\epsilon_2 = \frac{1}{2}\epsilon_0$, respectively. Thus we have two intervals with their associated tolerances to consider for further refinement and testing: $\{[a_1, b_1], \epsilon_1\}$ and $\{[a_2, b_2], \epsilon_2\}$, where $\epsilon_1 + \epsilon_2 = \epsilon_0$. If adaptive quadrature must be continued, the smaller intervals must be refined and tested, each with its own associated tolerance.

In the second step we first consider $\{[a_1, b_1], \epsilon_1\}$ and refine the interval $[a_1, b_1]$ into $[a_{11}, b_{11}]$ and $[a_{12}, b_{12}]$. If they pass the accuracy test (8) with the tolerance ϵ_1, quadrature formula (3) is applied to $[a_1, b_1]$ and accuracy has been achieved over this interval. If they fail the test in (8) with the tolerance ϵ_1, each subinterval $[a_{11}, b_{11}]$ and $[a_{12}, b_{12}]$ must be refined and tested in the third step with the reduced tolerance $\frac{1}{2}\epsilon_1$. Moreover, the second step involves looking at $\{[a_2, b_2], \epsilon_2\}$ and refining $[a_2, b_2]$ into $[a_{21}, b_{21}]$ and $[a_{22}, b_{22}]$. If they pass the accuracy test (8) with tolerance ϵ_2, quadrature formula (3) is applied to $[a_2, b_2]$ and accuracy is achieved over this interval. If they fail the test in (8) with the tolerance ϵ_2, each subinterval $[a_{21}, b_{21}]$ and $[a_{22}, b_{22}]$ must be refined and tested in the third step with the reduced tolerance $\frac{1}{2}\epsilon_2$. Therefore, the second step produces either three or four intervals, which we relabel consecutively. The three intervals would be relabeled to produce $\{\{[a_1, b_1], \epsilon_1\}, \{[a_2, b_2], \epsilon_2\}, \{[a_3, b_3], \epsilon_3\}\}$, where $\epsilon_1 + \epsilon_2 + \epsilon_3 = \epsilon_0$. In the case of four intervals, we would obtain $\{\{[a_1, b_1], \epsilon_1\}, \{[a_2, b_2], \epsilon_2\}, \{[a_3, b_3], \epsilon_3\}, \{[a_4, b_4], \epsilon_4\}\}$, where $\epsilon_1 + \epsilon_2 + \epsilon_3 + \epsilon_4 = \epsilon_0$.

If adaptive quadrature must be continued, the smaller intervals must be tested, each with its own associated tolerance. The error term in (4) shows that each time a refinement is made over a smaller subinterval there is a reduction of error by about

Table 7.8   Adaptive Quadrature Computations for $f(x) = 13(x - x^2)e^{-3x/2}$

a_k	b_k	$S(a_{k1}, b_{k1}) + S(a_{k2}, b_{k2})$	Error bound on the left side of (8)	Tolerance ϵ_k for $[a_k, b_k]$
0.0	0.0625	0.02287184840	0.00000001522	0.00000015625
0.0625	0.125	0.05948686456	0.00000001316	0.00000015625
0.125	0.1875	0.08434213630	0.00000001137	0.00000015625
0.1875	0.25	0.09969871532	0.00000000981	0.00000015625
0.25	0.375	0.21672136781	0.00000025055	0.0000003125
0.375	0.5	0.20646391592	0.00000018402	0.0000003125
0.5	0.625	0.17150617231	0.00000013381	0.0000003125
0.625	0.75	0.12433363793	0.00000009611	0.0000003125
0.75	0.875	0.07324515141	0.00000006799	0.0000003125
0.875	1.0	0.02352883215	0.00000004718	0.0000003125
1.0	1.125	−0.02166038952	0.00000003192	0.0000003125
1.125	1.25	−0.06065079384	0.00000002084	0.0000003125
1.25	1.5	−0.21080823822	0.00000031714	0.000000625
1.5	2.0	−0.60550965007	0.00000003195	0.00000125
2.0	2.25	−0.31985720175	0.00000008106	0.000000625
2.25	2.5	−0.30061749228	0.00000008301	0.000000625
2.5	2.75	−0.27009962412	0.00000007071	0.000000625
2.75	3.0	−0.23474721177	0.00000005447	0.000000625
3.0	3.5	−0.36389799695	0.00000103699	0.00000125
3.5	4.0	−0.24313827772	0.00000041708	0.00000125
	Totals	−1.54878823413	0.00000296809	0.00001

a factor of $\frac{1}{16}$. Thus the process will terminate after a finite number of steps. The bookkeeping for implementing the method includes a sentinel variable which indicates if a particular subinterval has passed its accuracy test. To avoid unnecessary additional evaluations of $f(x)$, the function values can be included in a data list corresponding to each subinterval. The details are shown in Program 7.6.

Example 7.16.   Use adaptive quadrature to numerically approximate the value of the definite integral $\int_0^4 13(x - x^2)e^{-3x/2} \, dx$ with the starting tolerance $\epsilon_0 = 0.00001$.

Implementation of the method revealed that 20 subintervals are needed. Table 7.8 lists each interval $[a_k, b_k]$, composite Simpson rule $S(a_{k1}, b_{k1}) + S(a_{k2}, b_{k2})$, the error bound for this approximation, and the associated tolerance ϵ_k. The approximate value of the integral is obtained by summing the Simpson rule approximations to get

$$(11) \qquad \int_0^4 13(x - x^2)e^{-3x/2} \, dx \approx -1.54878823413.$$

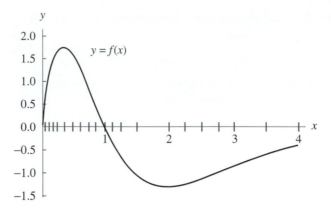

Figure 7.9 The subintervals of $[0, 4]$ used in adaptive quadrature.

The true value of the integral is

(12)
$$\int_0^4 13(x - x^2)e^{-3x/2}\, dx = \frac{4108e^{-6} - 52}{27}$$
$$= -1.5487883725279481333.$$

Therefore, the error for adaptive quadrature is

(13) $|-1.54878837253 - (-1.54878823413)| = 0.00000013840,$

which is smaller than the specified tolerance $\epsilon_0 = 0.00001$. The adaptive method involves 20 subintervals of $[0, 4]$, and 81 function evaluations were used. Figure 7.9 shows the graph of $y = f(x)$ and these 20 subintervals. The intervals are smaller where a larger functional variation occurs near the origin.

In the refinement and testing process in the adaptive method, the first four intervals of width 0.25 were bisected into eight subintervals of width 0.03125. If this uniform spacing is continued throughout the interval $[0, 4]$, $M = 128$ subintervals are required for the composite Simpson rule, which yields the approximation -1.54878844029, which is in error by the amount 0.00000006776. Although the composite Simpson method contains half the error of the adaptive quadrature method, 176 more function evaluations are required. This gain of accuracy is negligible; hence there is a considerable saving of computing effort with the adaptive method.   ■

Program 7.5, `srule`, is a modification of Simpson's rule from Section 7.1. The output is a vector Z that contains the results of Simpson's rule on the interval $[a0, b0]$. Program 7.6 calls `srule` as a subroutine to carry out Simpson's rule on each of the subintervals generated by the adaptive quadrature process.

Program 7.5 (Simpson's Rule). To approximate the integral

$$\int_{a0}^{b0} f(x)\, dx \approx \frac{h}{3}(f(a0) + 4f(c0) + f(b0))$$

by using Simpson's rule, where $c0 = (a0 + b0)/2$.

```
function Z=srule(f,a0,b0,tol0)
%Input   - f is the integrand input as a string 'f'
%         - a0 and b0 are upper and lower limits of integration
%         - tol0 is the tolerance
% Output - Z is a 1x6 vector [a0 b0 S S2 err tol1]
h=(b0-a0)/2;
C=zeros(1,3);
C=feval(f,[a0 (a0+b0)/2 b0]);
S=h*(C(1)+4*C(2)+C(3))/3;
S2=S;
tol1=tol0;
err=tol0;
Z=[a0 b0 S S2 err tol1];
```

Program 7.6 produces a matrix SRmat, quad (adaptive quadrature approximation to definite integral) and err (the error bound for the approximation). The rows of SRmat consist of the endpoints, the Simpson's rule approximation, and the error bound on each subinterval generated by the adaptive quadrature process.

Program 7.6 (Adaptive Quadrature Using Simpson's Rule). To approximate the integral

$$\int_{a}^{b} f(x)\, dx \approx \sum_{k=1}^{M}(f(x_{4k-4}) + 4f(x_{4k-3}) + 2f(x_{4k-2})$$

$$+ 4f(x_{4k-1}) + f(x_{4k})).$$

The composite Simpson rule is applied to the $4M$ subintervals $[x_{4k-4}, x_{4k}]$, where $[a, b] = [x_0, x_{4M}]$ and $x_{4k-4+j} = x_{4k-4} + jh_k$, for each $k = 1, \ldots, M$ and $j = 1, \ldots, 4$.

```
function [SRmat,quad,err]=adapt(f,a,b,tol)
%Input   - f is the integrand input as a string 'f'
%         - a and b are upper and lower limits of integration
%         - tol is the tolerance
%Output  - SRmat is the table of values
%         - quad is the quadrature value
```

```
%         - err is the error estimate
%Initialize values
SRmat = zeros(30,6);
iterating=0;
done=1;
SRvec=zeros(1,6);
SRvec=srule(f,a,b,tol);
SRmat(1,1:6)=SRvec;
m=1;
state=iterating;

while(state==iterating)
   n=m;
   for j=n:-1:1
      p=j;
      SR0vec=SRmat(p,:);
      err=SR0vec(5);
      tol=SR0vec(6);
      if (tol<=err)
         %Bisect interval,apply Simpson's rule
         %recursively, and determine error
         state=done;
         SR1vec=SR0vec;
         SR2vec=SR0vec;
         a=SR0vec(1);
         b=SR0vec(2);
         c=(a+b)/2;
         err=SR0vec(5);
         tol=SR0vec(6);
         tol2=tol/2;
         SR1vec=srule(f,a,c,tol2);
         SR2vec=srule(f,c,b,tol2);
         err=abs(SR0vec(3)-SR1vec(3)-SR2vec(3))/10;

         %Accuracy test
         if (err<tol)
            SRmat(p,:)=SR0vec;
            SRmat(p,4)=SR1vec(3)+SR2vec(3);
            SRmat(p,5)=err;
         else
            SRmat(p+1:m+1,:)=SRmat(p:m,:);
            m=m+1;
            SRmat(p,:)=SR1vec;
            SRmat(p+1,:)=SR2vec;
```

```
            state=iterating;
          end
        end
      end
    end
quad=sum(SRmat(:,4));
err=sum(abs(SRmat(:,5)));
SRmat=SRmat(1:m,1:6);
```

Algorithms and Programs

1. Use Program 7.6 to approximate the value of the definite integral. Use the starting tolerance $\epsilon_0 = 0.00001$.

   (a) $\displaystyle\int_0^3 \frac{\sin(2x)}{1+x^5}\,dx$ (b) $\displaystyle\int_0^3 \sin(4x)e^{-2x}\,dx$ (c) $\displaystyle\int_{0.04}^1 \frac{1}{\sqrt{x}}\,dx$

   (d) $\displaystyle\int_0^2 \frac{1}{x^2+\frac{1}{10}}\,dx$ (e) $\displaystyle\int_{1/(2\pi)}^2 \sin\left(\frac{1}{x}\right)\,dx$ (f) $\displaystyle\int_0^2 \sqrt{4x-x^2}\,dx$

2. For each of the definite integrals in Problem 1, construct a graph analogous to Figure 7.9. *Hint.* The first column of SRmat contains the endpoints (except for *b*) of the subintervals from the adaptive quadrature process. If T=SRmat(:,1) and Z=zeros(length(T))' then plot(T,Z,'.') will produce the subintervals (except for the right endpoint *b*).

3. Modify Program 7.6 so that Boole's rule is used in each subinterval $[a_k, b_k]$.

4. Use the modified program in Problem 3 to compute approximations and construct graphs analogous to Figure 7.9 for the definite integrals in Problem 1.

7.5   Gauss-Legendre Integration (Optional)

We wish to find the area under the curve

$$y = f(x), \qquad -1 \le x \le 1.$$

What method gives the best answer if only two function evaluations are to be made? We have already seen that the trapezoidal rule is a method for finding the area under the curve and that it uses two function evaluations at the endpoints $(-1, f(-1))$, and $(1, f(1))$. But if the graph of $y = f(x)$ is concave down, the error in approximation is the entire region that lies between the curve and the line segment joining the points; another instance is shown in Figure 7.10(a).

If we can use nodes x_1 and x_2 that lie inside the interval $[-1, 1]$, the line through the two points $(x_1, f(x_1))$ and $(x_2, f(x_2))$ crosses the curve, and the area under the line

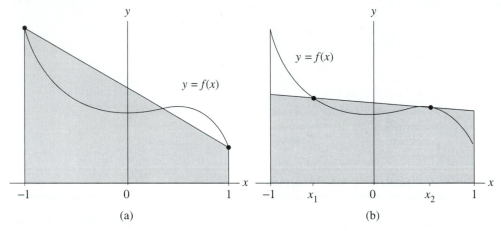

Figure 7.10 (a) Trapezoidal approximation using the abscissas -1 and 1. (b) Trapezoidal approximation using the abscissas x_1 and x_2.

more closely approximates the area under the curve (see Figure 7.10(b)). The equation of the line is

$$(1) \qquad y = f(x_1) + \frac{(x - x_1)(f(x_2) - f(x_1))}{x_2 - x_1}$$

and the area of the trapezoid under the line is

$$(2) \qquad A_{\text{trap}} = \frac{2x_2}{x_2 - x_1} f(x_1) - \frac{2x_1}{x_2 - x_1} f(x_2).$$

Notice that the trapezoidal rule is a special case of (2). When we choose $x_1 = -1$, $x_2 = 1$, and $h = 2$, then

$$T(f, h) = \frac{2}{2} f(x_1) - \frac{-2}{2} f(x_2) = f(x_1) + f(x_2).$$

We shall use the method of undetermined coefficients to find the abscissas x_1, x_2 and weights w_1, w_2 so that the formula

$$(3) \qquad \int_{-1}^{1} f(x)\, dx \approx w_1 f(x_1) + w_2 f(x_2)$$

is exact for cubic polynomials (i.e., $f(x) = a_3 x^3 + a_2 x^2 + a_1 x + a_0$). Since four coefficients w_1, w_2, x_1, and x_2 need to be determined in equation (3), we can select four conditions to be satisfied. Using the fact that integration is additive, it will suffice to require that (3) be exact for the four functions $f(x) = 1, x, x^2, x^3$. The four integral conditions are

$$f(x) = 1: \qquad \int_{-1}^{1} 1\,dx = 2 = w_1 + w_2$$

$$f(x) = x: \qquad \int_{-1}^{1} x\,dx = 0 = w_1 x_1 + w_2 x_2$$

(4)

$$f(x) = x^2: \qquad \int_{-1}^{1} x^2\,dx = \frac{2}{3} = w_1 x_1^2 + w_2 x_2^2$$

$$f(x) = x^3: \qquad \int_{-1}^{1} x^3\,dx = 0 = w_1 x_1^3 + w_2 x_2^3.$$

Now solve the system of nonlinear equations

(5) $$w_1 + w_2 = 2$$

(6) $$w_1 x_1 = -w_2 x_2$$

(7) $$w_1 x_1^2 + w_2 x_2^2 = \frac{2}{3}$$

(8) $$w_1 x_1^3 = -w_2 x_2^3$$

We can divide (8) by (6) and the result is

(9) $$x_1^2 = x_2^2 \qquad \text{or} \qquad x_1 = -x_2.$$

Use (9) and divide (6) by x_1 on the left and $-x_2$ on the right to get

(10) $$w_1 = w_2.$$

Substituting (10) into (5) results in $w_1 + w_2 = 2$. Hence

(11) $$w_1 = w_2 = 1.$$

Now using (11) and (9) in (7), we write

(12) $$w_1 x_1^2 + w_2 x_2^2 = x_2^2 + x_2^2 = \frac{2}{3} \qquad \text{or} \qquad x_2^2 = \frac{1}{3}.$$

Finally, from (12) and (9) we see that the nodes are

$$-x_1 = x_2 = 1/3^{1/2} \approx 0.5773502692.$$

We have found the nodes and weights that make up the two-point Gauss-Legendre rule. Since the formula is exact for cubic equations, the error term will involve the fourth derivative.

Theorem 7.8 (Gauss-Legendre Two-Point Rule). If f is continuous on $[-1, 1]$, then

$$(13) \qquad \int_{-1}^{1} f(x) \, dx \approx G_2(f) = f\left(\frac{-1}{\sqrt{3}}\right) + f\left(\frac{1}{\sqrt{3}}\right).$$

The Gauss-Legendre rule $G_2(f)$ has degree of precision $n = 3$. If $f \in C^4[-1, 1]$, then

$$(14) \qquad \int_{-1}^{1} f(x) \, dx = f\left(\frac{-1}{\sqrt{3}}\right) + f\left(\frac{1}{\sqrt{3}}\right) + E_2(f),$$

where

$$(15) \qquad E_2(f) = \frac{f^{(4)}(c)}{135}.$$

Example 7.17. Use the two-point Gauss-Legendre rule to approximate

$$\int_{-1}^{1} \frac{dx}{x + 2} = \ln(3) - \ln(1) \approx 1.09861$$

and compare the result with the trapezoidal rule $T(f, h)$ with $h = 2$ and Simpson's rule $S(f, h)$ with $h = 1$.

Let $G_2(f)$ denote the two-point Gauss-Legendre rule; then

$$G_2(f) = f(-0.57735) + f(0.57735)$$
$$= 0.70291 + 0.38800 = 1.09091,$$

$$T(f, 2) = f(-1.00000) + f(1.00000)$$
$$= 1.00000 + 0.33333 = 1.33333,$$

$$S(f, 1) = \frac{f(-1) + 4f(0) + f(1)}{3} = \frac{1 + 2 + \frac{1}{3}}{3} = 1.11111.$$

The errors are 0.00770, -0.23472, and -0.01250, respectively, so the Gauss-Legendre rule is seen to be best. Notice that the Gauss-Legendre rule required only two function evaluations and Simpson's rule required three. In this example the size of the error for $G_2(f)$ is about 61% of the size of the error for $S(f, 1)$. ∎

The general N-point Gauss-Legendre rule is exact for polynomial functions of degree $\leq 2N - 1$, and the numerical integration formula is

$$(16) \qquad G_N(f) = w_{N,1} f(x_{N,1}) + w_{N,2} f(x_{N,2}) + \cdots + w_{N,N} f(x_{N,N}).$$

Table 7.9 Gauss-Legendre Abscissas and Weights

$$\int_{-1}^{1} f(x)\, dx = \sum_{k=1}^{N} w_{N,k} f(x_{N,k}) + E_N(f)$$

N	Abscissas, $x_{N,k}$	Weights, $w_{N,k}$	Truncation error, $E_N(f)$
2	-0.5773502692 0.5773502692	1.0000000000 1.0000000000	$\dfrac{f^{(4)}(c)}{135}$
3	± 0.7745966692 0.0000000000	0.5555555556 0.8888888888	$\dfrac{f^{(6)}(c)}{15,750}$
4	± 0.8611363116 ± 0.3399810436	0.3478548451 0.6521451549	$\dfrac{f^{(8)}(c)}{3,472,875}$
5	± 0.9061798459 ± 0.5384693101 0.0000000000	0.2369268851 0.4786286705 0.5688888888	$\dfrac{f^{(10)}(c)}{1,237,732,650}$
6	± 0.9324695142 ± 0.6612093865 ± 0.2386191861	0.1713244924 0.3607615730 0.4679139346	$\dfrac{f^{(12)}(c)2^{13}(6!)^4}{(12!)^3 13!}$
7	± 0.9491079123 ± 0.7415311856 ± 0.4058451514 0.0000000000	0.1294849662 0.2797053915 0.3818300505 0.4179591837	$\dfrac{f^{(14)}(c)2^{15}(7!)^4}{(14!)^3 15!}$
8	± 0.9602898565 ± 0.7966664774 ± 0.5255324099 ± 0.1834346425	0.1012285363 0.2223810345 0.3137066459 0.3626837834	$\dfrac{f^{(16)}(c)2^{17}(8!)^4}{(16!)^3 17!}$

The abscissas $x_{N,k}$ and weights $w_{N,k}$ to be used have been tabulated and are easily available; Table 7.9 gives the values up to eight points. Also included in the table is the form of the error term $E_N(f)$ that corresponds to $G_N(f)$, and it can be used to determine the accuracy of the Gauss-Legendre integration formula.

The values in Table 7.9 in general have no easy representation. This fact makes the method less attractive for humans to use when hand calculations are required. But once the values are stored in a computer it is easy to call them up when needed. The nodes are actually roots of the Legendre polynomials, and the corresponding weights must be obtained by solving a system of equations. For the three-point Gauss-Legendre rule the nodes are $-(0.6)^{1/2}$, 0, and $(0.6)^{1/2}$, and the corresponding weights are 5/9, 8/9, and 5/9.

Theorem 7.9 (Gauss-Legendre Three-Point Rule).   If f is continuous on $[-1, 1]$, then

(17) $$\int_{-1}^{1} f(x)\,dx \approx G_3(f) = \frac{5f(-\sqrt{3/5}) + 8f(0) + 5f(\sqrt{3/5})}{9}.$$

The Gauss-Legendre rule $G_3(f)$ has degree of precision $n = 5$. If $f \in C^6[-1, 1]$, then

(18) $$\int_{-1}^{1} f(x)\,dx = \frac{5f(-\sqrt{3/5}) + 8f(0) + 5f(\sqrt{3/5})}{9} + E_3(f),$$

where

(19) $$E_3(f) = \frac{f^{(6)}(c)}{15,750}.$$

Example 7.18.   Show that the three-point Gauss-Legendre rule is exact for

$$\int_{-1}^{1} 5x^4\,dx = 2 = G_3(f).$$

Since the integrand is $f(x) = 5x^4$ and $f^{(6)}(x) = 0$, we can use (19) to see that $E_3(f) = 0$. But it is instructive to use (17) and do the calculations in this case.

$$G_3(f) = \frac{5(5)(0.6)^2 + 0 + 5(5)(0.6)^2}{9} = \frac{18}{9} = 2. \qquad \blacksquare$$

The next result shows how to change the variable of integration so that the Gauss-Legendre rules can be used on the interval $[a, b]$.

Theorem 7.10 (Gauss-Legendre Translation).   Suppose that the abscissas $\{x_{N,k}\}_{k=1}^{N}$ and weights $\{w_{N,k}\}_{k=1}^{N}$ are given for the N-point Gauss-Legendre rule over $[-1, 1]$. To apply the rule over the interval $[a, b]$, use the change of variable

(20) $$t = \frac{a+b}{2} + \frac{b-a}{2}x \qquad \text{and} \qquad dt = \frac{b-a}{2}\,dx.$$

Then the relationship

(21) $$\int_{a}^{b} f(t)\,dt = \int_{-1}^{1} f\left(\frac{a+b}{2} + \frac{b-a}{2}x\right)\frac{b-a}{2}\,dx$$

is used to obtain the quadrature formula

(22) $$\int_{a}^{b} f(t)\,dt = \frac{b-a}{2}\sum_{k=1}^{N} w_{N,k}\, f\left(\frac{a+b}{2} + \frac{b-a}{2}x_{N,k}\right).$$

Example 7.19.   Use the three-point Gauss-Legendre rule to approximate

$$\int_1^5 \frac{dt}{t} = \ln(5) - \ln(1) \approx 1.609438$$

and compare the result with Boole's rule $B(2)$ with $h = 1$.

Here $a = 1$ and $b = 5$, so the rule in (22) yields

$$G_3(f) = (2) \frac{5f(3 - 2(0.6)^{1/2}) + 8f(3 + 0) + 5f(3 + 2(0.6)^{1/2})}{9}$$

$$= (2) \frac{3.446359 + 2.666667 + 1.099096}{9} = 1.602694.$$

In Example 7.13 we saw that Boole's rule gave $B(2) = 1.617778$. The errors are 0.006744 and -0.008340, respectively, so that the Gauss-Legendre rule is slightly better in this case. Notice that the Gauss-Legendre rule requires three function evaluations and Boole's rule requires five. In this example the size of the two errors is about the same.   ■

Gauss-Legendre integration formulas are extremely accurate, and they should be considered seriously when many integrals of a similar nature are to be evaluated. In this case, proceed as follows. Pick a few representative integrals, including some with the worst behavior that is likely to occur. Determine the number of sample points N that is needed to obtain the required accuracy. Then fix the value N, and use the Gauss-Legendre rule with N sample points for all the integrals.

For a given value of N, Program 7.7 requires that the abscissas and weights from Table 7.9 be saved in $1 \times N$ matrices A and W, respectively. This can be done in the MATLAB command window or the matrices can be saved as M-files. It would be expedient to save Table 7.9 in a 35×2 matrix G. The first column of G would contain the abscissas and the second column the corresponding weights. Then, for a given value of N, the matrices A and W would be submatrices of G. For example, if $N = 3$, then A=G(3:5,1)' and W=G(3:5,2)'.

Program 7.7 (Gauss-Legendre Quadrature).   To approximate the integral

$$\int_a^b f(x)\,dx \approx \frac{b-a}{2} \sum_{k=1}^{N} w_{N,k} f(t_{N,k})$$

by sampling $f(x)$ at the N unequally spaced points $\{t_{N,k}\}_{k=1}^{N}$. The changes of variable

$$t = \frac{a+b}{2} + \frac{b-a}{2}x \quad \text{and} \quad dt = \frac{b-a}{2}\,dx$$

are used. The abscissas $\{x_{N,k}\}_{k=1}^{N}$ and the corresponding weights $\{w_{N,k}\}_{k=1}^{N}$ must be obtained from a table of known values.

```
function quad=gauss(f,a,b,A,W)
```

```
%Input   - f is the integrand input as a string 'f'
%        - a and b are upper and lower limits of integration
%        - A is the 1 x N vector of abscissas from Table 7.9
%        - W is the 1 x N vector of weights from Table 7.9
%Output - quad is the quadrature value
N=length(A);
T=zeros(1,N);
T=((a+b)/2)+((b-a)/2)*A;
quad=((b-a)/2)*sum(W.*feval(f,T));
```

Exercises for Gauss-Legendre Integration

In Exercises 1 through 4, **(a)** show that the two integrals are equivalent and **(b)** calculate $G_2(f)$.

1. $\displaystyle\int_0^2 6t^5\,dt = \int_{-1}^1 6(x+1)^5\,dx$

2. $\displaystyle\int_0^2 \sin(t)\,dt = \int_{-1}^1 \sin(x+1)\,dx$

3. $\displaystyle\int_0^1 \frac{\sin(t)}{t}\,dt = \int_{-1}^1 \frac{\sin((x+1)/2)}{x+1}\,dx$

4. $\displaystyle\frac{1}{\sqrt{2\pi}}\int_0^1 e^{-t^2/2}\,dt = \frac{1}{\sqrt{2\pi}}\int_{-1}^1 \frac{e^{-(x+1)^2/8}}{2}\,dx$

5. $\displaystyle\frac{1}{\pi}\int_0^\pi \cos(0.6\sin(t))\,dt = 0.5\int_{-1}^1 \cos\left(0.6\sin\left((x+1)\frac{\pi}{2}\right)\right)\,dx$

6. Use $E_N(f)$ in Table 7.9 and the change of variable given in Theorem 7.10 to find the smallest integer N so that $E_N(f) = 0$ for

    (a) $\int_0^2 8x^7\,dx = 256 = G_N(f)$.

    (b) $\int_0^2 11x^{10}\,dx = 2048 = G_N(f)$.

7. Find the roots of the following Legendre polynomials and compare them with the abscissa in Table 7.9.

    (a) $P_2(x) = (3x^2 - 1)/2$

    (b) $P_3(x) = (5x^3 - 3x)/2$

    (c) $P_4(x) = (35x^4 - 30x^2 + 3)/8$

8. The truncation error term for the two-point Gauss-Legendre rule on the closed interval $[-1, 1]$ is $f^{(4)}(c_1)/135$. The truncation error for Simpson's rule on $[a, b]$ is $-h^5 f^{(4)}(c_2)/90$. Compare the truncation error terms when $[a, b] = [-1, 1]$. Which method do you think is best? Why?

9. The three-point Gauss-Legendre rule is

$$\int_{-1}^1 f(x)\,dx \approx \frac{5f(-(0.6)^{1/2}) + 8f(0) + 5f((0.6)^{1/2})}{9}.$$

Show that the formula is exact for $f(x) = 1, x, x^2, x^3, x^4, x^5$. *Hint.* If f is an odd function (i.e., $f(-x) = f(x)$), the integral of f over $[-1, 1]$ is zero.

10. The truncation error term for the three-point Gauss-Legendre rule on the interval $[-1, 1]$ is $f^{(6)}(c_1)/15,750$. The truncation error term for Boole's rule on $[a, b]$ is $-8h^7 f^{(6)}(c_2)/945$. Compare the error terms when $[a, b] = [-1, 1]$. Which method is better? Why?

11. Derive the three-point Gauss-Legendre rule using the following steps. Use the fact that the abscissas are the roots of the Legendre polynomial of degree 3.

$$x_1 = -(0.6)^{1/2}, \qquad x_2 = 0, \qquad x_3 = (0.6)^{1/2}.$$

Find the weights w_1, w_2, w_3 so that the relation

$$\int_{-1}^{1} f(x)\, dx \approx w_1 f(-(0.6)^{1/2}) + w_2 f(0) + w_3 f((0.6)^{1/2})$$

is exact for the functions $f(x) = 1$, x, and x^2. *Hint.* First obtain and then solve the linear system of equations

$$w_1 + w_2 + w_3 = 2$$
$$-(0.6)^{1/2} w_1 + (0.6)^{1/2} w_3 = 0$$
$$0.6 w_1 + 0.6 w_3 = \frac{2}{3}.$$

12. In practice, if many integrals of a similar type are evaluated, a preliminary analysis is made to determine the number of function evaluations required to obtain the desired accuracy. Suppose that 17 function evaluations are to be made. Compare the Romberg answer $R(4, 4)$ with the Gauss-Legendre answer $G_{17}(f)$.

Algorithms and Programs

1. For each of the integrals in Exercises 1 through 5, use Program 7.7 to find $G_6(f)$, $G_7(f)$, and $G_8(f)$.

2. **(a)** Modify Program 7.7 so that it will compute $G_1(f), G_2(f), \ldots, G_8(f)$ and stop when the relative error in the approximations $G_{N-1}(f)$ and $G_N(f)$ is less than the preassigned value tol, that is,

$$\frac{2|G_{N-1}(f) - G_N(f)|}{|G_{N-1}(f) + G_N(f)|} < \text{tol}.$$

Hint. As discussed at the end of the section, save Table 7.9 in an M-file G as a 35×2 matrix **G**.

(b) Use your program from part (a) to approximate the integrals in Exercises 1 through 5 with an accuracy of five decimal places.

3. (a)   Use the six-point Gauss-Legendre rule to approximate the solution of the integral equation

$$v(x) = x^2 + 0.1 \int_0^3 (x^2 + t)v(t)\, dt.$$

Substitute your approximate solution into the right-hand side of the integral equation and simplify.

(b)   Repeat part (a) using an eight-point Gauss-Legendre rule.

8

Numerical
Optimization

The two-dimensional wave equation is used in mechanical engineering to model vibrations in rectangular plates. If the plates have all four edges clamped, the sinusoidal vibrations are described with a double Fourier series. Suppose that at a certain instant

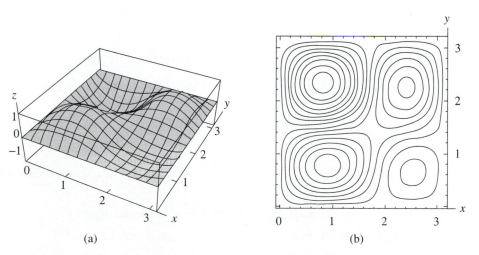

(a)   (b)

Figure 8.1   (a) The displacement $z = f(x, y)$ of a vibrating plate. (b) The contour plot $f(x, y) = C$ for a vibrating plate.

of time the height $z = f(x, y)$ over the point (x, y) is given by the function

$$z = f(x, y) = 0.02 \sin(x) \sin(y) - 0.03 \sin(2x) \sin(y)$$
$$+ 0.04 \sin(x) \sin(2y) + 0.08 \sin(2x) \sin(2y).$$

Where are the points of maximum deflection located? Looking at the three-dimensional graph and the companion contour plot in Figure 8.1(a) and (b), respectively, we see that there are two local minima and two local maxima over the square $0 \leq x \leq \pi$, $0 \leq y \leq \pi$. Numerical methods can be used to determine their approximate location:

$$f(0.8278, 2.3322) = -0.1200 \quad \text{and} \quad f(2.5351, 0.6298) = -0.0264$$

are the local minima, and

$$f(0.9241, 0.7640) = 0.0998 \quad \text{and} \quad f(2.3979, 2.2287) = 0.0853$$

are the local maxima.

In this chapter we give a brief introduction to some of the basic methods for locating extrema of functions of one or several variables.

8.1   Minimization of a Function of One Variable

Definition 8.1. The function f is said to have a *local minimum value* at $x = p$, if there exists an open interval I containing p so that $f(p) \leq f(x)$ for all $x \in I$. Similarly, f is said to have a *local maximum value* at $x = p$ if $f(x) \leq f(p)$ for all $x \in I$. If f has either a local minimum or maximum value at $x = p$, it is said to have a *local extremum* at $x = p$. ▲

Definition 8.2. Assume that $f(x)$ is defined on the interval I.

(i) If $x_1 < x_2$ implies that $f(x_1) < f(x_2)$ for all $x_1, x_2 \in I$, then f is said to be *increasing* on I.

(ii) If $x_1 < x_2$ implies that $f(x_1) > f(x_2)$ for all $x_1, x_2 \in I$, then f is said to be *decreasing* on I. ▲

Theorem 8.1. Suppose that $f(x)$ is continuous on $I = [a, b]$ and is differentiable on (a, b).

(i) If $f'(x) > 0$ for all $x \in (a, b)$, then $f(x)$ is increasing on I.

(ii) If $f'(x) < 0$ for all $x \in (a, b)$, then $f(x)$ is decreasing on I.

Theorem 8.2. Assume that $f(x)$ is defined on $I = [a, b]$ and has a local extremum at an interior point $p \in (a, b)$. If $f(x)$ is differentiable at $x = p$, then $f'(p) = 0$.

Theorem 8.3 (First Derivative Test).   Assume that $f(x)$ is continuous on $I = [a, b]$. Furthermore, suppose that $f'(x)$ is defined for all $x \in (a, b)$, except possibly at $x = p$.

   (i) If $f'(x) < 0$ on (a, p) and $f'(x) > 0$ on (p, b), then $f(p)$ is a local minimum.

   (ii) If $f'(x) > 0$ on (a, p) and $f'(x) < 0$ on (p, b), then $f(p)$ is a local maximum.

Theorem 8.4 (Second Derivative Test).   Assume that f is continuous on $[a, b]$ and f' and f'' are defined on (a, b). Also, suppose that $p \in (a, b)$ is a critical point where $f'(p) = 0$.

   (i) If $f''(p) > 0$, then $f(p)$ is a local minimum of f.

   (ii) If $f''(p) < 0$, then $f(p)$ is a local maximum of f.

   (iii) If $f''(p) = 0$, then this test is inconclusive.

Example 8.1.   Use the second derivative test to classify the local extrema of $f(x) = x^3 + x^2 - x + 1$ on the interval $[-2, 2]$.

The first derivative is $f'(x) = 3x^2 + 2x - 1 = (3x - 1)(x + 1)$, and the second derivative is $f''(x) = 6x + 2$. There are two points where $f'(x) = 0$ (i.e., $x = 1/3, -1$).

Case (i): At $x = 1/3$ we find that $f'(1/3) = 0$ and $f''(1/3) = 4 > 0$, so that $f(x)$ has a local minimum at $x = 1/3$.

Case (ii): At $x = -1$ we find that $f'(-1) = 0$ and $f''(-1) = -4 < 0$, so that $f(x)$ has a local maximum at $x = -1$.   ■

Bracketing Search Methods

Another approach for finding the minimum of $f(x)$ in a given interval is to evaluate the function many times and search for a local minimum. To reduce the number of function evaluations it is important to have a good strategy for determining where $f(x)$ is to be evaluated. Two efficient bracketing methods are the *golden ratio* and *fibonacci* searches. To use either bracketing method for finding the minimum of $f(x)$, a special condition must be met to ensure that there is a proper minimum in the given interval.

Definition 8.3.   The function $f(x)$ is *unimodal* on $I = [a, b]$, if there exists a unique number $p \in I$ such that

(1) $f(x)$ is decreasing on $[a, p]$

(2) $f(x)$ is increasing on $[p, b]$ ▲

Golden Ratio Search

If $f(x)$ is known to be unimodal on $[a, b]$, then it is possible to replace the interval with a subinterval on which $f(x)$ takes on its minimum value. One approach is to select two interior points $c < d$. This results in $a < c < d < b$. The condition

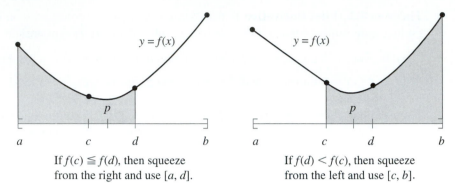

If $f(c) \leqq f(d)$, then squeeze   If $f(d) < f(c)$, then squeeze
from the right and use $[a, d]$.   from the left and use $[c, b]$.

Figure 8.2   The decision process for the golden ratio search.

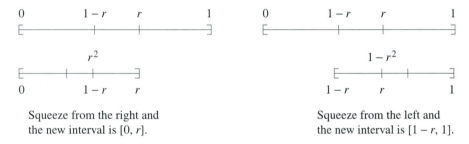

Squeeze from the right and   Squeeze from the left and
the new interval is $[0, r]$.   the new interval is $[1 - r, 1]$.

Figure 8.3   The intervals involved in the golden ratio search.

that $f(x)$ is unimodal guarantees that the function values $f(c)$ and $f(d)$ are less than $\max\{f(a), f(b)\}$. We have two cases to consider (see Figure 8.2).

If $f(c) \leq f(d)$, the minimum must occur in the subinterval $[a, d]$, and we replace b with d and continue the search in the new subinterval $[a, d]$. If $f(d) < f(c)$, the minimum must occur in $[c, b]$, and we replace a with c and continue the search in $[c, b]$

The interior points c and d are selected so that the resulting intervals $[a, c]$ and $[d, b]$ are symmetrical; that is, $b - d = c - a$, where

(3) $$c = a + (1 - r)(b - a) = ra + (1 - r)b,$$
(4) $$d = b - (1 - r)(b - a) = (1 - r)a + rb,$$

and $1/2 < r < 1$ (to preserve the ordering $c < d$).

We want the value of r to remain constant on each subinterval. Additionally, one of the old interior points will be used as an interior point of the new subinterval, while the other interior point will become an endpoint of the new subinterval (see Figure 8.3). Thus, on each iteration only one new point will have to be found and only one new function evaluation will have to be made. If $f(c) \leq f(d)$ and only one new function evaluation is to be made, then we must have

$$\frac{d-a}{b-a} = \frac{c-a}{d-a}$$

$$\frac{r(b-a)}{b-a} = \frac{(1-r)(b-a)}{r(b-a)}$$

$$\frac{r}{1} = \frac{1-r}{r}$$

$$r^2 + r - 1 = 0$$

$$r = \frac{-1 \pm \sqrt{5}}{2}.$$

Thus $r = (-1 + \sqrt{5})/2$ (the golden ratio). Similarly, if $f(d) < f(c)$, then $r = (-1 + \sqrt{5})/2$.

The next example compares the root-finding method with the golden search method.

Example 8.2. Find the minimum of the unimodal function $f(x) = x^2 - \sin(x)$ on the interval $[0, 1]$.

Solution by solving $f'(x) = 0$. A root-finding method can be used to determine where the derivative $f'(x) = 2x - \cos(x)$ is zero. Since $f'(0) = -1 < 0$ and $f'(1) = 1.4596977 > 0$, then by the intermediate value theorem a root of $f'(x)$ lies in the interval $[0, 1]$. The results of using the secant method with the initial values $p_0 = 0$ and $p_1 = 1$ are given in Table 8.1.

The conclusion from applying the secant method is that $f'(0.4501836) = 0$. The second derivative is $f''(x) = 2 + \sin(x)$ and we compute $f''(0.4501836) = 2.435131 > 0$. Hence, by Theorem 8.4 (second derivative test), the minimum is $f(0.4501836) = -0.2324656$.

Solution using the golden search. Let $a_0 = 0$ and $b_0 = 1$. Formulas (3) and (4) yield

$$c_0 = 0 + \left(1 - \frac{-1 + \sqrt{5}}{2}\right)(1 - 0) = \frac{3 - \sqrt{5}}{2} \approx 0.38919660,$$

$$d_0 = 1 - \left(1 - \frac{-1 + \sqrt{5}}{2}\right)(1 - 0) = \frac{-1 + \sqrt{5}}{2} \approx 0.6180340.$$

We calculate $f(c_0) = -0.22684748$ and $f(d_0) = -0.19746793$. Since $f(c_0) < f(d_0)$, the new subinterval is $[a_0, d_0] = [0.00000000, 0.6180340]$. We let $a_1 = a_0$, $b_1 = d_0$, $d_1 = c_0$ and use formula (3) to find c_1:

$$c_1 = a_1 + (1 - r)(b_1 - a_1)$$

$$= 0 + \left(1 - \frac{-1 + \sqrt{5}}{2}\right)(0.6180340 - 0)$$

$$\approx 0.2360680.$$

Table 8.1 Secant Method for
Solving $f'(x) = 2x - \cos(x) = 0$

k	p_k	$2p_k - \cos(p_k)$
0	0.0000000	-1.00000000
1	1.0000000	1.45969769
2	0.4065540	-0.10538092
3	0.4465123	-0.00893398
4	0.4502137	0.00007329
5	0.4501836	-0.00000005

Table 8.2 Golden Search for the Minimum of $f(x) = x^2 - \sin(x)$

k	a_k	c_k	d_k	b_k	$f(c_k)$	$f(d_k)$
0	0.0000000	0.3819660	0.6180340	1	-0.22684748	-0.19746793
1	0.0000000	0.2360680	0.3819660	0.6180340	-0.17815339	-0.22684748
2	0.2360680	0.3819660	0.4721360	0.6180340	-0.22684748	-0.23187724
3	0.3819660	0.4721360	0.5278640	0.6180340	-0.23187724	-0.22504882
4	0.3819660	0.4376941	0.4721360	0.5278640	-0.23227594	-0.23187724
5	0.3819660	0.4164079	0.4376941	0.4721360	-0.23108238	-0.23227594
6	0.4164079	0.4376941	0.4508497	0.4721360	-0.23227594	-0.23246503
$\vdots$	$\vdots$	$\vdots$	$\vdots$	$\vdots$	$\vdots$	$\vdots$
21	0.4501574	0.4501730	0.4501827	0.4501983	-0.23246558	-0.23246558
22	0.4501730	0.4501827	0.4501886	0.4501983	-0.23246558	-0.23246558
23	0.4501827	0.4501886	0.4501923	0.4501983	-0.23246558	-0.23246558

Now compute and compare $f(c_1)$ and $f(d_1)$ to determine the new subinterval and continue the iteration process. Some of the computations are shown in Table 8.2.

At the twenty-third iteration the interval has been narrowed down to $[a_{23}, b_{23}] = [0.4501827, 0.4501983]$. This interval has width 0.0000156. However, the computed function values at the endpoints agree to eight decimal places (i.e., $f(a_{23}) \approx -0.23246558 \approx f(b_{23})$); hence the algorithm is terminated. A problem in using search methods is that the function may be flat near the minimum, and this limits the accuracy that can be obtained. The secant method was able to find the more accurate answer $p_5 = 0.4501836$.

Although the golden ratio search is slower in this example, it has the desirable feature that it can be applied in cases where $f(x)$ is not differentiable. ∎

Fibonacci Search

In the golden ratio search two function evaluations are made at the first iteration and then only one function evaluation is made for each subsequent iteration. The value of

r remains constant on each subinterval and the search is terminated at the kth subinterval, provided that $|b_k - a_k|$ or $|f(b_k) - f(a_k)|$ satisfies predefined tolerances. The **Fibonacci search method** differs from the golden ratio method in that the value of r is not constant on each subinterval. Additionally, the number of subintervals (iterations) is predetermined and based on the specified tolerances.

The Fibonacci search is based on the sequence of Fibonacci numbers $\{F_k\}_{k=0}^{\infty}$ defined by the equations

$$(5) \qquad\qquad\qquad F_0 = 0, \ F_1 = 1$$

$$(6) \qquad\qquad\qquad F_n = F_{n-1} + F_{n-2}$$

for $n = 2, 3, \ldots$. Thus the Fibonacci numbers are $0, 1, 1, 2, 3, 5, 8, 13, 21, \ldots$.

Assume we are given a function $f(x)$ that is unimodal on the interval $[a_0, b_0]$. As in the golden ratio search a value r_0 $(1/2 < r_0 < 1)$ is selected so that both of the interior points c_0 and d_0 will be used in the next subinterval and there will be only one new function evaluation. Without loss of generality assume that $f(c_0) > f(d_0)$. It follows that $a_1 = a_0$, $b_1 = d_0$, and $d_1 = c_0$ (see Figure 8.4). If there is to be only one new function evaluation, then we select r_1 $(1/2 < r_1 < 1)$ for the subinterval $[a_1, b_1]$, such that

$$d_0 - c_0 = b_1 - d_1$$
$$(2r_0 - 1)(b_0 - a_0) = (1 - r_1)(b_1 - a_1)$$
$$(2r_0 - 1)(b_0 - a_0) = (1 - r_1)(r_0(b_0 - a_0))$$
$$2r_0 - 1 = (1 - r_1)r_0$$
$$r_1 = \frac{1 - r_0}{r_0}.$$

Substituting $r_0 = F_{n-1}/F_n$, $n \geq 4$, into this last equation yields

$$r_1 = \frac{1 - \dfrac{F_{n-1}}{F_n}}{\dfrac{F_{n-1}}{F_n}}$$
$$= \frac{F_n - F_{n-1}}{F_{n-1}}$$
$$= \frac{F_{n-2}}{F_{n-1}}$$

since, by equation (6), $F_n = F_{n-1} + F_{n-2}$.

Reasoning inductively, it follows that the Fibonacci search can be begun with $r_0 = F_{n-1}/F_n$ and continued using $r_k = F_{n-1-k}/F_{n-k}$ for $k = 1, 2, \ldots, n - 3$. Note that $r_{n-3} = F_2/F_3 = 1/2$, thus no new points can be added at this stage. Therefore, there are a total of $(n - 3) + 1 = n - 2$ steps in this process.

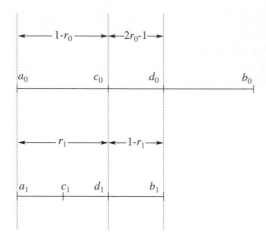

Figure 8.4 The Fibonacci search intervals $[a_0, b_0]$ and $[a_1, b_1]$.

The $(k + 1)$st subinterval is obtained by reducing the length of the kth subinterval by a factor of $r_k = F_{n-1-k}/F_{n-k}$. The length of the last subinterval is

$$\frac{F_{n-1} F_{n-2} \cdots F_2}{F_n F_{n-1} \cdots F_3}(b_0 - a_0) = \frac{F_2}{F_n}(b_0 - a_0)$$

$$= \frac{1}{F_n}(b_0 - a_0) = \frac{b_0 - a_0}{F_n}.$$

If the absissa of the minimum is to be found with a tolerance of ϵ, then we need to find the smallest value of n such that

(7) $$\frac{b_0 - a_0}{F_n} < \epsilon \quad \text{or} \quad F_n > \frac{b_0 - a_0}{\epsilon}.$$

The interior points c_k and d_k of the kth subinterval $[a_k, b_k]$ are found, as needed, using the formulas

(8) $$c_k = a_k + \left(1 - \frac{F_{n-k-1}}{F_{n-k}}\right)(b_k - a_k)$$

(9) $$d_k = a_k + \frac{F_{n-k-1}}{F_{n-k}}(b_k - a_k).$$

Note. the value of n used in formulas (8) and (9) is found using inequality (7).

Each iteration requires the determination of two new interior points, one from the previous iteration and the second from formula (8) or (9). When $r_0 = F_2/F_3 = 1/2$, the two interior points will be concurrent in the middle of the interval. To distinguish the two interior points a small distinguishability constant, e, is introduced. Thus when formula (8) or (9) is used, the coefficients of $(b_k - a_k)$ are $1/2 - e$ or $1/2 + e$, respectively.

Example 8.3.   Find the minimum of the function $f(x) = x^2 - \sin(x)$ on the interval $[0, 1]$ using the Fibonacci search method. Use a tolerance of $\epsilon = 10^{-4}$ and the distinguishability constant $e = 0.01$.

The smallest Fibonacci number satisfying

$$F_n > \frac{b_0 - a_0}{\epsilon} = \frac{1 - 0}{10^{-4}} = 10{,}000,$$

is $F_{21} = 10{,}946$. Thus $n = 21$. Let $a_0 = 0$ and $b_0 = 1$. Formulas (8) and (9) yield

$$c_0 = 0 + \left(1 - \frac{F_{20}}{F_{21}}\right)(1 - 0) \approx 0.3819660$$

$$d_0 = 0 + \frac{F_{20}}{F_{21}}(1 - 0) \approx 0.6180340.$$

We set $a_1 = a_0$, $b_1 = d_0$, and $d_1 = c_0$, since $f(0.3819660) = -0.2268475$ and $f(0.6180340) = -0.1974679$ ($f(d_0) \geq f(c_0)$). The new subinterval containing the abscissa of the minimum of f is $[a_1, b_1] = [0, 0.6180340]$. Now use formula (8) to calculate the interior point c_1:

$$c_1 = a_1 + \left(1 - \frac{F_{21-1-1}}{F_{21-1}}\right)(b_1 - a_1)$$

$$= 0 + \left(1 - \frac{F_{19}}{F_{20}}\right)(0.6180340 - 0)$$

$$\approx 0.2360680.$$

Now compute and compare $f(c_1)$ and $f(d_1)$ to determine the new subinterval $[a_2, b_2]$, and continue the iteration process. Some of the computations are shown in Table 8.3.

At the seventeenth iteration the interval has been narrowed down to $[a_{17}, b_{17}] = [0.4501188, 0.4503928]$, where $c_{17} = 0.4502101$, $d_{17} = 0.4503105$, and $f(d_{17}) \geq f(c_{17})$. Thus $[a_{18}, b_{18}] = [0.4501188, 0.4503015]$ and $d_{18} = 0.4502101$. At this stage the multiplier is $r_{18} = 1 - F_2/F_3 = 1 - 1/2 = 1/2$ and the distinguishability constant $e = 0.01$ is used to calculate c_{18}:

$$c_{18} = a_{18} + (0.5 - 0.01)(b_{18} - a_{18})$$

$$= 0.4501188 - 0.49(0.450315 - 0.4501188)$$

$$\approx 0.4502083.$$

Since $f(d_{18}) \geq f(c_{18})$, the final subinterval is $[a_{19}, b_{19}] = [0.4501188, 0.4502101]$. This interval has width 0.0000913. We choose to report the abscissa of the minimum as the midpoint of this interval. Therefore, the minimum value is $f(0.4501645) = -0.2324656$. ∎

Both the Fibonacci and golden ratio search methods can be applied in cases where $f(x)$ is not differentiable. It should be noted that when n is small the Fibonacci method is more efficient than the golden ratio method. However, for n large the two methods are almost identical.

Table 8.3 Fibonacci Search for the Minimum of $f(x) = x^2 - \sin(x)$

k	a_k	c_k	d_k	b_k
0	0.0000000	0.3819660	0.6180340	1.0000000
1	0.0000000	0.2360680	0.3819660	0.6180340
2	0.2360680	0.3819660	0.4721359	0.6180340
3	0.3819660	0.4721359	0.5278641	0.6180340
4	0.3819660	0.4376941	0.4721359	0.5278641
$\vdots$	$\vdots$	$\vdots$	$\vdots$	$\vdots$
16	0.4499360	0.4501188	0.4502102	0.4503928
17	0.4501188	0.4502101	0.4503015	0.4503928
18	0.4501188	0.4502083	0.4502101	0.4503015

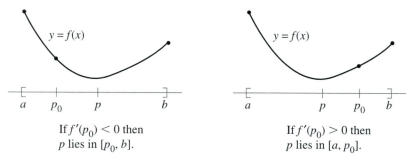

If $f'(p_0) < 0$ then
p lies in $[p_0, b]$.

If $f'(p_0) > 0$ then
p lies in $[a, p_0]$.

Figure 8.5 Using $f'(x)$ to find the minimum value of the unimodal function $f(x)$ on the interval $[a, b]$.

Minimization Using Derivatives

Suppose that $f(x)$ is unimodal over $[a, b]$ and has a unique minimum at $x = p$. Also, assume that $f'(x)$ is defined at all points in (a, b). Let the starting value p_0 lie in (a, b). If $f'(p_0) < 0$, the minimum point p lies to the right of p_0. If $f'(p_0) > 0$, p lies to the left of p_0 (see Figure 8.5).

Bracketing the Minimum

Our first task is to obtain three test values,

(10) $$p_0, \quad p_1 = p_0 + h \quad \text{and} \quad p_2 = p_0 + 2h,$$

so that

(11) $$f(p_0) > f(p_1) \quad \text{and} \quad f(p_1) < f(p_2).$$

Suppose that $f'(p_0) < 0$; then $p_0 < p$ and the step size h should be chosen positive. It is an easy task to find a value of h so that the three points in (10) satisfy (11). Start with $h = 1$ in formula (10) (provided that $a + 1 < b$); if not, take $h = 1/2$, and so on.

Case (i):   If (11) is satisfied we are done.

Case(ii):   If $f(p_0) > f(p_1)$ and $f(p_1) > f(p_2)$, then $p_2 < p$. We need to check points that lie farther to the right. Double the step size and repeat the process.

Case (iii):   If $f(p_0) \leq f(p_1)$, we have jumped over p and h is too large. We need to check values closer to p_0. Reduce the step size by a factor of $1/2$ and repeat the process.

When $f'(p_0) > 0$, the step size h should be chosen negative and then cases similar to (i), (ii), and (iii) can be used.

Quadratic Approximation to Find p

Finally, we have three points (10) that satisfy (11). We will use quadratic interpolation to find $p_{\min}$, which is an approximation to p. The Lagrange polynomial based on the nodes in (10) is

$$(12) \quad Q(x) = \frac{y_0(x - p_1)(x - p_2)}{2h^2} - \frac{y_1(x - p_0)(x - p_2)}{h^2} + \frac{y_2(x - p_0)(x - p_1)}{2h^2},$$

where $y_i = f(p_i)$ for $i = 0, 1, 2$. The derivative of $Q(x)$ is

$$(13) \quad Q'(x) = \frac{y_0(2x - p_1 - p_2)}{2h^2} - \frac{y_1(2x - p_0 - p_2)}{h^2} + \frac{y_2(2x - p_0 - p_1)}{2h^2}.$$

Solving $Q'(x) = 0$ in the form $Q'(p_0 + h_{\min})$ yields

$$
\begin{aligned}
(14) \quad 0 = {}& \frac{y_0(2(p_0 + h_{\min}) - p_1 - p_2)}{2h^2} - \frac{y_1(4(p_0 + h_{\min}) - 2p_0 - 2p_2)}{2h^2} \\
& + \frac{y_2(2(p_0 + h_{\min}) - p_0 - p_1)}{2h^2}.
\end{aligned}
$$

Multiply each term in (14) by $2h^2$ and collect terms involving $h_{\min}$:

$$
\begin{aligned}
-h_{\min}(2y_0 - 4y_1 + 2y_2) = {}& y_0(2p_0 - p_1 - p_2) \\
& - y_1(4p_0 - 2p_0 - 2p_2) + y_2(2p_0 - p_0 - p_1) \\
= {}& y_0(-3h) - y_1(-4h) + y_2(-h).
\end{aligned}
$$

This last quantity is easily solved for $h_{\min}$:

$$(15) \qquad\qquad\qquad h_{\min} = \frac{h(4y_1 - 3y_0 - y_2)}{4y_1 - 2y_0 - 2y_2}.$$

The value $p_{min} = p_o + h_{min}$ is a better approximation to p than p_0. Hence we can replace p_0 with p_{min} and repeat the two processes outlined above to determine a new h and a new h_{min}. Continue the iteration until the desired accuracy is achieved. The details are outlined in Program 8.3.

In this algorithm the derivative of the objective function f was used implicitly in (13) to locate the minimum of the interpolatory quadratic. The reader should note that Program 8.3 makes no explicit use of the derivative. We now consider an approach that utilizes functional evaluations of both f and f'.

Cubic Approximation to Find p

An alternative approach that uses both functional and derivative evaluations explicitly is to find the minimum of a third-degree polynomial that interpolates the objective function f at two points. Assume that f is unimodal and differentiable on $[a, b]$, and has a unique minimum at $x = p$. Let $p_0 = a$. The mean value theorem is used to estimate an initial step size h such that p_1 is close to p:

$$h = \frac{2(f(b) - f(a))}{f'(a)}.$$

Thus $p_1 = p_0 + h$. The cubic is expressed in terms of p_2, the abscissa of the minimum:

$$(16) \qquad P(x) = \frac{\alpha}{h^3}(x - p_2)^3 + \frac{\beta}{h^2}(x - p_2)^2 + f(p_2).$$

Note:

$$(17) \qquad P'(x) = \frac{3\alpha}{h^3}(x - p_2)^2 + \frac{2\beta}{h^2}(x - p_2).$$

The introduction of $h = x_1 - x_0$ in the denominators will make further calculations less tiresome. It is required that $P(p_0) = f(p_0)$, $P(p_1) = f(p_1)$, $P'(p_0) = f'(p_0)$, and $P'(p_1) = f'(p_1)$. To find p_2 we define

$$(18) \qquad p_2 = p_0 + h\gamma$$

(see Figure 8.5) and use (16) and (17) to show that

$$(19) \qquad F = f(p_1) - f(p_0) = \alpha(3\gamma^2 - 3\gamma + 1) + \beta(1 - 2\gamma)$$
$$(20) \qquad G = f'(p_1) - f'(p_0) = 3\alpha(1 - 2\gamma) + 2\beta$$
$$(21) \qquad hf'(p_0) = 3\alpha\gamma^2 - 2\beta\gamma.$$

The system represented by (19), (20), and (21) is solved for α:

$$(22) \qquad \alpha = G - 2(F - f'(p_0)h).$$

Now β is eliminated from (20) and (21), yielding

$$(23) \qquad\qquad 3\alpha\gamma^2 + (G - 3\alpha)\gamma + hf'(p_0) = 0.$$

Solving (23) gives us

$$\gamma = \frac{-2hf'(p_0)}{(G - 3\alpha) \pm \sqrt{(G - 3\alpha)^2 - 12\alpha hf'(p_0)}}$$

(see Section 1.3, Exercise 12). In general, the quadratic term in (16) should dominate and thus the value of α should be small. Since the smaller value of γ is desired, we let

$$(24) \qquad\qquad \gamma = \frac{-2hf'(p_0)}{(G - 3\alpha) + \sqrt{(G - 3\alpha)^2 - 12\alpha hf'(p_0)}}.$$

The value of p_2 is found by substituting the calculated value of γ into formula (18). To continue the iteration process, let $h = p_2 - p_1$ and replace p_0 and p_1 with p_1 and p_2, respectively, in formulas (18), (19), (20), (22), and (24). The algorithm outlined above is not a bracketing method. Thus determining stopping criteria becomes more problematic. One technique would be to require that $|f'(p_k)| < \epsilon$, since $f'(p) = 0$.

Example 8.4.   Find the minimum of the function $f(x) = x^2 - \sin(x)$ on the interval $[0, 1]$ using the cubic search method.

The derivative of f is $f'(x) = 2x - \cos(x)$. Substituting $f(0) = 0$, $f(1) = 0.5852902$, and $f'(0) = -1$ into $h_1 = 2(f(b) - f(a))/f'(a)$ yields $h_1 = -0.3170580$. Thus

$$p_1 = p_0 + h_1 = 0 + (-0.3170580) = -0.3170580$$
$$f(p_1) = f(-0.3170580) = 0.4122984$$
$$f'(p_1) = f'(-0.3170580) = -0.8496310.$$

Substituting h_1, $f(p_0)$, $f(p_1)$, $f'(p_0)$, and $f'(p_1)$ into formulas (19), (20), (22), and (24) yields

$$F = 0.4122984,$$
$$G = 0.1852484,$$
$$\alpha = -0.0052323,$$
$$\gamma = -1.4202625.$$

Thus

$$p_2 = p_1 + h_1\gamma = -0.3170580 + (-0.3170580)(-1.4202625) = 0.4503056.$$

Now set $h_2 = p_2 - p_1 = 0.7673637$ and continue the iteration process. The results in Table 8.4 were obtained using the stopping criterion $f'(p_k) < 10^{-7}$. The value of the function at $p_5 = 0.4501836$ is $f(p_5) = -0.2324656$, which compares favorably with the minimum value found by the secant method in Example 8.2. ∎

Table 8.4   Cubic Search for the Minimum of
$f(x) = x^2 - \sin(x)$

k	p_{k-1}	h_k	p_k
1	0.0000000	−0.3170580	−0.3170580
2	−0.3170580	0.7673637	0.4503056
3	0.4503056	0.0001217	0.4501810
4	0.4501810	0.0002433	0.4504272
5	0.4504272	0.0002436	0.4501836

Program 8.1   (Golden Search for a Minimum).   To approximate the minimum of $f(x)$ numerically on the interval $[a, b]$ by using a golden search. Proceed with the method only if $f(x)$ is a unimodal function on the interval $[a, b]$.

```
function[S,E,G]=golden(f,a,b,delta,epsilon)

%Input   - f is the object function input as a string 'f'
%         - a and b are the endpoints of the interval
%         - delta is the tolerance for the abscissas
%         - epsilon is the tolerance for the ordinates
%Output - S=(p,yp) contains the abscissa p and
%           the ordinate yp of the minimum
%         - E=(dp,dy) contains the error bounds for p and yp
%         - G is an n x 4 matrix:  the kth row contains
%           [ak ck dk bk]; the values of a, c, d, and b at the
%           kth iteration
r1=(sqrt(5)-1)/2;
r2=r1^2;
h=b-a;
ya=feval(f,a);
yb=feval(f,b);
c=a+r2*h;
d=a+r1*h;
yc=feval(f,c);
yd=feval(f,d);
k=1;
A(k)=a;B(k)=b;C(k)=c;D(k)=d;
while(abs(yb-ya)>epsilon)|(h>delta)
   k=k+1;
   if(yc<yd)
      b=d;
      yb=yd;
```

```
            d=c;
            yd=yc;
            h=b-a;
            c=a+r2*h;
            yc=feval(f,c);
        else
            a=c;
            ya=yc;
            c=d;
            yc=yd;
            h=b-a;
            d=a+r1*h;
            yd=feval(f,d);
        end
        A(k)=a;B(k)=b;C(k)=c;D(k)=d;
end

dp=abs(b-a);
dy=abs(yb-ya);
p=a;
yp=ya;
if(yb<ya)
    p=b;
    yp=yb;
end
G=[A' C' D' B'];
S=[p yp];
E=[dp dy];
```

Program 8.2 uses the following MATLAB M-function to calculate Fibonacci numbers.

```
function y=fib(n)
fz(1)=1; fz(2)=1;
for k=3:n      .
    fz(k)=fz(k-1)+fz(k-2);
end
y=fz(n);
```

Program 8.2 (Fibonacci Search for a Minimum).   To numerically approximate the minimum of $f(x)$ on the interval $[a, b]$ by using a Fibonacci search. Proceed with the method only if $f(x)$ is a unimodal function on the interval $[a.b]$.

```
function X=fibonacci(f,a,b,tol,e)
%Input- f, the object function as a string
```

```
%        a, the left endpoint of the interval
%        b, the right endpoint of the interval
%        tol, length of uncertainty
%        e, distinguishability constant
%Output-X, x and y coordinates of minimum

%Note:  this function calls the m-file fib.m
%Determine n
i=1;
F=1;
while F<=(b-a)/tol
   F=fib(i);
   i=i+1;
end

%Initialize values
n=i-1;
A=zeros(1,n-2);B=zeros(1,n-2);
A(1)=a;
B(1)=b;
c=A(1)+(fib(n-2)/fib(n))*(B(1)-A(1));
d=A(1)+(fib(n-1)/fib(n))*(B(1)-A(1));
k=1;

%Compute Iterates
while k<=n-3
   if feval(f,c)>feval(f,d)
      A(k+1)=c;
      B(k+1)=B(k);
      c=d;
      d=A(k+1)+(fib(n-k-1)/fib(n-k))*(B(k+1)-A(k+1));
   else
      A(k+1)=A(k);
      B(k+1)=d;
      d=c;
      c=A(k+1)+(fib(n-k-2)/fib(n-k))*(B(k+1)-A(k+1));
   end
   k=k+1;
end

%Last iteration using distinguishability constant e
if feval(f,c)>feval(f,d)
   A(n-2)=c;
   B(n-2)=B(n-3);
   c=d;
   d=A(n-2)+(0.5+e)*(B(n-2)-A(n-2));
```

```
else
    A(n-2)=A(n-3);
    B(n-2)=d;
    d=c;
    c=A(n-2)+(0.5-e)*(B(n-2)-A(n-2));
end
%Output:  Use midpoint of last interval for abscissa
if feval(f,c)>feval(f,d)
    a=c;b=B(n-2);
else
    a=A(n-2);b=d;
end
X=[(a+b)/2 feval(f,(a+b)/2)];
```

> **Program 8.3 (Local Minimum Search Using Quadratic Interpolation).** To find
> a local minimum of the function $f(x)$ over the interval $[a, b]$, by starting with one
> initial approximation p_0 and then searching the intervals $[a, p_0]$ and $[p_0, b]$.

```
function[p,yp,dp,dy,P]=quadmin(f,a,b,delta,epsilon)
%Input   - f is the object function input as a string 'f'
%         - a and b are the endpoints of the interval
%         - delta is the tolerance for the abscissas
%         - epsilon is the tolerance for the ordinates
%Output - p is the abscissa of the minimum
%         - yp is the ordinate of the minimum
%         - dp is the error bound for p
%         - dy is the error bound for yp
%         - P is the vector of iterations
p0=a;
maxj=20;
maxk=30;
big=1e6;
err=1;
k=1;
P(k)=p0;
cond=0;
h=1;
if (abs(p0)>1e4),h=abs(p0)/1e4;end
while(k<maxk&err>epsilon&cond~=5)
    f1=(feval(f,p0+0.00001)-feval(f,p0-0.00001))/0.00002;
    if(f1>0),h=-abs(h);end
    p1=p0+h;
    p2=p0+2*h;
```

```
pmin=p0;
y0=feval(f,p0);
y1=feval(f,p1);
y2=feval(f,p2);
ymin=y0;
cond=0;
j=0;
%Determine h so that y1<y0&y1<y2
while(j<maxj&abs(h)>delta&cond==0)
   if (y0<=y1),
      p2=p1;
      y2=y1;
      h=h/2;
      p1=p0+h;
      y1=feval(f,p1);
   else
      if(y2<y1),
         p1=p2;
         y1=y2;
         h=2*h;
         p2=p0+2*h;
         y2=feval(f,p2);
      else
         cond=-1;
      end
   end
j=j+1;
if(abs(h)>big|abs(p0)>big),cond=5;end
end
if(cond==5),
   pmin=p1;
   ymin=feval(f,p1);
else
   %Quadratic interpolation to find yp
   d=4*y1-2*y0-2*y2;
   if(d<0),
      hmin=h*(4*y1-3*y0-y2)/d;
   else
      hmin=h/3;
      cond=4;
   end
   pmin=p0+hmin;
   ymin=feval(f,pmin);
```

```
        h=abs(h);
        h0=abs(hmin);
        h1=abs(hmin-h);
        h2=abs(hmin-2*h);

        %Determine magnitude of next h
        if(h0<h),h=h0;end
        if(h1<h),h=h1;end
        if(h2<h),h=h2;end
        if(h==0),h=hmin;end
        if(h<delta),cond=1;end
        if (abs(h)>big|abs(pmin)>big),cond=5;end

        %Termination test for minimization
        e0=abs(y0-ymin);
        e1=abs(y1-ymin);
        e2=abs(y2-ymin);
        if(e0~=0 & e0<err),err=e0;end
        if(e1~=0 & e1<err),err=e1;end
        if(e2~=0 & 2<err),err=e2;end
        if(e0~=0 & e1==0 & e2==0),error=0;end
        if(err<epsilon),cond=2;end
        p0=pmin;
        k=k+1;
        P(k)=p0;
    end
    if(cond==2&h<delta),cond=3;end
end
p=p0;
dp=h;
yp=feval(f,p);
dy=err;
```

Exercises for Minimization of a Function of One Variable

1. Use Theorem 8.1 to determine where each of the following functions is increasing and where it is decreasing.

   (a) $f(x) = 2x^3 - 9x^2 + 12x - 5$

   (b) $f(x) = x/(x + 1)$

   (c) $f(x) = (x + 1)/x$

   (d) $f(x) = x^x$

2. Use Definition 8.3 to show that the following functions are unimodal on the given intervals.
   - (a) $f(x) = x^2 - 2x + 1$; $[0, 4]$
   - (b) $f(x) = \cos(x)$; $[0, 4]$
   - (c) $f(x) = x^x$; $[0.1, 10]$
   - (d) $f(x) = -x(3 - x)^{5/3}$; $[0, 3]$

3. Use Theorems 8.3 and 8.4, if possible, to find all local minima and maxima of each of the following functions on the given interval.
   - (a) $f(x) = 4x^3 - 8x^2 - 11x + 5$; $[0, 2]$
   - (b) $f(x) = x + 3/x^2$; $[0.5, 3]$
   - (c) $f(x) = (x + 2.5)/(4 - x^2)$; $[-1.9, 1.9]$
   - (d) $f(x) = e^x/x^2$; $[0.5, 3]$
   - (e) $f(x) = -\sin(x) - \sin(3x)/3$; $[0, 2]$
   - (f) $f(x) = -2\sin(x) + \sin(2x) - 2\sin(3x)/3$; $[1, 3]$

4. Find the point on the parabola $y = x^2$ that is closest to the point $(3, 1)$.

5. Find the point on the curve $y = \sin(x)$ that is closest to the point $(2, 1)$.

6. Find the point(s) on the circle $x^2 + y^2 = 25$ that is farthest from the chord AB if $A = (3, 4)$ and $B = (-1, \sqrt{24})$.

7. Use the golden ratio search and five-digit rounding arithmetic to find $[a_k, b_k]$ for $k = 0, 1, 2$, for each of the following functions. *Note.* Each function is unimodal on the given interval.
   - (a) $f(x) = e^x + 2x + \frac{x^2}{2}$; $[-2.4, -1.6]$
   - (b) $f(x) = -\sin(x) - x + \frac{x^2}{2}$; $[0.8, 1.6]$
   - (c) $f(x) = \frac{x^2}{2} - 4x - x\cos(x)$; $[0.5, 2.5]$
   - (d) $f(x) = x^3 - 5x^2 + 23$; $[1, 5]$

8. Use the Fibonacci search and five-digit rounding arithmetic to find $[a_k, b_k]$ for $k = 0, 1, 2$, for each of the functions in Exercise 7. In each case assume that F_{10} is the smallest Fibonacci number satisfying a given tolerance ϵ.

9. Carry out two iterations of the quadratic approximation method, using five-digit rounding arithmetic, for each of the functions in Exercise 7.

10. Use the cubic search method and five-digit rounding arithmetic to find p_1 and p_2 for each of the functions in Exercise 7.

11. The golden ratio search is applied to a function on the given interval. Determine the length of the kth subinterval.
    - (a) $[0, 1]$, $k = 4$
    - (b) $[-2.3, -1.6]$, $k = 5$
    - (c) $[-4.6, 3.5]$, $k = 10$

12. For each interval and value of ϵ find the smallest Fibonacci number F_n satisfying inequality (7).

    (a) $[-0.1, 3.4]$, $\epsilon = 10^{-4}$

    (b) $[-2.3, 5.3]$, $\epsilon = 10^{-6}$

    (c) $[3.33, 3.99]$, $\epsilon = 10^{-8}$

13. Algebraically establish the identity

$$1 - \frac{F_{n-k-1}}{F_{n-k}} = \frac{F_{n-k-2}}{F_{n-k}}.$$

14. Establish formulas (19), (20), and (21).

15. Establish formula (22).

16. Establish formula (23).

17. *Dichotomous search method.* The dichotomous search is another bracketing method for determining the minimum of a unimodal function f on a closed interval $[a_0, b_0]$ without using derivatives. The values c_0 and d_0 are placed symmetrically at a distance ϵ from the midpoint of the interval, $(a_0 + b_0)/2$. Depending on the values of $f(c_0)$ and $f(d_0)$ a new subinterval is obtained. The process is then repeated by determining c_1 and d_1.
Input: ϵ, the distinguishability constant; and *tol*, the length of the final subinterval. While $b_k - a_k \geq tol$, let

$$c_k = \frac{a_k + b_k}{2} - \epsilon \quad \text{and} \quad d_k = \frac{a_k + b_k}{2} + \epsilon.$$

If $f(c_k) < f(d_k)$, let $a_{k+1} = a_k$ and $b_{k+1} = d_k$. Otherwise, let $a_{k+1} = c_k$ and $b_{k+1} = b_k$. Let $k = k + 1$ and continue loop.

    (a) Use the dichotomous search and five-digit rounding arithmetic to find $[a_1, b_1]$ and $[a_2, b_2]$ for the function $f(x) = e^x + 2x + x^2/2$ on the interval $[-2.4, -1.6]$. Use the distinguishability constant $\epsilon = 0.1$.

    (b) Show that the length of the kth subinterval is given by

$$b_k - a_k = \frac{1}{2^k}(b_0 - a_0) + 2\epsilon \left(1 - \frac{1}{2^k}\right)$$

    (c) For the function in part (a) determine the value of k such that $b_k - a_k < 10^{-4}$, where $\epsilon = 10^{-6}$.

18. *Cubic bracketing search method.* Assume that f is unimodal and differentiable on the interval $[a_0, b_0]$. Again, we consider a search method that explicitly uses f'. We seek the abscissa of the minimum, $p_{\min}$, of a cubic polynomial that agrees with f and f' at the endpoints a_0 and b_0. Let

$$P(x) = \alpha(x - a_0)^3 + \beta(x - a_0)^2 + \gamma(x - a_0) + \rho,$$

where $P(a_0) = f(a_0)$, $P(b_0) = f(b_0)$, $P'(a_0) = f'(a_0)$, and $P'(b_0) = f'(b_0)$. If $f(p_{\min}) > 0$, then set $b_1 = p_{\min}$ and $a_1 = a_0$; else set $a_1 = p_{\min}$ and $b_1 = b_0$.

Continue the iteration process until the length of the kth subinterval is less than the desired error: $b_k - a_k < \epsilon$. As with the cubic search introduced in the text, it remains to find explicit formulas for the coefficients α, β, γ, and ρ.

(a) Show that $p_{\min} = a_0 + \dfrac{-\beta + \sqrt{\beta^2 - 3\alpha\gamma}}{3\alpha}$.

(b) Show that $\rho = P(a_0) = f(a_0)$ and $\gamma = P'(a_0) = f'(a_0)$.

(c) Show that $\alpha = \dfrac{G - 2D}{b_0 - a_0}$ and $\beta = 3D - G$, where $F = \dfrac{f(b_0) - f(a_0)}{b_0 - a_0}$,

$D = \dfrac{F - \gamma}{b_0 - a_0}$ and $G = \dfrac{f'(b_0) - f'(a_0)}{b_0 - a_0}$.

(d) Use the cubic bracketing search and five-digit rounding arithmetic to find $[a_1, b_1]$ and $[a_2, b_2]$ for the function $f(x) = e^x + 2x + x^2/2$ on the interval $[a_0, b_0] = [-2.4, -1.6]$.

Algorithms and Programs

1. Use Program 8.1 to find the local minimum of each of the functions in Exercise 7 with an accuracy of six decimal places.

2. Use Program 8.2 to find the local minimum of each of the functions in Exercise 7 with an accuracy of six decimal places.

3. Use Program 8.3 to find the local minimum of each of the functions in Exercise 7 with an accuracy of six decimal places. Start with the midpoint of the given interval.

4. Use Program 8.1 and/or 8.3 to find all local maxima, with an accuracy of six decimal places, of the function $f(x) = \cos^2(x) - \sin(x)$ on the interval $[0, 2\pi]$.

5. Use Program 8.1 and/or 8.3 to find all the local maxima and minima, with an accuracy of six decimal places of the following function in the interval $[0, 2]$.

$$f(x) = \frac{x^3 + x^2 - 12x - 12}{2x^6 - 3x^5 - 4x^4 + 9x^2 + 12x - 18}$$

6. Write a MATLAB program for the cubic approximation method presented in Section 8.1. Use the program to find the local minimum of each of the functions in Exercise 7 with an accuracy of six decimal places.

7. Write a MATLAB program for the dichotomous search method in Exercise 17. Use the program to find the local minimum of each of the functions in Exercise 7 with an accuracy of six decimal places.

8. Use Program 8.1 and/or 8.3 to find all the local maxima and minima with an accuracy of six decimal places, of the:
   (a) extrapolated cubic spline that passes through $(0.0, 0.0)$, $(1.0, 0.5)$, $(2.0, 2.0)$, and $(3.0, 1.5)$.
   (b) parabolically terminated cubic spline that passes through $(0.0, 0.0)$, $(1.0, 0.5)$, $(2.0, 2.0)$, and $(3.0, 1.5)$.

9. Use Program 8.1 and/or 8.3 to find all the local maxima and minima with an accuracy of six decimal places, of the trigonometric polynomial $T_7(x)$ from Section 5.4,
   Algorithms and Programs, Problem 5(b).

8.2   Nelder-Mead and Powell's Methods

The definitions in Section 8.1 extend naturally to functions of several variables. Suppose that $f(x_1, x_2, \ldots, x_N)$ is defined in the region

$$(1) \qquad R = \left\{ (x_1, x_2, \ldots, x_N) : \sum_{k=1}^{N} (x_k - p_k)^2 < r^2 \right\}.$$

The function $f(x_1, x_2, \ldots, x_N)$ has a local minimum at the point $(p_1, p_2, \ldots, p_N)$
provided that

$$(2) \qquad f(p_1, p_2, \ldots, p_N) \le f(x_1, x_2, \ldots, x_N)$$

for each point $(x_1, x_2, \ldots, x_N) \in R$. The function $f(x_1, x_2, \ldots, x_N)$ has a local maximum at the point $(p_1, p_2, \ldots, p_N)$ provided that

$$(3) \qquad f(p_1, p_2, \ldots, p_N) \ge f(x_1, x_2, \ldots, x_N)$$

or each point $(x_1, x_2, \ldots, x_N) \in R$.

   The introduction of minimization methods for multivariable functions will be simpi-
fied by considering functions of two independent variables, $f(x, y)$. The graph of a
function of two independent variables can be interpreted geometrically as a surface
(see Figure 8.1). The second partial derivative test for an extreme value of a function
$f(x, y)$ is an extension of Theorem 8.4.

Theorem 8.5 (Second Partial Derivative Test).   Assume that $f(x, y)$ and its first-
and second-order partial derivatives are continuous on a region R. Suppose that $(p, q) \in$
R is a critical point where both $f_x(p, q) = 0$ and $f_y(p, q) = 0$. The higher-order partial derivatives are used to determine the nature of the critical point.

(i) If $f_{xx}(p, q) f_{yy}(p, q) - f_{xy}^2(p, q) > 0$ and $f_{xx}(p, q) > 0$, then $f(p, q)$ is a
   local minimum of f.

(ii) If $f_{xx}(p, q) f_{yy}(p, q) - f_{xy}^2(p, q) > 0$ and $f_{xx}(p, q) < 0$, then $f(p, q)$ is a
   local maximum of f.

(iii) If $f_{xx}(p, q) f_{yy}(p, q) - f_{xy}^2(p, q) < 0$, then $f(x, y)$ does not have a local extremum at (p, q).

(iv) If $f_{xx}(p, q) f_{yy}(p, q) - f_{xy}^2(p, q) = 0$, then this test is inconclusive.

Example 8.5.   Find the minimum of $f(x, y) = x^2 - 4x + y^2 - y - xy$.
The first-order partial derivative are

$$f_x(x, y) = 2x - 4 - y \quad \text{and} \quad f_y(x, y) = 2y - 1 - x.$$

Setting these partial derivatives equal to zero yields the linear system

(4)
$$\begin{aligned} 2x - y &= 4 \\ -x + 2y &= 1. \end{aligned}$$

The solution to (4) is $(x, y) = (3, 2)$. The second-order partial derivatives of $f(x, y)$ are

$$f_{xx}(x, y) = 2, \quad f_{yy}(x, y) = 2, \quad \text{and} \quad f_{xy}(x, y) = -1.$$

It is easy to see that we have case (i) of Theorem 8.5, that is,

$$f_{xx}(3, 2) f_{yy}(3, 2) - f_{xy}^2(3, 2) = 3 > 0 \quad \text{and} \quad f_{xx}(3, 2) = 2 > 0.$$

Hence, $f(x, y)$ has a local minimum, $f(3, 2) = -7$, at the point $(3, 2)$.   ∎

Recall that the golden ratio and Fibonacci searches made no direct use of the derivative of the objective function $f(x)$. In both methods the objective function was used to compare function values. Direct searches for minimums of multivariable objective functions, $f(x_1, x_2, \ldots, x_N)$, share this characteristic. No implicit or explicit assumptions are made regarding the differentiability of the multivariable objective function. Thus direct methods are particularly useful for nonsmooth (nondifferentiable) objective functions.

Nelder-Mead Method

A simplex method for finding a local minimum of a function of several variables has been devised by Nelder and Mead. For two variables, a simplex is a triangle, and the method is a pattern search that compares function values at the three vertices of a triangle. The worst vertex, where $f(x, y)$ is largest, is rejected and replaced with a new vertex. A new triangle is formed and the search is continued. The process generates a sequence of triangles (which might have different shapes), for which the function values at the vertices get smaller and smaller. The size of the triangles is reduced and the coordinates of the minimum point are found.

The algorithm is stated using the term *simplex* (a generalized triangle in N dimensions) and will find the minimum of a function of N variables. It is effective and computationally compact.

Initial Triangle BGW

Let $f(x, y)$ be the function that is to be minimized. To start, we are given three vertices of a triangle: $V_k = (x_k, y_k)$, $k = 1, 2, 3$. The function $f(x, y)$ is then evaluated at each of the three points: $z_k = f(x_k, y_k)$ for $k = 1, 2, 3$. The subscripts are then reordered so that $z_1 \le z_2 \le z_3$. We use the notation

$$(5) \qquad B = (x_1, y_1), \qquad G = (x_2, y_2), \qquad \text{and} \qquad W = (x_3, y_3)$$

to help remember that B is the best vertex, G is good (next to best), and W is the worst vertex.

Midpoint of the Good Side

The construction process uses the midpoint of the line segment joining B and G. It is found by averaging the coordinates:

$$(6) \qquad M = \frac{B + G}{2} = \left(\frac{x_1 + x_2}{2}, \frac{y_1 + y_2}{2} \right).$$

Reflection Using the Point R

The function decreases as we move along the side of the triangle from W to B, and it decreases as we move along the side from W to G. Hence it is feasible that $f(x, y)$ takes on smaller values at points that lie away from W on the opposite side of the line between B and G. We choose a test point R that is obtained by "reflecting" the triangle through the side $\overline{BG}$. To determine R, we first find the midpoint M of the side $\overline{BG}$. Then draw the line segment from W to M and call its length d. This last segment is extended a distance d through M to locate the point R (see Figure 8.6). The vector formula for R is

$$(7) \qquad R = M + (M - W) = 2M - W.$$

Expansion Using the Point E

If the function value at R is smaller than the function value at W, then we have moved in the correct direction toward the minimum. Perhaps the minimum is just a bit farther than the point R. So we extend the line segment through M and R to the point E. This forms an expanded triangle BGE. The point E is found by moving an additional distance d along the line joining M and R (see Figure 8.7). If the function value at E is less than the function value at R, then we have found a better vertex than R. The vector formula for E is

$$(8) \qquad E = R + (R - M) = 2R - M.$$

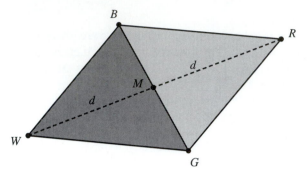

Figure 8.6 The triangle $\triangle BGW$ and midpoint M and reflected point R for the Nelder-Mead method.

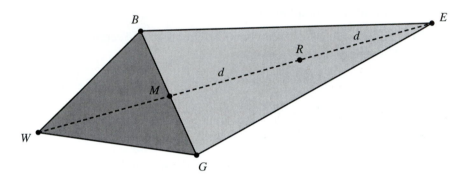

Figure 8.7 The triangle $\triangle BGW$ and point R and extended point E.

Contraction Using the Point C

If the function values at R and W are the same, another point must be tested. Perhaps the function is smaller at M, but we cannot replace W with M because we must have a triangle. Consider the two midpoints C_1 and C_2 of the line segments $\overline{WM}$ and $\overline{MR}$, respectively (see Figure 8.8). The point with the smaller function value is called C, and the new triangle is BGC. *Note.* The choice between C_1 and C_2 might seem inappropriate for the two-dimensional case, but it is important in higher dimensions.

Shrink toward B

If the function value at C is not less than the value at W, the points G and W must be shrunk toward B (see Figure 8.9). The point G is replaced with M, and W is replaced with S, which is the midpoint of the line segment joining B with W.

Logical Decisions for Each Step

A computationally efficient algorithm should perform function evaluations only if needed. In each step, a new vertex is found, which replaces W. As soon as it is

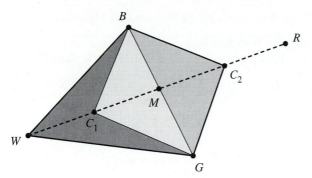

Figure 8.8 The contraction point C_1 or C_2 for Nelder-Mead method.

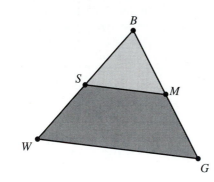

Figure 8.9 Shrinking the triangle toward B.

found, further investigation is not needed, and the iteration step is completed. The logical details for two-dimensional cases are explained in Table 8.5.

Example 8.6. Use the Nelder-Mead algorithm to find the minimum of $f(x, y) = x^2 - 4x + y^2 - y - xy$. Start with the three vertices

$$V_1 = (0, 0), \qquad V_2 = (1.2, 0.0), \qquad V_3 = (0.0, 0.8).$$

The function $f(x, y)$ takes on the values

$$f(0, 0) = 0.0, \qquad f(1.2, 0.0) = -3.36, \qquad f(0.0, 0.8) = -0.16.$$

The function values must be compared to determine B, G, and W;

$$B = (1.2, 0.0), \qquad G = (0.0, 0.8), \qquad W = (0, 0).$$

The vertex $W = (0, 0)$ will be replaced. The points M and R are

$$M = \frac{B + G}{2} = (0.6, 0.4) \quad \text{and} \quad R = 2M - W = (1.2, 0.8).$$

The function value $f(R) = f(1.2, 0.8) = -4.48$ is less than $f(G)$, so the situation is case (i). Since $f(R) \leq f(B)$, we have moved in the right direction, and the vertex E must

Table 8.5   Logical Decisions for the Nelder-Mead Algorithm

IF $f(R) < f(G)$, THEN Perform Case (i) {either reflect or extend}
ELSE Perform Case (ii) {either contract or shrink}

BEGIN {Case (i).}	BEGIN {Case (ii).}
IF $f(B) < f(R)$ THEN	IF $f(R) < f(W)$ THEN
replace W with R	∟ replace W with R
ELSE	Compute $C = (W + M)/2$
	or $C = (M + R)/2$ and $f(C)$
Compute E and $f(E)$	IF $f(C) < f(W)$ THEN
IF $f(E) < f(B)$ THEN	replace W with C
replace W with E	ELSE
ELSE	Compute S and $f(S)$
replace W with R	replace W with S
ENDIF	replace G with M
ENDIF	ENDIF
END {Case (i).}	END {Case (ii).}

be constructed:

$$E = 2R - M = 2(1.2, 0.8) - (0.6, 0.4) = (1.8, 1.2).$$

The function value $f(E) = f(1.8, 1.2) = -5.88$ is less than $f(B)$, and the new triangle has vertices

$$V_1 = (1.8, 1.2), \qquad V_2 = (1.2, 0.0), \qquad V_3 = (0.0, 0.8).$$

The process continues and generates a sequence of triangles that converges down on the solution point (3, 2) (see Figure 8.10). Table 8.6 gives the function values at vertices of the triangle for several steps in the iteration. A computer implementation of the algorithm continued until the thirty-third step, where the best vertex was $B = (2.99996456, 1.99983839)$ and $f(B) = -6.99999998$. These values are approximations to $f(3, 2) = -7$ found in Example 8.5. The reason that the iteration quit before (3, 2) was obtained is that the function is flat near the minimum. The function values $f(B)$, $f(G)$, and $f(W)$ were checked (see Table 8.6) and found to be the same (this is an example of round-off error), and the algorithm was terminated.   ∎

Powell's Method

Let $\mathbf{X}_0$ be an initial guess at the location of the minimum of the function $z = f(x_1, x_2, \ldots, x_N)$. Assume that the partial derivatives of the function are not available. An intuitively appealing approach to approximating a minimum of the function f is to generate the next approximation $\mathbf{X}_1$ by proceeding successively to a minimum of f along each of the N standard base vectors. The process generates the sequence of

Table 8.6   Function Values at Various Triangles for Example 8.6

k	Best point	Good point	Worst point
1	$f(1.2, 0.0) = -3.36$	$f(0.0, 0.8) = -0.16$	$f(0.0, 0.0) = 0.00$
2	$f(1.8, 1.2) = -5.88$	$f(1.2, 0.0) = -3.36$	$f(0.0, 0.8) = -0.16$
3	$f(1.8, 1.2) = -5.88$	$f(3.0, 0.4) = -4.44$	$f(1.2, 0.0) = -3.36$
4	$f(3.6, 1.6) = -6.24$	$f(1.8, 1.2) = -5.88$	$f(3.0, 0.4) = -4.44$
5	$f(3.6, 1.6) = -6.24$	$f(2.4, 2.4) = -6.24$	$f(1.8, 1.2) = -5.88$
6	$f(2.4, 1.6) = -6.72$	$f(3.6, 1.6) = -6.24$	$f(2.4, 2.4) = -6.24$
7	$f(3.0, 1.8) = -6.96$	$f(2.4, 1.6) = -6.72$	$f(2.4, 2.4) = -6.24$
8	$f(3.0, 1.8) = -6.96$	$f(2.55, 2.05) = -6.7725$	$f(2.4, 1.6) = -6.72$
9	$f(3.0, 1.8) = -6.96$	$f(3.15, 2.25) = -6.9525$	$f(2.55, 2.05) = -6.7725$
10	$f(3.0, 1.8) = -6.96$	$f(2.8125, 2.0375) = -6.95640625$	$f(3.15, 2.25) = -6.9525$

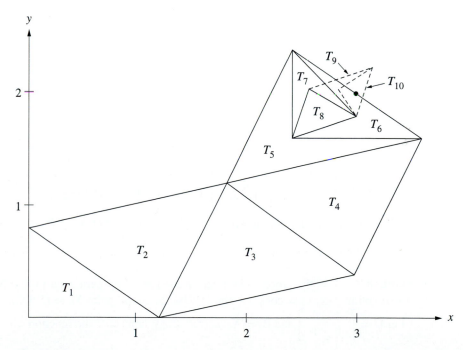

Figure 8.10   The sequence of triangles $\{T_k\}$ converging to the point $(3, 2)$ for the Nelder-Mead method.

points $\mathbf{X}_0 = \mathbf{P}_0$, $\mathbf{P}_1$, $\mathbf{P}_2$, $\ldots$, $\mathbf{P}_N = \mathbf{X}_1$. Along each standard base vector the function f is a function of one variable. Thus the minimization of f requires the application of either the golden ratio or Fibonacci searches (Section 8.1) on an interval over which the function is unimodal. The iteration is then repeated to generate a sequence of points $\{\mathbf{X}_k\}_{k=0}^{\infty}$. Unfortunately, the method is, in general, inefficient due to the geometry of multivariable functions. But the step from the point $\mathbf{X}_0$ to the point $\mathbf{X}_1$ is the first step of *Powell's method*.

The essence of Powell's method is to add two steps to the process described in the preceding paragraph. The vector $\mathbf{P}_N - \mathbf{P}_0$ represents, in some sense, the *average direction* moved during each iteration. Thus the point $\mathbf{X}_1$ is determined to be the point at which the minimum of the function f occurs along the vector $\mathbf{P}_N - \mathbf{P}_0$. As before, f is a function of one variable along this vector and the minimization requires an application of the golden ratio or Fibonacci searches. Finally, since the vector $\mathbf{P}_N - \mathbf{P}_0$ was such a *good* direction, it replaces one of the direction vectors for the next iteration. The iteration is then repeated using the new set of direction vectors to generate a sequence of points $\{\mathbf{X}_k\}_{k=0}^{\infty}$. The process is outlined below.

Let $\mathbf{X}_0$ be an initial guess at the location of the minimum of the function $z = f(x_1, x_2, \ldots, x_N)$, $\{\mathbf{E}_k = [0\,0\,\cdots\,0\,1_k\,0\,\cdots\,0] : k = 1, 2, \ldots, N\}$ be the set of standard base vectors,

$$(9) \qquad \mathbf{U} = [\mathbf{U}_1'\,\mathbf{U}_2'\,\cdots\,\mathbf{U}_N'] = [\mathbf{E}_1'\,\mathbf{E}_2'\,\cdots\,\mathbf{E}_N'],$$

and $i = 0$.

(i) Set $\mathbf{P}_0 = \mathbf{X}_i$.

(ii) For $k = 1, 2, \ldots, N$ find the value of γ_k that minimizes $f(\mathbf{P}_{k-1} + \gamma_k \mathbf{U}_k)$ and set $\mathbf{P}_k = \mathbf{P}_{k-1} + \gamma_k \mathbf{U}_k$.

(iii) Set $i = i + 1$.

(iv) Set $\mathbf{U}_j = \mathbf{U}_{j+1}$ for $j = 1, 2, \ldots, N - 1$. Set $\mathbf{U}_N = \mathbf{P}_N - \mathbf{P}_0$.

(v) Find the value of γ that minimizes $f(\mathbf{P}_0 + \gamma \mathbf{U}_N)$. Set $\mathbf{X}_i = \mathbf{P}_0 + \gamma \mathbf{U}_N$

(vi) Repeat steps (i) through (v).

Example 8.7.   Use the process described in the preceding paragraph to find $\mathbf{X}_1$ and $\mathbf{X}_2$ for the function $f(x, y) = \cos(x) + \sin(y)$. Use the initial point $\mathbf{X}_0 = (5.5, 2)$.

Let $\mathbf{U} = \begin{bmatrix} 1 & 0 \\ 0 & 1 \end{bmatrix}$ and $\mathbf{P}_0 = \mathbf{X}_0 = (5.5, 2)$. When $i = 1$ the function

$$
\begin{aligned}
f(\mathbf{P}_0 + \gamma_1 \mathbf{U}_1) &= f((5.5, 2) + \gamma_1(1, 0)) \\
&= f(5.5 + \gamma_1, 2) \\
&= \cos(5.5 + \gamma_1) + \sin(2)
\end{aligned}
$$

has a minimum at $\gamma_1 = -2.3584042$. Thus $\mathbf{P}_1 = (3.1415958, 2)$. When $i = 2$ the function

$$
\begin{aligned}
f(\mathbf{P}_1 + \gamma_2 \mathbf{U}_2) &= f((3.1415958, 2) + \gamma_2(0, 1)) \\
&= f(3.1415982, 2 + \gamma_2) \\
&= \cos(3.1415982) + \sin(2 + \gamma_2)
\end{aligned}
$$

has a minimum at $\gamma_2 = 2.7123803$. Thus $\mathbf{P}_2 = (3.1415958, 4.7123803)$. Set $\mathbf{U}'_2 = (\mathbf{P}_2 - \mathbf{P}_0)'$ and

$$
\mathbf{U} = \begin{bmatrix} 0 & -2.3584042 \\ 1 & 2.7123803 \end{bmatrix}.
$$

The function

$$
\begin{aligned}
f(\mathbf{P}_0 + \gamma \mathbf{U}_2) &= f((5.5, 2) + \gamma(-2.3584042, 2.7123803)) \\
&= f(5.5 - 2.3584042\gamma, 2 + 2.7123903\gamma) \\
&= \cos(5.5 - 2.3584042\gamma) + \sin(2 + 2.7123803\gamma)
\end{aligned}
$$

has a minimum at $\gamma = 0.9816697$. Thus $\mathbf{X}_1 = (3.1848261, 4.6626615)$.

Set $\mathbf{P}_0 = \mathbf{X}_1$. When $i = 1$ the function

$$
\begin{aligned}
f(\mathbf{P}_0 + \gamma_1 \mathbf{U}_1) &= f((3.1848261, 4.6626615) + \gamma_1(0, 1)) \\
&= f(3.1848261, 4.6626615 + \gamma_1) \\
&= \cos(3.1848261) + \sin(4.6626615 + \gamma_1)
\end{aligned}
$$

has a minimum at $\gamma_1 = 0.0497117$. Thus $\mathbf{P}_1 = (3.1848261, 4.7123732)$. When $i = 2$ the function

$$
\begin{aligned}
f(\mathbf{P}_1 + \gamma_2 \mathbf{U}_2) &= f((3.1848261, 4.7123732) + \gamma_2(-2.3584042, 2.7123809)) \\
&= f(3.1848261 - 2.3584042\gamma_2, 4.7123732 + 2.7123809\gamma_2) \\
&= \cos(3.1848261 - 2.3584042\gamma_2) + \sin(4.7123732 + 2.7123809\gamma_2)
\end{aligned}
$$

has a minimum at $\gamma_2 = 0.0078820$. Thus $\mathbf{P}_2 = (3.1662373, 4.7337521)$. Set $\mathbf{U}'_2 = (\mathbf{P}_2 - \mathbf{P}_0)'$ and

$$
\mathbf{U} = \begin{bmatrix} -2.3584042 & -0.0185889 \\ 2.7123803 & 0.0710906 \end{bmatrix}.
$$

The function

$$
\begin{aligned}
f(\mathbf{P}_0 + \gamma \mathbf{U}_2) &= f((3.1848261, 4.6626615) + \gamma(-0.0185889, 0.0710906)) \\
&= f(3.1848261 - 0.0185889\gamma, 4.6626615 + 0.0710906\gamma) \\
&= \cos(3.1848261 - 0.0185889\gamma) + \sin(4.6626615 + 0.0710906\gamma)
\end{aligned}
$$

has a minimum at $\gamma = 0.8035684$. Thus $\mathbf{X}_2 = (3.1698887, 4.7197876)$.

The function $f(x, y) = \cos(x) + \sin(y)$ has a relative minimum at the point $\mathbf{P} = (\pi, 3\pi/2)$. The graph of f is shown in Figure 8.11. Figure 8.12 shows a contour plot of the function f and the relative positions of the points $\mathbf{X}_0$, $\mathbf{X}_1$, and $\mathbf{X}_2$. ∎

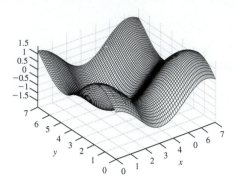

Figure 8.11 The graph of $f(x, y) = \cos(x) + \sin(y)$.

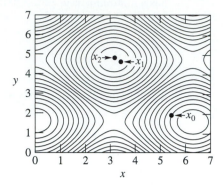

Figure 8.12 The contour graph of $f(x, y) = \cos(x) + \sin(y)$.

In step (iv) of the previous process the first vector U_1 was discarded and the average direction vector $P_N - P_0$ was added to the list of direction vectors. In fact, it would be better to discard the vector U_r along which the greatest decrease in f occurred. It seems reasonable that the vector U_r is a large component of the average direction vector $U_N = P_N - P_0$. Thus, as the number of iterations increase, the set of direction vectors will tend to become *linearly dependent*. When the set becomes linearly dependent one or more of the directions will be lost and it is likely that the set of points $\{X\}_{k=0}^{\infty}$ will not converge to the point at which the local minimum occurs. Furthermore, in step (iv) it was assumed that the average direction vector represented a good direction in which to continue the search. But that may not be the case.

Outline of Powell's Method

(i) Set $P_0 = X_i$.

(ii) For $k = 1, 2, \ldots, N$ find the value of γ_k that minimizes $f(P_{k-1} + \gamma_k U_k)$ and set $P_k = P_{k-1} + \gamma_k U_k$.

(iii) Set r and U_r equal to the maximum decrease in f and the direction of the maximum decrease, respectively, over all the direction vectors in step (ii).

(iv) Set $i = i + 1$.

(v) If $f(2P_N - P_0) \geq f(P_0)$ or

$$2(f(P_0) - 2f(P_N) + f(2P_N - P_0))(f(P_0) - f(P_N) - r)^2 \geq r(f(P_0) - f(2P_N - P_0))^2,$$

then set $X_i = P_N$ and return to step (i). Otherwise, go to step (vi).

(vi) Set $\mathbf{U}_r = \mathbf{P}_N - \mathbf{P}_0$.

(vii) Find the value of γ that minimizes $f(\mathbf{P}_0 + \gamma \mathbf{U}_r)$. Set $\mathbf{X}_i = \mathbf{P}_0 + \gamma \mathbf{U}_r$.

(viii) Repeat steps (i) through (vii).

If the conditions in step (v) are satisfied, then the set of direction vectors is left unchanged. The first inequality in step (v) indicates that there is no further decrease in the value of f in the average direction $\mathbf{P}_N - \mathbf{P}_0$. The second inequality indicates that the decrease in the function f in the direction of greatest decrease $\mathbf{U}_r$ was not a major part of the total decrease in f in step (ii). If the conditions in step (v) are not satisfied, then the direction of greatest decrease $\mathbf{U}_r$ is replaced with the average direction from step (ii); $\mathbf{P}_N - \mathbf{P}_0$. In step (vii) the function is minimized in this direction. Stopping criteria based on the magnitudes $\|\mathbf{X}_i - \mathbf{X}_{i-1}\|$ or $\|f(\mathbf{X}_i)\|$ are typically found in steps (v) and (vii).

Program 8.4 requires that the object function f be saved as an M-file. The argument of f needs to be a $1 \times N$ array. To illustrate, consider saving the function in Example 8.7 as an M-file.

```
function z=f(V)
z=0;x=V(1);y=V(2);
z=cos(x)+sin(y);
```

Program 8.4 (Nelder-Mead's Minimization Method).   To approximate a local minimum of $f(x_1, x_2, \ldots, x_N)$, where f is a continuous function of N real variables, and given the $N + 1$ initial starting points $V_k = (v_{k,1}, \ldots, v_{k,N})$ for $k = 0, 1, \ldots, N$.

```
function[V0,y0,dV,dy]=nelder(F,V,min1,max1,epsilon,show)
%Input   - F is the object function input as a string 'F'
%         - V is a 3 x n matrix containing starting simplex
%         - min1 & max1 are minimum and maximum number
%            of iterations
%         - epsilon is the tolerance
%         - show == 1 displays iterations (P and Q)
%Output - V0 is the vertex for the minimum
%         - y0 is the function value F(V0)
%         - dV is the size of the final simplex
%         - dy is the error bound for the minimum
%         - P is a matrix containing the vertex iterations
%         - Q is an array containing the iterations for F(P)
if nargin==5,
```

```
   show=0;
end
[mm n]=size(V);
% Order the vertices
for j=1:n+1
   Z=V(j,1:n);
   Y(j)=feval(F,Z);
end
[mm lo]=min(Y);
[mm hi]=max(Y);
li=hi;
ho=lo;
for j=1:n+1
   if(j~=lo&j~=hi&Y(j)<=Y(li))
      li=j;
   end
   if(j~=hi&j~=lo&Y(j)>=Y(ho))
      ho=j;
   end
end
cnt=0;
% Start of Nelder-Mead algorithm
while(Y(hi)>Y(lo)+epsilon&cnt<max1)|cnt<min1
   S=zeros(1,1:n);
   for j=1:n+1
      S=S+V(j,1:n);
   end
   M=(S-V(hi,1:n))/n;
   R=2*M-V(hi,1:n);
   yR=feval(F,R);
   if(yR<Y(ho))
      if(Y(li)<yR)
         V(hi,1:n)=R;
         Y(hi)=yR;
      else
         E=2*R-M;
         yE=feval(F,E);
         if(yE<Y(li))
            V(hi,1:n)=E;
            Y(hi)=yE;
         else
            V(hi,1:n)=R;
```

```
                Y(hi)=yR;
            end
        end
    else
        if(yR<Y(hi))
            V(hi,1:n)=R;
            Y(hi)=yR;
        end
        C=(V(hi,1:n)+M)/2;
        yC=feval(F,C);
        C2=(M+R)/2;
        yC2=feval(F,C2);
        if(yC2<yC)
            C=C2;
            yC=yC2;
        end
        if(yC<Y(hi))
            V(hi,1:n)=C;
            Y(hi)=yC;
        else
            for j=1:n+1
                if(j~=lo)
                    V(j,1:n)=(V(j,1:n)+V(lo,1:n))/2;
                    Z=V(j,1:n);
                    Y(j)=feval(F,Z);
                end
            end
        end
    end
    [mm lo]=min(Y);
    [mm hi]=max(Y);
    li=hi;
    ho=lo;
    for j=1:n+1
        if(j~=lo&j~=hi&Y(j)<=Y(li))
            li=j;
        end
        if(j~=hi&j~=lo&Y(j)>=Y(ho))
            ho=j;
        end
    end
    cnt=cnt+1;
    P(cnt,:)=V(lo,:);
```

```
      Q(cnt)=Y(lo);
end
% End of Nelder-Mead algorithm

%Determine size of simplex
snorm=0;
for j=1:n+1
    s=norm(V(j)-V(lo));
    if(s>=snorm)
        snorm=s;
    end
end

Q=Q';
V0=V(lo,1:n);
y0=Y(lo);
dV=snorm;
dy=abs(Y(hi)-Y(lo));
if (show==1)
    disp(P);
    disp(Q);
end
```

Exercises for Nelder-Mead and Powell's Methods

1. Use Theorem 8.5 to find the local minimum of each of the following functions.
   - (a) $f(x, y) = x^3 + y^3 - 3x - 3y + 5$
   - (b) $f(x, y) = x^2 + y^2 + x - 2y - xy + 1$
   - (c) $f(x, y) = x^2y + xy^2 - 3xy$
   - (d) $f(x, y) = (x - y)/(x^2 + y^2 + 2)$
   - (e) $f(x, y) = 100(y - x^2)^2 + (1 - x)^2$

   (Rosenbrock's parabolic valley, circa 1960)

2. Let $B = (2, -3)$, $G = (1, 1)$, and $W = (5, 2)$. Find the points M, R, and E and sketch the triangles that are involved.

3. Let $B = (-1, 2)$, $G = (-2, -5)$, and $W = (3, 1)$. Find the points M, R, and E and sketch the triangles that are involved.

4. Let $B = (0, 0, 0)$, $G = (1, 1, 0)$, $P = (0, 0, 1)$, and $W = (1, 0, 0)$.
   - (a) Sketch the tetrahedron $BGPW$.
   - (b) Find $M = (B + G + P)/3$.
   - (c) Find $R = 2M - W$ and sketch the tetrahedron $BGPR$.
   - (d) Find $E = 2R - M$ and sketch the tetrahedron $BGPE$.

5. Let $B = (0, 0, 0)$, $G = (0, 2, 0)$, $P = (0, 1, 1)$, and $W = (2, 1, 0)$. Follow the instructions in Exercise 4.

6. Follow the process in Example 8.7 and find X_1 for $f(x, y) = x^3 + y^3 - 3x - 3y + 5$. Use the initial point $P_0 = (1/2, 1/3)$.

7. Follow the process in Example 8.7 and find X_1 for $f(x, y) = x^2 y + xy^2 - 3xy$. Use the initial point $P_0 = (1/2, 1/3)$.

8. Give a vector proof that $M = (B + G)/2$ is the midpoint of the line segment joining the points B and G.

9. Give a vector proof of equation (7).

10. Give a vector proof of equation (8).

11. Give a vector proof that the medians of any triangle intersect at a point that is two-thirds of the distance from each vertex to the midpoint of the opposite side.

Algorithms and Programs

1. Use Program 8.4 to find the minimum of each of the functions in Exercise 1 with an accuracy of eight decimal places. Use the following starting vertices:
   (a) $(1, 2)$, $(2, 0)$, and $(2, 2)$
   (b) $(0, 0)$, $(2, 0)$, and $(2, 1)$
   (c) $(0, 0)$, $(2, 0)$, and $(2, 1)$
   (d) $(0, 0)$, $(0, 1)$, and $(1, 1)$
   (e) $(0, 0)$, $(1, 0)$, and $(0, 2)$

2. Use Program 8.4 to find the local minimum of each of the following functions with an accuracy of eight decimal places.
   (a) $f(x, y, z) = 2x^2 + 2y^2 + z^2 - 2xy + yz - 7y - 4z$
        Start with $(1, 1, 1)$, $(0, 1, 0)$, $(1, 0, 1)$, and $(0, 0, 1)$.
   (b) $f(x, y, z, u) = 2(x^2 + y^2 + z^2 + u^2) - x(y + z - u) + yz - 3x - 8y - 5z - 9u$
        Start the search near $(1, 1, 1, 1)$.
   (c) $f(x, y, z, u) = xyzu + \dfrac{1}{x} + \dfrac{1}{y} + \dfrac{1}{z} + \dfrac{1}{u}$
        Start the search near $(0.7, 0.7, 0.7, 0.7)$.

3. Write a MATLAB program to implement Powell's method.

4. Use the program for Powell's method (Problem 3) to find the local minimum of each of functions in Problem 1 with an accuracy of seven decimal places. Use a starting value near one of the given vertices.

5. Use the program for Powell's method (Problem 3) to find the local minimum of each of functions in Problem 2 with an accuracy of seven decimal places. Use the starting values or start near a vertex given in Problem 2.

6. Find the point on the surface $z = x^2 + y^2$ that is closest to the point $(2, 3, 1)$ with an accuracy of seven decimal places.

7. A company has five factories A, B, C, D, and E, located at the points $(10, 10)$, $(30, 50)$, $(16.667, 29)$, $(0.555, 29.888)$, and $(22.2221, 49.988)$, respectively, in the xy-plane. Assume that the distance between two points represents the driving distance, in miles, between the factories. The company plans to build a warehouse at some point in the plane. It is anticipated that during an average week there will be 10, 18, 20, 14, and 25 deliveries made to factories A, B, C, D, and E, respectively. Ideally, to minimize the weekly mileage of delivery vehicles, where should the warehouse be located?

8. In Problem 7, where should the warehouse be located if, due to zoning restrictions, it must be located at a point on the curve $y = x^2$?

8.3   Gradient and Newton's Methods

Now we turn to the minimization of a function $f(X)$ of N variables, where $X = (x_1, x_2, \ldots, x_N)$ and the partial derivatives of f are accessible.

Steepest Descent or Gradient Method

Definition 8.4.   Let $z = f(X)$ be a function of X such that $\partial f(X)/\partial x_k$ exists for $k = 1, 2, \ldots, N$. The **gradient** of f, denoted by $\nabla f(X)$, is the vector

$$(1) \qquad \nabla f(X) = \left(\frac{\partial f(X)}{\partial x_1}, \frac{\partial f(X)}{\partial x_2}, \ldots, \frac{\partial f(X)}{\partial x_N} \right). \qquad \blacktriangle$$

Example 8.8.   Find the gradient of $f(x, y) = \dfrac{x - y}{x^2 + y^2 + 2}$ at the point $(-3, -2)$.

Substituting $x = -3$ and $y = -2$ into

$$f_x(x, y) = \frac{-x^2 + 2xy + y^2 + 2}{(x^2 + y^2 + 2)^2} \qquad \text{and} \qquad f_y(x, y) = \frac{-x^2 - 2xy + y^2 - 2}{(x^2 + y^2 + 2)^2}$$

yields

$$\nabla f(-3, -2) = (f_x(-3, -2), f_y(-3, -2)) = \left(\frac{9}{225}, -\frac{19}{225} \right). \qquad \blacksquare$$

Recall that the gradient vector in (1) points locally in the direction of the greatest rate of increase of $f(X)$. Hence $-\nabla f(X)$ points locally in the direction of greatest decrease. Start at the point P_0 and search along the line through P_0 in the direction $S_0 = -\nabla f(P_0)/\| - \nabla f(P_0)\|$. You will arrive at a point P_1, where a local minimum occurs when the point X is constrained to lie on the line $X = P_0 + \gamma S_0$. Since partial derivatives are accessible, the minimization process should be executed using the quadratic or cubic approximation methods in Section 8.1.

Next we compute $-\nabla f(\boldsymbol{P}_1)$ and move in the search direction $\boldsymbol{S}_1 = -\nabla f(\boldsymbol{P}_1)/\|-\nabla f(\boldsymbol{P}_1)\|$. You will come to $\boldsymbol{P}_2$, where a local minimum occurs when $\boldsymbol{X}$ is constrained to lie on the line $\boldsymbol{X} = \boldsymbol{P}_1 + \gamma \boldsymbol{S}_1$. Iteration will produce a sequence, $\{\boldsymbol{P}_k\}_{k=0}^{\infty}$, of points with the property $f(\boldsymbol{P}_0) > f(\boldsymbol{P}_1) > \cdots > f(\boldsymbol{P}_k) > \cdots$. If $\lim_{k\to\infty} \boldsymbol{P}_k = \boldsymbol{P}$, then $f(\boldsymbol{P})$ will be a local minimum for $f(\boldsymbol{X})$.

Outline of the Gradient Method

Suppose that $\boldsymbol{P}_k$ has been obtained.

(i) Evaluate the gradient vector $\nabla f(\boldsymbol{P}_k)$.

(ii) Compute the search direction $\boldsymbol{S}_k = -\nabla f(\boldsymbol{P}_k)/\|-\nabla f(\boldsymbol{P}_k)\|$.

(iii) Perform a single parameter minimization of $\Phi(\gamma) = f(\boldsymbol{P}_k + \gamma \boldsymbol{S}_k)$ on the interval $[0, b]$, where b is large. This will produce a value $\gamma = h_{\min}$ where a local minimum for $\Phi(\gamma)$ occurs. The relation $\Phi(h_{\min}) = f(\boldsymbol{P}_k + h_{\min}\boldsymbol{S}_k)$ shows that this is a minimum for $f(\boldsymbol{X})$ along the search line $\boldsymbol{X} = \boldsymbol{P}_k + h_{\min}\boldsymbol{S}_k$.

(iv) Construct the next point $\boldsymbol{P}_{k+1} = \boldsymbol{P}_k + h_{\min}\boldsymbol{S}_k$.

(v) Perform the termination test for minimization; that is, are the function values $f(\boldsymbol{P}_k)$ and $f(\boldsymbol{P}_{k+1})$ sufficiently close and the distance $\|\boldsymbol{P}_{k+1} - \boldsymbol{P}_k\|$ small enough?

Repeat the process.

Example 8.9.   Use the gradient method to find $\boldsymbol{P}_1$ and $\boldsymbol{P}_2$ for the function $f(x, y) = \dfrac{x - y}{x^2 + y^2 + 2}$. Use the initial point $\boldsymbol{P}_0 = (-3, -2)$.

When $\boldsymbol{P}_0 = (-3, -2)$,

$$\begin{aligned}
\boldsymbol{S}_0 &= \frac{1}{\|-\nabla f(\boldsymbol{P}_0)\|}(-\nabla f(\boldsymbol{P}_0)) \\
&= \frac{1}{\|-\nabla f(-3, -2)\|}(-\nabla f(-3, -2)) \\
&= (-0.4280863, 0.9037378).
\end{aligned}$$

The function

$$\begin{aligned}
f(\boldsymbol{P}_0 + \gamma \boldsymbol{S}_0) &= f((-3, -2) + \gamma(-0.4280863, 0.9037378)) \\
&= f(-3 - 0.4280863\gamma, -2 + 0.9037378\gamma) \\
&= \frac{(-3 - 0.4280863\gamma) - (-2 + 0.9037378\gamma)}{(-3 - 0.4280863\gamma)^2 + (-2 + 0.9037378\gamma)^2 + 2}
\end{aligned}$$

has a minimum at $\gamma = h_{\min_0} = 4.8186760$ (Program 8.3, Quadratic Interpolation). Thus

$$\begin{aligned} \boldsymbol{P}_1 &= \boldsymbol{P}_0 + h_{\min_0}\boldsymbol{S}_0 \\ &= (-3, -2) + 4.8186760(-0.4280863, 0.9037378) \\ &= (-5.0628094, 2.3548199). \end{aligned}$$

When $\boldsymbol{P}_1 = (-5.0628094, 2.3548199)$,

$$\begin{aligned} \boldsymbol{S}_1 &= \frac{1}{\| -\nabla f(\boldsymbol{P}_1)\|}(-\nabla f(\boldsymbol{P}_1)) \\ &= \frac{1}{\| -\nabla f(-5.0628094, 2.3548199)\|}(-\nabla f(-5.0628094, 2.3548199)) \\ &= (0.9991231, -0.0418690). \end{aligned}$$

The function

$$\begin{aligned} f(\boldsymbol{P}_1 + \gamma\boldsymbol{S}_1) &= f((-5.0628094, 2.3548199) + \gamma(0.9991231, -0.0418690)) \\ &= f(-5.0628094 + 0.9991231\gamma, 2.3545199 - 0.0418690\gamma) \\ &= \frac{(-5.0628094 + 0.9991231\gamma) - (2.3545199 - 0.0418690\gamma)}{(-5.0628094 + 0.9991231\gamma)^2 + (2.3545199 - 0.0418690\gamma)^2 + 2} \end{aligned}$$

has a minimum at $\gamma = h_{\min_1} = 2.7708281$ (Program 8.3, Quadratic Interpolation). Thus

$$\begin{aligned} \boldsymbol{P}_2 &= \boldsymbol{P}_1 + h_{\min_1}\boldsymbol{S}_0 \\ &= (-5.0628094, 2.3548199) + 2.7708281(0.9991231, -0.0418690) \\ &= (-2.2944111, 2.2388080). \end{aligned}$$

The function $f(x, y) = (x - y)/(x^2 + y^2 + 2)$ has a relative minimum at $\boldsymbol{P} = (-1, 1)$. Figure 8.13 shows a contour plot of the function f and the relative positions of the points $\boldsymbol{P}_0$, $\boldsymbol{P}_1$, $\boldsymbol{P}_2$, and $\boldsymbol{P}$. Some additional computations are shown in Table 8.7.   ∎

The previous discussion supports the analytic and geometric appeal of the gradient method. The method is a natural extension of our geometric understanding of the gradient. Unfortunately, convergence to a minimum of a function of N variables, $f(x_1, x_2, \ldots, x_N)$, can be slow. In general, the geometry of a minimum of a function f will cause the value of $h_{\min}$ to be small. Subsequently, there will be a large number of returns to the minimization step (step (iii)) of the gradient method.

Newton's Method

The quadratic approximation method of Section 8.1 generated a sequence of second-degree Lagrange polynomials. It was implicitly assumed that near the minimum, the shape of the quadratics approximated the shape of the objective function $y = f(x)$. The resulting sequence of minimums of the quadratics produced a sequence converging

Table 8.7   Gradient Method for $f(x, y) = (x - y)/(x^2 + y^2 + 2)$

k	x_k	y_k	$f(x_k, y_k)$
0	-3.0000000	-2.0000000	-0.0666667
1	-5.0628094	2.3548199	-0.2235760
2	-2.2944111	2.2388080	-0.3692574
3	-1.3879337	1.3859313	-0.4743948
4	-1.0726050	1.0724933	-0.4987762
5	-1.0035351	1.0035334	-0.4999969
6	-1.0000091	1.0000091	-0.5000000
7	-1.0000000	1.0000000	-0.5000000

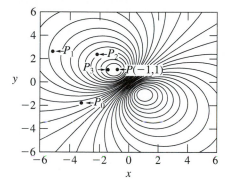

Figure 8.13   The countour graph of $f(x, y) = (x - y)/(x^2 + y^2 + 2)$ and the gradient method.

to the minimum of the objective function f. **Newton's method** extends this process to functions of N independent variables: $z = f(x_1, x_2, \ldots, x_N)$. Starting at an initial point P_0, a sequence of second-degree polynomials in N variables will be constructed recursively. If the objective function is well-behaved and the initial point is near the actual minimum, then the sequence of minimums of the quadratics will converge to the minimum of the objective function.

The process will use both the first- and second-order partial derivatives of the objective function. Recall that the gradient method used only the first partial derivatives. It is to be expected that Newton's method will be more efficient than the gradient method.

Definition 8.5. Let $z = f(X)$ be a function of X such that $\dfrac{\partial^2 f(X)}{\partial x_i \, \partial x_j}$ exists for $i, j = 1, 2, \ldots N$. The **Hessian matrix** for f at X, denoted by $H f(X)$, is the $N \times N$ matrix

$$(2) \qquad\qquad H f(X) = \left[\frac{\partial^2 f(X)}{\partial x_i \partial x_j} \right]_{N \times N},$$

where $i, j = 1, 2, \ldots, N$. ▲

It is appropriate to think of the Hessian matrix of a function f as representing the *second derivative* of the function (precisely the case when $N = 1$). It is not difficult to show that the Hessian matrix of a function f equals the Jacobian matrix (see Section 3.7) of the gradient of f;

$$(3) \qquad\qquad H f(X) = J \nabla f(X).$$

Example 8.10. Find the Hessian matrix at the point $(-3, -2)$ of the function $f(x, y) = (x - y)/(x^2 + y^2 + 2)$.
From Example 8.8,

$$f_x(x, y) = \frac{-x^2 + 2xy + y^2 + 2}{(x^2 + y^2 + 2)^2} \quad \text{and} \quad f_y(x, y) = \frac{-x^2 - 2xy + y^2 - 2}{(x^2 + y^2 + 2)^2}.$$

The second partials are

$$f_{xx}(x, y) = \frac{2(x^3 - 3x^2 y - 3x(y^2 + 2) + y(y^2 + 2))}{(x^2 + y^2 + 2)^3},$$

$$f_{xy}(x, y) = \frac{2(x^3 + 3x^2 y + x(2 - 3y^2) - y(y^2 + 2))}{(x^2 + y^2 + 2)^3},$$

$$f_{yx}(x, y) = \frac{2(x^3 + 3x^2 y + x(2 - 3y^2) - y(y^2 + 2))}{(x^2 + y^2 + 2)^3},$$

$$f_{yy}(x, y) = -\frac{2(2x + x^3 - 6y - 3x^2 y - 3xy^2 + y^3)}{(x^2 + y^2 + 2)^3}.$$

Evaluating the Hessian matrix

$$H f(x, y) = \begin{bmatrix} f_{xx}(x, y) & f_{xy}(x, y) \\ f_{yx}(x, y) & f_{yy}(x, y) \end{bmatrix}$$

at $(x, y) = (-3, -2)$ yields

$$H f(-3, -2) = \frac{1}{3375} \begin{bmatrix} 138 & -78 \\ -78 & -122 \end{bmatrix}. \qquad ■$$

Definition 8.6.   The *Taylor polynomial* of degree two for $f(X)$ centered at A is

$$(4) \quad Q(X) = f(A) + \nabla f(A) \cdot (X - A) + \frac{1}{2}(X - A)Hf(A)(X - A)'. \qquad \blacktriangle$$

Mathematical descriptions of Taylor polynomials of degree m can be found in most vector or advanced calculus textbooks.

Example 8.11.   Calculate the second-degree Taylor polynomial of $f(x, y) = (x-y)/(x^2 + y^2 + 2)$ centered at the point $A = (-3, -2)$. Treat the gradient of f as a 1×2 matrix.
From Examples 8.8 and 8.10,

$$\nabla f(-3, -2) = [f_x(-3, -2), f_y(-3, -2)] = \left[\frac{9}{225}, -\frac{19}{225}\right],$$

$$Hf(-3, -2) = \frac{1}{3375}\begin{bmatrix} 138 & -78 \\ -78 & -122 \end{bmatrix},$$

respectively. Thus

$$Q(x, y) = -\frac{1}{15} + \frac{1}{225}[\ 9 \quad -19\ ] \cdot [\ x+3 \quad y+2\ ]$$

$$+ \frac{1}{2}[\ x+3 \quad y+2\ ]\left(\frac{1}{3375}\right)\begin{bmatrix} 138 & -78 \\ -78 & -122 \end{bmatrix}[\ x+3 \quad y+2\ ]'$$

$$= \frac{69x^2 - 61y^2 + 393x - 763y - 78xy - 481}{3375}.$$

Without ambiguity the matrix notation is dropped from the resultant 1×1 matrix. $\blacksquare$

Assume that the first and second partial derivatives of $z = f(x_1, x_2, \ldots, x_N)$ exist and are continuous in a region containing the point P_0, and that there is a minimum at the point P. Substituting P_0 for A in formula (4) yields

$$(5) \quad Q(X) = f(P_0) + \nabla f(P_0) \cdot (X - P_0) + \frac{1}{2}(X - P_0)Hf(P_0)(X - P_0)',$$

a second-degree polynomial in N variables; where $X = [x_1\ x_2 \cdots x_N]$. A minimum of $Q(X)$ occurs where

$$(6) \qquad\qquad\qquad \nabla Q(X) = 0$$

or

$$(7) \qquad\qquad\qquad \nabla f(P_0) + (X - P_0)(Hf(P_0))' = 0.$$

If P_0 is close to the point P (where a minimum of f occurs), then $Hf(P_0)$ is invertible and equation (7) can be solved for X:

$$(8) \qquad\qquad\qquad X = P_0 - \nabla f(P_0)((Hf(P_0))^{-1})'.$$

Substituting P_1 for X in formula (8) yields

(9) $$P_1 = P_0 - \nabla f(P_0)((Hf(P_0))^{-1})'.$$

When P_{k-1} is used in place of P_0 in formula (9), the following general rule is established:

(10) $$P_k = P_{k-1} - \nabla f(P_{k-1})((Hf(P_{k-1}))^{-1})'.$$

In equation (7) the inverse of the Hessian matrix was used to solve for X. It would be better to solve the system of linear equations represented by equation (7) with one of the methods from Chapter 3. In general, the methods in Chapter 3 are more reliable and efficient. The reader should realize that the inverse is primarily a theoretical tool and the computation and use of inverses is inherently inefficient.

Example 8.12.   Use formula (10) to find P_1 and P_2 for the function $f(x, y) = (x - y)/(x^2 + y^2 + 2)$. Use the initial point $P_0 = [-0.3 \ 0.2]$.

If $P_0 = [-0.3 \ 0.2]$, then

$$\nabla f(P_0) = \begin{bmatrix} 0.4033591 & -0.4254006 \end{bmatrix},$$

$$Hf(P_0) = \begin{bmatrix} 0.4476594 & -0.1955793 \\ -0.1955793 & 0.3801897 \end{bmatrix},$$

$$(Hf(P_0))^{-1} = \begin{bmatrix} 2.8814429 & 1.4822882 \\ 1.4822882 & 3.3927931 \end{bmatrix}.$$

Substituting P_0, $\nabla f(P_0)$, and $(Hf(P_0))^{-1}$ into formula (10) yields

$$P_1 = \begin{bmatrix} -0.3 & 0.2 \end{bmatrix} - \begin{bmatrix} 0.4033591 & -0.4254006 \end{bmatrix} \begin{bmatrix} 2.8814429 & 1.4822882 \\ 1.4822882 & 3.3927931 \end{bmatrix}$$

$$= \begin{bmatrix} -0.8316899 & 1.0454017 \end{bmatrix}.$$

If $P_1 = \begin{bmatrix} -0.8316899 & 1.0454017 \end{bmatrix}$, then

$$\nabla f(P_1) = \begin{bmatrix} 0.0462373 & 0.0097785 \end{bmatrix},$$

$$Hf(P_1) = \begin{bmatrix} 0.3027529 & -0.0212462 \\ -0.0212462 & 0.2513046 \end{bmatrix},$$

$$(Hf(P_1))^{-1} = \begin{bmatrix} 3.3227373 & 0.2809163 \\ -0.2809163 & 4.0029851 \end{bmatrix}.$$

Substituting P_1, $\nabla f(P_1)$, and $(Hf(P_1))^{-1}$ into formula (10) yields

$$P_2 = \begin{bmatrix} -0.8316899 & 1.0454017 \end{bmatrix}$$

$$- \begin{bmatrix} 0.0462373 & 0.0097785 \end{bmatrix} \begin{bmatrix} 3.3227373 & 0.2809163 \\ -0.2809163 & 4.0029851 \end{bmatrix}$$

$$= \begin{bmatrix} -0.9880713 & 0.9932699 \end{bmatrix}.$$

The process appears to be converging to the point $P = [-1 \ 1]$, where the minimum occurs for the function f. At the fifth iteration $P_5 = [-1 \ 1]$.   ∎

It should be noted that formula (9) is equivalent (take the transpose of both sides) to formula (30) in the optional Section 3.7. Formula (10) is also equivalent to step (iv) in the outline of Newton's method in Section 3.7. Thus Program 3.7 (Newton-Raphson method) can be used to produce the sequence $\{\mathbf{P_k}\}_{k=0}^{\infty}$ (without using inverse matrices) that converges to $\mathbf{P}$.

Newton's method requires a good initial point if there is to be convergence. This is similar to the situation for the Newton-Raphson method for approximating a root of $f(x) = 0$. Unlike earlier examples, the initial point in Example 8.12 was not $\mathbf{P}_0 = [-3 \ -2]$. In fact, as the reader can easily verify, Newton's method diverges for that particular initial point.

Newton's method can be modified by treating the expression

$$-\nabla f(\mathbf{P}_{k-1})((\mathbf{H}f(\mathbf{P}_{k-1}))^{-1})'$$

in formula (10) as a search direction. This is analogous to the use of the search direction $\mathbf{S}_k$ in the gradient method. As with the gradient method a single parameter minimization (line search) is implemented in the search direction. In general, this modified Newton's method will be more reliable than Newton's method.

Outline of Modified Newton's Method

Suppose that $\mathbf{P}_k$ has been obtained.

(i) Compute the search direction $\mathbf{S}_k = -\nabla f(\mathbf{P}_{k-1})((\mathbf{H}f(\mathbf{P}_{k-1}))^{-1})'$.

(ii) Perform a single parameter minimization of $\Phi(\gamma) = f(\mathbf{P}_k + \gamma \mathbf{S}_k)$ on the interval $[0, b]$, where b is large. This will produce a value $\gamma = h_{\min}$ where a local minimum for $\Phi(\gamma)$ occurs. The relation $\Phi(h_{\min}) = f(\mathbf{P}_k + h_{\min}\mathbf{S}_k)$ shows that this is a minimum for $f(\mathbf{X})$ along the search line $\mathbf{X} = \mathbf{P}_k + h_{\min}\mathbf{S}_k$.

(iii) Construct the next point, $\mathbf{P}_{k+1} = \mathbf{P}_k + h_{\min}\mathbf{S}_k$.

(iv) Perform the termination test for minimization; that is, are the function values $f(\mathbf{P}_k)$ and $f(\mathbf{P}_{k+1})$ sufficiently close and the distance $\|\mathbf{P}_{k+1} - \mathbf{P}_k\|$ small enough?

Repeat the process.

The methods in this section require that the gradient and Hessian of a function $z = f(x_1, x_2, \ldots, x_N)$ be saved as M-files (a method to save f as an M-file was shown in Section 8.2). To illustrate, consider the function $f(x, y) = x^2 + y^2 - xy - 4x - y$. Appropriate M-files for the gradient and Hessian, respectively, are

```
function z=G(V)
z=zeros(1,2);
x=V(1);y=V(2);
g=[2x-4-y 2*y-1-x];
```

```
z=-(1/norm(g))*g;
function z=H(V)
z=zeros(2,2);
x=V(1);y=V(2);
z=[2 -1;-1 2];
```

Program 8.5 (Steepest Descent or Gradient Method).   To approximate a local minimum of $f(X)$ numerically, where f is a continuous function of N real variables and $X = (x_1, x_2, \ldots, x_N)$, by starting with one point P_0 and using the gradient method.

```
function[P0,y0,err]=grads(F,G,P0,max1,delta,epsilon,show)
%Input   - F is the object function input as a string 'F'
%         - G =-(1/norm(grad F))*grad F; the search direction
%           input as a string 'G'
%         - P0 is the initial starting point
%         - max1 is the maximum number of iterations
%         - delta is the tolerance for hmin in the single
%           parameter minimization in the search direction
%         - epsilon is the tolerance for the error in y0
%         - show; if show==1 the iterations are displayed
%Output  - P0 is the point for the minimum
%         - y0 is the function value F(P0)
%         - err is the error bound for y0
%         - P is a vector containing the iterations
if nargin==5,show=0;end
[mm n]=]size(P0);
maxj=10; big=1e8; h=1;
P=zeros(maxj,n+1);
len=norm(P0);
y0=feval(F,P0);
if (len>e4),h=len/1e4;end
err=1;cnt=0;cond=0;
P(cnt+1,:)=[P0 y0];
while(cnt<max1&cond~=5&(h>delta|err>epsilon))
    %Compute search direction
    S=feval(G,P0);

    %Start single parameter quadratic minimization
    P1=P0+h*S;
    P2=P0+2*h*S;
    y1=feval(F,P1);
    y2=feval(F,P2);
```

```
    cond=0;j=0;
    while(j<maxj&cond==0)
        len=norm(P0);
        if (y0<y1)
        P2=P1;
        y2=y1;
        h=h/2;
        P1=P0+h*S;
        y1=feval(F,P1);
    else
        if(y2<y1)
            P1=P2;
            y1=y2;
            h=2*h;
            P2=P0+2*h*S;
            y2=feval(F,P2);
        else
            cond=-1;
        end
    end
    j=j+1;
    if(h<delta),cond=1;end
    if(abs(h)>big|len>big),cond=5;end
end
if(cond==5)
    Pmin=P1;
    ymin=y1;
else
    d=4*y1-2*y0-2*y2;
    if(d<0)
        hmin=h*(4*y1-3*y0-y2)/d;
    else
        cond=4;
        hmin=h/3;
    end
    %Construct the next point
    Pmin=P0+hmin*S;
    ymin=feval(F,Pmin);
    %Determine magnitude of next h
    h0=abs(hmin);
    h1=abs(hmin-h);
```

```
      h2=abs(hmin-2*h);
      if(h0<h),h=h0;end
      if(h1<h),h=h1;end
      if(h2<h),h=h2;end
      if(h==0),h=hmin;end
      if(h<delta),cond=1;end

      %Termination test for minimization
      e0=abs(y0-ymin);
      e1=abs(y1-ymin);
      e2=abs(y2-ymin);
      if(e0~=0&e0<err),err=e0;end
      if(e1~=0&e1<err),err=e1;end
      if(e2~=0&e2<err),err=e2;end
      if(e0==0&e1==0&e2==0),err=0;end
      if(err<epsilon),cond=2;end
      if(cond==2&h<delta),cond=3;end
   end
   cnt=cnt+1;
   P(cnt+1,:)=[Pmin ymin];
   P0=Pmin;
   y0=ymin;
end
if(show==1)
   disp(P);
end
```

Exercises for Gradient and Newton's Methods

1. Find the gradient of each function at the given point.
   - (a) $f(x, y) = x^2 + y^3 - 3x - 3y + 5$ at $(-1, 2)$
   - (b) $f(x, y) = 100(y - x^2)^2 + (1 - x)^2$ at $(1/2, 4/3)$
     (Rosenbrock's parabolic valley, circa 1960)
   - (c) $f(x, y, z) = \cos(xy) - \sin(xz)$ at $(0, \pi, \pi/2)$

2. Use the gradient method to find P_1 and P_2 for the functions and initial points in Exercise 1.

3. Find the Hessian matrix for the functions and initial points in Exercise 1.

4. Calculate the second-degree Taylor polynomial for the functions in Exercise 1, centered at the given initial points.

5. Use formula (10) to find P_1 and P_2 for the functions and initial points in Exercise 1.

6. Use the modified Newton's method to find P_1 for the functions and initial points in Exercise 1.

7. Verify that formula (3) is true for the function in Example 8.10.

8. Establish formula (7) for the case $N = 2$ (i.e., $z = f(x_1, x_2)$).

9. Derive formula (8) from formula (7).

Algorithms and Programs

1. Use Program 8.5 to find the minimum of each of the functions in Exercise 1(a) and 1(b) with an accuracy of eight decimal places. Use the initial point $P_0 = (0.3, 0.4)$.

2. In Program 8.5 the x- and y-coordinates of the iterations are stored in the first two columns of the matrix P, respectively. Modify Program 8.5 so that it will plot the x- and y-coordinates of the iterations on the same coordinate system. *Hint.* Incorporate the command plot(P(:,1),P(:,2),'.') into your program. Use this program on the functions in Exercise 1(a) and 1(b). Use the initial point $P_0 = (-0.2, 0.3)$.

3. Write a MATLAB program for Newton's method (formula (10)). Use the program to find the minimum of each of the functions in Exercise 1(a) and 1(b) with an accuracy of eight decimal places. Use the initial point $P_0 = (0.3, 0.4)$.

4. Write a MATLAB program for the modified Newton's method.

5. Use the program for the modified Newton's method (Problem 4) to find the local minimum of each of the following functions with an accuracy of eight decimal places.

(a) $f(x, y, z) = 2x^2 + 2y^2 + z^2 - 2xy + yz - 7y - 4z$ with $P_0 = (0.5, 0.4, 0.5)$
(b) $f(x, y, z, u) = 2(x^2 + y^2 + z^2 + u^2) - x(y + z - u) + yz - 3x - 8y - 5z - 9u$ with $P_0 = (1, 1, 1, 1)$
(c) $f(x, y, z, u) = xyzu + \dfrac{1}{x} + \dfrac{1}{y} + \dfrac{1}{z} + \dfrac{1}{u}$ with $P_0 = (0.7, 0.7, 0.7, 0.7)$

6. Use Program 8.5 to find the local minimum of each of the functions in Problem 5 with an accuracy of eight decimal places. Use a starting value near one of the given vertices.

7. Find the point, with an accuracy of seven decimal places, on the surface $z = x^2 + y^2$ that is closest to the point $(2, 3, 1)$.

8. A company has five factories, A, B, C, D, and E, located at the points $(10, 10)$, $(30, 50)$, $(16.667, 29)$, $(0.555, 29.888)$, and $(22, 2221, 49.988)$, respectively, in the xy-plane. Assume that the distance between two points represents the driving distance, in miles, between the factories. The company plans to build a warehouse at some point in the plane. It is anticipated that during an average week there will be 10, 18, 20, 14, and 25 deliveries made to factories A, B, C, D, and E, respectively. Ideally, to minimize the weekly mileage of delivery vehicles, where in the xy-plane should the warehouse be located?

9. In Problem 8, where should the warehouse be located if due to zoning restrictions, it must be located at a point on the curve $y = x^2$?

9

Solution of Differential Equations

Differential equations are commonly used for mathematical modeling in science and engineering. Often, there is no known analytic solution and numerical approximations are required. As an illustration, we consider population dynamics and a nonlinear system that is a modification of the Lotka-Volterra equations:

$$x' = f(t, x, y) = x - xy - \frac{1}{10}x^2 \quad \text{and} \quad y' = g(t, x, y) = xy - y - \frac{1}{20}y^2,$$

with the initial condition $x(0) = 2$ and $y(0) = 1$ for $0 \leq t \leq 30$. Although the numerical solution is a list of numbers, it is helpful to plot the polygonal path joining

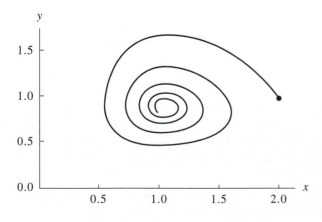

Figure 9.1 The trajectory for a nonlinear system of differential equations $x' = f(t, x, y)$ and $y' = g(t, x, y)$.

the approximation points $\{(x_k, y_k)\}$ and plot the trajectory shown in Figure 9.1. In this chapter we present the standard methods for solving ordinary differential equations, systems of differential equations, and boundary value problems.

9.1   Introduction to Differential Equations

Consider the equation

(1)
$$\frac{dy}{dt} = 1 - e^{-t}.$$

It is a differential equation because it involves the derivative dy/dt of the "unknown function" $y = y(t)$. Only the independent variable t appears on the right side of equation (1): hence a solution is an antiderivative of $1 - e^{-t}$. The rules of integration can be used to find $y(t)$:

(2)
$$y(t) = t + e^{-t} + C,$$

where C is the constant of integration. All the functions in (2) are solutions of (1) because they satisfy the requirement that $y'(t) = 1 - e^{-t}$. They form the family of curves in Figure 9.2.

Integration was the technique used to find the explicit formula for the functions in (2), and Figure 9.2 emphasizes that there is one degree of freedom involved in the solution, that is, the constant of integration C. By varying the value of C, we "move the solution curve" up or down, and a particular curve can be found that will pass through any desired point. The secrets of the world are seldom observed as explicit formulas. Instead, we usually measure how a change in one variable affects another variable.

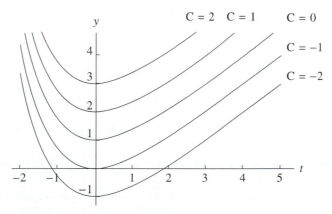

Figure 9.2   The solution curves $y(t) = t + e^{-t} + C$.

When this is translated into a mathematical model, the result is an equation involving the rate of change of the unknown function and the independent and/or dependent variable.

Consider the temperature $y(t)$ of a cooling object. It might be conjectured that the rate of change of the temperature of the body is related to the temperature difference between its temperature and that of the surrounding medium. Experimental evidence verifies this conjecture. Newton's law of cooling asserts that the rate of change is directly proportional to the difference in these temperatures. If A is the temperature of the surrounding medium and $y(t)$ is the temperature of the body at time t, then

$$(3) \qquad \frac{dy}{dt} = -k(y - A),$$

where k is a positive constant. The negative sign is required because dy/dt will be negative when the temperature of the body is greater than the temperature of the medium.

If the temperature of the object is known at time $t = 0$, we call this an initial condition and include this information in the statement of the problem. Usually, we are asked to solve

$$(4) \qquad \frac{dy}{dt} = -k(y - A) \quad \text{with} \quad y(0) = y_0.$$

The technique of separation of variables can be used to find the solution

$$(5) \qquad y = A + (y_0 - A)e^{-kt}.$$

For each choice of y_0, the solution curve will be different, and there is no simple way to move one curve around to get another one. The initial value is a point where the desired solution is "nailed down." Several solution curves are shown in Figure 9.3, and it can be observed that as t gets large the temperature of the object approaches room temperature. If $y_0 < A$, the body is warming instead of cooling.

Initial Value Problem

Definition 9.1.   A *solution* to the *initial value problem (I.V.P.)*

$$(6) \qquad y' = f(t, y) \quad \text{with} \quad y(t_0) = y_0$$

on an interval $[t_0, b]$ is a differentiable function $y = y(t)$ such that

$$(7) \qquad y(t_0) = y_0 \quad \text{and} \quad y'(t) = f(t, y(t)) \quad \text{for all } t \in [t_0, b].$$

Notice that the solution curve $y = y(t)$ must pass through the initial point (t_0, y_0).   ▲

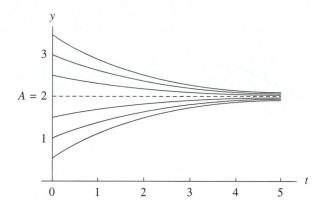

Figure 9.3   The solution curves
$y = A + (y_0 - A)e^{-kt}$ for Newton's
law of cooling (and warming).

Geometric Interpretation

At each point (t, y) in the rectangular region $R = \{(t, y) : a \le t \le b, c \le y \le d\}$, the slope of a solution curve $y = y(t)$ can be found using the implicit formula $m = f(t, y(t))$. Hence the values $m_{i,j} = f(t_i, y_j)$ can be computed throughout the rectangle, and each value $m_{i,j}$ represents the slope of the line tangent to a solution curve that passes through the point (t_i, y_j).

A slope field or direction field is a graph that indicates the slopes $\{m_{i,j}\}$ over the region. It can be used to visualize how a solution curve "fits" the slope constraint. To move along a solution curve, one must start at the initial point and check the slope field to determine in which direction to move. Then take a small step from t_0 to $t_0 + h$ horizontally and move the appropriate vertical distance $hf(t_0, y_0)$ so that the resulting displacement has the required slope. The next point on the solution curve is (t_1, y_1). Repeat the process to continue your journey along the curve. Since a finite number of steps will be used, the method will produce an approximation to the solution.

Example 9.1.   The slope field for $y' = (t - y)/2$ over the rectangle $R = \{(t, y) : 0 \le t \le 5, 0 \le y \le 4\}$ is shown in Figure 9.4. The solution curves with the following initial values are shown:
1. For $y(0) = 1$, the solution is $y(t) = 3e^{-t/2} - 2 + t$.
2. For $y(0) = 4$, the solution is $y(t) = 6e^{-t/2} - 2 + t$.   ■

Definition 9.2.   Given the rectangle $R = \{(t, y) : a \le t \le b, c \le y \le d\}$, assume that $f(t, y)$ is continuous on R. The function f is said to satisfy a *Lipschitz condition* in the variable y on R provided that a constant $L > 0$ exists with the property that

(8) $|f(t, y_1) - f(t, y_2)| \le L|y_1 - y_2|$

whenever $(t, y_1), (t, y_2) \in R$. The constant L is called a *Lipschitz constant* for f.   ▲

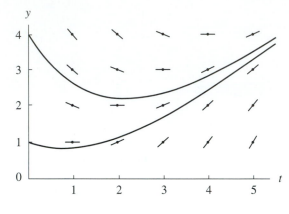

Figure 9.4   The slope field for the differential equation $y' = f(x, y) = (t - y)/2$.

Theorem 9.1.   Suppose that $f(t, y)$ is defined on the region R. If there exists a constant $L > 0$ so that

$$(9) \qquad\qquad |f_y(t, y)| \leq L \qquad \text{for all } (t, y) \in R,$$

then f satisfies a Lipschitz condition in the variable y with Lipschitz constant L over the rectangle R.

Proof.   Fix t and use the mean value theorem to get c_1 with $y_1 < c_1 < y_2$ so that

$$\begin{aligned}
|f(t, y_1) - f(t, y_2)| &= |f_y(t, c_1)(y_1 - y_2)| \\
&= |f_y(t, c_1)||y_1 - y_2| \leq L|y_1 - y_2|.
\end{aligned} \qquad\bullet$$

Theorem 9.2 (Existence and Uniqueness).   Assume that $f(t, y)$ is continuous in a region $R = \{(t, y) : t_0 \leq t \leq b, c \leq y \leq d\}$. If f satisfies a Lipschitz condition on R in the variable y and $(t_0, y_0) \in R$, then the initial value problem (6), $y' = f(t, y)$ with $y(t_0) = y_0$, has a unique solution $y = y(t)$ on some subinterval $t_0 \leq t \leq t_0 + \delta$.

Let us apply Theorems 9.1 and 9.2 to the function $f(t, y) = (t - y)/2$. The partial derivative is $f_y(t, y) = -1/2$. Hence $|f_y(t, y)| \leq \frac{1}{2}$ and, according to Theorem 9.1, the Lipschitz constant is $L = \frac{1}{2}$. Therefore, by Theorem 9.2 the I.V.P. has a unique solution.

Sketches of the slope field and solution curves can be constructed by using the `meshgrid` and `quiver` commands in MATLAB. The following M-file will generate a graph analogous to Figure 9.4. In general, care must be taken to avoid points (t, y) at which y' is undefined.

```
[t,y]=meshgrid(1:5,4:-1:1);
dt=ones(5,4);
dy=(t-y)/2;
quiver(t,y,dt,dy);
hold on
x=0:.01:5;
z1=3*exp(-x/2)-2+x;
z2=6*exp(-x/2)-2+x;
plot(x,z1,x,z2)
hold off
```

Exercises for Introduction to Differential Equations

In Exercises 1 through 5:

(a) Show that $y(t)$ is the solution to the differential equation by substituting $y(t)$ and $y'(t)$ into the differential equation $y'(t) = f(t, y(t))$.

(b) Use Theorem 9.1 to find a Lipschitz constant L for the rectangle $R = \{(t, y) : 0 \le t \le 3, 0 \le y \le 5\}$.

1. $y' = t^2 - y$, $y(t) = Ce^{-t} + t^2 - 2t + 2$

2. $y' = 3y + 3t$, $y(t) = Ce^{3t} - t - \frac{1}{3}$

3. $y' = -ty$, $y(t) = Ce^{-t^2/2}$

4. $y' = e^{-2t} - 2y$, $y(t) = Ce^{-2t} + te^{-2t}$

5. $y' = 2ty^2$, $y(t) = 1/(C - t^2)$

In Exercises 6 through 9, construct a graph of the slope field $m_{i,j} = f(t_i, y_j)$ over the rectangle $R = \{(t, y) : 0 < t \le 4, 0 < y \le 4\}$ and the indicated solution curves on the same coordinate system.

6. $y' = -t/y$, $y(t) = (C - t^2)^{1/2}$ for $C = 1, 2, 4, 9$

7. $y' = t/y$, $y(t) = (C + t^2)^{1/2}$ for $C = -4, -1, 1, 4$

8. $y' = 1/y$, $y(t) = (C + 2t)^{1/2}$ for $C = -4, -2, 0, 2$

9. $y' = y^2$, $y(t) = 1/(C - t)$ for $C = 1, 2, 3, 4$

10. Here is an example of an initial value problem that has "two solutions": $y' = \frac{3}{2}y^{1/3}$ with $y(0) = 0$.

   (a) Verify that $y(t) = 0$ for $t \ge 0$ is a solution.

   (b) Verify that $y(t) = t^{3/2}$ for $t \ge 0$ is a solution.

   (c) Does this violate Theorem 9.2? Why?

11. Consider the initial value problem

$$y' = (1 - y^2)^{1/2} \qquad y(0) = 0$$

(a)   Verify that $y(t) = \sin(t)$ is a solution on $[0, \pi/4]$.

(b)   Determine the largest interval over which the solution exists.

12. Show that the definite integral $\int_a^b f(t)\,dt$ can be computed by solving the initial value problem

$$y' = f(t) \qquad \text{for } a \le t \le b \qquad \text{with} \qquad y(a) = 0.$$

In Exercises 13 through 15, find the solution to the I.V.P.

13. $y' = 3t^2 + \sin(t)$, $y(0) = 2$

14. $y' = \dfrac{1}{1+t^2}$, $y(0) = 0$

15. $y' = e^{-t^2/2}$, $y(0) = 0$. *Hint.* This answer must be expressed as a certain integral.

16. Consider the first-order differential equation

$$y'(t) + p(t)y(t) = q(t).$$

Show that the general solution $y(t)$ can be found by using two special integrals. First define $F(t)$ as follows:

$$F(t) = e^{\int p(t)\,dt}.$$

Second, define $y(t)$ as follows:

$$y(t) = \frac{1}{F(t)}\left(\int F(t)q(t)\,dt + C\right).$$

Hint. Differentiate the product $F(t)y(t)$.

17. Consider the decay of a radioactive substance. If $y(t)$ is the amount of substance present at time t, then $y(t)$ decreases and experiments have verified that the rate of change of $y(t)$ is proportional to the amount of undecayed material. Hence the I.V.P. for the decay of a radioactive substance is

$$y' = -ky \qquad \text{with} \qquad y(0) = y_0.$$

(a)   Show that the solution is $y(t) = y_0 e^{-kt}$.

(b)   The half-life of a radioactive substance is the time required for half of an initial amount to decay. The half-life of ^{14}C is 5730 years. Find the formula $y(t)$ that gives the amount of ^{14}C present at time t. *Hint.* Find k so that $y(5730) = 0.5y_0$.

(c)   A piece of wood is analyzed and the amount of ^{14}C present is 0.712 of the amount that was present when the tree was alive. How old is the sample of wood?

(d)   At a certain instant, 10 mg of a radioactive substance is present. After 23 seconds, only 1 mg is present. What is the half-life of the substance?

In Exercises 18 and 19, derive an equation for the I.V.P. and find its solution.

18. Annual ticket sales for a new professional soccer league are projected to grow at a rate proportional to the difference between sales at time t and an upper bound of $300 million. Assume that annual ticket sales are initially $0 and must be $40 million after 3 years (or the league folds). Based on these assumptions, how long will it take for annual ticket sales to reach $220 million?

19. The interior volume of a new library is 5 millon cubic feet. The ventilation system introduces fresh air into the library at the rate of 45,000 cubic feet per minute. Before the ventilation system is turned on, the percents of carbon dioxide in the interior of the library and in the exterior fresh air are measured at 0.4% and 0.5%, respectively. Determine the percentage of carbon dioxide in the library 2 hours after the ventilation system is started.

9.2   Euler's Method

The reader should be convinced that not all initial value problems can be solved explicitly, and often it is impossible to find a formula for the solution $y(t)$; for example, there is no "closed-form expression" for the solution to $y' = t^3 + y^2$ with $y(0) = 0$. Hence for engineering and scientific purposes it is necessary to have methods for approximating the solution. If a solution with many significant digits is required, then more computing effort and a sophisticated algorithm must be used.

The first approach, called Euler's method, serves to illustrate the concepts involved in the advanced methods. It has limited use because of the larger error that is accumulated as the process proceeds. However, it is important to study because the error analysis is easier to understand.

Let $[a, b]$ be the interval over which we want to find the solution to the well-posed I.V.P. $y' = f(t, y)$ with $y(a) = y_0$. In actuality, we will not find a differentiable function that satisfies the I.V.P. Instead, a set of points $\{(t_k, y_k)\}$ is generated, and the points are used for an approximation (i.e., $y(t_k) \approx y_k$). How can we proceed to construct a "set of points" that will "satisfy a differential equation approximately"? First we choose the abscissas for the points. For convenience we subdivide the interval $[a, b]$ into M equal subintervals and select the mesh points

(1) $$t_k = a + kh \quad \text{for } k = 0, 1, \ldots, M \text{ where } h = \frac{b - a}{M}.$$

The value h is called the **step size**. We now proceed to solve approximately

(2) $$y' = f(t, y) \quad \text{over} \quad [t_0, t_M] \quad \text{with} \quad y(t_0) = y_0.$$

Assume that $y(t)$, $y'(t)$, and $y''(t)$ are continuous and use Taylor's theorem to expand $y(t)$ about $t = t_0$. For each value t there exists a value c_1 that lies between t_0 and t so that

$$(3) \qquad y(t) = y(t_0) + y'(t_0)(t - t_0) + \frac{y''(c_1)(t - t_0)^2}{2}.$$

When $y'(t_0) = f(t_0, y(t_0))$ and $h = t_1 - t_0$ are substituted in equation (3), the result is an expression for $y(t_1)$:

$$(4) \qquad y(t_1) = y(t_0) + hf(t_0, y(t_0)) + y''(c_1)\frac{h^2}{2}.$$

If the step size h is chosen small enough, then we may neglect the second-order term (involving h^2) and get

$$(5) \qquad y_1 = y_0 + hf(t_0, y_0),$$

which is **Euler's approximation**.

The process is repeated and generates a sequence of points that approximates the solution curve $y = y(t)$. The general step for Euler's method is

$$(6) \quad t_{k+1} = t_k + h, \quad y_{k+1} = y_k + hf(t_k, y_k) \quad \text{for } k = 0, 1, \ldots, M - 1.$$

Example 9.2. Use Euler's method to solve approximately the initial value problem

$$(7) \qquad y' = Ry \quad \text{over } [0, 1] \text{ with } y(0) = y_0 \text{ and } R \text{ constant.}$$

The step size must be chosen, and then the second formula in (6) can be determined for computing the ordinates. This formula is sometimes called a *difference equation*, and in this case it is

$$(8) \qquad y_{k+1} = y_k(1 + hR) \quad \text{for } k = 0, 1, \ldots, M - 1.$$

If we trace the solution values recursively, we see that

$$
\begin{aligned}
y_1 &= y_0(1 + hR) \\
y_2 &= y_1(1 + hR) = y_0(1 + hR)^2 \\
&\ \vdots \\
y_M &= y_{M-1}(1 + hR) = y_0(1 + hR)^M.
\end{aligned}
$$

(9)

For most problems there is no explicit formula for determining the solution points, and each new point must be computed successively from the previous point. However, for the initial value problem (7) we are fortunate; Euler's method has the explicit solution

$$(10) \qquad t_k = kh \quad y_k = y_0(1 + hR)^k \quad \text{for } k = 0, 1, \ldots, M.$$

Formula (10) can be viewed as the "compound interest" formula, and the Euler approximation gives the future value of a deposit. ∎

Table 9.1   Compound Interest in Example 9.3

Step size, h	Number of iterations, M	Approximation to $y(5)$, y_M
1	5	$1000\left(1 + \dfrac{0.1}{1}\right)^5 = 1610.51$
$\frac{1}{12}$	60	$1000\left(1 + \dfrac{0.1}{12}\right)^{60} = 1645.31$
$\frac{1}{360}$	1800	$1000\left(1 + \dfrac{0.1}{360}\right)^{1800} = 1648.61$

Example 9.3.   Suppose that \$1000 is deposited and earns 10% interest compounded continuously over 5 years. What is the value at the end of 5 years?

We choose to use Euler approximations with $h = 1$, $\frac{1}{12}$, and $\frac{1}{360}$ to approximate $y(5)$ for the I.V.P.:

$$y' = 0.1y \quad \text{over } [0, 5] \text{ with } y(0) = 1000.$$

Formula (10) with $R = 0.1$ produces Table 9.1.   ∎

Think about the different values y_5, y_{60}, and y_{1800} that are used to determine the future value after 5 years. These values are obtained using different step sizes and reflect different amounts of computing effort to obtain an approximation to $y(5)$. The solution to the I.V.P. is $y(5) = 1000e^{0.5} = 1648.72$. If we did not use the closed-form solution (10), then it would have required 1800 iterations of Euler's method to obtain y_{1800}, and we still have only five digits of accuracy in the answer!

If bankers had to approximate the solution to the I.V.P. (7), they would choose Euler's method because of the explicit formula in (10). The more sophisticated methods for approximating solutions do not have an explicit formula for finding y_k, but they will require less computing effort.

Geometric Description

If you start at the point (t_0, y_0) and compute the value of the slope $m_0 = f(t_0, y_0)$ and move horizontally the amount h and vertically $hf(t_0, y_0)$, then you are moving along the tangent line to $y(t)$ and will end up at the point (t_1, y_1) (see Figure 9.5). Notice that (t_1, y_1) is not on the desired solution curve! But this is the approximation that we are generating. Hence we must use (t_1, y_1) as though it were correct and proceed by computing the slope $m_1 = f(t_1, y_1)$ and using it to obtain the next vertical displacement $hf(t_1, y_1)$ to locate (t_2, y_2), and so on.

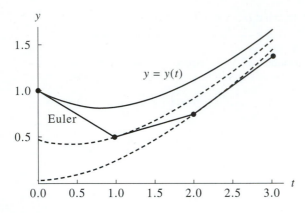

Figure 9.5 Euler's approximations $y_{k-1} = y_k + hf(t_k, y_k)$.

Step Size versus Error

The methods we introduce for approximating the solution of an initial value problem are called **difference methods** or **discrete variable methods**. The solution is approximated at a set of discrete points called a *grid* (or *mesh*) of points. An elementary single-step method has the form $y_{k+1} = y_k + h\Phi(t_k, y_k)$ for some function Φ called an **increment function**.

When using any discrete variable method to solve an initial value problem approximately, there are two sources of error: discretization and round off.

Definition 9.3. Assume that $\{(t_k, y_k)\}_{k=0}^M$ is the set of discrete approximations and that $y = y(t)$ is the unique solution to the initial value problem.

The **global discretization error** e_k is defined by

$$(11) \qquad e_k = y(t_k) - y_k \quad \text{for } k = 0, 1, \ldots, M.$$

It is the difference between the unique solution and the solution obtained by the discrete variable method.

The **local discretization error** ϵ_{k+1} is defined by

$$(12) \qquad \epsilon_{k+1} = y(t_{k+1}) - y_k - h\Phi(t_k, y_k) \quad \text{for } k = 0, 1, \ldots, M - 1.$$

It is the error committed in the single step from t_k to t_{k+1}. ▲

When we obtained equation (6) for Euler's method, the neglected term for each step was $y^{(2)}(c_k)(h^2/2)$. If this was the only error at each step, then at the end of the interval $[a, b]$, after M steps have been made, the accumulated error would be

$$\sum_{k=1}^{M} y^{(2)}(c_k) \frac{h^2}{2} \approx M y^{(2)}(c) \frac{h^2}{2} = \frac{hM}{2} y^{(2)}(c)h = \frac{(b-a)y^{(2)}(c)}{2} h = \mathbf{O}(h^1).$$

There could be more error, but this estimate predominates. A detailed discussion on this topic can be found in advanced texts on numerical methods for differential equations.

Theorem 9.3 (Precision of Euler's Method).   Assume that $y(t)$ is the solution to the I.V.P. given in (2). If $y(t) \in C^2[t_0, b]$ and $\{(t_k, y_k)\}_{k=0}^{M}$ is the sequence of approximations generated by Euler's method, then

(13)
$$|e_k| = |y(t_k) - y_k| = \boldsymbol{O}(h),$$

$$|\epsilon_{k+1}| = |y(t_{k+1}) - y_k - hf(t_k, y_k)| = \boldsymbol{O}(h^2).$$

The error at the end of the interval is called the *final global error (F.G.E.)*:

(14)
$$E(y(b), h) = |y(b) - y_M| = \boldsymbol{O}(h).$$

Remark. The final global error $E(y(b), h)$ is used to study the behavior of the error for various step sizes. It can be used to give us an idea of how much computing effort must be done to obtain an accurate approximation.

Examples 9.4 and 9.5 illustrate the concepts in Theorem 9.3. If approximations are computed using the step sizes h and $h/2$, we should have

(15)
$$E(y(b), h) \approx Ch$$

for the larger step size, and

(16)
$$E\left(y(b), \frac{h}{2}\right) \approx C\frac{h}{2} = \frac{1}{2}Ch \approx \frac{1}{2}E(y(b), h).$$

Hence the idea in Theorem 9.3 is that if the step size in Euler's method is reduced by a factor of $\frac{1}{2}$, we can expect that the overall F.G.E. will be reduced by a factor of $\frac{1}{2}$.

Example 9.4.   Use Euler's method to solve the I.V.P.

$$y' = \frac{t - y}{2} \quad \text{on } [0, 3] \text{ with } y(0) = 1.$$

Compare solutions for $h = 1, \frac{1}{2}, \frac{1}{4}$, and $\frac{1}{8}$.

Figure 9.6 shows graphs of the four Euler solutions and the exact solution curve $y(t) = 3e^{-t/2} - 2 + t$. Table 9.2 gives the values for the four solutions at selected abscissas. For the step size $h = 0.25$, the calculations are

$$y_1 = 1.0 + 0.25\left(\frac{0.0 - 1.0}{2}\right) = 0.875,$$

$$y_2 = 0.875 + 0.25\left(\frac{0.25 - 0.875}{2}\right) = 0.796875, \quad \text{etc.}$$

This iteration continues until we arrive at the last step:

$$y(3) \approx y_{12} = 1.440573 + 0.25\left(\frac{2.75 - 1.440573}{2}\right) = 1.604252. \qquad \blacksquare$$

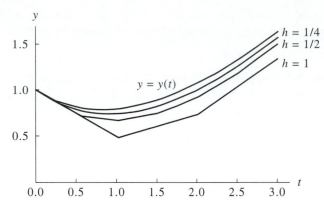

Figure 9.6 Comparison of Euler solutions with different step sizes for $y' = (t - y)/2$ over $[0, 3]$ with the initial condition $y(0) = 1$.

Example 9.5. Compare the F.G.E. when Euler's method is used to solve the I.V.P.

$$y' = \frac{t - y}{2} \quad \text{over } [0, 3] \text{ with } y(0) = 1,$$

using step sizes $1, \frac{1}{2}, \ldots, \frac{1}{64}$.

Table 9.3 gives the F.G.E. for several step sizes and shows that the error in the approximation to $y(3)$ decreases by about $\frac{1}{2}$ when the step size is reduced by a factor of $\frac{1}{2}$. For the smaller step sizes the conclusion of Theorem 9.3 is easy to see:

$$E(y(3), h) = y(3) - y_M = \mathbf{O}(h^1) \approx Ch, \quad \text{where} \quad C = 0.256. \qquad \blacksquare$$

Program 9.1 (Euler's Method). To approximate the solution of the initial value problem $y' = f(t, y)$ with $y(a) = y_0$ over $[a, b]$ by computing

$$y_{k+1} = y_k + hf(t_k, y_k) \quad \text{for } k = 0, 1, \ldots, M - 1.$$

```
function E=euler(f,a,b,ya,M)
%Input   - f is the function entered as a string 'f'
%         - a and b are the left and right endpoints
%         - ya is the initial condition y(a)
%         - M is the number of steps
%Output - E=[T' Y'] where T is the vector of abscissas and
%         Y is the vector of ordinates
h=(b-a)/M;
T=zeros(1,M+1);
Y=zeros(1,M+1);
```

Table 9.2 Comparison of Euler Solutions with Different Step Sizes for $y' = (t - y)/2$ over $[0, 3]$ with $y(0) = 1$

t_k	y_k				$y(t_k)$ Exact
	$h = 1$	$h = \frac{1}{2}$	$h = \frac{1}{4}$	$h = \frac{1}{8}$	
0	1.0	1.0	1.0	1.0	1.0
0.125				0.9375	0.943239
0.25			0.875	0.886719	0.897491
0.375				0.846924	0.862087
0.50		0.75	0.796875	0.817429	0.836402
0.75			0.759766	0.786802	0.811868
1.00	0.5	0.6875	0.758545	0.790158	0.819592
1.50		0.765625	0.846386	0.882855	0.917100
2.00	0.75	0.949219	1.030827	1.068222	1.103638
2.50		1.211914	1.289227	1.325176	1.359514
3.00	1.375	1.533936	1.604252	1.637429	1.669390

Table 9.3 Relation between Step Size and F.G.E. for Euler Solutions to $y' = (t - y)/2$ over $[0, 3]$ with $y(0) = 1$

Step size, h	Number of steps, M	Approximation to $y(3)$, y_M	F.G.E. Error at $t = 3$, $y(3) - y_M$	$O(h) \approx Ch$ where $C = 0.256$
1	3	1.375	0.294390	0.256
$\frac{1}{2}$	6	1.533936	0.135454	0.128
$\frac{1}{4}$	12	1.604252	0.065138	0.064
$\frac{1}{8}$	24	1.637429	0.031961	0.032
$\frac{1}{16}$	48	1.653557	0.015833	0.016
$\frac{1}{32}$	96	1.661510	0.007880	0.008
$\frac{1}{64}$	192	1.665459	0.003931	0.004

```
T=a:h:b;
Y(1)=ya;
for j=1:M
    Y(j+1)=Y(j)+h*feval(f,T(j),Y(j));
end
E=[T' Y'];
```

Exercises for Euler's Method

In Exercises 1 through 5 solve the differential equations by the Euler method.

(a) Let $h = 0.2$ and do two steps by hand calculation. Then let $h = 0.1$ and do four steps by hand calculation.

(b) Compare the exact solution $y(0.4)$ with the two approximations in part (a).

(c) Does the F.G.E. in part (a) behave as expected when h is halved?

1. $y' = t^2 - y$ with $y(0) = 1$, $y(t) = -e^{-t} + t^2 - 2t + 2$

2. $y' = 3y + 3t$ with $y(0) = 1$, $y(t) = \frac{4}{3}e^{3t} - t - \frac{1}{3}$

3. $y' = -ty$ with $y(0) = 1$, $y(t) = e^{-t^2/2}$

4. $y' = e^{-2t} - 2y$ with $y(0) = \frac{1}{10}$, $y(t) = \frac{1}{10}e^{-2t} + te^{-2t}$

5. $y' = 2ty^2$ with $y(0) = 1$, $y(t) = 1/(1 - t^2)$

6. *Logistic population growth.*   The population curve $P(t)$ for the United States is assumed to obey the differential equation for a logistic curve $P' = aP - bP^2$. Let t denote the year past 1900, and let the step size be $h = 10$. The values $a = 0.02$ and $b = 0.00004$ produce a model for the population. Using hand calculations, find the Euler approximations to $P(t)$ and fill in the following table. Round off each value P_k to the nearest tenth.

Year	t_k	$P(t_k)$ Actual	P_k Euler approximation
1900	0.0	76.1	76.1
1910	10.0	92.4	89.0
1920	20.0	106.5	_____
1930	30.0	123.1	
1940	40.0	132.6	138.2
1950	50.0	152.3	
1960	60.0	180.7	_____
1970	70.0	204.9	202.8
1980	80.0	226.5	_____

7. Show that when Euler's method is used to solve the I.V.P.

$$y' = f(t) \quad \text{over } [a, b] \text{ with } y(a) = y_0 = 0$$

the result is

$$y(b) \approx \sum_{k=0}^{M-1} f(t_k)h,$$

which is a Riemann sum that approximates the definite integral of $f(t)$ taken over the interval $[a, b]$.

8. Show that Euler's method fails to approximate the solution $y(t) = t^{3/2}$ of the I.V.P.

$$y' = f(t, y) = 1.5y^{1/3} \quad \text{with} \quad y(0) = 0.$$

Justify your answer. What difficulties were encountered?

9. Can Euler's method be used to solve the I.V.P.

$$y' = 1 + y^2 \quad \text{over } [0, 3] \text{ with } y(0) = 0?$$

Hint. The exact solution curve is $y(t) = \tan(t)$.

Algorithms and Programs

In Problems 1 through 5, solve the differential equations by the Euler method.

(a) Let $h = 0.1$ and do 20 steps with Program 9.1. Then let $h = 0.05$ and do 40 steps with Program 9.1.

(b) Compare the exact solution $y(2)$ with the two approximations in part (a).

(c) Does the F.G.E. in part (a) behave as expected when h is halved?

(d) Plot the two approximations and the exact solution on the same coordinate system. *Hint.* The output matrix E from Program 9.1 contains the x and y coordinates of the approximations. The command plot(E(:,1),E(:,2)) will produce a graph analogous to Figure 9.6.

1. $y' = t^2 - y$ with $y(0) = 1$, $y(t) = -e^{-t} + t^2 - 2t + 2$

2. $y' = 3y + 3t$ with $y(0) = 1$, $y(t) = \frac{4}{3}e^{3t} - t - \frac{1}{3}$

3. $y' = -ty$ with $y(0) = 1$, $y(t) = e^{-t^2/2}$

4. $y' = e^{-2t} - 2y$ with $y(0) = \frac{1}{10}$, $y(t) = \frac{1}{10}e^{-2t} + te^{-2t}$

5. $y' = 2ty^2$ with $y(0) = 1$, $y(t) = 1/(1 - t^2)$

6. Consider $y' = 0.12y$ over $[0, 5]$ with $y(0) = 1000$.

   (a) Apply formula (10) to find Euler's approximation to $y(5)$ using the step sizes $h = 1, \frac{1}{12}$, and $\frac{1}{360}$.

   (b) What is the limit in part (a) when h goes to zero?

7. *Exponential population growth.* The population of a certain species grows at a rate that is proportional to the current population and obeys the I.V.P.

$$y' = 0.02y \quad \text{over } [0, 5] \text{ with } y(0) = 5000.$$

  (a) Apply formula (10) to find Euler's approximation to $y(5)$ using the step sizes $h = 1, \frac{1}{12},$ and $\frac{1}{360}$.
  (b) What is the limit in part (a) when h goes to zero?

8. A skydiver jumps from a plane, and up to the moment he opens the parachute the air resistance is proportional to $v^{3/2}$ (v represents velocity). Assume that the time interval is $[0, 6]$ and that the differential equation for the downward direction is

$$v' = 32 - 0.032v^{3/2} \quad \text{over } [0, 6] \text{ with } v(0) = 0.$$

Use Euler's method with $h = 0.05$ and estimate $v(6)$.

9. *Epidemic model.* The mathematical model for epidemics is described as follows. Assume that there is a community of L members that contains P infected individuals and Q uninfected individuals. Let $y(t)$ denote the number of infected individuals at time t. For a mild illness, such as the common cold, everyone continues to be active, and the epidemic spreads from those who are infected to those uninfected. Since there are PQ possible contacts between these two groups, the rate of change of $y(t)$ is proportional to PQ. Hence the problem can be stated as the I.V.P.

$$y' = ky(L - y) \quad \text{with} \quad y(0) = y_0.$$

  (a) Use $L = 25,000$, $k = 0.00003$, and $h = 0.2$ with the initial condition $y(0) = 250$, and use Program 9.1 to compute Euler's approximate solution over $[0, 60]$.
  (b) Plot the graph of the approximate solution from part (a).
  (c) Estimate the average number of individuals infected by finding the average of the ordinates from Euler's method in part (a).
  (d) Estimate the average number of individuals infected by fitting a curve to the data from part (a) and using Theorem 1.10 (mean value theorem for integrals).

10. Consider the first-order integro-ordinary differential equation

$$y' = 1.3y - 0.25y^2 - 0.0001y \int_0^t y(\tau)\,d\tau.$$

  (a) Use Euler's method with $h = 0.2$, and $y(0) = 250$ over the interval $[0, 20]$, and the trapezoidal rule to find an approximate solution to the equation. *Hint.* The general step for Euler's method (6) is

$$y_{k+1} = y_k + h(1.3y_k - 0.25y_k^2 - 0.0001y_k \int_0^{t_k} y(\tau)\,d\tau).$$

If the trapezoidal rule is used to approximate the integral, then this expression becomes
$$y_{k+1} = y_k + h(1.3y_k - 0.25y_k^2 - 0.0001y_k T_k(h)),$$

where $T_0(h) = 0$ and

$$T_k(h) = T_{k-1}(h) + \frac{h}{2}(y_{k-1} + y_k) \quad \text{for } k = 0, 1, \ldots, 99.$$

(b)   Repeat part (a) using the initial values $y(0) = 200$ and $y(0) = 300$.

(c)   Plot the approximate solutions from parts (a) and (b) on the same coordinate system.

9.3   Heun's Method

The next approach, Heun's method, introduces a new idea for constructing an algorithm to solve the I.V.P.

$$(1) \qquad\qquad y'(t) = f(t, y(t)) \quad \text{over} \quad [a, b] \quad \text{with} \quad y(t_0) = y_0.$$

To obtain the solution point (t_1, y_1), we can use the fundamental theorem of calculus and integrate $y'(t)$ over $[t_0, t_1]$ to get

$$(2) \qquad\qquad \int_{t_0}^{t_1} f(t, y(t))\, dt = \int_{t_0}^{t_1} y'(t)\, dt = y(t_1) - y(t_0),$$

where the antiderivative of $y'(t)$ is the desired function $y(t)$. When equation (2) is solved for $y(t_1)$, the result is

$$(3) \qquad\qquad y(t_1) = y(t_0) + \int_{t_0}^{t_1} f(t, y(t))\, dt.$$

Now a numerical integration method can be used to approximate the definite integral in (3). If the trapezoidal rule is used with the step size $h = t_1 - t_0$, then the result is

$$(4) \qquad\qquad y(t_1) \approx y(t_0) + \frac{h}{2}(f(t_0, y(t_0)) + f(t_1, y(t_1))).$$

Notice that the formula on the right-hand side of (4) involves the yet to be determined value $y(t_1)$. To proceed, we use an estimate for $y(t_1)$. Euler's solution will suffice for this purpose. After it is substituted into (4), the resulting formula for finding (t_1, y_1) is called **Heun's method**:

$$(5) \qquad\qquad y_1 = y(t_0) + \frac{h}{2}(f(t_0, y_0) + f(t_1, y_0 + hf(t_0, y_0))).$$

The process is repeated and generates a sequence of points that approximates the solution curve $y = y(t)$. At each step, Euler's method is used as a prediction, and then

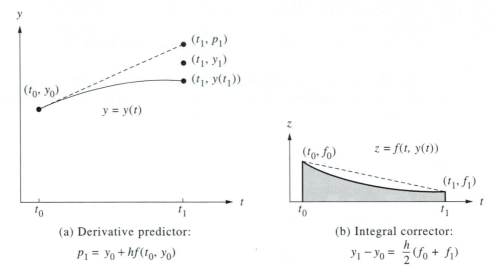

(a) Derivative predictor:

$$p_1 = y_0 + hf(t_0, y_0)$$

(b) Integral corrector:

$$y_1 - y_0 = \frac{h}{2}(f_0 + f_1)$$

Figure 9.7   The graphs $y = y(t)$ and $z = f(t, y(t))$ in the derivation of Heun's method.

the trapezoidal rule is used to make a correction to obtain the final value. The general step for Heun's method is

(6)
$$p_{k+1} = y_k + hf(t_k, y_k), \qquad t_{k+1} = t_k + h,$$
$$y_{k+1} = y_k + \frac{h}{2}(f(t_k, y_k) + f(t_{k+1}, p_{k+1})).$$

Notice the role played by differentiation and integration in Heun's method. Draw the line tangent to the solution curve $y = y(t)$ at the point (t_0, y_0) and use it to find the predicted point (t_1, p_1). Now look at the graph $z = f(t, y(t))$ and consider the points (t_0, f_0) and (t_1, f_1), where $f_0 = f(t_0, y_0)$ and $f_1 = f(t_1, p_1)$. The area of the trapezoid with vertices (t_0, f_0) and (t_1, f_1) is an approximation to the integral in (3), which is used to obtain the final value in equation (5). The graphs are shown in Figure 9.7.

Step Size versus Error

The error term for the trapezoidal rule used to approximate the integral in (3) is

(7)
$$-y^{(2)}(c_k)\frac{h^3}{12}.$$

If the only error at each step is that given in (7), after M steps the accumulated error for Heun's method would be

(8)
$$-\sum_{k=1}^{M} y^{(2)}(c_k)\frac{h^3}{12} \approx \frac{b-a}{12}y^{(2)}(c)h^2 = \boldsymbol{O}(h^2).$$

The next theorem is important, because it states the relationship between F.G.E. and step size. It is used to give us an idea of how much computing effort must be done to obtain an accurate approximation using Heun's method.

Theorem 9.4 (Precision of Heun's Method).   Assume that $y(t)$ is the solution to the I.V.P. (1). If $y(t) \in C^3[t_0, b]$ and $\{(t_k, y_k)\}_{k=0}^M$ is the sequence of approximations generated by Heun's method, then

(9)
$$|e_k| = |y(t_k) - y_k| = \mathbf{O}(h^2),$$
$$|\epsilon_{k+1}| = |y(t_{k+1}) - y_k - h\Phi(t_k, y_k)| = \mathbf{O}(h^3),$$

where $\Phi(t_k, y_k) = y_k + (h/2)(f(t_k, y_k) + f(t_{k+1}, y_k + hf(t_k, y_k)))$.

In particular, the final global error (F.G.E.) at the end of the interval will satisfy

(10)
$$E(y(b), h) = |y(b) - y_M| = \mathbf{O}(h^2).$$

Examples 9.6 and 9.7 illustrate Theorem 9.4. If approximations are computed using the step sizes h and $h/2$, we should have

(11)
$$E(y(b), h) \approx Ch^2$$

for the larger step size, and

(12)
$$E\left(y(b), \frac{h}{2}\right) \approx C\frac{h^2}{4} = \frac{1}{4}Ch^2 \approx \frac{1}{4}E(y(b), h).$$

Hence the idea in Theorem 9.4 is that if the step size in Heun's method is reduced by a factor of $\frac{1}{2}$ we can expect that the overall F.G.E. will be reduced by a factor of $\frac{1}{4}$.

Example 9.6.   Use Heun's method to solve the I.V.P.

$$y' = \frac{t - y}{2} \quad \text{on } [0, 3] \text{ with } y(0) = 1.$$

Compare solutions for $h = 1, \frac{1}{2}, \frac{1}{4}$, and $\frac{1}{8}$.

Figure 9.8 shows the graphs of the first two Heun solutions and the exact solution curve $y(t) = 3e^{-t/2} - 2 + t$. Table 9.4 gives the values for the four solutions at selected abscissas. For the step size $h = 0.25$, a sample calculation is

$$f(t_0, y_0) = \frac{0 - 1}{2} = -0.5$$
$$p_1 = 1.0 + 0.25(-0.5) = 0.875,$$
$$f(t_1, p_1) = \frac{0.25 - 0.875}{2} = -0.3125,$$
$$y_1 = 1.0 + 0.125(-0.5 - 0.3125) = 0.8984375.$$

This iteration continues until we arrive at the last step:

$$y(3) \approx y_{12} = 1.511508 + 0.125(0.619246 + 0.666840) = 1.672269. \quad \blacksquare$$

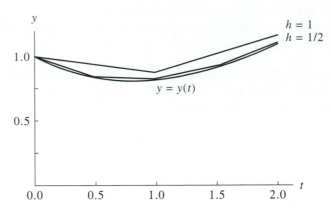

Figure 9.8   Comparison of Heun solutions with different step sizes for $y' = (t - y)/2$ over $[0, 2]$ with the initial condition $y(0) = 1$.

Table 9.4   Comparison of Heun Solutions with Different Step Sizes for $y' = (t - y)/2$ over $[0, 3]$ with $y(0) = 1$

t_k	y_k				
	$h = 1$	$h = \frac{1}{2}$	$h = \frac{1}{4}$	$h = \frac{1}{8}$	$y(t_k)$ Exact
0	1.0	1.0	1.0	1.0	1.0
0.125				0.943359	0.943239
0.25			0.898438	0.897717	0.897491
0.375				0.862406	0.862087
0.50		0.84375	0.838074	0.836801	0.836402
0.75			0.814081	0.812395	0.811868
1.00	0.875	0.831055	0.822196	0.820213	0.819592
1.50		0.930511	0.920143	0.917825	0.917100
2.00	1.171875	1.117587	1.106800	1.104392	1.103638
2.50		1.373115	1.362593	1.360248	1.359514
3.00	1.732422	1.682121	1.672269	1.670076	1.669390

Example 9.7.   Compare the F.G.E. when Heun's method is used to solve

$$y' = \frac{t - y}{2} \quad \text{over } [0, 3] \text{ with } y(0) = 1,$$

using step sizes $1, \frac{1}{2}, \ldots, \frac{1}{64}$.

Table 9.5 Relation between Step Size and F.G.E. for Heun Solutions to $y' = (t - y)/2$ over $[0, 3]$ with $y(0) = 1$

Step size, h	Number of steps, M	Approximation to $y(3)$, y_M	F.G.E. Error at $t = 3$, $y(3) - y_M$	$O(h^2) \approx Ch^2$ where $C = -0.0432$
1	3	1.732422	−0.063032	−0.043200
$\frac{1}{2}$	6	1.682121	−0.012731	−0.010800
$\frac{1}{4}$	12	1.672269	−0.002879	−0.002700
$\frac{1}{8}$	24	1.670076	−0.000686	−0.000675
$\frac{1}{16}$	48	1.669558	−0.000168	−0.000169
$\frac{1}{32}$	96	1.669432	−0.000042	−0.000042
$\frac{1}{64}$	192	1.669401	−0.000011	−0.000011

Table 9.5 gives the F.G.E. and shows that the error in the approximation to $y(3)$ decreases by about $\frac{1}{4}$ when the step size is reduced by a factor of $\frac{1}{2}$:

$$E(y(3), h) = y(3) - y_M = O(h^2) \approx Ch^2, \qquad \text{where } C = -0.0432. \qquad \blacksquare$$

Program 9.2 (Heun's Method). To approximate the solution of the initial value problem $y' = f(t, y)$ with $y(a) = y_0$ over $[a, b]$ by computing

$$y_{k+1} = y_k + \frac{h}{2}(f(t_k, y_k) + f(t_{k+1}, y_k + hf(t_k, y_k)))$$

for $k = 0, 1, \ldots, M - 1$.

```
function H=heun(f,a,b,ya,M)
%Input   - f is the function entered as a string 'f'
%         - a and b are the left and right endpoints
%         - ya is the initial condition y(a)
%         - M is the number of steps
%Output - H=[T'Y'] where T is the vector of abscissas and
%           Y is the vector of ordinates
h=(b-a)/M;
T=zeros(1,M+1);
Y=zeros(1,M+1);
```

```
T=a:h:b;
Y(1)=ya;
for j=1:M
    k1=feval(f,T(j),Y(j));
    k2=feval(f,T(j+1),Y(j)+h*k1);
    Y(j+1)=Y(j)+(h/2)*(k1+k2);
end
H=[T'Y'];
```

Exercises for Heun's Method

In Exercises 1 through 5, solve the differential equations by Heun's method.

(a) Let $h = 0.2$ and do two steps by hand calculation. Then let $h = 0.1$ and do four steps by hand calculation.

(b) Compare the exact solution $y(0.4)$ with the two approximations in part (a).

(c) Does the F.G.E. in part (a) behave as expected when h is halved?

1. $y' = t^2 - y$ with $y(0) = 1$, $y(t) = -e^{-t} + t^2 - 2t + 2$

2. $y' = 3y + 3t$ with $y(0) = 1$, $y(t) = \frac{4}{3}e^{3t} - t - \frac{1}{3}$

3. $y' = -ty$ with $y(0) = 1$, $y(t) = e^{-t^2/2}$

4. $y' = e^{-2t} - 2y$ with $y(0) = \frac{1}{10}$, $y(t) = \frac{1}{10}e^{-2t} + te^{-2t}$

5. $y' = 2ty^2$ with $y(0) = 1$, $y(t) = 1/(1 - t^2)$
   Notice that Heun's method will generate an approximation to $y(1)$ even though the solution curve is not defined at $t = 1$.

6. Show that when Heun's method is used to solve the I.V.P. $y' = f(t)$ over $[a, b]$ with $y(a) = y_0 = 0$ the result is

$$y(b) = \frac{h}{2} \sum_{k=0}^{M-1} (f(t_k) + f(t_{k+1})),$$

which is the trapezoidal rule approximation for the definite integral of $f(t)$ taken over the interval $[a, b]$.

7. The Richardson improvement method discussed in Lemma 7.1 (Section 7.3) can be used in conjunction with Heun's method. If Heun's method is used with step size h, then we have

$$y(b) \approx y_h + Ch^2.$$

If Heun's method is used with step size $2h$, we have

$$y(b) \approx y_{2h} + 4Ch^2.$$

The terms involving Ch^2 can be eliminated to obtain an improved approximation for $y(b)$, and the result is

$$y(b) \approx \frac{4y_h - y_{2h}}{3}.$$

The improvement scheme can be used with the values in Example 9.7 to obtain better approximations to $y(3)$. Find the missing entries in the table below.

h	y_h	$(4y_h - y_{2h})/3$
1	1.732422	_____
1/2	1.682121	1.665354
1/4	1.672269	_____
1/8	1.670076	_____
1/16	1.669558	1.669385
1/32	1.669432	_____
1/64	1.669401	_____

8. Show that Heun's method fails to approximate the solution $y(t) = t^{3/2}$ of the I.V.P.

$$y' = f(t, y) = 1.5y^{1/3} \quad \text{with } y(0) = 0.$$

Justify your answer. What difficulties were encountered?

Algorithms and Programs

In Problems 1 through 5 solve the differential equations by Heun's method.

(a) Let $h = 0.1$ and do 20 steps with Program 9.2. Then let $h = 0.05$ and do 40 steps with Program 9.2.

(b) Compare the exact solution $y(2)$ with the two approximations in part (a).

(a) Does the F.G.E. in part (a) behave as expected when h is halved?

(a) Plot the two approximations and the exact solution on the same coordinate system. *Hint.* The output matrix H from Program 9.2 contains the x- and y-coordinates of the approximations. The command `plot(H(:,1),H(:,2))` will produce a graph analogous to Figure 9.8.

1. $y' = t^2 - y$ with $y(0) = 1$, $y(t) = -e^{-t} + t^2 - 2t + 2$

2. $y' = 3y + 3t$ with $y(0) = 1$, $y(t) = \frac{4}{3}e^{3t} - t - \frac{1}{3}$

3. $y' = -ty$ with $y(0) = 1$, $y(t) = e^{-t^2/2}$

4. $y' = e^{-2t} - 2y$ with $y(0) = \frac{1}{10}$, $y(t) = \frac{1}{10}e^{-2t} + te^{-2t}$

5. $y' = 2ty^2$ with $y(0) = 1$, $y(t) = 1/(1 - t^2)$

6. Consider a projectile that is fired straight up and falls straight down. If air resistance is proportional to the velocity, the I.V.P. for the velocity $v(t)$ is

$$v' = -32 - \frac{K}{M}v \quad \text{with} \quad v(0) = v_0,$$

where v_0 is the initial velocity, M is the mass, and K the coefficient of air resistance. Suppose that $v_0 = 160$ ft/sec and $K/M = 0.1$. Use Heun's method with $h = 0.5$ to solve

$$v' = -32 - 0.1v \quad \text{over } [0, 30] \text{ with } v(0) = 160.$$

Graph your computer solution and the exact solution $v(t) = 480e^{-t/10} - 320$ on the same coordinate system. Observe that the limiting velocity is -320 ft/sec.

7. In psychology, the Wever-Fechner law for stimulus-response states that the rate of change dR/dS of the reaction R is inversely proportional to the stimulus. The threshold value is the lowest level of the stimulus that can be detected consistently. The I.V.P. for this model is

$$R' = \frac{k}{S} \quad \text{with } R(S_0) = 0.$$

Suppose that $S_0 = 0.1$ and $R(0.1) = 0$. Use Heun's method with $h = 0.1$ to solve

$$R' = \frac{1}{S} \quad \text{over } [0.1, 5.1] \text{ with } R(0.1) = 0.$$

8. (a) Write a program to implement the Richardson improvement method discussed in Exercise 7.

(b) Use your program to approximate $y(2)$ for each of the differential equations in Problems 1 through 5 over the interval $[0, 2]$. Use the initial step size $h = 0.05$. The program should terminate when the absolute value of the difference between two consecutive Richardson improvements is $< 10^{-6}$.

9.4   Taylor Series Method

The Taylor series method is of general applicability, and it is the standard to which we compare the accuracy of the various other numerical methods for solving an I.V.P. It can be devised to have any specified degree of accuracy. We start by reformulating Taylor's theorem in a form that is suitable for solving differential equations.

Theorem 9.5 (Taylor's Theorem). Assume that $y(t) \in C^{N+1}[t_0, b]$ and that $y(t)$ has a Taylor series expansion of order N about the fixed value $t = t_k \in [t_0, b]$:

(1) $$y(t_k + h) = y(t_k) + hT_N(t_k, y(t_k)) + O(h^{N+1}),$$

where

(2) $$T_N(t_k, y(t_k)) = \sum_{j=1}^{N} \frac{y^{(j)}(t_k)}{j!} h^{j-1}$$

and $y^{(j)}(t) = f^{(j-1)}(t, y(t))$ denotes the $(j - 1)$st total derivative of the function f with respect to t. The formulas for the derivatives can be computed recursively:

$$
\begin{aligned}
y'(t) &= f \\
y''(t) &= f_t + f_y y' = f_t + f_y f \\
y^{(3)}(t) &= f_{tt} + 2f_{ty} y' + f_y y'' + f_{yy}(y')^2 \\
&= f_{tt} + 2f_{ty} f + f_{yy} f^2 + f_y(f_t + f_y f) \\
y^{(4)}(t) &= f_{ttt} + 3f_{tty} y' + 3f_{tyy}(y')^2 + 3f_{ty} y'' \\
&\quad + f_y y''' + 3f_{yy} y' y'' + f_{yyy}(y')^3 \\
&= (f_{ttt} + 3f_{tty} f + 3f_{tyy} f^2 + f_{yyy} f^3) + f_y(f_{tt} + 2f_{ty} f + f_{yy} f^2) \\
&\quad + 3(f_t + f_y f)(f_{ty} + f_{yy} f) + f_y^2(f_t + f_y f)
\end{aligned}
$$

(3)

and, in general,

(4) $$y^{(N)}(t) = P^{(N-1)} f(t, y(t)),$$

where P is the derivative operator

$$P = \left(\frac{\partial}{\partial t} + f \frac{\partial}{\partial y} \right).$$

The approximate numerical solution to the I.V.P. $y'(t) = f(t, y)$ over $[t_0, t_M]$ is derived by using formula (1) on each subinterval $[t_k, t_{k+1}]$. The general step for Taylor's method of order N is

(5) $$y_{k+1} = y_k + d_1 h + \frac{d_2 h^2}{2!} + \frac{d_3 h^3}{3!} + \cdots + \frac{d_N h^N}{N!},$$

where $d_j = y^{(j)}(t_k)$ for $j = 1, 2, \ldots, N$ at each step $k = 0, 1, \ldots, M - 1$.

The Taylor method of order N has the property that the final global error (F.G.E.) is of the order $O(h^{N+1})$; hence N can be chosen as large as necessary to make this error as small as desired. If the order N is fixed, it is theoretically possible to a priori determine the step size h so that the F.G.E. will be as small as desired. However, in practice we usually compute two sets of approximations using step sizes h and $h/2$ and compare the results.

Theorem 9.6 (Precision of Taylor's Method of Order N). Assume that $y(t)$ is the solution to the I.V.P. If $y(t) \in C^{N+1}[t_0, b]$ and $\{(t_k, y_k)\}_{k=0}^{M}$ is the sequence of approximations generated by Taylor's method of order N, then

(6)
$$|e_k| = |y(t_k) - y_k| = \boldsymbol{O}(h^N),$$

$$|\epsilon_{k+1}| = |y(t_{k+1}) - y_k - hT_N(t_k, y_k)| = \boldsymbol{O}(h^{N+1}).$$

In particular, the F.G.E. at the end of the interval will satisfy

(7)
$$E(y(b), h) = |y(b) - y_M| = \boldsymbol{O}(h^N).$$

Examples 9.8 and 9.9 illustrate Theorem 9.6 for the case $N = 4$. If approximations are computed using the step sizes h and $h/2$, we should have

(8)
$$E(y(b), h) \approx Ch^4$$

for the larger step size, and

(9)
$$E\left(y(b), \frac{h}{2}\right) \approx C\frac{h^4}{16} = \frac{1}{16}Ch^4 \approx \frac{1}{16}E(y(b), h).$$

Hence the idea in Theorem 9.6 is that if the step size in the Taylor method of order 4 is reduced by a factor of $\frac{1}{2}$, the overall F.G.E. will be reduced by about $\frac{1}{16}$.

Example 9.8. Use the Taylor method of order $N = 4$ to solve $y' = (t - y)/2$ on $[0, 3]$ with $y(0) = 1$. Compare solutions for $h = 1, \frac{1}{2}, \frac{1}{4}$, and $\frac{1}{8}$.

The derivatives of $y(t)$ must first be determined. Recall that the solution $y(t)$ is a function of t, and differentiate the formula $y'(t) = f(t, y(t))$ with respect to t to get $y^{(2)}(t)$. Then continue the process to obtain the higher derivatives.

$$y'(t) = \frac{t - y}{2},$$

$$y^{(2)}(t) = \frac{d}{dt}\left(\frac{t - y}{2}\right) = \frac{1 - y'}{2} = \frac{1 - (t - y)/2}{2} = \frac{2 - t + y}{4},$$

$$y^{(3)}(t) = \frac{d}{dt}\left(\frac{2 - t + y}{4}\right) = \frac{0 - 1 + y'}{4} = \frac{-1 + (t - y)/2}{4} = \frac{-2 + t - y}{8},$$

$$y^{(4)}(t) = \frac{d}{dt}\left(\frac{-2 + t - y}{8}\right) = \frac{-0 + 1 - y'}{8} = \frac{1 - (t - y)/2}{8} = \frac{2 - t + y}{16}.$$

To find y_1, the derivatives given above must be evaluated at the point $(t_0, y_0) = (0, 1)$.

Calculation reveals that

$$d_1 = y'(0) = \frac{0.0 - 1.0}{2} = -0.5,$$

$$d_2 = y^{(2)}(0) = \frac{2.0 - 0.0 + 1.0}{4} = 0.75,$$

$$d_3 = y^{(3)}(0) = \frac{-2.0 + 0.0 - 1.0}{8} = -0.375,$$

$$d_4 = y^{(4)}(0) = \frac{2.0 - 0.0 + 1.0}{16} = 0.1875.$$

Next the derivatives $\{d_j\}$ are substituted into (5) with $h = 0.25$, and nested multiplication is used to compute the value y_1:

$$y_1 = 1.0 + 0.25 \left(-0.5 + 0.25 \left(\frac{0.75}{2} + 0.25 \left(\frac{-0.375}{6} + 0.25 \left(\frac{0.1875}{24} \right) \right) \right) \right)$$

$$= 0.8974915.$$

The computed solution point is $(t_1, y_1) = (0.25, 0.8974915)$.

To determine y_2, the derivatives $\{d_j\}$ must now be evaluated at the point $(t_1, y_1) = (0.25, 0.8974915)$. The calculations are starting to require a considerable amount of computational effort and are tedious to do by hand. Calculation reveals that

$$d_1 = y'(0.25) = \frac{0.25 - 0.8974915}{2} = -0.3237458,$$

$$d_2 = y^{(2)}(0.25) = \frac{2.0 - 0.25 + 0.8974915}{4} = 0.6618729,$$

$$d_3 = y^{(3)}(0.25) = \frac{-2.0 + 0.25 - 0.8974915}{8} = -0.3309364,$$

$$d_4 = y^{(4)}(0.25) = \frac{2.0 - 0.25 + 0.8974915}{16} = 0.1654682.$$

Now these derivatives $\{d_j\}$ are substituted into (5) with $h = 0.25$, and nested multiplication is used to compute the value y_2:

$$y_2 = 0.8974915 + 0.25 \Bigg(-0.3237458$$

$$+ 0.25 \left(\frac{0.6618729}{2} + 0.25 \left(\frac{-0.3309364}{6} + 0.25 \left(\frac{0.1654682}{24} \right) \right) \right) \Bigg)$$

$$= 0.8364037.$$

The solution point is $(t_2, y_2) = (0.50, 0.8364037)$. Table 9.6 gives solution values at selected abscissas using various step sizes. ∎

Table 9.6   Comparison of the Taylor Solutions of Order $N = 4$ for $y' = (t - y)/2$ over $[0, 3]$ with $y(0) = 1$

| t_k | y_k | | | | $y(t_k)$ Exact |
	$h = 1$	$h = \frac{1}{2}$	$h = \frac{1}{4}$	$h = \frac{1}{8}$	
0	1.0	1.0	1.0	1.0	1.0
0.125				0.9432392	0.9432392
0.25			0.8974915	0.8974908	0.8974917
0.375				0.8620874	0.8620874
0.50		0.8364258	0.8364037	0.8364024	0.8364023
0.75			0.8118696	0.8118679	0.8118678
1.00	0.8203125	0.8196285	0.8195940	0.8195921	0.8195920
1.50		0.9171423	0.9171021	0.9170998	0.9170997
2.00	1.1045125	1.1036826	1.1036408	1.1036385	1.1036383
2.50		1.3595575	1.3595168	1.3595145	1.3595144
3.00	1.6701860	1.6694308	1.6693928	1.6693906	1.6693905

Table 9.7   Relation between Step Size and F.G.E. for the Taylor Solutions to $y' = (t - y)/2$ over $[0, 3]$

Step size, h	Number of steps, M	Approximation to $y(3)$, y_M	F.G.E. Error at $t = 3$, $y(3) - y_M$	$O(h^2) \approx Ch^4$ where $C = -0.000614$
1	3	1.6701860	−0.0007955	−0.0006140
$\frac{1}{2}$	6	1.6694308	−0.0000403	−0.0000384
$\frac{1}{4}$	12	1.6693928	−0.0000023	−0.0000024
$\frac{1}{8}$	24	1.6693906	−0.0000001	−0.0000001

Example 9.9.   Compare the F.G.E. for the Taylor solutions to $y' = (t - y)/2$ over $[0, 3]$ with $y(0) = 1$ given in Example 9.8.

Table 9.7 gives the F.G.E. for these step sizes and shows that the error in the approximation $y(3)$ decreases by about $\frac{1}{16}$ when the step size is reduced by a factor of $\frac{1}{2}$:

$$E(y(3), h) = y(3) - y_M = O(h^4) \approx Ch^4, \quad \text{where } C = -0.000614. \qquad \blacksquare$$

The following program requires that the derivatives y', y'', y''', and y'''' be saved in an M-file named df. For example, the following M-file would save the derivatives from Example 9.8 in the format required by Program 9.3.

```
function z=df(t,y)
z=[(t-y)/2 (2-t+y)/4 (-2+t-y)/8 (2-t+y)/16];
```

Program 9.3 (Taylor's Method of Order 4). To approximate the solution of the
initial value problem $y' = f(t, y)$ with $y(a) = y_0$ over $[a, b]$ by evaluating y'', y''',
and y'''' and using the Taylor polynomial at each step.

```
function T4=taylor(df,a,b,ya,M)
%Input   - df=[y' y'' y''' y''''] entered as a string 'df'
%           where y'=f(t,y)
%         - a and b are the left and right endpoints
%         - ya is the initial condition y(a)
%         - M is the number of steps
%Output  - T4=[T' Y'] where T is the vector of abscissas and
%           Y is the vector of ordinates
h=(b-a)/M;
T=zeros(1,M+1);
Y=zeros(1,M+1);
T=a:h:b;
Y(1)=ya;
for j=1:M
   D=feval(df,T(j),Y(j));
   Y(j+1)=Y(j)+h*(D(1)+h*(D(2)/2+h*(D(3)/6+h*D(4)/24)));
end
T4=[T' Y'];
```

Exercises for Taylor Series Method

In Exercises 1 through 5, solve the differential equations by Taylor's method of order $N = 4$.

(a) Let $h = 0.2$ and do two steps by hand calculation. Then let $h = 0.1$ and do four
steps by hand calculation.

(b) Compare the exact solution $y(0.4)$ with the two approximations in part (a).

(c) Does the F.G.E. in part (a) behave as expected when h is halved?

1. $y' = t^2 - y$ with $y(0) = 1$, $y(t) = -e^{-t} + t^2 - 2t + 2$

2. $y' = 3y + 3t$ with $y(0) = 1$, $y(t) = \frac{4}{3}e^{3t} - t - \frac{1}{3}$

3. $y' = -ty$ with $y(0) = 1$, $y(t) = e^{-t^2/2}$

4. $y' = e^{-2t} - 2y$ with $y(0) = \frac{1}{10}$, $y(t) = \frac{1}{10}e^{-2t} + te^{-2t}$

5. $y' = 2ty^2$ with $y(0) = 1$, $y(t) = 1/(1 - t^2)$

6. The Richardson improvement method discussed in Lemma 7.1 (Section 7.3) can be used in conjunction with Taylor's method. If Taylor's method of order $N = 4$ is used with step size h, then $y(b) \approx y_h + Ch^4$. If Taylor's method of order $N = 4$ is used with step size $2h$, then $y(b) \approx y_{2h} + 16Ch^4$. The terms involving Ch^4 can be eliminated to obtain an improved approximation for $y(b)$:

$$y(b) \approx \frac{16y_h - y_{2h}}{15}.$$

This improvement scheme can be used with the values in Example 9.9 to obtain better approximations to $y(3)$. Find the missing entries in the table below.

h	y_h	$(16y_h - y_{2h})/15$
1.0	1.6701860	_____
0.5	1.6694308	_____
0.25	1.6693928	_____
0.125	1.6693906	_____

7. Show that when Taylor's method of order N is used with step sizes h and $h/2$, then the overall F.G.E. will be reduced by a factor of about 2^{-N} for the smaller step size.

8. Show that Taylor's method fails to approximate the solution $y(t) = t^{3/2}$ of the I.V.P. $y' = f(t, y) = 1.5y^{1/3}$ with $y(0) = 0$. Justify your answer. What difficulties were encountered?

9. (a) Verify that the solution to the I.V.P. $y' = y^2$, $y(0) = 1$ over the interval $[0, 1)$ is $y(t) = 1/(1 - t)$.

(b) Verify that the solution to the I.V.P. $y' = 1 + y^2$, $y(0) = 1$ over the interval $[0, \pi/4)$ is $y(t) = \tan(t + \pi/4)$.

(c) Use the results of parts (a) and (b) to argue that the solution to the I.V.P. $y' = t^2 + y^2$, $y(0) = 1$ has a vertical asymptote between $\pi/4$ and 1. (Its location is near $t = 0.96981$.)

10. Consider the I.V.P. $y' = 1 + y^2$, $y(0) = 1$.

(a) Find an expression for $y^{(2)}(t)$, $y^{(3)}(t)$, and $y^{(4)}(t)$.

(b) Evaluate the derivatives at $t = 0$, and use them to find the first five terms in the Maclaurin expansion for $\tan(t)$.

Algorithms and Programs

In Problems 1 through 5, solve the differential equations by Taylor's method of order $N = 4$.

(a) Let $h = 0.1$ and do 20 steps with Program 9.3. Then let $h = 0.05$ and do 40 steps with Program 9.3.

(b) Compare the exact solution $y(2)$ with the two approximations in part (a).

(c) Does the F.G.E. in part (a) behave as expected when h is halved?

(d) Plot the two approximations and the exact solution on the same coordinate system. *Hint.* The output matrix T4 from Program 9.3 contains the x- and y-coordinates of the approximations. The command `plot(T4(:,1),T4(:,2))` will produce a graph analogous to Figure 9.6.

1. $y' = t^2 - y$ with $y(0) = 1$, $y(t) = -e^{-t} + t^2 - 2t + 2$

2. $y' = 3y + 3t$ with $y(0) = 1$, $y(t) = \frac{4}{3}e^{3t} - t - \frac{1}{3}$

3. $y' = -ty$ with $y(0) = 1$, $y(t) = e^{-t^2/2}$

4. $y' = e^{-2t} - 2y$ with $y(0) = \frac{1}{10}$, $y(t) = \frac{1}{10}e^{-2t} + te^{-2t}$

5. $y' = 2ty^2$ with $y(0) = 1$, $y(t) = 1/(1 - t^2)$

6. **(a)**   Write a program to implement the Richardson improvement method discussed in Exercise 6.

   (b)   Use your program from part (a) to approximate $y(0.8)$ for the I.V.P. $y' = t^2 + y^2$, $y(0) = 1$ over $[0, 0.8]$. The true solution at $t = 0.8$ is known to be $y(0.8) = 5.8486168$. Start with the step size $h = 0.05$. The program should terminate when the absolute value of the difference between two consecutive Richardson improvements is $< 10^{-6}$.

7. **(a)**   Modify Program 9.3 to carry out Taylor's method of order $N = 3$.

   (b)   Use your program from part (a) to solve the I.V.P. $y' = t^2 + y^2$, $y(0) = 1$ over $[0, 0.8]$. Find approximate solutions for the step sizes $h = 0.05, 0.025, 0.0125$, and 0.00625. Plot the four approximations on the same coordinate system.

9.5   Runge-Kutta Methods

The Taylor methods in the preceding section have the desirable feature that the F.G.E. is of order $O(h^N)$, and N can be chosen large so that this error is small. However, the shortcomings of the Taylor methods are the a priori determination of N and the computation of the higher derivatives, which can be very complicated. Each Runge-Kutta method is derived from an appropriate Taylor method in such a way that the F.G.E. is of order $O(h^N)$. A trade-off is made to perform several function evaluations at each step and eliminate the necessity to compute the higher derivatives. These methods can be constructed for any order N. The Runge-Kutta method of order $N = 4$ is most popular. It is a good choice for common purposes because it is quite accurate, stable, and easy to program. Most authorities proclaim that it is not necessary to go to a higher-order method because the increased accuracy is offset by additional computational effort. If more accuracy is required, then either a smaller step size or an adaptive method should be used.

The fourth-order Runge-Kutta method (RK4) simulates the accuracy of the Taylor series method of order $N = 4$. The method is based on computing y_{k+1} as follows:

$$
(1) \qquad y_{k+1} = y_k + w_1 k_1 + w_2 k_2 + w_3 k_3 + w_4 k_4,
$$

where k_1, k_2, k_3, and k_4 have the form

$$
(2) \qquad
\begin{aligned}
k_1 &= hf(t_k, y_k), \\
k_2 &= hf(t_k + a_1 h, y_k + b_1 k_1), \\
k_3 &= hf(t_k + a_2 h, y_k + b_2 k_1 + b_3 k_2), \\
k_4 &= hf(t_k + a_3 h, y_k + b_4 k_1 + b_5 k_2 + b_6 k_3).
\end{aligned}
$$

By matching coefficients with those of the Taylor series method of order $N = 4$ so that the local truncation error is of order $O(h^5)$, Runge and Kutta were able to obtain the following system of equations:

$$
(3) \qquad
\begin{aligned}
b_1 &= a_1, \\
b_2 + b_3 &= a_2, \\
b_4 + b_5 + b_6 &= a_3, \\
w_1 + w_2 + w_3 + w_4 &= 1, \\
w_2 a_1 + w_3 a_2 + w_4 a_3 &= \frac{1}{2}, \\
w_2 a_1^2 + w_3 a_2^2 + w_4 a_3^2 &= \frac{1}{3}, \\
w_2 a_1^3 + w_3 a_2^3 + w_4 a_3^3 &= \frac{1}{4}, \\
w_3 a_1 b_3 + w_4 (a_1 b_5 + a_2 b_6) &= \frac{1}{6}, \\
w_3 a_1 a_2 b_3 + w_4 a_3 (a_1 b_5 + a_2 b_6) &= \frac{1}{8}, \\
w_3 a_1^2 b_3 + w_4 (a_1^2 b_5 + a_2^2 b_6) &= \frac{1}{12}, \\
w_4 a_1 b_3 b_6 &= \frac{1}{24}.
\end{aligned}
$$

The system involves 11 equations in 13 unknowns. Two additional conditions must be supplied to solve the system. The most useful choice is

$$
(4) \qquad a_1 = \frac{1}{2} \quad \text{and} \quad b_2 = 0.
$$

Then the solution for the remaining variables is

$$
(5) \quad
\begin{aligned}
&a_2 = \frac{1}{2}, \quad a_3 = 1, \quad b_1 = \frac{1}{2}, \quad b_3 = \frac{1}{2}, \quad b_4 = 0, \quad b_5 = 0, \quad b_6 = 1, \\
&w_1 = \frac{1}{6}, \quad w_2 = \frac{1}{3}, \quad w_3 = \frac{1}{3}, \quad w_4 = \frac{1}{6}.
\end{aligned}
$$

The values in (4) and (5) are substituted into (2) and (1) to obtain the formula for the standard Runge-Kutta method of order $N = 4$, which is stated as follows. Start with the initial point (t_0, y_0) and generate the sequence of approximations using

$$
(6) \quad y_{k+1} = y_k + \frac{h(f_1 + 2f_2 + 2f_3 + f_4)}{6},
$$

where

$$
(7) \quad
\begin{aligned}
f_1 &= f(t_k, y_k), \\
f_2 &= f\left(t_k + \frac{h}{2}, y_k + \frac{h}{2}f_1\right), \\
f_3 &= f\left(t_k + \frac{h}{2}, y_k + \frac{h}{2}f_2\right), \\
f_4 &= f(t_k + h, y_k + hf_3).
\end{aligned}
$$

Discussion about the Method

The complete development of the equations in (7) is beyond the scope of this book and can be found in advanced texts, but we can get some insights. Consider the graph of the solution curve $y = y(t)$ over the first subinterval $[t_0, t_1]$. The function values in (7) are approximations for slopes to this curve. Here f_1 is the slope at the left, f_2 and f_3 are two estimates for the slope in the middle, and f_4 is the slope at the right (see Figure 9.9(a)). The next point (t_1, y_1) is obtained by integrating the slope function

$$
(8) \quad y(t_1) - y(t_0) = \int_{t_0}^{t_1} f(t, y(t))\, dt.
$$

If Simpson's rule is applied with step size $h/2$, the approximation to the integral in (8) is

$$
(9) \quad \int_{t_0}^{t_1} f(t, y(t))\, dt \approx \frac{h}{6}(f(t_0, y(t_0)) + 4f(t_{1/2}, y(t_{1/2})) + f(t_1, y(t_1))),
$$

where $t_{1/2}$ is the midpoint of the interval. Three function values are needed; hence we make the obvious choice $f(t_0, y(t_0)) = f_1$ and $f(t_1, y(t_1)) \approx f_4$. For the value in the middle we chose the average of f_2 and f_3:

$$
f(t_{1/2}, y(t_{1/2})) \approx \frac{f_2 + f_3}{2}.
$$

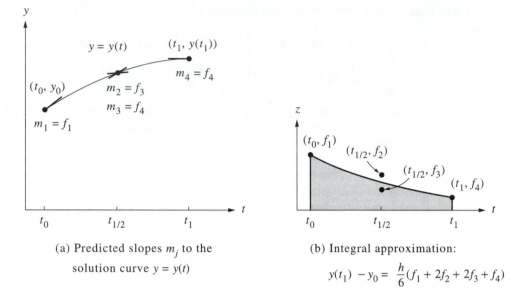

(a) Predicted slopes m_j to the
solution curve $y = y(t)$

(b) Integral approximation:

$$y(t_1) - y_0 = \frac{h}{6}(f_1 + 2f_2 + 2f_3 + f_4)$$

Figure 9.9   The graphs $y = y(t)$ and $z = f(t, y(t))$ in the discussion of the Runge-Kutta method of order $N = 4$.

These values are substituted into (9), which is used in equation (8) to get y_1:

$$(10) \qquad y_1 = y_0 + \frac{h}{6}\left(f_1 + \frac{4(f_2 + f_3)}{2} + f_4\right).$$

When this formula is simplified, it is seen to be equation (6) with $k = 0$. The graph for the integral in (9) is shown in Figure 9.9(b).

Step Size versus Error

The error term for Simpson's rule with step size $h/2$ is

$$(11) \qquad -y^{(4)}(c_1)\frac{h^5}{2880}.$$

If the only error at each step is that given in (11), after M steps the accumulated error for the RK4 method would be

$$(12) \qquad -\sum_{k=1}^{M} y^{(4)}(c_k)\frac{h^5}{2880} \approx \frac{b - a}{5760}y^{(4)}(c)h^4 \approx O(h^4).$$

The next theorem states the relationship between F.G.E. and step size. It is used to give us an idea of how much computing effort must be done when using the RK4 method.

Theorem 9.7 (Precision of the Runge-Kutta Method). Assume that $y(t)$ is the solution to the I.V.P. If $y(t) \in C^5[t_0, b]$ and $\{(t_k, y_k)\}_{k=0}^{M}$ is the sequence of approximations generated by the Runge-Kutta method of order 4, then

(13)
$$|e_k| = |y(t_k) - y_k| = O(h^4),$$
$$|\epsilon_{k+1}| = |y(t_{k+1}) - y_k - hT_N(t_k, y_k)| = O(h^5).$$

In particular, the F.G.E. at the end of the interval will satisfy

(14)
$$E(y(b), h) = |y(b) - y_M| = O(h^4).$$

Examples 9.10 and 9.11 illustrate Theorem 9.7. If approximations are computed using the step sizes h and $h/2$, we should have

(15)
$$E(y(b), h) \approx Ch^4$$

for the larger step size, and

(16)
$$E\left(y(b), \frac{h}{2}\right) \approx C\frac{h^4}{16} = \frac{1}{16}Ch^4 \approx \frac{1}{16}E(y(b), h).$$

Hence the idea in Theorem 9.7 is that if the step size in the RK4 method is reduced by a factor of $\frac{1}{2}$ we can expect that the overall F.G.E. will be reduced by a factor of $\frac{1}{16}$.

Example 9.10. Use the RK4 method to solve the I.V.P. $y' = (t - y)/2$ on $[0, 3]$ with $y(0) = 1$. Compare solutions for $h = 1, \frac{1}{2}, \frac{1}{4},$ and $\frac{1}{8}$.

Table 9.8 gives the solution values at selected abscissas. For the step size $h = 0.25$, a sample calculation is

$$f_1 = \frac{0.0 - 1.0}{2} = -0.5,$$
$$f_2 = \frac{0.125 - (1 + 0.25(0.5)(-0.5))}{2} = -0.40625,$$
$$f_3 = \frac{0.125 - (1 + 0.25(0.5)(-0.40625))}{2} = -0.4121094,$$
$$f_4 = \frac{0.25 - (1 + 0.25(-0.4121094))}{2} = -0.3234863,$$
$$y_1 = 1.0 + 0.25\left(\frac{-0.5 + 2(-0.40625) + 2(-0.4121094) - 0.3234863}{6}\right)$$
$$= 0.8974915. \qquad \blacksquare$$

Example 9.11. Compare the F.G.E. when the RK4 method is used to solve $y' = (t - y)/2$ over $[0, 3]$ with $y(0) = 1$ using step sizes $1, \frac{1}{2}, \frac{1}{4},$ and $\frac{1}{8}$.

Table 9.8   Comparison of the RK4 Solutions with Different Step Sizes for $y' = (t - y)/2$ over $[0, 3]$ with $y(0) = 1$

	y_k				
t_k	$h = 1$	$h = \frac{1}{2}$	$h = \frac{1}{4}$	$h = \frac{1}{8}$	$y(t_k)$ Exact
0	1.0	1.0	1.0	1.0	1.0
0.125				0.9432392	0.9432392
0.25			0.8974915	0.8974908	0.8974917
0.375				0.8620874	0.8620874
0.50		0.8364258	0.8364037	0.8364024	0.8364023
0.75			0.8118696	0.8118679	0.8118678
1.00	0.8203125	0.8196285	0.8195940	0.8195921	0.8195920
1.50		0.9171423	0.9171021	0.9170998	0.9170997
2.00	1.1045125	1.1036826	1.1036408	1.1036385	1.1036383
2.50		1.3595575	1.3595168	1.3595145	1.3595144
3.00	1.6701860	1.6694308	1.6693928	1.6693906	1.6693905

Table 9.9   Relation between Step Size and F.G.E. for the RK4 Solutions to $y' = (t - y)/2$ over $[0, 3]$ with $y(0) = 1$

Step size, h	Number of steps, M	Approximation to $y(3)$, y_M	F.G.E. Error at $t = 3$, $y(3) - y_M$	$O(h^4) \approx Ch^4$ where $C = -0.000614$
1	3	1.6701860	-0.0007955	-0.0006140
$\frac{1}{2}$	6	1.6694308	-0.0000403	-0.0000384
$\frac{1}{4}$	12	1.6693928	-0.0000023	-0.0000024
$\frac{1}{8}$	24	1.6693906	-0.0000001	-0.0000001

Table 9.9 gives the F.G.E. for the various step sizes and shows that the error in the approximation to $y(3)$ decreases by about $\frac{1}{16}$ when the step size is reduced by a factor of $1/2$.

$$E(y(3), h) = y(3) - y_M = O(h^4) \approx Ch^4 \quad \text{where } C = -0.000614. \qquad \blacksquare$$

A comparison of Examples 9.10 and 9.11 and Examples 9.8 and 9.9 shows what is meant by the statement "The RK4 method simulates the Taylor series method of order $N = 4$." For these examples, the two methods generate identical solution sets $\{(t_k, y_k)\}$ over the given interval. The advantage of the RK4 method is obvious; no formulas for the higher derivatives need to be computed nor do they have to be in the program.

It is not easy to determine the accuracy to which a Runge-Kutta solution has been computed. We could estimate the size of $y^{(4)}(c)$ and use formula (12). Another way is to repeat the algorithm using a smaller step size and compare results. A third way is to adaptively determine the step size, which is done in Program 9.5. In Section 9.6 we will see how to change the step size for a multistep method.

Runge-Kutta Methods of Order $N = 2$

The second-order Runge-Kutta method (denoted RK2) simulates the accuracy of the Taylor series method of order 2. Although this method is not as good to use as the RK4 method, its proof is easier to understand and illustrates the principles involved. To start, we write down the Taylor series formula for $y(t + h)$:

$$(17) \qquad y(t + h) = y(t) + hy'(t) + \frac{1}{2}h^2 y''(t) + C_T h^3 + \cdots ,$$

where C_T is a constant involving the third derivative of $y(t)$ and the other terms in the series involve powers of h^j for $j > 3$.

The derivatives $y'(t)$ and $y''(t)$ in equation (17) must be expressed in terms of $f(t, y)$ and its partial derivatives. Recall that

$$(18) \qquad y'(t) = f(t, y).$$

The chain rule for differentiating a function of two variables can be used to differentiate (18) with respect to t, and the result is

$$y''(t) = f_t(t, y) + f_y(t, y)y'(t).$$

Using (18), this can be written

$$(19) \qquad y''(t) = f_t(t, y) + f_y(t, y)f(t, y).$$

The derivatives (18) and (19) are substituted in (17) to give the Taylor expression for $y(t + h)$:

$$(20) \qquad \begin{aligned} y(t + h) &= y(t) + hf(t, y) + \frac{1}{2}h^2 f_t(t, y) \\ &\quad + \frac{1}{2}h^2 f_y(t, y)f(t, y) + C_T h^3 + \cdots . \end{aligned}$$

Now consider the Runge-Kutta method of order $N = 2$, which uses a linear combination of two function values to express $y(t + h)$:

$$(21) \qquad y(t + h) = y(t) + Ahf_0 + Bhf_1,$$

where

(22)
$$f_0 = f(t, y),$$
$$f_1 = f(t + Ph, y + Qhf_0).$$

Next the Taylor polynomial approximation for a function of two independent variables is used to expand $f(t, y)$ (see the Exercises). This gives the following representation for f_1:

(23) $$f_1 = f(t, y) + Phf_t(t, y) + Qhf_y(t, y)f(t, y) + C_P h^2 + \cdots,$$

where C_P involves the second-order partial derivatives of $f(t, y)$. Then (23) is used in (21) to get the RK2 expression for $y(t + h)$:

(24)
$$y(t + h) = y(t) + (A + B)hf(t, y) + BPh^2 f_t(t, y)$$
$$+ BQh^2 f_y(t, y)f(t, y) + BC_P h^3 + \cdots.$$

A comparison of similar terms in equations (20) and (24) will produce the following conclusions:

$$hf(t, y) = (A + B)hf(t, y) \qquad \text{implies that } 1 = A + B,$$

$$\frac{1}{2}h^2 f_t(t, y) = BPh^2 f_t(t, y) \qquad \text{implies that } \frac{1}{2} = BP,$$

$$\frac{1}{2}h^2 f_y(t, y)f(t, y) = BQh^2 f_y(t, y)f(t, y) \quad \text{implies that } \frac{1}{2} = BQ.$$

Hence, if we require that A, B, P, and Q satisfy the relations

(25) $$A + B = 1 \qquad BP = \frac{1}{2} \qquad BQ = \frac{1}{2},$$

then the RK2 method in (24) will have the same order of accuracy as the Taylor's method in (20).

Since there are only three equations in four unknowns, the system of equations (25) is underdetermined, and we are permitted to choose one of the coefficients. There are several special choices that have been studied in the literature; we mention two of them.

Case (i): Choose $A = \frac{1}{2}$. This choice leads to $B = \frac{1}{2}$, $P = 1$, and $Q = 1$. If equation (21) is written with these parameters, the formula is

(26) $$y(t + h) = y(t) + \frac{h}{2}(f(t, y) + f(t + h, y + hf(t, y))).$$

When this scheme is used to generate $\{(t_k, y_k)\}$, the result is Heun's method.

Case (ii): Choose $A = 0$. This choice leads to $B = 1$, $P = \frac{1}{2}$, and $Q = \frac{1}{2}$. If equation (21) is written with these parameters, the formula is

(27) $$y(t + h) = y(t) + hf\left(t + \frac{h}{2}, y + \frac{h}{2}f(t, y)\right).$$

When this scheme is used to generate $\{(t_k, y_k)\}$, it is called the **modified Euler-Cauchy method**.

Runge-Kutta-Fehlberg Method (RKF45)

One way to guarantee accuracy in the solution of an I.V.P. is to solve the problem twice using step sizes h and $h/2$ and compare answers at the mesh points corresponding to the larger step size. But this requires a significant amount of computation for the smaller step size and must be repeated if it is determined that the agreement is not good enough.

The Runge-Kutta-Fehlberg method (denoted RKF45) is one way to try to resolve this problem. It has a procedure to determine if the proper step size h is being used. At each step, two different approximations for the solution are made and compared. If the two answers are in close agreement, the approximation is accepted. If the two answers do not agree to a specified accuracy, the step size is reduced. If the answers agree to more significant digits than required, the step size is increased.

Each step requires the use of the following six values:

$$
\begin{aligned}
k_1 &= hf(t_k, y_k), \\
k_2 &= hf\left(t_k + \frac{1}{4}h, \, y_k + \frac{1}{4}k_1\right), \\
k_3 &= hf\left(t_k + \frac{3}{8}h, \, y_k + \frac{3}{32}k_1 + \frac{9}{32}k_2\right), \\
k_4 &= hf\left(t_k + \frac{12}{13}h, \, y_k + \frac{1932}{2197}k_1 - \frac{7200}{2197}k_2 + \frac{7296}{2197}k_3\right), \\
k_5 &= hf\left(t_k + h, \, y_k + \frac{439}{216}k_1 - 8k_2 + \frac{3680}{513}k_3 - \frac{845}{4104}k_4\right), \\
k_6 &= hf\left(t_k + \frac{1}{2}h, \, y_k - \frac{8}{27}k_1 + 2k_2 - \frac{3544}{2565}k_3 + \frac{1859}{4104}k_4 - \frac{11}{40}k_5\right).
\end{aligned}
$$

(28)

Then an approximation to the solution of the I.V.P. is made using a Runge-Kutta method of order 4:

(29)
$$
y_{k+1} = y_k + \frac{25}{216}k_1 + \frac{1408}{2565}k_3 + \frac{2197}{4101}k_4 - \frac{1}{5}k_5,
$$

where the four function values f_1, f_3, f_4, and f_5 are used. Notice that f_2 is not used in formula (29). A better value for the solution is determined using a Runge-Kutta method of order 5:

(30)
$$
z_{k+1} = y_k + \frac{16}{135}k_1 + \frac{6656}{12{,}825}k_3 + \frac{28{,}561}{56{,}430}k_4 - \frac{9}{50}k_5 + \frac{2}{55}k_6.
$$

The optimal step size sh can be determined by multiplying the scalar s times the current step size h. The scalar s is

(31)
$$
s = \left(\frac{\text{tol } h}{2|z_{k+1} - y_{k+1}|}\right)^{1/4} \approx 0.84 \left(\frac{\text{tol } h}{|z_{k+1} - y_{k+1}|}\right)^{1/4}.
$$

Table 9.10 RKF45 Solution to $y' = 1 + y^2$, $y(0) = 0$

k	t_k	RK45 approximation y_k	True solution, $y(t_k) = \tan(t_k)$	Error $y(t_k) - y_k$
0	0.0	0.0000000	0.0000000	0.0000000
1	0.2	0.2027100	0.2027100	0.0000000
2	0.4	0.4227933	0.4227931	−0.0000002
3	0.6	0.6841376	0.6841368	−0.0000008
4	0.8	1.0296434	1.0296386	−0.0000048
5	1.0	1.5574398	1.5774077	−0.0000321
6	1.1	1.9648085	1.9647597	−0.0000488
7	1.2	2.5722408	2.5721516	−0.0000892
8	1.3	3.6023295	3.6021024	−0.0002271
9	1.35	4.4555714	4.4552218	−0.0003496
10	1.4	5.7985045	5.7978837	−0.0006208

where tol is the specified error control tolerance.

The derivation of formula (31) can be found in advanced books on numerical analysis. It is important to learn that a fixed step size is not the best strategy even though it would give a nicer-appearing table of values. If values are needed that are not in the table, polynomial interpolation should be used.

Example 9.12. Compare RKF45 and RK4 solutions to the I.V.P.

$$y' = 1 + y^2 \quad \text{with} \quad y(0) = 0 \quad \text{on} \quad [0, 1.4].$$

An RKF45 program was used with the value tol $= 2 \times 10^{-5}$ for the error control tolerance. It changed the step size automatically and generated the 10 approximations to the solution in Table 9.10. An RK4 program was used with the a priori step size of $h = 0.1$, which required the computer to generate 14 approximations at the equally spaced points in Table 9.11. The approximations at the right endpoint are

$$y(1.4) \approx y_{10} = 5.7985045 \quad \text{and} \quad y(1.4) \approx y_{14} = 5.7919748$$

and the errors are

$$E_{10} = -0.0006208 \quad \text{and} \quad E_{14} = 0.0059089$$

for the RKF45 and RK4 methods, respectively. The RKF45 method has the smaller error. ∎

Table 9.11   RK4 Solution to $y' = 1 + y^2$, $y(0) = 0$

k	t_k	RK4 approximation y_k	True solution, $y(t_k) = \tan(t_k)$	Error $y(t_k) - y_k$
0	0.0	0.0000000	0.0000000	0.0000000
1	0.1	0.1003346	0.1003347	0.0000001
2	0.2	0.2027099	0.2027100	0.0000001
3	0.3	0.3093360	0.3093362	0.0000002
4	0.4	0.4227930	0.4227932	0.0000002
5	0.5	0.5463023	0.5463025	0.0000002
6	0.6	0.6841368	0.6841368	0.0000000
7	0.7	0.8422886	0.8422884	−0.0000002
8	0.8	1.0296391	1.0296386	−0.0000005
9	0.9	1.2601588	1.2601582	−0.0000006
10	1.0	1.5574064	1.5574077	0.0000013
11	1.1	1.9647466	1.9647597	0.0000131
12	1.2	2.5720718	2.5721516	0.0000798
13	1.3	3.6015634	3.6021024	0.0005390
14	1.4	5.7919748	5.7978837	0.0059089

Program 9.4 (Runge-Kutta Method of Order 4).   To approximate the solution of the initial value problem $y' = f(t, y)$ with $y(a) = y_0$ over $[a, b]$ by using the formula

$$y_{k+1} = y_k + \frac{h}{6}(k_1 + 2k_2 + 2k_3 + k_4).$$

```
function R=rk4(f,a,b,ya,M)
%Input   - f is the function entered as a string 'f'
%         - a and b are the left and right endpoints
%         - ya is the initial condition y(a)
%         - M is the number of steps
%Output - R=[T' Y'] where T is the vector of abscissas
%          and Y is the vector of ordinates
h=(b-a)/M;
T=zeros(1,M+1);
Y=zeros(1,M+1);
T=a:h:b;
Y(1)=ya;
for j=1:M
   k1=h*feval(f,T(j),Y(j));
   k2=h*feval(f,T(j)+h/2,Y(j)+k1/2);
   k3=h*feval(f,T(j)+h/2,Y(j)+k2/2);
   k4=h*feval(f,T(j)+h,Y(j)+k3);
```

```
    Y(j+1)=Y(j)+(k1+2*k2+2*k3+k4)/6;
end
R=[T' Y'];
```

The following program implements the Runge-Kutta-Fehlberg Method (RKF45) described in (28) through (31).

> **Program 9.5 (Runge-Kutta-Fehlberg Method (RKF45)).** To approximate the solution of the initial value problem $y' = f(t, y)$ with $y(a) = y_0$ over $[a, b]$ with an error control and step-size method.

```
function R=rkf45(f,a,b,ya,M,tol)
%Input   - f is the function entered as a string 'f'
%         - a and b are the left and right endpoints
%         - ya is the initial condition y(a)
%         - M is the number of steps
%         - tol is the tolerance
%Output  - R=[T' Y'] where T is the vector of abscissas
%           and Y is the vector of ordinates
%Enter the coefficients necessary to calculate the
%values in (28) and (29)
a2=1/4;b2=1/4;a3=3/8;b3=3/32;c3=9/32;a4=12/13;
b4=1932/2197;c4=-7200/2197;d4=7296/2197;a5=1;
b5=439/216;c5=-8;d5=3680/513;e5=-845/4104;a6=1/2;
b6=-8/27;c6=2;d6=-3544/2565;e6=1859/4104;
f6=-11/40;r1=1/360;r3=-128/4275;r4=-2197/75240;r5=1/50;
r6=2/55;n1=25/216;n3=1408/2565;n4=2197/4104;n5=-1/5;
big=1e15;
h=(b-a)/M;
hmin=h/64;
hmax=64*h;
max1=200;
Y(1)=ya;
T(1)=a;
j=1;
br=b-0.00001*abs(b);
while (T(j)<b)
    if ((T(j)+h)>br)
        h=b-T(j);
    end

    %Calculation of values in (28) and (29)
    k1=h*feval(f,T(j),Y(j));
    y2=Y(j)+b2*k1;
```

```
if big<abs(y2)break,end
k2=h*feval(f,T(j)+a2*h,y2);
y3=Y(j)+b3*k1+c3*k2;
if big<abs(y3)break,end
k3=h*feval(f,T(j)+a3*h,y3);
y4=Y(j)+b4*k1+c4*k2+d4*k3;
if big<abs(y4)break,end
k4=h*feval(f,Y(j)+a4*h,y4);
y5=Y(j)+b5*k1+c5*k2+d5*k3+e5*k4;
if big<abs(y5)break,end
k5=h*feval(f,T(j)+a5*h,y5);
y6=Y(j)+b6*k1+c6*k2+d6*k3+e6*k4+f6*k5;
if big<abs(y6)break,end
k6=h*feval(f,Y(j)+a6*h,y6);
err=abs(r1*k1+r3*k3+r4*k4+r5*k5+r6*k6);
ynew=Y(j)+n1*k1+n3*k3+n4*k4+n5*k5;
%Error and step size control
if((err<tol)|(h<2*hmin))
    Y(j+1)=ynew;
    if((T(j)+h)>br)
        T(j+1)=b;
    else
        T(j+1)=T(j)+h;
    end
    j=j+1;
end
if (err==0)
    s=0;
else
    s=0.84*(tol*h/err)^(0.25);
end
if((s<0.75)&(h>2*hmin))
    h=h/2;
end
if((s>1.50)&(2*h<hmax))
h=2*h;
end
if((big<abs(Y(j)))|(max1==j)),break,end
M=j;
if (b>T(j))
    M=j+1;
else
    M=j;
```

```
    end
end
R=[T' Y'];
```

Exercises for Runge-Kutta Methods

In Exercises 1 through 5, solve the differential equations by the Runge-Kutta method of order $N = 4$.

    (a) Let $h = 0.2$ and do two steps by hand calculation. Then let $h = 0.1$ and do four steps by hand calculation.

    (b) Compare the exact solution $y(0.4)$ with the two approximations in part (a).

    (c) Does the F.G.E. in part (a) behave as expected when h is halved?

    1. $y' = t^2 - y$ with $y(0) = 1$, $y(t) = -e^{-t} + t^2 - 2t + 2$

    2. $y' = 3y + 3t$ with $y(0) = 1$, $y(t) = \frac{4}{3}e^{3t} - t - \frac{1}{3}$

    3. $y' = -ty$ with $y(0) = 1$, $y(t) = e^{-t^2/2}$

    4. $y' = e^{-2t} - 2y$ with $y(0) = \frac{1}{10}$, $y(t) = \frac{1}{10}e^{-2t} + te^{-2t}$

    5. $y' = 2ty^2$ with $y(0) = 1$, $y(t) = 1/(1 - t^2)$

    6. Show that when the Runge-Kutta method of order $N = 4$ is used to solve the I.V.P. $y' = f(t)$ over $[a, b]$ with $y(a) = 0$ the result is

$$y(b) \approx \frac{h}{6} \sum_{k=0}^{M-1} (f(t_k) + 4f(t_{k+1/2}) + f(t_{k+1})),$$

where $h = (b - a)/M$, and $t_k = a + kh$, and $t_{k+1/2} = a + \left(k + \frac{1}{2}\right)h$, which is Simpson's approximation (with step size $h/2$) for the definite integral of $f(t)$ taken over the interval $[a, b]$.

    7. The Richardson improvement method discussed in Lemma 7.1 (Section 7.3) can be used in conjunction with the Runge-Kutta method. If the Runge-Kutta method of order $N = 4$ is used with step size h, we have

$$y(b) \approx y_h + Ch^4.$$

If the Runge-Kutta method of order $N = 4$ is used with step size $2h$, we have

$$y(b) \approx y_{2h} + 16Ch^4.$$

The terms involving Ch^4 can be eliminated to obtain an improved approximation for $y(b)$, and the result is

$$y(b) \approx \frac{16y_h - y_{2h}}{15}.$$

This improvement scheme can be used with the values in Example 9.11 to obtain better approximations to $y(3)$. Find the missing entries in the following table.

h	y_h	$(16y_h - y_{2h})/15$
1	1.6701860	_____
$\frac{1}{2}$	1.6694308	_____
$\frac{1}{4}$	1.6693928	_____
$\frac{1}{8}$	1.6693906	_____

For Exercises 8 and 9, the Taylor polynomial of degree $N = 2$ for a function $f(t, y)$ of two variables t and y expanded about the point (a, b) is

$$P_2(t, y) = f(a, b) + f_t(a, b)(t - a) + f_y(a, b)(y - b)$$
$$+ \frac{f_{tt}(a, b)(t - a)^2}{2} + f_{ty}(a, b)(t - a)(y - b) + \frac{f_{yy}(a, b)(y - b)^2}{2}.$$

8. (a) Find the Taylor polynomial of degree $N = 2$ for $f(t, y) = y/t$ expanded about $(1, 1)$.

   (b) Find $P_2(1.05, 1.1)$ and compare with $f(1.05, 1.1)$.

9. (a) Find the Taylor polynomial of degree $N = 2$ for $f(t, y) = (1 + t - y)^{1/2}$ expanded about $(0, 0)$.

   (b) Find $P_2(0.04, 0.08)$ and compare with $f(0.04, 0.08)$.

Algorithms and Programs

In Problems 1 through 5, solve the differential equations by the Runge-Kutta method of order $N = 4$.

(a) Let $h = 0.1$ and do 20 steps with Program 9.4. Then let $h = 0.05$ and do 40 steps with Program 9.4.

(b) Compare the exact solution $y(2)$ with the two approximations in part (a).

(c) Does the F.G.E. in part (a) behave as expected when h is halved?

(d) Plot the two approximations and the exact solution on the same coordinate system. Hint. The output matrix R from Program 9.4 contains the x- and y-coordinates of the approximations. The command plot(R(:,1),R(:,2)) will produce a graph analogous to Figure 9.6.

1. $y' = t^2 - y$ with $y(0) = 1$, $y(t) = -e^{-t} + t^2 - 2t + 2$

2. $y' = 3y + 3t$ with $y(0) = 1$, $y(t) = \frac{4}{3}e^{3t} - t - \frac{1}{3}$

3. $y' = -ty$ with $y(0) = 1$, $y(t) = e^{-t^2/2}$

4. $y' = e^{-2t} - 2y$ with $y(0) = \frac{1}{10}$, $y(t) = \frac{1}{10}e^{-2t} + te^{-2t}$

5. $y' = 2ty^2$ with $y(0) = 1$, $y(t) = 1/(1 - t^2)$

In Problems 6 and 7, solve the differential equations by the Runge-Kutta-Fehlberg method.

(a) Use Program 9.5 with initial step size $h = 0.1$ and tol $= 10^{-7}$.

(b) Compare the exact solution $y(b)$ with the approximation.

(c) Plot the approximation and the exact solution on the same coordinate system.

6. $y' = 9te^{3t}$, $y(0) = 0$ over $[0, 3]$, $y(t) = 3te^{3t} - e^{3t} + 1$

7. $y' = 2 \tan^{-1}(t)$, $y(0) = 0$ over $[0, 1]$, $y(t) = 2t \tan^{-1}(t) - \ln(1 + t^2)$

8. In a chemical reaction, one molecule of A combines with one molecule of B to form one molecule of the chemical C. It is found that the concentration $y(t)$ of C at time t is the solution to the I.V.P.

$$y' = k(a - y)(b - y) \quad \text{with} \quad y(0) = 0,$$

where k is a positive constant and a and b are the initial concentrations of A and B, respectively. Suppose that $k = 0.01$, $a = 70$ millimoles/liter, and $b = 50$ millimoles/liter. Use the Runge-Kutta method of order $N = 4$ with $h = 0.5$ to find the solution over $[0, 20]$. *Remark.* You can compare your computer solution with the exact solution $y(t) = 350(1 - e^{-0.2t})/(7 - 5e^{-0.2t})$. Observe that the limiting value is 50 as $t \to +\infty$.

9. By solving an appropriate initial value problem, make a table of values of the function $f(t)$ given by the following integral:

$$f(x) = \frac{1}{2} + \frac{1}{\sqrt{2\pi}} \int_0^x e^{-t^2/2} \, dt \quad \text{for } 0 \le x \le 3.$$

Use the Runge-Kutta method of order $N = 4$ with $h = 0.1$ for your computations. Your solution should agree with the values in the following table. *Remark.* This is a good way to generate the table of areas for a standard normal distribution.

x	$f(x)$
0.0	0.5
0.5	0.6914625
1.0	0.8413448
1.5	0.9331928
2.0	0.9772499
2.5	0.9937903
3.0	0.9986501

10. (a) Write a program to implement the Richardson improvement method discussed in Exercise 7.

(b) Use your program from part (a) to approximate $y(0.8)$ for the I.V.P. $y' = t^2 + y^2$, $y(0) = 1$ over $[0, 0.8]$. The true solution at $t = 0.8$ is known to be $y(0.8) = 5.8486168$. Start with the step size $h = 0.05$. The program should terminate when the absolute value of the difference between two consecutive Richardson improvements is $< 10^{-7}$.

11. Consider the first-order integro-ordinary differential equation:

$$y' = 1.3y - 0.25y^2 - 0.0001y \int_0^t y(\tau)\, d\tau.$$

(a) Use the Runge-Kutta method of order 4 with $h = 0.2$ and $y(0) = 250$ over the interval $[0, 20]$, and the trapezoidal rule to find an approximate solution to the equation (see Problem 10 in the Algorithms and Programs in Section 9.2).

(b) Repeat part (a) using the initial values $y(0) = 200$ and $y(0) = 300$.

(c) Plot the approximate solutions from parts (a) and (b) on the same coordinate system.

9.6 Predictor-Corrector Methods

The methods of Euler, Heun, Taylor, and Runge-Kutta are called *single-step methods* because they use only the information from one previous point to compute the successive point; that is, only the initial point (t_0, y_0) is used to compute (t_1, y_1), and in general, y_k is needed to compute y_{k+1}. After several points have been found, it is feasible to use several prior points in the calculation. For illustration, we develop the Adams-Bashforth four-step method, which requires y_{k-3}, y_{k-2}, y_{k-1}, and y_k in the calculation of y_{k+1}. This method is not self-starting; four initial points, (t_0, y_0), (t_1, y_1), (t_2, y_2), and (t_3, y_3), must be given in advance in order to generate the points $\{(t_k, y_k) : k \geq 4\}$ (this can be done with one of the methods from the previous sections).

A desirable feature of a multistep method is that the local truncation error (L.T.E.) can be determined and a correction term can be included, which improves the accuracy of the answer at each step. Also, it is possible to determine if the step size is small enough to obtain an accurate value for y_{k+1}, yet large enough so that unnecessary and time-consuming calculations are eliminated. Using the combinations of a predictor and corrector requires only two function evaluations of $f(t, y)$ per step.

Adams-Bashforth-Moulton Method

The Adams-Bashforth-Moulton predictor-corrector method is a multistep method derived from the fundamental theorem of calculus:

$$(1) \qquad\qquad y(t_{k+1}) = y(t_k) + \int_{t_k}^{t_{k+1}} f(t, y(t))\, dt.$$

The predictor uses the Lagrange polynomial approximation for $f(t, y(t))$ based on the points (t_{k-3}, f_{k-3}), (t_{k-2}, f_{k-2}), (t_{k-1}, f_{k-1}), and (t_k, f_k). It is integrated over the interval $[t_k, t_{k+1}]$ in (1). This process produces the Adams-Bashforth predictor:

$$(2) \qquad\qquad p_{k+1} = y_k + \frac{h}{24}(-9f_{k-3} + 37f_{k-2} - 59f_{k-1} + 55f_k).$$

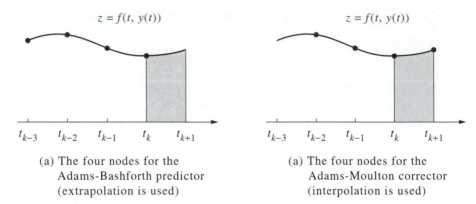

(a) The four nodes for the
Adams-Bashforth predictor
(extrapolation is used)

(a) The four nodes for the
Adams-Moulton corrector
(interpolation is used)

Figure 9.10 Integration over $[t_k, t_{k-1}]$ in the Adams-Bashforth method.

The corrector is developed similarly. The value p_{k+1} just computed can now be used. A second Lagrange polynomial for $f(t, y(t))$ is constructed, which is based on the points (t_{k-2}, f_{k-2}), (t_{k-1}, f_{k-1}), (t_k, f_k), and the new point $(t_{k+1}, f_{k+1}) = (t_{k+1}, f(t_{k+1}, p_{k+1}))$. This polynomial is then integrated over $[t_k, t_{k+1}]$, producing the Adams-Moulton corrector:

$$(3) \qquad y_{k+1} = y_k + \frac{h}{24}(f_{k-2} - 5f_{k-1} + 19f_k + 9f_{k+1}).$$

Figure 9.10 shows the nodes for the Lagrange polynomials that are used in developing formulas (2) and (3), respectively.

Error Estimation and Correction

The error terms for the numerical integration formulas used to obtain both the predictor and corrector are of the order $O(h^5)$. The L.T.E. for formulas (2) and (3) are

$$(4) \qquad y(t_{k+1}) - p_{k+1} = \frac{251}{720}y^{(5)}(c_{k+1})h^5 \qquad \text{(L.T.E. for the predictor)},$$

$$(5) \qquad y(t_{k+1}) - y_{k+1} = \frac{-19}{720}y^{(5)}(d_{k+1})h^5 \qquad \text{(L.T.E. for the corrector)}.$$

Suppose that h is small and $y^{(5)}(t)$ is nearly constant over the interval; then the terms involving the fifth derivative in (4) and (5) can be eliminated, and the result is

$$(6) \qquad y(t_{k+1}) - y_{k+1} \approx \frac{-19}{270}(y_{k+1} - p_{k+1}).$$

The importance of the predictor-corrector method should now be evident. Formula (6) gives an approximate error estimate based on the two computed values p_{k+1} and y_{k+1} and does not use $y^{(5)}(t)$.

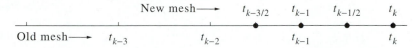

Figure 9.11   Reduction of the step size to $h/2$ in an adaptive method.

Practical Considerations

The corrector (3) used the approximation $f_{k+1} \approx f(t_{k+1}, p_{k+1})$ in the calculation of y_{k+1}. Since y_{k+1} is also an estimate for $y(t_{k+1})$, it could be used in the corrector (3) to generate a new approximation for f_{k+1}, which in turn will generate a new value for y_{k+1}. However, when this iteration on the corrector is continued, it will converge to a fixed point of (3) rather than the differential equation. It is more efficient to reduce the step size if more accuracy is needed.

Formula (6) can be used to determine when to change the step size. Although elaborate methods are available, we show how to reduce the step size to $h/2$ or increase it to $2h$. Let RelErr $= 5 \times 10^{-6}$ be our relative error criterion, and let Small $= 10^{-5}$.

$$(7) \qquad \text{If} \qquad \frac{19}{270} \frac{|y_{k+1} - p_{k+1}|}{|y_{k+1}| + \text{Small}} > \text{RelErr}, \qquad \text{then set } h = \frac{h}{2}.$$

$$(8) \qquad \text{If} \qquad \frac{19}{270} \frac{|y_{k+1} - p_{k+1}|}{|y_{k+1}| + \text{Small}} < \frac{\text{RelErr}}{100}, \qquad \text{then set } h = 2h.$$

When the predicted and corrected values do not agree to five significant digits, then (7) reduces the step size. If they agree to seven or more significant digits, then (8) increases the step size. Fine-tuning of these parameters should be made to suit your particular computer.

Reducing the step size requires four new starting values. Interpolation of $f(t, y(t))$ with a fourth-degree polynomial is used to supply the missing values that bisect the intervals $[t_{k-2}, t_{k-1}]$ and $[t_{k-1}, t_k]$. The four mesh points $t_{k-3/2}, t_{k-1}, t_{k-1/2}$, and t_k used in the successive calculations are shown in Figure 9.11.

The interpolation formulas needed to obtain the new starting values for the step size $h/2$ are

$$(9) \qquad \begin{aligned} f_{k-1/2} &= \frac{-5f_{k-4} + 28f_{k-3} - 70f_{k-2} + 140f_{k-1} + 35f_k}{128}, \\[2mm] f_{k-3/2} &= \frac{3f_{k-4} - 20f_{k-3} + 90f_{k-2} + 60f_{k-1} - 5f_k}{128}. \end{aligned}$$

Increasing the step size is an easier task. Seven prior points are needed to double the step size. The four new points are obtained by omitting every second one, as shown in Figure 9.12.

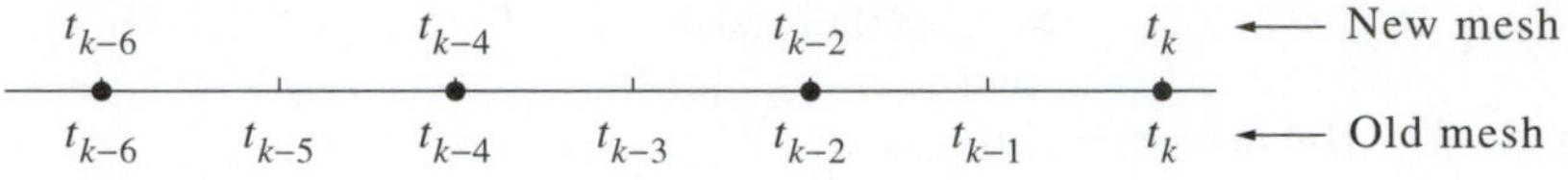

Figure 9.12   Increasing the step size to $2h$ in an adaptive method.

Milne-Simpson Method

Another popular predictor-corrector scheme is known as the Milne-Simpson method. Its predictor is based on integration of $f(t, y(t))$ over the interval $[t_{k-3}, t_{k+1}]$:

$$(10) \qquad y(t_{k+1}) = y(t_{k-3}) + \int_{t_{k-3}}^{t_{k+1}} f(t, y(t))\, dt.$$

The predictor uses the Lagrange polynomial approximation for $f(t, y(t))$ based on the points (t_{k-3}, f_{k-3}), (t_{k-2}, f_{k-2}), (t_{k-1}, f_{k-1}), and (t_k, f_k). It is integrated over the interval $[t_{k-3}, t_{k+1}]$. This produces the Milne predictor:

$$(11) \qquad p_{k+1} = y_{k-3} + \frac{4h}{3}(2f_{k-2} - f_{k-1} + 2f_k).$$

The corrector is developed similarly. The value p_{k+1} can now be used. A second Lagrange polynomial for $f(t, y(t))$ is constructed, which is based on the points (t_{k-1}, f_{k-1}), (t_k, f_k), and the new point $(t_{k+1}, f_{k+1}) = (t_{k+1}, f(t_{k+1}, p_{k+1}))$. The polynomial is integrated over $[t_{k-1}, t_{k+1}]$, and the result is the familiar Simpson's rule:

$$(12) \qquad y_{k+1} = y_{k-1} + \frac{h}{3}(f_{k-1} + 4f_k + f_{k+1}).$$

Error Estimation and Correction

The error terms for the numerical integration formulas used to obtain both the predictor and corrector are of the order $O(h^5)$. The L.T.E. for the formulas in (11) and (12) are

$$(13) \qquad y(t_{k+1}) - p_{k+1} = \frac{28}{90} y^{(5)}(c_{k+1})h^5 \qquad \text{(L.T.E. for the predictor)},$$

$$(14) \qquad y(t_{k+1}) - y_{k+1} = \frac{-1}{90} y^{(5)}(d_{k+1})h^5 \qquad \text{(L.T.E. for the corrector)}.$$

Suppose that h is small enough so that $y^{(5)}(t)$ is nearly constant over the interval $[t_{k-3}, t_{k+1}]$. Then the terms involving the fifth derivative can be eliminated in (13) and (14) and the result is

$$(15) \qquad y(t_{k+1}) - p_{k+1} \approx \frac{28}{29}(y_{k+1} - p_{k+1}).$$

Formula (15) gives an error estimate for the predictor that is based on the two computed values p_{k+1} and y_{k+1} and does not use $y^{(5)}(t)$. It can be used to improve the predicted value. Under the assumption that the difference between the predicted and corrected values at each step changes slowly, we can substitute p_k and y_k for p_{k+1} and y_{k+1} in (15) and get the following modifier:

$$(16) \qquad m_{k+1} = p_{k+1} + 28\frac{y_k - p_k}{29}.$$

This modified value is used in place of p_{k+1} in the correction step, and equation (12) becomes

$$(17) \qquad y_{k+1} = y_{k-1} + \frac{h}{3}(f_{k-1} + 4f_k + f(t_{k+1}, m_{k+1})).$$

Therefore, the improved (modified) Milne-Simpson method is

$$(18) \qquad \begin{aligned} p_{k+1} &= y_{k-3} + \frac{4h}{3}(2f_{k-2} - f_{k-1} + 2f_k) & \text{(predictor)} \\ m_{k+1} &= p_{k+1} + 28\frac{y_k - p_k}{29} & \text{(modifier)} \\ f_{k+1} &= f(t_{k+1}, m_{k+1}) & \\ y_{k+1} &= y_{k-1} + \frac{h}{3}(f_{k-1} + 4f_k + f_{k+1}) & \text{(corrector)}. \end{aligned}$$

Hamming's method is another important method. We shall omit its derivation, but furnish a program at the end of the section. As a final precaution we mention that all the predictor-corrector methods have stability problems. Stability is an advanced topic and the serious reader should research this subject.

Example 9.13. Use the Adams-Bashforth-Moulton, Milne-Simpson, and Hamming methods with $h = \frac{1}{8}$ and compute approximations for the solution of the I.V.P.

$$y' = \frac{t - y}{2}, \qquad y(0) = 1 \qquad \text{over } [0, 3].$$

A Runge-Kutta method was used to obtain the starting values

$$y_1 = 0.94323919, \qquad y_2 = 0.89749071, \qquad \text{and} \qquad y_3 = 0.86208736.$$

Then a computer implementation of Programs 9.6 through 9.8 produced the values in Table 9.12. The error for each entry in the table is given as a multiple of 10^{-8}. In all entries there are at least six digits of accuracy. In this example, the best answers were produced by Hamming's method. ∎

Table 9.12   Comparison of the Adams-Bashforth-Moulton, Milne-Simpson, and Hamming Methods for Solving $y' = (t - y)/2$, $y(0) = 1$

k	Adams-Bashforth-Moulton	Error	Milne-Simpson	Error	Hamming's method	Error
0.0	1.00000000	$0E - 8$	1.00000000	$0E - 8$	1.00000000	$0E - 8$
0.5	0.83640227	$8E - 8$	0.83640231	$4E - 8$	0.83640234	$1E - 8$
0.625	0.81984673	$16E - 8$	0.81984687	$2E - 8$	0.81984688	$1E - 8$
0.75	0.81186762	$22E - 8$	0.81186778	$6E - 8$	0.81186783	$1E - 8$
0.875	0.81194530	$28E - 8$	0.81194555	$3E - 8$	0.81194558	$0E - 8$
1.0	0.81959166	$32E - 8$	0.81959190	$8E - 8$	0.81959198	$0E - 8$
1.5	0.91709920	$46E - 8$	0.91709957	$9E - 8$	0.91709967	$-1E - 8$
2.0	1.10363781	$51E - 8$	1.10363822	$10E - 8$	1.10363834	$-2E - 8$
2.5	1.35951387	$52E - 8$	1.35951429	$10E - 8$	1.35951441	$-2E - 8$
2.625	1.43243853	$52E - 8$	1.43243899	$6E - 8$	1.43243907	$-2E - 8$
2.75	1.50851827	$52E - 8$	1.50851869	$10E - 8$	1.50851881	$-2E - 8$
2.875	1.58756195	$51E - 8$	1.58756240	$6E - 8$	1.58756248	$-2E - 8$
3.0	1.66938998	$50E - 8$	1.66939038	$10E - 8$	1.66939050	$-2E - 8$

The Right Step

Our selection of methods has a purpose. First, their development is easy enough for a first course; second, more advanced methods have a similar development; third, most undergraduate problems can be solved by one of these methods. However, when a predictor-corrector method is used to solve the I.V.P. $y' = f(t, y)$, where $y(t_0) = y_0$, over a large interval, difficulties sometimes occur.

If $f_y(t, y) < 0$ and the step size is too large, a predictor-corrector method might be unstable. As a rule of thumb, stability exists when a small error is propagated as a decreasing error, and instability exists when a small error is propagated as an increasing error. When too large a step size is used over a large interval, instability will result and is sometimes manifested by oscillations in the computed solution. They can be attenuated by changing to a smaller step size. Formulas (7) through (9) suggest how to modify the algorithm(s). When step-size control is included, the following error estimate(s) should be used:

$$(19) \qquad y(t_k) - y_k \approx 19\frac{p_k - y_k}{270} \qquad \text{(Adams-Bashforth-Moulton)},$$

$$(20) \qquad y(t_k) - y_k \approx \frac{p_k - y_k}{29} \qquad \text{(Milne-Simpson)},$$

$$(21) \qquad y(t_k) - y_k \approx 9\frac{p_k - y_k}{121} \qquad \text{(Hamming)}.$$

In all methods, the corrector step is a type of fixed-point iteration. It can be proved that the step size h for the methods must satisfy the following conditions:

$$(22) \qquad h \ll \frac{2.66667}{|f_y(t, y)|} \qquad \text{(Adams-Bashforth-Moulton)},$$

$$(23) \qquad h \ll \frac{3.00000}{|f_y(t, y)|} \qquad \text{(Milne-Simpson)},$$

$$(24) \qquad h \ll \frac{2.66667}{|f_y(t, y)|} \qquad \text{(Hamming)}.$$

The notation $\ll$ in (22) through (24) means "much smaller than." The next example shows that more stringent inequalities should be used:

$$(25) \qquad h < \frac{0.75}{|f_y(t, y)|} \qquad \text{(Adams-Bashforth-Moulton)},$$

$$(26) \qquad h < \frac{0.45}{|f_y(t, y)|} \qquad \text{(Milne-Simpson)},$$

$$(27) \qquad h < \frac{0.69}{|f_y(t, y)|} \qquad \text{(Hamming)}.$$

Inequalities (25)–(27) are found in advanced books on numerical analysis.

Example 9.14.   Use the Adams-Bashforth-Moulton, Milne-Simpson, and Hamming methods and compute approximations for the solution of

$$y' = 30 - 5y, \qquad y(0) = 1 \qquad \text{over the interval } [0, 10].$$

All three methods are of the order $O(h^4)$. When $N = 120$ steps was used for all three methods, the maximum error for each method occurred at a different place:

$$y(0.41666667) - y_5 \approx -0.00277037 \qquad \text{(Adams-Bashforth-Moulton)},$$
$$y(0.33333333) - y_4 \approx -0.00139255 \qquad \text{(Milne-Simpson)},$$
$$y(0.33333333) - y_4 \approx -0.00104982 \qquad \text{(Hamming)}.$$

At the right endpoints $t = 10$, the error was

$$y(10) - y_{120} \approx 0.00000000 \qquad \text{(Adams-Bashforth-Moulton)},$$
$$y(10) - y_{120} \approx 0.00001015 \qquad \text{(Milne-Simpson)},$$
$$y(10) - y_{120} \approx 0.00000000 \qquad \text{(Hamming)}.$$

Both the Adams-Bashforth-Moulton and Hamming methods gave approximate solutions with eight digits of accuracy at the right endpoint.   ■

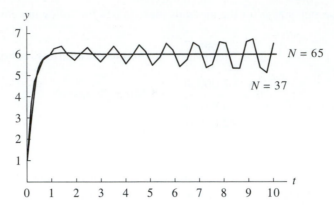

Figure 9.13 (a) The Adams-Bashforth-Moulton solution to $y' = 30 - 5y$ with $N = 37$ steps produces oscillation. It is stabilized when $N = 65$ because $h = 10/65 = 0.1538 \approx 0.15 = 0.75/5 = 0.75/|f_y(t, y)|$.

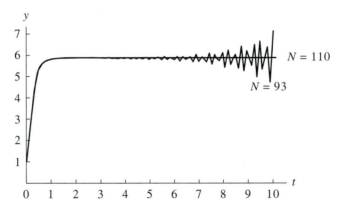

Figure 9.13 (b) The Milne-Simpson solution to $y' = 30 - 5y$ with $N = 93$ steps produces oscillation. It is stabilized when $N = 110$ because $h = 10/110 = 0.0909 \approx 0.09 = 0.45/5 = 0.45/|f_y(t, y)|$.

It is instructive to see that if the step size is too large, the computed solution oscillates about the true solution. Figure 9.13 illustrates this phenomenon. The small number of steps was determined experimentally so that the oscillations was about the same magnitude. The large number of steps required to attenuate the oscillations were determined with equations (25) through (27).

Each of the following three programs requires that the first four coordinates of T and Y be initial starting values obtained by another method. Consider Example 9.13,

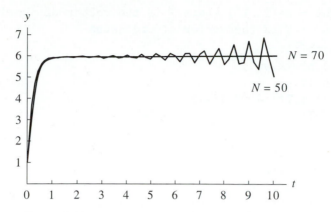

Figure 9.13 (c) Hamming's solution to $y' = 30 - 5y$ with $N = 50$ steps produces oscillation. It is stabilized when $N = 70$ because $h = 10/70 = 0.1428 \approx 0.138 = 0.69/5 = 0.69/|f_y(t, y)|$.

where the step size was $h = \frac{1}{8}$ and the interval was $[0, 3]$. The following string of commands in the MATLAB command window will produce appropriate input vectors T and Y.

```
>>T=zeros(1,25);
>>Y=zeros(1,25);
>>T=0:1/8:3;
>>Y(1:4)=[1 0.94323919 0.89749071 0.86208736];
```

Program 9.6 (Adams-Bashforth-Moulton Method). To approximate the solution of the initial value problem $y' = f(t, y)$ with $y(a) = y_0$ over $[a, b]$ by using the predictor

$$p_{k+1} = y_k + \frac{h}{24}(-9f_{k-3} + 37f_{k-2} - 59f_{k-1} + 55f_k)$$

and the corrector

$$y_{k+1} = y_k + \frac{h}{24}(f_{k-2} - 5f_{k-1} + 19f_k + 9f_{k+1}).$$

```
function A=abm(f,T,Y)
%Input   - f is the function entered as a string 'f'
%         - T is the vector of abscissas
%         - Y is the vector of ordinates
%Remark.  The first four coordinates of T and Y must
%          have starting values obtained with RK4
```

```
%Output - A=[T' Y'] where T is the vector of abscissas and
%          Y is the vector of ordinates
n=length(T);
if n<5,break,end;
F=zeros(1,4);
F=feval(f,T(1:4),Y(1:4));
h=T(2)-T(1);
for k=4:n-1
    %Predictor
    p=Y(k)+(h/24)*(F*[-9 37 -59 55]');
    T(k+1)=T(1)+h*k;
    F=[F(2) F(3) F(4) feval(f,T(k+1),p)];
    %Corrector
    Y(k+1)=Y(k)+(h/24)*(F*[1 -5 19 9]');
    F(4)=feval(f,T(k+1),Y(k+1));
end
A=[T' Y'];
```

Program 9.7 (Milne-Simpson Method). To approximate the solution of the initial value problem $y' = f(t, y)$ with $y(a) = y_0$ over $[a, b]$ by using the predictor

$$p_{k+1} = y_{k-3} + \frac{4h}{3}(2f_{k-2} - f_{k-1} + 2f_k)$$

and the corrector

$$y_{k+1} = y_{k-1} + \frac{h}{3}(f_{k-1} + 4f_k + f_{k+1}).$$

```
function M=milne(f,T,Y)
%Input  - f is the function entered as a string 'f'
%        - T is the vector of abscissas
%        - Y is the vector of ordinates
%Remark.  The first four coordinates of T and Y must
%          have starting values obtained with RK4
%Output - M=[T' Y'] where T is the vector of abscissas and
%          Y is the vector of ordinates
n=length(T);
if n<5,break,end;
F=zeros(1,4);
F=feval(f,T(1:4),Y(1:4));
h=T(2)-T(1);
pold=0;
yold=0;
```

```
for k=4:n-1
    %Predictor
    pnew=Y(k-3)+(4*h/3)*(F(2:4)*[2 -1 2]');
    %Modifier
    pmod=pnew+28*(yold-pold)/29;
    T(k+1)=T(1)+h*k;
    F=[F(2) F(3) F(4) feval(f,T(k+1),pmod)];
    %Corrector
    Y(k+1)=Y(k-1)+(h/3)*(F(2:4)*[1 4 1]');
    pold=pnew;
    yold=Y(k+1);
    F(4)=feval(f,T(k+1),Y(k+1));
end
M=[T' Y'];
```

Program 9.8 (Hamming Method). To approximate the solution of the initial value problem $y' = f(t, y)$ with $y(a) = y_0$ over $[a, b]$ by using the predictor

$$p_{k+1} = y_{k-3} + \frac{4h}{3}(2f_{k-2} - f_{k-1} + 2f_k)$$

and the corrector

$$y_{k+1} = \frac{-y_{k-2} + 9y_k}{8} + \frac{3h}{8}(-f_{k-1} + 2f_k + f_{k+1}).$$

```
function H=hamming(f,T,Y)
%Input   - f is the function entered as a string 'f'
%         - T is the vector of abscissas
%         - Y is the vector of ordinates
%Remark.  The first four coordinates of T and Y must
%         have starting values obtained with RK4
%Output - H=[T' Y'] where T is the vector of abscissas and
%         Y is the vector of ordinates
n=length(T);
if n<5,break,end;
F=zeros(1,4);
F=feval(f,T(1:4),Y(1:4));
h=T(2)-T(1);
pold=0;
cold=0;
for k=4:n-1
    %Predictor
    pnew=Y(k-3)+(4*h/3)*(F(2:4)*[2 -1 2]');
```

```
%Modifier
pmod=pnew+112*(cold-pold)/121;
T(k+1)=T(1)+h*k;
F=[F(2) F(3) F(4) feval(f,T(k+1),pmod)];
%Corrector
cnew=(9*Y(k)-Y(k-2)+3*h*(F(2:4)*[-1 2 1]'))/8;
Y(k+1)=cnew+9*(pnew-cnew)/121;
pold=pnew;
cold=cnew;
F(4)=feval(f,T(k+1),Y(k+1));
end
H=[T' Y'];
```

Exercises for Predictor-Corrector Methods

In Exercises 1 through 3, use the Adams-Bashforth-Moulton method, the three starting values y_1, y_2, and y_3, and the step size $h = 0.05$ to calculate by hand the next two values y_4 and y_5 for the I.V.P. Compare your solution with the exact solution $y(t)$.

1. $y' = t^2 - y$, $y(0) = 1$ over $[0, 5]$, $y(t) = -e^{-t} + t^2 - 2t + 2$

$y(0.05) = 0.95127058$
$y(0.10) = 0.90516258$
$y(0.15) = 0.86179202$

2. $y' = y + 3t - t^2$, $y(0) = 1$ over $[0, 5]$, $y(t) = 2e^t + t^2 - t - 1$

$y(0.05) = 1.0550422$
$y(0.10) = 1.1203418$
$y(0.15) = 1.1961685$

3. $y' = -t/y$, $y(1) = 1$ over $[1, 1.4]$, $y(t) = (2 - t^2)^{1/2}$

$y(1.05) = 0.94736477$
$y(1.10) = 0.88881944$
$y(1.15) = 0.82310388$

In Exercises 4 through 6, use the Milne-Simpson method, the three starting values y_1, y_2, and y_3, and the step size $h = 0.05$ to calculate by hand the next two values y_4 and y_5 for the I.V.P. Compare your solution with the exact solution $y(t)$.

4. $y' = e^{-t} - y$, $y(0) = 1$ over $[0, 5]$, $y(t) = te^{-t} + e^{-t}$

$y(0.05) = 0.99879090$
$y(0.10) = 0.99532116$
$y(0.15) = 0.98981417$

5. $y' = 2ty^2$, $y(0) = 1$ over $[0, 0.95]$, $y(t) = 1/(1 - t^2)$

   $y(0.05) = 1.0025063$
   $y(0.10) = 1.0101010$
   $y(0.15) = 1.0230179$

6. $y' = 1 + y^2$, $y(0) = 1$ over $[0, 0.75]$, $y(t) = \tan(t + \pi/4)$

   $y(0.05) = 1.1053556$
   $y(0.10) = 1.2230489$
   $y(0.15) = 1.3560879$

In Exercises 7 through 9, use the Hamming method, the three starting values y_1, y_2, and y_3, and the step size $h = 0.05$ to calculate by hand the next two values y_4 and y_5 for the I.V.P. Compare your solution with the exact solution $y(t)$.

7. $y' = 2y - y^2$, $y(0) = 1$ over $[0, 5]$, $y(t) = 1 + \tanh(t)$

   $y(0.05) = 1.0499584$
   $y(0.10) = 1.0996680$
   $y(0.15) = 1.1488850$

8. $y' = (1 - y^2)^{1/2}$, $y(0) = 0$ over $[0, 1.55]$, $y(t) = \sin(t)$

   $y(0.05) = 0.049979169$
   $y(0.10) = 0.099833417$
   $y(0.15) = 0.14943813$

9. $y' = y^2 \sin(t)$, $y(0) = 1$ over $[0, 1.55]$, $y(t) = \sec(t)$

   $y(0.05) = 1.0012513$
   $y(0.10) = 1.0050209$
   $y(0.15) = 1.0113564$

Algorithms and Programs

1. (a) Use Program 9.6 to solve the differential equations in Exercises 1 through 3.
   (b) Plot your approximation and the exact solution on the same coordinate system.

2. (a) Use Program 9.7 to solve the differential equations in Exercises 4 through 6.
   (b) Plot your approximation and the exact solution on the same coordinate system.

3. (a) Use Program 9.8 to solve the differential equations in Exercises 7 through 9.
   (b) Plot your approximation and the exact solution on the same coordinate system.

4. Produce a graph analogous to Figure 9.13 by using Program 9.6 with $N = 37$ and $N = 65$ to solve the I.V.P.

$$y' = 30 - 5y, \quad y(0) = 1 \quad \text{over } [0, 10].$$

5. For the I.V.P. $y' = 45 - 9y$, $y(1) = 0$ over $[1, 20]$:
   (a) Use inequality (22) to determine for which step sizes the Adams-Bashforth-Moulton method might be unstable.

(b) Based on your results from part (a), select step sizes h_s and h_u for which the Adams-Bashforth-Moulton method should be stable and unstable, respectively. Use a Runge-Kutta method to generate three starting values y_1, y_2, and y_3 for each of the step sizes.

(c) Use Program 9.6 to generate two approximations, one for each step size, to the I.V.P.

(d) Use your results from part (c) to produce a graph analogous to Figure 9.13. You may find it necessary to experiment with several sets of step sizes.

9.7 Systems of Differential Equations

This section is an introduction to systems of differential equations. To illustrate the concepts, we consider the initial value problem

(1)
$$\frac{dx}{dt} = f(t, x, y) \qquad \text{with} \qquad \begin{cases} x(t_0) = x_0, \\ y(t_0) = y_0. \end{cases}$$
$$\frac{dy}{dt} = g(t, x, y)$$

A solution to (1) is a pair of differentiable functions $x(t)$ and $y(t)$ with the property that when t, $x(t)$, and $y(t)$ are substituted in $f(t, x, y)$ and $g(t, x, y)$, the result is equal to the derivative $x'(t)$ and $y'(t)$, respectively; that is,

(2)
$$x'(t) = f(t, x(t), y(t)) \qquad \text{with} \qquad \begin{cases} x(t_0) = x_0, \\ y(t_0) = y_0. \end{cases}$$
$$y'(t) = g(t, x(t), y(t))$$

For example, consider the system of differential equations

(3)
$$\frac{dx}{dt} = x + 2y \qquad \text{with} \qquad \begin{cases} x(0) = 6, \\ y(0) = 4. \end{cases}$$
$$\frac{dy}{dt} = 3x + 2y$$

The solution to the I.V.P. (3) is

(4)
$$x(t) = 4e^{4t} + 2e^{-t},$$
$$y(t) = 6e^{4t} - 2e^{-t}.$$

This is verified by directly substituting $x(t)$ and $y(t)$ into the right-hand side of (3), computing the derivatives of (4), and substituting them in the left side of (3) to get

$$16e^{4t} - 2e^{-t} = (4e^{4t} + 2e^{-t}) + 2(6e^{4t} - 2e^{-t}),$$
$$24e^{4t} + 2e^{-t} = 3(4e^{4t} + 2e^{-t}) + 2(6e^{4t} - 2e^{-t}).$$

Numerical Solutions

A numerical solution to (1) over the interval $a \leq t \leq b$ is found by considering the differentials

$$(5) \qquad\qquad dx = f(t, x, y)\, dt \quad \text{and} \quad dy = g(t, x, y)\, dt.$$

Euler's method for solving the system is easy to formulate. The differentials $dt = t_{k+1} - t_k$, $dx = x_{k+1} - x_k$, and $dy = y_{k+1} - y_k$ are substituted into (5) to get

$$(6) \qquad\qquad \begin{aligned} x_{k+1} - x_k &\approx f(t_k, x_k, y_k)(t_{k+1} - t_k), \\ y_{k+1} - y_k &\approx g(t_k, x_k, y_k)(t_{k+1} - t_k). \end{aligned}$$

The interval is divided into M subintervals of width $h = (b - a)/M$, and the mesh points are $t_{k+1} = t_k + h$. This is used in (6) to get the recursive formulas for Euler's method:

$$(7) \qquad\qquad \begin{aligned} t_{k+1} &= t_k + h, \\ x_{k+1} &= x_k + hf(t_k, x_k, y_k), \\ y_{k+1} &= y_k + hg(t_k, x_k, y_k) \quad \text{for } k = 0,\ 1,\ \ldots,\ M-1. \end{aligned}$$

A higher-order method should be used to achieve a reasonable amount of accuracy. For example, the Runge-Kutta formulas of order 4 are

$$(8) \qquad\qquad \begin{aligned} x_{k+1} &= x_k + \frac{h}{6}(f_1 + 2f_2 + 2f_3 + f_4), \\ y_{k+1} &= y_k + \frac{h}{6}(g_1 + 2g_2 + 2g_3 + g_4), \end{aligned}$$

where

$$f_1 = f(t_k, x_k, y_k), \qquad\qquad g_1 = g(t_k, x_k, y_k),$$

$$f_2 = f\left(t_k + \frac{h}{2}, x_k + \frac{h}{2}f_1, y_k + \frac{h}{2}g_1\right), \quad g_2 = g\left(t_k + \frac{h}{2}, x_k + \frac{h}{2}f_1, y_k + \frac{h}{2}g_1\right),$$

$$f_3 = f\left(t_k + \frac{h}{2}, x_k + \frac{h}{2}f_2, y_k + \frac{h}{2}g_2\right), \quad g_3 = g\left(t_k + \frac{h}{2}, x_k + \frac{h}{2}f_2, y_k + \frac{h}{2}g_2\right),$$

$$f_4 = f(t_k + h, x_k + hf_3, y_k + hg_3), \qquad g_4 = g(t_k + h, x_k + hf_3, y_k + hg_3).$$

Example 9.15.   Use the Runge-Kutta method given in (8) and compute the numerical solution to (3) over the interval $[0.0, 0.2]$ using 10 subintervals and the step size $h = 0.02$. For the first point we have $t_1 = 0.02$, and the intermediate calculations required to

Table 9.13   Runge-Kutta Solution to $x'(t) = x + 2y$, $y'(t) = 3x + 2y$ with the Initial Values $x(0) = 6$ and $y(0) = 4$

k	t_k	x_k	y_k
0	0.00	6.00000000	4.00000000
1	0.02	6.29354551	4.53932490
2	0.04	6.61562213	5.11948599
3	0.06	6.96852528	5.74396525
4	0.08	7.35474319	6.41653305
5	0.10	7.77697287	7.14127221
6	0.12	8.23813750	7.92260406
7	0.14	8.74140523	8.76531667
8	0.16	9.29020955	9.67459538
9	0.18	9.88827138	10.6560560
10	0.20	10.5396230	11.7157807

compute x_1 and y_1 are

$$f_1 = f(0.00, 6.0, 4.0) = 14.0 \qquad\qquad g_1 = g(0.00, 6.0, 4.0) = 26.0$$

$$x_0 + \frac{h}{2}f_1 = 6.14 \qquad\qquad y_0 + \frac{h}{2}g_1 = 4.26$$

$$f_2 = f(0.01, 6.14, 4.26) = 14.66 \qquad g_2 = g(0.01, 6.14, 4.26) = 26.94$$

$$x_0 + \frac{h}{2}f_2 = 6.1466 \qquad\qquad y_0 + \frac{h}{2}g_2 = 4.2694$$

$$f_3 = f(0.01, 6.1466, 4.2694) = 14.6854$$

$$g_3 = f(0.01, 6.1466, 4.2694) = 26.9786$$

$$x_0 + hf_3 = 6.293708 \qquad y_0 + hg_3 = 4.539572$$

$$f_4 = f(0.02, 6.293708, 4.539572) = 15.372852$$

$$g_4 = f(0.02, 6.293708, 4.539572) = 27.960268.$$

These values are used in the final computation:

$$x_1 = 6 + \frac{0.02}{6}(14.0 + 2(14.66) + 2(14.6854) + 15.372852) = 6.29354551,$$

$$y_1 = 4 + \frac{0.02}{6}(26.0 + 2(26.94) + 2(26.9786) + 27.960268) = 4.53932490.$$

The calculations are summarized in Table 9.13.   ∎

The numerical solutions contain a certain amount of error at each step. For the example above, the error grows, and at the right end point $t = 0.2$ it reaches its maximum:

$$x(0.2) - x_{10} = 10.5396252 - 10.5396230 = 0.0000022,$$
$$y(0.2) - y_{10} = 11.7157841 - 11.7157807 = 0.0000034.$$

Higher-Order Differential Equations

Higher-order differential equations involve the higher derivatives $x''(t)$, $x'''(t)$, and so on. They arise in mathematical models for problems in physics and engineering. For example,

$$mx''(t) + cx'(t) + kx(t) = g(t)$$

represents a mechanical system in which a spring with spring constant k restores a displaced mass m. Damping is assumed to be proportional to the velocity, and the function $g(t)$ is an external force. It is often the case that the position $x(t_0)$ and velocity $x'(t_0)$ are known at a certain time t_0.

By solving for the second derivative, we can write a second-order initial value problem in the form

$$(9) \qquad x''(t) = f(t, x(t), x'(t)) \quad \text{with } x(t_0) = x_0 \text{ and } x'(t_0) = y_0.$$

The second-order differential equation can be reformulated as a system of two first-order equations if we use the substitution

$$(10) \qquad\qquad\qquad\qquad x'(t) = y(t).$$

Then $x''(t) = y'(t)$ and the differential equation in (9) becomes a system:

$$(11) \qquad\qquad \begin{aligned} \frac{dx}{dt} &= y \\ \frac{dy}{dt} &= f(t, x, y) \end{aligned} \quad \text{with} \quad \begin{cases} x(t_0) = x_0, \\ y(t_0) = y_0. \end{cases}$$

A numerical procedure such as the Runge-Kutta method can be used to solve (11) and will generate two sequences $\{x_k\}$ and $\{y_k\}$. The first sequence is the numerical solution to (9). The next example can be interpreted as damped harmonic motion.

Table 9.14   Runge-Kutta Solution to $x''(t) + 4x'(t) + 5x(t) = 0$ with the Initial Conditions $x(0) = 3$ and $x'(0) = -5$

k	t_k	x_k	$x(t_k)$
0	0.0	3.00000000	3.00000000
1	0.1	2.52564583	2.52565822
2	0.2	2.10402783	2.10404686
3	0.3	1.73506269	1.73508427
4	0.4	1.41653369	1.41655509
5	0.5	1.14488509	1.14490455
10	1.0	0.33324302	0.33324661
20	2.0	−0.00620684	−0.00621162
30	3.0	−0.00701079	−0.00701204
40	4.0	−0.00091163	−0.00091170
48	4.8	−0.00004972	−0.00004969
49	4.9	−0.00002348	−0.00002345
50	5.0	−0.00000493	−0.00000490

Example 9.16.   Consider the second-order initial value problem

$$x''(t) + 4x'(t) + 5x(t) = 0 \quad \text{with } x(0) = 3 \text{ and } x'(0) = -5.$$

(a) Write down the equivalent system of two first-order equations.

(b) Use the Runge-Kutta method to solve the reformulated problem over $[0, 5]$ using $M = 50$ subintervals of width $h = 0.1$.

(c) Compare the numerical solution with the true solution:

$$x(t) = 3e^{-2t} \cos(t) + e^{-2t} \sin(t).$$

(a) The differential equation has the form

$$x''(t) = f(t, x(t), x'(t)) = -4x'(t) - 5x(t).$$

(b) Using the substitution in (10), we get the reformulated problem:

$$\frac{dx}{dt} = y \qquad \text{with} \qquad \begin{cases} x(0) = 3, \\ y(0) = -5. \end{cases}$$
$$\frac{dy}{dt} = -5x - 4y$$

(c) Samples of the numerical computations are given in Table 9.14. The values $\{y_k\}$ are extraneous and are not included. Instead, the true solution values $\{x(t_k)\}$ are included for comparison.   ∎

Exercises for Systems of Differential Equations

In Exercises 1 through 4, use $h = 0.05$ and

   (a) Euler's method (7) by hand to find (x_1, y_1) and (x_2, y_2).

   (b) the Runge-Kutta method (8) by hand to find (x_1, y_1).

  1. Solve the system $x' = 2x + 3y$, $y' = 2x + y$ with the initial condition $x(0) = -2.7$ and $y(0) = 2.8$ over the interval $0 \le t \le 1.0$ using the step size $h = 0.05$. The polygonal path formed by the solution set is given in Figure 9.14 and can be compared with the analytic solution:

$$x(t) = -\frac{69}{25}e^{-t} + \frac{3}{50}e^{4t} \quad \text{and} \quad y(t) = \frac{69}{25}e^{-t} + \frac{1}{25}e^{4t}.$$

  2. Solve the system $x' = 3x - y$, $y' = 4x - y$ with the initial condition $x(0) = 0.2$ and $y(0) = 0.5$ over the interval $0 \le t \le 2$ using the step size $h = 0.05$. The polygonal path formed by the solution set is given in Figure 9.15 and can be compared with the analytic solution:

$$x(t) = \frac{1}{5}e^{t} - \frac{1}{10}te^{t} \quad \text{and} \quad y(t) = \frac{1}{2}e^{t} - \frac{1}{5}te^{t}.$$

  3. Solve the system $x' = x - 4y$, $y' = x + y$ with the initial condition $x(0) = 2$ and $y(0) = 3$ over the interval $0 \le t \le 2$ using the step size $h = 0.05$. The polygonal path formed by the solution set is given in Figure 9.16 and can be compared with the analytic solution:

$$x(t) = -2e^{t} + 4e^{t}\cos^{2}(t) - 12e^{t}\cos(t)\sin(t)$$

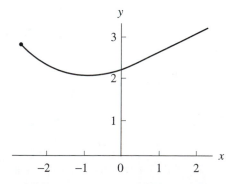

Figure 9.14 The solution to the system $x' = 2x + 3y$ and $y' = 2x + y$ over $[0.0, 1.0]$.

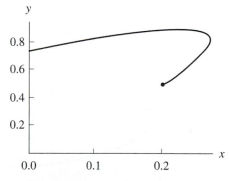

Figure 9.15 The solution to the system $x' = 3x - y$ and $y' = 4x - y$ over $[0.0, 2.0]$.

and

$$y(t) = -3e^t + 6e^t \cos^2(t) + 2e^t \cos(t) \sin(t).$$

4. Solve the system $x' = y - 4x$, $y' = x + y$ with the initial condition $x(0) = 1$ and $y(0) = 1$ over the interval $0 \le t \le 1.2$ using the step size $h = 0.05$. The polygonal path formed by the solution set is given in Figure 9.17 and can be compared with the analytic solution:

$$x(t) = \frac{3e^{-\sqrt{29}\,t/2} - 3e^{\sqrt{29}\,t/2}}{2\sqrt{29}e^{3t/2}} + \frac{e^{-\sqrt{29}\,t/2} + e^{\sqrt{29}\,t/2}}{2e^{3t/2}}$$

and

$$y(t) = \frac{-7e^{-\sqrt{29}\,t/2} + 7e^{\sqrt{29}\,t/2}}{2\sqrt{29}e^{3t/2}} + \frac{e^{-\sqrt{29}\,t/2} + e^{\sqrt{29}\,t/2}}{2e^{3t/2}}.$$

In Exercises 5 through 8:

(a) Verify that the function $x(t)$ is the solution.

(b) Reformulate the second-order differential equation as a system of two first-order equations.

(c) Use $h = 0.1$ and Euler's method by hand to find x_1 and x_2.

(d) Use $h = 0.05$ and the Runge-Kutta method by hand to find x_1.

5. $2x''(t) - 5x'(t) - 3x(t) = 45e^{2t}$ with $x(0) = 2$ and $x'(0) = 1$
$x(t) = 4e^{-t/2} + 7e^{3t} - 9e^{2t}$

6. $x''(t) + 6x'(t) + 9x(t) = 0$ with $x(0) = 4$ and $x'(0) = -4$
$x(t) = 4e^{-3t} + 8te^{-3t}$

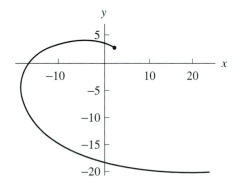

Figure 9.16   The solution to the system $x' = x - 4y$ and $y' = x + y$ over $[0.0, 2.0]$.

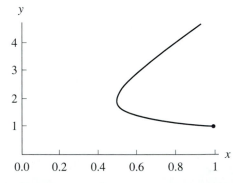

Figure 9.17   The solution to the system $x' = y - 4x$ and $y' = x + y$ over $[0.0, 1.2]$.

7. $x''(t) + x(t) = 6\cos(t)$ with $x(0) = 2$ and $x'(0) = 3$
   $x(t) = 2\cos(t) + 3\sin(t) + 3t\sin(t)$

8. $x''(t) + 3x'(t) = 12$ with $x(0) = 5$ and $x'(0) = 1$
   $x(t) = 4 + 4t + e^{-3t}$

Algorithms and Programs

1. Write a program to solve a system of equations by the Runge -Kutta method of order $N = 4$ (8).

In Problems 2 through 5, use your computer implementation of the Runge-Kutta method for systems to solve each system using the step size $h = 0.05$. Plot your approximation and the analytic solution on the same coordinate system.

2. $x' = 2x + 3y$, $y' = 2x + y$, with $x(0) = -2.7$, $y(0) = 2.8$ over $0 \le t \le 1.0$
   $x(t) = -\frac{69}{25}e^{-t} + \frac{3}{50}e^{4t}$ and $y(t) = \frac{69}{25}e^{-t} + \frac{1}{25}e^{4t}$

3. $x' = 3x - y$, $y' = 4x - y$, with $x(0) = 0.2$, $y(0) = 0.5$ over $0 \le t \le 2$
   $x(t) = \frac{1}{5}e^t - \frac{1}{10}te^t$ and $y(t) = \frac{1}{2}e^t - \frac{1}{5}te^t$

4. $x' = x - 4y$, $y' = x + y$, with $x(0) = 2$, $y(0) = 3$ over $0 \le t \le 2$
   $x(t) = -2e^t + 4e^t\cos^2(t) - 12e^t\cos(t)\sin(t)$
   $y(t) = -3e^t + 6e^t\cos^2(t) + 2e^t\cos(t)\sin(t)$

5. $x' = y - 4x$, $y' = x + y$, with $x(0) = 1$, $y(0) = 1$ over $0 \le t \le 1.2$
   $$x(t) = \frac{3e^{-\sqrt{29}\,t/2} - 3e^{\sqrt{29}\,t/2}}{2\sqrt{29}\,e^{3t/2}} + \frac{e^{-\sqrt{29}\,t/2} + e^{\sqrt{29}\,t/2}}{2e^{3t/2}}$$
   $$y(t) = \frac{-7e^{-\sqrt{29}\,t/2} + 7e^{\sqrt{29}\,t/2}}{2\sqrt{29}\,e^{3t/2}} + \frac{e^{-\sqrt{29}\,t/2} + e^{\sqrt{29}\,t/2}}{2e^{3t/2}}$$

In Problems 6 through 9:

(a) Reformulate the second-order differential equation as a system of two first-order equations.

(b) Use your computer implementation of the Runge-Kutta method for systems to solve each system over the interval $[0, 2]$ with the step size $h = 0.05$.

(c) Plot your approximation and the analytic solution on the same coordinate system.

6. $2x''(t) - 5x'(t) - 3x(t) = 45e^{2t}$ with $x(0) = 2$ and $x'(0) = 1$
   $x(t) = 4e^{-t/2} + 7e^{3t} - 9e^{2t}$

7. $x''(t) + 6x'(t) + 9x(t) = 0$ with $x(0) = 4$ and $x'(0) = -4$
   $x(t) = 4e^{-3t} + 8te^{-3t}$

8. $x''(t) + x(t) = 6\cos(t)$ with $x(0) = 2$ and $x'(0) = 3$
   $x(t) = 2\cos(t) + 3\sin(t) + 3t\sin(t)$

9. $x''(t) + 3x'(t) = 12$ with $x(0) = 5$ and $x'(0) = 1$
$x(t) = 4 + 4t + e^{-3t}$

In Problems 10 through 19, use your computer implementation of the Runge-Kutta method of order $N = 4$ to solve the given differential equation or system of equations. Plot each approximation.

10. A certain resonant spring system with a periodic forcing function is modeled by

$$x''(t) + 25x(t) = 8\sin(5t) \quad \text{with } x(0) = 0 \text{ and } x'(0) = 0.$$

Use the Runge-Kutta method to solve the differential equation over the interval $[0, 2]$ using $M = 40$ steps and $h = 0.05$.

11. The mathematical model of a certain RLC electrical circuit is

$$Q''(t) + 20Q'(t) + 125Q(t) = 9\sin(5t)$$

with $Q(0) = 0$ and $Q'(0) = 0$. Use the Runge-Kutta method to solve the differential equation over the interval $[0, 2]$ using $M = 40$ steps and $h = 0.05$. *Remark.* $I(t) = Q'(t)$ is the current at time t.

12. At time t, a pendulum makes an angle $x(t)$ with the vertical axis. Assuming that there is no friction, the equation of motion is

$$mlx''(t) = -mg\sin(x(t)),$$

where m is the mass and l is the length of the string. Use the Runge-Kutta method to solve the differential equation over the interval $[0, 2]$ using $M = 40$ steps and $h = 0.05$ if $g = 32$ ft/sec^2 and
(a) $l = 3.2$ ft and $x(0) = 0.3$ and $x'(0) = 0$.
(b) $l = 0.8$ ft and $x(0) = 0.3$ and $x'(0) = 0$.

13. *Predator-prey model.*   An example of a system of nonlinear differential equations is the predator-prey problem. Let $x(t)$ and $y(t)$ denote the population of rabbits and foxes, respectively, at time t. The predator-prey model asserts that $x(t)$ and $y(t)$ satisfy

$$x'(t) = Ax(t) - Bx(t)y(t),$$
$$y'(t) = Cx(t)y(t) - Dy(t).$$

A typical computer simulation might use the coefficients

$$A = 2, \quad B = 0.02, \quad C = 0.0002, \quad D = 0.8.$$

Use the Runge-Kutta method to solve the system of differential equations over the interval $[0, 5]$ using $M = 50$ steps and $h = 0.2$ if
(a) $x(0) = 3000$ rabbits and $y(0) = 120$ foxes.
(b) $x(0) = 5000$ rabbits and $y(0) = 100$ foxes.

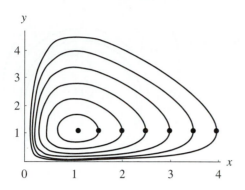

Figure 9.18   Solutions to the system $x' = x - xy$ and $y' = -y + xy$.

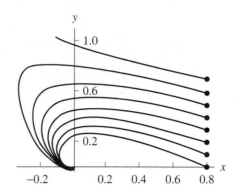

Figure 9.19   Solutions to the system $x' = -3x - 2y - 2xy^2$ and $y' = 2x - y + 2y^3$.

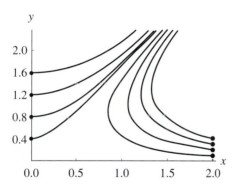

Figure 9.20   Solutions to the system $x' = y^2 - x^2$ and $y' = 2xy$.

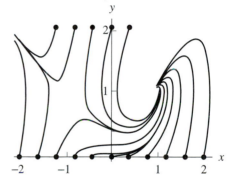

Figure 9.21   Solutions to the system $x' = 1 - y$ and $y' = x^2 - y^2$.

14. Solve $x' = x - xy$, $y' = -y + xy$ with $x(0) = 4$ and $y(0) = 1$ over $[0, 8]$ using $h = 0.1$. The trajectories of this system form closed paths. The polygonal path formed by the solution set is one of the curves shown in Figure 9.18.

15. Solve $x' = -3x - 2y - 2xy^2$, $y' = 2x - y + 2y^3$ with $x(0) = 0.8$ and $y(0) = 0.6$ over $[0, 4]$ using $h = 0.1$. For this system, the origin is classified as a spiral point that is asymptotically stable. The polygonal path formed by the solution set is one of the curves shown in Figure 9.19.

16. Solve $x' = y^2 - x^2$, $y' = 2xy$ with $x(0) = 2.0$ and $y(0) = 0.1$ over $[0.0, 1.5]$ using $h = 0.05$. For this system, there is an unstable saddle point at the origin. The polygonal path formed by the solution set is one of the curves shown in Figure 9.20.

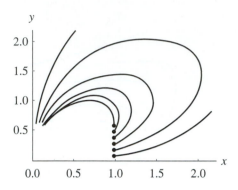

Figure 9.22 Solutions to the system $x' = x^3 - 2xy^2$ and $y' = 2x^2y - y^3$.

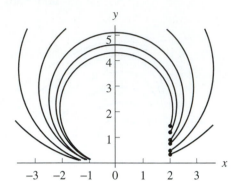

Figure 9.23 Solutions to the system $x' = x^2 - y^2$ and $y' = 2xy$.

17. Solve $x' = 1 - y$, $y' = x^2 - y^2$ with $x(0) = -1.2$ and $y(0) = 0.0$ over $[0, 5]$ using $h = 0.1$. The point $(1, 1)$ is a spiral point that is asymptotically stable, and the point $(-1, 1)$ is an unstable saddle point. The polygonal path formed by the solution set is one of the curves shown in Figure 9.21.

18. Solve $x' = x^3 - 2xy^2$, $y' = 2x^2y - y^3$ with $x(0) = 1.0$ and $y(0) = 0.2$ over $[0, 2]$ using $h = 0.025$. This system has an unstable critical point at the origin. The polygonal path formed by the solution set is one of the curves shown in Figure 9.22.

19. Solve $x' = x^2 - y^2$, $y' = 2xy$ with $x(0) = 2.0$ and $y(0) = 0.6$ over $[0.0, 1.6]$ using $h = 0.02$. The origin is an unstable critical point. The polygonal path formed by the solution set is one of the curves shown in Figure 9.23.

9.8 Boundary Value Problems

Another type of differential equation has the form

(1) $$x'' = f(t, x, x') \quad \text{for } a \leq t \leq b,$$

with the boundary conditions

(2) $$x(a) = \alpha \quad \text{and} \quad x(b) = \beta.$$

This is called a ***boundary value problem***.

The conditions that guarantee that a solution to (1) exists should be checked before any numerical scheme is applied; otherwise, a list of meaningless output may be generated. The general conditions are stated in the following theorem.

Theorem 9.8 (Boundary Value Problem).   Assume that $f(t, x, y)$ is continuous on the region $R = \{(t, x, y) : a \leq t \leq b, -\infty < x < \infty, -\infty < y < \infty\}$ and that $\partial f/\partial x = f_x(t, x, y)$ and $\partial f/\partial y = f_y(t, x, y)$ are continuous on R. If there exists a constant $M > 0$ for which f_x and f_y satisfy

$$(3) \hspace{3cm} f_x(t, x, y) > 0 \hspace{1cm} \text{for all} \ \ (t, x, y) \in R \ \ \text{and}$$

$$(4) \hspace{3cm} |f_y(t, x, y)| \leq M \hspace{1cm} \text{for all} \ \ (t, x, y) \in R,$$

then the boundary value problem

$$(5) \hspace{2.5cm} x'' = f(t, x, x') \hspace{1cm} \text{with} \ x(a) = \alpha \ \text{and} \ x(b) = \beta$$

has a unique solution $x = x(t)$ for $a \leq t \leq b$.

The notation $y = x'(t)$ has been used to distinguish the third variable of the function $f(t, x, x')$. Finally, the special case of linear differential equations is worthy of mention.

Corollary 9.1 (Linear Boundary Value Problem).   Assume that f in Theorem 9.8 has the form $f(t, x, y) = p(t)y + q(t)x + r(t)$ and that f and its partial derivatives $\partial f/\partial x = q(t)$ and $\partial f/\partial y = p(t)$ are continuous on R. If there exists a constant $M > 0$ for which $p(t)$ and $q(t)$ satisfy

$$(6) \hspace{3cm} q(t) > 0 \hspace{1cm} \text{for all} \ t \in [a, b]$$

and

$$(7) \hspace{2.5cm} |p(t)| \leq M = \max_{a \leq t \leq b} \{|p(t)|\},$$

then the *linear boundary value problem*

$$(8) \hspace{1.5cm} x'' = p(t)x'(t) + q(t)x(t) + r(t) \hspace{1cm} \text{with} \ x(a) = \alpha \ \text{and} \ x(b) = \beta$$

has a unique solution $x = x(t)$ over $a \leq t \leq b$.

Reduction to Two I.V.P.s: Linear Shooting Method

Finding the solution of a linear boundary problem is assisted by the linear structure of the equation and the use of two special initial value problems. Suppose that $u(t)$ is the unique solution to the I.V.P.

$$(9) \hspace{1.5cm} u'' = p(t)u'(t) + q(t)u(t) + r(t) \hspace{1cm} \text{with} \ u(a) = \alpha \ \text{and} \ u'(a) = 0.$$

Furthermore, suppose that $v(t)$ is the unique solution to the I.V.P.

(10) $$v'' = p(t)v'(t) + q(t)v(t) \quad \text{with } v(a) = 0 \text{ and } v'(a) = 1.$$

Then the linear combination

(11) $$x(t) = u(t) + Cv(t)$$

is a solution to $x'' = p(t)x'(t) + q(t)x(t) + r(t)$ as seen by the computation

$$
\begin{aligned}
x'' = u'' + Cv'' &= p(t)u'(t) + q(t)u(t) + r(t) + p(t)Cv'(t) + q(t)Cv(t) \\
&= p(t)(u'(t) + Cv'(t)) + q(t)(u(t) + Cv(t)) + r(t) \\
&= p(t)x'(t) + q(t)x(t) + r(t).
\end{aligned}
$$

The solution $x(t)$ in equation (11) takes on the boundary values

(12) $$
\begin{aligned}
x(a) &= u(a) + Cv(a) = \alpha + 0 = \alpha, \\
x(b) &= u(b) + Cv(b).
\end{aligned}
$$

Imposing the boundary condition $x(b) = \beta$ in (12) produces $C = (\beta - u(b))/v(b)$. Therefore, if $v(b) \neq 0$, the unique solution to (8) is

(13) $$x(t) = u(t) + \frac{\beta - u(b)}{v(b)} v(t).$$

Remark. If q fulfills the hypotheses of Corollary 9.1, this rules out the troublesome solution $v(t) \equiv 0$, so that (13) is the form of the required solution. The details are left for the reader to investigate in the exercises.

Example 9.17.   Solve the boundary value problem

$$x''(t) = \frac{2t}{1+t^2} x'(t) - \frac{2}{1+t^2} x(t) + 1$$

with $x(0) = 1.25$ and $x(4) = -0.95$ over the interval $[0, 4]$.
    The functions p, q, and r are $p(t) = 2t/(1+t^2)$, $q(t) = -2/(1+t^2)$, and $r(t) = 1$, respectively. The Runge-Kutta method of order 4 with step size $h = 0.2$ is used to construct numerical solutions $\{u_j\}$ and $\{v_j\}$ to equations (9) and (10), respectively. The approximations $\{u_j\}$ for $u(t)$ are given in the first column of Table 9.15. Then $u(4) \approx u_{20} = -2.893535$ and $v(4) \approx v_{20} = 4$ are used with (13) to construct

$$w_j = \frac{b - u(4)}{v(4)} v_j = 0.485884 v_j.$$

Table 9.15   Approximate Solutions $\{x_j\} = \{u_j + w_j\}$ to the Equation $x''(t) = \dfrac{2t}{1+t^2}x'(t) - \dfrac{2}{1+t^2} + 1$

t_j	u_j	w_j	$x_j = u_j + w_j$
0.0	1.250000	0.000000	1.250000
0.2	1.220131	0.097177	1.317308
0.4	1.132073	0.194353	1.326426
0.6	0.990122	0.291530	1.281652
0.8	0.800569	0.388707	1.189276
1.0	0.570844	0.485884	1.056728
1.2	0.308850	0.583061	0.891911
1.4	0.022522	0.680237	0.702759
1.6	−0.280424	0.777413	0.496989
1.8	−0.592609	0.874591	0.281982
2.0	−0.907039	0.971767	0.064728
2.2	−1.217121	1.068944	−0.148177
2.4	−1.516639	1.166121	−0.350518
2.6	−1.799740	1.263297	−0.536443
2.8	−2.060904	1.360474	−0.700430
3.0	−2.294916	1.457651	−0.837265
3.2	−2.496842	1.554828	−0.942014
3.4	−2.662004	1.652004	−1.010000
3.6	−2.785960	1.749181	−1.036779
3.8	−2.864481	1.846358	−1.018123
4.0	−2.893535	1.943535	−0.950000

Then the required approximate solution is $\{x_j\} = \{u_j + w_j\}$. Sample computations are given in Table 9.15, and Figure 9.24 shows their graphs. The reader can verify that $v(t) = t$ is the analytic solution for boundary value problem (10); that is,

$$v''(t) = \frac{2t}{1+t^2}v'(t) - \frac{2}{1+t^2}v(t)$$

with the initial conditions $v(0) = 0$ and $v'(0) = 1$.

The approximations in Table 9.16 compare numerical solutions obtained with the linear shooting method with the step sizes $h = 0.2$ and $h = 0.1$ and the analytic solution

$$x(t) = 1.25 + 0.4860896526t - 2.25t^2 + 2t\arctan(t) - \frac{1}{2}\ln(1 + t^2) + \frac{1}{2}t^2\ln(1 + t^2).$$

A graph of the approximate solution when $h = 0.2$ is given in Figure 9.25. Included in the table are columns for the error. Since the Runge-Kutta solutions have error of order $O(h^4)$, the error in the solution with the smaller step size $h = 0.1$ is about $\frac{1}{16}$ the error of the solution with the large step size $h = 0.2$.   ∎

Program 9.10 will call Program 9.9 to solve the initial value problems (9) and (10). Program 9.9 approximates solutions of systems of differential equations using a modification of the Runge-Kutta method of order $N = 4$. Thus, it is necessary to save

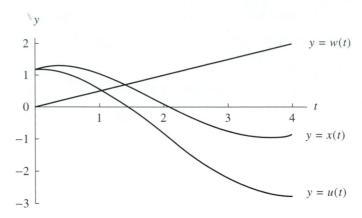

Figure 9.24 The numerical approximations $u(t)$ and $w(t)$ used to form $x(t) = u(t) + w(t)$, which is the solution to

$$x''(t) = \frac{2t}{1+t^2}x'(t) - \frac{2}{1+t^2}x(t) + 1.$$

Table 9.16 Numerical Approximations for $x''(t) = \dfrac{2t}{1+t^2}x'(t) - \dfrac{2}{1+t^2}x(t) + 1$

t_j	x_j $h = 0.2$	$x(t_j)$ exact	$x(t_j) - x_j$ error	t_j	x_j $h = 0.1$	$x(t_j)$ exact	$x(t_j) - x_j$ error
0.0	1.250000	1.250000	0.000000	0.0	1.250000	1.250000	0.000000
				0.1	1.291116	1.291117	0.000001
0.2	1.317308	1.317350	0.000042	0.2	1.317348	1.317350	0.000002
				0.3	1.328986	1.328990	0.000004
0.4	1.326426	1.326505	0.000079	0.4	1.326500	1.326505	0.000005
				0.5	1.310508	1.310514	0.000006
0.6	1.281652	1.281762	0.000110	0.6	1.281756	1.281762	0.000006
0.8	1.189276	1.189412	0.000136	0.8	1.189404	1.189412	0.000008
1.0	1.056728	1.056886	0.000158	1.0	1.056876	1.056886	0.000010
1.2	0.891911	0.892086	0.000175	1.2	0.892076	0.892086	0.000010
1.6	0.496989	0.497187	0.000198	1.6	0.497175	0.497187	0.000012
2.0	0.064728	0.064931	0.000203	2.0	0.064919	0.064931	0.000012
2.4	-0.350518	-0.350325	0.000193	2.4	-0.350337	-0.350325	0.000012
2.8	-0.700430	-0.700262	0.000168	2.8	-0.700273	-0.700262	0.000011
3.2	-0.942014	-0.941888	0.000126	3.2	-0.941895	-0.941888	0.000007
3.6	-1.036779	-1.036708	0.000071	3.6	-1.036713	-1.036708	0.000005
4.0	-0.950000	-0.950000	0.000000	4.0	-0.950000	-0.950000	0.000000

the equations (9) and (10) in the form of the system of equations (11) of Section 9.7. As an illustration, consider the boundary value problem in Example 9.17. The follow-

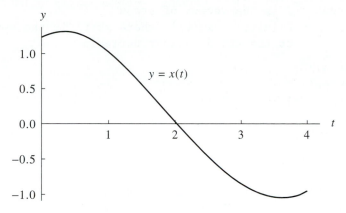

Figure 9.25 The graph of the numerical approximation for

$$x''(t) = \frac{2t}{1+t^2}x'(t) - \frac{2}{1+t^2}x(t) + 1$$

(using $h = 0.2$).

ing M-file, named F1, will save the I.V.P. (9) in the form of a system of differential equations.

```
function Z=F1(t,Z)
x=Z(1);y=Z(2);
Z=[y,2*t*y/(1+t^2)-2*x/(1+t^2)+1];
```

A similar M-file, named F2, will save the I.V.P. (10) (just let $r(t) = 0$ in F1) in the appropriate form.

A plot of the approximation obtained from Program 9.10 can be constructed by using the command `plot(L(:,1), L(:,2))`.

Program 9.9 (Runge-Kutta Method of Order $N = 4$ for Systems). To approximate the solution of the system of differential equations

$$x_1'(t) = f_1(t, x_1(t), \ldots, x_n(t))$$

$$\vdots \qquad\qquad \vdots$$

$$x_n'(t) = f_n(t, x_1(t), \ldots, x_n(t))$$

with $x_1(a) = \alpha_1, \ldots, x_n(a) = \alpha_n$ over the interval $[a, b]$.

```
function [T,Z]=rks4(F,a,b,Za,M)
%Input   - F is the system input as a string 'F'
%         - a and b are the endpoints of the interval
%         - Za=[x(a) y(a)] are the initial conditions
%         - M is the number of steps
```

```
%Output - T is the vector of steps
%        - Z=[x1(t)...xn(t)]; where xk(t) is the approximation
%          to the kth dependent variable

h=(b-a)/M;
T=zeros(1,M+1);
Z=zeros(M+1,length(Za));
T=a:h:b;
Z(1,:)=Za;

for j=1:M
   k1=h*feval(F,T(j),Z(j,:));
   k2=h*feval(F,T(j)+h/2,Z(j,:)+k1/2);
   k3=h*feval(F,T(j)+h/2,Z(j,:)+k2/2);
   k4=h*feval(F,T(j)+h,Z(j,:)+k3);
   Z(j+1,:)=Z(j,:)+(k1+2*k2+2*k3+k4)/6;

end
```

Program 9.10 (Linear Shooting Method).   To approximate the solution of the boundary value problem $x'' = p(t)x'(t) + q(t)x(t) + r(t)$ with $x(a) = \alpha$ and $x(b) = \beta$ over the interval $[a, b]$ by using the Runge-Kutta method of order $N = 4$.

```
function L=linsht(F1,F2,a,b,alpha,beta,M)

%Input  - F1 and F2 are the systems of first-order equations
%          representing the I.V.P.s (9) and (10), respectively;
%          input as strings 'F1', 'F2'
%        - a and b are the endpoints of the interval
%        - alpha = x(a) and beta = x(b); boundary conditions
%        - M is the number of steps
%Output - L =[T' X]; where T' is the (M+1)x1 vector of
%          abscissas and X is the (M+1)x1 vector of ordinates

%Solve the system F1
Za=[alpha,0];
[T,Z]=rks4(F1,a,b,Za,M);
U=Z(:,1);
%Solve the system F2
Za=[0,1];
[T,Z]=rks4(F2,a,b,Za,M);
V=Z(:,1);

%Calculate the solution to the boundary value problem
X=U+(beta-U(M+1))*V/V(M+1);
L=[T' X];
```

Exercises for Boundary Value Problems

1. Verify that the function $x(t)$ is the solution to the boundary value problem.

   (a) $x'' = (-2/t)x' + (2/t^2)x + (10\cos(\ln(t)))/t^2$ over [1, 3] with $x(1) = 1$ and $x(3) = -1$.

   $$x(t) = \frac{4.335950689 - 0.3359506908t^3 - 3t^2\cos(\ln(t)) + t^2\sin(\ln(t))}{t^2}$$

   (b) $x'' = -2x' - 2x + e^{-t} + \sin(2t)$ over [0, 4] with $x(0) = 0.6$ and $x(4) = -0.1$.

   $$x(t) = \frac{1}{5} + e^{-t} - \frac{1}{5}e^{-t}\cos(t) - \frac{2}{5}\cos^2(t)$$
   $$+ 3.670227413e^{-t}\sin(t) - \frac{1}{5}\cos(t)\sin(t)$$

   (c) $x'' = -4x' - 4x + 5\cos(4t) + \sin(2t)$ over [0, 2] with $x(0) = 0.75$ and $x(2) = 0.25$.

   $$x(t) = -\frac{1}{40} + 1.025e^{-2t} - 1.915729975te^{-2t} + \frac{19}{20}\cos^2(t)$$
   $$- \frac{6}{5}\cos^4(t) - \frac{4}{5}\cos(t)\sin(t) + \frac{8}{5}\cos^3(t)\sin(t)$$

   (d) $x'' + (1/t)x' + (1 - 1/(4t^2))x = 0$ over [1, 6] with $x(1) = 1$ and $x(6) = 0$.

   $$x(t) = \frac{0.2913843206\cos(t) + 1.001299385\sin(t)}{\sqrt{t}}$$

   (e) $x'' - (1/t)x' + (1/t^2)x = 1$ over [0.5, 4.5] with $x(0.5) = 1$ and $x(4.5) = 2$.

   $$x(t) = t^2 - 0.2525826491t - 2.528442297t\ln(t)$$

2. Does the boundary value problem in Exercise 1(e) satisfy the hypotheses of Corollary 9.1? Explain.

3. If q fulfills the hypothesis of Corollary 9.1, show that $v(t) \equiv 0$ is the unique solution to the boundary value problem

   $$v'' = p(t)v'(t) + q(t)v(t) \quad \text{with } v(a) = 0 \text{ and } v(b) = 0.$$

Algorithms and Programs

1. (a) Use Programs 9.9 and 9.10 to solve each of the boundary value problems in Exercise 1, using the step size $h = 0.05$.

   (b) Graph your solution and the actual solution on the same coordinate system.

2. Construct programs analogous to Program 9.9 based on

   (a) Heun's method,

   (b) the Adams-Bashforth-Moulton method, and

   (c) Hamming's method.

3. (a) Modify Program 9.10 to call each of your programs from Problem 2.

   (b) Use your programs to solve each of the five boundary value problems in Exercise 1 using the step size $h = 0.05$.

   (c) Graph your solutions and the actual solution on the same coordinate system.

9.9 Finite-Difference Method

Methods involving difference quotient approximations for derivatives can be used for solving certain second-order boundary value problems. Consider the linear equation

$$(1) \qquad x'' = p(t)x'(t) + q(t)x(t) + r(t)$$

over $[a, b]$ with $x(a) = \alpha$ and $x(b) = \beta$. Form a partition of $[a, b]$ using the points $a = t_0 < t_1 < \cdots < t_N = b$, where $h = (b - a)/N$ and $t_j = a + jh$ for $j = 0, 1, \ldots, N$. The central-difference formulas discussed in Chapter 6 are used to approximate the derivatives

$$(2) \qquad x'(t_j) = \frac{x(t_{j+1}) - x(t_{j-1})}{2h} + O(h^2)$$

and

$$(3) \qquad x''(t_j) = \frac{x(t_{j+1}) - 2x(t_j) + x(t_{j-1})}{h^2} + O(h^2).$$

To start the derivation, we replace each term $x(t_j)$ on the right side of (2) and (3) with x_j, and the resulting equations are substituted into (1) to obtain the relation

$$(4) \qquad \frac{x_{j+1} - 2x_j + x_{j-1}}{h^2} + O(h^2) = p(t_j)\left(\frac{x_{j+1} - x_{j-1}}{2h} + O(h^2)\right)$$
$$+ q(t_j)x_j + r(t_j).$$

Next, we drop the two terms $O(h^2)$ in (4) and introduce the notation $p_j = p(t_j)$, $q_j = q(t_j)$, and $r_j = r(t_j)$; this produces the difference equation

$$(5) \qquad \frac{x_{j+1} - 2x_j + x_{j-1}}{h^2} = p_j \frac{x_{j+1} - x_{j-1}}{2h} + q_j x_j + r_j,$$

which is used to compute numerical approximations to the differential equation (1). This is carried out by multiplying each side of (5) by h^2 and then collecting terms involving $x_{j-1}, x_j,$ and x_{j+1} and arranging them in a system of linear equations:

$$(6) \qquad \left(\frac{-h}{2}p_j - 1\right)x_{j-1} + (2 + h^2 q_j)x_j + \left(\frac{h}{2}p_j - 1\right)x_{j+1} = -h^2 r_j,$$

for $j = 1, 2, \ldots, N - 1$, where $x_0 = \alpha$ and $x_N = \beta$. The system in (6) has the familiar tridiagonal form, which is more visible when displayed with matrix notation:

$$
\begin{bmatrix}
2 + h^2 q_1 & \frac{h}{2}p_1 - 1 & & & & \\
\frac{-h}{2}p_2 - 1 & 2 + h^2 q_2 & \frac{h}{2}p_2 - 1 & & \mathbf{0} & \\
& \frac{-h}{2}p_j - 1 & 2 + h^2 q_j & \frac{h}{2}p_j - 1 & & \\
\mathbf{0} & & \frac{-h}{2}p_{N-2} - 1 & 2 + h^2 q_{N-2} & \frac{h}{2}p_{N-2} - 1 & \\
& & & \frac{-h}{2}p_{N-1} - 1 & 2 + h^2 q_{N-1} &
\end{bmatrix}
\begin{bmatrix}
x_1 \\
x_2 \\
x_j \\
x_{N-2} \\
x_{N-1}
\end{bmatrix}
$$

$$
=
\begin{bmatrix}
-h^2 r_1 + e_0 \\
-h^2 r_2 \\
-h^2 r_j \\
-h^2 r_{N-2} \\
-h^2 r_{N-1} + e_N
\end{bmatrix},
$$

where

$$
e_0 = \left(\frac{h}{2}p_1 + 1\right)\alpha \quad \text{and} \quad e_N = \left(\frac{-h}{2}p_{N-1} + 1\right)\beta.
$$

When computations with step size h are used, the numerical approximation to the solution is a set of discrete points $\{(t_j, x_j)\}$; if the analytic solution $x(t_j)$ is known, we can compare x_j and $x(t_j)$.

Example 9.18.   Solve the boundary value problem

$$
x''(t) = \frac{2t}{1 + t^2}x'(t) - \frac{2}{1 + t^2}x(t) + 1
$$

with $x(0) = 1.25$ and $x(4) = -0.95$ over the interval $[0, 4]$.

The functions p, q, and r are $p(t) = 2t/(1 + t^2)$, $q(t) = -2/(1 + t^2)$, and $r(t) = 1$, respectively. The finite-difference method is used to construct numerical solutions $\{x_j\}$ using the system of equations (6). Sample values of the approximations $\{x_{j,1}\}$, $\{x_{j,2}\}$, $\{x_{j,3}\}$, and $\{x_{j,4}\}$ corresponding to the step sizes $h_1 = 0.2$, $h_2 = 0.1$, $h_3 = 0.05$, and $h_4 = 0.025$ are given in Table 9.17. Figure 9.26 shows the graph of the polygonal path formed from $\{(t_j, x_{j,1})\}$ for the case $h_1 = 0.2$. There are 41 terms in the sequence generated with $h_2 = 0.1$, and the sequence $\{x_{j,2}\}$ only includes every other term from these computations; they correspond to the 21 values of $\{t_j\}$ given in Table 9.17. Similarly, the sequences $\{x_{j,3}\}$ and $\{x_{j,4}\}$ are a portion of the values generated with step sizes $h_3 = 0.05$ and $h_4 = 0.025$, respectively, and they correspond to the 21 values of $\{t_j\}$ in Table 9.17.

Next we compare numerical solutions in Table 9.17 with the analytic solution: $x(t) = 1.25 + 0.486089652t - 2.25t^2 + 2t\arctan(t) - \frac{1}{2}\ln(1 + t^2) + \frac{1}{2}t^2\ln(1 + t^2)$. The numerical

Table 9.17   Numerical Approximations for $x''(t) = \frac{2t}{1+t^2} x'(t) - \frac{2}{1+t^2} x(t) + 1$

t_j	$x_{j,1}$ $h = 0.2$	$x_{j,2}$ $h = 0.1$	$x_{j,3}$ $h = 0.05$	$x_{j,4}$ $h = 0.025$	$x(t_j)$ exact
0.0	1.250000	1.250000	1.250000	1.250000	1.250000
0.2	1.314503	1.316646	1.317174	1.317306	1.317350
0.4	1.320607	1.325045	1.326141	1.326414	1.326505
0.6	1.272755	1.279533	1.281206	1.281623	1.281762
0.8	1.177399	1.186438	1.188670	1.189227	1.189412
1.0	1.042106	1.053226	1.055973	1.056658	1.056886
1.2	0.874878	0.887823	0.891023	0.891821	0.892086
1.4	0.683712	0.698181	0.701758	0.702650	0.702947
1.6	0.476372	0.492027	0.495900	0.496865	0.497187
1.8	0.260264	0.276749	0.280828	0.281846	0.282184
2.0	0.042399	0.059343	0.063537	0.064583	0.064931
2.2	−0.170616	−0.153592	−0.149378	−0.148327	−0.147977
2.4	−0.372557	−0.355841	−0.351702	−0.350669	−0.350325
2.6	−0.557565	−0.541546	−0.537580	−0.536590	−0.536261
2.8	−0.720114	−0.705188	−0.701492	−0.700570	−0.700262
3.0	−0.854988	−0.841551	−0.838223	−0.837393	−0.837116
3.2	−0.957250	−0.945700	−0.942839	−0.942125	−0.941888
3.4	−1.022221	−1.012958	−1.010662	−1.010090	−1.009899
3.6	−1.045457	−1.038880	−1.037250	−1.036844	−1.036709
3.8	−1.022727	−1.019238	−1.018373	−1.018158	−1.018086
4.0	−0.950000	−0.950000	−0.950000	−0.950000	−0.950000

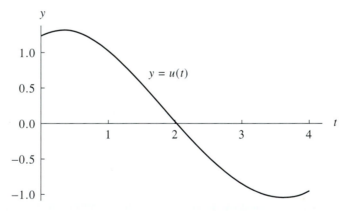

Figure 9.26   The graph of the numerical approximation for $x(t) = u(t) + w(t)$, which is the solution to

$$x''(t) = \frac{2t}{1+t^2} x'(t) - \frac{2}{1+t^2} x(t) + 1$$

(using $h = 0.2$).

Table 9.18 Errors in Numerical Approximations Using the Finite-Difference Method

t_j	$x(t_j) - x_{j,1}$ $= e_{j,1}$	$x(t_j) - x_{j,2}$ $= e_{j,2}$	$x(t_j) - x_{j,3}$ $= e_{j,3}$	$x(t_j) - x_{j,4}$ $= e_{j,4}$
	$h_1 = 0.2$	$h_2 = 0.1$	$h_3 = 0.05$	$h_4 = 0.025$
0.0	0.000000	0.000000	0.000000	0.000000
0.2	0.002847	0.000704	0.000176	0.000044
0.4	0.005898	0.001460	0.000364	0.000091
0.6	0.009007	0.002229	0.000556	0.000139
0.8	0.012013	0.002974	0.000742	0.000185
1.0	0.014780	0.003660	0.000913	0.000228
1.2	0.017208	0.004263	0.001063	0.000265
1.4	0.019235	0.004766	0.001189	0.000297
1.6	0.020815	0.005160	0.001287	0.000322
1.8	0.021920	0.005435	0.001356	0.000338
2.0	0.022533	0.005588	0.001394	0.000348
2.2	0.022639	0.005615	0.001401	0.000350
2.4	0.022232	0.005516	0.001377	0.000344
2.6	0.021304	0.005285	0.001319	0.000329
2.8	0.019852	0.004926	0.001230	0.000308
3.0	0.017872	0.004435	0.001107	0.000277
3.2	0.015362	0.003812	0.000951	0.000237
3.4	0.012322	0.003059	0.000763	0.000191
3.6	0.008749	0.002171	0.000541	0.000135
3.8	0.004641	0.001152	0.000287	0.000072
4.0	0.000000	0.000000	0.000000	0.000000

solutions can be shown to have error of order $O(h^2)$. Hence reducing the step size by a factor of $\frac{1}{2}$ results in the error being reduced by about $\frac{1}{4}$. A careful scrutiny of Table 9.18 will reveal that this is happening. For instance, at $t_j = 1.0$ the errors incurred with step sizes h_1, h_2, h_3, and h_4 are $e_{j,1} = 0.014780$, $e_{j,2} = 0.003660$, $e_{j,3} = 0.000913$, and $e_{j,4} = 0.000228$, respectively. Their successive ratios $e_{j,2}/e_{j,1} = 0.003660/0.014780 = 0.2476$, $e_{j,3}/e_{j,2} = 0.000913/0.003660 = 0.2495$, and $e_{j,4}/e_{j,3} = 0.000228/0.000913 = 0.2497$ are approaching $\frac{1}{4}$.

Finally, we show how Richardson's improvement scheme can be used to extrapolate the seemingly inaccurate sequences $\{x_{j,1}\}$, $\{x_{j,2}\}$, $\{x_{j,3}\}$, and $\{x_{j,4}\}$ and obtain six digits of precision. Eliminate the error terms $O(h^2)$ and $O((h/2)^2)$ in the approximations $\{x_{j,1}\}$ and $\{x_{j,2}\}$ by generating the extrapolated sequence $\{z_{j,1}\} = \{(4x_{j,2} - x_{j,1})/3\}$. Similarly, the error terms $O((h/2)^2)$ and $O((h/4)^2)$ for $\{x_{j,2}\}$ and $\{x_{j,3}\}$ are eliminated by generating $\{z_{j,2}\} = \{(4x_{j,3} - x_{j,2})/3\}$. It has been shown that the second level of Richardson's improvement scheme applies to the sequences $\{z_{j,1}\}$ and $\{z_{j,2}\}$, so the third improvement is $\{(16z_{j,2} - z_{j,1})/15\}$. Let us illustrate the situation by finding the extrapolated values that

Table 9.19   Extrapolation of the Numerical Approximations $\{x_{j,1}\}, \{x_{j,2}\}, \{x_{j,3}\}$ Obtained with the Finite-Difference Method

t_j	$\dfrac{4x_{j,2}-x_{j,1}}{3}$ $= z_{j,1}$	$\dfrac{4x_{j,3}-x_{j,2}}{3}$ $= z_{j,2}$	$\dfrac{16z_{j,2}-z_{j,1}}{3}$	$x(t_j)$ Exact solution
0.0	1.250000	1.250000	1.250000	1.250000
0.2	1.317360	1.317351	1.317350	1.317350
0.4	1.326524	1.326506	1.326504	1.326505
0.6	1.281792	1.281764	1.281762	1.281762
0.8	1.189451	1.189414	1.189412	1.189412
1.0	1.056932	1.056889	1.056886	1.056886
1.2	0.892138	0.892090	0.892086	0.892086
1.4	0.703003	0.702951	0.702947	0.702948
1.6	0.497246	0.497191	0.497187	0.497187
1.8	0.282244	0.282188	0.282184	0.282184
2.0	0.064991	0.064935	0.064931	0.064931
2.2	−0.147918	−0.147973	−0.147977	−0.147977
2.4	−0.350268	−0.350322	−0.350325	−0.350325
2.6	−0.536207	−0.536258	−0.536261	−0.536261
2.8	−0.700213	−0.700259	−0.700263	−0.700262
3.0	−0.837072	−0.837113	−0.837116	−0.837116
3.2	−0.941850	−0.941885	−0.941888	−0.941888
3.4	−1.009870	−1.009898	−1.009899	−1.009899
3.6	−1.036688	−1.036707	−1.036708	−1.036708
3.8	−1.018075	−1.018085	−1.018086	−1.018086
4.0	−0.950000	−0.950000	−0.950000	−0.950000

correspond to $t_j = 1.0$. The first extrapolated value is

$$\frac{4x_{j,2} - x_{j,1}}{3} = \frac{4(1.053226) - 1.042106}{3} = 1.056932 = z_{j,1}.$$

The second extrapolated value is

$$\frac{4x_{j,3} - x_{j,2}}{3} = \frac{4(1.055973) - 1.053226}{3} = 1.056889 = z_{j,2}.$$

Finally, the third extrapolation involves the terms $z_{j,1}$ and $z_{j,2}$:

$$\frac{16z_{j,2} - z_{j,1}}{15} = \frac{16(1.056889) - 1.056932}{15} = 1.056886.$$

This last computation contains six decimal places of accuracy. The values at the other points are given in Table 9.19.   ■

Program 9.12 will call Program 9.11 to solve the tridiagonal system (6). Program 9.12 requires that the coefficient functions $p(t)$, $q(t)$, and $r(t)$ (boundary value problem (1)) be saved in M-files p.m, q.m, and r.m, respectively.

Program 9.11 (Tridiagonal Systems). To solve the tridiagonal system $CX = B$, where C is a tridiagonal matrix.

```
function X=trisys(A,D,C,B)

%Input  - A is the subdiagonal of the coefficient matrix
%        - D is the main diagonal of the coefficient matrix
%        - C is the superdiagonal of the coefficient matrix
%        - B is the constant vector of the linear system
%Output - X is the solution vector
N=length(B);
for k=2:N
   mult=A(k-1)/D(k-1);
   D(k)=D(k)-mult*C(k-1);
   B(k)=B(k)-mult*B(k-1);
end
X(N)=B(N)/D(N);
for k= N-1:-1:1
   X(k)=(B(k)-C(k)*X(k+1))/D(k);
end
```

Program 9.12 (Finite-Difference Method). To approximate the solution of the boundary value problem $x'' = p(t)x'(t) + q(t)x(t) + r(t)$ with $x(a) = \alpha$ and $x(b) = \beta$ over the interval $[a, b]$ by using the finite-difference method of order $O(h^2)$.

Remark. The mesh is $a = t_1 < \cdots < t_{N+1} = b$ and the solution points are $\{(t_j, x_j)\}_{j=1}^{N+1}$.

```
function F=findiff(p,q,r,a,b,alpha,beta,N)

%Input  - p,q,and r are the coefficient functions of (1)
%          input as strings; 'p','q','r'
%        - a and b are the left and right endpoints
%        - alpha=x(a) and beta=x(b)
%        - N is the number of steps
%Output - F=[T' X']:where T' is the 1xN vector of abscissas
%          and X' is the 1xN vector of ordinates

%Initialize vectors and h
T=zeros(1,N+1);
X=zeros(1,N-1);
Va=zeros(1,N-2);
Vb=zeros(1,N-1);
Vc=zeros(1,N-2);
Vd=zeros(1,N-1);
h=(b-a)/N;
```

```
%Calculate the constant vector B in AX=B
Vt=a+h:h:a+h*(N-1);
Vb=-h^2*feval(r,Vt);
Vb(1)=Vb(1)+(1+h/2*feval(p,Vt(1)))*alpha;
Vb(N-1)=Vb(N-1)+(1-h/2*feval(p,Vt(N-1)))*beta;

%Calculate the main diagonal of A in AX=B
Vd=2+h^2*feval(q,Vt);

%Calculate the superdiagonal of A in AX=B
Vta=Vt(1,2:N-1);
Va=-1-h/2*feval(p,Vta);

%Calculate the subdiagonal of A in AX=B
Vtc=Vt(1,1:N-2);
Vc=-1+h/2*feval(p,Vtc);

%Solve AX=B using trisys
X=trisys(Va,Vd,Vc,Vb);
T=[a,Vt,b];
X=[alpha,X,beta];
F=[T' X'];
```

Exercises for Finite-Difference Method

In Exercises 1 through 3, use the finite-difference method to approximate $x(a + 0.5)$.

(a) Let $h_1 = 0.5$ and do one step by hand calculation. Then let $h_2 = 0.25$ and do two steps by hand calculation.

(b) Use extrapolation of the values in part (a) to obtain a better approximation (i.e., $z_{j,1} = (4x_{j,2} - x_{j,1})/3$).

(c) Compare your results from parts (a) and (b) with the exact value $x(a + 0.5)$.

1. $x'' = 2x' - x + t^2 - 1$ over $[0, 1]$ with $x(0) = 5$ and $x(1) = 10$
   $x(t) = t^2 + 4t + 5$

2. $x'' + (1/t)x' + (1 - 1/(4t^2))x = 0$ over $[1, 6]$ with $x(1) = 1$ and $x(6) = 0$
   $$x(t) = \frac{0.2913843206 \cos(t) + 1.001299385 \sin(t)}{\sqrt{t}}$$

3. $x'' - (1/t)x' + (1/t^2)x = 1$ over $[0.5, 4.5]$ with $x(0.5) = 1$ and $x(4.5) = 2$
   $x(t) = t^2 - 0.2525826491t - 2.528442297t \ln(t)$

4. Assume that p, q, and r are continuous over the interval $[a, b]$ and that $q(t) \geq 0$ for $a \leq t \leq b$. If h satisfies $0 < h < 2/M$, where $M = \max_{a \leq t \leq b}\{|p(t)|\}$, prove that the coefficient matrix of (6) is strictly diagonally dominant and that there is a unique solution.

5. Assume that $p(t) \equiv C_1 > 0$ and $q(t) \equiv C_2 > 0$. **(a)** Write out the tridiagonal linear system for this situation. **(b)** Prove that the tridiagonal system is strictly diagonally dominant and hence has a unique solution, provided that $C_1/C_2 \le h$.

Algorithms and Programs

1. Use Programs 9.11 and 9.12 to solve the given boundary problem using step sizes $h = 0.1$ and $h = 0.01$. Plot your two approximate solutions and the actual solution on the same coordinate system.
   (a) $x'' = 2x' - x + t^2 - 1$ over $[0, 1]$ with $x(0) = 5$ and $x(1) = 10$
   $x(t) = t^2 + 4t + 5$
   (b) $x'' + (1/t)x' + (1 - 1/(4t^2))x = 0$ over $[1, 6]$ with $x(1) = 1$ and $x(6) = 0$
   $$x(t) = \frac{0.2913843206 \cos(t) + 1.001299385 \sin(t)}{\sqrt{t}}$$
   (c) $x'' - (1/t)x' + (1/t^2)x = 1$ over $[0.5, 4.5]$ with $x(0.5) = 1$ and $x(4.5) = 2$
   $x(t) = t^2 - 0.2525826491t - 2.528442297t \ln(t)$

In Problems 2 through 7, use Programs 9.11 and 9.12 to solve the given boundary problem using step sizes $h = 0.2$, $h = 0.1$, and $h = 0.05$. For each problem, graph the three solutions on the same coordinate system.

2. $x'' = (-2/t)x' + (2/t^2)x + (10 \cos(\ln(t)))/t^2$ over $[1, 3]$ with $x(1) = 1$ and $x(3) = -1$

3. $x'' = -5x' - 6x + te^{-2t} + 3.9 \cos(3t)$ over $[0, 3]$ with $x(0) = 0.95$ and $x(3) = 0.15$

4. $x'' = -4x' - 4x + 5 \cos(4t) + \sin(2t)$ over $[0, 2]$ with $x(0) = 0.75$ and $x(2) = 0.25$

5. $x'' = -2x' - 2x + e^{-t} + \sin(2t)$ over $[0, 4]$ with $x(0) = 0.6$ and $x(4) = -0.1$

6. $x'' + (2/t)x' - (2/t^2)x = \sin(t)/t^2$ over $[1, 6]$ with $x(1) = -0.02$ and $x(6) = 0.02$

7. $x'' + (1/t)x' + (1 - 1/(4t^2))x = \sqrt{t} \cos(t)$ over $[1, 6]$ with $x(1) = 1.0$ and $x(6) = -0.5$

8. Construct a program that will call Programs 9.11 and 9.12 and carry out the extrapolation process illustrated in Example 9.18 and Table 9.19.

9. For each of the given boundary value problems, use your program from Problem 8 and the step sizes $h = 0.1$, $h = 0.05$, and $h = 0.025$ to construct a table analogous to Table 9.19. Plot your extrapolated solution and the actual solution on the same coordinate system.
   (a) $x'' = 2x' - x + t^2 - 1$ over $[0, 1]$ with $x(0) = 5$ and $x(1) = 10$
   $x(t) = t^2 + 4t + 5$
   (b) $x'' + (1/t)x' + (1 - 1/(4t^2))x = 0$ over $[1, 6]$ with $x(1) = 1$ and $x(6) = 0$
   $$x(t) = \frac{0.2913843206 \cos(t) + 1.001299385 \sin(t)}{\sqrt{t}}$$
   (c) $x'' - (1/t)x' + (1/t^2)x = 1$ over $[0.5, 4.5]$ with $x(0.5) = 1$ and $x(4.5) = 2$
   $x(t) = t^2 - 0.2525826491t - 2.528442297t \ln(t)$

10

Solution of Partial Differential Equations

Many problems in applied science, physics, and engineering are modeled mathematically with partial differential equations. A differential equation involving more than one independent variable is called a **partial differential equation** (PDE). It is not necessary to have taken a specialized course in PDEs to understand the rudimentary principles involved in obtaining computer solutions. In this chapter we will study finite-difference methods which are based on formulas for approximating the first and second derivatives of a function. We start by classifying the three types of equations under investigation and introduce a physical problem for each case. A partial differential equation of the form

(1) $$A\Phi_{xx} + B\Phi_{xy} + C\Phi_{yy} = f(x, y, \Phi, \Phi_x, \Phi_y),$$

where A, B, and C are constants, is called **quasilinear**. There are three types of quasilinear equations:

(2)   If $B^2 - 4AC < 0$, the equation is called **elliptic**.

(3)   If $B^2 - 4AC = 0$, the equation is called **parabolic**.

(4)   If $B^2 - 4AC > 0$, the equation is called **hyperbolic**.

As an example of a hyperbolic equation, we consider the one-dimensional model for a vibrating string. The displacement $u(x, t)$ is governed by the wave equation

(5) $$\rho u_{tt}(x, y) = T u_{xx}(x, t) \quad \text{for } 0 < x < L \text{ and } 0 < t < \infty,$$

544

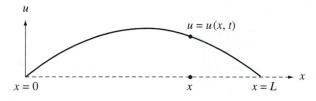

Figure 10.1 The wave equation models a vibrating string.

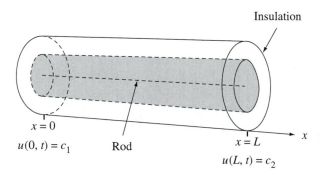

Figure 10.2 The heat equation models the temperature in an insulated rod.

with the given initial position and velocity functions

(6)
$$u(x, 0) = f(x) \qquad \text{for } t = 0 \text{ and } 0 \le x \le L,$$
$$u_t(x, 0) = g(x) \qquad \text{for } t = 0 \text{ and } 0 < x < L,$$

and the boundary values

(7)
$$u(0, t) = 0 \quad \text{for } x = 0 \text{ and } 0 \le t < \infty,$$
$$u(L, t) = 0 \quad \text{for } x = L \text{ and } 0 \le t < \infty.$$

The constant ρ is the mass of the string per unit length and T is the tension in the string. A diagram of a string with fixed ends at the locations $(0, 0)$ and $(L, 0)$ is shown in Figure 10.1.

As an example of a parabolic equation, we consider the one-dimensional model for heat flow in an insulated rod of length L (see Figure 10.2). The heat equation, which involves the temperature $u(x, t)$ in the rod at the position x and time t, is

(8)
$$\kappa u_{xx}(x, t) = \sigma \rho u_t(x, t) \qquad \text{for } 0 < x < L \text{ and } 0 < t < \infty,$$

the initial temperature distribution at $t = 0$ is

(9)
$$u(x, 0) = f(x) \qquad \text{for } t = 0 \text{ and } 0 \le x \le L,$$

and the boundary values at the ends of the rod are

(10)
$$u(0, t) = c_1 \quad \text{for } x = 0 \text{ and } 0 \le t < \infty,$$
$$u(L, t) = c_2 \quad \text{for } x = L \text{ and } 0 \le t < \infty.$$

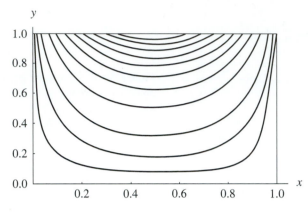

Figure 10.3   Solution curves $u(x, y) = C$ to Laplace's equation.

The constant κ is the coefficient of thermal conductivity, σ is the specific heat, and ρ is the density of the material in the rod.

As an example of an elliptic equation, consider the potential function $u(x, y)$, which might represent a steady-state electrostatic potential or a steady-state temperature distribution in a rectangular region in the plane. These situations are modeled with Laplace's equation in a rectangle:

(11) $u_{xx}(x, y) + u_{yy}(x, y) = 0$ for $0 < x < 1$ and $0 < y < 1$,

with boundary conditions specified:

$$u(x, 0) = f_1(x) \quad \text{for } y = 0 \text{ and } 0 \le x \le 1 \text{ (on the bottom)},$$
$$u(x, 1) = f_2(x) \quad \text{for } y = 1 \text{ and } 0 \le x \le 1 \text{ (on the top)},$$
$$u(0, y) = f_3(y) \quad \text{for } x = 0 \text{ and } 0 \le y \le 1 \text{ (on the left)},$$
$$u(1, y) = f_4(y) \quad \text{for } x = 1 \text{ and } 0 \le y \le 1 \text{ (on the right)}.$$

A contour plot for $u(x, y)$ with boundary functions $f_1(x) = 0$, $f_2(x) = \sin(\pi x)$, $f_3(y) = 0$, and $f_4(y) = 0$ over the square $R = \{(x, y) : 0 \le x \le 1, 0 \le y \le 1\}$ is shown in Figure 10.3.

10.1   Hyperbolic Equations

Wave Equation

As an example of a hyperbolic partial differential equation, we consider the wave equation

(1) $u_{tt}(x, t) = c^2 u_{xx}(x, t)$ for $0 < x < a$ and $0 < t < b$,

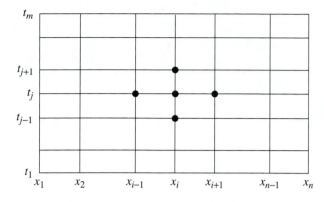

Figure 10.4 The grid for solving $u_{tt}(x, t) = c^2 u_{xx}(x, t)$ over R.

with the boundary conditions

(2)

$$u(0, t) = 0 \quad \text{and} \quad u(a, t) = 0 \quad \text{for } 0 \leq t \leq b,$$
$$u(x, 0) = f(x) \qquad\qquad\qquad \text{for } 0 \leq x \leq a,$$
$$u_t(x, 0) = g(x) \qquad\qquad\qquad \text{for } 0 < x < a.$$

The wave equation models the displacement u of a vibrating elastic string with fixed ends at $x = 0$ and $x = a$. Although analytic solutions to the wave equation can be obtained with Fourier series, we use the problem as a prototype of a hyperbolic equation.

Derivation of the Difference Equation

Partition the rectangle $R = \{(x, t) : 0 \leq x \leq a, 0 \leq t \leq b\}$ into a grid consisting of $n-1$ by $m-1$ rectangles with sides $\Delta x = h$ and $\Delta t = k$, as shown in Figure 10.4. Start at the bottom row, where $t = t_1 = 0$ and the solution is known to be $u(x_i, t_1) = f(x_i)$. We shall use a difference-equation method to compute approximations

$$\{u_{i,j} : i = 1, 2, \ldots, n\} \text{ in successive rows} \quad \text{for } j = 2, 3, \ldots, m.$$

The true solution value at the grid points is $u(x_i, t_j)$.

The central-difference formulas for approximating $u_{tt}(x, t)$ and $u_{xx}(x, t)$ are

(3)
$$u_{tt}(x, t) = \frac{u(x, t + k) - 2u(x, t) + u(x, t - k)}{k^2} + O(k^2)$$

and

(4)
$$u_{xx}(x, t) = \frac{u(x + h, t) - 2u(x, t) + u(x - h, t)}{h^2} + O(h^2).$$

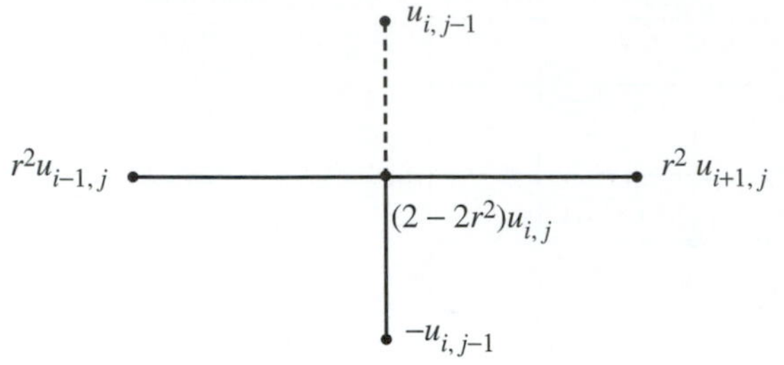

Figure 10.5   The wave equation stencil.

The grid spacing is uniform in every row: $x_{i+1} = x_i + h$ (and $x_{i-1} = x_i - h$); and it is uniform in every column: $t_{j+1} = t_j + k$ (and $t_{j-1} = t_j - k$). Next, we drop the terms $O(k^2)$ and $O(h^2)$ and use the approximation $u_{i,j}$ for $u(x_i, t_j)$ in equations (3) and (4), which in turn are substituted into (1); this produces the difference equation

$$(5) \qquad \frac{u_{i,j+1} - 2u_{i,j} + u_{i,j-1}}{k^2} = c^2 \frac{u_{i+1,j} - 2u_{i,j} + u_{i-1,j}}{h^2},$$

which approximates equation (1). For convenience, the substitution $r = ck/h$ is introduced in (5), and we obtain the relation

$$(6) \qquad u_{i,j+1} - 2u_{i,j} + u_{i,j-1} = r^2(u_{i+1,j} - 2u_{i,j} + u_{i-1,j}).$$

Equation (6) is employed to find row $j + 1$ across the grid, assuming that approximations in both rows j and $j - 1$ are known:

$$(7) \qquad u_{i,j+1} = (2 - 2r^2)u_{i,j} + r^2(u_{i+1,j} + u_{i-1,j}) - u_{i,j-1},$$

for $i = 2, 3, \ldots, n - 1$. The four known values on the right side of equation (7), which are used to create the approximation $u_{i,j+1}$, are shown in Figure 10.5.

   Caution must be taken when using formula (7). If the error made at one stage of the calculations is eventually dampened out, the method is called *stable*. To guarantee stability in formula (7), it is necessary that $r = ck/h \leq 1$. There are other schemes, called *implicit* methods, that are more complicated to implement, but do not have stability restrictions for r.

Starting Values

Two starting rows of values corresponding to $j = 1$ and $j = 2$ must be supplied in order to use formula (7) to compute the third row. Since the second row is not usually given, the boundary function $g(x)$ is used to help produce starting approximations in the second row. Fix $x = x_i$ at the boundary and apply Taylor's formula of order 1 for expanding $u(x, t)$ about $(x_i, 0)$. The value $u(x_i, k)$ satisfies

$$(8) \qquad u(x_i, k) = u(x_i, 0) + u_t(x_i, 0)k + O(k^2).$$

Then use $u(x_i, 0) = f(x_i) = f_i$ and $u_t(x_i, 0) = g(x_i) = g_i$ in (8) to produce the formula for computing the numerical approximations in the second row:

$$(9) \qquad\qquad u_{i,2} = f_i + kg_i \qquad \text{for } i = 2, 3, \ldots, n - 1.$$

Usually, $u(x_i, t_2) \neq u_{i,2}$, and such errors introduced by formula (9) will propagate throughout the grid and will not be dampened out when the scheme in (7) is implemented. Hence it is prudent to use a very small step size for k so that the values for $u_{i,2}$ given in (9) do not contain a large amount of truncation error.

Often, the boundary function $f(x)$ has a second derivative $f''(x)$ over the interval. In this case we have $u_{xx}(x, 0) = f''(x)$, and it is beneficial to use the Taylor formula of order $n = 2$ to help construct the second row. To do this, we go back to the wave equation and use the relationship between the second-order partial derivatives to obtain

$$(10) \qquad u_{tt}(x_i, 0) = c^2 u_{xx}(x_i, 0) = c^2 f''(x_i) = c^2 \frac{f_{i+1} - 2f_i + f_{i-1}}{h^2} + O(h^2).$$

Recall that Taylor's formula of order 2 is

$$(11) \qquad\qquad u(x, k) = u(x, 0) + u_t(x, 0)k + \frac{u_{tt}(x, 0)k^2}{2} + O(k^3).$$

Applying formula (11) at $x = x_i$, together with (9) and (10), we get

$$(12) \qquad u(x_i, k) = f_i + kg_i + \frac{c^2 k^2}{2h^2}(f_{i+1} - 2f_i + f_{i-1}) + O(h^2)O(k^2) + O(k^3).$$

Using $r = ck/h$, formula (12) can be simplified to obtain a difference formula for the improved numerical approximations in the second row:

$$(13) \qquad\qquad u_{i,2} = (1 - r^2)f_i + kg_i + \frac{r^2}{2}(f_{i+1} + f_{i-1})$$

for $i = 2, 3, \ldots, n - 1$.

D'Alembert's Solution

The French mathematician Jean Le Rond d'Alembert (1717–1783) discovered that

$$(14) \qquad\qquad u(x, t) = F(x + ct) + G(x - ct)$$

is a solution to the wave equation (1) over the interval $0 \leq x \leq a$, provided that F', F'', G', and G'' all exist and F and G have period $2a$ and obey the relationships $F(-z) = -F(z)$, $F(z + 2a) = F(z)$, $G(-z) = -G(z)$, and $G(z + 2a) = G(z)$ for all z. We can check this out by direct substitution. The second-order partial derivatives of the solution (14) are

$$(15) \qquad u_{tt}(x,t) = c^2 F''(x+ct) + c^2 G''(x-ct),$$
$$(16) \qquad u_{xx}(x,t) = F''(x+ct) + G''(x-ct).$$

Substitution of these quantities into (1) produces the desired relationship:

$$
\begin{aligned}
u_{tt}(x,t) &= c^2 F''(x+ct) + c^2 G''(x-ct) \\
&= c^2(F''(x+ct) + G''(x-ct)) \\
&= c^2 u_{xx}(x,t).
\end{aligned}
$$

The particular solution that has the boundary values $u(x,0) = f(x)$ and $u_t(x,0) = 0$ requires that $F(x) = G(x) = f(x)/2$ and is left for the reader to verify.

Two Exact Rows Given

The accuracy of the numerical approximations produced by the equations in (7) depends on the truncation errors in the formulas used to convert the partial differential equation into a difference equation. Although it is unlikely to know values of the exact solution for the second row of the grid, if such knowledge were available, using the increment $k = ch$ along the t-axis will generate an exact solution at all the other points throughout the grid.

Theorem 10.1.   Assume that the two rows of values $u_{i,1} = u(x_i, 0)$ and $u_{i,2} = u(x_i, k)$, for $i = 1, 2, \ldots, n$, are the exact solutions to the wave equation (1). If the step size $k = h/c$ is chosen along the t-axis, then $r = 1$ and formula (7) becomes

$$(17) \qquad u_{i,j+1} = u_{i+1,j} + u_{i-1,j} - u_{i,j-1}.$$

Furthermore, the finite-difference solutions produced by (17) throughout the grid are exact solution values to the differential equation (neglecting computer round-off error).

Proof.   Use d'Alembert's solution and the relation $ck = h$. The calculation $x_i - ct_j = (i-1)h - c(j-1)k = (i-1)h - (j-1)h = (i-j)h$ and a similar one producing $x_i + ct_j = (i+j-2)h$ are used in equation (14) to produce the following special form of $u_{i,j}$:

$$(18) \qquad u_{i,j} = F((i-j)h) + G((i+j-2)h)$$

for $i = 1, 2, \ldots, n$ and $j = 1, 2, \ldots, m$. Applying this formula to the terms

$u_{i+1,j}$, $u_{i-1,j}$, and $u_{i,j-1}$ on the right side of (17) yields

$$u_{i+1,j} + u_{i-1,j} - u_{i,j-1}$$
$$= F((i+1-j)h) + F((i-1-j)h)$$
$$- F((i-(j-1))h) + G((i+1+j-2)h)$$
$$+ G((i-1+j-2)h) - G((i+j-1-2)h)$$
$$= F((i-(j+1))h) + G((i+j+1-2)h) = u_{i,j+1},$$

for $i = 1, 2, \ldots, n$ and $j = 1, 2, \ldots, m$.   ●

Warning.   Theorem 10.1 does not guarantee that the numerical solutions are exact when numerical calculations based on (9) and (13) are used to construct approximations $u_{i,2}$ in the second row. Indeed, truncation error will be introduced if $u_{i,2} \neq u(x_i, k)$ for some i, where $1 \leq i \leq n$. This is why we endeavor to obtain the best possible values for the second row by using the second-order Taylor approximations in equation (13).

Example 10.1.   Use the finite-difference method to solve the wave equation for a vibrating string:

(19) $u_{tt}(x, t) = 4u_{xx}(x, t)$ for $0 < x < 1$ and $0 < t < 0.5$,

with the boundary conditions

$$u(0, t) = 0 \quad \text{and} \quad u(1, t) = 0 \qquad \text{for } 0 \leq t \leq 0.5,$$

(20) $u(x, 0) = f(x) = \sin(\pi x) + \sin(2\pi x)$ for $0 \leq x \leq 1$,

$$u_t(x, 0) = g(x) = 0 \qquad\qquad\qquad \text{for } 0 \leq x \leq 1.$$

For convenience we choose $h = 0.1$ and $k = 0.05$. Since $c = 2$, this yields $r = ck/h = 2(0.05)/0.1 = 1$. Since $g(x) = 0$ and $r = 1$, formula (13) for creating the second row is

(21) $u_{i,2} = \dfrac{f_{i-1} + f_{i+1}}{2}$ for $i = 2, 3, \ldots, 9$.

Substituting $r = 1$ into equation (7) gives the simplified difference equation

(22) $u_{i,j+1} = u_{i+1,j} + u_{i-1,j} - u_{i,j-1}$.

Applying formulas (21) and (22) successively to generate rows will produce the approximations to $u(x, t)$ given in Table 10.1 for $0 < x_i < 1$ and $0 \leq t_j \leq 0.50$.

The numerical values in Table 10.1 agree to more than six decimal places of accuracy with those obtained with the analytic solution

$$u(x, t) = \sin(\pi x)\cos(2\pi t) + \sin(2\pi x)\cos(4\pi t).$$

Table 10.1   Solution of the Wave Equation (19) with Boundary Conditions (20)

t_j	x_2	x_3	x_4	x_5	x_6	x_7	x_8	x_9	x_{10}
0.00	0.896802	1.538842	1.760074	1.538842	1.000000	0.363271	−0.142040	−0.363271	−0.278768
0.05	0.769421	1.328438	1.538842	1.380037	0.951056	0.428980	0.000000	−0.210404	−0.181636
0.10	0.431636	0.769421	0.948401	0.951056	0.809017	0.587785	0.360616	0.181636	0.068364
0.15	0.000000	0.051599	0.181636	0.377381	0.587785	0.740653	0.769421	0.639384	0.363271
0.20	−0.380037	−0.587785	−0.519421	−0.181636	0.309017	0.769421	1.019421	0.951056	0.571020
0.25	−0.587785	−0.951056	−0.951056	−0.587785	0.000000	0.587785	0.951056	0.951056	0.587785
0.30	−0.571020	−0.951056	−1.019421	−0.769421	−0.309017	0.181636	0.519421	0.587785	0.380037
0.35	−0.363271	−0.639384	−0.769421	−0.740653	−0.587785	−0.377381	−0.181636	−0.051599	0.000000
0.40	−0.068364	−0.181636	−0.360616	−0.587785	−0.809017	−0.951056	−0.948401	−0.769421	−0.431636
0.45	0.181636	0.210404	0.000000	−0.428980	−0.951056	−1.380037	−1.538842	−1.328438	−0.769421
0.50	0.278768	0.363271	0.142040	−0.363271	−1.000000	−1.538842	−1.760074	−1.538842	−0.896802

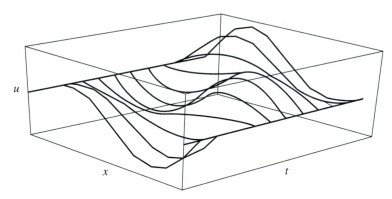

Figure 10.6   The vibrating string for equations (19) and (20).

A three-dimensional presentation of the data in Table 10.1 is given in Figure 10.6.   ∎

Example 10.2.   Use the finite-difference method to solve the wave equation for a vibrating string:

$$(23) \qquad u_{tt}(x, t) = 4u_{xx}(x, t) \qquad \text{for } 0 < x < 1 \text{ and } 0 < t < 0.5,$$

with the boundary conditions

$$u(0, t) = 0 \quad \text{and} \quad u(1, t) = 0 \quad \text{for } 0 \le t \le 1,$$

$$(24) \qquad u(x, 0) = f(x) = \begin{cases} x & \text{for } 0 \le x \le \frac{3}{5} \\ 1.5 - 1.5x & \text{for } \frac{3}{5} \le x \le 1, \end{cases}$$

$$u_t(x, 0) = g(x) = 0 \qquad \text{for } 0 < x < 1.$$

For convenience we choose $h = 0.1$ and $k = 0.05$. Since $c = 2$, this again yields $r = 1$. Applying formulas (21) and (22) successively to generate rows will produce the

Table 10.2   Solution of the Wave Equation (23) with Boundary Conditions (24)

t_j	x_2	x_3	x_4	x_5	x_6	x_7	x_8	x_9	x_{10}
0.00	0.100	0.200	0.300	0.400	0.500	0.600	0.450	0.300	0.150
0.05	0.100	0.200	0.300	0.400	0.500	0.475	0.450	0.300	0.150
0.10	0.100	0.200	0.300	0.400	0.375	0.350	0.325	0.300	0.150
0.15	0.100	0.200	0.300	0.275	0.250	0.225	0.200	0.175	0.150
0.20	0.100	0.200	0.175	0.150	0.125	0.100	0.075	0.050	0.025
0.25	0.100	0.075	0.050	0.025	0.000	−0.025	−0.050	−0.075	−0.100
0.30	−0.025	−0.050	−0.075	−0.100	−0.125	−0.150	−0.175	−0.200	−0.100
0.35	−0.150	−0.175	−0.200	−0.225	−0.250	−0.275	−0.300	−0.200	−0.100
0.40	−0.150	−0.300	−0.325	−0.350	−0.375	−0.400	−0.300	−0.200	−0.100
0.45	−0.150	−0.300	−0.450	−0.475	−0.500	−0.400	−0.300	−0.200	−0.100
0.50	−0.150	−0.300	−0.450	−0.600	−0.500	−0.400	−0.300	−0.200	−0.100

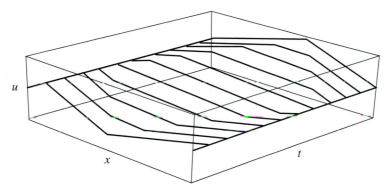

Figure 10.7   The vibrating string for equations (23) and (24).

approximations to $u(x, t)$ given in Table 10.2 for $0 \le x_i \le 1$ and $0 \le t_j \le 0.50$. A three-dimensional presentation of the data in Table 10.2 is given in Figure 10.7.   ∎

Program 10.1 approximates the solution of the wave equation ((1) and (2)). A three-dimensional presentation of the output matrix U can be obtained by using the commands `mesh(U)` or `surf(U)`. Additionally, the command `contour(U)` will produce a graph analogous to Figure 10.3, while the command `contour3(U)` will produce the three-dimensional analogy of Figure 10.3.

> **Program 10.1 (Finite-Difference Solution for the Wave Equation).** To approx-
> imate the solution of $u_{tt}(x,t) = c^2 u_{xx}(x,t)$ over $R = \{(x,t) : 0 \le x \le a, 0 \le t \le b\}$ with $u(0,t) = 0$, $u(a,t) = 0$, for $0 \le t \le b$, and $u(x,0) = f(x)$,
> $u_t(x,0) = g(x)$, for $0 \le x \le a$.

```
function U = finedif(f,g,a,b,c,n,m)

%Input    - f=u(x,0) as a string 'f'
%          - g=ut(x,0) as a string 'g'
%          - a and b right endpoints of [0,a] and [0,b]
%          - c the constant in the wave equation
%          - n and m number of grid points over [0,a] and [0,b]
%Output - U solution matrix; analogous to Table 10.1

%Initialize parameters and U
h=a/(n-1);
k=b/(m-1);
r=c*k/h;
r2=r^2;
r22=r^2/2;
s1=1-r^2;
s2=2-2*r^2;
U=zeros(n,m);

%Compute first and second rows
for i=2:n-1
   U(i,1)=feval(f,h*(i-1));
   U(i,2)=s1*feval(f,h*(i-1))+k*feval(g,h*(i-1)) ...
      +r22*(feval(f,h*i)+feval(f,h*(i-2)));
end

%Compute remaining rows of U
for j=3:m,
   for i=2:(n-1),
      U(i,j) = s2*U(i,j-1)+r2*(U(i-1,j-1)+U(i+1,j-1))-U(i,j-2);
   end
end

U=U';
```

Exercises for Hyperbolic Equations

1. (a)   Verify by direct substitution that $u(x, t) = \sin(n\pi x)\cos(2n\pi t)$ is a solution to the wave equation $u_{tt}(x, t) = 4u_{xx}(x, t)$ for each positive integer $n = 1, 2, \ldots$.

    (b)   Verify by direct substitution that $u(x, t) = \sin(n\pi x)\cos(cn\pi t)$ is a solution to the wave equation $u_{tt}(x, t) = c^2 u_{xx}(x, t)$ for each positive integer $n = 1, 2, \ldots$.

2. Assume that the initial position and velocity are $u(x, 0) = f(x)$ and $u_t(x, 0) \equiv 0$, respectively. Show that the d'Alembert solution for this case is

$$u(x, t) = \frac{f(x + ct) + f(x - ct)}{2}.$$

3. Obtain a simplified form of the difference equation (7) in the case $h = 2ck$.

In Exercises 4 and 5, use the finite-difference method to calculate the first three rows of the approximate solution for the given wave equation. Carry out your calculations by hand (calculator).

4. $u_{tt}(x, t) = 4u_{xx}(x, t)$, for $0 \leq x \leq 1$ and $0 \leq t \leq 0.5$, with the boundary conditions

$$u(0, t) = 0 \quad \text{and} \quad u(1, t) = 0 \qquad \text{for } 0 \leq t \leq 0.5,$$
$$u(x, 0) = f(x) = \sin(\pi x) \qquad \text{for } 0 \leq x \leq 1,$$
$$u_t(x, 0) = g(x) = 0 \qquad \text{for } 0 \leq x \leq 1.$$

   Let $h = 0.2$, $k = 0.1$, and $r = 1$.

5. $u_{tt}(x, t) = 4u_{xx}(x, t)$, for $0 \leq x \leq 1$ and $0 \leq t \leq 0.5$, with the boundary conditions

$$u(0, t) = 0 \quad \text{and} \quad u(1, t) = 0 \qquad \text{for } 0 \leq t \leq 0.5,$$

$$u(x, 0) = f(x) = \begin{cases} \dfrac{5x}{2} & \text{for } 0 \leq x \leq \frac{3}{5}, \\[2mm] \dfrac{15 - 15x}{4} & \text{for } \frac{3}{5} \leq x \leq 1, \end{cases}$$

$$u_t(x, 0) = g(x) = 0 \qquad \text{for } 0 < x < 1.$$

   Let $h = 0.2$, $k = 0.1$, and $r = 1$.

6. Assume that the initial position and velocity are $u(x, 0) = f(x)$ and $u_t(x, 0) = g(x)$, respectively. Show that the d'Alembert solution for this case is

$$u(x, t) = \frac{f(x + ct) + f(x - ct)}{2} + \frac{1}{2c} \int_{x-ct}^{x+ct} g(s)\, ds.$$

7. For the equation $u_{tt}(x, t) = 9u_{xx}(x, t)$, what relationship between h and k must occur in order to produce the difference equation $u_{i,j+1} = u_{i+1,j} + u_{i-1,j} - u_{i,j-1}$?

8. What difficulty might occur when trying to use the finite-difference method to solve $u_{tt}(x, t) = 4u_{xx}(x, t)$ with the choice $k = 0.02$ and $h = 0.03$?

Algorithms and Programs

In Problems 1 to 8, use Program 10.1 to solve the wave equation $u_{tt}(x, t) = c^2 u_{xx}(x, t)$, for $0 \le x \le a$ and $0 \le t \le b$, with the boundary conditions

$$u(0, t) = 0 \quad \text{and} \quad u(a, t) = 0 \qquad \text{for } 0 \le t \le b,$$
$$u(x, 0) = f(x) \qquad\qquad\qquad\qquad \text{for } 0 \le x \le a,$$
$$u_t(x, 0) = g(x) \qquad\qquad\qquad\qquad \text{for } 0 \le x \le a,$$

for the given values. Use the surf and contour commands to plot your approximate solutions.

1. Use $a = 1$, $b = 1$, $c = 1$, $f(x) = \sin(\pi x)$, and $g(x) = 0$. For convenience, choose $h = 0.1$ and $k = 0.1$.

2. Use $a = 1$, $b = 1$, $c = 1$, $f(x) = x - x^2$, and $g(x) = 0$. For convenience, choose $h = 0.1$ and $k = 0.1$.

3. Use $a = 1$, $b = 1$, $c = 1$, $f(x) = \begin{cases} 2x & \text{for } 0 \le x \le \frac{1}{2}, \\ 2 - 2x & \text{for } \frac{1}{2} \le x \le 1. \end{cases}$

   $g(x) = 0$, $h = 0.1$, and $k = 0.1$.

4. Use $a = 1$, $b = 1$, $c = 2$, $f(x) = \sin(\pi x)$, $g(x) = 0$, $h = 0.1$, and $k = 0.05$.

5. Use $a = 1$, $b = 1$, $c = 2$, $f(x) = x - x^2$, $g(x) = 0$, $h = 0.1$, and $k = 0.05$.

6. Repeat Problem 3, but with $c = 2$ and $k = 0.05$.

7. Repeat Problem 1, but with $f(x) = \sin(2\pi x) + \sin(4\pi x)$.

8. Repeat Problem 1, but with $c = 2$, $f(x) = \sin(2\pi x) + \sin(4\pi x)$, and $k = 0.05$.

10.2   Parabolic Equations

Heat Equation

As an example of parabolic differential equations, we consider the one-dimensional heat equation

$$(1) \qquad u_t(x, t) = c^2 u_{xx}(x, t) \qquad \text{for } 0 \le x < a \text{ and } 0 < t < b,$$

with the initial condition

$$(2) \qquad u(x, 0) = f(x) \qquad \text{for } t = 0 \text{ and } 0 \le x \le a,$$

and the boundary conditions

$$(3) \qquad \begin{aligned} u(0, t) &= g_1(t) \equiv c_1 & \text{for } x = 0 \text{ and } 0 \le t \le b, \\ u(a, t) &= g_2(t) \equiv c_2 & \text{for } x = a \text{ and } 0 \le t \le b. \end{aligned}$$

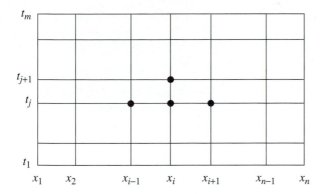

Figure 10.8 The grid for solving $u_t(x, t) = c^2 u_{xx}(x, t)$ over R.

The heat equation models the temperature in an insulated rod with ends held at constant temperatures c_1 and c_2 and the initial temperature distribution along the rod being $f(x)$. Although analytic solutions to the heat equation can be obtained with Fourier series, we use the problem as a prototype of a parabolic equation for numerical solution.

Derivation of the Difference Equation

Assume that the rectangle $R = \{(x, t) : 0 \le x \le a, 0 \le t \le b\}$ is subdivided into $n - 1$ by $m - 1$ rectangles with sides $\Delta x = h$ and $\Delta t = k$, as shown in Figure 10.8. Start at the bottom row, where $t = t_1 = 0$, and the solution is $u(x_i, t_1) = f(x_i)$. A method for computing the approximations to $u(x, t)$ at grid points in successive rows $\{u(x_i, t_j) : i = 1, 2, \ldots, n\}$, for $j = 2, 3, \ldots, m$, will be developed.
     The difference formulas used for $u_t(x, t)$ and $u_{xx}(x, t)$ are

$$(4) \qquad\qquad u_t(x, t) = \frac{u(x, t + k) - u(x, t)}{k} + O(k)$$

and

$$(5) \qquad u_{xx}(x, t) = \frac{u(x - h, t) - 2u(x, t) + u(x + h, t)}{h^2} + O(h^2).$$

The grid spacing is uniform in every row: $x_{i+1} = x_i + h$ (and $x_{i-1} = x_i - h$), and it is uniform in every column: $t_{j+1} = t_j + k$. Next, we drop the terms $O(k)$ and $O(h^2)$ and use the approximation $u_{i,j}$ for $u(x_i, t_j)$ in equations (4) and (5), which are in turn substituted into equation (1) to obtain

$$(6) \qquad\qquad \frac{u_{i,j+1} - u_{i,j}}{k} = c^2 \frac{u_{i-1,j} - 2u_{i,j} + u_{i+1,j}}{h^2},$$

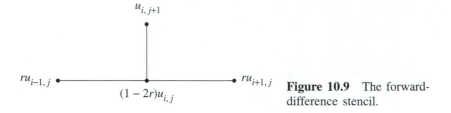

Figure 10.9   The forward-difference stencil.

which approximates the solution to (1). For convenience, the substitution $r = c^2 k / h^2$ is introduced in (6), and the result is the explicit forward-difference equation

$$(7) \qquad u_{i,j+1} = (1 - 2r)u_{i,j} + r(u_{i-1,j} + u_{i+1,j}).$$

Equation (7) is employed to create the $(j + 1)$th row across the grid, assuming that approximations in the jth row are known. Notice that this formula explicitly gives the value $u_{i,j+1}$ in terms of $u_{i-1,j}$, $u_{i,j}$, and $u_{i+1,j}$. The computational stencil representing the situation in formula (7) is given in Figure 10.9.

The simplicity of formula (7) makes it appealing to use. However, it is important to use numerical techniques that are stable. If any error made at one stage of the calculations is eventually dampened out, the method is called *stable*. The explicit forward-difference equation (7) is stable if and only if r is restricted to the interval $0 \le r \le \frac{1}{2}$. This means that the step size k must satisfy $k \le h^2/(2c^2)$. If this condition is not fulfilled, errors committed in one line $\{u_{i,j}\}$ might be magnified in subsequent lines $\{u_{i,p}\}$ for some $p > j$. The next example illustrates this point.

Example 10.3.   Use the forward-difference method to solve the heat equation

$$(8) \qquad u_t(x, t) = u_{xx}(x, t) \qquad \text{for } 0 < x < 1 \text{ and } 0 < t < 0.20,$$

with the initial condition

$$(9) \qquad u(x, 0) = f(x) = 4x - 4x^2 \qquad \text{for } t = 0 \text{ and } 0 \le x \le 1,$$

and the boundary conditions

$$(10) \qquad \begin{aligned} u(0, t) &= g_1(t) \equiv 0 \qquad \text{for } x = 0 \text{ and } 0 \le t \le 0.20, \\ u(1, t) &= g_2(t) \equiv 0 \qquad \text{for } x = 1 \text{ and } 0 \le t \le 0.20. \end{aligned}$$

For the first illustration, we use the step sizes $\Delta x = h = 0.2$ and $\Delta t = k = 0.02$ and $c = 1$, so the ratio is $r = 0.5$. The grid will be $n = 6$ columns wide by $m = 11$ rows high. In this case, formula (7) becomes

$$(11) \qquad u_{i,j+1} = \frac{u_{i-1,j} + u_{i+1,j}}{2}.$$

Table 10.3   Using the Forward-difference Method with $r = 0.5$

	$x_1 = 0.00$	$x_2 = 0.20$	$x_3 = 0.40$	$x_4 = 0.60$	$x_5 = 0.80$	$x_6 = 1.00$
$t_1 = 0.00$	0.000000	0.640000	0.960000	0.960000	0.640000	0.000000
$t_2 = 0.02$	0.000000	0.480000	0.800000	0.800000	0.480000	0.000000
$t_3 = 0.04$	0.000000	0.400000	0.640000	0.640000	0.400000	0.000000
$t_4 = 0.06$	0.000000	0.320000	0.520000	0.520000	0.320000	0.000000
$t_5 = 0.08$	0.000000	0.260000	0.420000	0.420000	0.260000	0.000000
$t_6 = 0.10$	0.000000	0.210000	0.340000	0.340000	0.210000	0.000000
$t_7 = 0.12$	0.000000	0.170000	0.275000	0.275000	0.170000	0.000000
$t_8 = 0.14$	0.000000	0.137500	0.222500	0.222500	0.137500	0.000000
$t_9 = 0.16$	0.000000	0.111250	0.180000	0.180000	0.111250	0.000000
$t_{10} = 0.18$	0.000000	0.090000	0.145625	0.145625	0.090000	0.000000
$t_{11} = 0.20$	0.000000	0.072812	0.117813	0.117813	0.072812	0.000000

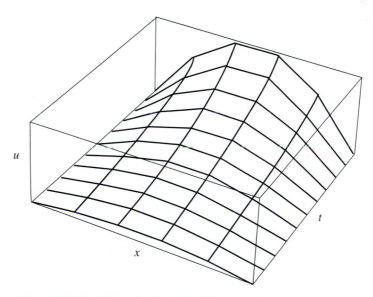

Figure 10.10   Using the forward-difference method with $r = 0.5$.

Formula (11) is stable for $r = 0.5$ and can be used successfully to generate reasonably accurate approximations to $u(x, t)$. Successive rows in the grid are given in Table 10.3. A three-dimensional presentation of the data in Table 10.3 is given in Figure 10.10.

For our second illustration, we use the step sizes $\Delta x = h = 0.2$ and $\Delta t = k = \frac{1}{30} \approx 0.033333$, so that the ratio is $r = 0.833333$. In this case, formula (7) becomes

(12) $$u_{i,j+1} = -0.666665 u_{i,j} + 0.833333(u_{i-1,j} + u_{i+1,j}).$$

Table 10.4 Using the Forward-difference Method with $r = 0.833333$

	$x_1 = 0.00$	$x_2 = 0.20$	$x_3 = 0.40$	$x_4 = 0.60$	$x_5 = 0.80$	$x_6 = 1.00$
$t_1 = 0.000000$	0.000000	0.640000	0.960000	0.960000	0.640000	0.000000
$t_2 = 0.033333$	0.000000	0.373333	0.693333	0.693333	0.373333	0.000000
$t_3 = 0.066667$	0.000000	0.328889	0.426667	0.426667	0.328889	0.000000
$t_4 = 0.100000$	0.000000	0.136296	0.345185	0.345185	0.136296	0.000000
$t_5 = 0.133333$	0.000000	0.196790	0.171111	0.171111	0.196790	0.000000
$t_6 = 0.166667$	0.000000	0.011399	0.192510	0.192510	0.011399	0.000000
$t_7 = 0.200000$	0.000000	0.152826	0.041584	0.041584	0.152826	0.000000
$t_8 = 0.233333$	0.000000	−0.067230	0.134286	0.134286	−0.067230	0.000000
$t_9 = 0.266667$	0.000000	0.156725	−0.033644	−0.033644	0.156725	0.000000
$t_{10} = 0.300000$	0.000000	−0.132520	0.124997	0.124997	−0.132520	0.000000
$t_{11} = 0.333333$	0.000000	0.192511	−0.089601	−0.089601	0.192511	0.000000

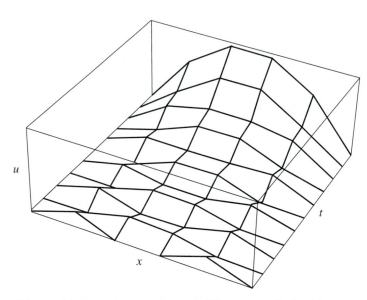

Figure 10.11 Using the forward-difference method with $r = 0.833333$.

Formula (12) is unstable in this case, because $r > \frac{1}{2}$, and errors committed at one row will be magnified in successive rows. Numerical values that turn out to be imprecise approximations to $u(x, t)$, for $0 \le t \le 0.33333$, are given in Table 10.4. A three-dimensional presentation of the data in Table 10.4 is given in Figure 10.11. ∎

The difference equation (7) has accuracy of the order $O(k) + O(h^2)$. Because the term $O(k)$ decreases linearly as k tends to zero, it is not surprising that it must be made small to produce good approximations. However, the stability requirement introduces further considerations. Suppose that the solutions over the grid are not sufficiently accurate and that both the increments $\Delta x = h_0$ and $\Delta t = k_0$ must be reduced. For simplicity, suppose that the new x increment is $\Delta x = h_1 = h_0/2$. If the same ratio r is used, k_1 must satisfy

$$k_1 = \frac{r(h_1)^2}{c^2} = \frac{r(h_0)^2}{4c^2} = \frac{k_0}{4}.$$

This results in a doubling and quadrupling of the number of grid points along the x-axis and t-axis, respectively. Consequently, there must be an eightfold increase in the total computational effort when reducing the grid size in this manner. This extra effort is usually prohibitive and demands that we explore a more efficient method that does not have stability restrictions. The method proposed will be implicit rather than explicit. The apparent rise in the level of complexity will have the immediate payoff of being unconditionally stable.

Crank-Nicholson Method

An implicit scheme, invented by John Crank and Phyllis Nicholson, is based on numerical approximations for solutions of equation (1) at the point $(x, t + k/2)$ that lies between the rows in the grid. Specifically, the approximation used for $u_t(x, t + k/2)$ is obtained from the central-difference formula,

$$(13) \qquad u_t\left(x, t + \frac{k}{2}\right) = \frac{u(x, t + k) - u(x, t)}{k} + O(k^2).$$

The approximation used for $u_{xx}(x, t + k/2)$ is the average of the approximations $u_{xx}(x, t)$ and $u_{xx}(x, t + k)$, which has an accuracy of the order $O(h^2)$:

$$(14) \qquad u_{xx}\left(x, t + \frac{k}{2}\right) = \frac{1}{2h^2}(u(x - h, t + k) - 2u(x, t + k) + u(x + h, t + k)$$
$$+ u(x - h, t) - 2u(x, t) + u(x + h, t)) + O(h^2).$$

In a fashion similar to the previous derivation, we substitute (13) and (14) into (1) and neglect the error terms $O(h^2)$ and $O(k^2)$. Then employing the notation $u_{i,j} = u(x_i, t_j)$ will produce the difference equation

$$(15) \qquad \frac{u_{i,j+1} - u_{i,j}}{k} = c^2 \frac{u_{i-1,j+1} - 2u_{i,j+1} + u_{i+1,j+1} + u_{i-1,j} - 2u_{i,j} + u_{i+1,j}}{2h^2}.$$

Also, the substitution $r = c^2 k/h^2$ is used in (15). But this time we must solve for the three "yet to be computed" values $u_{i-1,j+1}, u_{i,j+1}$, and $u_{i+1,j+1}$. This is accomplished by placing them all on the left side of the equation. Then rearrangement of the terms in equation (15) results in the implicit difference formula

$$(16) \qquad -ru_{i-1,j+1} + (2 + 2r)u_{i,j+1} - ru_{i+1,j+1}$$
$$= (2 - 2r)u_{i,j} + r(u_{i-1,j} + u_{i+1,j}).$$

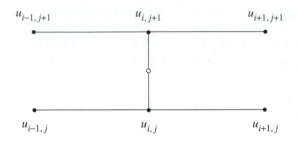

Figure 10.12 The Crank-Nicholson stencil.

for $i = 2, 3, \ldots, n - 1$. The terms on the right-hand side of equation (16) are all known. Hence the equations in (16) form a tridiagonal linear system $AX = B$. The six points used in the Crank-Nicholson formula (16), together with the intermediate grid point where the numerical approximations are based, are shown in Figure 10.12.

Implementation of formula (16) is sometimes done by using the ratio $r = 1$. In this case the increment along the t-axis is $\Delta t = k = h^2/c^2$, and the equations in (16) simplify and become

$$(17) \qquad -u_{i-1,j+1} + 4u_{i,j+1} - u_{i+1,j+1} = u_{i-1,j} + u_{i+1,j},$$

for $i = 2, 3, \ldots, n-1$. The boundary conditions are used in the first and last equations (i.e., $u_{1,j} = u_{1,j+1} = c_1$ and $u_{n,j} = u_{n,j+1} = c_2$, respectively). Equations (17) are especially pleasing to view in their tridiagonal matrix form $AX = B$.

$$\begin{bmatrix} 4 & -1 & & & & & \\ -1 & 4 & -1 & & & O & \\ & & \ddots & & & & \\ & & -1 & 4 & -1 & & \\ & & & & \ddots & & \\ O & & & -1 & 4 & -1 \\ & & & & -1 & 4 \end{bmatrix} \begin{bmatrix} u_{2,j+1} \\ u_{3,j+1} \\ \vdots \\ u_{p,j+1} \\ \vdots \\ u_{n-2,j+1} \\ u_{n-1,j+1} \end{bmatrix} = \begin{bmatrix} 2c_1 + u_{3,j} \\ u_{2,j} + u_{4,j} \\ \vdots \\ u_{p-1,j} + u_{p+1,j} \\ \vdots \\ u_{n-3,j} + u_{n-1,j} \\ u_{n-2,j} + 2c_2 \end{bmatrix}.$$

When the Crank-Nicholson method is implemented with a computer, the linear system $AX = B$ can be solved by either direct means or by iteration.

Example 10.4. Use the Crank-Nicholson method to solve the equation

$$(18) \qquad u_t(x, t) = u_{xx}(x, t) \qquad \text{for } 0 < x < 1 \text{ and } 0 < t < 0.1,$$

with the initial condition

$$(19) \qquad u(x, 0) = f(x) = \sin(\pi x) + \sin(3\pi x) \qquad \text{for } t = 0 \text{ and } 0 \le x \le 1,$$

Table 10.5   Values $u(x_i, t_i)$ Using the Crank-Nicholson Method with $t_j = (j-1)/100$

	$x_2 = 0.1$	$x_3 = 0.2$	$x_4 = 0.3$	$x_5 = 0.4$	$x_6 = 0.5$	$x_7 = 0.6$	$x_8 = 0.7$	$x_9 = 0.8$	$x_{10} = 0.9$
t_1	1.118034	1.538842	1.118034	0.363271	0.000000	0.363271	1.118034	1.538842	1.118034
t_2	0.616905	0.928778	0.862137	0.617659	0.490465	0.617659	0.862137	0.928778	0.616905
t_3	0.394184	0.647957	0.718601	0.680009	0.648834	0.680009	0.718601	0.647957	0.394184
t_4	0.288660	0.506682	0.625285	0.666493	0.673251	0.666493	0.625285	0.506682	0.288660
t_5	0.233112	0.425766	0.556006	0.625082	0.645788	0.625082	0.556006	0.425766	0.233112
t_6	0.199450	0.372035	0.499571	0.575402	0.600242	0.575402	0.499571	0.372035	0.199450
t_7	0.175881	0.331490	0.451058	0.525306	0.550354	0.525306	0.451058	0.331490	0.175881
t_8	0.157405	0.298131	0.408178	0.477784	0.501545	0.477784	0.408178	0.298131	0.157405
t_9	0.141858	0.269300	0.369759	0.433821	0.455802	0.433821	0.369759	0.269300	0.141858
t_{10}	0.128262	0.243749	0.335117	0.393597	0.413709	0.393597	0.335117	0.243749	0.128262
t_{11}	0.116144	0.220827	0.303787	0.356974	0.375286	0.356974	0.303787	0.220827	0.116144

and the boundary conditions

$$u(0, t) = g_1(t) \equiv 0 \quad \text{for } x = 0 \text{ and } 0 \le t \le 0.1,$$
$$u(1, t) = g_2(t) \equiv 0 \quad \text{for } x = 1 \text{ and } 0 \le t \le 0.1.$$

For simplicity, we use the step sizes $\Delta x = h = 0.1$ and $\Delta t = k = 0.01$ so that the ratio is $r = 1$. The grid will be $n = 11$ columns wide by $m = 11$ rows high. Applying the algorithm generates the values in Table 10.5 for $0 < x_i < 1$ and $0 \le t_j \le 0.1$.

The values obtained with the Crank-Nicholson method compare favorably with the analytic solution $u(x, t) = \sin(\pi x)e^{-\pi^2 t} + \sin(3\pi x)e^{-9\pi^2 t}$, the true values for the final row being

t_{11}	0.115285	0.219204	0.301570	0.354385	0.372569	0.354385	0.301570	0.219204	0.115285

A three-dimensional presentation of the data in Table 10.5 is given in Figure 10.13. ∎

Program 10.2 (Forward-Difference Method for the Heat Equation).   To approximate the solution of $u_t(x, t) = c^2 u_{xx}(x, t)$ over $R = \{(x, t) : 0 \le x \le a, 0 \le t \le b\}$ with $u(x, 0) = f(x)$, for $0 \le x \le a$, and $u(0, t) = c_1$, $u(a, t) = c_2$, for $0 \le t \le b$.

```
function U=forwdif(f,c1,c2,a,b,c,n,m)

%Input   - f=u(x,0) as a string 'f'
%         - c1=u(0,t) and c2=u(a,t)
%         - a and b right endpoints of [0,a] and [0,b]
%         - c the constant in the heat equation
%         - n and m number of grid points over [0,a] and [0,b]
%Output  - U solution matrix; analogous to Table 10.4
```

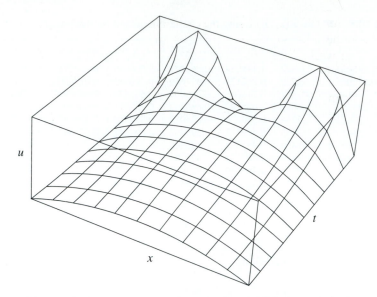

Figure 10.13 $u = u(x_i, t_j)$ from the Crank-Nicholson method.

```
%Initialize parameters and U
h=a/(n-1);
k=b/(m-1);
r=c^2*k/h^2;
s=1-2*r;
U=zeros(n,m);

%Boundary conditions
U(1,1:m)=c1;
U(n,1:m)=c2;

%Generate first row
U(2:n-1,1)=feval(f,h:h:(n-2)*h)';

%Generate remaining rows of U
for j=2:m
    for i=2:n-1
        U(i,j)=s*U(i,j-1)+r*(U(i-1,j-1)+U(i+1,j-1));
    end
end

U=U';
```

> **Program 10.3 (Crank-Nicholson Method for the Heat Equation).** To approximate the solution of $u_t(x, t) = c^2 u_{xx}(x, t)$ over $R = \{(x, t) : 0 \le x \le a, 0 \le t \le b\}$ with $u(x, 0) = f(x)$, for $0 \le x \le a$, and $u(0, t) = c_1$, $u(a, t) = c_2$, for $0 \le t \le b$.

```
function U=crnich(f,c1,c2,a,b,c,n,m)
%Input   - f=u(x,0) as a string 'f'
%         - c1=u(0,t) and c2=u(a,t)
%         - a and b right endpoints of [0,a] and [0,b]
%         - c the constant in the heat equation
%         - n and m number of grid points over [0,a] and [0,b]
%Output - U solution matrix; analogous to Table 10.5
%Initialize parameters and U
h=a/(n-1);
k=b/(m-1);
r=c^2*k/h^2;
s1=2+2/r;
s2=2/r-2;
U=zeros(n,m);

%Boundary conditions
U(1,1:m)=c1;
U(n,1:m)=c2;

%Generate first row
U(2:n-1,1)=feval(f,h:h:(n-2)*h)';

%Form the diagonal and off-diagonal elements of A and
%the constant vector B and solve tridiagonal system AX=B
Vd(1,1:n)=s1*ones(1,n);
Vd(1)=1;
Vd(n)=1;
Va=-ones(1,n-1);
Va(n-1)=0;
Vc=-ones(1,n-1);
Vc(1)=0;
Vb(1)=c1;
Vb(n)=c2;
for j=2:m
   for i=2:n-1
      Vb(i)=U(i-1,j-1)+U(i+1,j-1)+s2*U(i,j-1);
   end
   X=trisys(Va,Vd,Vc,Vb);
   U(1:n,j)=X';
end
U=U'
```

Exercises for Parabolic Equations

1. **(a)** Verify by direct substitution that $u(x, t) = \sin(n\pi x)e^{-4n^2\pi^2 t}$ is a solution to the heat equation $u_t(x, t) = 4u_{xx}(x, t)$ for each positive integer $n = 1, 2, \ldots$.

   (b) Verify by direct substitution that $u(x, t) = \sin(n\pi x)e^{-(cn\pi)^2 t}$ is a solution to the heat equation $u_t(x, t) = c^2 u_{xx}(x, t)$ for each positive integer $n = 1, 2, \ldots$.

2. What difficulty might occur if $\Delta t = k = h^2/c^2$ is used with formula (7)?

In Exercises 3 and 4, use the forward-difference method to calculate the first three rows of the approximate solution for the given heat equation. Carry out your calculations by hand (calculator).

3. $u_t(x, t) = u_{xx}(x, t)$, for $0 < x < 1$ and $0 \le t \le 0.1$, with the initial condition $u(x, 0) = f(x) = \sin(\pi x)$, for $t = 0$ and $0 \le x \le 1$, and the boundary conditions

$$u(0, t) = c_1 = 0 \quad \text{for } x = 0 \text{ and } 0 \le t \le 0.1,$$
$$u(1, t) = c_2 = 0 \quad \text{for } x = 1 \text{ and } 0 \le t \le 0.1.$$

   Let $h = 0.2$, $k = 0.02$, and $r = 0.5$.

4. $u_t(x, t) = u_{xx}(x, t)$, for $0 < x < 1$ and $0 \le t \le 0.1$, with the initial condition $u(x, 0) = f(x) = 1 - |2x - 1|$, for $t = 0$ and $0 \le x \le 1$, and the boundary conditions

$$u(0, t) = c_1 = 0 \quad \text{for } x = 0 \text{ and } 0 \le t \le 0.1,$$
$$u(1, t) = c_2 = 0 \quad \text{for } x = 1 \text{ and } 0 \le t \le 0.1.$$

5. Suppose that $\Delta t = k = h^2/(2c^2)$.
   (a) Use this in formula (16) and simplify.
   (b) Express the equations in part (a) in the matrix form $AX = B$.
   (c) Is the matrix in part (b) strictly diagonally dominant? Why?

6. Show that $u(x, t) = \sum_{j=1}^{N} a_j e^{-(j\pi)^2 t} \sin(j\pi x)$ is a solution to $u_t(x, t) = u_{xx}(x, t)$, for $0 \le x \le 1$ and $0 < t$, and has the boundary values $u(0, t) = 0$, $u(1, t) = 0$, and $u(x, 0) = \sum_{j=1}^{N} a_j \sin(j\pi x)$.

7. Consider the analytic solution $u(x, t) = \sin(\pi x)e^{-\pi^2 t} + \sin(3\pi x)e^{-(3\pi)^2 t}$ that was discussed in Example 10.4.
   (a) Hold x fixed and determine $\lim_{t \to \infty} u(x, t)$.
   (b) What does this mean physically?

8. Suppose that we wish to solve the parabolic equation $u_t(x, t) - u_{xx}(x, t) = h(x)$.
   (a) Derive the explicit forward-difference equation for this situation.
   (b) Derive the implicit difference formula for this situation.

9. Suppose that equation (11) is used and that $f(x) \ge 0$, $g_1(t) = 0$, and $g_2(t) = 0$.
   (a) Show that the maximum value of $u(x_i, t_{j+1})$ in row $j + 1$ is less than or equal to the maximum of $u(x_i, t_j)$ in row j.

(b) Make a conjecture concerning the maximum of $u(x_i, t_n)$ in row n as n tends to infinity.

Algorithms and Programs

In Problems 1 and 2, use Program 10.3 to solve the heat equation $u_t(x, t) = c^2 u_{xx}(x, t)$, for $0 < x < 1$ and $0 < t < 0.1$, with the initial condition $u(x, 0) = f(x)$, for $t = 0$ and $0 \le x \le 1$, and the boundary conditions

$$u(0, t) = c_1 = 0 \quad \text{for } x = 0 \text{ and } 0 \le t \le 0.1,$$
$$u(1, t) = c_2 = 0 \quad \text{for } x = 1 \text{ and } 0 \le t \le 0.1,$$

for the given values. Use the surf and contour commands to plot your approximate solutions.

1. Use $f(x) = \sin(\pi x) + \sin(2\pi x)$, $h = 0.1$, $k = 0.01$, and $r = 1$.

2. Use $f(x) = 3 - |3x - 1| - |3x - 2|$, $h = 0.1$, $k = 0.01$ and $r = 1$.

3. **(a)** Modify Programs 10.2 and 10.3 to accept the boundary conditions $u(0, t) = g_1(t) \ne 0$ and $u(a, t) = g_2(t) \ne 0$.

   (b) Use your modified Program 10.3 to solve the heat equations in Problems 1 and 2, but use the boundary conditions

   $$u(0, t) = g_1(t) = t^2 \quad \text{for } x = 0 \text{ and } 0 \le t < 0.1,$$
   $$u(1, t) = g_2(t) = e^t \quad \text{for } x = 1 \text{ and } 0 \le t \le 0.1,$$

   in place of $c_1 = c_2 = 0$.

   (c) Use the surf and contour commands to plot your approximate solutions.

4. Construct programs to implement your explicit forward-difference equations and implicit difference formula from parts (a) and (b) of Exercise 8, respectively.

5. Use your programs from Problem 4 to solve the heat equation $u_t(x, t) - u_{xx}(x, t) = \sin(x)$, for $0 < x < 1$ and $0 < t < 0.20$, with the initial condition $u(x, 0) = f(x) = \sin(\pi x) + \sin(3\pi x)$ and the boundary conditions

$$u(0, t) = c_2 = 0 \quad \text{for } x = 0 \text{ and } 0 \le t \le 0.20,$$
$$u(1, t) = c_2 = 0 \quad \text{for } x = 1 \text{ and } 0 \le t \le 0.20.$$

Let $h = 0.2$, $k = 0.02$, and $r = 0.5$.

10.3   Elliptic Equations

As examples of elliptic partial differential equations, we consider the Laplace, Poisson, and Helmholtz equations. Recall that the Laplacian of the function $u(x, y)$ is

$$(1) \qquad\qquad \nabla^2 u = u_{xx} + u_{yy}.$$

With this notation, we can write the Laplace, Poisson, and Helmholtz equations in the following forms:

$$(2) \qquad\qquad \nabla^2 u = 0 \qquad\qquad\qquad\qquad \text{Laplace's equation,}$$

$$(3) \qquad\qquad \nabla^2 u = g(x, y) \qquad\qquad\qquad \text{Poisson's equation,}$$

$$(4) \qquad\qquad \nabla^2 u + f(x, y)u = g(x, y) \qquad \text{Helmholtz's equation.}$$

It is often the case that the boundary values for the function u are known at all points on the sides of a rectangular region R in the plane. In this case, each of these equations can be solved by the numerical technique known as the finite-difference method.

Laplacian Difference Equation

The Laplacian operator must be expressed in a discrete form suitable for numerical computations. The formula for approximating $f''(x)$ is obtained from

$$(5) \qquad\qquad f''(x) = \frac{f(x + h) - 2f(x) + f(x - h)}{h^2} + O(h^2).$$

When this is applied to the function $u(x, y)$ to approximate $u_{xx}(x, y)$ and $u_{yy}(x, y)$ and the results are added, we obtain

$$(6) \quad \nabla^2 u = \frac{u(x + h, y) + u(x - h, y) + u(x, y + h) + u(x, y - h) - 4u(x, y)}{h^2} + O(h^2).$$

Assume that the rectangle $R = \{(x, y) : 0 \le x \le a, 0 \le y \le b, \text{ where } b/a = m/n\}$ is subdivided into $n - 1 \times m - 1$ squares with side h (i.e., $a = nh$ and $b = mh$), as shown in Figure 10.14.

To solve Laplace's equation, we impose the approximation

$$(7) \qquad \frac{u(x + h, y) + u(x - h, y) + u(x, y + h) + u(x, y - h) - 4u(x, y)}{h^2} = 0,$$

which has order of accuracy $O(h^2)$ at all interior grid points $(x, y) = (x_i, y_j)$ for $i = 2, \ldots, n - 1$ and $j = 2, \ldots, m - 1$. The grid points are uniformly spaced: $x_{i+1} = x_i + h$, $x_{i-1} = x_i - h$, $y_{j+1} = y_i + h$, and $y_{j-1} = y_i - h$. Using the approximation $u_{i,j}$ for $u(x_i, y_j)$, equation (7) can be written in the form

$$(8) \qquad\qquad \nabla^2 u_{i,j} \approx \frac{u_{i+1,j} + u_{i-1,j} + u_{i,j+1} + u_{i,j-1} - 4u_{i,j}}{h^2} = 0,$$

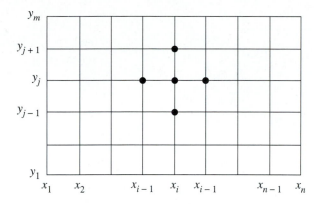

Figure 10.14 The grid used with Laplace's difference equation.

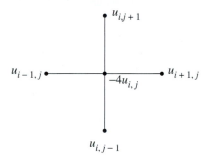

Figure 10.15 The Laplace stencil.

which is known as the *five-point difference formula* for Laplace's equation. This formula relates the function value $u_{i,j}$ to its four neighboring values $u_{i+1,j}$, $u_{i-1,j}$, $u_{i,j+1}$, and $u_{i,j-1}$, as shown in Figure 10.15. The term h^2 can be eliminated in (8) to obtain the Laplacian computational formula

$$(9) \qquad u_{i+1,j} + u_{i-1,j} + u_{i,j+1} + u_{i,j-1} - 4u_{i,j} = 0.$$

Setting Up the Linear System

Assume that the values $u(x, y)$ are known at the following boundary grid points:

$$u(x_1, y_j) = u_{1,j} \quad \text{for } 2 \le j \le m - 1 \quad \text{(on the left)},$$
$$u(x_i, y_1) = u_{i,1} \quad \text{for } 2 \le i \le n - 1 \quad \text{(on the bottom)},$$
$$u(x_n, y_j) = u_{n,j} \quad \text{for } 2 \le j \le m - 1 \quad \text{(on the right)},$$
$$u(x_i, y_m) = u_{i,m} \quad \text{for } 2 \le i \le n - 1 \quad \text{(on the top)}.$$

Then applying the Laplacian computational formula (9) at each of the interior points of R will create a linear system of $(n - 2)$ equations in $(n - 2)$ unknowns, which is

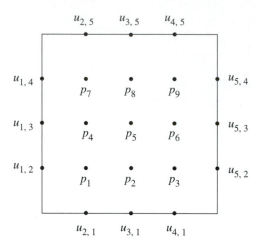

Figure 10.16   A 5×5 grid for boundary values only.

solved to obtain approximations to $u(x, y)$ at the interior points of R. For example, suppose that the region is a square, that $n = m = 5$, and that the unknown values of $u(x_i, y_j)$ at the nine interior grid points are labeled $p_1, p_2, \ldots, p_9$ and positioned in the grid as shown in Figure 10.16.

The Laplacian computational formula (9) is applied at each of the interior grid points, and the result is the system $AP = B$ of nine linear equations:

$$
\begin{array}{rcl}
-4p_1 + \; p_2 \qquad\quad + \; p_4 \qquad\qquad\qquad\qquad\qquad\qquad &=& -u_{2,1} - u_{1,2} \\
p_1 - 4p_2 + \; p_3 \qquad\quad + \; p_5 \qquad\qquad\qquad\qquad &=& -u_{3,1} \\
p_2 - 4p_3 \qquad\qquad\quad + \; p_6 \qquad\qquad\qquad &=& -u_{4,1} - u_{5,2} \\
p_1 \qquad\qquad\quad - 4p_4 + \; p_5 \qquad\quad + \; p_7 \qquad\qquad &=& -u_{1,3} \\
p_2 \qquad\quad + \; p_4 - 4p_5 + \; p_6 \qquad\quad + \; p_8 \qquad &=& 0 \\
p_3 \qquad\quad + \; p_5 - 4p_6 \qquad\qquad\quad + \; p_9 &=& -u_{5,3} \\
p_4 \qquad\qquad\qquad - 4p_7 + \; p_8 \qquad\quad &=& -u_{2,5} - u_{1,4} \\
p_5 \qquad\qquad\quad + \; p_7 - 4p_8 + \; p_9 &=& -u_{3,5} \\
p_6 \qquad\qquad\quad + \; p_8 - 4p_9 &=& -u_{4,5} - u_{5,4}.
\end{array}
$$

Example 10.5.   Find an approximate solution to Laplace's equation $\nabla^2 u = 0$ in the rectangle $R = \{(x, y) : 0 \le x \le 4, 0 \le y \le 4\}$, where $u(x, y)$ denotes the temperature at the point (x, y) and the boundary values are

$$u(x, 0) = 20 \quad \text{and} \quad u(x, 4) = 180 \quad \text{for} \quad 0 < x < 4,$$

and

$$u(0, y) = 80 \quad \text{and} \quad u(4, y) = 0 \quad \text{for} \quad 0 < y < 4.$$

See Figure 10.17 for the grid to be used.

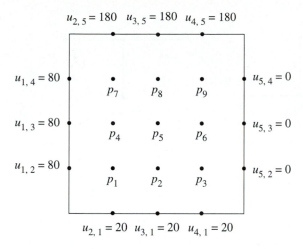

$u_{2,5} = 180$ $u_{3,5} = 180$ $u_{4,5} = 180$

$u_{1,4} = 80$ · · · $u_{5,4} = 0$
p_7 p_8 p_9

$u_{1,3} = 80$ · · · $u_{5,3} = 0$
p_4 p_5 p_6

$u_{1,2} = 80$ · · · $u_{5,2} = 0$
p_1 p_2 p_3

$u_{2,1} = 20$ $u_{3,1} = 20$ $u_{4,1} = 20$

Figure 10.17 The 5×5 grid in Example 10.5.

Applying formula (9) in this case, the linear system $AP = B$ is

$$
\begin{array}{rcl}
-4p_1 + p_2 + p_4 & = & -100 \\
p_1 - 4p_2 + p_3 + p_5 & = & -20 \\
p_2 - 4p_3 + p_6 & = & -20 \\
p_1 - 4p_4 + p_5 + p_7 & = & -80 \\
p_2 + p_4 - 4p_5 + p_6 + p_8 & = & 0 \\
p_3 + p_5 - 4p_6 + p_9 & = & 0 \\
p_4 - 4p_7 + p_8 & = & -260 \\
p_5 + p_7 - 4p_8 + p_9 & = & -180 \\
p_6 + p_8 - 4p_9 & = & -180
\end{array}
$$

The solution vector P can be obtained by Gaussian elimination (or more efficient schemes can be devised, such as the extension of the tridiagonal algorithm to pentadiagonal systems). The temperatures at the interior grid points are expressed in vector form

$$
\begin{aligned}
P &= \begin{bmatrix} p_1 & p_2 & p_3 & p_4 & p_5 & p_6 & p_7 & p_8 & p_9 \end{bmatrix}' \\
&= [55.7143 \quad 43.2143 \quad 27.1429 \quad 79.6429 \quad 70.0000 \\
&\qquad 45.3571 \quad 112.857 \quad 111.786 \quad 84.2857]'.
\end{aligned}
$$
∎

Derivative Boundary Conditions

The Neumann boundary conditions specify the directional derivative of $u(x, y)$ normal to an edge. For our illustration we will use the zero normal derivative condition,

(10)
$$
\frac{\partial}{\partial N} u(x, y) = 0.
$$

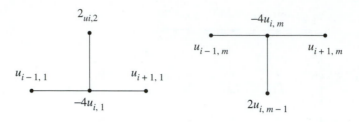

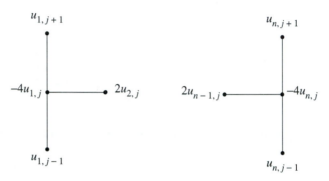

Figure 10.18 The Neumann stencils.

For applications in the area of heat flow, this means that the edge is thermally insulated and the heat flux throughout the edge is zero.

Suppose that $x = x_n$ is held fixed and that we are considering the right edge $x = a$ of the rectangle $R = \{(x, y) : 0 \le x \le a, 0 \le y \le b\}$. The normal boundary condition to be used along this edge is

$$(11) \qquad \frac{\partial}{\partial x} u(x_n, y_j) = u_x(x_n, y_j) = 0.$$

Then the Laplace difference equation for the point (x_n, y_j) is

$$(12) \qquad u_{n+1,j} + u_{n-1,j} + u_{n,j+1} + u_{n,j-1} - 4u_{n,j} = 0.$$

The value $u_{n+1,j}$ is unknown, because it lies outside the region R. However, we can use the numerical differentiation formula

$$(13) \qquad \frac{u_{n+1,j} - u_{n-1,j}}{2h} \approx u_x(x_n, y_j) = 0$$

and obtain the approximation $u_{n+1,j} \approx u_{n-1,j}$, which has order of accuracy $O(h^2)$. When this approximation is used in (12), the result is

$$2u_{n-1,j} + u_{n,j+1} + u_{n,j-1} - 4u_{n,j} = 0.$$

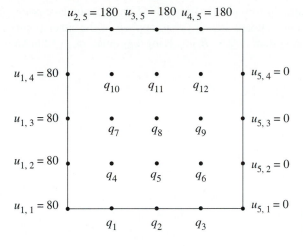

Figure 10.19   The 5×5 grid in Example 10.6.

This formula relates the function value $u_{n,j}$ to its three neighboring values $u_{n-1,j}$, $u_{n,j+1}$, and $u_{n,j-1}$.

The computational stencils for the other edges can be derived similarly (see Figure 10.18). The four cases for the Neumann computational stencils are summarized next:

$$(14) \qquad 2u_{i,2} + u_{i-1,1} + u_{i+1,1} - 4u_{i,1} = 0 \qquad \text{(bottom edge)},$$

$$(15) \qquad 2u_{i,m-1} + u_{i-1,m} + u_{i+1,m} - 4u_{i,m} = 0 \qquad \text{(top edge)},$$

$$(16) \qquad 2u_{2,j} + u_{1,j-1} + u_{1,j+1} - 4u_{1,j} = 0 \qquad \text{(left edge)},$$

$$(17) \qquad 2u_{n-1,j} + u_{n,j-1} + u_{n,j+1} - 4u_{n,j} = 0 \qquad \text{(right edge)}.$$

Suppose that the derivative condition $\partial u(x, y)/\partial N = 0$ is used along part of the boundary of R, and that known boundary values of $u(x, y)$ are used on the other portions of the boundary; then we have a mixed problem. The equations for determining approximations for $u(x_i, y_j)$ at boundary points will involve appropriate Neumann computational stencils (14) to (17). The Laplacian computational formula (9) is still used to determine approximations for $u(x_i, y_j)$ at the interior points of R.

Example 10.6.   Find an approximate solution to Laplace's equation $\nabla^2 u = 0$ in the rectangle $R = \{(x, y) : 0 \le x \le 4, 0 \le y \le 4\}$, where $u(x, y)$ denotes the temperature at the point (x, y) and the boundary values are shown in Figure 10.19:

$$
\begin{aligned}
u(x, 4) &= 180 && \text{for } 0 < x < 4, \\
u_y(x, 0) &= 0 && \text{for } 0 < x < 4, \\
u(0, y) &= 80 && \text{for } 0 \le y < 4, \\
u(4, y) &= 0 && \text{for } 0 \le y < 4.
\end{aligned}
$$

The Neumann computational formula (14) is applied at the boundary points q_1, q_2, and q_3, and the Laplace computational stencil (9) is applied at the other points q_4, q_5, ..., q_{12}. The result is a linear system $AQ = B$ involving 12 equations in 12 unknowns:

$$
\begin{array}{rcrcrcrcrcrcrcl}
-4q_1 + & q_2 & & + 2q_4 & & & & & & & & & & = & -80 \\
q_1 - & 4q_2 + & q_3 & & + 2q_5 & & & & & & & & & = & 0 \\
& q_2 - & 4q_3 & & & + 2q_6 & & & & & & & & = & 0 \\
q_1 & & & - 4q_4 + & q_5 & & + q_7 & & & & & & & = & -80 \\
& q_2 & & + q_4 - & 4q_5 + & q_6 & & + q_8 & & & & & & = & 0 \\
& & q_3 & & + q_5 - & 4q_6 & & & + q_9 & & & & & = & 0 \\
& & & q_4 & & & - 4q_7 + & q_8 & & + q_{10} & & & & = & -80 \\
& & & & q_5 & & + q_7 - & 4q_8 + & q_9 & & + q_{11} & & & = & 0 \\
& & & & & q_6 & & + q_8 - & 4q_9 & & & + q_{12} & = & 0 \\
& & & & & & q_7 & & & - 4q_{10} + & q_{11} & & & = & -260 \\
& & & & & & & q_8 & & + q_{10} - & 4q_{11} + & q_{12} & = & -180 \\
& & & & & & & & q_9 & & + q_{11} - & 4q_{12} & = & -180
\end{array}
$$

The solution vector Q can be obtained by Gaussian elimination (or more efficient schemes can be devised, such as the extension of the tridiagonal algorithm to pentadiagonal systems). The temperatures at the interior grid points and along the lower edge are expressed in vector form as

$$
\begin{aligned}
Q &= \begin{bmatrix} q_1 & q_2 & q_3 & q_4 & q_5 & q_6 & q_7 & q_8 & q_9 & q_{10} & q_{11} & q_{12} \end{bmatrix}' \\
&= [71.8218 \quad 56.8543 \quad 32.2342 \quad 75.2165 \quad 61.6806 \quad 36.0412 \\
&\qquad 87.3636 \quad 78.6103 \quad 50.2502 \quad 115.628 \quad 115.147 \quad 86.3492]'.
\end{aligned}
$$

$\blacksquare$

Iterative Methods

The preceding method showed how to solve Laplace's difference equation by constructing a certain system of linear equations and solving it. The shortcoming of this method is storage; each interior grid point introduces an equation to be solved. Since better approximations require a finer mesh grid, many equations might be needed. For example, the solution of Laplace's equation with the Dirichlet boundary conditions requires solving a system of $(n-2)(m-2)$ equations. If R is divided into a modest number of squares, say 10 by 10, there would be 91 equations involving 91 unknowns. Hence it is sensible to develop techniques that will reduce the amount of storage. An iterative method would require only the storage of the 100 numerical approximations $\{u_{i,j}\}$ throughout the grid.

Let us start with Laplace's difference equation

$$
(18) \qquad u_{i+1,j} + u_{i-1,j} + u_{i,j+1} + u_{i,j-1} - 4u_{i,j} = 0
$$

and suppose that the boundary values $u(x, y)$ are known at the following grid points:

(19)
$$
\begin{aligned}
u(x_1, y_j) &= u_{1,j} & \text{for } 2 \le j \le m-1 & \quad \text{(on the left)}, \\
u(x_i, y_1) &= u_{i,1} & \text{for } 2 \le i \le n-1 & \quad \text{(on the bottom)}, \\
u(x_n, y_j) &= u_{n,j} & \text{for } 2 \le j \le m-1 & \quad \text{(on the right)}, \\
u(x_i, y_m) &= u_{i,m} & \text{for } 2 \le i \le n-1 & \quad \text{(on the top)}.
\end{aligned}
$$

Equation (18) is rewritten in the following form that is suitable for iteration:

(20)
$$ u_{i,j} = u_{i,j} + r_{i,j}, $$

where

(21)
$$ r_{i,j} = \frac{u_{i+1,j} + u_{i-1,j} + u_{i,j+1} + u_{i,j-1} - 4u_{i,j}}{4} $$

for $2 \le i \le n-1$ and $2 \le j \le m-1$.

Starting values for all interior grid points must be supplied. The constant K, which is the average of the $2n + 2m - 4$ boundary values given in (19), can be used for this purpose. One iteration consists of sweeping formula (20) throughout all of the interior points of the grid. Successive iterations sweep the interior of the grid with the Laplace iterative operator (20) until the residual term $r_{i,j}$ on the right side of equation (20) is "reduced to zero" (i.e., $|r_{i,j}| < \epsilon$ holds for each $2 \le i \le n-1$ and $2 \le j \le m-1$). The speed of convergence for reducing all the residuals $\{r_{i,j}\}$ to zero is increased by using the method called *successive overrelaxation* (SOR). The SOR method uses the iteration formula

(22)
$$
\begin{aligned}
u_{i,j} &= u_{i,j} + \omega \left(\frac{u_{i+1,j} + u_{i-1,j} + u_{i,j+1} + u_{i,j-1} - 4u_{i,j}}{4} \right) \\
&= u_{i,j} + \omega r_{i,j},
\end{aligned}
$$

where the parameter ω lies in the range $1 \le \omega < 2$. In the SOR method, formula (22) is swept across the grid until $|r_{i,j}| < \epsilon$. The optimal choice for ω is based on the study of eigenvalues of iteration matrices for linear systems and is given in this case by the formula

(23)
$$ \omega = \frac{4}{2 + \sqrt{4 - \left(\cos\left(\dfrac{\pi}{n-1} \right) + \cos\left(\dfrac{\pi}{m-1} \right) \right)^2}}. $$

If the Neumann boundary condition is specified on some portion of the boundary, we must rewrite equations (14) through (17) in a form that is suitable for iteration. The four cases are summarized next and include the relaxation parameter ω:

$$(24) \quad u_{i,1} = u_{i,1} + \omega \left(\frac{2u_{i,2} + u_{i-1,1} + u_{i+1,1} - 4u_{i,1}}{4} \right) \qquad \text{(bottom edge)},$$

$$(25) \quad u_{i,m} = u_{i,m} + \omega \left(\frac{2u_{i,m-1} + u_{i-1,m} + u_{i+1,m} - 4u_{i,m}}{4} \right) \qquad \text{(top edge)},$$

$$(26) \quad u_{i,j} = u_{i,j} + \omega \left(\frac{2u_{2,j} + u_{1,j-1} + u_{1,j+1} - 4u_{1,j}}{4} \right) \qquad \text{(left edge)},$$

$$(27) \quad u_{n,j} = u_{n,j} + \omega \left(\frac{2u_{n-1,j} + u_{n,j-1} + u_{n,j+1} - 4u_{n,j}}{4} \right) \qquad \text{(right edge)}.$$

Example 10.7.   Use an iterative method to compute an approximate solution to Laplace's equation $\nabla^2 = 0$ in $R = \{(x, y) : 0 \le x \le 4, 0 \le y \le 4\}$, where the boundary values are

$$u(x, 0) = 20 \quad \text{and} \quad u(x, 4) = 180 \quad \text{for } 0 < x < 4,$$

and

$$u(0, y) = 80 \quad \text{and} \quad u(4, y) = 0 \quad \text{for } 0 < y < 4.$$

For illustration, the square is divided into 64 squares with sides $\Delta x = h = 0.5$ and $\Delta y = h = 0.5$. The initial value at the interior grid points was set at $u_{i,j} = 70$ for each $i = 2, \ldots, 8$ and $j = 2, \ldots, 8$. The SOR method was used with the parameter $\omega = 1.44646$ (substitute $n = 9$ and $m = 9$ in formula (23)). After 19 iterations, the residual was uniformly reduced (i.e., $|r_{i,j}| \le 0.000606 < 0.001$). The resulting approximations are given in Table 10.6. Because of the discontinuity of the boundary function at the corners, the boundary values $u_{1,1} = 50$, $u_{9,1} = 10$, $u_{1,9} = 130$, and $u_{9,9} = 90$ have been introduced in Table 10.6 and Figure 10.20; they were not used in the computations at the interior grid points. A three-dimensional presentation of the data in Table 10.6 is given in Figure 10.20.   ∎

Example 10.8.   Use an iterative method to compute an approximate solution to Laplace's equation $\nabla^2 u = 0$ in $R = \{(x, y) : 0 \le x \le 4, 0 \le y \le 4\}$, where the boundary values are

$$
\begin{aligned}
u(x, 4) &= 180 & \text{for} \quad y &= 4 & \text{and} \quad & 0 < x < 4, \\
u_y(x, 0) &= 0 & \text{for} \quad y &= 0 & \text{and} \quad & 0 < x < 4, \\
u(0, y) &= 80 & \text{for} \quad x &= 0 & \text{and} \quad & 0 \le y < 4, \\
u(4, y) &= 0 & \text{for} \quad x &= 4 & \text{and} \quad & 0 \le y < 4.
\end{aligned}
$$

For illustration, the square is divided into 64 squares with sides $\Delta x = h = 0.5$ and $\Delta y = h = 0.5$. Starting values using linear interpolation were used along the edge where $y = y_1 = 0$. The initial value at the interior grid points was set at $u_{i,j} = 70$ for each $i = 2, \ldots, 8$ and $j = 2, \ldots, 8$. Then the SOR method was employed with the parameter $\omega = 1.44646$ (as in Example 10.7). After 29 iterations, the residual was reduced uniformly; (i.e., $|r_{i,j}| \le 0.000998 < 0.001$). The resulting approximations are given in Table 10.7. Because of the discontinuity of the boundary functions at the corners, the boundary values

Table 10.6   Approximate Solution to Laplace's Equation with Dirichlet Conditions

	x_1	x_2	x_3	x_4	x_5	x_6	x_7	x_8	x_9
y_9	130.000	180.000	180.000	180.000	180.000	180.000	180.000	180.000	90.0000
y_8	80.000	124.821	141.172	145.414	144.005	137.478	122.642	88.6070	0.0000
y_7	80.000	102.112	113.453	116.479	113.126	103.266	84.4844	51.7856	0.0000
y_6	80.000	89.1736	94.0499	93.9210	88.7553	77.9737	60.2439	34.0510	0.0000
y_5	80.000	80.5319	79.6515	76.3999	70.0003	59.6301	44.4667	24.1744	0.0000
y_4	80.000	73.3023	67.6241	62.0267	55.2159	46.0796	33.8184	18.1798	0.0000
y_3	80.000	65.0528	55.5159	48.8671	42.7568	35.6543	26.5473	14.7266	0.0000
y_2	80.000	51.3931	40.5195	35.1691	31.2899	27.2335	21.9900	14.1791	0.0000
y_1	50.000	20.0000	20.0000	20.0000	20.0000	20.0000	20.0000	20.0000	10.0000

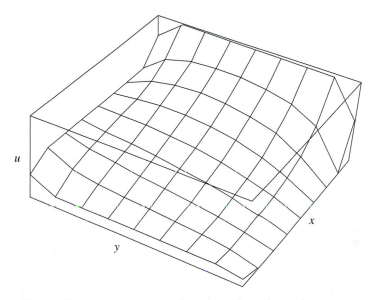

Figure 10.20 $u = u(x, y)$ with Dirichlet boundary values.

$u_{1,9} = 130$ and $u_{9,9} = 90$ have been introduced in Table 10.7 and Figure 10.21; they were not used in the computations at the interior grid points. A three-dimensional presentation of the data in Table 10.7 is given in Figure 10.21.   ■

Poisson's and Helmholtz's Equations

Consider Poisson's equation

$$(28) \qquad\qquad\qquad \nabla^2 u = g(x, y).$$

Table 10.7   Approximate Solution to Laplace's Equation with Mixed Boundary Conditions

	x_1	x_2	x_3	x_4	x_5	x_6	x_7	x_8	x_9
y_9	130.000	180.000	180.000	180.000	180.000	180.000	180.000	180.000	90.0000
y_8	80.000	126.457	142.311	146.837	145.468	138.762	123.583	89.1008	0.0000
y_7	80.000	103.518	115.951	119.568	116.270	105.999	86.4683	52.8201	0.0000
y_6	80.000	91.6621	98.4053	99.2137	94.0461	82.4936	63.4715	35.7113	0.0000
y_5	80.000	84.7247	86.7936	84.8347	78.2063	66.4578	49.2124	26.5538	0.0000
y_4	80.000	80.4424	79.2089	75.1245	67.4860	55.9185	40.3665	21.2915	0.0000
y_3	80.000	77.8354	74.4742	68.9677	60.6944	49.3635	35.0435	18.2459	0.0000
y_2	80.000	76.4244	71.8842	65.5772	56.9600	45.7972	32.1981	16.6485	0.0000
y_1	80.000	75.9774	71.0605	64.4964	55.7707	44.6670	31.3032	16.1500	0.0000

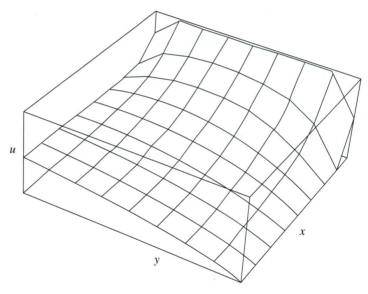

Figure 10.21 $u = u(x, y)$ for a mixed problem.

Using the notation $g_{i,j} = g(x_i, y_j)$, the generalization of formula (20) for solving (28) over the rectangular grid is

$$(29) \qquad u_{i,j} = u_{i,j} + \frac{u_{i+1,j} + u_{i-1,j} + u_{i,j+1} + u_{i,j-1} - 4u_{i,j} - h^2 g_{i,j}}{4}.$$

Consider Helmholtz's equation

$$(30) \qquad \nabla^2 u + f(x, y)u = g(x, y).$$

Using the notation $f_{i,j} = f(x_i, y_j)$, the generalization of formula (20) for solving (30) over the rectangular grid is

$$(31) \quad u_{i,j} = u_{i,j} + \frac{u_{i+1,j} + u_{i-1,j} + u_{i,j+1} + u_{i,j-1} - (4 - h^2 f_{i,j}) u_{i,j} - h^2 g_{i,j}}{4 - h^2 f_{i,j}}.$$

These formulas are explored in greater detail in the exercises.

Improvements

A modification of (8) that can be employed is the ***nine-point difference formula*** for Laplace's equation:

$$\nabla^2 u_{i,j} \approx \frac{1}{6h^2} (u_{i+1,j-1} + u_{i-1,j-1} + u_{i+1,j+1} + u_{i-1,j+1}$$
$$+ 4u_{i+1,j} + 4u_{i-1,j} + 4u_{i,j+1} + 4u_{i,j-1} - 20u_{i,j}) = 0.$$

The truncation errors for the nine- and five-point formulas (see formula (8)) are $O(h^4)$ and $O(h^2)$, respectively. Thus there is an advantage to using the nine-point difference formula.

Program 10.4 (Dirichlet Method for Laplace's Equation). To approximate the solution of $u_{xx}(x, y) + u_{yy}(x, y) = 0$ over $R = \{(x, y) : 0 \le x \le a, 0 \le y \le b\}$ with $u(x, 0) = f_1(x)$, $u(x, b) = f_2(x)$, for $0 \le x \le a$, and $u(0, y) = f_3(y)$, $u(a, y) = f_4(y)$, for $0 \le y \le b$. It is assumed that $\Delta x = \Delta y = h$ and that integers n and m exist so that $a = nh$ and $b = mh$.

```
function U=dirich(f1,f2,f3,f4,a,b,h,tol,max1)

%Input   - f1,f2,f3,f4 are boundary functions input as strings
%         - a and b right endpoints of [0,a] and [0,b]
%         - h step size
%         - tol is the tolerance
%Output - U solution matrix; analogous to Table 10.6

%Initialize parameters and U
n=fix(a/h)+1;
m=fix(b/h)+1;
ave=(a*(feval(f1,0)+feval(f2,0)) ...
   +b*(feval(f3,0)+feval(f4,0)))/(2*a+2*b);
U=ave*ones(n,m);

%Boundary conditions
U(1,1:m)=feval(f3,0:h:(m-1)*h)';
U(n,1:m)=feval(f4,0:h:(m-1)*h)';
U(1:n,1)=feval(f1,0:h:(n-1)*h);
U(1:n,m)=feval(f2,0:h:(n-1)*h);
```

```
U(1,1)=(U(1,2)+U(2,1))/2;
U(1,m)=(U(1,m-1)+U(2,m))/2;
U(n,1)=(U(n-1,1)+U(n,2))/2;
U(n,m)=(U(n-1,m)+U(n,m-1))/2;

%SOR parameter
w=4/(2+sqrt(4-(cos(pi/(n-1))+cos(pi/(m-1)))^2));

%Refine approximations and sweep operator throughout
%the grid
err=1;
cnt=0;
while((err>tol)&(cnt<=max1))
   err=0;
   for j=2:m-1
      for i=2:n-1
         relx=w*(U(i,j+1)+U(i,j-1)+U(i+1,j)+U(i-1,j)-4*U(i,j))/4;
         U(i,j)=U(i,j)+relx;
         if (err<=abs(relx))
         err=abs(relx);
         end
      end
   end
cnt=cnt+1;
end
U=flipud(U');
```

Exercises for Elliptic Equations

1. **(a)** Determine the system of four equations in the four unknowns p_1, p_2, p_3, and p_4 for computing approximations for the harmonic function $u(x, y)$ in the rectangle $R = \{(x, y) : 0 \leq x \leq 3, 0 \leq y \leq 3\}$ (see Figure 10.22). The boundary values are

$$u(x, 0) = 10 \quad \text{and} \quad u(x, 3) = 90 \quad \text{for} \quad 0 < x < 3,$$
$$u(0, y) = 70 \quad \text{and} \quad u(3, y) = 0 \quad \text{for} \quad 0 < y < 3.$$

   (b) Solve the equations in part (a) for p_1, p_2, p_3, and p_4.

2. **(a)** Determine the system of six equations in the six unknowns q_1, q_2, ..., q_6 for computing approximations for the harmonic function $u(x, y)$ in the rectangle $R = \{(x, y) : 0 \leq x \leq 3, 0 \leq y \leq 3\}$ (see Figure 10.23). The boundary values

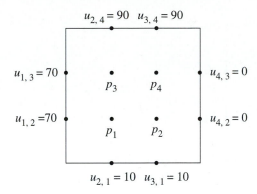

Figure 10.22
The grid for Exercise 1.

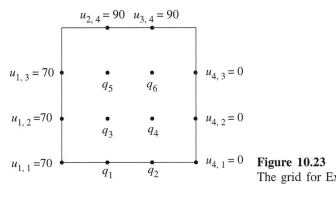

Figure 10.23
The grid for Exercise 2.

are

$$u(x, 3) = 90 \quad \text{and} \quad u_y(x, 0) = 90 \quad \text{for} \quad 0 < x < 3,$$
$$u(0, y) = 70 \quad \text{and} \quad u(3, y) = 0 \quad \text{for} \quad 0 \le y < 3.$$

(b) Solve the equations in part (a) for $q_1, q_2, \ldots, q_6$.

3. (a) Show that $u(x, y) = a_1 \sin(x) \sinh(y) + b_1 \sinh(x) \sin(y)$ is a solution of Laplace's equation.

(b) Show that $u(x, y) = a_n \sin(nx) \sinh(ny) + b_n \sinh(nx) \sin(ny)$ is a solution of Laplace's equation for each positive integer $n = 1, 2, \ldots$.

4. Let $u(x, y) = x^2 - y^2$. Determine the quantities $u(x+h, y)$, $u(x-h, y)$, $u(x, y+h)$, and $u(x, y-h)$, substitute them into equation (7), and simplify.

5. (a) Suppose that u has the form $u(x, y) = ax^2 + bxy + cy^2 + dx + ey + f$. Find a relationship among the coefficients which guarantees that $u_{xx} + u_{yy} = 0$.

(b) Suppose that u has the form given in part (a). Find a relationship among the coefficients which guarantees that $u_{xx} + u_{yy} = -1$.

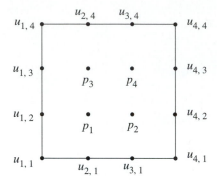

Figure 10.24
The grid for Exercise 7.

(c) Find the coefficients of the polynomial $u(x, y)$ given in part (a) that satisfy the partial differential equation in part (a) and also the boundary conditions $u(x, 0) = 0$ and $u(x, \beta) = 0$.

(d) Find the coefficients of the polynomial $u(x, y)$ given in part (a) that satisfy the partial differential equation in part (b) and also the boundary conditions $u(x, 0) = 0$ and $u(x, \beta) = 0$.

6. Solve $u_{xx} + u_{yy} = -4u$ over $R = \{(x, y) : 0 \le x \le 1, 0 \le y \le 1\}$ with the boundary values

$$u(x, y) = \cos(2x) + \sin(2y).$$

7. Determine the system of four equations in four unknowns p_1, p_2, p_2, and p_4 for implementing the Laplace nine-point difference equation on the 4×4 grid shown in Figure 10.24.

Algorithms and Programs

1. (a) Use Program 10.4 to compute approximations for the harmonic function $u(x, y)$ in the rectangle $R = \{(x, y) : 0 \le x \le 1.5, 0 \le y \le 1.5\}$; use $h = 0.5$. The boundary values are

$$u(x, 0) = x^4 \quad \text{and} \quad u(x, 1.5) = x^4 - 13.5x^2 + 5.0625 \quad \text{for } 0 \le x \le 1.5,$$
$$u(0, y) = y^4 \quad \text{and} \quad u(1.5, y) = y^4 - 13.5y^2 + 5.0625 \quad \text{for } 0 \le y \le 1.5.$$

(b) Use the surf command to plot your approximation from part (a) and compare it with the exact solution $u(x, y) = x^4 - 6x^2y^2 + y^4$.

2. Modify Program 9.11 (Tridiagonal Systems) to solve a pentadiagonal system.

3. **(a)** Use a 5×5 grid similar to that in Example 10.5 and determine the system of nine equations in the nine unknowns $p_1, p_2, p_3, \ldots, p_9$ for computing approximations for the harmonic function $u(x, y)$ in the rectangle $R = \{(x, y) : 0 \le x \le 4, 0 \le y \le 4\}$. The boundary values are

$$u(x, 0) = 10 \quad \text{and} \quad u(x, 4) = 120 \quad \text{for} \quad 0 < x < 4,$$
$$u(0, y) = 90 \quad \text{and} \quad u(4, y) = 40 \quad \text{for} \quad 0 < y < 4.$$

    (b) Use your modification of Program 9.11 to solve for $p_1, p_2, \ldots, p_9$.

    (c) Use Program 10.4 to solve for the approximations.

    (d) Use a 9×9 grid similar to that in Example 10.7 and Program 10.4 to solve for the approximations.

4. **(a)** Use a 5×5 grid similar to that in Example 10.6 and determine the system of 12 equations in the 12 unknowns $q_1, q_2, \ldots, q_{12}$ for computing approximations for the harmonic function $u(x, y)$ in the rectangle $R = \{(x, y) : 0 \le x \le 4, 0 \le y \le 4\}$. The boundary values are

$$u(x, 4) = 120 \quad \text{and} \quad u_y(x, y) = 0 \quad \text{for} \quad 0 < x < 4,$$
$$u(0, y) = 90 \quad \text{and} \quad u(4, y) = 40 \quad \text{for} \quad 0 \le y < 4.$$

    (b) Use your modification of Program 9.11 to solve for $q_1, q_2, \ldots, q_{12}$.

    (c) Modify Program 10.4 to solve for the approximations.

    (d) Use a 9×9 grid similar to that in Example 10.8 and a modification of Program 10.4 to solve for the approximations.

5. **(a)** Using a 5×5 grid, derive the nine equations involving the nine unknowns $p_1, p_2, p_3, \ldots, p_9$ for computing approximations for the solution $u(x, y)$ to Poisson's equation with $g(x, y) = 2$ in the rectangle $R = \{(x, y) : 0 \le x \le 1, 0 \le y \le 1\}$. The boundary values are

$$u(x, 0) = x^2 \quad \text{and} \quad u(x, 1) = (x - 1)^2 \quad \text{for} \quad 0 \le x \le 1,$$
$$u(0, y) = y^2 \quad \text{and} \quad u(1, y) = (y - 1)^2 \quad \text{for} \quad 0 \le y \le 1.$$

    (b) Use your modification of Program 9.11 to solve for $p_1, p_2, \ldots, p_9$.

    (c) Modify Program 10.4 to solve for the approximations.

    (d) Use a 9×9 grid and your modification of Program 10.4 to solve for the approximations.

6. **(a)** Using a 5×5 grid, derive the nine equations involving the nine unknowns $p_1, p_2, p_3, \ldots, p_9$ for computing approximations for the solution $u(x, y)$ to Poisson's equation with $g(x, y) = y$ in the rectangle $R = \{(x, y) : 0 \le x \le 1, 0 \le y \le 1\}$. The boundary values are

$$u(x, 0) = x^3 \quad \text{and} \quad u(x, 1) = x^3 \quad \text{for} \quad 0 \le x \le 1,$$
$$u(0, y) = 0 \quad \text{and} \quad u(1, y) = 1 \quad \text{for} \quad 0 \le y \le 1.$$

    (b) Use your modification of Program 9.11 to solve for $p_1, p_2, \ldots, p_9$.

    (c) Modify Program 10.4 to solve for the approximations.

    (d) Use a 9×9 grid and your modification of Program 10.4 to solve for the approximations.

11

Eigenvalues and Eigenvectors

The design of certain engineering systems involves the ***maximum stress theory of failure***. This theory is based on the assumption that the maximum principal stress acting on a body determines its failure. The related mathematical result is the principal axes theorem for a linear transformation $Y = AX$. In two dimensions there exists basis vectors U_1 and U_2 so that the effect of this transformation is to stretch space in the directions parallel to U_1 and U_2 by the amount λ_1 and λ_2, respectively. Consider the symmetric matrix

$$\begin{bmatrix} 3.8 & 0.6 \\ 0.6 & 2.2 \end{bmatrix};$$

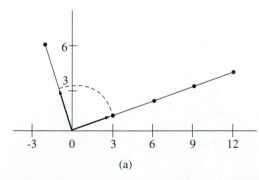

(a)

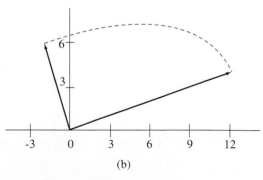

(b)

Figure 11.1 (a) Preimages $U_1 = \begin{bmatrix} 3 & 1 \end{bmatrix}'$ and $U_2 = \begin{bmatrix} -1 & 3 \end{bmatrix}'$ for the transformation $Y = AX$. (b) The image vectors $V_1 = AU_1 = \begin{bmatrix} 12 & 4 \end{bmatrix}'$ and $V_2 = AU_2 = \begin{bmatrix} -2 & 6 \end{bmatrix}'$.

the principal directions are $U_1 = \begin{bmatrix} 3 & 1 \end{bmatrix}'$ and $U_2 = \begin{bmatrix} -1 & 3 \end{bmatrix}'$, with corresponding eigenvalues $\lambda_1 = 4$ and $\lambda_2 = 2$, respectively. Images of these vectors are $V_1 = AU_1 = \begin{bmatrix} 12 & 4 \end{bmatrix}' = 4\begin{bmatrix} 3 & 1 \end{bmatrix}'$ and $V_2 = AU_2 = \begin{bmatrix} -2 & 6 \end{bmatrix}' = 2\begin{bmatrix} -1 & 3 \end{bmatrix}'$. This transformation stretches the quarter-circle shown in Figure 11.1(a) into the quarter ellipse shown in Figure 11.11(b).

11.1 Homogeneous Systems: Eigenvalue Problem

Background

We will now review some ideas from linear algebra. Proofs of the theorems are either left as exercises or can be found in any standard text on linear algebra.

In Chapter 3 we saw how to solve n linear equations in n unknowns. It was assumed that the determinant of the matrix was nonzero and hence that the solution was unique. In the case of a homogeneous system $AX = 0$, if $\det(A) \neq 0$, the unique solution is the trivial solution $X = 0$. If $\det(A) = 0$, there exist nontrivial solutions to $AX = 0$. Suppose that $\det(A) = 0$, and consider solutions to the homogeneous linear system

$$
\begin{aligned}
a_{11}x_1 + a_{12}x_2 + \cdots + a_{1n}x_n &= 0 \\
a_{21}x_1 + a_{22}x_2 + \cdots + a_{2n}x_n &= 0 \\
\vdots \qquad \vdots \qquad\qquad \vdots \qquad \vdots& \\
a_{n1}x_1 + a_{n2}x_2 + \cdots + a_{nn}x_n &= 0.
\end{aligned}
$$

(1)

The system of equations (1) always has the trivial solution $x_1 = 0, x_2 = 0, \ldots, x_n = 0$. Gaussian elimination can be used to obtain a solution by forming a set of relationships between the variables.

Example 11.1. Find the nontrivial solutions to the homogeneous system

$$
\begin{aligned}
x_1 + 2x_2 - x_3 &= 0 \\
2x_1 + x_2 + x_3 &= 0 \\
5x_1 + 4x_2 + x_3 &= 0.
\end{aligned}
$$

Use Gaussian elimination to eliminate x_1 and the result is

$$
\begin{aligned}
x_1 + 2x_2 - x_3 &= 0 \\
-3x_2 + 3x_3 &= 0 \\
-6x_2 + 6x_3 &= 0.
\end{aligned}
$$

Since the third equation is a multiple of the second equation, this system reduces to two equations in three unknowns:

$$x_1 + x_2 \qquad = 0$$
$$-x_2 + x_3 = 0.$$

We can select one unknown and use it as a parameter. For instance, let $x_3 = t$; then the second equation implies that $x_2 = t$ and the first equation is used to compute $x_1 = -t$. Therefore, the solution can be expressed as the set of relations:

$$\begin{matrix} x_1 = -t \\ x_2 = t \\ x_3 = t \end{matrix} \quad \text{or} \quad X = \begin{bmatrix} -t \\ t \\ t \end{bmatrix} = t \begin{bmatrix} -1 \\ 1 \\ 1 \end{bmatrix},$$

where t is any real number.   ■

Definition 11.1.   The vectors $U_1, U_2, \ldots, U_n$ are said to be *linearly independent* if the equation

$$(2) \qquad\qquad\qquad c_1 U_1 + c_2 U_2 + \cdots + c_n U_n = 0$$

implies that $c_1 = 0, c_2 = 0, \ldots, c_n = 0$. If the vectors are not linearly independent they are said to be linearly dependent. In other words, the vectors are *linearly dependent* if there exists a set of numbers $\{c_1, c_2, \ldots, c_n\}$ not all zero, such that equation (2) holds.   ▲

Two vectors in $\Re^2$ are linearly independent if and only if they are not parallel. Three vectors in $\Re^3$ are linearly independent if and only if they do not lie in the same plane.

Theorem 11.1.   The vectors $U_1, U_2, \ldots, U_n$ are linearly dependent if and only if at least one of them is a linear combination of the others.

A desirable feature for a vector space is the ability to express each vector as a linear combination of vectors chosen from a small subset of vectors. This motivates the next definition.

Definition 11.2.   Suppose that $S = \{U_1, U_2, \ldots, U_m\}$ is a set of m vectors in $\Re^n$. The set S is called a *basis* for $\Re^n$ if for every vector X in $\Re^n$ there exists a unique set of scalars $\{c_1, c_2, \ldots, c_m\}$ so that X can be expressed as the linear combination

$$(3) \qquad\qquad\qquad X = c_1 U_1 + c_2 U_2 + \cdots + c_m U_m.$$ ▲

Theorem 11.2.   In $\Re^n$, any set of n linearly independent vectors forms a basis of $\Re^n$. Each vector X in $\Re^n$ is uniquely expressed as a linear combination of the basis vectors, as shown in equation (3).

Theorem 11.3. Let $K_1, K_2, ldots, K_m$ be vectors in $\Re^n$.

(4)   If $m > n$, then the vectors are linearly dependent.

(5)   If $m = n$, the vectors are linearly dependent if and only if $\det(K) = 0$,
where $K = \begin{bmatrix} K_1 & K_2 & \cdots & K_m \end{bmatrix}$.

Eigenvalues

Applications of mathematics sometimes encounter the following equations: What are the singularities of $A - \lambda I$, where λ is a parameter? What is the behavior of the sequence of vectors $\{A^j X_0\}_{j=0}^{\infty}$? What are the geometric features of a linear transformation? Solutions for problems in many different disciplines, such as economics, engineering, and physics, can involve ideas related to these equations. The theory of eigenvalues and eigenvectors is powerful enough to help solve these otherwise intractable problems.

Let A be a square matrix of dimension $n \times n$ and let X be a vector of dimension n. The product $Y = AX$ can be viewed as a linear transformation from n-dimensional space into itself. We want to find scalars λ for which there exists a nonzero vector X such that

$$(6) \qquad\qquad\qquad AX = \lambda X;$$

that is, the linear transformation $T(X) = AX$ maps X onto the multiple λX. When this occurs, we call X an eigenvector that corresponds to the eigenvalue λ, and together they form the eigenpair λ, X for A. In general, the scalar λ and vector X can involve complex numbers. For simplicity, most of our illustrations will involve real calculations. However, the techniques are easily extended to the complex case. The identity matrix I can be used to express equation (6) as $AX = \lambda I X$, which is then rewritten in the standard form for a linear system as

$$(7) \qquad\qquad\qquad (A - \lambda I)X = \mathbf{0}.$$

The significance of equation (7) is that the product of the matrix $(A - \lambda I)$ and the nonzero vector X is the zero vector! According to Theorem 3.5, this linear system has nontrivial solutions if and only if the matrix $A - \lambda I$ is singular, that is,

$$(8) \qquad\qquad\qquad \det(A - \lambda I) = 0.$$

This determinant can be written in the form

$$(9) \qquad\qquad \begin{vmatrix} a_{11} - \lambda & a_{12} & \cdots & a_{1n} \\ a_{21} & a_{22} - \lambda & \cdots & a_{2n} \\ \vdots & \vdots & \cdots & \vdots \\ a_{n1} & a_{n2} & \cdots & a_{nn} - \lambda \end{vmatrix} = 0.$$

When the determinant in (9) is expanded, it becomes a polynomial of degree n, which is called the *characteristic polynomial*

(10)
$$p(\lambda) = \det(A - \lambda I)$$
$$= (-1)^n (\lambda^n + c_1 \lambda^{n-1} + c_2 \lambda^{n-2} + \cdots + c_{n-1} \lambda + c_n).$$

There exist exactly n roots (not necessarily distinct) of a polynomial of degree n. Each root λ can be substituted into equation (7) to obtain an underdetermined system of equations that has a corresponding nontrivial solution vector X. If λ is real, a real eigenvector X can be constructed. For emphasis, we state the following definitions.

Definition 11.3.   If A is an $n \times n$ real matrix, then its n **eigenvalues** $\lambda_1, \lambda_2, \ldots, \lambda_n$ are the real and complex roots of the characteristic polynomial

(11)
$$p(\lambda) = \det(A - \lambda I). \qquad \blacktriangle$$

Definition 11.4.   If λ is an eigenvalue of A and the nonzero vector V has the property that

(12)
$$AV = \lambda V,$$

then V is called an **eigenvector** of A corresponding to the eigenvalue λ. $\blacktriangle$

The characteristic polynomial (11) can be factored in the form

(13)
$$p(\lambda) = (-1)^n (\lambda - \lambda_1)^{m_1} (\lambda - \lambda_2)^{m_2} \cdots (\lambda - \lambda_k)^{m_k},$$

where m_j is called the *multiplicity* of the eigenvalue λ_j. The sum of the multiplicities of all eigenvalues is n; that is,

$$n = m_1 + m_2 + \cdots + m_k.$$

The next three results concern the existence of eigenvectors.

Theorem 11.4.   (a) For each distinct eigenvalue λ there exists at least one eigenvector V corresponding to λ.

(b) If λ has multiplicity r, then there exist at most r linearly independent eigenvectors $V_1, V_2, \ldots, V_r$ that correspond to λ.

Theorem 11.5.   Suppose that A is a square matrix and $\lambda_1, \lambda_2, \ldots, \lambda_k$ are distinct eigenvalues of A, with associated eigenvectors $V_1, V_2, \ldots, V_k$, respectively; then $\{V_1, V_2, \ldots, V_k\}$ is a set of linearly independent vectors.

Theorem 11.6.   If the eigenvalues of the $n \times n$ matrix A are all distinct, then there exist n linearly independent eigenvectors V_j, for $j = 1, 2, \ldots, n$.

Theorem 11.4 is usually applied for hand computations in the following manner. The eigenvalue λ of multiplicity $r \geq 1$ is substituted into the equation

$$(14) \qquad\qquad (A - \lambda I)V = 0.$$

Then Gaussian elimination can be performed to obtain the Gauss reduced form, which will involve $n - k$ equations in n unknowns, where $1 \leq k \leq r$. Hence there are k free variables to choose. The free variables can be selected in a judicious manner to produce k linearly independent solution vectors $V_1, V_2, \ldots, V_k$ that correspond to λ.

Example 11.2. Find the eigenpairs λ_j, V_j for the matrix

$$A = \begin{bmatrix} 3 & -1 & 0 \\ -1 & 2 & -1 \\ 0 & -1 & 3 \end{bmatrix}.$$

Also, show that the eigenvectors are linearly independent.

The characteristic equation $\det(A - \lambda I) = 0$ is

$$(15) \qquad \begin{vmatrix} 3 - \lambda & -1 & 0 \\ -1 & 2 - \lambda & -1 \\ 0 & -1 & 3 - \lambda \end{vmatrix} = -\lambda^3 + 8\lambda^2 - 19\lambda + 12 = 0,$$

which can be written as $-(\lambda - 1)(\lambda - 3)(\lambda - 4) = 0$. Therefore, the three eigenvalues are $\lambda_1 = 1$, $\lambda_2 = 3$, and $\lambda_3 = 4$.

Case (i): Substitute $\lambda_1 = 1$ into equation (14) and obtain

$$\begin{aligned} 2x_1 - x_2 \qquad\ &= 0 \\ -x_1 + x_2 - x_3 &= 0 \\ -x_2 + 2x_3 &= 0. \end{aligned}$$

Since the sum of the first equation plus two times the second equation plus the third equation is identically zero, the system can be reduced to two equations in three unknowns:

$$\begin{aligned} 2x_1 - x_2 \qquad\ &= 0 \\ -x_2 + 2x_3 &= 0. \end{aligned}$$

Choose $x_2 = 2a$, where a is an arbitrary constant; then the first and second equations are used to compute $x_1 = a$ and $x_3 = a$, respectively. Thus the first eigenpair is $\lambda_1 = 1$, $V_1 = \begin{bmatrix} a & 2a & a \end{bmatrix}' = a \begin{bmatrix} 1 & 2 & 1 \end{bmatrix}'$.

Case (ii): Substitute $\lambda_2 = 3$ into equation (14) and obtain

$$\begin{aligned} -x_2 \qquad\quad &= 0 \\ -x_1 - x_2 - x_3 &= 0 \\ -x_2 \qquad\quad &= 0. \end{aligned}$$

This is equivalent to the system of two equations

$$x_1 \qquad + x_3 = 0$$
$$\quad x_2 \qquad = 0.$$

Choose $x_1 = b$, where b is an arbitrary constant, and compute $x_3 = -b$. Hence the second eigenpair is $\lambda_2 = 3$, $V_2 = \begin{bmatrix} b & 0 & -b \end{bmatrix}' = b \begin{bmatrix} 1 & 0 & -1 \end{bmatrix}'$.

Case (iii): Substitute $\lambda_3 = 4$ into (14); the result is

$$-x_1 - \quad x_2 \qquad = 0$$
$$-x_1 - 2x_2 - x_3 = 0$$
$$-x_2 - x_3 = 0.$$

This is equivalent to the two equations

$$x_1 + x_2 \qquad = 0$$
$$x_2 + x_3 = 0.$$

Choose $x_3 = c$, where c is a constant, then use the second equation to compute $x_2 = -c$. Then use the first equation to get $x_1 = c$. Thus the third eigenpair is $\lambda_3 = 4$, $V_3 = \begin{bmatrix} c & -c & c \end{bmatrix}' = c \begin{bmatrix} 1 & -1 & 1 \end{bmatrix}'$.

To prove that the vectors are linearly independent, it suffices to apply Theorem 11.5. However, it is beneficial to review techniques from linear algebra and use Theorem 11.3. Form the determinant

$$\det(\begin{bmatrix} V_1 & V_2 & V_3 \end{bmatrix}) = \begin{vmatrix} a & b & c \\ 2a & 0 & -c \\ a & -b & c \end{vmatrix} = -6abc.$$

Since $\det(\begin{bmatrix} V_1 & V_2 & V_3 \end{bmatrix}) \neq 0$, Theorem 11.3 implies that the vectors V_1, V_2, and V_3 are linearly independent.   ∎

Example 11.2 shows how hand computations are used to find eigenvalues when the dimension n is small: (1) find the coefficients of the characteristic polynomial; (2) find its roots; (3) find the nonzero solutions of the homogeneous linear system $(A - \lambda I)V = 0$. We will take the prevalent approach of studying the power and Jacobi methods and the QR algorithm. The QR algorithm and its improvements are used in professional software packages such as EISPACK and MATLAB.

Since V in (12) is multiplied on the right side of the matrix A, it is called a ***right eigenvector*** corresponding to λ. There also exists a left eigenvector Y such that

$$(16) \qquad\qquad Y'A = \lambda Y'.$$

In general, the left eigenvector Y is not equal to the right eigenvector V. However, if A is real and symmetric $(A' = A)$, then

$$(17) \qquad\qquad \begin{aligned} (AV)' &= V'A' = V'A, \\ (\lambda V)' &= \lambda V' \end{aligned}$$

Therefore, the right eigenvector V is a left eigenvector when A is symmetric. In the remainder of the book we consider only right eigenvectors.

An eigenvector V is unique only up to a constant multiple. Suppose that c is a scalar; then the following calculation shows that cV is an eigenvector:

$$(18) \qquad A(cV) = c(AV) = c(\lambda V) = \lambda(cV).$$

To regain some semblance of uniqueness, we normalize the eigenvector in one of the following ways. Use one of the vector norms

$$(19) \qquad \|X\|_{\infty} = \max_{1 \le k \le n} \{|x_k|\}$$

or

$$(20) \qquad \|X\|_2 = \left(\sum_{k=1}^{n} |x_k|^2 \right)^{1/2}$$

and require that either $\|X\|_{\infty} = 1$ or $\|X\|_2 = 1$.

Diagonalizability

The eigenvalue situation is easiest to understand for a diagonal matrix D that has the form

$$(21) \qquad D = \operatorname{diag}(\lambda_1, \lambda_2, \ldots, \lambda_n) = \begin{bmatrix} \lambda_1 & 0 & \cdots & 0 \\ 0 & \lambda_2 & \cdots & 0 \\ \vdots & \vdots & \cdots & \vdots \\ 0 & 0 & \cdots & \lambda_n \end{bmatrix}.$$

Let $E_j = \begin{bmatrix} 0 & 0 & \cdots & 0 & 1 & 0 & \cdots & 0 \end{bmatrix}'$ be the standard base vector, where the jth component is 1 and all other components are 0. Then

$$(22) \qquad DE_j = \begin{bmatrix} 0 & 0 & \cdots & 0 & \lambda_j & 0 & \cdots & 0 \end{bmatrix}' = \lambda_j E_j,$$

which implies that the eigenpairs of D are λ_j, E_j for $j = 1, 2, \ldots, n$. It is desirable to invent a simple way of transforming the matrix A into diagonal form so that the eigenvalues are left invariant. This is the motivation for the following definition.

Definition 11.5. Two $n \times n$ matrices A and B are said to be *similar* if there exists a nonsingular matrix K so that

$$(23) \qquad B = K^{-1}AK. \qquad\qquad \blacktriangle$$

Theorem 11.7. Suppose that A and B are similar matrices and that λ is an eigenvalue of A with corresponding eigenvector V. Then λ is also an eigenvalue of B. If $K^{-1}AK = B$, then $Y = K^{-1}V$ is an eigenvector of B associated with the eigenvalue λ.

An $n \times n$ matrix A is called ***diagonalizable*** if it is similar to a diagonal matrix. The next theorem illuminates the intimate role of eigenvectors in this process.

Theorem 11.8 (Diagonalization).   The matrix A is similar to a diagonal matrix D if and only if it has n linearly independent eigenvectors. If A is similar to D, then

(24)
$$V^{-1}AV = D = \text{diag}(\lambda_1, \lambda_2, \ldots, \lambda_n)$$
$$V = \begin{bmatrix} V_1 & V_2 & \cdots & V_n \end{bmatrix},$$

where the n eigenpairs are λ_j, V_j, for $j = 1, 2, \ldots, n$.

Theorem 11.8 implies that every matrix A that has n distinct eigenvalues is diagonalizable.

Example 11.3.   Show that the following matrix is diagonalizable.

$$A = \begin{bmatrix} 3 & -1 & 0 \\ -1 & 2 & -1 \\ 0 & -1 & 3 \end{bmatrix}.$$

In Example 11.2 we found the eigenvalues $\lambda_1 = 1$, $\lambda_2 = 3$, and $\lambda_3 = 4$ and the matrix of eigenvectors

$$V = \begin{bmatrix} V_1 & V_2 & V_3 \end{bmatrix} = \begin{bmatrix} 1 & 1 & 1 \\ 2 & 0 & -1 \\ 1 & -1 & 1 \end{bmatrix}.$$

The inverse matrix V^{-1} is

$$V^{-1} = \begin{bmatrix} \frac{1}{6} & \frac{1}{3} & \frac{1}{6} \\ \frac{1}{2} & 0 & -\frac{1}{2} \\ \frac{1}{3} & -\frac{1}{3} & \frac{1}{3} \end{bmatrix}.$$

It is left to the reader to check the details in computing the product in (24):

$$\begin{bmatrix} \frac{1}{6} & \frac{1}{3} & \frac{1}{6} \\ \frac{1}{2} & 0 & -\frac{1}{2} \\ \frac{1}{3} & -\frac{1}{3} & \frac{1}{3} \end{bmatrix} \begin{bmatrix} 3 & -1 & 0 \\ -1 & 2 & -1 \\ 0 & -1 & 3 \end{bmatrix} \begin{bmatrix} 1 & 1 & 1 \\ 2 & 0 & -1 \\ 1 & -1 & 1 \end{bmatrix} = \begin{bmatrix} 1 & 0 & 0 \\ 0 & 3 & 0 \\ 0 & 0 & 4 \end{bmatrix}.$$

Hence we have shown that A can be diagonalized; that is, $V^{-1}AV = D = \text{diag}(1, 3, 4)$.
∎

A more general result relating the structure of a matrix to its eigenvalues is the following theorem.

Theorem 11.9 (Schur).   Suppose that A is an arbitrary $n \times n$ matrix. A nonsingular matrix P exists with the property that $T = P^{-1}AP$, where T is an upper-triangular matrix whose diagonal entries consist of the eigenvalues of A.

Certain types of structural analysis in engineering require that a basis of $\Re^n$ be selected that consists of the eigenvectors of A. This choice makes it easier to visualize how space is transformed by the mapping $Y = T(X) = AX$. Recall that the eigenpair λ_j, V_j has the property that T maps V_j onto the multiple of $\lambda_j V_j$. This characteristic is exploited in the following theorem.

Theorem 11.10.   Suppose that A is an $n \times n$ matrix that possesses n linearly independent eigenpairs λ_j, V_j for $j = 1, 2, \ldots, n$; then any vector X in $\Re^n$ has a unique representation as a linear combination of the eigenvectors:

(25)
$$X = c_1 V_1 + c_2 V_2 + \cdots + c_n V_n.$$

The linear transformation $T(X) = AX$ maps X onto the vector

(26)
$$Y = T(X) = c_1 \lambda_1 V_1 + c_2 \lambda_2 V_2 + \cdots + c_n \lambda_n V_n.$$

Example 11.4.   Suppose that the 3×3 matrix A has eigenvalues $\lambda_1 = 2$, $\lambda_2 = -1$, and $\lambda_3 = 4$, which correspond to the eigenvectors $V_1 = \begin{bmatrix} 1 & 2 & -2 \end{bmatrix}'$, $V_2 = \begin{bmatrix} -2 & 1 & 1 \end{bmatrix}'$, and $V_3 = \begin{bmatrix} 1 & 3 & -4 \end{bmatrix}'$, respectively. If $X = \begin{bmatrix} -1 & 2 & 1 \end{bmatrix}'$, find the image of X under the mapping $T(X) = AX$.

We must first express X as a linear combination of the eigenvectors. This is accomplished by solving the equation

$$\begin{bmatrix} -1 & 2 & 1 \end{bmatrix}' = c_1 \begin{bmatrix} 1 & 2 & -2 \end{bmatrix}' + c_2 \begin{bmatrix} -2 & 1 & 1 \end{bmatrix}' + c_3 \begin{bmatrix} 1 & 3 & -4 \end{bmatrix}'$$

for c_1, c_2, and c_3. Observe that this is equivalent to solving the linear system

$$
\begin{aligned}
c_1 - 2c_2 + c_3 &= -1 \\
2c_1 + c_2 + 3c_3 &= 2 \\
-2c_1 + c_2 - 4c_3 &= 1.
\end{aligned}
$$

The solution is $c_1 = 2$, $c_2 = 1$, and $c_3 = -1$. Using Definition 11.4, for eigenvectors, $T(X)$ is found by the computation

$$
\begin{aligned}
T(X) &= A(2V_1 + V_2 - V_3) \\
&= 2AV_1 + AV_2 - AV_3 \\
&= 2(2V_1) - V_2 - 4V_3 \\
&= \begin{bmatrix} 2 & -5 & 7 \end{bmatrix}'.
\end{aligned}
$$ ∎

Virtues of Symmetry

There is no easy way to determine how many linearly independent eigenvectors a matrix possesses without resorting to using the most effective algorithms in a professional software package such as EISPACK or MATLAB. However, it is known that a real symmetric matrix has n real eigenvectors and that for each eigenvalue of multiplicity m_j there corresponds m_j linearly independent eigenvectors. Hence every real symmetric matrix is diagonalizable.

Definition 11.6. A set of vectors $\{V_1, V_2, \ldots, V_n\}$ is said to be *orthogonal* provided that

$$(27) \qquad\qquad V_j' V_k = 0 \quad \text{whenever} \quad j \neq k. \qquad\qquad \blacktriangle$$

Definition 11.7. Suppose that $\{V_1, V_2, \ldots, V_n\}$ is a set of orthogonal vectors; then we say that they are *orthonormal* if they are all of unit norm, that is,

$$(28) \qquad \begin{aligned} V_j' V_k &= 0 \quad \text{whenever} \quad j \neq k. \\ V_j' V_j &= 1 \quad \text{for all} \quad j = 1, 2, \ldots, n. \end{aligned} \qquad \blacktriangle$$

Theorem 11.11. An orthonormal set of vectors is linearly independent.

Remark. The zero vector cannot belong to an orthonormal set of vectors.

Definition 11.8. An $n \times n$ matrix A is said to be an *orthogonal matrix* provided that A' is the inverse of A; that is,

$$(29) \qquad\qquad A'A = I,$$

which is equivalent to

$$(30) \qquad\qquad A^{-1} = A'.$$

Also, A is orthogonal if and only if the columns (and rows) of A form a set of orthonormal vectors. $\qquad\qquad \blacktriangle$

Theorem 11.12. If A is a real symmetric matrix, there exists an orthogonal matrix K such that

$$(31) \qquad\qquad K'AK = K^{-1}AK = D,$$

where D is a diagonal matrix consisting of the eigenvalues of A.

Corollary 11.1. If A is an $n \times n$ real symmetric matrix, there exist n linearly independent eigenvectors for A, and they form an orthogonal set.

Corollary 11.2. The eigenvalues of a real symmetric matrix are all real numbers.

Theorem 11.13. Eigenvectors corresponding to distinct eigenvalues of a symmetric matrix are orthogonal.

Theorem 11.14. A symmetric matrix A is positive definite if and only if all the eigenvalues of A are positive.

Estimates for the Size of Eigenvalues

It is useful to find a bound for the magnitude of the eigenvalues of A. The following results will give some insights.

Definition 11.9.   Let $\|X\|$ be a vector norm. Then a corresponding natural *matrix norm* is

$$(32) \qquad \|A\| = \max_{\|X\|=1} \left\{ \frac{\|AX\|}{\|X\|} \right\}.$$

For the norm $\|A\|_\infty$ the following formula holds:

$$(33) \qquad \|A\|_\infty = \max_{1 \le i \le n} \left\{ \sum_{j=1}^{n} |a_{ij}| \right\}. \qquad\qquad \blacktriangle$$

Theorem 11.15.   If λ is any eigenvalue of A, then

$$(34) \qquad |\lambda| \le \|A\|,$$

for any natural matrix norm $\|A\|$.

Theorem 11.16 (Gerschgorin's Circle Theorem).   Assume that A is an $n \times n$ matrix, and let C_j denote the disk in the complex plane with center a_{jj} and radius

$$(35) \qquad r_j = \sum_{k=1, k \ne j}^{n} |a_{jk}| \quad \text{for each } j = 1, 2, \ldots, n;$$

that is, C_j consists of all complex numbers $z = x + iy$ such that

$$(36) \qquad C_j = \{z : |z - a_{jj}| \le r_j\}.$$

If $S = \bigcup_{i=1}^{n} C_i$, then all the eigenvalues of A lie in the set S. Moreover, the union of any k of these disks that do not intersect the remaining $n - k$ must contain precisely k (counting multiplicities) of the eigenvalues.

Theorem 11.17 (Spectral Radius Theorem).   Let A be a symmetric matrix. The spectral radius of A is $\|A\|_2$ and obeys the relationship

$$(37) \qquad \|A\|_2 = \max\{|\lambda_1|, |\lambda_2|, \ldots, |\lambda_n|\}.$$

Overview of Methods

For problems involving moderate-sized symmetric matrices, it is safe to use Jacobi's method. For problems involving large symmetric matrices (for n up to several hundred), it is best to use Householder's method to produce a tridiagonal form, followed by the QR algorithm. Unlike real symmetric matrices, real unsymmetric matrices can have complex eigenvalues and eigenvectors.

For matrices that possess a dominant eigenvalue, the power method can be used to find the dominant eigenvector. Deflation techniques can be used thereafter to find the first few subdominant eigenvectors. For real unsymmetric matrices, Householder's method is used to produce a Hessenberg matrix, followed by the LR or QR algorithm.

Exercises for Homogeneous Systems: Eigenvalue Problem

1. For each of the following matrices, find (i) the characteristic polynomial $p(\lambda)$, (ii) the eigenvalues, and (iii) an eigenvector for each eigenvalue.

   (a) $A = \begin{bmatrix} 1 & 2 \\ 3 & 2 \end{bmatrix}$
   (b) $A = \begin{bmatrix} 1 & 6 \\ 9 & 2 \end{bmatrix}$
   (c) $A = \begin{bmatrix} -2 & 3 \\ 3 & -2 \end{bmatrix}$

   (d) $A = \begin{bmatrix} 1 & 2 & 1 \\ 0 & 1 & 2 \\ -1 & 3 & 2 \end{bmatrix}$
   (e) $A = \begin{bmatrix} 1 & 1 & 1 & 1 \\ 0 & 2 & 2 & 3 \\ 0 & 0 & 3 & 2 \\ 0 & 0 & 0 & 4 \end{bmatrix}$

2. Determine the spectral radius of each of the matrices in Exercise 1.

3. Determine the $\|A\|_2$ and $\|A\|_\infty$ norms of each of the matrices in Exercise 1.

4. Determine which, if any, of the matrices in Exercise 1 are diagonalizable. For each diagonalizable matrix in Exercise 1, find the matrices V and D from Theorem 11.8 and carry out the matrix product in (24).

5. (a)   For any fixed θ, show that

$$R = \begin{bmatrix} \cos\theta & -\sin\theta \\ \sin\theta & \cos\theta \end{bmatrix}$$

   is an orthogonal matrix.

   Remark. The matrix R is called a *rotation matrix*.

   (b)   Determine all values of θ for which all the eigenvalues of R are real.

6. In Section 3.2 the plane rotations $R_x(\alpha)$, $R_y(\beta)$, and $R_z(\gamma)$ were introduced.

   (a)   For any fixed α, β, and γ, show that $R_x(\alpha)$, $R_y(\beta)$, and $R_z(\gamma)$, respectively, are orthogonal matrices.

   (b)   Determine all values of α, β, and γ for which all the eigenvalues of $R_x(\alpha)$, $R_y(\beta)$, and $R_z(\gamma)$, respectively, are real.

7. Let $A = \begin{bmatrix} a+3 & 2 \\ 2 & a \end{bmatrix}$.

   (a) Show that the characteristic polynomial is $p(\lambda) = \lambda^2 - (3+2a)\lambda + a^2 + 3a - 4$.
   (b) Show that the eigenvalues of A are $\lambda_1 = a+4$ and $\lambda_2 = a-1$.
   (c) Show that the eigenvectors of A are $V_1 = \begin{bmatrix} 2 & 1 \end{bmatrix}'$ and $V_2 = \begin{bmatrix} -1 & 2 \end{bmatrix}'$.

8. Assume that λ, V form an eigenpair of the matrix A. If k is a positive integer, prove that λ^k, V are an eigenpair of the matrix A^k.

9. Suppose that V is an eigenvector of A that corresponds to the eigenvalue $\lambda = 3$. Prove that $\lambda = 9$ is an eigenvalue of the matrix A^2 corresponding to V.

10. Suppose that V is an eigenvector of A that corresponds to the eigenvalue $\lambda = 2$. Prove that $\lambda = \frac{1}{2}$ is an eigenvalue of the matrix A^{-1} corresponding to V.

11. Suppose that V is an eigenvector of A that corresponds to the eigenvalue $\lambda = 5$. Prove that $\lambda = 4$ is an eigenvalue of the matrix $A - I$ corresponding to V.

12. Let A be an $n \times n$ square matrix with characteristic polynomial $p(\lambda)$ given by

$$p(\lambda) = \det(A - \lambda I)$$
$$= (-1)^n (\lambda^n + c_1 \lambda^{n-1} + c_2 \lambda^{n-2} + \cdots + c_{n-1}\lambda + c_n).$$

   (a) Show that the constant term of $p(\lambda)$ is $c_n = (-1)^n \det(A)$.
   (b) Show that the coefficient of λ^{n-1} is $c_1 = -(a_{11} + a_{22} + \cdots + a_{nn})$.

13. Assume that A is similar to a diagonal matrix; that is,

$$V^{-1}AV = D = \operatorname{diag}(\lambda_1, \lambda_2, \ldots, \lambda_n).$$

   If k is a positive integer, prove that

$$A^k = V \operatorname{diag}(\lambda_1^k, \lambda_2^k, \ldots, \lambda_n^k)V^{-1}.$$

11.2 Power Method

We now describe the power method for computing the dominant eigenpair. Its extension to the inverse power method is practical for finding any eigenvalue provided that a good initial approximation is known. Some schemes for finding eigenvalues use other methods that converge fast, but have limited precision. The inverse power method is then invoked to refine the numerical values and gain full precision. To discuss the situation, we will need the following definitions.

Definition 11.10. If λ_1 is an eigenvalue of A that is larger in absolute value than any other eigenvalue, it is called the ***dominant eigenvalue***. An eigenvector V_1 corresponding to λ_1 is called a ***dominant eigenvector***. ▲

Definition 11.11.   An eigenvector V is said to be *normalized* if the coordinate of largest magnitude is equal to unity (i.e., the largest coordinate in the vector V is the number 1).   ▲

It is easy to normalize an eigenvector $\begin{bmatrix} v_1 & v_2 & \cdots & v_n \end{bmatrix}'$ by forming a new vector $V = (1/c)\begin{bmatrix} v_1 & v_2 & \cdots & v_n \end{bmatrix}'$, where $c = v_j$ and $|v_j| = \max_{1 \le i \le n}\{|v_i|\}$.

Suppose that the matrix A has a dominant eigenvalue λ and that there is a unique normalized eigenvector V that corresponds to λ. This eigenpair λ, V can be found by the following iterative procedure called the *power method*. Start with the vector

$$(1) \qquad\qquad X_0 = \begin{bmatrix} 1 & 1 & \cdots & 1 \end{bmatrix}'.$$

Generate the sequence $\{X_k\}$ recursively, using

$$
(2) \qquad\qquad
\begin{aligned}
Y_k &= AX_k, \\
X_{k+1} &= \frac{1}{c_{k+1}}Y_k,
\end{aligned}
$$

where c_{k+1} is the coordinate of Y_k of largest magnitude (in the case of a tie, choose the coordinate that comes first). The sequences $\{X_k\}$ and $\{c_k\}$ will converge to V and λ, respectively:

$$(3) \qquad\qquad \lim_{k \to \infty} X_k = V \quad \text{and} \quad \lim_{k \to \infty} c_k = \lambda.$$

Remark. If X_0 is an eigenvector and $X_0 \ne V$, then some other starting vector must be chosen.

Example 11.5.   Use the power method to find the dominant eigenvalue and eigenvector for the matrix

$$A = \begin{bmatrix} 0 & 11 & -5 \\ -2 & 17 & -7 \\ -4 & 26 & -10 \end{bmatrix}.$$

Start with $X_0 = \begin{bmatrix} 1 & 1 & 1 \end{bmatrix}'$ and use the formulas in (2) to generate the sequence of vectors $\{X_k\}$ and constants $\{c_k\}$. The first iteration produces

$$\begin{bmatrix} 0 & 11 & -5 \\ -2 & 17 & -7 \\ -4 & 26 & -10 \end{bmatrix}\begin{bmatrix} 1 \\ 1 \\ 1 \end{bmatrix} = \begin{bmatrix} 6 \\ 8 \\ 12 \end{bmatrix} = 12\begin{bmatrix} \frac{1}{2} \\ \frac{2}{3} \\ 1 \end{bmatrix} = c_1 X_1.$$

The second iteration produces

$$\begin{bmatrix} 0 & 11 & -5 \\ -2 & 17 & -7 \\ -4 & 26 & -10 \end{bmatrix}\begin{bmatrix} \frac{1}{2} \\ \frac{2}{3} \\ 1 \end{bmatrix} = \begin{bmatrix} \frac{7}{3} \\ \frac{10}{3} \\ \frac{16}{3} \end{bmatrix} = \frac{16}{3}\begin{bmatrix} \frac{7}{16} \\ \frac{5}{8} \\ 1 \end{bmatrix} = c_2 X_2.$$

Table 11.1   Power Method Used in Example 11.5 to Find the Normalized Dominant Eigenvector $V = \begin{bmatrix} \frac{2}{5} & \frac{3}{5} & 1 \end{bmatrix}'$ and Corresponding Eigenvalue $\lambda = 4$

$AX_k =$			Y_k		$=$	$c_{k+1}X_{k+1}$			
$AX_0 = [6.000000$	8.000000	$12.00000]'$	$=$	$12.00000[0.500000$	0.666667	$1]'$	$= c_1 X_1$
$AX_1 = [2.333333$	3.333333	$5.333333]'$	$=$	$5.333333[0.437500$	0.625000	$1]'$	$= c_2 X_2$
$AX_2 = [1.875000$	2.750000	$4.500000]'$	$=$	$4.500000[0.416667$	0.611111	$1]'$	$= c_3 X_3$
$AX_3 = [1.722222$	2.555556	$4.222222]'$	$=$	$4.222222[0.407895$	0.605263	$1]'$	$= c_4 X_4$
$AX_4 = [1.657895$	2.473684	$4.105263]'$	$=$	$4.105263[0.403846$	0.602564	$1]'$	$= c_5 X_5$
$AX_5 = [1.628205$	2.435897	$4.051282]'$	$=$	$4.051282[0.401899$	0.601266	$1]'$	$= c_6 X_6$
$AX_6 = [1.613924$	2.417722	$4.025316]'$	$=$	$4.025316[0.400943$	0.600629	$1]'$	$= c_7 X_7$
$AX_7 = [1.606918$	2.408805	$4.012579]'$	$=$	$4.012579[0.400470$	0.600313	$1]'$	$= c_8 X_8$
$AX_8 = [1.603448$	2.404389	$4.006270]'$	$=$	$4.006270[0.400235$	0.600156	$1]'$	$= c_9 X_9$
$AX_9 = [1.601721$	2.402191	$4.003130]'$	$=$	$4.003130[0.400117$	0.600078	$1]'$	$= c_{10} X_{10}$
$AX_{10} = [1.600860$	2.401095	$4.001564]'$	$=$	$4.001564[0.400059$	0.600039	$1]'$	$= c_{11} X_{11}$

Iteration generates the sequence $\{X_k\}$ (where X_k is a normalized vector):

$$12\begin{bmatrix} \frac{1}{2} \\ \frac{2}{3} \\ 1 \end{bmatrix}, \quad 16\begin{bmatrix} \frac{7}{16} \\ \frac{5}{8} \\ 1 \end{bmatrix}, \quad 9\begin{bmatrix} \frac{5}{12} \\ \frac{11}{18} \\ 1 \end{bmatrix}, \quad 38\begin{bmatrix} \frac{31}{76} \\ \frac{23}{38} \\ 1 \end{bmatrix}, \quad 78\begin{bmatrix} \frac{21}{52} \\ \frac{47}{78} \\ 1 \end{bmatrix}, \quad 158\begin{bmatrix} \frac{127}{316} \\ \frac{95}{158} \\ 1 \end{bmatrix}, \quad \cdots$$

The sequence of vectors converges to $V = \begin{bmatrix} \frac{2}{5} & \frac{3}{5} & 1 \end{bmatrix}'$, and the sequence of constants converges to $\lambda = 4$ (see Table 11.1). It can be proved that the rate of convergence is linear. ∎

Theorem 11.18 (Power Method).   Assume that the $n \times n$ matrix A has n distinct eigenvalues $\lambda_1, \lambda_2, \ldots, \lambda_n$ and that they are ordered in decreasing magnitude; that is,

$$(4) \qquad |\lambda_1| > |\lambda_2| \geq |\lambda_3| \geq \cdots \geq |\lambda_n|.$$

If X_0 is chosen appropriately, then the sequences $\{X_k = \begin{bmatrix} x_1^{(k)} & x_2^{(k)} & \ldots & x_n^{(k)} \end{bmatrix}'\}$ and $\{c_k\}$ generated recursively by

$$(5) \qquad Y_k = AX_k$$

and

$$(6) \qquad X_{k+1} = \frac{1}{c_{k+1}}Y_k,$$

where

$$(7) \qquad c_{k+1} = x_j^{(k)} \quad \text{and} \quad x_j^{(k)} = \max_{1 \leq i \leq n}\{|x_i^{(k)}|\},$$

will converge to the dominant eigenvector V_1 and eigenvalue λ_1, respectively. That is,

$$(8) \qquad \lim_{k \to \infty} X_k = V_1 \quad \text{and} \quad \lim_{k \to \infty} c_k = \lambda_1.$$

Proof. Since A has n eigenvalues, there are n corresponding eigenvectors V_j, for $j = 1, 2, \ldots, n$, that are linearly independent, normalized, and form a basis for n-dimensional space. Hence the starting vector X_0 can be expressed as the linear combination

$$(9) \qquad X_0 = b_1 V_1 + b_2 V_2 + \cdots + b_n V_n.$$

Assume that $X_0 = \begin{bmatrix} x_1 & x_2 & \ldots & x_n \end{bmatrix}'$ was chosen in such a manner that $b_1 \neq 0$. Also, assume that the coordinates of X_0 are scaled so that $\max_{1 \le j \le n}\{|x_j|\} = 1$. Because $\{V_j\}_{j=1}^n$ are eigenvectors of A, the multiplication AX_0, followed by normalization, produces

$$
\begin{aligned}
(10) \qquad Y_0 = AX_0 &= A(b_1 V_1 + b_2 V_2 + \cdots + b_n V_n) \\
&= b_1 AV_1 + b_2 AV_2 + \cdots + b_n AV_n \\
&= b_1 \lambda_1 V_1 + b_2 \lambda_2 V_2 + \cdots + b_n \lambda_n V_n \\
&= \lambda_1 \left(b_1 V_1 + b_2 \left(\frac{\lambda_2}{\lambda_1} \right) V_2 + \cdots + b_n \left(\frac{\lambda_n}{\lambda_1} \right) V_n \right)
\end{aligned}
$$

and

$$X_1 = \frac{\lambda_1}{c_1} \left(b_1 V_1 + b_2 \left(\frac{\lambda_2}{\lambda_1} \right) V_2 + \cdots + b_n \left(\frac{\lambda_n}{\lambda_1} \right) V_n \right).$$

After k iterations we arrive at

$$
\begin{aligned}
(11) \\
Y_{k-1} = AX_{k-1} \\
&= A \frac{\lambda_1^{k-1}}{c_1 c_2 \cdots c_{k-1}} \left(b_1 V_1 + b_2 \left(\frac{\lambda_2}{\lambda_1} \right)^{k-1} V_2 + \cdots + b_n \left(\frac{\lambda_n}{\lambda_1} \right)^{k-1} V_n \right) \\
&= \frac{\lambda_1^{k-1}}{c_1 c_2 \cdots c_{k-1}} \left(b_1 AV_1 + b_2 \left(\frac{\lambda_2}{\lambda_1} \right)^{k-1} AV_2 + \cdots + b_n \left(\frac{\lambda_n}{\lambda_1} \right)^{k-1} AV_n \right) \\
&= \frac{\lambda_1^{k-1}}{c_1 c_2 \cdots c_{k-1}} \left(b_1 \lambda_1 V_1 + b_2 \left(\frac{\lambda_2}{\lambda_1} \right)^{k-1} \lambda_2 V_2 + \cdots + b_n \left(\frac{\lambda_n}{\lambda_1} \right)^{k-1} \lambda_n V_n \right) \\
&= \frac{\lambda_1^{k}}{c_1 c_2 \cdots c_{k-1}} \left(b_1 V_1 + b_2 \left(\frac{\lambda_2}{\lambda_1} \right)^{k} V_2 + \cdots + b_n \left(\frac{\lambda_n}{\lambda_1} \right)^{k} V_n \right)
\end{aligned}
$$

and

$$X_k = \frac{\lambda_1^{k}}{c_1 c_2 \cdots c_k} \left(b_1 V_1 + b_2 \left(\frac{\lambda_2}{\lambda_1} \right)^{k-1} V_2 + \cdots + b_n \left(\frac{\lambda_n}{\lambda_1} \right)^{k-1} V_n \right).$$

Since we assumed that $|\lambda_j|/|\lambda_1| < 1$ for each $j = 2, 3, \ldots, n$, we have

$$(12) \qquad \lim_{k \to \infty} b_j \left(\frac{\lambda_j}{\lambda_1}\right)^k V_j = 0 \qquad \text{for each } j = 2, 3, \ldots, n.$$

Hence it follows that

$$(13) \qquad \lim_{k \to \infty} X_k = \lim_{k \to \infty} \frac{b_1 \lambda_1^k}{c_1 c_2 \cdots c_k} V_1.$$

We have required that both X_k and V_1 be normalized and their largest component be 1. Hence the limiting vector on the left side of (13) will be normalized, with its largest component being 1. Consequently, the limit of the scalar multiple of V_1 on the right side of (13) exists and its value must be 1; that is,

$$(14) \qquad \lim_{k \to \infty} \frac{b_1 \lambda_1^k}{c_1 c_2 \cdots c_k} = 1.$$

Therefore, the sequence of vectors $\{X_k\}$ converges to the dominant eigenvector:

$$(15) \qquad \lim_{k \to \infty} X_k = V_1.$$

Replacing k with $k - 1$ in the terms of the sequence in (14) yields

$$\lim_{k \to \infty} \frac{b_1 \lambda_1^{k-1}}{c_1 c_2 \cdots c_{k-1}} = 1,$$

and dividing both sides of this result into (14) yields

$$\lim_{k \to \infty} \frac{\lambda_1}{c_k} = \lim_{k \to \infty} \frac{b_1 \lambda_1^k / (c_1 c_2 \cdots c_k)}{b_1 \lambda_1^{k-1} / (c_1 c_2 \cdots c_{k-1})} = \frac{1}{1} = 1.$$

Therefore, the sequence of constants $\{c_k\}$ converges to the dominant eigenvalue:

$$(16) \qquad \lim_{k \to \infty} c_k = \lambda_1,$$

and the proof of the theorem is complete.   ●

Speed of Convergence

In the light of equation (12) we see that the coefficient of V_j in X_k goes to zero in proportion to $(\lambda_j/\lambda_1)^k$ and that the speed of convergence of $\{X_k\}$ to V_1 is governed by the terms $(\lambda_2/\lambda_1)^k$. Consequently, the rate of convergence is linear. Similarly, the

Table 11.2   Comparison of the Rate of Convergence of the Power Method and Acceleration of the Power Method Using Aitken's Δ^2 Technique

	$c_k Y_k$				$\widehat{c}_k \widehat{X}_k$		
$c_1 X_1$	$= 12.000000[0.5000000$	0.6666667	$1]'$;	$4.3809524[0.4062500$	0.6041667	$1]' = \widehat{c}_1 \widehat{X}_1$
$c_2 X_2$	$= 5.3333333[0.4375000$	0.6250000	$1]'$;	$4.0833333[0.4015152$	0.6010101	$1]' = \widehat{c}_2 \widehat{X}_2$
$c_3 X_3$	$= 4.5000000[0.4166667$	0.6111111	$1]'$;	$4.0202020[0.4003759$	0.6002506	$1]' = \widehat{c}_3 \widehat{X}_3$
$c_4 X_4$	$= 4.2222222[0.4078947$	0.6052632	$1]'$;	$4.0050125[0.4000938$	0.6000625	$1]' = \widehat{c}_4 \widehat{X}_4$
$c_5 X_5$	$= 4.1052632[0.4038462$	0.6025641	$1]'$;	$4.0012508[0.4000234$	0.6000156	$1]' = \widehat{c}_5 \widehat{X}_5$
$c_6 X_6$	$= 4.0512821[0.4018987$	0.6012658	$1]'$;	$4.0003125[0.4000059$	0.6000039	$1]' = \widehat{c}_6 \widehat{X}_6$
$c_7 X_7$	$= 4.0253165[0.4009434$	0.6006289	$1]'$;	$4.0000781[0.4000015$	0.6000010	$1]' = \widehat{c}_7 \widehat{X}_7$
$c_8 X_8$	$= 4.0125786[0.4004702$	0.6003135	$1]'$;	$4.0000195[0.4000004$	0.6000002	$1]' = \widehat{c}_8 \widehat{X}_8$
$c_9 X_9$	$= 4.0062696[0.4002347$	0.6001565	$1]'$;	$4.0000049[0.4000001$	0.6000001	$1]' = \widehat{c}_9 \widehat{X}_9$
$c_{10} X_{10}$	$= 4.0031299[0.4001173$	0.6000782	$1]'$;	$4.0000012[0.4000000$	0.6000000	$1]' = \widehat{c}_{10} \widehat{X}_{10}$

convergence of the sequence of constants $\{c_k\}$ to λ_1 is linear. The Aitken Δ^2 method can be used for any linearly convergent sequence $\{p_k\}$ to form a new sequence,

$$\left\{ \widehat{p}_k = \frac{(p_{k+1} - p_k)^2}{p_{k+2} - 2p_{k+1} + p_k} \right\},$$

that converges faster. In Example 11.4 this Aitken Δ^2 method can be applied to speed up convergence of the sequence of constants $\{c_k\}$, as well as the first two components of the sequence of vectors $\{X_k\}$. A comparison of the results obtained with this technique and the original sequences is shown in Table 11.2.

Shifted-Inverse Power Method

We will now discuss the shifted inverse power method. It requires a good starting approximation for an eigenvalue, and then iteration is used to obtain a precise solution. Other procedures such as the QM and Givens' method are used first to obtain the starting approximations. Cases involving complex eigenvalues, multiple eigenvalues, or the presence of two eigenvalues with the same magnitude or approximately the same magnitude will cause computational difficulties and require more advanced methods. Our illustrations will focus on the case where the eigenvalues are distinct. The shifted inverse power method is based on the following three results (the proofs are left as exercises).

Theorem 11.19 (Shifting Eigenvalues).   Suppose that λ, V is an eigenpair of A. If α is any constant, then $\lambda - \alpha$, V is an eigenpair of the matrix $A - \alpha I$.

Theorem 11.20 (Inverse Eigenvalues).   Suppose that λ, V is an eigenpair of A. If $\lambda \neq 0$, then $1/\lambda$, V is an eigenpair of the matrix A^{-1}.

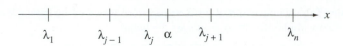

Figure 11.2   The location of α for the shifted-inverse power method.

Theorem 11.21.   Suppose that λ, V is an eigenpair of A. If $\alpha \neq \lambda$, then $1/(\lambda - \alpha)$, V is an eigenpair of the matrix $(A - \alpha I)^{-1}$.

Theorem 11.22 (Shifted-Inverse Power Method).   Assume that the $n \times n$ matrix A has distinct eigenvalues λ_1, λ_2, ..., λ_n and consider the eigenvalue λ_j. Then a constant α can be chosen so that $\mu_1 = 1/(\lambda_j - \alpha)$ is the dominant eigenvalue of $(A - \alpha I)^{-1}$. Furthermore, if X_0 is chosen appropriately, then the sequences $\{X_k = \left[x_1^{(k)} \; x_2^{(k)} \; \ldots \; x_n^{(k)}\right]'\}$ and $\{c_k\}$ are generated recursively by

$$(17) \qquad\qquad Y_k = (A - \alpha I)^{-1} X_k$$

and

$$(18) \qquad\qquad X_{k+1} = \frac{1}{c_{k+1}} Y_k,$$

where

$$(19) \qquad c_{k+1} = x_j^{(k)} \quad \text{and} \quad x_j^{(k)} = \max_{1 \leq j \leq n} \{|x_i^{(k)}|\}$$

will converge to the dominant eigenpair μ_1, V_j of the matrix $(A - \alpha I)^{-1}$. Finally, the corresponding eigenvalue for the matrix A is given by the calculation

$$(20) \qquad\qquad \lambda_j = \frac{1}{\mu_1} + \alpha.$$

Remark. For practical implementations of Theorem 11.22, a linear system solver is used to compute Y_k in each step by solving the linear system $(A - \alpha I)Y_k = X_k$.

Proof.   Without loss of generality, we may assume that $\lambda_1 < \lambda_2 < \cdots < \lambda_n$. Select a number α ($\alpha \neq \lambda_j$) that is closer to λ_j than any of the other eigenvalues (see Figure 11.2), that is,

$$(21) \qquad |\lambda_j - \alpha| < |\lambda_i - \alpha| \quad \text{for each } i = 1, 2, \ldots, j-1, j+1, \ldots, n.$$

According to Theorem 11.21, $1/(\lambda_j - \alpha)$, V is an eigenpair of the matrix $(A - \alpha I)^{-1}$. Relation (21) implies that $1/|\lambda_i - \alpha| < 1/|\lambda_j - \alpha|$ for each $i \neq j$ so that $\mu_1 = 1/(\lambda_j - \alpha)$ is the dominant eigenvalue of the matrix $(A - \alpha I)^{-1}$. The shifted-inverse power method uses a modification of the power method to determine the eigenpair μ_1, V_j. Then the calculation $\lambda_j = 1/\mu_1 + \alpha$ produces the desired eigenvalue of the matrix A. $\qquad\qquad\bullet$

Table 11.3   Shifted-Inverse Power Method for the Matrix $(A - 4.2I)^{-1}$ in Example 11.6: Convergence to the Eigenvector $V = \begin{bmatrix} \frac{2}{5} & \frac{3}{5} & 1 \end{bmatrix}'$ and $\mu_1 = -5$

$(A - \alpha I)^{-1} X_k =$	$c_{k+1} X_{k+1}$
$(A - \alpha I)^{-1} X_0 = -23.18181818 \; [0.4117647059 \quad 0.6078431373 \quad 1]' = c_1 X_1$	
$(A - \alpha I)^{-1} X_1 = -5.356506239 \; [0.4009983361 \quad 0.6006655574 \quad 1]' = c_2 X_2$	
$(A - \alpha I)^{-1} X_2 = -5.030252609 \; [0.4000902120 \quad 0.6000601413 \quad 1]' = c_3 X_3$	
$(A - \alpha I)^{-1} X_3 = -5.002733697 \; [0.4000081966 \quad 0.6000054644 \quad 1]' = c_4 X_4$	
$(A - \alpha I)^{-1} X_4 = -5.000248382 \; [0.4000007451 \quad 0.6000004967 \quad 1]' = c_5 X_5$	
$(A - \alpha I)^{-1} X_5 = -5.000022579 \; [0.4000000677 \quad 0.6000000452 \quad 1]' = c_6 X_6$	
$(A - \alpha I)^{-1} X_6 = -5.000002053 \; [0.4000000062 \quad 0.6000000041 \quad 1]' = c_7 X_7$	
$(A - \alpha I)^{-1} X_7 = -5.000000187 \; [0.4000000006 \quad 0.6000000004 \quad 1]' = c_8 X_8$	
$(A - \alpha I)^{-1} X_8 = -5.000000017 \; [0.4000000001 \quad 0.6000000000 \quad 1]' = c_9 X_9$	

Example 11.6.   Employ the shifted-inverse power method to find the eigenpairs of the matrix

$$A = \begin{bmatrix} 0 & 11 & -5 \\ -2 & 17 & -7 \\ -4 & 26 & -10 \end{bmatrix}.$$

Use the fact that the eigenvalues of A are $\lambda_1 = 4$, $\lambda_2 = 2$, and $\lambda_3 = 1$, and select an appropriate α and starting vector for each case.

   Case (i):   For the eigenvalue $\lambda_1 = 4$, we select $\alpha = 4.2$ and the starting vector $X_0 = \begin{bmatrix} 1 & 1 & 1 \end{bmatrix}'$. First, form the matrix $A - 4.2I$, compute the solution to

$$\begin{bmatrix} -4.2 & 11 & -5 \\ -2 & 12.8 & -7 \\ -4 & 26 & -14.2 \end{bmatrix} Y_0 = X_0 = \begin{bmatrix} 1 \\ 1 \\ 1 \end{bmatrix},$$

and get the vector $Y_0 = \begin{bmatrix} -9.545454545 & -14.09090909 & -23.18181818 \end{bmatrix}'$. Then compute $c_1 = -23.18181818$ and $X_1 = \begin{bmatrix} 0.4117647059 & 0.6078431373 & 1 \end{bmatrix}'$. Iteration generates the values given in Table 11.3. The sequence $\{c_k\}$ converges to $\mu_1 = -5$, which is the dominant eigenvalue of $(A - 4.2I)^{-1}$, and $\{X_k\}$ converges to $V_1 = \begin{bmatrix} \frac{2}{5} & \frac{3}{5} & 1 \end{bmatrix}'$. The eigenvalue λ_1 of A is given by the computation $\lambda_1 = 1/\mu_1 + \alpha = 1/(-5) + 4.2 = -0.2 + 4.2 = 4$.

   Case (ii):   For the eigenvalue $\lambda_2 = 2$, we select $\alpha = 2.1$ and the starting vector $X_0 = \begin{bmatrix} 1 & 1 & 1 \end{bmatrix}'$. Form the matrix $A - 2.1I$, compute the solution to

$$\begin{bmatrix} -2.1 & 11 & -5 \\ -2 & 14.9 & -7 \\ -4 & 26 & -12.1 \end{bmatrix} Y_0 = X_0 = \begin{bmatrix} 1 \\ 1 \\ 1 \end{bmatrix},$$

and obtain the vector $Y_0 = \begin{bmatrix} 11.05263158 & 21.57894737 & 42.63157895 \end{bmatrix}'$. Then $c_1 = 42.63157895$ and vector $X_1 = \begin{bmatrix} 0.2592592593 & 0.5061728395 & 1 \end{bmatrix}'$. Iteration produces the

Table 11.4 Shifted-Inverse Power Method for the Matrix $(A - 2.1I)^{-1}$ in Example 11.6: Convergence to the Dominant Eigenvector $V = \begin{bmatrix} \frac{1}{4} & \frac{1}{2} & 1 \end{bmatrix}$ and $\mu_1 = -10$

$(A - \alpha I)^{-1} X_k =$		$c_{k+1} X_{k+1}$	
$(A - \alpha I)^{-1} X_0 =$ 42.63157895	[0.2592592593	0.5061728395	1]$' = c_1 X_1$
$(A - \alpha I)^{-1} X_1 =$ -9.350227420	[0.2494788047	0.4996525365	1]$' = c_2 X_2$
$(A - \alpha I)^{-1} X_2 =$ -10.03657511	[0.2500273314	0.5000182209	1]$' = c_3 X_3$
$(A - \alpha I)^{-1} X_3 =$ -9.998082009	[0.2499985612	0.4999990408	1]$' = c_4 X_4$
$(A - \alpha I)^{-1} X_4 =$ -10.00010097	[0.2500000757	0.5000000505	1]$' = c_5 X_5$
$(A - \alpha I)^{-1} X_5 =$ -9.999994686	[0.2499999960	0.4999999973	1]$' = c_6 X_6$
$(A - \alpha I)^{-1} X_6 =$ -10.00000028	[0.2500000002	0.5000000001	1]$' = c_7 X_7$

Table 11.5 Shifted-Inverse Power Method for the Matrix $(A - 0.875I)^{-1}$ in Example 11.6: Convergence to the Dominant Eigenvector $V = \begin{bmatrix} \frac{1}{2} & \frac{1}{2} & 1 \end{bmatrix}'$ and $\mu_1 = 8$

$(A - \alpha I)^{-1} X_k =$		$c_{k+1} X_{k+1}$	
$(A - \alpha I)^{-1} X_0 =$ -30.40000000	[0.5052631579	0.4947368421	1]$' = c_1 X_1$
$(A - \alpha I)^{-1} X_1 =$ 8.404210526	[0.5002004008	0.4997995992	1]$' = c_2 X_2$
$(A - \alpha I)^{-1} X_2 =$ 8.015390782	[0.5000080006	0.4999919994	1]$' = c_3 X_3$
$(A - \alpha I)^{-1} X_3 =$ 8.000614449	[0.5000003200	0.4999996800	1]$' = c_4 X_4$
$(A - \alpha I)^{-1} X_4 =$ 8.000024576	[0.5000000128	0.4999999872	1]$' = c_5 X_5$
$(A - \alpha I)^{-1} X_5 =$ 8.000000983	[0.5000000005	0.4999999995	1]$' = c_6 X_6$
$(A - \alpha I)^{-1} X_6 =$ 8.000000039	[0.5000000000	0.5000000000	1]$' = c_7 X_7$

values given in Table 11.4. The dominant eigenvalue of $(A - 2.1I)^{-1}$ is $\mu_1 = -10$, and the eigenpair of the matrix A is $\lambda_2 = 1/(-10) + 2.1 = -0.1 + 2.1 = 2$ and $V_2 = \begin{bmatrix} \frac{1}{4} & \frac{1}{2} & 1 \end{bmatrix}'$.

Case (iii): For the eigenvalue $\lambda_3 = 1$, we select $\alpha = 0.875$ and the starting vector $X_0 = \begin{bmatrix} 0 & 1 & 1 \end{bmatrix}'$. Iteration produces the values given in Table 11.5. The dominant eigenvalue of $(A - 0.875I)^{-1}$ is $\mu_1 = 8$, and the eigenpair of matrix A is $\lambda_3 = 1/8 + 0.875 = 0.125 + 0.875 = 1$ and $V_3 = \begin{bmatrix} \frac{1}{2} & \frac{1}{2} & 1 \end{bmatrix}'$. The sequence $\{X_k\}$ of vectors with the starting vector $\begin{bmatrix} 0 & 1 & 1 \end{bmatrix}'$ converged in seven iterations. (Computational difficulties were encountered when $X_0 = \begin{bmatrix} 1 & 1 & 1 \end{bmatrix}'$ was used, and convergence took significantly longer.) ∎

Program 11.1 (Power Method). To compute the dominant eigenvalue λ_1 and its associated eigenvector V_1 for the $n \times n$ matrix A. It is assumed that the n eigenvalues have the dominance property $|\lambda_1| > |\lambda_2| \geq |\lambda_3| \geq \cdots \geq |\lambda_n| > 0$.

```
function [lambda,V]=power1(A,X,epsilon,max1)
```

```
%Input   - A is an nxn matrix
%          - X is the nx1 starting vector
%          - epsilon is the tolerance
%          - max1 is the maximum number of iterations
%Output - lambda is the dominant eigenvalue
%          - V is the dominant eigenvector
%Initialize parameters
lambda=0;
cnt=0;
err=1;
state=1;
while ((cnt<=max1)&(state==1))
    Y=A*X;
    %Normalize Y
    [m j]=max(abs(Y));
    c1=m;
    dc=abs(lambda-c1);
    Y=(1/c1)*Y;
    %Update X and lambda and check for convergence
    dv=norm(X-Y);
    err=max(dc,dv);
    X=Y;
    lambda=c1;
    state=0;
    if(err>epsilon)
        state=1;
    end
    cnt=cnt+1;
end
V=X;
```

Program 11.2 (Shifted-Inverse Power Method). To compute the dominant eigen-value λ_j and its associated eigenvector V_j for the $n \times n$ matrix A. It is assumed that the n eigenvalues have the property $\lambda_1 < \lambda_2 < \cdots < \lambda_n$ and that α is a real number such that $|\lambda_j - \alpha| < |\lambda_i - \alpha|$, for each $i = 1, 2, \ldots, j-1, j+1, \ldots, n$.

```
function [lambda,V]=invpow(A,X,alpha,epsilon,max1)
%Input   - A is an nxn matrix
%          - X is the nx1 starting vector
%          - alpha is the given shift
%          - epsilon is the tolerance
%          - max1 is the maximum number of iterations
%Output - lambda is the dominant eigenvalue
```

```
%          - V is the dominant eigenvector
%Initialize the matrix A-alphaI and parameters
[n n]=size(A);
A=A-alpha*eye(n);
lambda=0;
cnt=0;
err=1;
state=1;

while ((cnt<=max1)&(state==1))
    %Solve system AY=X
    Y=A\X;
    %Normalize Y
    [m j]=max(abs(Y));
    c1=m;
    dc=abs(lambda-c1);
    Y=(1/c1)*Y;
    %Update X and lambda and check for convergence
    dv=norm(X-Y);
    err=max(dc,dv);
    X=Y;
    lambda=c1;
    state=0;
    if (err>epsilon)
        state=1;
    end
    cnt=cnt+1;
end
lambda=alpha+1/c1;
V=X;
```

Exercises for Power Method

1. Let λ, V be an eigenpair of A. If α is any constant, show that $\lambda - \alpha$, V is an eigenpair of the matrix $A - \alpha I$.

2. Let λ, V be an eigenpair of A. If $\lambda \neq 0$, show that $1/\lambda$, V is an eigenpair of the matrix A^{-1}.

3. Let λ, V be an eigenpair of A. If $\alpha \neq \lambda$, show that $1/(\lambda - \alpha)$, V is an eigenpair of the matrix $(A - \alpha I)^{-1}$.

4. *Deflation techniques.* Suppose that $\lambda_1, \lambda_2, \lambda_3, \ldots, \lambda_n$ are the eigenvalues of A with associated eigenvectors $V_1, V_2, V_3, \ldots, V_n$ and that λ_1 has multiplicity 1. If X is

any vector with the property that $X'V_1 = 1$, prove that the matrix

$$B = A - \lambda_1 V_1 X'$$

has eigenvalues $0, \lambda_2, \lambda_3, \ldots, \lambda_n$ with associated eigenvectors $V_1, W_2, W_3, \ldots, W_n$, where V_j and W_j are related by the equation

$$V_j = (\lambda - \lambda_1)W_j + \lambda_1(X'W_j)V_1 \quad \text{for each } j = 2, 3, \ldots, n.$$

5. *Markov processes and eigenvalues.* A Markov process can be described by a square matrix A whose entries are all positive and the column sums all equal 1. For illustration, let $P_0 = \begin{bmatrix} x^{(0)} & y^{(0)} \end{bmatrix}'$ record the number of people in a certain city who use brands X and Y, respectively. Each month people decide to keep using the same brand or switch brands. The probability that a user of brand X will switch to brand Y is 0.3. The probability that a user of brand Y will switch to brand X is 0.2. The transition matrix for this process is

$$P_{k+1} = AP_k = \begin{bmatrix} 0.8 & 0.3 \\ 0.2 & 0.7 \end{bmatrix} \begin{bmatrix} x^{(k)} \\ y^{(k)} \end{bmatrix}.$$

If $AP_j = P_j$ for some j, then $P_j = V$ is said to be the steady-state distribution for the Markov process. Thus, if there is a steady-state distribution, then $\lambda = 1$ must be an eigenvalue of A. Additionally, the steady-state distribution V is an eigenvector associated with $\lambda = 1$ (i.e., solve $(A - I)V = 0$).

(a) For the example given above; verify that $\lambda = 1$ is an eigenvalue of the transition matrix A.

(b) Verify that the set of eigenvectors associated with $\lambda = 1$ is $\{t\begin{bmatrix} 3/2 & 1 \end{bmatrix}' : t \in \Re, t \neq 0\}$.

(c) Assume that the population of the city was 50,000. Use your results from part (b) to verify that the steady-state distribution is $\begin{bmatrix} 30,000 & 20,000 \end{bmatrix}'$.

Algorithms and Programs

In Problems 1 through 4, use:
(a) Program 11.1 to find the dominant eigenpair of the given matrices.
(b) Program 11.2 to find the other eigenpairs.

1. $A = \begin{bmatrix} 7 & 6 & -3 \\ -12 & -20 & 24 \\ -6 & -12 & 16 \end{bmatrix}.$

2. $A = \begin{bmatrix} -14 & -30 & 42 \\ 24 & 49 & -66 \\ 12 & 24 & -32 \end{bmatrix}.$

3. $A = \begin{bmatrix} 2.5 & -2.5 & 3.0 & 0.5 \\ 0.0 & 5.0 & -2.0 & 2.0 \\ -0.5 & -0.5 & 4.0 & 2.5 \\ -2.5 & -2.5 & 5.0 & 3.5 \end{bmatrix}.$

4. $A = \begin{bmatrix} 2.5 & -2.0 & 2.5 & 0.5 \\ 0.5 & 5.0 & -2.5 & -0.5 \\ -1.5 & 1.0 & 3.5 & -2.5 \\ 2.0 & 3.0 & -5.0 & 3.0 \end{bmatrix}.$

5. Suppose that the probability that a user of brand X will switch to brand Y or Z is 0.4 and 0.2, respectively. The probability that a user of brand Y will switch to brand X or Z is 0.2 and 0.2, respectively. The probability that a user of brand Z will switch to brand X or Y is 0.1 and 0.1, respectively. The transition matrix for this process is

$$P_{k+1} = AP_k = \begin{bmatrix} 0.4 & 0.2 & 0.1 \\ 0.4 & 0.6 & 0.1 \\ 0.2 & 0.2 & 0.8 \end{bmatrix} \begin{bmatrix} x^{(k)} \\ y^{(k)} \\ z^{(k)} \end{bmatrix}.$$

(a)   Verify that $\lambda = 1$ is an eigenvalue of A.

(b)   Determine the steady-state distribution for a population of 80,000.

6. Suppose that the coffee industry consists of five brands B_1, B_2, B_3, B_4, and B_5. Assume that each customer purchases a 3-pound can of coffee each month and 60 million pounds of coffee is sold each month. Regardless of brand, each pound of coffee represents a profit of one dollar. The coffee industry has empirically determined the following transition matrix A for monthly coffee sales, where a_{ij} represents the probability that a customer will purchase brand B_i given that their previous purchase was brand B_j.

$$A = \begin{bmatrix} 0.1 & 0.2 & 0.2 & 0.6 & 0.2 \\ 0.1 & 0.1 & 0.1 & 0.1 & 0.2 \\ 0.1 & 0.3 & 0.4 & 0.1 & 0.2 \\ 0.3 & 0.3 & 0.1 & 0.1 & 0.2 \\ 0.4 & 0.1 & 0.2 & 0.1 & 0.2 \end{bmatrix}$$

An advertising agency guarantees the manufacturer of brand B_1 that, for $40 million a year, they can change the first column of A to $\begin{bmatrix} 0.3 & 0.1 & 0.1 & 0.2 & 0.3 \end{bmatrix}'$. Should the manufacturer of brand B_1 hire the advertising agency?

7. Write a program, based on the deflation technique in Exercise 4, to find all the eigenvalues of a given matrix. Your program should call Program 11.1 as a subroutine to determine the dominant eigenvalue and eigenvector at each iteration.

8. Use your program from Problem 7 to find all the eigenvalues of the following matrices.

(a) $A = \begin{bmatrix} 1 & 2 & -1 \\ 1 & 0 & 1 \\ 4 & -4 & 5 \end{bmatrix}$

(b) $A = [a_{ij}]$, where $a_{ij} = \begin{cases} i + j & i = j \\ ij & i \neq j \end{cases}$ and $i, j = 1, 2, \ldots, 15$.

11.3   Jacobi's Method

Jacobi's method is an easily understood algorithm for finding all eigenpairs for a symmetric matrix. It is a reliable method that produces uniformly accurate answers for the results. For matrices of order up to 10, the algorithm is competitive with more sophisticated ones. If speed is not a major consideration, it is quite acceptable for matrices up to order 20.

A solution is guaranteed for all real symmetric matrices when Jacobi's method is used. This limitation is not severe since many practical problems of applied mathematics and engineering involve symmetric matrices. From a theoretical viewpoint, the method embodies techniques that are found in more sophisticated algorithms. For instructive purposes, it is worthwhile to investigate the details of Jacobi's method.

Plane Rotations

We start with some geometrical background about coordinate transformations. Let X denote a vector in n-dimensional space and consider the linear transformation $Y = RX$, where R is an $n \times n$ matrix:

$$R = \begin{bmatrix} 1 & \cdots & 0 & \cdots & 0 & \cdots & 0 \\ \vdots & & \vdots & & & & \vdots \\ 0 & \cdots & \cos\phi & \cdots & \sin\phi & \cdots & 0 \\ \vdots & & \vdots & & & & \vdots \\ 0 & \cdots & -\sin\phi & \cdots & \cos\phi & \cdots & 0 \\ \vdots & & \vdots & & & & \vdots \\ 0 & \cdots & 0 & \cdots & 0 & \cdots & 1 \end{bmatrix} \begin{matrix} \\ \\ \leftarrow \text{row } p \\ \\ \leftarrow \text{row } q \\ \\ \\ \end{matrix}$$

$$\underset{\text{col } p}{\uparrow} \qquad \underset{\text{col } q}{\uparrow}$$

Here all off-diagonal elements of R are zero except for the values $\pm\sin\phi$, and all diagonal elements are 1 except for $\cos\phi$. The effect of the transformation $Y = RX$ is easy to grasp:

$$y_j = x_j \qquad \text{when } j \neq p \text{ and } j \neq q,$$
$$y_p = x_p \cos\phi + x_q \sin\phi,$$
$$y_q = -x_p \sin\phi + x_q \cos\phi.$$

The transformation is seen to be a rotation of n-dimensional space in the $x_p x_q$-plane through the angle ϕ. By selecting an appropriate angle ϕ, we could make either $y_p = 0$ or $y_q = 0$ in the image. The inverse transformation $X = R^{-1}Y$ rotates space in the same $x_p x_q$-plane through the angle $-\phi$. Observe that R is an orthogonal matrix; that is,

$$R^{-1} = R' \quad \text{or} \quad R'R = I.$$

Similarity and Orthogonal Transformations

Consider the eigenproblem

$$(1) \qquad\qquad AX = \lambda X.$$

Suppose that K is a nonsingular matrix and that B is defined by

$$(2) \qquad\qquad B = K^{-1}AK.$$

Multiply both members of (2) on the right side by the quantity $K^{-1}X$. This produces

$$(3) \qquad BK^{-1}X = K^{-1}AKK^{-1}X = K^{-1}AX$$
$$= K^{-1}\lambda X = \lambda K^{-1}X.$$

We define the change of variable

$$(4) \qquad\qquad Y = K^{-1}X \quad \text{or} \quad X = KY.$$

When (4) is used in (3), the new eigenproblem is

$$(5) \qquad\qquad BY = \lambda Y.$$

Comparing (1) and (5), we see that the similarity transformation (2) preserved the eigenvalue λ and that the eigenvectors are different, but are related by the change of variable in (4).

Suppose that the matrix R is an orthogonal matrix (i.e., $R^{-1} = R'$) and that D is defined by

$$(6) \qquad\qquad D = R'AR.$$

Multiply both terms in (6) on the right by $R'X$ to obtain

$$(7) \qquad DR'X = R'ARR'X = R'AX = R'\lambda X = \lambda R'X.$$

We define the change of variable

$$(8) \qquad\qquad Y = R'X \quad \text{or} \quad X = RY.$$

Now use (8) in (7) to obtain a new eigenproblem,

$$(9) \qquad\qquad DY = \lambda Y.$$

As before, the eigenvalues of (1) and (9) are the same. However, for equation (9) the change of variable (8) makes it easier to convert X to Y and Y back into X because $R^{-1} = R'$.

In addition, suppose that A is a symmetric matrix (i.e., $A = A'$). Then we find that

$$(10) \qquad D' = (R'AR)' = R'A(R')' = R'AR = D.$$

Hence D is a symmetric matrix. Therefore, we conclude that if A is a symmetric matrix and R is an orthogonal matrix, the transformation of A to D given by (6) preserves symmetry as well as eigenvalues. The relationship between their eigenvectors is given by the change of variable (8).

Jacobi Series of Transformations

Start with the real symmetric matrix A. Then construct the sequence of orthogonal matrices $R_1, R_2, \ldots, R_n$ as follows:

$$
(11) \qquad
\begin{aligned}
D_0 &= A, \\
D_j &= R_j' D_{j-1} R_j \quad \text{for } j = 1, 2, \ldots.
\end{aligned}
$$

We will show how to construct the sequence $\{R_j\}$ so that

$$
(12) \qquad \lim_{j \to \infty} D_j = D = \operatorname{diag}(\lambda_1, \lambda_2, \ldots, \lambda_n).
$$

In practice we will stop when the off-diagonal elements are close to zero. Then we will have

$$
(13) \qquad D_n \approx D.
$$

The construction produces

$$
(14) \qquad D_n = R_n' R_{n-1}' \cdots R_1' A R_1 R_2 \cdots R_{n-1} R_n.
$$

If we define

$$
(15) \qquad R = R_1 R_2 \cdots R_{n-1} R_n,
$$

then $R^{-1} A R = D_k$, which implies that

$$
(16) \qquad A R = R D_k \approx R \operatorname{diag}(\lambda_1, \lambda_2, \ldots, \lambda_n).
$$

Let the columns of R be denoted by the vectors $X_1, X_2, \ldots, X_n$. Then R can be expressed as a row vector of column vectors:

$$
(17) \qquad R = \begin{bmatrix} X_1 & X_2 & \cdots & X_n \end{bmatrix}.
$$

The columns of the products in (16) now take on the form

$$
(18) \qquad \begin{bmatrix} A X_1 & A X_2 & \cdots & A X_n \end{bmatrix} \approx \begin{bmatrix} \lambda_1 X_1 & \lambda_2 X_2 & \cdots & \lambda_n X_n \end{bmatrix}.
$$

From (17) and (18) we see that the vector X_j, which is the jth column of R, is an eigenvector that corresponds to the eigenvalue λ_j.

General Step

Each step in the Jacobi iteration will accomplish the limited objective of reduction of the two off-diagonal elements d_{pq} and d_{qp} to zero. Let $\boldsymbol{R}_1$ denote the first orthogonal matrix used. Suppose that

$$(19) \qquad \boldsymbol{D}_1 = \boldsymbol{R}_1' \boldsymbol{A} \boldsymbol{R}_1$$

reduces the elements d_{pq} and d_{qp} to zero, where $\boldsymbol{R}_1$ has the form

$$(20) \qquad \boldsymbol{R}_1 = \begin{bmatrix} 1 & \cdots & 0 & \cdots & 0 & \cdots & 0 \\ \vdots & & & & & & \vdots \\ 0 & \cdots & c & \cdots & s & \cdots & 0 \\ \vdots & & & & & & \vdots \\ 0 & \cdots & -s & \cdots & c & \cdots & 0 \\ \vdots & & & & & & \vdots \\ 0 & \cdots & 0 & \cdots & 0 & \cdots & 1 \end{bmatrix} \begin{matrix} \\ \\ \leftarrow \text{row } p \\ \\ \leftarrow \text{row } q \\ \\ \\ \end{matrix}$$

$$\qquad\qquad\qquad \underset{\text{col } p}{\uparrow} \qquad \underset{\text{col } q}{\uparrow}$$

Here all off-diagonal elements of $\boldsymbol{R}_1$ are zero except for the element s located in row p, column q, and the element $-s$ located in row q, column p. Also note that all diagonal elements are 1 except for the element c, which appears at two locations, in row p, column p, and in row q, column q. The matrix is a plane rotation where we have used the notation $c = \cos\phi$ and $s = \sin\phi$.

We must verify that the transformation (19) will produce a change only to rows p and q and columns p and q. Consider postmultiplication of $\boldsymbol{A}$ by $\boldsymbol{R}_1$ and the product $\boldsymbol{B} = \boldsymbol{A}\boldsymbol{R}_1$:

$$(21)$$

$$\boldsymbol{B} = \begin{bmatrix} a_{11} & \cdots & a_{1p} & \cdots & a_{1q} & \cdots & a_{1n} \\ a_{p1} & \cdots & a_{pp} & \cdots & a_{pq} & \cdots & a_{pn} \\ a_{q1} & \cdots & a_{qp} & \cdots & a_{qq} & \cdots & a_{qn} \\ a_{n1} & \cdots & a_{np} & \cdots & a_{nq} & \cdots & a_{nn} \end{bmatrix} \begin{bmatrix} 1 & \cdots & 0 & \cdots & 0 & \cdots & 0 \\ 0 & \cdots & c & \cdots & s & \cdots & 0 \\ 0 & \cdots & -s & \cdots & c & \cdots & 0 \\ 0 & \cdots & 0 & \cdots & 0 & \cdots & 1 \end{bmatrix}$$

The row by column rule for multiplication applies, and we observe that there is no change to columns 1 to $p-1$ and $p+1$ to $q-1$ and $q+1$ to n. Hence only columns p and q are altered.

$$(22) \qquad \begin{aligned} b_{jk} &= a_{jk} && \text{when } k \neq p \text{ and } k \neq q, \\ b_{jp} &= c a_{jp} - s a_{jq} && \text{for } j = 1, 2, \ldots, n, \\ b_{jq} &= s a_{jp} + c a_{jq} && \text{for } j = 1, 2, \ldots, n. \end{aligned}$$

A similar argument shows that premultiplication of A by R_1' will only alter rows p and q. Therefore, the transformation

$$(23) \qquad\qquad D_1 = R_1' A R_1$$

will alter only columns p and q and rows p and q of A. The elements d_{jk} of D_1 are computed with the formulas

$$(24) \qquad \begin{aligned} d_{jp} &= ca_{jp} - sa_{jq} & \text{when } j \neq p \text{ and } j \neq q, \\ d_{jq} &= sa_{jp} + ca_{jq} & \text{when } j \neq p \text{ and } j \neq q, \\ d_{pp} &= c^2 a_{pp} + s^2 a_{qq} - 2cs a_{pq}, \\ d_{qq} &= s^2 a_{pp} + c^2 a_{qq} + 2cs a_{pq}, \\ d_{pq} &= (c^2 - s^2) a_{pq} + cs(a_{pp} - a_{qq}), \end{aligned}$$

and the other elements of D_1 are found by symmetry.

Zeroing Out d_{pq} and d_{qp}

The goal for each step of Jacobi's iteration is to make the two off-diagonal elements d_{pq} and d_{qp} zero. The obvious strategy would be to observe the fact that

$$(25) \qquad\qquad c = \cos\phi \quad \text{and} \quad s = \sin\phi,$$

where ϕ is the angle of rotation that produces the desired effect. However, some ingenious maneuvers with trigonometric identities are now required. The identity for $\cot\phi$ is used with (25) to define

$$(26) \qquad\qquad \theta = \cot 2\phi = \frac{c^2 - s^2}{2cs}.$$

Suppose that $a_{pq} \neq 0$ and we want to produce $d_{pq} = 0$. Then using the last equation in (24), we obtain

$$(27) \qquad\qquad 0 = (c^2 - s^2) a_{pq} + cs(a_{pp} - a_{qq}).$$

This can be rearranged to yield $(c^2 - s^2)/(cs) = (a_{qq} - a_{pp})/a_{pq}$, which is used in (26) to solve for θ:

$$(28) \qquad\qquad \theta = \frac{a_{qq} - a_{pp}}{2a_{pq}}.$$

Although we can use (28) with formulas (25) and (26) to compute c and s, less round-off error is propagated if we compute $\tan \phi$ and use it in later computations. So we define

$$(29) \qquad t = \tan \phi = \frac{s}{c}.$$

Now divide the numerator and denominator in (26) by c^2 to obtain

$$\theta = \frac{1 - s^2/c^2}{2s/c} = \frac{1 - t^2}{2t},$$

which yields the equation

$$(30) \qquad t^2 + 2t\theta - 1 = 0.$$

Since $t = \tan \phi$, the smaller root of (30) corresponds to the smaller angle of rotation with $|\phi| \leq \pi/4$. The special form of the quadratic formula for finding this root is

$$(31) \qquad t = -\theta \pm (\theta^2 + 1)^{1/2} = \frac{\text{sign}(\theta)}{|\theta| + (\theta^2 + 1)^{1/2}},$$

where $\text{sign}(\theta) = 1$ when $\theta \geq 0$ and $\text{sign}(\theta) = -1$ when $\theta < 0$. Then c and s are computed with the formulas

$$(32) \qquad \begin{aligned} c &= \frac{1}{(t^2 + 1)^{1/2}} \\ s &= ct. \end{aligned}$$

Summary of the General Step

We can now outline the calculations required to zero out the element d_{pq}. First, select row p and column q for which $a_{pq} \neq 0$. Second, form the preliminary quantities

$$(33) \qquad \begin{aligned} \theta &= \frac{a_{qq} - a_{pp}}{2a_{pq}}, \\ t &= \frac{\text{sign}(\theta)}{|\theta| + (\theta^2 + 1)^{1/2}}, \\ c &= \frac{1}{(t^2 + 1)^{1/2}}, \\ s &= ct. \end{aligned}$$

Third, to construct $D = D_1$, use

$$d_{pq} = 0;$$
$$d_{qp} = 0;$$
$$d_{pp} = c^2 a_{pp} + s^2 a_{qq} - 2cs a_{pq};$$
$$d_{qq} = s^2 a_{pp} + c^2 a_{qq} + 2cs a_{pq};$$

(34)

$$\begin{aligned}
&\text{for}\quad j = 1:n \\
&\quad\text{if}\quad (j \sim= p)\quad\text{and}\quad(j \sim= q) \\
&\qquad d_{jp} = c a_{jp} - s a_{jq}; \\
&\qquad d_{pj} = d_{jp}; \\
&\qquad d_{jq} = c a_{jq} + s a_{jp}; \\
&\qquad d_{qj} = d_{jq}; \\
&\quad\text{end} \\
&\text{end}
\end{aligned}$$

Updating the Matrix of Eigenvectors

We need to keep track of the matrix product $R_1 R_2 \cdots R_n$. When we stop at the nth iteration, we will have computed

(35)
$$V_n = R_1 R_2 \cdots R_n,$$

where V_n is an orthogonal matrix. We need only keep track of the current matrix V_j, for $j = 1, 2, \ldots, n$. Start by initializing $V = I$. Use the vector variables **XP** and **XQ** to store columns p and q of V, respectively. Then for each step perform the calculation

(36)

$$\begin{aligned}
&\text{for}\quad j = 1:n \\
&\quad \mathbf{XP}_j = v_{jp}; \\
&\quad \mathbf{XQ}_j = v_{jq}; \\
&\text{end} \\
&\text{for}\quad j = 1:n \\
&\quad v_{jp} = c\mathbf{XP}_j - s\mathbf{XQ}_j; \\
&\quad v_{jq} = s\mathbf{XP}_j + c\mathbf{XQ}_j; \\
&\text{end}
\end{aligned}$$

Strategy for Eliminating a_{pq}

The speed of convergence of Jacobi's method is seen by considering the sum of the squares of the off-diagonal elements:

$$(37) \qquad S_1 = \sum_{\substack{j,k=1 \\ k \neq j}}^{n} |a_{jk}|^2$$

$$(38) \qquad S_2 = \sum_{\substack{j,k=1 \\ k \neq j}}^{n} |d_{jk}|^2, \qquad \text{where} \qquad \mathbf{D}_1 = \mathbf{R}'\mathbf{A}\mathbf{R}.$$

The reader can verify that the equations given in (34) can be used to prove that

$$(39) \qquad S_2 = S_1 - 2|a_{pq}|^2.$$

At each step we let S_j denote the sum of the squares of the off-diagonal elements of $\mathbf{D}_j$. Then the sequence $\{S_j\}$ decreases monotonically and is bounded below by zero. Jacobi's original algorithm of 1846 selected, at each step, the off-diagonal element a_{pq} of largest magnitude to zero out and involved a search to compute the value

$$(40) \qquad \max\{\mathbf{A}\} = \max_{p<q}\{|a_{pq}|\}.$$

This choice will guarantee that $\{S_j\}$ converges to zero. As a consequence, this proves that $\{\mathbf{D}_j\}$ converges to $\mathbf{D}$ and $\{\mathbf{V}_j\}$ converges to the matrix $\mathbf{V}$ of eigenvectors.

Jacobi's search can become time consuming since it requires an order of $(n^2 - n)/2$ comparisons in a loop. It is prohibitive for larger values of n. A better strategy is the cyclic Jacobi method, where one annihilates elements in a strict order across the rows. A tolerance value ϵ is selected; then a sweep is made throughout the matrix, and if an element a_{pq} is found to be larger than ϵ, it is zeroed out. For one sweep through the matrix the elements are checked in row 1, $a_{12}, a_{13}, \ldots, a_{1n}$; then row 2, $a_{23}, a_{24}, \ldots,$ a_{2n}; and so on. It has been proved that the convergence rate is quadratic for both the original and cyclic Jacobi methods. An implementation of the cyclic Jacobi method starts by observing that the sum of the squares of the diagonal elements increases with each iteration; that is, if

$$(41) \qquad T_0 = \sum_{j=1}^{n} |a_{jj}|^2$$

and

$$T_1 = \sum_{j=1}^{n} |d_{jj}|^2,$$

then

$$T_1 = T_0 + 2|a_{pq}|^2.$$

Consequently, the sequence $\{D_j\}$ converges to the diagonal matrix D. Notice that the average size of a diagonal element can be computed with the formula $(T_0/n)^{1/2}$. The magnitudes of the off-diagonal elements are compared to $\epsilon(T_0/n)^{1/2}$, where ϵ is the preassigned tolerance. Therefore, the element a_{pq} is zeroed out if

$$(42) \qquad\qquad |a_{pq}| > \epsilon \left(\frac{T_0}{n}\right)^{1/2}.$$

Another variation of the method, called the *threshold Jacobi method*, is left for the reader to investigate.

Example 11.7.   Use Jacobi iteration to transform the following symmetric matrix into diagonal form.

$$\begin{bmatrix} 8 & -1 & 3 & -1 \\ -1 & 6 & 2 & 0 \\ 3 & 2 & 9 & 1 \\ -1 & 0 & 1 & 7 \end{bmatrix}$$

The computational details are left for the reader. The first rotation matrix that will zero out $a_{13} = 3$ is

$$R_1 = \begin{bmatrix} 0.763020 & 0.000000 & 0.646375 & 0.000000 \\ 0.000000 & 0.000000 & 0.000000 & 0.000000 \\ -0.646375 & 0.000000 & 0.763020 & 0.000000 \\ 0.000000 & 0.000000 & 0.000000 & 0.000000 \end{bmatrix}.$$

Calculation reveals that $A_2 = R_1 A_1 R_1$ is

$$A_2 = \begin{bmatrix} 5.458619 & -2.055770 & 0.000000 & -1.409395 \\ -2.055770 & 6.000000 & 0.879665 & 0.000000 \\ 0.000000 & 0.879665 & 11.541381 & 0.116645 \\ -1.409395 & 0.000000 & 0.116645 & 7.000000 \end{bmatrix}.$$

Next, the element $a_{12} = -2.055770$ is zeroed out and we get

$$A_3 = \begin{bmatrix} 3.655795 & 0.000000 & 0.579997 & -1.059649 \\ 0.000000 & 7.802824 & 0.661373 & 0.929268 \\ 0.579997 & 0.661373 & 11.541381 & 0.116645 \\ -1.059649 & 0.929268 & 0.116645 & 7.000000 \end{bmatrix}.$$

After 10 iterations we arrive at

$$A_{10} = \begin{bmatrix} 3.295870 & 0.002521 & 0.037859 & 0.000000 \\ 0.002521 & 8.405210 & -0.004957 & 0.066758 \\ 0.037859 & -0.004957 & 11.704123 & -0.001430 \\ 0.000000 & 0.066758 & -0.001430 & 6.594797 \end{bmatrix}.$$

It will take six more iterations for the diagonal elements to get close to the diagonal matrix

$$D = \text{diag}(3.295699, 8.407662, 11.704301, 6.592338).$$

However, the off-diagonal elements are not small enough, and it will take three more iterations for them to be less than 10^{-6} in magnitude. Then the eigenvectors are the columns of the matrix $V = R_1 R_2 \cdots R_{18}$, which is

$$V = \begin{bmatrix} 0.528779 & -0.573042 & 0.582298 & 0.230097 \\ 0.591967 & 0.472301 & 0.175776 & -0.628975 \\ -0.536039 & 0.282050 & 0.792487 & -0.071235 \\ 0.287454 & 0.607455 & 0.044680 & 0.739169 \end{bmatrix}. \quad \blacksquare$$

Program 11.3 (Jacobi Iteration for Eigenvalues and Eigenvectors). To compute the full set of eigenpairs $\{\lambda_j, V_j\}_{j=1}^n$ of the $n \times n$ real symmetric matrix A. Jacobi iteration is used to find all eigenpairs.

```
function [V,D]=jacobi1(A,epsilon)

%Input   - A is an nxn matrix
%         - epsilon is the tolerance
%Output - V is the nxn matrix of eigenvectors
%         - D is the diagonal nxn matrix of eigenvalues
%Initialize V,D,and parameters
D=A;
[n,n]=size(A);
V=eye(n);
state=1;

%Calculate row p and column q of the off-diagonal element
%of greatest magnitude in A
[m1 p]=max(abs(D-diag(diag(D))));
[m2 q]=max(m1);
p=p(q);

while(state==1)
    %Zero out Dpq and Dqp
    t=D(p,q)/(D(q,q)-D(p,p));
    c=1/sqrt(t^2+1);
    s=c*t;
    R=[c s;-s c];
    D([p q],:)=R'*D([p q],:);
    D(:,[p q])=D(:,[p q])*R;
    V(:,[p q])=V(:,[p q])*R;
```

```
[m1 p]=max(abs(D-diag(diag(D))));
[m2 q]=max(m1);
p=p(q);
if (abs(D(p,q))<epsilon*sqrt(sum(diag(D).^2)/n))
    state=0;
end
```
end
```
D=diag(diag(D));
```

Exercises for Jacobi's Method

1. *Mass-spring systems.*   Consider the undamped mass-spring system shown in Figure 11.3. The mathematical model describing the displacements from static equilibrium is

$$
\begin{bmatrix} k_1 + k_2 & -k_2 & 0 \\ -k_2 & k_2 + k_3 & -k_3 \\ 0 & -k_3 & k_3 \end{bmatrix} \begin{bmatrix} x_1(t) \\ x_2(t) \\ x_3(t) \end{bmatrix} + \begin{bmatrix} m_1 & 0 & 0 \\ 0 & m_2 & 0 \\ 0 & 0 & m_3 \end{bmatrix} \begin{bmatrix} x_1''(t) \\ x_2''(t) \\ x_3''(t) \end{bmatrix} = \begin{bmatrix} 0 \\ 0 \\ 0 \end{bmatrix}
$$

(a)   Use the substitutions $x_j(t) = v_j \sin(\omega t + \theta)$ for $j = 1, 2, 3$, where θ is a constant, and show that the solution to the mathematical model can be reformulated as follows:

$$
\begin{bmatrix} \dfrac{k_1 + k_2}{m_1} & \dfrac{-k_2}{m_1} & 0 \\[2mm] \dfrac{-k_2}{m_2} & \dfrac{k_2 + k_3}{m_2} & \dfrac{-k_3}{m_2} \\[2mm] 0 & \dfrac{-k_3}{m_3} & \dfrac{k_3}{m_3} \end{bmatrix} \begin{bmatrix} v_1 \\ v_2 \\ v_3 \end{bmatrix} = \omega^2 \begin{bmatrix} v_1 \\ v_2 \\ v_3 \end{bmatrix}.
$$

(b)   Set $\lambda = \omega^2$; then the three solutions to part (a) are the eigenpairs λ_j, $V_j = \begin{bmatrix} v_1^{(j)} & v_2^{(j)} & v_3^{(j)} \end{bmatrix}'$, for $j = 1, 2, 3$. Show that they are used to form the three

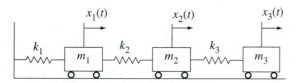

Figure 11.3   An undamped mass-spring system.

fundamental solutions:

$$X_j(t) = \begin{bmatrix} v_1^{(j)} \sin(\omega_j t + \theta) \\ v_2^{(j)} \sin(\omega_j t + \theta) \\ v_3^{(j)} \sin(\omega_j t + \theta) \end{bmatrix} = \sin(\omega_j t + \theta) \begin{bmatrix} v_1^{(j)} \\ v_2^{(j)} \\ v_3^{(j)} \end{bmatrix},$$

where $\omega_j = \sqrt{\lambda_j}$, for $j = 1, 2, 3$.

Remark. These three solutions are referred to as the ***three principal modes of vibration***.

2. The ***homogeneous linear system*** of differential equations

$$\begin{aligned} x_1'(t) &= x_1(t) + x_2(t) \\ x_2'(t) &= -2x_1(t) + 4x_2(t) \end{aligned}$$

can be written in the matrix form

$$X'(t) = \begin{bmatrix} x_1'(t) \\ x_2'(t) \end{bmatrix} = \begin{bmatrix} 1 & 1 \\ -2 & 4 \end{bmatrix} \begin{bmatrix} x_1(t) \\ x_2(t) \end{bmatrix} = AX(t).$$

(a) Verify that 2, $\begin{bmatrix} 1 & 1 \end{bmatrix}'$ and 3, $\begin{bmatrix} 1 & 2 \end{bmatrix}'$ are eigenpairs of the matrix A.

(b) By direct substitution into the matrix form of the system, verify that both $X(t) = e^{2t}\begin{bmatrix} 1 & 1 \end{bmatrix}'$ and $X(t) = e^{3t}\begin{bmatrix} 1 & 2 \end{bmatrix}'$ are solutions of the system of differential equations.

(c) By direct substitution into the matrix form of the system, verify that $X(t) = c_1 e^{2t}\begin{bmatrix} 1 & 1 \end{bmatrix}' + c_2 e^{3t}\begin{bmatrix} 1 & 2 \end{bmatrix}'$ is the general solution of the system of differential equations.

Remark. If the matrix A has n distinct eigenvalues, then it will have n linearly independent eigenvectors. In this case the general solution of a homogeneous system of differential equations can be written as a linear combination: that is, $X(t) = c_1 e^{\lambda_1 t} V_1 + c_2 e^{\lambda_2 t} V_2 + \cdots + c_n e^{\lambda_n t} V_n$.

3. Use the technique (by hand) outlined in Exercise 2 to solve each of the following initial value problems.

(a) $\begin{aligned} x_1' &= 4x_1 + 2x_2 \\ x_2' &= 3x_1 - x_2 \end{aligned}$ with $\begin{cases} x_1(0) = 1 \\ x_2(0) = 2 \end{cases}$

(b) $\begin{aligned} x_1' &= 2x_1 - 12x_2 \\ x_2' &= x_1 - 5x_2 \end{aligned}$ with $\begin{cases} x_1(0) = 2 \\ x_2(0) = 2 \end{cases}$

(c) $\begin{aligned} x_1' &= x_2 \\ x_2' &= x_3 \\ x_3' &= 8x_1 - 14x_2 + 7x_3 \end{aligned}$ with $\begin{cases} x_1(0) = 1 \\ x_2(0) = 2 \\ x_3(0) = 3 \end{cases}$

Algorithms and Programs

1. Use Program 11.3 to find the eigenpairs of the given matrix with a tolerance of $\epsilon = 10^{-7}$. Compare your results with those obtained from the MATLAB command `eig` by entering `[V,D]=eig(A)` in the MATLAB command window.

   (a) $A = \begin{bmatrix} 4 & 3 & 2 & 1 \\ 3 & 4 & 3 & 2 \\ 2 & 3 & 4 & 3 \\ 1 & 2 & 3 & 4 \end{bmatrix}$

   (b) $A = \begin{bmatrix} 2.25 & -0.25 & -1.25 & 2.75 \\ -0.25 & 2.25 & 2.75 & 1.25 \\ -1.25 & 2.75 & 2.25 & -0.25 \\ 2.75 & 1.25 & -0.25 & 2.25 \end{bmatrix}$

   (c) $A = [a_{ij}]$, where $a_{ij} = \begin{cases} i + j & i = j \\ ij & i \neq j \end{cases}$ and $i, j = 1, 2, \ldots, 30$.

   (d) $A = [a_{ij}]$, where $a_{ij} = \begin{cases} \cos(\sin(i + j)) & i = j \\ i + ij + j & i \neq j \end{cases}$ and $i, j = 1, 2, \ldots, 40$.

2. Use the technique outlined in Exercise 1 and Program 11.3 to find the eigenpairs and the three principal modes of vibration for the undamped mass-spring systems with the following coefficients.

   (a) $k_1 = 3, k_2 = 2, k_3 = 1, m_1 = 1, m_2 = 1, m_3 = 1$
   (b) $k_1 = \frac{1}{2}, k_2 = \frac{1}{4}, k_3 = \frac{1}{4}, m_1 = 4, m_2 = 4, m_3 = 4$
   (c) $k_1 = 0.2, k_2 = 0.4, k_3 = 0.3, m_1 = 2.5, m_2 = 2.5, m_3 = 2.5$

3. Use the technique outlined in Exercise 2 and Program 11.3 to find the general solution of the given homogeneous system of differential equations.

   (a) $x_1' = 4x_1 + 3x_2 + 2x_3 + x_4$
        $x_2' = 3x_1 + 4x_2 + 3x_3 + 2x_4$
        $x_3' = 2x_1 + 3x_2 + 4x_3 + 3x_4$
        $x_4' = x_1 + 2x_2 + 3x_3 + 4x_4$

   (b) $x_1' = 5x_1 + 4x_2 + 3x_3 + 2x_4 + x_5$
        $x_2' = 4x_1 + 5x_2 + 4x_3 + 3x_4 + 2x_5$
        $x_3' = 3x_1 + 4x_2 + 5x_3 + 4x_4 + 3x_5$
        $x_4' = 2x_1 + 3x_2 + 4x_3 + 5x_4 + 4x_5$
        $x_5' = x_1 + 2x_2 + 3x_3 + 4x_4 + 5x_5$

4. Modify Program 11.3 to implement the "cyclic" Jacobi method.

5. Use your program from Problem 4 on the symmetric matrices in Problem 1. In particular, compare the number of iterations required by your cyclic program and Program 11.3 to satisfy the given tolerance.

11.4   Eigenvalues of Symmetric Matrices

Householder's Method

Each transformation in Jacobi's method produced two zero off-diagonal elements, but subsequent iterations might make them nonzero. Hence many iterations are required to make the off-diagonal entries sufficiently close to zero. We now develop a method that produces several zero off-diagonal elements in each iteration, and they remain zero in subsequent iterations. We start by developing an important step in the process.

Theorem 11.23 (Householder Reflection).   If X and Y are vectors with the same norm, there exists an orthogonal symmetric matrix P such that

$$(1) \qquad\qquad Y = PX,$$

where

$$(2) \qquad\qquad P = I - 2WW'$$

and

$$(3) \qquad\qquad W = \frac{X - Y}{\|X - Y\|_2}.$$

Since P is both orthogonal and symmetric, it follows that

$$(4) \qquad\qquad P^{-1} = P.$$

Proof.   Equation (3) is used and defines W to be the unit vector in the direction $X - Y$; hence

$$(5) \qquad\qquad W'W = 1$$

and

$$(6) \qquad\qquad Y = X + cW,$$

where $c = -\|X - Y\|_2$. Since X and Y have the same norm, the parallelogram rule for vector addition can be used to see that $Z = (X+Y)/2 = X+(c/2)W$ is orthogonal to vector W (see Figure 11.4). This implies that

$$W'\left(X + \frac{c}{2}W\right) = 0.$$

Now we can use (5) to expand the preceding equation and get

$$(7) \qquad\qquad W'X + \frac{c}{2}W'W = W'X + \frac{c}{2} = 0.$$

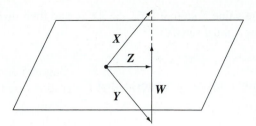

Figure 11.4 The vectors W, X, Y, and Z involved in the Householder reflection.

The crucial step is to use (7) and express c in the form

(8) $$c = -2(W'X).$$

Now (8) can be used in (6) to see that

$$Y = X + cW = X - 2W'XW.$$

Since the quantity $W'X$ is a scalar, the last equation can be written as

(9) $$Y = X - 2WW'X = (I - 2WW')X.$$

Looking at (9), we see that $P = I - 2WW'$. The matrix P is symmetric because

$$\begin{aligned} P' &= (I - 2WW')' = I - 2(WW')' \\ &= I - 2WW' = P. \end{aligned}$$

The following calculation shows that P is orthogonal:

$$\begin{aligned} P'P &= (I - 2WW')(I - 2WW') \\ &= I - 4WW' + 4WW'WW' \\ &= I - 4WW' + 4WW' = I, \end{aligned}$$

and the proof is complete. •

It should be observed that the effect of the mapping $Y = PX$ is to reflect X through the line whose direction is Z, hence the name *Householder reflection*.

Corollary 11.3 (kth Householder Matrix). Let A be an $n \times n$ matrix, and X any vector. If k is an integer with $1 \le k \le n - 2$, we can construct a vector W_k and matrix $P_k = I - 2W_kW_k'$ so that

(10) $$P_kX = P_k \begin{bmatrix} x_1 \\ \vdots \\ x_k \\ x_{k+1} \\ x_{k+2} \\ \vdots \\ x_n \end{bmatrix} = \begin{bmatrix} x_1 \\ \vdots \\ x_k \\ -S \\ 0 \\ \vdots \\ 0 \end{bmatrix} = Y.$$

Proof. The key is to define the value S so that $\|X\|_2 = \|Y\|_2$ and then invoke Theorem 11.23. The proper value for S must satisfy

$$
(11) \qquad S^2 = x_{k+1}^2 + x_{k+2}^2 + \cdots + x_n^2,
$$

which is readily verified by computing the norms of X and Y:

$$
(12) \qquad
\begin{aligned}
\|X\|_2 &= x_1^2 + x_2^2 + \cdots + x_n^2 \\
&= x_1^2 + x_2^2 + \cdots + x_k^2 + S^2 \\
&= \|Y\|_2.
\end{aligned}
$$

The vector W is found by using equation (3) of Theorem 11.23:

$$
(13) \qquad
\begin{aligned}
W &= \frac{1}{R}(X - Y) \\
&= \frac{1}{R}\begin{bmatrix} 0 & \cdots & 0 & (x_{k+1} + S) & x_{k+2} & \cdots & x_n \end{bmatrix}'.
\end{aligned}
$$

Less round-off error is propagated when the sign of S is chosen to be the same as the sign of x_{k+1}; hence we compute

$$
(14) \qquad S = \mathrm{sign}(x_{k+1})(x_{k+1}^2 + x_{k+2}^2 + \cdots + x_n^2)^{1/2}.
$$

The number R in (13) is chosen so that $\|W\|_2 = 1$ and must satisfy

$$
(15) \qquad
\begin{aligned}
R^2 &= (x_{k+1} + S)^2 + x_{k+2}^2 + \cdots + x_n^2 \\
&= 2x_{k+1}S + S^2 + x_{k+1}^2 + x_{k+2}^2 + \cdots + x_n^2 \\
&= 2x_{k+1}S + 2S^2.
\end{aligned}
$$

Therefore, the matrix P_k is given by the formula

$$
(16) \qquad P_k = I - 2WW',
$$

and the proof is complete. ●

Householder Transformation

Suppose that A is a symmetric $n \times n$ matrix. Then a sequence of $n - 2$ transformations of the form PAP will reduce A to a symmetric tridiagonal matrix. Let us visualize the process when $n = 5$. The first transformation is defined to be $P_1 A P_1$, where P_1 is constructed by applying Corollary 11.3, with the vector X being the first column of the matrix A. The general form of P_1 is

$$
(17) \qquad
P_1 = \begin{bmatrix}
1 & 0 & 0 & 0 & 0 \\
0 & p & p & p & p \\
0 & p & p & p & p \\
0 & p & p & p & p \\
0 & p & p & p & p
\end{bmatrix},
$$

where the letter p stands for some element in P_1. As a result, the transformation $P_1 A P_1$ does not affect the element a_{11} of A:

$$(18) \qquad P_1 A P_1 = \begin{bmatrix} a_{11} & v_1 & 0 & 0 & 0 \\ u_1 & w_1 & w & w & w \\ 0 & w & w & w & w \\ 0 & w & w & w & w \\ 0 & w & w & w & w \end{bmatrix} = A_1.$$

The element denoted u_1 is changed because of premultiplication by P_1, and v_1 is changed because of postmultiplication by P_1; since A_1 is symmetric, we have $u_1 = v_1$. The changes to the elements denoted w have been affected by both premultiplication and postmultiplication. Also, since X is the first column of A, equation (10) implies that $u_1 = -S$.

The second Householder transformation is applied to the matrix A_1 defined in (18) and is denoted $P_2 A P_2$, where P_2 is constructed by applying Corollary 11.3, with the vector X being the second column of the matrix A_1. The form of P_2 is

$$(19) \qquad P_2 = \begin{bmatrix} 1 & 0 & 0 & 0 & 0 \\ 0 & 1 & 0 & 0 & 0 \\ 0 & 0 & p & p & p \\ 0 & 0 & p & p & p \\ 0 & 0 & p & p & p \end{bmatrix},$$

where p stands for some element in P_2. The 2×2 identity block in the upper-left corner ensures that the partial tridiagonalization achieved in the first step will not be altered by the second transformation $P_2 A_1 P_2$. The outcome of this transformation is

$$(20) \qquad P_2 A_1 P_2 = \begin{bmatrix} a_{11} & v_1 & 0 & 0 & 0 \\ u_1 & w_1 & v_2 & 0 & 0 \\ 0 & u_2 & w_2 & w & w \\ 0 & 0 & w & w & w \\ 0 & 0 & w & w & w \end{bmatrix} = A_2.$$

The elements u_2 and v_2 were affected by premultiplication and postmultiplication by P_2. Additional changes have been introduced to the other elements w by the transformation.

The third Householder transformation, $P_3 A_2 P_3$, is applied to the matrix A_2 defined in (20), where the corollary is used with X being the third column of A_2. The form of P_3 is

$$(21) \qquad P_3 = \begin{bmatrix} 1 & 0 & 0 & 0 & 0 \\ 0 & 1 & 0 & 0 & 0 \\ 0 & 0 & 1 & 0 & 0 \\ 0 & 0 & 0 & p & p \\ 0 & 0 & 0 & p & p \end{bmatrix}.$$

Again, the 3×3 identity block ensures that $P_3 A_2 P_3$ does not affect the elements of A_2, which lie in the upper 3×3 corner, and we obtain

(22)
$$P_3 A_2 P_3 = \begin{bmatrix} a_{11} & v_1 & 0 & 0 & 0 \\ u_1 & w_1 & v_2 & 0 & 0 \\ 0 & u_2 & w_2 & v_3 & 0 \\ 0 & 0 & u_3 & w & w \\ 0 & 0 & 0 & w & w \end{bmatrix} = A_3.$$

Thus it has taken three transformations to reduce A to tridiagonal form.

For efficiency, the transformation PAP is not performed in matrix form. The next result shows that it is more efficiently carried out via some clever vector manipulations.

Theorem 11.24 (Computation of One Householder Transformation). If P is a Householder matrix, the transformation PAP is accomplished as follows. Let

(23)
$$V = AW$$

and compute

(24)
$$c = W'V$$

and

(25)
$$Q = V - cW.$$

Then

(26)
$$PAP = A - 2WQ' - 2QW'.$$

Proof. First, form the product

$$AP = A(I - 2WW') = A - 2AWW'.$$

Using equation (23), this is written as

(27)
$$AP = A - 2VW'.$$

Now use (27) and write

(28)
$$PAP = (I - 2WW')(A - 2VW').$$

When this quantity is expanded, the term $2(2WW'VW')$ is divided into two portions and (28) can be rewritten as

(29)
$$PAP = A - 2W(W'A) + 2W(W'VW') - 2VW' + 2W(W'V)W'.$$

Under the assumption that A is symmetric, we can use the identity $(W'A) = (W'A') = V'$. The tricky part is to observe that $(W'V)$ is a scalar quantity; hence it can commute freely about in any term. Another scalar identity, $W'V = (W'V)'$, is used to obtain the relation $W'VW' = (W'V)W' = W'(W'V) = W'(W'V)' = ((W'V)W)' = (W'VW)'$. These results are used in the terms of (29) in parentheses to get

$$(30) \qquad PAP = A - 2WV' + 2W(W'VW)' - 2VW' + 2W'VWW'.$$

Now the distributive law is used in (30) and we obtain

$$(31) \qquad PAP = A - 2W(V' - (W'VW)') - 2(V - W'VW)W'.$$

Finally, the definition for Q given in (25) is used in (31) and the outcome is equation (26), and the proof is complete.   ●

Reduction to Tridiagonal Form

Suppose that A is a symmetric $n \times n$ matrix. Start with

$$(32) \qquad\qquad\qquad A_0 = A.$$

Construct the sequence $P_1, P_2, \ldots, P_{n-1}$ of Householder matrices, so that

$$(33) \qquad\qquad A_k = P_k A_{k-1} P_k \quad\text{for } k = 1, 2, \ldots, n - 2,$$

where A_k has zeros below the subdiagonal in columns 1, 2, ..., k. Then A_{n-2} is a symmetric tridiagonal matrix that is similar to A. This process is called **Householder's method**.

Example 11.8.   Use Householder's method to reduce the following matrix to symmetric tridiagonal form:

$$A_0 = \begin{bmatrix} 4 & 2 & 2 & 1 \\ 2 & -3 & 1 & 1 \\ 2 & 1 & 3 & 1 \\ 1 & 1 & 1 & 2 \end{bmatrix}.$$

The details are left for the reader. The constants $S = 3$ and $R = 30^{1/2} = 5.477226$ are used to construct the vector

$$W' = \frac{1}{\sqrt{30}}[0 \;\; 5 \;\; 2 \;\; 1] = [0.000000 \;\; 0.912871 \;\; 0.365148 \;\; 0.182574].$$

Then matrix multiplication $V = AW$ is used to form

$$V' = \frac{1}{\sqrt{30}}[0 \;\; -12 \;\; 12 \;\; 9]$$
$$= [0.000000 \;\; -2.190890 \;\; 2.190890 \;\; 1.643168].$$

The constant $c = W'V$ is then found to be

$$c = -0.9.$$

Then the vector $Q = V - cW = V + 0.9W$ is formed:

$$Q' = \frac{1}{\sqrt{30}} \begin{bmatrix} 0.000000 & -7.500000 & 13.800000 & 9.900000 \end{bmatrix}$$
$$= \begin{bmatrix} 0.000000 & -1.369306 & 2.519524 & 1.807484 \end{bmatrix}.$$

The computation $A_1 = A_0 - 2WQ' - 2QW'$ produces

$$A_1 = \begin{bmatrix} 4.0 & -3.0 & 0.0 & 0.0 \\ -3.0 & 2.0 & -2.6 & -1.8 \\ 0.0 & -2.6 & -0.68 & -1.24 \\ 0.0 & -1.8 & -1.24 & 0.68 \end{bmatrix}.$$

The final step uses the constants $S = -3.1622777$, $R = 6.0368737$, $c = -1.2649111$ and the vectors

$$W' = \begin{bmatrix} 0.000000 & 0.000000 & -0.954514 & -0.298168 \end{bmatrix},$$
$$V' = \begin{bmatrix} 0.000000 & 0.000000 & 1.018797 & 0.980843 \end{bmatrix},$$
$$Q' = \begin{bmatrix} 0.000000 & 0.000000 & -0.188578 & 0.603687 \end{bmatrix}.$$

The tridiagonal matrix $A_2 = A_1 - 2WQ' - 2QW'$ is

$$A_2 = \begin{bmatrix} 4.0 & -3.0 & 0.0 & 0.0 \\ -3.0 & 2.0 & 3.162278 & 0.0 \\ 0.0 & 3.162278 & -1.4 & -0.2 \\ 0.0 & 0.0 & -0.2 & 1.4 \end{bmatrix}. \qquad \blacksquare$$

Program 11.4 (Reduction to Tridiagonal Form).   To reduce the $n \times n$ symmetric matrix A to tridiagonal form by using $n - 2$ Householder transformations.

```
function T=house (A)
%Input   - A is an nxn symmetric matrix
%Output  - T is a tridiagonal matrix
[n,n]=size(A);
for k=1:n-2
    %Construct W
    s=norm(A(k+1:n,k));
    if (A(k+1,k)<0)
        s=-s;
    end
    r=sqrt(2*s*(A(k+1,k)+s));
```

```
    W(1:k)=zeros(1,k);
    W(k+1)=(A(k+1,k)+s)/r;
    W(k+2:n)=A(k+2:n,k)'/r;
    %Construct V
    V(1:k)=zeros(1,k);
    V(k+1:n)=A(k+1:n,k+1:n)*W(k+1:n)';
    %Construct Q
    c=W(k+1:n)*V(k+1:n)';
    Q(1:k)=zeros(1,k);
    Q(k+1:n)=V(k+1:n)-c*W(k+1:n);
    %Form Ak
    A(k+2:n,k)=zeros(n-k-1,1);
    A(k,k+2:n)=zeros(1,n-k-1);
    A(k+1,k)=-s;
    A(k,k+1)=-s;
    A(k+1:n,k+1:n)=A(k+1:n,k+1:n) ...
    -2*W(k+1:n)'*Q(k+1:n)-2*Q(k+1:n)'*W(k+1:n);
end
T=A;
```

QR Method

Suppose that A is a real symmetric matrix. In the preceding section we saw how Householder's method is used to construct a similar tridiagonal matrix. The QR method is used to find all eigenvalues of a tridiagonal matrix. Plane rotations similar to those that were introduced in Jacobi's method are used to construct an orthogonal matrix $Q_1 = Q$ and an upper-triangular matrix $U_1 = U$ so that $A_1 = A$ has the factorization

$$(34) \qquad\qquad A_1 = Q_1 U_1.$$

Then form the product

$$(35) \qquad\qquad A_2 = U_1 Q_1.$$

Since Q_1 is orthogonal, we can use (34) to see that

$$(36) \qquad\qquad Q_1' A_1 = Q_1' Q_1 U_1 = U_1.$$

Therefore, A_2 can be computed with the formula

$$(37) \qquad\qquad A_2 = Q_1' A_1 Q_1.$$

Since $Q_1' = Q_1^{-1}$, it follows that A_2 is similar to A_1 and has the same eigenvalues. In general, construct the orthogonal matrix Q_k and upper-triangular matrix U_k so that

$$(38) \qquad\qquad A_k = Q_k U_k.$$

Then define

$$(39) \qquad A_{k+1} = U_k Q_k = Q'_k A_k Q_k.$$

Again, we have $Q'_k = Q_k^{-1}$, which implies that A_{k+1} and A_k are similar. An important consequence is that A_k is similar to A and hence has the same structure. Specifically, we can conclude that if A is tridiagonal then A_k is also tridiagonal for all k. Now suppose that A is written as

$$(40) \qquad A = \begin{bmatrix} d_1 & e_1 & & & & & \\ e_1 & d_2 & e_2 & & & & \\ & e_2 & d_3 & \cdots & & & \\ & & & \vdots & d_{n-2} & e_{n-2} & \\ & & & & e_{n-2} & d_{n-1} & e_{n-1} \\ & & & & & e_{n-1} & d_n \end{bmatrix}.$$

We can find a plane rotation P_{n-1} that reduces to zero the element of A in location $(n, n-1)$, that is,

$$(41) \qquad P_{n-1}A = \begin{bmatrix} d_1 & e_1 & & & & & \\ e_1 & d_2 & e_2 & & & & \\ & e_2 & d_3 & \cdots & & & \\ & & & \vdots & d_{n-2} & q_{n-2} & r_{n-2} \\ & & & & e_{n-2} & p_{n-1} & q_{n-1} \\ & & & & & 0 & p_n \end{bmatrix}.$$

Continuing in a similar fashion, we can construct a plane rotation P_{n-2} that will reduce to zero the element of $P_{n-1}A$ located in position $(n-1, n-2)$. After $n-1$ steps we arrive at

$$(42) \qquad P_1 \cdots P_{n-1}A = \begin{bmatrix} p_1 & q_1 & r_1 & \cdots & & & & \\ 0 & p_2 & q_2 & \ddots & & & & \\ 0 & 0 & p_3 & \ddots & r_{n-4} & & & \\ & & \vdots & \ddots & q_{n-3} & r_{n-3} & & \\ & & & & p_{n-2} & q_{n-2} & r_{n-2} \\ & & & & 0 & p_{n-1} & q_{n-1} \\ & & & & 0 & 0 & p_n \end{bmatrix} = U.$$

Since each plane rotation is represented by an orthogonal matrix, equation (42) implies that

$$(43) \qquad Q = P'_{n-1} P'_{n-2} \cdots P'_1.$$

Direct multiplication of U by Q will produce all zero elements below the lower second diagonal. The tridiagonal form of A_2 implies that it also has zeros above the upper second diagonal. Investigation will reveal that the terms r_j are used only to compute these zero elements. Consequently, the numbers $\{r_j\}$ do not need to be stored or used in the computer.

For each plane rotation P_j it is assumed that we store the coefficients c_j and s_j that define it. Then we do not need to compute and store Q explicitly; instead, we can use the sequences $\{c_j\}$ and $\{s_j\}$ together with the correct formulas to unravel the product

$$(44) \qquad A_2 = U Q = U P'_{n-1} P'_{n-2} \cdots P'_1.$$

Acceleration Shifts

As outlined above the QR method will work, but convergence is slow even for matrices of small dimension. We can add a shifting technique that speeds up the rate of convergence. Recall that if λ_j is an eigenvalue of A, then $\lambda_j - s_i$ is an eigenvalue of the matrix $B = A - s_i I$. This idea is incorporated in the modified step

$$(45) \qquad A_i - s_i I = U_i Q_i;$$

then form

$$(46) \qquad A_{i+1} = U_i Q_i \quad \text{for } i = 1,\ 2,\ \ldots,\ k_j,$$

where $\{s_i\}$ is a sequence whose sum is λ_j; that is, $\lambda_j = s_1 + s_2 + \cdots + s_{k_j}$.

At each stage the correct amount of shift is found by using the four elements in the lower-right corner of the matrix. Start by finding λ_1 and compute the eigenvalues of the 2×2 matrix

$$(47) \qquad \begin{bmatrix} d_{n-1} & e_{n-1} \\ e_{n-1} & d_n \end{bmatrix}.$$

They are x_1 and x_2 and are the roots of the quadratic equation

$$(48) \qquad x^2 - (d_{n-1} + d_n)x + d_{n-1}d_n - e_{n-1}e_{n-1} = 0.$$

The value s_i in equation (45) is chosen to be the root of (48) that is closest to d_n.

Then QR iterating with shifting is repeated until we have $e_{n-1} \approx 0$. This will produce the first eigenvalue $\lambda_1 = s_1 + s_2 + \cdots + s_{k_1}$. A similar process is repeated with the upper $n - 1$ rows to obtain $e_{n-2} \approx 0$, and the next eigenvalue is λ_2. Successive iteration is applied to smaller submatrices until we obtain $e_2 \approx 0$ and the eigenvalue λ_{n-2}. Finally, the quadratic formula is used to find the last two eigenvalues. The details can be gleaned from Program 11.5

Example 11.9. Find the eigenvalues of the matrix

$$M = \begin{bmatrix} 4 & 2 & 2 & 1 \\ 2 & -3 & 1 & 1 \\ 2 & 1 & 3 & 1 \\ 1 & 1 & 1 & 2 \end{bmatrix}.$$

In Example 11.8, a tridiagonal matrix A_1 was constructed that is similar to M. We start our diagonalization process with this matrix:

$$A_1 = \begin{bmatrix} 4 & -3 & 0 & 0 \\ -3 & 2 & 3.16228 & 0 \\ 0 & 3.16228 & -1.4 & -0.2 \\ 0 & 0 & -0.2 & 1.4 \end{bmatrix}.$$

The four elements in the lower right corner are $d_3 = -1.4$, $d_4 = 1.4$, and $e_3 = -0.2$ and are used to form the quadratic equation

$$x^2 - (-1.4 + 1.4)x + (-1.4)(1.4) - (-0.2)(-0.2) = x^2 - 2 = 0.$$

Calculation produces the roots $x_1 = -1.41421$ and $x_2 = 1.41421$. The root closest to d_4 is chosen as the first shift $s_1 = 1.41421$, and the first shifted matrix is

$$A_1 - s_1 I = \begin{bmatrix} 2.58579 & -3 & 0 & 0 \\ -3 & 0.58579 & 1.74806 & 0 \\ 0 & 1.74806 & -2.81421 & -1.61421 \\ 0 & 0 & -1.61421 & -0.01421 \end{bmatrix}.$$

Next, the factorization $A_1 - s_1 I = Q_1 U_1$ is computed:

$$Q_1 U_1 = \begin{bmatrix} -0.65288 & -0.38859 & -0.55535 & 0.33814 \\ 0.75746 & -0.33494 & -0.47867 & 0.29145 \\ 0 & 0.85838 & -0.43818 & 0.26610 \\ 0 & 0 & 0.52006 & 0.85413 \end{bmatrix}$$

$$\times \begin{bmatrix} -3.96059 & 2.40235 & 2.39531 & 0 \\ 0 & 3.68400 & -3.47483 & -0.17168 \\ 0 & 0 & -0.38457 & 0.08024 \\ 0 & 0 & 0 & -0.06550 \end{bmatrix}.$$

Then the matrix product is computed in the reverse order to obtain

$$A_2 = U_1 Q_1 = \begin{bmatrix} 4.40547 & 2.79049 & 0 & 0 \\ 2.79049 & -4.21663 & -0.33011 & 0 \\ 0 & -0.33011 & 0.21024 & -0.03406 \\ 0 & 0 & -0.03406 & -0.05595 \end{bmatrix}.$$

The second shift is $s_2 = -0.06024$, the second shifted matrix is $A_2 - s_2 I = Q_2 U_2$, and

$$A_3 = U_2 Q_2 = \begin{bmatrix} 4.55257 & -2.65725 & 0 & 0 \\ -2.65725 & -4.26047 & 0.01911 & 0 \\ 0 & 0.01911 & 0.29171 & 0.00003 \\ 0 & 0 & 0.00003 & 0.00027 \end{bmatrix}.$$

The third shift is $s_3 = 0.00027$, the third shifted matrix is $A_3 - s_3 I = Q_3 U_3$, and

$$A_4 = U_3 Q_3 = \begin{bmatrix} 4.62640 & 2.53033 & 0 & 0 \\ 2.53033 & -4.33489 & -0.00111 & 0 \\ 0 & -0.00111 & 0.29150 & 0 \\ 0 & 0 & 0 & 0 \end{bmatrix}.$$

The first eigenvalue, rounded to five decimal places is given in the calculation

$$\lambda_1 = s_1 + s_2 + s_3 = 1.41421 - 0.06023 + 0.00027 = 1.35425.$$

Next λ_1 is placed in the last diagonal position of A_4 and the process is repeated, but changes are made only in the upper 3×3 corner of the matrix

$$A_4 = \begin{bmatrix} 4.62640 & 2.53033 & 0 & 0 \\ 2.53033 & -4.33489 & -0.00111 & 0 \\ 0 & -0.00111 & 0.29150 & 0 \\ 0 & 0 & 0 & 1.35425 \end{bmatrix}.$$

In a similar manner, one more shift reduces the entry in the second row and third column to zero (to 10 decimal places):

$$s_4 = 0.29150, \qquad A_4 - s_4 I = Q_4 U_4, \qquad A_5 = U_4 Q_4.$$

Hence the second eigenvalue is

$$\lambda_2 = \lambda_1 + s_4 = 1.35425 + 0.29150 = 1.64575.$$

Finally, λ_2 is placed on the diagonal of A_5 in the third row and column to obtain

$$A_5 = \begin{bmatrix} 4.26081 & -2.65724 & 0 & 0 \\ -2.65724 & -4.55232 & 0 & 0 \\ 0 & 0 & 1.64575 & 0 \\ 0 & 0 & 0 & 1.35425 \end{bmatrix}.$$

The final computation requires finding the eigenvalues of the 2×2 matrix in the upper-left corner of A_5. The characteristic equation is

$$x^2 - (-4.26081 + 4.55232)x + (4.26081)(-4.55232) - (2.65724)(2.65724) = 0,$$

which reduces to

$$x^2 + 0.29151x - 26.45749 = 0.$$

The roots are $x_1 = 5.00000$ and $x_2 = -5.29150$, and the last two eigenvalues are computed with the calculations

$$\lambda_3 = \lambda_2 + x_1 = 1.64575 + 5.0000 = 6.64575$$

and

$$\lambda_4 = \lambda_2 + x_2 = 1.64575 - 5.29150 = -3.64575. \qquad \blacksquare$$

Program 11.5 can be used to approximate all the eigenvalues of a symmetric tridi-agonal matrix. The program follows directly from the previous discussion, but with two notable exceptions. First, the MATLAB command `eig` is used to find the roots of the characteristic equation (48) of each 2×2 submatrix (47). Second, the QR factorization of the matrix $A_i - s_i I$ (45) is executed using the MATLAB command `[Q,R]=qr(B)`, which produces an orthogonal matrix Q and an upper-triangular matrix R, such that B=Q*R (readers will be asked to write their own QR factorization program).

Program 11.5 (QR Method with Shifts). To approximate the eigenvalues of a symmetric tridiagonal matrix A using the QR method with shifts.

```
function D=qr2(A,epsilon)

%Input   - A is a symmetric tridiagonal nxn matrix
%         - epsilon is the tolerance
%Output  - D is the nx1 vector of eigenvalues

%Initialize parameters
[n,n]=size(A);
m=n;
D=zeros(n,1);
B=A;

while (m>1)
   while (abs(B(m,m-1))>=epsilon)

      %Calculate shift
      S=eig(B(m-1:m,m-1:m));
      [j,k]=min([abs(B(m,m)*[1 1]'-S)]);

      %QR factorization of B
      [Q,U]=qr(B-S(k)*eye(m));

      %Calculate next B
      B=U*Q+S(k)*eye(m);
   end

   %Place mth eigenvalue in A(m,m)
   A(1:m,1:m)=B;

   %Repeat process on the m-1 x m-1 submatrix of A
   m=m-1;
   B=A(1:m,1:m);
end
D=diag(A);
```

Exercises for Eigenvalues of Symmetric Matrices

1. In the proof of Theorem 11.23, carefully explain why Z is perpendicular to W.

2. If X is any vector and $P = I - 2XX'$, show that P is a symmetric matrix.

3. Let X be any vector and set $P = I - 2XX'$.
   - (a) Find the quantity $P'P$.
   - (b) What additional condition is necessary in order that P be an orthogonal matrix?

Algorithms and Programs

In Problems 1 through 6, use:
(a) Program 11.4 to reduce the given matrix to tridiagonal form.
(b) Program 11.5 to find the eigenvalues of the given matrix.

1. $\begin{bmatrix} 3 & 2 & 1 \\ 2 & 3 & 2 \\ 1 & 2 & 3 \end{bmatrix}$

2. $\begin{bmatrix} 4 & 3 & 2 & 1 \\ 3 & 4 & 3 & 2 \\ 2 & 3 & 4 & 3 \\ 1 & 2 & 3 & 4 \end{bmatrix}$

3. $\begin{bmatrix} 2.75 & -0.25 & -0.75 & 1.25 \\ -0.25 & 2.75 & 1.25 & -0.75 \\ -0.75 & 1.25 & 2.75 & -0.25 \\ 1.25 & -0.75 & -0.25 & 2.75 \end{bmatrix}$

4. $\begin{bmatrix} 3.6 & 4.4 & 0.8 & -1.6 & -2.8 \\ 4.4 & 2.6 & 1.2 & -0.4 & 0.8 \\ 0.8 & 1.2 & 0.8 & -4.0 & -2.8 \\ -1.6 & -0.4 & -4.0 & 1.2 & 2.0 \\ -2.8 & 0.8 & -2.8 & 2.0 & 1.8 \end{bmatrix}$

5. $A = [a_{ij}]$, where $a_{ij} = \begin{cases} i + j & i = j \\ ij & i \neq j \end{cases}$ and $i, j = 1, 2, \ldots, 30$.

6. $A = [a_{ij}]$, where $a_{ij} = \begin{cases} \cos(\sin(i + j)) & i = j \\ i + ij + j & i \neq j \end{cases}$ and $i, j = 1, 2, \ldots, 40$.

7. Write a program to carry out the QR method on a symmetric matrix.

8. Modify Program 11.5 to call your program from Problem 7 as a subroutine. Use this modified program to find the eigenvalues of the matrices in Problems 1 through 6.

Appendix:
Introduction to MATLAB

This appendix introduces the reader to programming with the software package MAT-LAB. It is assumed that the reader has had previous experience with a high-level programming language and is familiar with the techniques of writing loops, branching using logical relations, calling subroutines, and editing. These techniques are directly applicable in the windows-type environment of MATLAB.

MATLAB is a mathematical software package based on matrices. The package consists of an extensive library of numerical routines, easily accessed two- and three-dimensional graphics, and a high-level programming format. The ability to implement and modify programs quickly makes MATLAB an appropriate format for exploring and executing the algorithms in this textbook.

The reader should work through the following tutorial introduction to MATLAB (MATLAB commands are in `typewriter` type). The examples illustrate typical input and output from the MATLAB Command Window. To find additional information about commands, options, and examples, the reader is urged to make use of the on-line help facility and the Reference and User's Guides that accompany the software.

Arithmetic Operations

`+`	Addition
`-`	Subtraction
`*`	Multiplication
`/`	Division
`^`	Power
`pi, e, i`	Constants

```
Ex. >>(2+3*pi)/2
    ans =
        5.7124
```

Built-in Functions

Below is a short list of some of the functions available in MATLAB. The following example illustrates how functions and arithmetic operations are combined. Descriptions of other available functions may be found by using the on-line help facility.

```
    abs(#)      cos(#)      exp(#)      log(#)      log10(#)    cosh(#)
    sin(#)      tan(#)      sqrt(#)     floor(#)    acos(#)     tanh(#)
Ex. >>3*cos(sqrt(4.7))
    ans =
        -1.6869
```

The default format shows approximately five significant decimal figures. Entering the command format long will display approximately 15 significant decimal figures.

```
Ex. >>format long
    3*cos(sqrt(4.7))
    ans =
        -1.68686892236893
```

Assignment Statements

Variable names are assigned to expressions by using an equal sign.

```
Ex. >>a=3-floor(exp(2.9))
    a=
        -15
```

A semicolon placed at the end of an expression suppresses the computer echo (output).

```
Ex. >>b=sin(a);              Note. b was not displayed.
    >>2*b^2
    ans=
        0.8457
```

Defining Functions

In MATLAB the user can define a function by constructing an M-file (a file ending in .m) in the M-file Editor/Debugger. Once defined, a user-defined function is called in the same manner as built-in functions.

Ex. Place the function fun$(x) = 1 + x - x^2/4$ in the M-file `fun.m`. In the Editor/Debugger one would enter the following:

```
function y=fun(x)
y=1+x-x.^2/4;
```

We will explain the use of ".^" shortly. Different letters could be used for the variables and a different name could be used for the function, but the same format would have to be followed. Once this function has been saved as an M-file named `fun.m`, it can be called in the MATLAB Command Window in the same manner as any function.

```
>>cos(fun(3))
ans=
      -0.1782
```

A useful and efficient way to evaluate functions is to use the `feval` command. This command requires that the function be called as a string.

```
Ex. >>feval('fun',4)
    ans=
          1
```

Matrices

All variables in MATLAB are treated as matrices or arrays. Matrices can be entered directly:

```
Ex. >>A=[1 2 3;4 5 6;7 8 9]
    A=
          1 2 3
          4 5 6
          7 8 9
```

Semicolons are used to separate the rows of a matrix. Note that the entries of the matrix must be separated by a single space. Alternatively, a matrix can be entered row by row.

```
Ex. >>A=[1 2 3
         4 5 6
         7 8 9]
    A =
          1 2 3
          4 5 6
          7 8 9
```

Matrices can be generated using built-in functions.

```
Ex. >>Z=zeros(3,5);        creates a 3 × 5 matrix of zeros
    >>X=ones(3,5);         creates a 3 × 5 matrix of ones
    >>Y=0:0.5:2            creates the displayed 1 × 5 matrix
    Y=
    0 0.5000 1.0000 1.5000 2.0000
```

>>cos(Y)   creates a 1×5 matrix by taking the cosine of each entry of Y

ans=
            1.0000 0.8776 0.5403 0.0707 −0.4161

The components of matrices can be manipulated in several ways.

Ex. >>A(2,3)   select a single entry of A

ans=
            6

>>A(1:2,2:3)   select a submatrix of A

ans=
            2 3
            5 6

>>A([1 3],[1 3])   another way to select a submatrix of A

ans=
            1 3
            7 9

>>A(2,2)=tan(7.8);   assign a new value to an entry of A

Additional commands for matrices can be found by using the on-line help facility or consulting the documentation accompanying the software.

Matrix Operations

+	Addition
−	Subtraction
*	Multiplication
^	Power
'	Conjugate transpose

Ex. >>B=[1 2;3 4];

>>C=B'   C is the transpose of B

C=
            1 3
            2 4

>>3*(B*C)^3 $3(BC)^3$

ans=
            13080 29568
            29568 66840

Array Operations

One of the most useful characteristics of the MATLAB package is the number of functions that can operate on the individual elements of a matrix. This was demonstrated earlier when the cosine of the entries of a 1×5 matrix was taken. The matrix operations of addition, subtraction, and scalar multiplication already operate elementwise, but the matrix operations of multiplication, division, and power do not. These three operations can be made to operate elementwise by preceding them with a period: `.*`, `./`, and `.^`. It is important to understand how and when to use these operations. Array operations are crucial to the efficient construction and execution of MATLAB programs and graphics.

```
Ex.  >>A=[1 2;3 4];
     >>A^2                        produces the matrix product AA
     ans=
           7 10
           15 22
     >>A.^2                       squares each entry of A
     ans=
           1 4
           9 16
     >>cos(A./2)                  divides each entry of A by 2, then takes
                                  the cosine of each entry
     ans=
           0.8776  0.5403
           0.0707 -0.4161
```

Graphics

MATLAB can produce two- and three-dimensional plots of curves and surfaces. Options and additional features of graphics in MATLAB can be found in the on-line facility and the documentation accompanying the software.

The `plot` command is used to generate graphs of two-dimensional functions. The following example will create the plot of the graphs of $y = \cos(x)$ and $y = \cos^2(x)$ over the interval $[0, \pi]$.

```
Ex.  >>x=0:0.1:pi;
     >>y=cos(x);
     >>z=cos(x).^2;
     >>plot(x,y,x,z,'o')
```

The first line specifies the domain with a step size of 0.1. The next two lines define the two functions. Note that the first three lines all end in a semicolon. The semicolon is necessary to suppress the echoing of the matrices x, y, and z on the command screen. The fourth line contains the plot command that produces the graph. The first two terms in the plot command, x and y, plot the function $y = \cos(x)$. The third and fourth terms, x and z, produce the plot of $y = \cos^2(x)$. The last term, `'o'`, results in o's being plotted at each point (x_k, z_k) where $z_k = \cos^2(x_k)$.

In the third line the use of the array operation ".^" is critical. First the cosine of each entry in the matrix x is taken, and then each entry in the matrix cos(x) is squared using the .^ command.

The graphics command fplot is a useful alternative to the plot command. The form of the command is fplot('name', [a,b], n). This command creates a plot of the function name.m by sampling n points in the interval $[a, b]$. The default number for n is 25.

Ex. >>fplot('tanh', [-2,2])   plots $y = \tanh(x)$ over $[-2, 2]$

The plot and plot3 commands are used to graph parametric curves in two- and three-dimensional space, respectively. These commands are particularly useful in the visualization of the solutions of differential equations in two and three dimensions.

Ex. The plot of the ellipse $c(t) = (2\cos(t), 3\sin(t))$, where $0 \le t \le 2\pi$, is produced with the following commands:

```
>>t=0:0.2:2*pi;
>>plot(2*cos(t),3*sin(t))
```

Ex. The plot of the curve $c(t) = (2\cos(t), t^2, 1/t)$, where $0.1 \le t \le 4\pi$, is produced with the following commands:

```
>>t=0.1:0.1:4*pi;
>>plot3(2*cos(t),t.^2,1./t)
```

Three-dimensional surface plots are obtained by specifying a rectangular subset of the domain of a function with the meshgrid command and then using the mesh or surf commands to obtain a graph. These graphs are helpful in visualizing the solutions of partial differential equations.

```
Ex.  >>x=-pi:0.1:pi;
     >>y=x;
     >>[x,y]=meshgrid(x,y);
     >>z=sin(cos(x+y));
     >>mesh(z)
```

Loops and Conditionals

Relational Operators

==	Equal to
~=	Not equal to
<	Less than
>	Greater than
<=	Less than or equal to
>=	Greater than or equal to

Logical Operators

~	Not	(complement)
&	And	(true if both operands are true)
|	Or	(true if either or both operands are true)

Boolean Values

1	True
0	False

The `for`, `if`, and `while` statements in MATLAB operate in a manner analogous to their counterparts in other programming languages. These statements have the following basic form:

```
for (loop-variable = loop-expression)
        executable-statements
end

if (logical-expression)
        executable-statements
else (logical- expression)
        executable-statements
end

while (while-expression)
        executable-statements
end
```

The following example shows how to use nested loops to generate a matrix. The following file was saved as a M-file named `nest.m`. Typing `nest` in the MATLAB Command Window produces the matrix A. Note that when viewed from the upper-left corner, the entries of the matrix A are the entries in Pascal's triangle.

```
Ex. for i=1:5
       A(i,1)=1;A(1,i)=1;
    end
    for i=2:5
      for j=2:5
        A(i,j)=A(i,j-1)+A(i-1,j);
      end
    end
    A
```

The `break` command is used to exit from a loop.

```
Ex. for k=1:100
       x=sqrt(k);
       if ((k>10)&(x-floor(x)==0))
         break
       end
    end
```

```
k
```

The `disp` command can be used to display text or a matrix.

```
Ex. n=10;
    k=0;
    while k<=n
      x=k/3;
      disp([x x^2 x^3])
      k=k+1;
    end
```

Programs

An efficient way to construct programs is to use user-defined functions. These functions are saved as M-files. These programs allow the user to specify the input and output parameters. They are easily called as subroutines in other programs. The following example allows one to visualize the effects of moding out Pascal's triangle with a prime number. Type the following function in the MATLAB Editor/Debugger and then save it as an M-file named `pasc.m`.

```
Ex. function P=pasc(n,m)
    %Input   - n is the number of rows
    %         - m is the prime number
    %Output  - P is Pascal's triangle

    for j=1:n
      P(j,1)=1;P(1,j)=1;
    end
    for k=2:n
      for j=2:n
        P(k,j)=rem(P(k,j-1)+P(k-1,j),m);
      end
    end
```

Now in the MATLAB Command Window enter P=`pasc(5,3)` to see the first five rows of Pascal's triangle mod 3. Or try P=`pasc(175,3);` (note the semicolon) and then type `spy(P)` (generates a sparse matrix for large values of n).

Conclusion

At this point the reader should be able to create and modify programs based on the algorithms in this textbook. Additional information on commands and information regarding the use of MATLAB on your particular platform can be found in the on-line help facility or in the documentation accompanying the software.

Answers to Selected Exercises

Section 1.1   Review of Calculus

1. **(a)** $L = 2$, $\{\epsilon_n\} = \left\{ \dfrac{1}{2n + 1} \right\}$, $\lim_{n \to \infty} \epsilon_n = 0$

3. **(a)** $c = 1 - \sqrt{2}$

4. **(a)** $M_1 = -5/4$, $M_2 = 5$

5. **(a)** $c = 0$

6. **(a)** $c = 1$

7. $c = 4/3$

9. **(a)** $x^2 \cos(x)$

10. **(a)** $c = \pm\sqrt{13/3}$

11. **(a)** 2   **(b)** 1

15. $13\pi/3$, apply the mean value theorem for integrals

16. Let the n roots of $P(x)$ be $x_0, x_1, \ldots, x_{n-1}$. Verify that the hypotheses of the generalized Rolle's theorem are satisfied. Therefore, there exists $c \in (a, b)$ such that $P^{(n-1)}(c) = 0$.

Section 1.2   Binary Numbers

1. **(a)** The computer's answer is not 0 because 0.1 is not an exact binary fraction.

    (b) 0 (exactly)

2. (a) 21   **(c)** 254

3. (a) 0.84375   **(c)** 0.6640625

4. (a) 1.4140625

5. (a) $\sqrt{2} - 1.4140625 = 0.000151062\ldots$

6. (a) 10111_{two} **(c)** 101111010_{two}

7. (a) 0.0111_{two} **(c)** 0.10111_{two}

8. (a) $0.0\overline{0011}_{\text{two}}$ **(c)** $0.\overline{001}_{\text{two}}$

9. (a) $0.006250000\ldots$

11. Use $c = \frac{3}{16}$ and $r = \frac{1}{16}$ to get $S = \frac{\frac{3}{16}}{1-\frac{1}{16}} = \frac{1}{5}$

13. (a)
$$
\begin{array}{lll}
\frac{1}{3} & \approx 0.1011_{\text{two}} \times 2^{-1} & = & 0.1011_{\text{two}} \times 2^{-1} \\
\frac{1}{5} & \approx 0.1101_{\text{two}} \times 2^{-2} & = & 0.01101_{\text{two}} \times 2^{-1} \\
\hline
\frac{8}{15} & & & 0.100011_{\text{two}} \times 2^{-0}
\end{array}
$$

$$
\begin{array}{lll}
\frac{8}{15} & \approx 0.1001_{\text{two}} \times 2^{-0} & = & 0.1001_{\text{two}} \times 2^{0} \\
\frac{1}{6} & \approx 0.1011_{\text{two}} \times 2^{-2} & = & 0.001011_{\text{two}} \times 2^{-0} \\
\hline
\frac{7}{10} & & & 0.101111_{\text{two}} \times 2^{-0} \approx \boxed{0.1100_{\text{two}}}
\end{array}
$$

14. (a) $10 = 101_{\text{three}}$ **(c)** $421 = 120121_{\text{three}}$

15. (a) $\frac{1}{3} = 0.1_{\text{three}}$ **(b)** $\frac{1}{2} = 0.\overline{1}_{\text{three}}$

16. (a) $10 = 20_{\text{five}}$ **(c)** $721 = 10341_{\text{five}}$

17. (b) $\frac{1}{2} = 0.\overline{2}_{\text{five}}$

Section 1.3   Error Analysis

1. (a) $x = 2.71828182, \widehat{x} = 2.7182, (x - \widehat{x}) = 0.00008182,$
$(x - \widehat{x})/x = 0.00003010$, four significant digits

2. $\dfrac{1}{4} + \dfrac{1}{4^3 3} + \dfrac{1}{4^5 5(2!)} + \dfrac{1}{4^7 7(3!)} = \dfrac{292{,}807}{1{,}146{,}880} = 0.2553074428 = \widehat{p},$
$p - \widehat{p} = 0.0000000178, (p - \widehat{p})/p = 0.0000000699$

3. (a) $p_1 + p_2 = 1.414 + 0.09125 = 1.505, p_1 p_2 = (1.414)(0.09125) = 0.1290$

4. The error involves loss of significance.
(a) $\dfrac{0.70711385222 - 0.70710678119}{0.00001} = \dfrac{0.00000707103}{0.000001} = 0.707103$

5. (a) $\ln((x+2)/x)$ or $\ln(1+1/x)$ **(c)** $\cos(2x)$

6. (a) $P(2.72) = (2.72)^3 - 3(2.72)^2 + 3(2.72) - 1 = 20.12 - 22.19 + 8.16 - 1$

$$= -2.07 + 8.16 - 1 = 6.09 - 1 = 5.09$$

$Q(2.72) = ((2.72 - 3)2.72 + 3)2.72 - 1 = ((-0.28)2.72 + 3)2.72 - 1$

$$= (-0.7616 + 3)2.72 - 1 = (2.238)2.72 - 1 = 6.087 - 1$$

$$= 5.087$$

$R(2.72) = (2.72 - 1)^3 = (1.72)^3 = 5.088$

7. (a) 0.498   **(b)** 0.499

9. $\dfrac{1}{1-h} + \cos(h) = 2 + h + \dfrac{h^2}{2}h^3 + O(h^4)$

$\dfrac{1}{1-h} \cos(h) = 1 + h + \dfrac{h^2}{2} + \dfrac{h^3}{2} + O(h^4)$

Section 2.1   Iteration for Solving $x = g(x)$

1. (a) $g \in C[0, 1]$, g maps $[0, 1]$ onto $[3/4, 1] \subseteq [0, 1]$, and $|g'(x)| = |-x/2| = x/2 \le 1/2 < 1$ on $[0, 1]$. Therefore, the hypotheses of Theorem 2.2 are satisfied and g has a unique fixed point on $[0, 1]$.

2. (a) $g(2) = -4 + 8 - 2 = 2$, $g(4) = -4 + 16 - 8 = 4$

(b)

$p_0 = 1.9$	$E_0 = 0.1$	$R_0 = 0.05$
$p_1 = 1.795$	$E_1 = 0.205$	$R_1 = 0.1025$
$p_2 = 1.5689875$	$E_2 = 0.4310125$	$R_2 = 0.21550625$
$p_3 = 1.04508911$	$E_3 = 0.95491089$	$R_3 = 0.477455444$

(e) The sequence in part (b) does not converge to $P = 2$. The sequence in part (c) converges to $P = 4$.

4. $P = 2$, $g'(2) = 5$, iteration will not converge to $P = 2$.

5. $P = 2n\pi$ where n is any integer, $g'(P) = 1$; Theorem 2.3 gives no information regarding convergence.

9. (a) $g(3) = 0.5(3) + 1.5 = 3$

(c) Proof by mathematical induction. If $n = 1$, then $|P - p_1| = |P - p_0|/2^1$, by part (b). Induction hypothesis: Assume that $|P - p_k| = |P - p_0|/2^k$. Show statement is true for $n = k + 1$:

$$|P - p_{k+1}| = |P - p_k|/2 \qquad \text{(by part (b))}$$
$$= (|P - p_0|/2^k)/2 \qquad \text{(induction hypothesis)}$$
$$= |P - p_0|/2^{k+1}.$$

10. (a) $\dfrac{|p_{k+1} - p_k|}{|p_{k+1}|} = \left| \dfrac{\dfrac{p_k}{2} - p_k}{\dfrac{p_k}{2}} \right| = 1$

Section 2.2 Bracketing Methods for Locating a Root

1. $I_0 = (0.11 + 0.12)/2 = 0.115$ $A(0.115) = 254{,}403$
   $I_1 = (0.11 + 0.115)/2 = 0.1125$ $A(0.1125) = 246{,}072$
   $I_2 = (0.1125 + 0.115)/2 = 0.11375$ $A(0.11375) = 250{,}198$

3. There are many choices for intervals $[a, b]$ on which $f(a)$ and $f(b)$ have opposite sign. The following answers are one such choice.

   (a) $f(1) < 0$ and $f(2) > 0$, so there is a root in $[1, 2]$; also, $f(-1) < 0$ and $f(-2) > 0$, so there is a root in $[-2, -1]$.

   (c) $f(3) < 0$ and $f(4) > 0$, so there is a root in $[3, 4]$.

4. $c_0 = -1.8300782$, $c_1 = -1.8409252$, $c_2 = -1.8413854$, $c_3 = -1.8414048$

6. $c_0 = 3.6979549$, $c_1 = 3.6935108$, $c_2 = 3.6934424$, $c_3 = 3.6934414$

11. Find N such that $\dfrac{7 - 2}{2^{N+1}} < 5 \times 10^{-9}$.

14. The bisection method will never converge (assuming that $c_n \neq 2$) to $x = 2$.

Section 2.3 Initial Approximation and Convergence Criteria

1. There is a root near $x = -0.7$. The interval $[-1, 0]$ could be used.

3. There is a root near $x = 1$. The interval $[-2, 2]$ could be used.

5. There is one root near $x = 1.4$. The interval $[1, 2]$ could be used. There is a second root near $x = 3$. The interval $[2, 4]$ could be used.

Section 2.4 Newton-Raphson and Secant Methods

1. **(a)** $p_k = g(p_{k-1}) = \dfrac{p_{k-1}^2 - 2}{2p_{k-1} - 1}$.
   (b) $p_0 = -1.5$, $p_1 = 0.125$, $p_2 = 2.6458$, $p_3 = 1.1651$

3. **(a)** $p_k = g(p_{k-1}) = \frac{3}{4}p_{k-1} + \frac{1}{2}$.
   (b) $p_0 = 2.1$, $p_1 = 2.075$, $p_2 = 2.0561$, $p_3 = 2.0421$, $p_4 = 2.0316$

5. **(a)** $p_k = g(p_{k-1}) = p_{k-1} + \cos(p_{k-1})$

7. **(a)** $g(p_{k-1}) = p_{k-1}^2/(p_{k-1} - 1)$

   (b) $p_0 = 0.20$ **(c)** $p_0 = 20.0$
   $p_1 = -0.05$ $p_1 = 21.05263158$
   $p_2 = -0.002380953$ $p_2 = 22.10250034$
   $p_3 = -0.000005655$ $p_3 = 23.14988809$
   $p_4 = -0.000000000$ $p_4 = 24.19503505$
   $\displaystyle\lim_{n \to \infty} p_k = 0.0$ $\displaystyle\lim_{n \to \infty} p_k = \infty$

8. $p_0 = 2.6$, $p_1 = 2.5$, $p_2 = 2.41935484$, $p_3 = 2.41436464$

14. No, because $f'(x)$ is not continuous at the root $p = 0$. You could also try computing terms with $g(p_{k-1}) = -2p_{k-1}$ and see that the sequence diverges.

22. (a) $g(x) = x - \dfrac{x^2 - a}{2x}\left(1 - \dfrac{(x^2 - a)2}{2(2x)^2}\right)^{-1} = \dfrac{x(x^2 + 3a)}{3x^2 + a}$

$$g(x) = \dfrac{15x + x^3}{5 + 3x^2}$$

$p_1 = 2.2352941176$, $p_2 = 2.2360679775$, $p_3 = 2.2360679775$

(b) $g(x) = \dfrac{2 + 4x + 2x^2 + x^3}{3 + 4x + 2x^2}$

$p_1 = -2.0130081301$, $p_2 = -2.0000007211$, $p_3 = -2.0000000000$

Section 2.5   Aitken's Process and Steffensen's and Muller's Methods (Optional)

2. (a) $\Delta^2 p_n = \Delta(\Delta p_n) = \Delta(p_{n+1} - p_n) = (p_{n+2} - p_{n+1}) - (p_{n+1} - p_n)$

$$= p_{n+2} - 2p_{n+1} + p_n = 2(n + 2)^2 + 1 - 2(2(n + 1)^2 + 1)$$

$$+ 2n^2 + 1 = 4$$

6. $p_n = 1/(4^n + 4^{-n})$

n	p_n	q_n Aitken's
0	0.5	-0.26437542
1	0.23529412	-0.00158492
2	0.06225681	-0.00002390
3	0.01562119	-0.00000037
4	0.00390619	
5	0.00097656	

7. $g(x) = (6 + x)^{1/2}$

n	p_n	q_n Aitken's
0	2.5	3.00024351
1	2.91547595	3.00000667
2	2.98587943	3.00000018
3	2.99764565	3.00000001
4	2.99960758	
5	2.99993460	

9. Solution of $\cos(x) - 1 = 0$.

n	p_n Steffensen's
0	0.5
1	0.24465808
2	0.12171517
3	0.00755300
4	0.00377648
5	0.00188824
6	0.00000003

11. The sum of the infinite series is $S = 99$.

n	S_n	T_n
1	0.99	98.9999988
2	1.9701	99.0000017
3	2.940399	98.9999988
4	3.90099501	98.9999992
5	4.85198506	
6	5.79346521	

13. The sum of the infinite series is $S = 4$.

15. Muller's method for $f(x) = x^3 - x - 2$.

n	p_n	$f(p_n)$
0	1.0	−2.0
1	1.2	−1.472
2	1.4	−0.656
3	1.52495614	0.02131598
4	1.52135609	−0.00014040
5	1.52137971	−0.00000001

Section 3.1   Introduction to Vectors and Matrices

1. (i) (a) $(1, 4)$ **(b)** $(5, -12)$ **(c)** $(9, -12)$ **(d)** 5   **(e)** $(-26, 72)$
(f) -38 **(g)** $2\sqrt{1465}$

2. $\theta = \arccos(-16/21) \approx 2.437045$ radians

3. (a) Assume that $X, Y \neq 0$. $X \cdot Y = 0$ iff $\cos(\theta) = 0$ iff $\theta = (2n + 1)\dfrac{\pi}{2}$ iff X and Y are orthogonal.

6. (c) $a_{ji} = \begin{cases} ji & j = i \\ j - ji + i & j \neq i \end{cases} = \begin{cases} ij & i = j \\ i - ij + j & i \neq j \end{cases} = a_{ij}$

Section 3.2   Properties of Vectors and Matrices

1. $AB = \begin{bmatrix} -11 & -12 \\ 13 & -24 \end{bmatrix}$, $\quad BA = \begin{bmatrix} -15 & 10 \\ -12 & -20 \end{bmatrix}$

3. (a) $(AB)C = A(BC) = \begin{bmatrix} 2 & -5 \\ -88 & -56 \end{bmatrix}$

5. (a) 33   **(c)** The determinant does not exist because the matrix is not square.

8. $(AB)(B^{-1}A^{-1}) = A(BB^{-1})A^{-1} = (AI)A^{-1} = AA^{-1} = I$. Similarly, $(B^{-1}A^{-1})(AB) = I$. Therefore, $(AB)^{-1} = B^{-1}A^{-1}$.

10. (a) MN **(b)** $M(N-1)$

13. $XX' = [6]$, $\quad X'X = \begin{bmatrix} 1 & -1 & 2 \\ -1 & 1 & -2 \\ 2 & -2 & 4 \end{bmatrix}$

Section 3.3   Upper-Triangular Linear Systems

1. $x_1 = 2$, $x_2 = -2$, $x_3 = 1$, $x_4 = 3$, and $\det A = 120$

5. $x_1 = 3$, $x_2 = 2$, $x_3 = 1$, $x_4 = -1$, and $\det A = -24$

Section 3.4   Gaussian Elimination and Pivoting

1. $x_1 = -3$, $x_2 = 2$, $x_3 = 1$

5. $y = 5 - 3x + 2x^2$

10. $x_1 = 1$, $x_2 = 3$, $x_3 = 2$, $x_4 = -2$

15. (a) Solution for Hilbert matrix A:
$x_1 = 16$, $x_2 = -120$, $x_3 = 240$, $x_4 = -140$

(b) Solution for the other matrix A:
$x_1 = 18.73$, $x_2 = -149.6$, $x_3 = 310.1$, $x_4 = -185.1$

Section 3.5   Triangular Factorization

1. (a) $Y' = \begin{bmatrix} -4 & 12 & 3 \end{bmatrix}$, $\quad X' = \begin{bmatrix} -3 & 2 & 1 \end{bmatrix}$

(b) $Y' = \begin{bmatrix} 20 & 39 & 9 \end{bmatrix}$, $\quad X' = \begin{bmatrix} 5 & 7 & 3 \end{bmatrix}$

3. (a) $\begin{bmatrix} -5 & 2 & -1 \\ 1 & 0 & 3 \\ 3 & 1 & 6 \end{bmatrix} = \begin{bmatrix} 1 & 0 & 0 \\ -0.2 & 1 & 0 \\ -0.6 & 5.5 & 1 \end{bmatrix} \begin{bmatrix} -5 & 2 & -1 \\ 0 & 0.4 & 2.8 \\ 0 & 0 & -10 \end{bmatrix}$

5. (a) $Y' = \begin{bmatrix} 8 & -6 & 12 & 2 \end{bmatrix}$, $\quad X' = \begin{bmatrix} 3 & -1 & 1 & 2 \end{bmatrix}$

(b) $Y' = \begin{bmatrix} 28 & 6 & 12 & 1 \end{bmatrix}$, $\quad X' = \begin{bmatrix} 3 & 1 & 2 & 1 \end{bmatrix}$

6. The triangular factorization $A = LU$ is

$$LU = \begin{bmatrix} 1 & 0 & 0 & 0 \\ 2 & 1 & 0 & 0 \\ 5 & 1 & 1 & 0 \\ -3 & -1 & -1.75 & 1 \end{bmatrix} \begin{bmatrix} 1 & 1 & 0 & 4 \\ 0 & -3 & 5 & -8 \\ 0 & 0 & -4 & -10 \\ 0 & 0 & 0 & -7.5 \end{bmatrix}$$

Section 3.6   Iterative Methods for Linear Systems

1. (a) Jacobi iteration

$P_1 = (3.75, 1.8)$

$P_2 = (4.2, 1.05)$

$P_3 = (4.0125, 0.96)$

Iteration will converge to $(4, 1)$.

(b) Gauss-Seidel Iteration

$P_1 = (3.75, 1.05)$

$P_2 = (4.0125, 0.9975)$

$P_3 = (3.999375, 1.000125)$

Iteration will converge to $(4, 1)$.

3. (a) Jacobi iteration

$P_1 = (-1, -1)$

$P_2 = (-4, -4)$

$P_3 = (-13, -13)$

The iteration diverges away

from the solution $P = (0.5, 0.5)$.

(b) Gauss-Seidel iteration

$P_1 = (-1, -4)$

$P_2 = (-13, -40)$

$P_3 = (-121, -361)$

The iteration diverges away

from the solution $P = (0.5, 0.5)$.

5. (a) Jacobi iteration

$P_1 = (2, 1.375, 0.75)$

$P_2 = (2.125, 0.96875, 0.90625)$

$P_3 = (2.0125, 0.95703125, 1.0390625)$

Iteration will converge to $P = (2, 1, 1)$.

(b) Gauss-Seidel iteration

$P_1 = (2, 0.875, 1.03125)$

$P_2 = (1.96875, 1.01171875, 0.989257813)$

$P_3 = (2.00449219, 0.99753418, 1.0017395)$

Iteration will converge to $P = (2, 1, 1)$.

9. (15): $\|X\|_1 = \sum_{k=1}^{N} |x_k| = 0$ iff $|x_k| = 0$ for $k = 0, 1, \ldots, N$ iff $X = 0$

(16): $\|cX\|_1 = \sum_{k=1}^{N} |cx_k| = \sum_{k=1}^{N} |c||x_k| = |c| \sum_{k=1}^{N} |x_k| = |c| \|X\|_1$

Section 3.7   Iteration for Nonlinear Systems: Seidel and Newton's Methods (Optional)

1. (a) $x = 0, y = 0$ **(c)** $x = 0, y = n\pi$

2. (a) $x = 4, y = -2$ **(c)** $x = 0, y = (2n + 1)\pi/2; x = 2(-1)^n, y = n\pi$

5. $J(x, y) = \begin{bmatrix} 1 - x & y/4 \\ (1-x)/2 & (2-y)/2 \end{bmatrix}$, $\quad J(1.1, 2.0) = \begin{bmatrix} -0.1 & 0.5 \\ -0.05 & 0.0 \end{bmatrix}$

	Fixed-point iteration		Seidel iteration	
k	p_k	q_k	p_k	q_k
0	1.1	2.0	1.1	2.0
1	1.12	1.9975	1.12	1.9964
2	1.1165508	1.9963984	1.1160016	1.9966327
∞	1.1165151	1.9966032	1.1165151	1.9966032

7. $0 = x^2 - y - 0.2$, $0 = y^2 - x - 0.3$

P_k	Solution of the linear system: $J(P_k)\,dP = -F(P_k)$	$P_k + dP$
$\begin{bmatrix} 1.2 \\ 1.2 \end{bmatrix}$	$\begin{bmatrix} 2.4 & -1.0 \\ -1.0 & 2.4 \end{bmatrix} \begin{bmatrix} -0.0075630 \\ 0.0218487 \end{bmatrix} = -\begin{bmatrix} 0.04 \\ -0.06 \end{bmatrix}$	$\begin{bmatrix} 1.192437 \\ 1.221849 \end{bmatrix}$
$\begin{bmatrix} 1.192437 \\ 1.221849 \end{bmatrix}$	$\begin{bmatrix} 2.384874 & -1.0 \\ -1.0 & 2.443697 \end{bmatrix} \begin{bmatrix} -0.0001278 \\ -0.0002476 \end{bmatrix} = -\begin{bmatrix} 0.0000572 \\ 0.0004774 \end{bmatrix}$	$\begin{bmatrix} 1.192309 \\ 1.221601 \end{bmatrix}$

(a) Therefore, $(p_1, q_1) = (1.192437, 1.221849)$ and
$(p_2, q_2) = (1.192309, 1.221601)$.

P_k	Solution of the linear system: $J(P_k)\,dP = -F(P_k)$	$P_k + dP$
$\begin{bmatrix} -0.2 \\ -0.2 \end{bmatrix}$	$\begin{bmatrix} -0.4 & -1.0 \\ -1.0 & -0.4 \end{bmatrix} \begin{bmatrix} -0.0904762 \\ 0.0761905 \end{bmatrix} = -\begin{bmatrix} 0.04 \\ -0.06 \end{bmatrix}$	$\begin{bmatrix} -0.2904762 \\ -0.1238095 \end{bmatrix}$
$\begin{bmatrix} -0.2904762 \\ -0.1238095 \end{bmatrix}$	$\begin{bmatrix} -0.5809524 & -1.0 \\ -1.0 & -0.2476190 \end{bmatrix} \begin{bmatrix} 0.0044128 \\ 0.0056223 \end{bmatrix} = -\begin{bmatrix} 0.0081859 \\ 0.0058050 \end{bmatrix}$	$\begin{bmatrix} -0.2860634 \\ -0.1181872 \end{bmatrix}$

(b) Therefore, $(p_1, q_1) = (-0.2904762, -0.1238095)$ and
$(p_2, q_2) = (-0.2860634, -0.1181872)$.

8. (b) The values of the Jacobian determinant at the solution points are $|J(1, 1)| = 0$ and $|J(-1, -1)| = 0$. Newton's method depends on being able to solve a linear system where the matrix is $J(p_n, q_n)$ and (p_n, q_n) is near a solution. For this example, the system equations are ill conditioned and thus hard to solve with precision. In fact, for some values near a solution we have $J(x_0, y_0) = 0$, for example, $J(1.0001, 1.0001) = 0$.

12. (a) *Note.* As with derivatives, we have $\dfrac{\partial}{\partial x}(cf(x, y)) = c\dfrac{\partial}{\partial x} f(x, y)$. $F(X)$ was defined as $F(X) = [f_1(x_1, \ldots, x_n) \cdots f_m(x_1, \ldots, x_n)]'$; thus, by scalar multiplication, $cF(X) = [cf_1(x_1, \ldots, x_n) \cdots cf_m(x_1, \ldots, x_n)]'$. $J(cF(X)) = [j_{ik}]_{m \times n}$, where $j_{ik} = \dfrac{\partial}{\partial x_k}(cf_i(x_1, \ldots, x_n)) = c\dfrac{\partial}{\partial x_k} f_i(x_1, \ldots, x_n)$. Therefore, by the definition of scalar multiplication, we have $J(cF(X)) = cJ(F(X))$.

Section 4.1   Taylor Series and Calculation of Functions

1. **(a)** $P_5(x) = x - x^3/3! + x^5/5!$

   $P_7(x) = x - x^3/3! + x^5/5! - x^7/7!$

   $P_9(x) = x - x^3/3! + x^5/5! - x^7/7! + x^9/9!$

   (b) $|E_9(x)| = |\sin(c)x^{10}/10!| \leq (1)(1)^{10}/10! = 0.0000002755$

   (c) $P_5(x) = 2^{-1/2}(1 + (x - \pi/4) - (x - \pi/4)^2/2 - (x - \pi/4)^3/6$

   $\qquad + (x - \pi/4)^4/24 + (x - \pi/4)^5/120)$

3. At $x_0 = 0$ the derivatives of $f(x)$ are undefined. But at $x_0 = 1$ the derivatives are defined.

5. $P_3(x) = 1 + 0x - x^2/2 + 0x^3 = 1 - x^2/2$

8. **(a)** $f(2) = 2$, $f'(2) = \frac{1}{4}$, $f''(2) = -\frac{1}{32}$, $f^{(3)}(2) = \frac{3}{256}$

   $P_3(x) = 2 + (x - 2)/4 - (x - 2)^2/64 + (x - 2)^3/512$

   (b) $P_3(1) = 1.732421875$; compare with $3^{1/2} = 1.732050808$

   (c) $f^{(4)}(x) = -15(2 + x)^{-7/2}/16$; the minimum of $|f^{(4)}(x)|$ on the interval $1 \leq x \leq 3$ occurs when $x = 1$ and $|f^{(4)}(x)| \leq |f^{(4)}(1)| \leq 3^{-7/2}(15/16) \approx$

   0.020046. Therefore, $|E_3(x)| \leq \dfrac{(0.020046)(1)^4}{4!} = 0.00083529$

13. **(d)** $P_3(0.5) = 0.41666667$

    $P_6(0.5) = 0.40468750$

    $P_9(0.5) = 0.40553230$

    $\ln(1.5) = 0.40546511$

14. **(d)** $P_2(0.5) = 1.21875000$

    $P_4(0.5) = 1.22607422$

    $P_6(0.5) = 1.22660828$

    $(1.5)^{1/2} = 1.22474487$

Section 4.2   Introduction to Interpolation

1. **(a)** Use $x = 4$ and get $b_3 = -0.02$, $b_2 = 0.02$, $b_1 = -0.12$, $b_0 = 1.18$. Hence $P(4) = 1.18$.

   (b) Use $x = 4$ and get $d_2 = -0.06$, $d_1 = -0.04$, $d_0 = -0.36$. Hence $P'(4) = -0.36$.

   (c) Use $x = 4$ and get $i_4 = -0.005$, $i_3 = 0.01333333$, $i_2 = -0.04666667$, $i_1 = 1.47333333$, $i_0 = 5.89333333$. Hence $I(4) = 5.89333333$. Similarly, use $x = 1$ and get $I(1) = 1.58833333$.

   $\int_1^4 P(x)\,dx = I(4) - I(1) = 5.89333333 - 1.58833333 = 4.305$

   (d) Use $x = 5.5$ and get $b_3 = -0.02$, $b_2 = -0.01$, $b_1 = -0.255$, $b_0 = 0.2575$. Hence $P(5.5) = 0.2575$.

Section 4.3   Lagrange Approximation

1. (a) $P_1(x) = -1(x - 0)/(-1 - 0) + 0 = x + 0 = x$

   (b) $P_2(x) = -1\dfrac{(x - 0)(x - 1)}{(-1 - 0)(-1 - 1)} + 0 + \dfrac{(x + 1)(x - 0)}{(1 + 1)(1 - 0)}$

   $= -0.5(x)(x - 1) + 0.5(x)(x + 1) = 0x^2 + x + 0 = x$

   (c) $P_3(x) = -1\dfrac{(x)(x - 1)(x - 2)}{(-1)(-2)(-3)} + 0 + \dfrac{(x + 1)(x)(x - 2)}{(2)(1)(-1)}$

   $+ 8\dfrac{(x + 1)(x)(x - 1)}{(3)(2)(1)} = x^3 + 0x^2 + 0x + 0 = x^3$

   (d) $P_1(x) = 1(x - 2)/(1 - 2) + 8(x - 1)/(2 - 1) = 7x - 6$

   (e) $P_2(x) = 0 + \dfrac{(x)(x - 2)}{(1)(-1)} + 8\dfrac{(x)(x - 1)}{(2)(1)} = 3x^2 - 2x$

5. (c) $f^{(4)}(c) = 120(c - 1)$ for all c; thus $E_3(x) = 5(x + 1)(x)(x - 3)(x - 4)(c - 1)$

10. $|f^{(2)}(c)| \le |-\sin(1)| = 0.84147098 = M_2$
   (a) $h^2 M_2/8 = h^2(0.84147098)/8 < 5 \times 10^{-7}$

12. (a) $z = 3 - 2x + 4y$

Section 4.4   Newton Polynomials

1. $P_1(x) = 4 - (x - 1)$

   $P_2(x) = 4 - (x - 1) + 0.4(x - 1)(x - 3)$

   $P_3(x) = P_2(x) + 0.01(x - 1)(x - 3)(x - 4)$

   $P_4(x) = P_3(x) - 0.002(x - 1)(x - 3)(x - 4)(x - 4.5)$

   $P_1(2.5) = 2.5,\ P_2(2.5) = 2.2,\ P_3(2.5) = 2.21125,\ P_4(2.2) = 2.21575$

5. $f(x) = x^{1/2}$

   $P_4(x) = 2.0 + 2.3607(x - 4) - 0.01132(x - 4)(x - 5)$

   $+ 0.00091(x - 4)(x - 5)(x - 6)$

   $- 0.00008(x - 4)(x - 5)(x - 6)(x - 7)$

   $P_1(4.5) = 2.11804,\ P_2(4.5) = 2.12086,\ P_3(4.5) = 2.12121,\ P_4(4.5) = 2.12128$

6. $f(x) = 3.6/x$

   $P_4(x) = 3.6 - 1.8(x - 1) + 0.6(x - 1)(x - 2) - 0.15(x - 1)(x - 2)(x - 3)$

   $+ 0.03(x - 1)(x - 2)(x - 3)(x - 4)$

   $P_1(2.5) = 0.9,\ P_2(2.5) = 1.35,\ P_3(2.5) = 1.40625,\ P_4(2.5) = 1.423125$

Section 4.5   Chebyshev Polynomials (Optional)

9. (a) $\ln(x + 2) \approx 0.69549038 + 0.49905042x - 0.14334605x^2 + 0.04909073x^3$

   (b) $|f^{(4)}(x)|/(2^3(4!)) \le |-6|/(2^3(4!)) = 0.03125000$

11. (a) $\cos(x) \approx 1 - 0.46952087x^2$

(b) $|f^{(3)}(x)|/(2^2(3!)) \leq |\sin(1)|/(2^2(3!)) = 0.03506129$

13. The error bound for Taylor's polynomial is

$$\frac{|f^{(8)}(x)|}{8!} \leq \frac{|\sin(1)|}{8!} = 0.00002087.$$

The error bound for the minimax approximation is

$$\frac{|f^{(8)}(x)|}{2^7(8!)} \leq \frac{|\sin(1)|}{2^7(8!)} = 0.00000016.$$

Section 4.6   Padé Approximations

1. $1 = p_0,\ 1 + q_1 = p_1,\ \dfrac{1}{2} + q_1 = 0,\ q_1 = -\dfrac{1}{2},\ p_1 = \dfrac{1}{2}$
$e^x \approx R_{1,1}(x) = (2 + x)/(2 - x)$

3. $1 = p_0,\ \dfrac{1}{3} + 2q_1/15 = p_1,\ \dfrac{2}{15} + q_1/3 = 0,\ q_1 = -\dfrac{2}{5},\ p_1 = -\dfrac{1}{15}$

5. $1 = p_0,\ 1 + q_1 = p_1,\ \dfrac{1}{2} + q_1 + q_2 = p_2.$

First solve the system $\begin{cases} \dfrac{1}{6} + \dfrac{q_1}{2} + q_2 = 0 \\[2mm] \dfrac{1}{24} + \dfrac{q_1}{6} + \dfrac{q_2}{2} = 0. \end{cases}$

Then $q_1 = -\dfrac{1}{2},\ q_2 = \dfrac{1}{12},\ p_1 = \dfrac{1}{2},\ p_2 = \dfrac{1}{12}.$

7. (a) $1 = p_0,\ \dfrac{1}{3} + q_1 = p_1,\ \dfrac{2}{15} + q_1/3 + q_2 = p_2.$

First solve the system $\begin{cases} \dfrac{17}{315} + \dfrac{2q_1}{15} + \dfrac{q_2}{3} = 0 \\[2mm] \dfrac{62}{2835} + \dfrac{17q_1}{315} + \dfrac{2q_2}{15} = 0. \end{cases}$

Then $q_1 = -\dfrac{4}{9},\ q_2 = \dfrac{1}{63},\ p_1 = -\dfrac{1}{9},\ p_2 = \dfrac{1}{945}.$

Section 5.1   Least-Squares Line

1. (a) $10A + 0B = 7$
$0A + 5B = 13$
$y = 0.70x + 2.60,\ E_2(f) \approx 0.2449$

2. (a) $40A + 0B = 58$
$0A + 5B = 31.2$
$y = 1.45x + 6.24,\ E_2(f) \approx 0.8958$

3. (c) $\displaystyle\sum_{k=1}^{5} x_k y_k \Big/ \sum_{k=1}^{5} x_k^2 = 86.9/55 = 1.58$

$y = 1.58x,\ E_2(f) \approx 0.1720$

11. (a) $y = 1.6866x^2,\ E_2(f) \approx 1.3$

$y = 0.5902x^3,\ E_2(f) \approx 0.29.$ This is the best fit.

Section 5.2   Methods of Curve Fitting

1. (a)

$$164A \qquad\quad + 20C = \ 186$$
$$20B \qquad\quad = -34$$
$$20A \qquad\quad + \ 4C = \ \ 26$$
$$y = 0.875x^2 - 1.70x + 2.125 = 7/8x^2 - 17/10x + 17/8$$

3. (a)

$$15A + 5B = -0.8647$$
$$5A + 5B = \ \ 4.2196$$
$$y = 3.8665e^{-0.5084x},\ E_1(f) \approx 0.10$$

6.

	Using linearization	Minimizing least squares
(a)	$\dfrac{1000}{1 + 4.3018e^{-1.0802t}}$	$\dfrac{1000}{1 + 4.2131e^{-1.0456t}}$
(b)	$\dfrac{5000}{1 + 8.9991e^{-0.81138t}}$	$\dfrac{5000}{1 + 8.9987e^{-0.81157t}}$

18. (a)

$$14A + 15B + 8C = 82$$
$$15A + 19B + 9C = 93$$
$$8A + \ 9B + 5C = 49$$
$$A = 2.4,\ B = 1.2,\ C = 3.8 \text{ yields } z = 2.4x + 1.2y + 3.8.$$

Section 5.3   Interpolation by Spline Functions

4. $h_0 = 1 \qquad d_0 = -2$

$h_1 = 3 \qquad d_1 = 1 \qquad\quad u_1 = 18$

$h_2 = 3 \qquad d_2 = -2/3 \qquad u_2 = -10$

Solve the system $\begin{cases} \frac{15}{2}m_1 + m_2 = 21 \\ 3m_1 + \frac{21}{2}m_2 = -15 \end{cases}$ to get $m_1 = \frac{314}{101}$ and $m_2 = -\frac{234}{101}$.

Then $m_0 = -\frac{460}{101}$ and $m_3 = \frac{856}{303}$. The cubic spline is

$$S_0(x) = \frac{129}{101}(x+3)^3 - \frac{230}{101}(x+3)^2 - (x+3) + 2 \qquad -3 \le x \le -2$$

$$S_1(x) = -\frac{274}{909}(x+2)^3 + \frac{157}{101}(x+2)^2 - \frac{96}{101}(x+2) \qquad -2 \le x \le 1$$

$$S_2(x) = \frac{779}{2727}(x-1)^3 - \frac{117}{101}(x-1)^2 + \frac{72}{303}(x-1) + 3 \qquad 1 \le x \le 4$$

5. $h_0 = 1 \qquad d_0 = -2$

$h_1 = 3 \qquad d_1 = 1 \qquad u_1 = 18$

$h_2 = 3 \qquad d_2 = -2/3 \qquad u_2 = -10$

Solve the system $\begin{cases} 8m_1 + 3m_2 = 18 \\ 3m_1 + 12m_2 = -10 \end{cases}$ to get $m_1 = \frac{82}{29}$ and $m_2 = -\frac{134}{87}$.

Set $m_0 = 0 = m_3$. The cubic spline is

$$S_0(x) = \frac{41}{87}(x+3)^3 - \frac{215}{87}(x+3) + 2 \qquad -3 \le x \le -2$$

$$S_1(x) = -\frac{190}{783}(x+2)^3 + \frac{41}{29}(x+2)^2 - \frac{92}{87}(x+2) \qquad -2 \le x \le 1$$

$$S_2(x) = \frac{67}{783}(x-1)^3 - \frac{67}{87}(x-1)^2 + \frac{76}{87}(x-1) + 3 \qquad 1 \le x \le 4$$

6. $h_0 = 1 \qquad d_0 = -2$

$h_1 = 3 \qquad d_1 = 1 \qquad u_1 = 18$

$h_2 = 3 \qquad d_2 = -2/3 \qquad u_2 = -10$

Solve the system $\begin{cases} \frac{28}{3}m_1 + \frac{8}{3}m_2 = 18 \\ 0m_1 + 18m_2 = -10 \end{cases}$ to get $m_1 = \frac{263}{126}$ and $m_2 = -\frac{5}{9}$.

Then $m_0 = \frac{187}{63}$ and $m_3 = -\frac{403}{126}$. The cubic spline is

$$S_0(x) = -\frac{37}{252}(x+3)^3 + \frac{187}{126}(x+3)^2 - \frac{841}{252}(x+3) + 2 \qquad -3 \le x \le -2$$

$$S_1(x) = -\frac{37}{252}(x+2)^3 + \frac{263}{252}(x+2)^2 - \frac{17}{21}(x+2) \qquad -2 \le x \le 1$$

$$S_2(x) = -\frac{37}{252}(x-1)^3 - \frac{5}{18}(x-1)^2 + \frac{125}{84}(x-1) + 3 \qquad 1 \le x \le 4$$

Section 5.4 Fourier Series and Trigonometric Polynomials

1. $f(x) = \frac{4}{\pi}\left(\sin(x) + \frac{\sin(3x)}{3} + \frac{\sin(5x)}{5} + \frac{\sin(7x)}{7} + \cdots\right)$

3. $f(x) = \frac{\pi}{4} + \sum_{j=1}^{\infty}\left(\frac{(-1)^j - 1}{\pi j^2}\right)\cos(jx) - \sum_{j=1}^{\infty}\left(\frac{(-1)^j}{j}\right)\sin(jx)$

5. $f(x) = \dfrac{4}{\pi}\left(\sin(x) - \dfrac{\sin(3x)}{3^2} + \dfrac{\sin(5x)}{5^2} - \dfrac{\sin(7x)}{7^2} + \cdots\right)$

12. $f(x) = 6 + \dfrac{36}{\pi^2}\sum_{j=1}^{\infty}\left(\dfrac{(-1)^{j+1}}{j^2}\right)\cos\left(\dfrac{j\pi x}{3}\right)$

Section 5.5 Bézier Curves

1. $B_{2,4}(t) = 6t^2 - 12t^3 + 6t^4$

$B_{3,5}(t) = 10t^3 - 20t^4 + 10t^5$

$B_{5,7}(t) = 21t^5 - 42t^6 + 21t^7$

3. *Note.* The binomial coefficients are nonnegative, and t^i and $(1 - t)^{N-i}$ are nonnegative for $t \in [0, 1]$. Can also be established using formula (4) and mathematical induction.

5. $\frac{d}{dt}B_{3,5}(t) = 5(B_{2,4}(t) - B_{3,4}(t)) = 5(6t^2(1 - t)^2 - 4t^3(1 - 2))$

$\frac{d}{dt}B_{3,5}(1/3) = 80/81$ and $\frac{d}{dt}B_{3,5}(2/3) = -40/81$.

7. $t B_{i,N}(t) = \binom{N}{i}t^{i+1}(1 - t)^{N-i}$

$\phantom{t B_{i,N}(t)} = \binom{N}{i}t^{i+1}(1 - t)^{(N+1)-(i+1)}$

$\phantom{t B_{i,N}(t)} = \dfrac{\binom{N}{i}}{\binom{N+1}{i+1}}B_{i+1,N+1}(t)$

$\phantom{t B_{i,N}(t)} = \dfrac{i + 1}{N + 1}B_{i+1,N+1}(t)$

8. **(a)** $P(t) = (1 + 6t - 9t^2 + 5t^3,\ 3 - 12t + 27t^2 - 18t^3)$

(b) $P(t) = (-2 + 4t + 18t^2 - 28t^3 + 10t^4,\ 3 + 12t^2 - 20t^3 + 8t^4)$

(c) $P(t) = (1 + 5t,\ 1 + 5t + 10t^2 - 30t^3 + 15t^4)$

9. $P(t) = (1 + 3t,\ 1 + 6t)$

Section 6.1 Approximating the Derivative

1. $f(x) = \sin(x)$

h	Approximate $f'(x)$, formula (3)	Error in the approximation	Bound for the truncation error
0.1	0.695546112	0.001160597	0.001274737
0.01	0.696695100	0.000011609	0.000012747
0.001	0.696706600	0.000000109	0.000000127

3. $f(x) = \sin(x)$

h	Approximate $f'(x)$, formula (10)	Error in the approximation	Bound for the truncation error
0.1	0.696704390	0.000002320	0.000002322
0.01	0.696706710	−0.000000001	0.000000000

5. $f(x) = x^3$ **(a)** $f'(2) \approx 12.0025000$ **(b)** $f'(2) \approx 12.0000000$
(c) For part (a): $O(h^2) = -(0.05)^2 f^{(3)}(c)/6 = -0.0025000$. For part (b): $O(h^4) = -(0.05)^4 f^{(3)}(c)/30 = -0.0000000$

7. $f(x, y) = xy/(x + y)$
(a) $f_x(x, y) = (y/(x + y))^2$, $f_x(2, 3) = 0.36$

h	Approximation to $f_x(2, 3)$	Error in the approximation
0.1	0.360144060	−0.000144060
0.01	0.360001400	−0.000001400
0.001	0.360000000	0.000000000

$f_y(x, y) = (x/(x + y))^2$, $f_y(2, 3) = 0.16$

h	Approximation to $f_y(2, 3)$	Error in the approximation
0.1	0.160064030	−0.000064030
0.01	0.160000600	−0.000000600
0.001	0.160000000	0.000000000

10. (a) Formula (3) gives $I'(1.2) \approx -13.5840$ and $E(1.2) \approx 11.3024$. Formula (10) gives $I'(1.2) \approx -13.6824$ and $E(1.2) \approx 11.2975$.
(b) Using differentiation rules from calculus, we obtain $I'(1.2) \approx -13.6793$ and $E(1.2) \approx 11.2976$.

12.

h	App. $f'(x)$, equation (17)	Error in the approximation	Equation (19), total error bound |round-off| + |trunc.|
0.1	−0.93050	−0.00154	$0.00005 + 0.00161 = 0.00166$
0.01	−0.93200	−0.00004	$0.00050 + 0.00002 = 0.00052$
0.001	−0.93000	−0.00204	$0.00500 + 0.00000 = 0.00500$

15. $f(x) = \cos(x), f^{(5)}(x) = -\sin(x)$
Use the bound $|f^{(5)}(x)| \le \sin(1.4) \approx 0.98545$.

h	App. $f'(x)$, equation (22)	Error in the approximation	Equation (24), total error bound $\lvert$round-off$\rvert + \lvert$trunc.$\rvert$
0.1	−0.93206	0.00002	$0.00008 + 0.00000 = 0.00008$
0.01	−0.93208	0.00004	$0.00075 + 0.00000 = 0.00075$
0.001	−0.92917	−0.00287	$0.00750 + 0.00000 = 0.00750$

Section 6.2   Numerical Differentiation Formulas

1. $f(x) = \ln(x)$

(a) $f''(5) \approx -0.040001600$ (b) $f''(5) \approx -0.040007900$

(c) $f''(5) \approx -0.039999833$ (d) $f''(5) = -0.04000000 = -1/5^2$

The answer in part (b) is most accurate.

3. $f(x) = \ln(x)$

(a) $f''(5) \approx 0.0000$ (b) $f''(5) \approx -0.0400$

(c) $f''(5) \approx 0.0133$ (d) $f''(5) = -0.0400 = -1/5^2$

The answer in part (b) is most accurate.

5. (a) $f(x) = x^2$, $f''(1) \approx 2.0000$

   (b) $f(x) = x^4$, $f''(1) \approx 12.0002$

9. (a)

x	$f'(x)$
0.0	0.141345
0.1	0.041515
0.2	−0.058275
0.3	−0.158025

Section 7.1   Introduction to Quadrature

1. (a) $f(x) = \sin(\pi x)$ trapezoidal rule   0.0

Simpson's rule   0.666667

Simpson's $\frac{3}{8}$ rule   0.649519

Boole's rule   0.636165

(c) $f(x) = \sin(\sqrt{x})$ trapezoidal rule   0.420735

Simpson's rule   0.573336

Simpson's $\frac{3}{8}$ rule   0.583143

Boole's rule   0.593376

2. (a) $f(x) = \sin(\pi x)$ composite trapezoidal rule   0.603553

                                          composite Simpson rule   0.638071

                                          Boole's rule   0.636165

(b) $f(x) = \sin(\sqrt{x})$ composite trapezoidal rule   0.577889

                                          composite Simpson rule   0.592124

                                          Boole's rule   0.593376

Section 7.2   Composite Trapezoidal and Simpson's Rule

1. (a) $F(x) = \arctan(x)$, $F(1) - F(-1) = \pi/2 \approx 1.57079632679$
(i) $M = 10$, $h = 0.2$, $T(f, h) = 1.56746305691$, $E_T(f, h) = 0.00333326989$
(ii) $M = 5$, $h = 0.2$, $S(f, h) = 1.57079538809$, $E_S(f, h) = 0.00000093870$
(c) $F(x) = 2\sqrt{x}$, $F(4) - F(\frac{1}{2}) = 3$
(i) $M = 10$, $h = 0.375$, $T(f, h) = 3.04191993765$,
$E_T(f, h) = -0.04191993765$
(ii) $M = 5$, $h = 0.375$, $S(f, h) = 3.00762208163$, $E_S(f, h) = -0.00762208163$

2. (a) $\int_0^1 \sqrt{1 + 9x^4}\, dx = 1.54786565469019$
(i) $M = 10$, $T(f, 1/10) = 1.55260945$
(ii) $M = 5$, $S(f, 1/10) = 1.54786419$

3. (a) $2\pi \int_0^1 x^3 \sqrt{1 + 9x^4}\, dx = 3.5631218520124$
(i) $M = 10$, $T(f, 1/10) = 3.64244664$
(ii) $M = 5$, $S(f, 1/10) = 3.56372816$

8. (a) Use the bound $|f^{(2)}(x)| = |-\cos(x)| \le |\cos(0)| = 1$, and obtain
$((\pi/3 - 0)h^2)/12 \le 5 \times 10^{-9}$; then substitute $h = \pi/(3M)$ and get $\pi^3/162 \times 10^8 \le M^2$. Solve and get $4374.89 \le M$; since M must be an integer, $M = 4375$ and $h = 0.000239359$.

9. (a) Use the bound $|f^{(4)}(x)| = |\cos(x)| \le |\cos(0)| = 1$, and obtain
$((\pi/3-0)h^4)/180 \le 5 \times 10^{-9}$; then substitute $h = \pi/(6M)$ and get $\pi^5/34{,}992 \times 10^7 \le M^4$; since M must be an integer, $M = 18$ and $h = 0.029088821$.

10.

M	h	$T(f, h)$	$E_T(f, h) = O(h^2)$
1	0.2	0.1990008	0.0006660
2	0.1	0.1995004	0.0001664
4	0.05	0.1996252	0.0000416
8	0.025	0.1996564	0.0000104
16	0.0125	0.1996642	0.0000026

Section 7.3   Recursive Rules and Romberg Integration

1. (a)

J	$R(J, 0)$	$R(J, 1)$	$R(J, 2)$
0	−0.00171772		
1	0.02377300	0.03226990	
2	0.60402717	0.79744521	0.84845691

(c)

J	$R(J, 0)$	$R(J, 1)$	$R(J, 2)$
0	2.88		
1	2.10564024	1.84752031	
2	1.78167637	1.67368841	1.66209962

10. (ii) For $\int_0^1 \sqrt{x}\, dx$, Romberg integration converges slowly because the higher derivatives of the integrand $f(x) = \sqrt{x}$ are not bounded near $x = 0$.

Section 7.5   Gauss-Legendre Integration

1. $\int_0^2 6t^5\, dt = 64$ **(b)** $G(f, 2) = 58.6666667$

3. $\int_0^1 \sin(t)/t\, dt \approx 0.9460831$ **(b)** $G(f, 2) = 0.9460411$

6. (a) $N = 4$ **(b)** $N = 6$

8. If the fourth derivative does not change too much, then $\left| \dfrac{f^{(4)}(c_1)}{135} \right| < \left| \dfrac{-f^{(4)}(c_2)}{90} \right|$.

The truncation error term for the Gauss-Legendre rule will be less than the truncation error term for Simpson's rule.

Section 8.1   Minimization of a Function of One Variable

1. (a) $f'(x) = 6x^2 - 18x + 12 = 6(x - 1)(x - 2)$
On $(-\infty, 1)$: $f'(x) > 0$, thus f is increasing.
On $(1, 2)$: $f'(x) < 0$, thus f is decreasing.
On $(2, \infty)$: $f'(x) > 0$: thus f is increasing.

(b) $f'(x) = \dfrac{1}{x^2 + 1} > 0$ for all x in the domain of f, thus f is increasing for all x in the domain of f.

(c) $f'(x) = -1/x^2 < 0$ for all x in the domain of f, thus f is decreasing for all x in the domain of f.

(d) $f'(x) = x^x(a + \ln(x))$
On $(0, e^{-1})$: $f'(x) < 0$, thus f is decreasing.
On (e^{-1}, ∞): $f'(x) > 0$, thus f is increasing.

3. **(a)** $f'(x) = 12x^3 - 16x - 11$; local minimum at $x = 11/6$
   (b) $f'(x) = 1 - 6/x^3$; local minimum at $x = \sqrt[3]{6}$
   (c) $f'(x) = (x^2 + 5x + 4)/((4 - x^2)^2)$; local minimum at $x = -1$
   (d) $f'(x) = e^x(x - 2)/x^3$; local minimum at $x = 2$
   (e) $f'(x) = -\cos(x) - \cos(3x)$; local minimum at $x = 0.785398163$

5. Minimize the distance squared: $d(x) = (x - 2)^2 + (\sin(x) - 1)^2$;
   $d'(x) = 2(x - 2 + \sin(x)\cos(x) - \cos(x))$. The minimum occurs at $x = 1.96954061$.

7. **(a)** $[a_0, b_0] = [-2.4000, -1.6000]$, $[a_1, b_1] = [-2.4000, -1.9056]$, $[a_2, b_2] = [-2.4000, -1.6000]$
   (b) $[a_0, b_0] = [0.8000, 1.6000]$, $[a_1, b_1] = [1.1056, 1.6000]$, $[a_2, b_2] = [1.1056, 1.4111]$
   (c) $[a_0, b_0] = [0.5000, 2.5000]$, $[a_1, b_1] = [1.2639, 2.5000]$, $[a_2, b_2] = [1.7361, 2.5000]$
   (d) $[a_0, b_0] = [1.000, 5.0000]$, $[a_1, b_1] = [2.5279, 5.0000]$, $[a_2, b_2] = [2.5279, 4.0557]$

9. **(a)** $p_0 = -2.4000$, $p_{\min_1} = -2.1220$, $p_{\min_2} = -2.1200$
   (b) $p_0 = 0.8000$, $p_{\min_1} = 1.2776$, $p_{\min_2} = 1.2834$
   (c) $p_0 = 0.5000$, $p_{\min_1} = 1.9608$, $p_{\min_2} = 1.8920$
   (d) $p_0 = 1.0000$, $p_{\min_1} = 2.8750$, $p_{\min_2} = 3.3095$

11. **(a)** $b_k - a_k = \left(\frac{-1+\sqrt{5}}{2}\right)^4 (1 - 0) = 0.14590$

   (b) $b_k - a_k = \left(\frac{-1+\sqrt{5}}{2}\right)^5 (-1.6 - (-2.3)) = 0063119$

Section 8.2 Nelder-Mead and Powell's Methods

1. **(a)** $f_x(x, y) = 3x^2 - 3$, $f_y(x, y) = 3y^2 - 3$
   Critical points: $(1, 1)$, $(1, -1)$, $(-1, 1)$, $(-1, -1)$
   Local minimum at $(1, 1)$
   (b) $f_x(x, y) = 2x - y + 1$, $f_y(x, y) = 2y - x - 2$
   Critical point: $(0, 1)$. Local minimum at $(0, 1)$.
   (c) $f_x(x, y) = 2xy + y^2 - 3y$, $f_y(x, y) = x^2 + 2xy - 3x$
   Critical point: $(0, 0)$, $(0, 3)$, $(3, 0)$, $(1, 1)$
   Local minimum at $(1, 1)$

3. $M = \dfrac{1}{2}(B + G) = (-3/2, -3/2)$
   $R = 2M - W = (-6, -4)$
   $E = 2R - M = (-21/2, -13/2)$

5. $M = \dfrac{1}{3}(B + G + P) = \dfrac{1}{3}(0, 3, 1)$
   $R = 2M - W = (-2, 1, 2/3)$
   $E = 2R - M = (-4, 1, 1)$

9. "Reflecting" the triangle through the side $\overline{BG}$ implies that the terminal points of of the vectors W, M, and R all lie on the same line segment. Thus, by the definition of scalar multiplication and vector addition, we have $R - W = 2(M - W)$ or $R = 2M - W$.

Section 8.3 Gradient and Newton's Methods

1. (a) $\nabla f(x, y) = (2x-3, 3y^2-3) \ \nabla f(-1, 2) = (2(-1)-3, 3(2)^2-3) = (-5, 9)$
(b) $\nabla f(x, y) = (200(y - x^2)(-2x) - 2(1 - x), 200(y - x^2))$
$\nabla f(1/2, 4/3) = (200(\frac{4}{3} - \left(\frac{1}{2}\right)^2)(-2(\frac{1}{2})) - 2(1 - \frac{1}{2}), 200(\frac{4}{3} - (\frac{1}{2})^2))$
(c) $\nabla f(x, y, z) = (-y\sin(xy) - z\cos(xz), -x\sin(xy), -x\cos(xz))$
$\nabla f(0, \pi, \pi/2) = (-\pi\sin(0) - \frac{\pi}{2}\cos\cos(0), -0\sin(0), -0\cos(0)) = (-\pi/2, 0, 0)$

3. (a) $\begin{bmatrix} 2 & 0 \\ 0 & 12 \end{bmatrix}$

(a) $\begin{bmatrix} -\frac{694}{3} & -200 \\ -200 & 200 \end{bmatrix}$

(c) $\begin{bmatrix} -\pi^2 & 0 & -1 \\ 0 & 0 & 0 \\ -1 & 0 & 0 \end{bmatrix}$

5. (a) If $P_0 = (-1, 2)$, then

$$P_1 = P_0 - \nabla f(P_0)((Hf(P_0))^{-1})' = \left(\frac{3}{2}, \frac{5}{4}\right)$$

$$P_2 = P_1 - \nabla f(P_1)((Hf(P_1))^{-1})' = \left(\frac{3}{2}, \frac{41}{40}\right)$$

(b) If $P_0 = (0.5, 1.33333)$, then

$$P_1 = P_0 - \nabla f(P_0)((Hf(P_0))^{-1})' = (0.498424, 0.248424)$$

$$P_2 = P_1 - \nabla f(P_1)((Hf(P_1))^{-1})' = (0.493401, 0.24342)$$

(c) The matrix $Hf(P_0)$ is not invertible.

9. Solve formula (7)

$$\nabla(P_0) + (X - P_0)(Hf(P_0))' = 0$$

for X:

$$(X - P_0)(Hf(P_0))' = -\nabla f(P_0),$$

assume that $(Hf(P_0))'$ is invertible,

$$X - P_0 = -\nabla f(P_0((Hf(P_0))')^{-1}$$

$$X = P - \nabla f(P_0((Hf(P_0))^{-1})'$$

Note. If a matrix A is invertible, then $(A')^{-1} = (A^{-1})'$.

Section 9.1   Introduction to Differential Equations

1. (b) $L = 1$ **3. (b)** $L = 3$ **5. (b)** $L = 60$

10. (c) No, because $f_y(t, y) = \frac{1}{2}y^{-2/3}$ is not continuous when $t = 0$, and $\lim_{y \to 0} f_y(t, y) = \infty$.

13. $y(t) = t^3 - \cos(t) + 3$

15. $y(t) = \int_0^t e^{-s^2/2}\, ds$

17. (b) $y(t) = y_0 e^{-0.000120968t}$ **(c)** 2808 years   **(d)** 6.9237 seconds

Section 9.2   Euler's Method

1. (a)

t_k	y_k ($h = 0.1$)	y_k ($h = 0.2$)
0.0	1	1
0.1	0.90000	
0.2	0.81100	0.80000
0.3	0.73390	
0.4	0.66951	0.64800

3. (a)

t_k	y_k ($h = 0.1$)	y_k ($h = 0.2$)
0.0	1	1
0.1	1.00000	
0.2	0.99000	1.00000
0.3	0.97020	
0.4	0.94109	0.96000

6. $P_{k+1} = P_k + (0.02P_k - 0.00004P_k^2)10$ for $k = 1, 2, \ldots, 8$.

Year	t_k	Actual population at t_k, $P(t_k)$	P_k Euler rounded at each step	P_k Euler with more digits carried
1900	0.0	76.1	76.1	76.1
1910	10.0	92.4	89.0	89.0035
1920	20.0	106.5	103.6	103.6356
1930	30.0	123.1	120.0	120.0666
1940	40.0	132.6	138.2	138.3135
1950	50.0	152.3	158.2	158.3239
1960	60.0	180.7	179.8	179.9621
1970	70.0	204.9	202.8	203.0000
1980	80.0	226.5	226.9	227.1164

9. No. For any M, Euler's method produces $0 < y_1 < y_2 < \cdots < y_M$. The mathematical solution is $y(t) = \tan(t)$ and $y(3) < 0$.

Section 9.3   Heun's Method

1. (a)

t_k	y_k $(h = 0.1)$	y_k $(h = 0.2)$
0	1	1
0.1	0.90550	
0.2	0.82193	0.82400
0.3	0.75014	
0.4	0.69093	0.69488

3. (a)

t_k	y_k $(h = 0.1)$	y_k $(h = 0.2)$
0	1	1
0.1	0.99500	
0.2	0.98107	0.98000
0.3	0.95596	
0.4	0.92308	0.92277

7. Richardson improvement for solving $y' = (t - y)/2$ over $[0, 3]$ with $y(0) = 1$. The table entries are approximations to $y(3)$.

k	y_k	$(4y_k - y_{2k})/3$
1	1.732422	
1/2	1.682121	1.665354
1/4	1.672269	1.668985
1/8	1.670076	1.669345
1/16	1.669558	1.669385
1/32	1.669432	1.669390
1/64	1.669401	1.669391

8. $y' = f(t, y) = 1.5y^{1/3}$, $f_y(t, t) = 0.5y^{-2/3}$. $f_y(0, 0)$ does not exist. The I.V.P. is not well-posed on any rectangle that contains $(0, 0)$.

Section 9.4 Taylor Series Method

1. (a)

t_k	y_k $(h = 0.1)$	y_k $(h = 0.2)$
0	1	1
0.1	0.90516	
0.2	0.82127	0.82127
0.3	0.74918	
0.4	0.68968	0.68968

3. (a)

t_k	y_k $(h = 0.1)$	y_k $(h = 0.2)$
0	1	1
0.1	0.99501	
0.2	0.98020	0.98020
0.3	0.96000	
0.4	0.92312	0.92313

6. Richardson improvement for the Taylor solution $y' = (t - y)/2$ over $[0, 3]$ with $y(0) = 1$. The table entries are approximations to $y(3)$.

h	y_k	$(16y_h - y_{2h})/15$
1	1.6701860	
1/2	1.6694308	1.6693805
1/4	1.6693928	1.6693903
1/8	1.6693906	1.6693905

Section 9.5 Runge-Kutta Methods

1. (a)

t_k	$y_k(h = 0.1)$	$y_k = (h = 0.2)$
0	1	1
0.1	0.90516	
0.2	0.82127	0.82127
0.3	0.74918	
0.4	0.68968	0.68969

3. (a)

t_k	$y_k \, (h = 0.1)$	$y_k = (h = 0.2)$
0	1	1
0.1	0.99501	
0.2	0.98020	0.98020
0.3	0.95600	
0.4	0.92312	0.92312

Section 9.6 Predictor-Corrector Methods

1. $y_4 = 0.82126825$, $y_5 = 0.78369923$

3. $y_4 = 0.74832050$, $y_5 = 0.66139979$

4. $y_4 = 0.98247692$, $y_5 = 0.97350099$

7. $y_4 = 1.1542232$, $y_5 = 1.2225213$

Section 9.7 Systems of Differential Equations

1. (a) $(x_1, y_1) = (-2.5500000, 2.6700000)$

$(x_2, y_2) = (-2.4040735, 2.5485015)$

(b) $(x_1, y_1) = (-2.5521092, 2.6742492)$

5. (b) $x' = y$

$y' = 1.5x + 2.5y + 22.5e^{2t}$

(c) $x_1 = 2.05, x_2 = 2.17$

(d) $x_1 = 2.0875384$

Section 9.8 Boundary Value Problems

2. No; $q(t) = -1/t^2 < 0$ for all $t \in [0.5, 4.5]$.

Section 9.9 Finite-Difference Method

1. (a) $h_1 = 0.5, x_1 = 7.2857149$

$h_2 = 0.25, x_1 = 6.0771913, x_2 = 7.2827443$

2. (a) $h_1 = 0.5, x_1 = 0.85414295$

$h_2 = 0.25, x_1 = 0.93524622, x_2 = 0.83762911$

Section 10.1 Hyperbolic Equations

4.

t_j	x_2	x_3	x_4	x_5
0.0	0.587785	0.951057	0.951057	0.587785
0.1	0.475528	0.769421	0.769421	0.475528
0.2	0.181636	0.293893	0.293893	0.181636

5.

t_j	x_2	x_3	x_4	x_5
0.0	0.500	1.000	1.500	0.750
0.1	0.500	1.000	0.875	0.800
0.2	0.500	0.375	0.300	0.125

Section 10.2   Parabolic Equations

3.

$x_1 = 0.0$	$x_2 = 0.2$	$x_3 = 0.4$	$x_4 = 0.6$	$x_5 = 0.8$	$x_6 = 1.0$
0.0	0.587785	0.951057	0.951057	0.587785	0.0
0.0	0.475528	0.769421	0.769421	0.475528	0.0
0.0	0.384710	0.622475	0.622475	0.384710	0.0

Section 10.3   Elliptic Equations

1. (a)
$$
\begin{aligned}
-4p_1 + p_2 + p_3 \quad\quad &= -80 \\
p_1 - 4p_2 \quad\quad + p_4 &= -10 \\
p_1 \quad\quad - 4p_3 + p_4 &= -160 \\
p_2 + p_3 - 4p_4 &= -90
\end{aligned}
$$
   (b) $p_1 = 41.25$, $p_2 = 23.75$, $p_3 = 61.25$, $p_4 = 43.75$

5. (a) $u_{xx} + u_{yy} = 2a + 2c = 0$, if $a = -c$

6. Determine if $u(x, y) = \cos(2x) + \sin(2y)$ is a solution, since it is also defined on the interior of R; that is, $u_{xx} + u_{yy} = -4\cos(2x) - 4\sin(2y) = -4(\cos(2x) + \sin(2y)) = -4u$.

Section 11.1   Homogeneous Systems: Eigenvalue Problem

1. (a) $|A - \lambda I| = \lambda^2 - 3\lambda - 4 = 0$ implies that $\lambda_1 = -1$ and $\lambda_2 = 4$. Substituting each eigenvalue into $|A - \lambda I| = 0$ and solving gives $V_1 = \begin{bmatrix} -1 & 1 \end{bmatrix}'$ and $V_2 = \begin{bmatrix} 2/3 & 1 \end{bmatrix}'$, respectively.

10. If $\lambda = 2$ is an eigenvalue of A corresponding to the vector V, then $AV = 2V$. Premultiply both sides by A^{-1}: $A^{-1}AV = A^{-1}(2V)$ or $V = 2A^{-1}V$. Thus $A^{-1}V = \frac{1}{2}V$.

Section 11.2   Power Method

1. $(A - \alpha I)V = AV - \alpha IV = AV - \alpha V = \lambda V - \alpha V = (\lambda - \alpha)V$. Thus $(\lambda - \alpha)$, V is an eigenpair of $A - \alpha I$.

5. (a) $|A - 1I| = \begin{vmatrix} -0.2 & 0.3 \\ 0.2 & -0.3 \end{vmatrix} = 0$

(b) $\begin{bmatrix} -0.2 & 0.3 & 0 \\ 0.2 & -0.3 & 0 \end{bmatrix}$ is equivalent to $\begin{bmatrix} -0.2 & 0.3 & 0 \\ 0 & 0 & 0 \end{bmatrix}$, thus $-0.2x + 0.3y = 0$.

Let $y = t$, then $x = 3/2$. Thus the eigenvectors associated with $\lambda = 1$ are $\{t[3/2 \ 1]' : t \in \mathfrak{R}, t \neq 0\}$.

(c) The eigenvector from part (b) implies that in the long run the 50,000 members of the population will be divided 3 to 2 in their preference for brands X and Y, respectively; that is, $[30{,}000 \ 20{,}000]'$.

Section 11.3   Jacobi's Method

3. (a) The eigenpairs of $A = \begin{bmatrix} 4 & 2 \\ 3 & -1 \end{bmatrix}$ are 5, $[2 \ 1]'$, and -2, $[-1/3 \ 1]$. Thus the general solution is $X(t) = c_1 e^{5t}[2 \ 1]' + c_2 e^{-2t}[-1/3 \ 1]'$. Set $t = 0$ to solve for c_1 and c_2; that is, $[1 \ 2]' = c_1[2 \ 1]' + c_2[-1/3 \ 1]'$. Thus $c_1 = 0.7143$ and $c_2 = 1.2857$.

Section 11.4   Eigenvalues of Symmetric Matrices

1. From (3) we have $W = \dfrac{X - Y}{\|X - Y\|_2}$ and, from Figure 11.4, $Z = \frac{1}{2}(X + Y)$.

Taking the dot product,

$$\frac{X - Y}{\|X - Y\|_2} \cdot \frac{1}{2}(X + Y) = \frac{(X - Y) \cdot (X + Y)}{2\|X - Y\|_2}$$

$$= \frac{X \cdot X + X \cdot Y - Y \cdot X - Y \cdot Y}{2\|X - Y\|_2} = \frac{\|X\|^2 - \|Y\|^2}{2\|X - Y\|_2} = 0,$$

since X and Y have the same norm.

2. $P' = (I - 2XX')' = I' - 2(XX')' = I - 2(X')'X' = I - 2XX' = P$

Index